## PUBLISHING

G000097952

# THIS COMPLETE TEXT COMES WITH FREE ONLINE ACCESS SO THAT YOU CAN STUDY ANYTIME, ANYWHERE

**IN ADDITION TO THE CONTENTS OF THE TEXT, EN-gage ALSO ENABLES YOU TO BENEFIT FROM EXTRA ONLINE TESTING AND OTHER USEFUL STUDY MATERIALS:**

- An online version of the Text which allows you to click in and out of the expandable content and view the answers to the Test Your Understanding exercises
- Fixed Online Tests with instant answers
- Test History and Reports to allow you to track and compare your results
- Interim and Final Assessment Questions and Answers

And you can access all of these extra resources anytime, anywhere using your EN-gage account.

## How to access your online resources

If you are a Kaplan Financial student

You will already have an EN-gage account and these extra resources will be available to you online. You do not need to register again, as this process was completed when you enrolled. If you are having problems accessing online materials, please ask your course administrator.

If you purchased through Kaplan Flexible Learning or via the Kaplan Publishing website

You will automatically receive an e-mail invitation to EN-gage online. Please register your details using this e-mail to gain access to your content. If you do not receive the e-mail or book content, please contact Kaplan Flexible Learning.

If you are already a registered EN-gage user

Go to www.EN-gage.co.uk and log in. Select the 'add a book' feature and enter the ISBN number of this book and the unique pass key at the bottom of this card. Then click 'finished' or 'add another book'. You may add as many books as you have purchased from this screen.

If you are a new EN-gage user

Register at www.EN-gage.co.uk and click on the link contained in the e-mail we sent you to activate your account. Then select the 'add a book' feature, enter the ISBN number of this book and the unique pass key at the bottom of this card. Then click 'finished' or 'add another book'.

Your Code and Information

**This code can only be used once** for the registration of one book online. This registration will expire when the final sittings for the examinations covered by this book have taken place. Please allow one hour from the time you submitted your book details for us to process your request.

C07p-isXX-weF2-Gclo

For technical support, please visit www.EN-gage.co.uk

# ACCA

Paper P6

Advanced Taxation

Complete Text

Finance Act 2009 for 2010 examination sittings

# British library cataloguing-in-publication data

A catalogue record for this book is available from the British Library.

Published by:
Kaplan Publishing
Unit 2 The Business Centre
Molly Millars Lane
Wokingham
Berkshire
RG41 2QZ

ISBN  978 1 84710 739 8

The text in this material and any others made available by any Kaplan Group company does not amount to advice on a particular matter and should not be taken as such. No reliance should be placed on the content as the basis for any investment or other decision or in connection with any advice given to third parties. Please consult your appropriate professional adviser as necessary. Kaplan Publishing Limited and all other Kaplan group companies  expressly disclaim all liability to any person in respect of any losses or other claims, whether direct, indirect, incidental, consequential or otherwise arising in  relation to the use of such materials.

Printed in the UK by CPI William Clowes Beccles NR34 7TL.

Acknowledgements

We are grateful to the Association of Chartered Certified Accountants and the Chartered Institute of Management Accountants for permission to reproduce past examination questions.  The answers have been prepared by Kaplan Publishing.

# Contents

# Paper Introduction

# How to Use the Materials

These Kaplan Publishing learning materials have been carefully designed to make your learning experience as easy as possible and to give you the best chances of success in your examinations.

The product range contains a number of features to help you in the study process. They include:

(1) Detailed study guide and syllabus objectives

(2) Description of the examination

(3) Study skills and revision guidance

(4) Complete text or essential text

(5) Question practice

The sections on the study guide, the syllabus objectives, the examination and study skills should all be read before you commence your studies. They are designed to familiarise you with the nature and content of the examination and give you tips on how to best to approach your learning.

The **complete text or essential text** comprises the main learning materials and gives guidance as to the importance of topics and where other related resources can be found. Each chapter includes:

- The **learning objectives** contained in each chapter, which have been carefully mapped to the examining body's own syllabus learning objectives or outcomes. You should use these to check you have a clear understanding of all the topics on which you might be assessed in the examination.

- The **chapter diagram** provides a visual reference for the content in the chapter, giving an overview of the topics and how they link together.

- The **content** for each topic area commences with a brief explanation or definition to put the topic into context before covering the topic in detail. You should follow your studying of the content with a review of the illustration/s. These are worked examples which will help you to understand better how to apply the content for the topic.

- **Test your understanding** sections provide an opportunity to assess your understanding of the key topics by applying what you have learned to short questions. Answers can be found at the back of each chapter.

- **Summary diagrams** complete each chapter to show the important links between topics and the overall content of the paper. These diagrams should be used to check that you have covered and understood the core topics before moving on.

- **Question practice** is provided at the back of each text.

## Icon Explanations

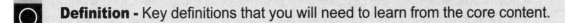

**Definition** - Key definitions that you will need to learn from the core content.

**Key Point** - Identifies topics that are key to success and are often examined.

**Expandable Text** - Expandable text provides you with additional information about a topic area and may help you gain a better understanding of the core content. Essential text users can access this additional content on-line (read it where you need further guidance or skip over when you are happy with the topic)

**Illustration** - Worked examples help you understand the core content better.

**Test Your Understanding** - Exercises for you to complete to ensure that you have understood the topics just learned.

**Tricky topic** - When reviewing these areas care should be taken and all illustrations and test your understanding exercises should be completed to ensure that the topic is understood.

**New topic** – This symbol indicates new areas of study, building on knowledge gained from previous studies or the introduction of a completely new topic.

## On-line subscribers

Our on-line resources are designed to increase the flexibility of your learning materials and provide you with immediate feedback on how your studies are progressing.

If you are subscribed to our on-line resources you will find:

(1) On-line referenceware: reproduces your Complete or Essential Text on-line, giving you anytime, anywhere access.

(2) On-line testing: provides you with additional on-line objective testing so you can practice what you have learned further.

(3) On-line performance management: immediate access to your on-line testing results. Review your performance by key topics and chart your achievement through the course relative to your peer group.

Ask your local customer services staff if you are not already a subscriber and wish to join.

## Syllabus

## Paper background

The aim of ACCA Paper P6, **Advanced taxation**, is to apply relevant knowledge and skills and to exercise professional judgement in providing relevant information and advice to individuals and businesses on the impact of the major taxes on financial decisions and situations.

## Objectives of the syllabus

- Apply further knowledge and understanding of the UK tax system through the study of further capital taxes, together with more advanced topics within the taxes studied previously.

- Evaluate and explain the importance of taxation to personal and corporate financial management.

- Identify and evaluate the impact of relevant taxes on various situations and courses of action, including the interaction of taxes.

- Provide advice on minimising and/or deferring tax liabilities by the use of standard tax planning measures.

- Communicate with clients, HM Revenue and Customs and other professionals in an appropriate manner.

## Core areas of the syllabus

- Further capital taxes.

- The importance of taxation to personal and corporate financial management.

- The impact of relevant taxes on various situations and courses of action, including the interaction of taxes.

- Minimising and/or deferring tax liabilities by the use of standard tax planning measures.

- Communicating with clients, HM Revenue and Customs and other professionals.

## Syllabus objectives

We have reproduced the ACCA's syllabus below, showing where the objectives are explored within this book. Within the chapters, we have broken down the extensive information found in the syllabus into easily digestible and relevant sections, called Content Objectives. These correspond to the objectives at the beginning of each chapter.

| Syllabus learning objective | Chapter reference |
|---|---|

**A APPLY FURTHER KNOWLEDGE AND UNDERSTANDING OF THE UK TAX SYSTEM THROUGH THE STUDY OF FURTHER CAPITAL TAXES, TOGETHER WITH MORE ADVANCED TOPICS WITHIN THE TAXES STUDIED PREVIOUSLY**

(1) **Income and income tax liabilities in situations involving further overseas aspects and in relation to trusts, and the application of exemptions and reliefs**

    (a) The contents of the Paper F6 study guide for income tax, under headings: [2]

        – B1 The scope of income tax

        – B2 Income from employment

        – B3 Income from self employment

        – B4 Property and investment income

        – B5 The comprehensive computation of taxable income and the income tax liability

        – B6 The use of exemptions and reliefs in deferring and minimising income tax liabilities

    The following additional material is also examinable:

    (b) The scope of income tax: [3]     **1,10**

       (i) Explain and apply the concepts of residence, ordinary residence and domicile and advise on the relevance to income tax   **10**

       (ii) Advise on the availability of the remittance basis to UK resident individuals [2]   **10**

       (iii) Advise on the tax position of individuals coming to and leaving the UK   **10**

       (iv) Determine the income tax treatment of overseas income   **10**

       (v) Understand the relevance of the OECD model double tax treaty to given situations   **10**

       (vi) Calculate and advise on the double taxation relief available to individuals   **10**

    (c) Income from employment: [3]

       (i) Advise on the tax treatment of share option and share incentive schemes   **2**

(ii) Advise on the tax treatment of lump sum receipts **2**

(iii) Advise on the overseas aspects of income from employment, including travelling and subsistence expenses **10**

(iv) Identify personal service companies and advise on the tax consequences of providing services via a personal service company **26**

(d) Income from self employment:

(i) Recognise the tax treatment of overseas trade travelling expenses [3] **10**

(ii) Advise on the allocation of the annual investment allowance between related businesses **17**

(iii) Identify the enhanced capital allowances available in respect of expenditure on green technologies [2] **17**

(iv) Recognise the tax treatment of the investment income and reliefs of a partnership [2] **19**

(e) Property and investment income: [3]

(i) Assess the tax implications of pre-owned assets **13**

(ii) Recognise income subject to the accrued income scheme **3**

(iii) Advise on the tax implications of jointly held assets **6**

(iv) Income from trusts and settlements: Understand the income tax position of trust beneficiaries **14**

(f) The comprehensive computation of taxable income and the income tax liability:[3]

(i) Advise on the income tax position of the income of minor children **1**

(g) The use of exemptions and reliefs in deferring and minimising income tax liabilities:

(i) Understand and apply the rules relating to investments in the enterprise investment scheme [3] **3**

(ii) Understand and apply the rules relating to investments in venture capital trusts [3] **3**

KAPLAN PUBLISHING

(iii) Explain the conditions that need to be satisfied for **4**
pension schemes to be approved by HM Revenue
and Customs [2]

(2) **Corporation tax liabilities in situations involving
further overseas and group aspects and in relation
to special types of company, and the application of
additional exemptions and reliefs**

(a) The contents of the Paper F6 study guide, for
corporation tax, under headings: [2]

- C1 The scope of corporation tax

- C2 Profits chargeable to corporation tax

- C3 The comprehensive computation of corporation
tax liability

- C4 The effect of a group structure for corporation tax
purposes

- C5 The use of exemptions and reliefs in deferring and
minimising corporation tax liabilities

The following additional material is also examinable:

(b) The scope of corporation tax: [3]

(i) Identify and calculate corporation tax for companies **23**
with investment business.

(ii) Close companies:

- Apply the definition of a close company to given
situations
**26**
- Conclude on the  tax implications of a company being
a close company or a close investment holding
company

(iii) Identify and evaluate the significance of accounting **22**
periods on administration or winding up

(iv) Conclude on the tax treatment of returns to **26**
shareholders after winding up has commenced

(v) Advise on the tax implications of a purchase by a **26**
company of its own shares

(vi) Identify personal service companies and advise on **26**
the tax consequences of services being provided via
a personal service company

(e) The effect of a group structure for corporation tax purposes: [3]

    (i) Advise on the allocation of the annual investment allowance between group or related companies   **23**

    (ii) Advise on the tax consequences of a transfer of intangible assets   **27**

    (iii) Advise on the tax consequences of a transfer of a trade and assets where there is common control   **27**

    (iv) Understand the meaning of consortium owned company and consortium member [2]   **27**

    (v) Advise on the operation of consortium relief   **27**

    (vi) Determine pre-entry gains and losses and understand their tax treatment   **27**

    (vii) Determine the degrouping charge where a company leaves a group within six years of receiving an asset by way of a no gain/no loss transfer   **27**

    (viii) Determine the effects of the anti-avoidance provisions, where arrangements exist for a company to leave a group   **27**

    (ix) Advise on the relief for trading losses incurred by an overseas subsidiary   **27**

(f) The use of exemptions and reliefs in deferring and minimising corporation tax liabilities:   **24,27,29**

No additional material at this level.

(3) **Chargeable gains and capital gains tax liabilities in situations involving further overseas aspects and in relation to closely related persons and trusts together with the application of additional exemptions and reliefs**

(a) The contents of the Paper F6 study guide for chargeable gains under headings: [2]

    – D1 The scope of the taxation of capital gains

    – D2 The basic principles of computing gains and losses

    – D3 Gains and losses on the disposal of movable and immovable property

- D4 Gains and losses on the disposal of shares and securities

- D5 The computation of capital gains tax payable by individuals

- D6 The use of exemptions and reliefs in deferring and minimising tax liabilities arising on the disposal of capital assets

The following additional material is also examinable

(b) The scope of the taxation of capital gains: [3]

(i) Determine the tax implications of independent taxation and transfers between spouses — **6**

(ii) Identify the concepts of residence, ordinary residence and domicile and determine their relevance to capital gains tax — **10**

(iii) Advise on the availability of the remittance basis to non-UK domiciled individuals [2] — **10**

(iv) Determine the UK taxation of foreign gains, including double taxation relief — **10**

(v) Conclude on the capital gains tax position of individuals coming to and leaving the UK — **10**

(vi) Identify the occasions when a capital gain would arise on a partner in a partnership — **19**

(c) Capital gains tax and trusts: — **14**

(i) Advise on the capital gains tax implications of transfers of property into trust [3]

(ii) Advise on the capital gains tax implications of property passing absolutely from a trust to a beneficiary [2]

(d) The basic principles of computing gains and losses: [3]

(i) Identify connected persons for capital gains tax purposes and advise on the tax implications of transfers between connected persons. — **6**

(ii) Advise on the impact of dates of disposal and conditional contracts — **6**

(iii) Evaluate the use of capital losses in the year of death — **6**

KAPLAN PUBLISHING

(e) Gains and losses on the disposal of movable and immovable property: [3]

   (i)  Advise on the tax implications of a part disposal, including small part disposals of land     **7**

   (ii)  Determine the gain on the disposal of leases and wasting assets     **7**

   (iii)  Establish the tax effect of appropriations to and from trading stock     **7**

   (iv)  Establish the tax effect of capital sums received in respect of the loss, damage or destruction of an asset     **7**

   (v)  Advise on the tax effect of making negligible value claims     **7**

   (vi)  Determine when capital gains tax can be paid by instalments and evaluate when this would be advantageous to taxpayers     **6**

(f) Gains and losses on the disposal of shares and securities: [3]

   (i)  Extend the explanation of the treatment of rights issues to include the small part disposal rules applicable to rights issues     **8**

   (ii)  Determine the application of the substantial shareholdings exemption     **23**

   (iii)  Define a qualifying corporate bond (QCB), and understand what makes a corporate bond non-qualifying. Understand the capital gains tax implications of the disposal of QCBs in exchange for cash or shares     **8**

   (iv)  Apply the rules relating to reorganisations, reconstructions and amalgamations and advise on the most tax efficient options available in given circumstances     **8,27**

   (v)  Establish the relief for capital losses on shares in unquoted trading companies     **8**

(g) The use of exemptions and reliefs in deferring and minimising tax liabilities arising on the disposal of capital assets: [3]

(i) Understand and apply enterprise investment scheme reinvestment relief   **3,9**

(ii) Advise on the availability of entrepreneurs' relief in relation to associated disposals   **9**

(iii) Understand the capital gains tax implications of the variation of wills   **13**

**(4)**   **Inheritance tax**

(a) The scope of inheritance tax: [2]

     (i) Identify and explain the persons chargeable   **11**

     (ii) Explain the concepts of domicile and deemed domicile and understand the application of these concepts to inheritance tax   **11**

(b) The basic principles for computing transfers of value: [3]

     (i) State, explain and apply the meaning of transfers of value, chargeable transfers and potentially exempt transfers   **11**

     (ii) Demonstrate the fall in value principle   **11**

     (iii) Demonstrate the seven year accumulation principle   **11**

     (iv) Identify excluded property [2]   **11**

     (v) Identify and advise on the tax implications of the location of assets   **11**

     (vi) Identify and advise on gifts with reservation of benefit   **12**

     (vii) Identify and advise on the tax implications of associated operations   **12**

(c) The liabilities arising on chargeable lifetime transfers and death transfers by individuals: [3]

     (i) Advise on the tax implications of chargeable lifetime transfers   **11**

     (ii) Advise on the tax implications of transfers within seven years of death   **11**

     (iii) Compute the death estate [2]   **13**

     (iv) Advise on the relief for the fall in value of lifetime gifts   **12**

(5) **Stamp duties (stamp duty and stamp duty land tax)**

    (a)  The scope of stamp duty and stamp duty land tax: [3]

        (i)  identify the property in respect of which stamp duty and stamp duty land tax is payable.   **6,8**

    (b)  Identify and advise on the liabilities arising on documented transfers. [3]

        (i)  Advise on the stamp duties payable on transfers of shares and securities   **8**

        (ii)  Advise on the stamp duties payable on transfers of land   **6**

    (c)  The use of exemptions and reliefs in deferring and minimising stamp duties: [3]

        (i)  Identify transfers involving no consideration   **6,8**

        (ii)  Advise on group transactions   **27**

    (d)  Understand and explain the systems by which stamp duties are administered.[2]   **6,8**

(6) **National insurance, value added tax, tax administration and the UK tax system:**

    (a)  The contents of the Paper F6 study guide for national insurance under headings:[2]

      –  E1 The scope of national insurance

      –  E2 Class 1 and class 1A contributions for employed persons

      –  E3 Class 2 and class 4 contributions for self-employed persons

    No additional material at this level.

    (b)  The contents of the Paper F6 study guide for value added tax (VAT) under headings:

      –  F1 The scope of value added tax (VAT)

      –  F2 The VAT registration requirements

      –  F3 The computation of VAT liabilities

      –  F4 The effect of special schemes

    The following additional material is also examinable:

(i) Advise on the impact of the disaggregation of business activities for VAT purposes [3] **20**

(ii) Advise on the impact of group registration and divisional registration [3] **20**

(iii) Advise on the VAT implications of the supply of land and buildings in the UK **20**

(iv) Advise on the VAT implications of imports and exports **21**

(v) Advise on the VAT implications of acquisitions and supplies within the EU **21**

(vi) Advise on the VAT implications of partial exemption **20**

(vii) Advise on the application of the capital goods scheme **20**

(c) The contents of the Paper F6 study guide for the obligations of taxpayers and/or their agents under headings:

– G1 The systems for self assessment and the making of returns

– G2 The time limits for the submission of information, claims and payment of tax, including payments on account

– G3 The procedures relating to enquiries appeals and disputes

– G4 Penalties for non-compliance

No additional material at this level

(d) The contents of the Paper F6 study guide for the UK tax system under headings:

– A1 The overall function and purpose of taxation in a modern economy

– A2 Different types of taxes

– A3 Principal sources of revenue law and practice

– A4 Tax avoidance and tax evasion

**B THE IMPORTANCE OF TAXATION TO PERSONAL AND CORPORATE FINANCIAL MANAGEMENT**

(1) **The principles underlying personal financial management,**

    (a) Calculate the receipts from a transaction, net of tax and compare the results of alternative scenarios and advise on the most tax efficient course of action.[3]     **6,15,17 18,13**

(2) **How an individual's personal financial objectives may differ depending on their circumstances and expectations**

    (a) Understand and apply the effect of age, family commitments, aspirations and the economy on personal financial objectives.[3]     **15**

(3) **The common forms of personal finance and investment products in a given set of circumstances, including ethical considerations**

    (a) Understand and be able to compare and contrast the tax treatment of the sources of finance available to individuals.[3]     **15**

    (b) Understand and be able to compare and contrast the tax treatment of investment products: [3]     **15**

        (i) Deposit based investments

        (ii) Fixed interest securities

        (iii) Packaged investments

        (iv) Collective investments

        (v) Equities

        (vi) Enterprise investment scheme

        (vii) Venture capital trusts

        (viii) Fixed interest securities

(4) **How a business' financial objectives may differ depending on its circumstances and the business environment**

    (a) Understand and be able to explain the effect of profitability, future plans, actions of competitors and the economy on a business' financial objectives.[3]     **15,25**

(5) **How taxation can affect the financial decisions made by businesses (corporate and unincorporated) and by individuals**

| | | |
|---|---|---|
| (a) | Understand and explain the tax implications of the effect of the raising of equity and loan finance.[3] | **15,25** |
| (b) | Explain the tax differences between decisions to lease, use hire purchase or purchase outright.[3] | **15,25** |
| (c) | Understand and explain the impact of taxation on the cash flows of a business.[3] | **15,25** |
| (d) | Other considerations, personal and commercial, which might affect a financial decision.[3] | **15,25** |

**C   THE IMPACT OF RELEVANT TAXES ON VARIOUS SITUATIONS AND COURSES OF ACTION, INCLUDING THE INTERACTION OF TAXES**

| | | |
|---|---|---|
| (1) | Identifying and advising on the taxes applicable to a given course of action and their impact.[3] | **13,15,17 18,26,29** |
| (2) | Identifying and understanding that the alternative ways of achieving personal or business outcomes may lead to different tax consequences. [3] | **17,18,26 29** |
| (3) | Assessing the tax advantages and disadvantages of alternative courses of action.[3] | **6,13,17 18,26,29** |
| (4) | Understanding the statutory obligations imposed in a given situation, including any time limits for action and advising on the implications of non-compliance.[3] | **16,17,24 25,26,27 29** |

**D   MINIMISING AND/OR DEFERRING TAX LIABILITIES BY THE USE OF STANDARD TAX PLANNING MEASURES**

| | | |
|---|---|---|
| (1) | Identifying and advising on the types of investment and other expenditure that will result in a reduction in tax liabilities for an individual and/or a business.[3] | **3,15,17 25,29** |
| (2) | Advising on legitimate tax planning measures, by which the tax liabilities arising from a particular situation or course of action can be mitigated. [3] | **6,13,17 18,24,26 27,29** |
| (3) | Advising on the appropriateness of such investment, expenditure or measures given a particular taxpayer's circumstances or stated objectives.[3] | **6,17,25 26,27,29** |
| (4) | Advise on the mitigation of tax in the manner recommended by reference to numerical analysis and/or reasoned argument.[3] | **6,17,24 26,27,29** |
| (5) | Be aware of the ethical and professional issues arising from the giving of tax planning advice.[3] | **6,15,16 26,29** |
| (6) | Be aware of and give advice on current issues in taxation.[3] | **6,16,26 29** |

## E COMMUNICATING WITH CLIENTS, HM REVENUE AND CUSTOMS AND OTHER PROFESSIONALS IN AN APPROPRIATE MANNER

(1) Communication of advice, recommendations and information in the required format:[3]                    **6**

For example the use of:

- Reports
- Letters
- Memoranda
- Meeting notes

(2) Presentation of written information, in language appropriate to the purpose of the communication and the intended recipient.[3]

(3) Communicating conclusions reached, together, where necessary with relevant supporting computations.[3]

(4) Stating and explaining assumptions made or limitations in the analysis provided; together with any inadequacies in the information available and/or additional information required to provide a fuller analysis.[3]

(5) Identifying and explaining other, non-tax, factors that should be considered.[3]

The superscript numbers in square brackets indicate the intellectual depth at which the subject area could be assessed within the examination.

Level 1 (knowledge and comprehension) broadly equates with the Knowledge module.

Level 2 (application and analysis) with the Skills module.

Level 3 (synthesis and evaluation) to the Professional level.

However, lower level skills can continue to be assessed as you progress through each module and level.

## The Examination

### Examination format

The paper consists of two sections:

Section A consists of two compulsory questions for a total of between 50 and 70 marks. Marks may not be allocated evenly between the two questions.

Section B consists of three questions, two of which must be answered. Each question will have the same number of marks, ranging from 15 marks each to 25 marks each.

Questions will be scenario based and will normally involve consideration of more than one tax together with some elements of planning and the interaction of taxes. Computations will normally only be required in support of explanations or advice and not in isolation.

Tax rates, allowances and information on certain reliefs will be given in the examination paper.

|  | Number of marks |
|---|---|
| **Section A** | |
| Two compulsory questions | 50-70 |
| **Section B** | |
| Choice of two from three questions | 30-50 |
| | |
| | 100 |
| | |

Total time allowed: 3 hours

There is an additional 15 minutes of reading and planning time at the start of the examination during which you can annotate the question paper.

## Paper-based examination tips

Spend the first few minutes of the examination reading the paper.

Where you have a choice of questions, decide which ones you will do.

**Divide the time** you spend on questions in proportion to the marks on offer. One suggestion **for this examination** is to allocate 1.8 minutes to each mark available, so a 10-mark question should be completed in approximately 18 minutes.

Unless you know exactly how to answer the question, spend some time **planning** your answer. Stick to the question and **tailor your answer** to what you are asked. Pay particular attention to the verbs in the question.

Spend the last five minutes reading through your answers and making any additions or corrections.

If you **get completely stuck** with a question, leave space in your answer book and **return to it later**.

If you do not understand what a question is asking, state your assumptions. Even if you do not answer in precisely the way the examiner hoped, you should be given some credit, if your assumptions are reasonable.

You should do everything you can to make things easy for the marker. The marker will find it easier to identify the points you have made if your answers are legible.

**Essay questions**: Your essay should have a clear structure. It should contain a brief introduction, a main section and a conclusion. Be concise. It is better to write a little about a lot of different points than a great deal about one or two points.

**Computations**: It is essential to include all your workings in your answers. Many computational questions require the use of a standard format. Be sure you know these formats thoroughly before the exam and use the layouts that you see in the answers given in this book and in model answers.

**Reports, memos and other documents**: some questions ask you to present your answer in the form of a report or a memo or other document. So use the correct format - there could be easy marks to gain here.

## Study skills and revision guidance

This section aims to give guidance on how to study for your ACCA exams and to give ideas on how to improve your existing study techniques.

### Preparing to study

### Set your objectives

Before starting to study decide what you want to achieve - the type of pass you wish to obtain. This will decide the level of commitment and time you need to dedicate to your studies.

### Devise a study plan

Determine which times of the week you will study.at least one hour for study of new material. Any shorter periods could be used for revision or practice.

Split these times into sessions of

Put the times you plan to study onto a study plan for the weeks from now until the exam and set yourself targets for each period of study - in your sessions make sure you cover the course, course assignments and revision.

If you are studying for more than one paper at a time, try to vary your subjects as this can help you to keep interested and see subjects as part of wider knowledge.

When working through your course, compare your progress with your plan and, if necessary, re-plan your work (perhaps including extra sessions) or, if you are ahead, do some extra revision/practice questions.

**Effective studying**

**Active reading**

You are not expected to learn the text by rote, rather, you must understand what you are reading and be able to use it to pass the exam and develop good practice. A good technique to use is SQ3Rs - Survey, Question, Read, Recall, Review:

(1) **Survey the chapter** - look at the headings and read the introduction, summary and objectives, so as to get an overview of what the chapter deals with.

(2) **Question** - whilst undertaking the survey, ask yourself the questions that you hope the chapter will answer for you.

(3) **Read** through the chapter thoroughly, answering the questions and making sure you can meet the objectives. Attempt the exercises and activities in the text, and work through all the examples.

(4) **Recall** - at the end of each section and at the end of the chapter, try to recall the main ideas of the section/chapter without referring to the text. This is best done after a short break of a couple of minutes after the reading stage.

(5) **Review** - check that your recall notes are correct.

You may also find it helpful to re-read the chapter to try to see the topic(s) it deals with as a whole.

**Note-taking**

Taking notes is a useful way of learning, but do not simply copy out the text. The notes must:

- be in your own words
- be concise
- cover the key points
- be well-organised
- be modified as you study further chapters in this text or in related ones.

Trying to summarise a chapter without referring to the text can be a useful way of determining which areas you know and which you don't.

**Three ways of taking notes:**

**Summarise the key points of a chapter.**

**Make linear notes** - a list of headings, divided up with subheadings listing the key points. If you use linear notes, you can use different colours to highlight key points and keep topic areas together. Use plenty of space to make your notes easy to use.

**Try a diagrammatic form** - the most common of which is a mind-map. To make a mind-map, put the main heading in the centre of the paper and put a circle around it. Then draw short lines radiating from this to the main sub-headings, which again have circles around them. Then continue the process from the sub-headings to sub-sub-headings, advantages, disadvantages, etc.

**Highlighting and underlining**

You may find it useful to underline or highlight key points in your study text - but do be selective. You may also wish to make notes in the margins.

**Revision**

The best approach to revision is to revise the course as you work through it. Also try to leave four to six weeks before the exam for final revision. Make sure you cover the whole syllabus and pay special attention to those areas where your knowledge is weak. Here are some recommendations:

Read through the text and your notes again and condense your notes into key phrases. It may help to put key revision points onto index cards to look at when you have a few minutes to spare.

Review any assignments you have completed and look at where you lost marks - put more work into those areas where you were weak.

Practise exam standard questions under timed conditions. If you are short of time, list the points that you would cover in your answer and then read the model answer, but do try to complete at least a few questions under exam conditions.

Also practise producing answer plans and comparing them to the model answer.

If you are stuck on a topic find somebody (a tutor) to explain it to you.

Read good newspapers and professional journals, especially ACCA's Student Accountant - this can give you an advantage in the exam.

Ensure you know the structure of the exam - how many questions and of what type you will be expected to answer. During your revision attempt all the different styles of questions you may be asked.

### Further reading

You can find further reading and technical articles under the student section of ACCA's website.

# RATES AND ALLOWANCES

**Supplementary instructions given in the examination**

1.  Calculations and workings need only be made to the nearest £.

2.  All apportionments should be made to the nearest month.

3.  All workings should be shown.

**The following tax rates and allowances are to be used**

## INCOME TAX

|  |  | % |
|---|---|---|
| Basic rate | £1 – £37,400 | 20 |
| Higher rate | £37,401 and above | 40 |

A starting rate of 10% applies to savings income where it falls within the first £2,440 of taxable income.

## Personal allowances

| Personal allowance | Standard | £6,475 |
|---|---|---|
| Personal allowance | 65 – 74 | £9,490 |
| Personal allowance | 75 and over | £9,640 |

| Income limit for age related allowances | £22,900 |
|---|---|

## Car benefit percentage

The base level of $CO_2$ emission is 135 grams per kilometre.

A lower rate of 10% applies to cars with $CO_2$ emissions of 120 grams per kilometre or less.

## Car fuel benefit

The base level figure for calculating car fuel benefit is £16,900.

## Pension scheme limits

| Annual allowance | £245,000 |
|---|---|
| Lifetime allowance | £1,750,000 |

The maximum contribution that can qualify for tax relief without any earnings is £3,600.

## Authorised mileage rates: cars

| Up to 10,000 miles | 40p |
|---|---|
| Over 10,000 miles | 25p |

## Capital allowances

| | | % |
|---|---|---|
| *Plant and machinery* | | |
| Writing down allowance | – General rate | 20 |
| | – Special rate pool | 10 |
| | | |
| First year allowance | – Low emission cars (CO$_2$ emissions of less than 110 grams per kilometre) | 100 |
| | – Expenditure in excess of annual investment allowance that would normally be allocated to the main pool | 40 |
| | | |
| Annual investment allowance for the first £50,000 of expenditure | | 100 |

| *Motor cars* | | |
|---|---|---|
| CO$_2$ emissions up to 110 gm/km | FYA | 100 |
| CO$_2$ emissions between 111 and 160 gm/km | WDA | 20 |
| CO$_2$ emissions above 160 gm/km | WDA | 10 |

| *Industrial buildings* | |
|---|---|
| Writing down allowance | 2 |

## CORPORATION TAX

| Financial Year | 2007 | 2008 | 2009 |
|---|---|---|---|
| Small companies rate | 20% | 21% | 21% |
| Full rate | 30% | 28% | 28% |
| | | | |
| Lower limit | £300,000 | £300,000 | £300,000 |
| Upper limit | £1,500,000 | £1,500,000 | £1,500,000 |
| Marginal relief fraction | 1/40 | 7/400 | 7,400 |

### Marginal relief

$(M - P) \times I/P \times$ Marginal relief fraction

## VALUE ADDED TAX

| | | |
|---|---|---|
| Standard rate | Up to 31 December 2009 | 15.0% |
| | From 1 January 2010 | 17.5% |
| | | |
| Registration limit | | £68,000 |
| Deregistration limit | | £66,000 |

## INHERITANCE TAX

| | |
|---|---|
| £1 - £325,000 | Nil |
| Excess | 40% |

## CAPITAL GAINS TAX

| | | |
|---|---|---|
| Rate of tax | | 18% |
| Annual exemption | | £10,100 |
| Entrepreneurs' relief | – Lifetime limit | £1,000,000 |
| | – Relief factor | 4/9ths |

## NATIONAL INSURANCE CONTRIBUTIONS
### (not contracted out rates)

| | | % |
|---|---|---|
| Class 1 Employee | £1 – £5,715 per year | Nil |
| | £5,716 – £43,875 per year | 11.0 |
| | £43,876 and above | 1.0 |
| Class 1 Employer | £1 – £5,715 per year | Nil |
| | £5,876 and above per year | 12.8 |
| Class 1A | | 12.8 |

**Self employed**

| | | |
|---|---|---|
| Class 2 | £2.40 per week | |
| Class 4 | £1 – £5,715 per year | Nil |
| | £5,716 – £43,875 per year | 8.0 |
| | £43,876 and above per year | 1.0 |

## RATES OF INTEREST

| | |
|---|---|
| Official rate of interest: | 4.75% |
| Interest on underpaid tax | 2.50% (assumed) |
| Interest on overpaid tax | Nil% (assumed) |

## STAMP DUTY LAND TAX

| **Ad Valorem Duty** | Rate |
|---|---|
| Residential property | |
| £175,000 or less (1) | Nil |
| £175,001 – £250,000 | 1% |
| £250,001 – £500,000 | 3% |
| £500,001 or more | 4% |

1    For non-residential property, the nil rate is extended to £150,000.

## STAMP DUTY

| | |
|---|---|
| Shares | 0.5% |

## RETAIL PRICES INDEX

The following tax rates and allowances are not given in the examination paper as shown below but the relevant information will be given within the questions where necessary.

These tables are reproduced for use in the questions within this workbook.

### Retail prices indices

|     | 1982 | 1983 | 1984 | 1985 | 1986 | 1987 | 1988 | 1989 | 1990 |
|-----|------|------|------|------|------|------|------|------|------|
| Jan | –    | 82.61 | 86.84 | 91.20 | 96.25 | 100.0 | 103.3 | 111.0 | 119.5 |
| Feb | –    | 82.97 | 87.20 | 91.94 | 96.60 | 100.4 | 103.7 | 111.8 | 120.2 |
| Mar | 79.44 | 83.12 | 87.48 | 92.80 | 96.73 | 100.6 | 104.1 | 112.3 | 121.4 |
| Apr | 81.04 | 84.28 | 88.64 | 94.78 | 97.67 | 101.8 | 105.8 | 114.3 | 125.1 |
| May | 81.62 | 84.64 | 88.97 | 95.21 | 97.85 | 101.9 | 106.2 | 115.0 | 126.2 |
| Jun | 81.85 | 84.84 | 89.20 | 95.41 | 97.79 | 101.9 | 106.6 | 115.4 | 126.7 |
| Jul | 81.88 | 85.30 | 89.10 | 95.23 | 97.52 | 101.8 | 106.7 | 115.5 | 126.8 |
| Aug | 81.90 | 85.68 | 89.94 | 95.49 | 97.82 | 102.1 | 107.9 | 115.8 | 128.1 |
| Sep | 81.85 | 86.06 | 90.11 | 95.44 | 98.30 | 102.4 | 108.4 | 116.6 | 129.3 |
| Oct | 82.26 | 86.36 | 90.67 | 95.59 | 98.45 | 102.9 | 109.5 | 117.5 | 130.3 |
| Nov | 82.66 | 86.67 | 90.95 | 95.92 | 99.29 | 103.4 | 110.0 | 118.5 | 130.0 |
| Dec | 82.51 | 86.89 | 90.87 | 96.05 | 99.62 | 103.3 | 110.3 | 118.8 | 129.9 |

|     | 1991 | 1992 | 1993 | 1994 | 1995 | 1996 | 1997 | 1998 | 1999 |
|-----|------|------|------|------|------|------|------|------|------|
| Jan | 130.2 | 135.6 | 137.9 | 141.3 | 146.0 | 150.2 | 154.4 | 159.5 | 163.4 |
| Feb | 130.9 | 136.3 | 138.8 | 142.1 | 146.9 | 150.9 | 155.0 | 160.3 | 163.7 |
| Mar | 131.4 | 136.7 | 139.3 | 142.5 | 147.5 | 151.5 | 155.4 | 160.8 | 164.1 |
| Apr | 133.1 | 138.8 | 140.6 | 144.2 | 149.0 | 152.6 | 156.3 | 162.6 | 165.2 |
| May | 133.5 | 139.3 | 141.1 | 144.7 | 149.6 | 152.9 | 156.9 | 163.5 | 165.6 |
| Jun | 134.1 | 139.3 | 141.0 | 144.7 | 149.8 | 153.0 | 157.5 | 163.4 | 165.6 |
| Jul | 133.8 | 138.8 | 140.7 | 144.0 | 149.1 | 152.4 | 157.5 | 163.0 | 165.1 |
| Aug | 134.1 | 138.9 | 141.3 | 144.7 | 149.9 | 153.1 | 158.5 | 163.7 | 165.5 |
| Sep | 134.6 | 139.4 | 141.9 | 145.0 | 150.6 | 153.8 | 159.3 | 164.4 | 166.2 |
| Oct | 135.1 | 139.9 | 141.8 | 145.2 | 149.8 | 153.8 | 159.5 | 164.5 | 166.5 |
| Nov | 135.6 | 139.7 | 141.6 | 145.3 | 149.8 | 153.9 | 159.6 | 164.4 | 166.7 |
| Dec | 135.7 | 139.2 | 141.9 | 146.0 | 150.7 | 154.4 | 160.0 | 164.4 | 167.3 |

|      | 2000  | 2001  | 2002  | 2003  | 2004  | 2005  | 2006  | 2007  | 2008  |
|------|-------|-------|-------|-------|-------|-------|-------|-------|-------|
| Jan  | 166.6 | 171.1 | 173.3 | 178.4 | 183.1 | 188.9 | 193.4 | 201.6 | 209.8 |
| Feb  | 167.5 | 172.0 | 173.8 | 179.3 | 183.8 | 189.6 | 194.2 | 203.1 | 211.4 |
| Mar  | 168.4 | 172.2 | 174.5 | 179.9 | 184.6 | 190.5 | 195.0 | 204.4 | 212.1 |
| Apr  | 170.1 | 173.1 | 175.7 | 181.2 | 185.7 | 191.6 | 196.5 | 205.4 | 214.0 |
| May  | 170.7 | 174.2 | 176.2 | 181.5 | 186.5 | 192.0 | 197.7 | 206.2 | 215.1 |
| Jun  | 171.1 | 174.4 | 176.2 | 181.3 | 186.8 | 192.2 | 198.5 | 207.3 | 216.8 |
| Jul  | 170.5 | 173.3 | 175.9 | 181.3 | 186.8 | 192.2 | 198.5 | 206.1 | 216.5 |
| Aug  | 170.5 | 174.0 | 176.4 | 181.6 | 187.4 | 192.6 | 199.2 | 207.3 | 217.2 |
| Sep  | 171.7 | 174.6 | 177.6 | 182.5 | 188.1 | 193.1 | 200.1 | 208.0 | 218.4 |
| Oct  | 171.6 | 174.3 | 177.9 | 182.6 | 188.6 | 193.3 | 200.4 | 208.9 | 217.7 |
| Nov  | 172.1 | 173.6 | 178.2 | 182.7 | 189.0 | 193.6 | 201.1 | 209.7 | 216.0 |
| Dec  | 172.2 | 173.4 | 178.5 | 183.5 | 189.9 | 194.1 | 202.7 | 210.9 | 212.9 |

|      | 2009   | 2010   | 2011 | 2012 | 2013 | 2014 | 2015 | 2016 | 2017 |
|------|--------|--------|------|------|------|------|------|------|------|
| Jan  | 209.8  | 213.3e |      |      |      |      |      |      |      |
| Feb  | 211.4  | 213.5e |      |      |      |      |      |      |      |
| Mar  | 211.3  | 213.7e |      |      |      |      |      |      |      |
| Apr  | 211.5  | 213.9e |      |      |      |      |      |      |      |
| May  | 211.7e |        |      |      |      |      |      |      |      |
| Jun  | 211.9e |        |      |      |      |      |      |      |      |
| Jul  | 212.1e |        |      |      |      |      |      |      |      |
| Aug  | 212.3e |        |      |      |      |      |      |      |      |
| Sep  | 212.5e |        |      |      |      |      |      |      |      |
| Oct  | 212.7e |        |      |      |      |      |      |      |      |
| Nov  | 212.9e |        |      |      |      |      |      |      |      |
| Dec  | 213.1e |        |      |      |      |      |      |      |      |

e – estimated

## LEASE DEPRECIATION PERCENTAGES

| Years | % | Years | % |
|---|---|---|---|
| 50 + | 100.00 | 25 | 81.100 |
| 49 | 99.657 | 24 | 79.622 |
| 48 | 99.289 | 23 | 78.055 |
| 47 | 98.902 | 22 | 76.399 |
| 46 | 98.490 | 21 | 74.635 |
| 45 | 98.059 | 20 | 72.770 |
| 44 | 97.595 | 19 | 70.791 |
| 43 | 97.107 | 18 | 68.697 |
| 42 | 96.593 | 17 | 66.470 |
| 41 | 96.041 | 16 | 64.116 |
| 40 | 95.457 | 15 | 61.617 |
| 39 | 94.842 | 14 | 58.971 |
| 38 | 94.189 | 13 | 56.167 |
| 37 | 93.497 | 12 | 53.191 |
| 36 | 92.761 | 11 | 50.038 |
| 35 | 91.981 | 10 | 46.695 |
| 34 | 91.156 | 09 | 43.154 |
| 33 | 90.280 | 08 | 39.399 |
| 32 | 89.354 | 07 | 35.414 |
| 31 | 88.371 | 06 | 31.195 |
| 30 | 87.330 | 05 | 26.722 |
| 29 | 86.226 | 04 | 21.983 |
| 28 | 85.053 | 03 | 16.959 |
| 27 | 83.816 | 02 | 11.629 |
| 26 | 82.496 | 01 | 05.983 |

KAPLAN PUBLISHING

## TIME LIMITS FOR ELECTIONS AND CLAIMS

The following tables summarise the key time limits for elections and claims. These tables are not given in the examination.

**Income Tax**

| Election / claim | Time limit | For 2009/10 |
|---|---|---|
| Agree the amount of trading losses to carry forward | 4 years from 31 January following the end of the tax year in which the loss arose | 5 April 2014 |
| Current and prior year set-off of trading losses against total income | 12 months from 31 January following the end of the tax year in which the loss arose | 31 January 2012 |
| Current and prior year set-off trading losses against capital gains | 12 months from 31 January following the end of the tax year in which the loss arose | 31 January 2012 |
| Three year carry back of trading losses in the opening years | 12 months from 31 January following the end of the tax year in which the loss arose | 31 January 2012 |
| Three year carry back of terminal trading losses in the closing years | 4 years from the end of the last tax year of trading | 5 April 2014 |
| Set-off of loss on the disposal of unquoted trading company shares against income | 12 months from 31 January following the end of the tax year in which the loss arose | 31 January 2012 |
| Transfer of assets eligible for capital allowances between connected parties at TWDV | 2 years from the date of sale | |

**Capital gains tax**

| Election / claim | Time limit | For 2009/10 |
|---|---|---|
| Replacement of business asset relief for individuals (Rollover relief) | 4 years from the end of the tax year in which the disposal occurred | 5 April 2014 |
| Holdover relief of gain on the gift of a business asset (Gift relief) | 4 years from the end of the tax year in which the disposal occurred | 5 April 2014 |
| Disapplication of incorporation relief | 2 years from the 31 January following the end of the tax year in which the business is transferred | 31 January 2013 |
| EIS Reinvestment relief | 5 years from 31 January following the end of the tax year in which the disposal occurred | 31 January 2016 |
| Entrepreneurs' relief | 12 months from 31 January following the end of the tax year in which the disposal occurred | 31 January 2012 |
| Determination of principal private residence | 2 years from the acquisition of the second property | |

KAPLAN PUBLISHING

## National Insurance Contributions

| Election / claim | Time limit | For 2009/10 |
|---|---|---|
| Class 1 primary and secondary – pay days | 14 days after the end of each tax month under PAYE system | $19^{th}$ of each month |
| Class 1 A NIC – pay day | 19 July following end of tax year | 19 July 2010 |
| Class 2 NICs – pay days | Monthly by direct debit or quarterly invoicing | |
| Class 4 NICs – pay days | Paid under self assessment with income tax | |

## Self assessment — individuals

| Election / claim | Time limit | For 2009/10 |
|---|---|---|
| Self assessment<br>– Pay days for income tax and Class 4 NIC | 1st instalment:<br>31 January in the tax year | 31 January 2010 |
| | 2nd instalment:<br>31 July following the end of the tax year | 31 July 2010 |
| | Balancing payment:<br>31 January following the end of the tax year | 31 January 2011 |
| Self assessment<br>– Pay day for capital gains tax | 31 January following the end of the tax year | 31 January 2011 |

| Election / claim | Time limit | For 2009/10 |
|---|---|---|
| Self assessment<br>– Filing dates<br>  If return issued by 31 October<br>  in the tax year | Paper return:<br>31 October following<br>end of tax year<br><br>Electronic return:<br>31 January following<br>end of tax year | 31 October 2010<br><br><br><br>31 January 2011 |
| – Filing dates<br>  If return issued after 31<br>  October in the tax year | 3 months from the<br>date of issue of the<br>return | |
| Retention of records<br>– Business records | 5 years from 31<br>January following the<br>end of the tax year | 31 January 2016 |
| – Personal records | 12 months from 31<br>January following the<br>end of the tax year | 31 January 2012 |
| HMRC right of repair<br>(i.e. to correct mistakes) | 9 months from the<br>date the return was<br>filed | |
| Tax payers right to amend a<br>return | 12 months from 31<br>January following the<br>end of the tax year | 31 January 2012 |
| Tax payers error or mistake<br>claim | 4 years from the end<br>of the tax year | 5 April 2014 |
| HMRC can open an enquiry | 12 months from the<br>actual submission of<br>the return | |
| HMRC can raise a discovery<br>assessment<br><br>– No careless or deliberate<br>behaviour | <br><br><br>4 years from the end<br>of the tax year | <br><br><br>5 April 2014 |
| – Tax lost due to careless<br>behaviour | 6 years from the end<br>of the tax year | 5 April 2016 |
| – Tax lost due to deliberate<br>behaviour | 20 years from the<br>end of the tax year | 5 April 2030 |
| Taxpayers right of appeal<br>against an assessment | 30 days from the<br>assessment<br>– appeal in writing | |

## Inheritance tax

| Election / claim | Time limit | For 2009/10 |
|---|---|---|
| Lifetime IHT on CLTs – pay day | Gift before 1 October in tax year: – following 30 April<br><br>Gift on/after 1 October in tax year – 6 months after the end of the month of the gift | 30 April 2010 |
| Death IHT on lifetime gifts within seven years of death (CLTs and PETs) | 6 months after the end of the month of death | |
| IHT on estate | 6 months after the end of the month of death | |
| Deed of variation | 2 years from the date of death – in writing | |
| Transfer of unused nil rate band to spouse or civil partner | 2 years from the date of the second death | |

## Corporation tax

| Election / claim | Time limit |
|---|---|
| Replacement of business asset relief for companies (Rollover relief) | 4 years from the end of the chargeable accounting period in which the disposal occurred |
| Agree the amount of trading losses to carry forward | 4 years from the end of the chargeable accounting period in which the loss arose |
| Current year set-off of trading losses against total profits (income and gains) and 12 month carry back of trading losses against total profits (income and gains) | 2 years from the end of the chargeable accounting period in which the loss arose |

| Election / claim | Time limit |
|---|---|
| Surrender of current period trading losses to other group companies (Group relief) | 2 years after the claimant company's chargeable accounting period |
| Election for transfer of capital gains or losses to another group company | 2 years from the end of the chargeable accounting period in which the disposal occurred by the company actually making the disposal |

## Self assessment – companies

| Election / claim | Time limit |
|---|---|
| Self assessment<br>– pay day for small and medium companies | 9 months and one day after the end of the chargeable accounting period |
| Self assessment<br>– pay day for large companies | Instalments due on 14th day of:<br>– Seventh<br>– Tenth<br>– Thirteenth, and<br>– Sixteenth month<br>after the start of the chargeable accounting period |
| Self assessment<br>– Filing dates | Later of:<br>– 12 months from the end of the chargeable accounting period<br>– 3 months form the issue of a notice to deliver a corporation tax return |
| HMRC right to repair<br>(i.e. to correct mistakes) | 9 months from the date the return was filed |
| Companies right to amend a return | 12 months from the filing date |
| Companies error or mistake claim | 4 years from the end of the chargeable accounting period |
| HMRC can open an enquiry | 12 months from the actual submission of the return |
| Retention of records | 6 years from the end of the chargeable accounting period |

**Value added tax**

| Election / claim | Time limit |
|---|---|
| Compulsory registration<br><br>– Historic test<br><br><br><br><br>Charge VAT<br><br><br><br><br><br>– Future test | Notify HMRC<br>– 30 days from end of the month in which the threshold was exceeded<br><br>Charge VAT<br>– Beginning of the month following the month in which the threshold was exceeded<br><br>Notify HMRC<br>– 30 days from the date it is anticipated that the threshold will be exceeded<br><br>Charge VAT<br>– the date it is anticipated that the threshold will be exceeded (i.e. the beginning of the 30 day period) |
| Compulsory deregistration | 30 days from cessation |
| Filing of VAT return and payment of VAT | End of month following the return period |

# Income tax: Computation

## Chapter learning objectives

Upon completion of this chapter you will be able to:

- prepare an income tax computation for an individual given a range of different types of income/payments
- determine the taxability of the income of minor children

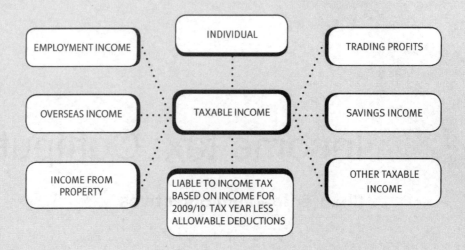

## 1 A revision of basic income tax

### Introduction

This and the following two chapters deal with the basic charge to income tax and national insurance, concentrating on an employed individual with property and investment income.

Much of this chapter is a revision of rules covered at F6 but there are some changes in the Finance Act 2009 that affect the operation of the income tax legislation.

A brief reminder of the F6 rules are given in expandable text and revision examples are provided to check your retention of the required F6 knowledge.

### Basis of assessment

Income tax is payable on an individual's taxable income for a tax year.

The 2010 examinations are based on the tax year 2009/10, which is from 6 April 2009 to 5 April 2010.

Individual taxpayers, married or single, are taxed separately on their own taxable income.

### Taxable income

A reminder of the computation of taxable income, the classification of income and the rates of income tax is given in the proforma income tax computation below.

Remember that in the taxable income computation:

- all income is included **gross** in the income tax computation
- any exempt income is excluded.

## Exempt income

The following income is exempt from income tax:

- income from Individual Savings Accounts (ISAs)
- interest on National Savings Certificates
- interest on repayment of tax
- redundancy payments under the Employment Protection Act 1978
- scholarship income
- gaming, lottery and premium bond winnings
- state benefits paid in the event of accident, sickness, disability or infirmity
- working tax credit and child tax credit.

## Proforma income tax computation

**Name of individual**
**Income tax computation – 2009/10**

| | Notes | £ |
|---|---|---|
| Earned income | | |
|     Employment income | | x |
|     Trading profits | | x |
|     Other earned income | 1 | x |
| Savings income | | |
|     Interest received net (× 100/80) | 2 | x |
|     Other interest | 3 | x |
| Other investment income | | |
|     Property income | | x |
|     Other types of investment income | 4 | x |
| Dividend income | | |
|     Dividends received from UK companies (× 100/90) | | x |
|     Other dividends | 5 | x |
| | | ___ |
| **Total income** | | x |
| Less **Reliefs** | | |
|     Qualifying loan interest (gross amount paid) | 6 | (x) |
|     Loss reliefs | 7 | (x) |
| | | ___ |
| **Net income** | | x |
| Less Personal Allowance (PA) | 8 | (6,475) |
| | | ___ |
| **Taxable income** | | x |
| | | ___ |

| | Notes | £ |
|---|---|---|
| Income tax (calculated at relevant rates) | 9 | x |
| Less EIS and VCT relief (20%/30%) | 10 | (x) |
|     Double taxation relief (DTR) | 11 | (x) |
| | | ___ |
| **Income tax liability** | | x |
| Less Tax credits | 12 | (x) |
| | | ___ |
| **Income tax payable by self assessment** | | x |
| | | ___ |

KAPLAN PUBLISHING

**Notes to computation:**

(1) **Other earned income** includes:

    –    pensions from former employment

    –    state pensions

    –    profits from furnished holiday lettings (Chapter 3).

(2) **Interest received net** includes:

    –    bank and building society interest

    –    corporate bond interest (e.g. debenture and loan stock interest)

    –    interest from an 'interest in possession' (IIP) trust (Chapter 14).

(3) **Other interest income** includes:

    –    interest received gross (e.g. gilt-edged security interest, NSB interest)

    –    foreign interest (gross of overseas tax suffered) (Chapter 10)

(4) **Other types of investment income** includes:

    –    annuity income (income element only)

    –    other income from an IIP trust (× 100/80) (Chapter 14)

    –    discretionary trust income (× 100/60) (Chapter 14)

    –    other foreign income (gross of overseas tax suffered) (Chapter 10)

    –    dividends from a real estate investment trust (REIT) (× 100/80) (Chapter 3)

(5) **Other dividend income** includes:

    –    dividends from an IIP trust (Chapter 14)

    –    foreign dividends (Chapter 10)

(6) **Reliefs:**

    –    The term 'charges on income' no longer exists. Former 'charges on income' are renamed 'reliefs' but are still treated in the same way (i.e. the gross amount paid in the tax year is an allowable deduction).

    –    Qualifying loan interest payments are the only former 'charge on income' which are relevant allowable reliefs for the P6 examination.

    –    Note that the rules for patent royalties have changed with the introduction of ITA 2007.

(7) **Loss reliefs** are covered in detail in Chapters 17 and 18.

(8) If the taxpayer is aged 65 or over at the end of the tax year, the **personal age allowance** may be available.

(9) The following **rates of incometax** apply in 2009/10:

| Income level | Band | Applicable rate | | |
|---|---|---|---|---|
| | | Other income | Savings (see note below) | Dividends |
| First £37,400 | Basic rate | 20% | 20% | 10% |
| £37,401 and over | Higher rate | 40% | 40% | 32.5% |

**Savings income** is normally taxed in the same way as 'other income' at the basic and higher rates of tax (20% and 40%).

However, a starting rate of tax of 10% applies to the first £2,440 of savings income in certain limited circumstances.

Savings income is treated as the next slice of taxpayer's income after 'other income' (i.e. employment income, trading income and property income) has been taxed.

The 10% starting rate only applies where savings income falls into the first £2,440 of taxable income.

Therefore, a taxpayer with taxable savings income will be taxed according to the level of their 'other income' as follows:

| 'Other income' | | Taxed at |
|---|---|---|
| None | First £2,440 of taxable savings income<br>Next £34,960<br>Balance above £37,400 | 10%<br>20%<br>40% |
| Below £2,440 | Taxable savings income falling into the first £2,440<br>Next £34,960<br>Balance above £37,400 | 10%<br>20%<br>40% |
| In excess of £2,440 | The 10% rate is not applicable<br>Taxable savings income falling into the first £37,400<br>Balance above £37,400 | <br>20%<br>40% |

Remember to:

–   tax income in the following order:

    –   other income

    –   savings

    –   dividends

KAPLAN PUBLISHING

- extend the basic rate band by the **gross amount paid** in the tax year of:

    - **personal pension plan** (PPP) contributions and free standing additional voluntary contributions paid into a registered pension scheme (Chapter 4), and

    - **Gift Aid donations.**(However, note that although donations to charity by an individual are examinable at F6, they are not examinable at P6).

(10) Relief under EIS and VCTs is covered in Chapter 3.

(11) Double taxation relief (DTR) and the treatment of overseas income is covered in Chapter 10.

(12) The tax credit on dividends is not repayable. The tax credit on dividends is deducted first to ensure the maximum benefit of relief is obtained.

## Example 1 – Income tax computation

Jeremy has trading income of £8,000 in 2009/10. In addition he received bank interest of £800 and dividend income of £1,800.

**Calculate his income tax payable for 2009/10.**

**Solution**

| Income tax computation – 2009/10 | £ |
| --- | --- |
| Trading Income | 8,000 |
| Bank interest received (£800 × 100/80) | 1,000 |
| UK Dividends received (£1,800 × 100/90) | 2,000 |
| | |
| Total Income | 11,000 |
| Less PA | (6,475) |
| | |
| Taxable income | 4,525 |

**Analysis of income**

| Dividends | Savings | Other income |
| --- | --- | --- |
| £2,000 | £1,000 | (£4,525– £2,000 – £1,000) = £1,525 |

**Income tax**

| | £ | £ |
|---|---|---|
| 1,525 × 20% (other income) | | 305 |
| 915 × 10% (savings income) (Note) | | 91 |
| **2,440** | | |
| 85 × 20% (savings income) | | 17 |
| 2,000 × 10% (dividend income) | | 200 |
| **4,525** | | |
| Income tax liability | | 613 |
| Less Tax credits: | | |
| Dividends | | (200) |
| Bank interest | | (200) |
| Income tax payable | | 213 |

**Note:** As 'other income' is less than £2,440, savings income up to £2,440 is taxed at 10%.

### Test your understanding 1

Tony has earnings from his employment of £37,000, from which PAYE of £6,105 was deducted.

He owns two let properties showing a total profit for the year of £3,000.

His investment income comprises of dividends from UK companies of £3,600 and bank interest of £800.

**Calculate Tony's tax payable for 2009/10.**

### Qualifying loan interest

A reminder of the types of loan interest qualifying for relief as an allowable deduction in an income tax computation is given in expandable text and is summarised in the diagram in section 2.

KAPLAN PUBLISHING

## Qualifying loan interest

- Relief is given for interest paid on loans incurred to finance expenditure for a qualifying purpose.

- Relief may be claimed for any payment of interest other than interest paid in excess of a reasonable commercial rate.

Note that qualifying loan interest is paid gross and the gross amount paid in the tax year is an allowable relief against total income.

The main types of qualifying purposes to which the loan must be applied are as follows:

### (1) Partnerships

The contribution of capital into a partnership.

A loan made by a partner for the purchase of plant or machinery for use in the partnership – year of purchase and next three years.

### (2) Close Companies

The purchase of ordinary shares in, or loans to, a 'close' trading company (Chapter 26).

The following conditions must be satisfied:

- the individual owns at least 5% of the ordinary share capital at the time the interest is paid; or

- they own some shares in the company at the time the interest is paid and, during the period from the purchase of the shares until the payment of the interest, they must have worked for the greater part of their time in the actual management of the company.

### (3) Employee-controlled companies

Relief is available to full-time employees for loans taken out to acquire ordinary shares in an employee-controlled, UK resident, unquoted trading company.

### (4) Personal Representatives

The payment of inheritance tax on the deceased's personal estate. Relief is available for one year only.

### The treatment of royalties paid by an individual

Patent and copyright royalties payable for trading purposes (calculated on an accruals basis) are an allowable deduction in calculating the adjusted trading profits of a business.

Copyright royalties are paid gross and patent royalties continue to be paid net of the basic rate of income tax (20%), but the income tax retained at source by the business is collected by HMRC under the self assessment rules.

The collection of the basic rate tax on patent royalties is not examinable at P6.

### Personal allowances

### Personal Allowance (PA)

All individuals (including children) are entitled to a personal allowance to be set against net income.

- The amount for 2009/10 is £6,475.
- The PA is deducted from other income first, then savings, then dividends.
- Unused PA is lost, it can not be transferred to any other tax payer.

### Personal age allowance (PAA)

- Taxpayers aged 65 and over **at any time** in the year of assessment are entitled to a higher rate of personal allowance.
- Those aged 65 – 74 get a higher rate (£9,490).
- Those aged 75 and over get the highest rate (£9,640).
- The PAA is given in the tax year in which the 65th or 75th birthday falls, even if the taxpayer dies before their birthday.
- If the taxpayer's 'net income (after reliefs)' is above £22,900, there is a reduction in the age related allowance, calculated as follows:
    - **50% × (net income less £22,900)**
    - the reduction cannot reduce the allowance to less than the minimum PA allowance of £6,475.
- If applicable, the 'net income (after reliefs)' must be reduced by the gross amount of any PPP contributions and Gift Aid donations paid in the tax year before comparing to the £22,900 limit to decide the amount of PAA available.

**Test your understanding 2**

Mr Brown, a widower who was born in 1936, is employed by the local bank.

For 2009/10 he received a salary of £39,850 and benefits of £4,750. PAYE of £7,700 was deducted at source.

Mr Brown also received the following amounts from his investments in 2009/10:

|  | £ |
|---|---|
| Building society interest | 1,568 |
| Interest on holding of £10,000 of 13% Treasury Stock 2011 | 1,300 (gross) |
| Dividends | 900 |

Mr Brown cashed in some National Savings Certificates, which he had purchased for £1,200 in 2000, from which he received £2,490.

In April 2009 Mr Brown invested £3,600 in an Individual Savings Account. The account was credited with £150 of interest by 5 April 2010.

Mr Brown also paid £600 of interest on a loan taken out to purchase shares in an employee controlled company.

**Calculate the income tax payable by Mr Brown for 2009/10.**

## The taxation of families

### The taxation of couples

Each partner in the couple is taxed separately.

However, there are special rules governing the allocation of income between the partners where assets are jointly owned:

- Generally, income generated from assets owned jointly will be split 50:50 regardless of the actual percentage ownership.

- Where jointly owned assets are held other than in a 50:50 ratio, an election can be made to HMRC for the income to be taxed on the individual partners according to their actual ownership.

- Where the jointly owned asset is shares in a close company, income is automatically taxed on the individual partners according to their actual ownership.

These rules apply to husband and wife couples, and civil partnerships.

## The taxation of children

All income of a child is assessable to income tax.

- The child has their own income tax computation.
- The child also has full entitlement to a PA, even in the year of birth.
- Returns and claims would be completed on behalf of the child by a parent or guardian.

Where the child has received taxed income, a repayment of tax will probably arise.

To avoid having to make repayment claims it is usual to complete a form R85 on each bank or building society account held by a child to authorise interest to be paid gross. The child's income, however, must be fully covered by the PA.

Income derived from a source set up by a parent is assessed on the parent, not the child, unless the income is £100 or less in a year assessment and the child is under 18 (and unmarried).

Full details regarding parental dispositions is given in expandable text.

### Parental disposition

There is an exception to income received by a child being treated as the child's income:

- where a child under the age of 18 (and unmarried) has investment income that is derived from capital provided by a parent, the income is treated as belonging to the parent (if the parent is still alive) rather than the child
- the capital could be provided by means of a formal trust or settlement or could simply be a gift of money (e.g. opening an NSB account in the child's name) or shares
- if the income does not exceed £100 in a year of assessment, then it is not taxed on the parent and is taxed as the child's income.

### Test your understanding 3

Kate, aged 38, has the following income, outgoings and allowances for the year ended 5 April 2010. She is married to Norman.

|  | £ |
|---|---|
| Salary | 38,600 |
| Benefits, assessable as employment income | 1,875 |
| Allowable expenses of employment | (95) |
| Bank interest received | 520 |
| Building society interest received | 892 |
| Interest from an ISA account | 500 |

Norman and Kate have a daughter, Ashleigh, aged 10. Ashleigh was given £5,000 of 3½% War loan on 6 April 2009 as a birthday present by Kate. Interest is received gross.

On 15 November 2009 Norman and Kate jointly bought a property that has been let out as unfurnished accommodation. The assessable property income for 2009/10 is £4,100. No declaration has been made in respect of this source of income.

**Calculate the income tax payable by Kate for 2009/10.**

## 2 Chapter Summary

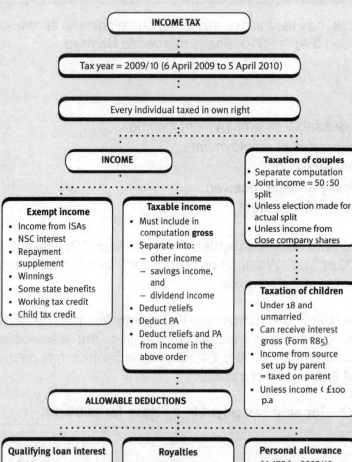

**INCOME TAX**

Tax year = 2009/10 (6 April 2009 to 5 April 2010)

Every individual taxed in own right

**INCOME**

**Taxation of couples**
- Separate computation
- Joint income = 50 : 50 split
- Unless election made for actual split
- Unless income from close company shares

**Exempt income**
- Income from ISAs
- NSC interest
- Repayment supplement
- Winnings
- Some state benefits
- Working tax credit
- Child tax credit

**Taxable income**
- Must include in computation **gross**
- Separate into:
  - other income
  - savings income, and
  - dividend income
- Deduct reliefs
- Deduct PA
- Deduct reliefs and PA from income in the above order

**Taxation of children**
- Under 18 and unmarried
- Can receive interest gross (Form R85)
- Income from source set up by parent = taxed on parent
- Unless income ‹ £100 p.a

**ALLOWABLE DEDUCTIONS**

**Qualifying loan interest**
- Paid gross
- Deduct gross amount paid in tax year
- Qualifying loan = loan to:
  - Contribute into a partnership
  - Buy shares in a close company
  - Buy shares in an employee controlled company
  - Enable an executor to pay IHT on an estate

**Royalties**
- Not an allowable deduction against total income
- Treat as an allowable deduction from trading income on an accruals basis
- Patent royalties paid net of 20% tax
- Copyright royalties paid gross

**Personal allowance**
- £6,475 for 2009/10
- unused amount = lost

**Personal age allowance**
- Available if 65 and over
- Amount depends on age at end of tax year
- Reduce allowance if 'net income (after reliefs)' is > £22,900
- Reduce by: 50% x (Net income less £22,900)
- Deduct gross PPP and GA payments from net income to calculate PAA

## Test your understanding answers

### Test your understanding 1

**Tony**

| **Income tax computation – 2009/10** | £ |
|---|---|
| Employment income | 37,000 |
| Bank interest (£800 × 100/80) | 1,000 |
| UK dividends (£3,600 × 100/90) | 4,000 |
| Property income | 3,000 |
| Total income | 45,000 |
| Less: PA | (6,475) |
| Taxable income | 38,525 |

Analysis of income:

| **Dividends** | **Savings** | **Other income** |
|---|---|---|
| £4,000 | £1,000 | (£38,525 - £4,000 - £1,000) = £33,525 |

| | £ | £ |
|---|---|---|
| Other income | 33,525 × 20% | 6,705 |
| Savings income | 1,000 × 20% | 200 |
| Dividend income | 2,875 × 10% | 287 |
| | 1,125 × 32.5% | 366 |
| | 38,525 | |
| Income tax liability | | 7,558 |
| Less Tax credits | | |
| Dividends | | (400) |
| Interest | | (200) |
| PAYE | | (6,105) |
| Income tax payable | | 853 |

**Note:** The starting rate for saving income is not applicable as 'other income' exceeds the £2,440 band limit.

## Test your understanding 2

**Mr Brown**

### Income tax computation – 2009/10

|  | £ |
|---|---|
| Employment income (£39,850 + £4,750) | 44,600 |
| Building society interest (× 100/80) | 1,960 |
| Government stock interest | 1,300 |
| Dividends (× 100/90) | 1,000 |
|  | ——— |
| Total income | 48,860 |
| Less: Reliefs – loan interest | (600) |
|  | ——— |
| Net income | 48,260 |
| Less: PA (Note 2) | (6,475) |
|  | ——— |
| Taxable income | 41,785 |
|  | ——— |

Analysis of income:

| **Dividends** | **Savings** | **Other income** |
|---|---|---|
| £1,000 | £3,260 | (£41,785 – £1,000 – £3,260) = £37,525 |

|  |  | £ | £ |
|---|---|---|---|
| Other income |  | 37,400 × 20% | 7,480 |
|  |  | 125 × 40% | 50 |
| Savings income |  | 3,260 × 40% | 1,304 |
| Dividend income |  | 1,000 × 32.5% | 325 |
|  |  | ——— |  |
|  |  | 41,785 |  |
|  |  | ——— |  |
| Income tax liability |  |  | 9,159 |
| Less Tax credits: |  |  |  |
| Dividends (£1,000 × 10%) |  |  | (100) |
| Savings (£1960 × 20%) |  |  | (392) |
| PAYE |  |  | (7,700) |
|  |  |  | ——— |
| Income tax payable |  |  | 967 |
|  |  |  | ——— |

**Notes:**

(1) Income from ISAs and encashments of National Savings Certificates are exempt from income tax.

(2) Mr Brown is entitled to the age allowance of £9,490, but as his net income (after reliefs) is £48,260, the PAA is restricted to the basic PA of £6,475.

(3) The starting rate for savings income is not applicable as taxable 'other income' exceeds the £2,440 band limit.

### Test your understanding 3

**Kate**

**Income tax computation – 2009/10**

|  | £ | £ |
|---|---:|---:|
| Employment income (£38,600 + £1,875 – £95) |  | 40,380 |
| Bank interest (£520 × 100/80) | 650 |  |
| Building society interest (£892 × 100/80) | 1,115 |  |
| War loan interest (Note 2) (3.5% × £5,000) | 175 |  |
| Interest from an ISA account (exempt) | Nil |  |
|  |  | 1,940 |
| Property income (Note 1) |  | 2,050 |
|  |  |  |
| Total income |  | 44,370 |
| Less PA |  | (6,475) |
|  |  |  |
| Taxable income |  | 37,895 |

**Analysis of income:**

| Dividends | Savings | Other income |
|---|---|---|
| £NIL | £1,940 | (£37,895 – £1,940) = £35,955 |

**Income tax**

| £ | | £ |
|---|---|---|
| 35,955 | × 20% (other income) | 7,191 |
| 1,445 | × 20% (savings) | 289 |
| —— | | |
| 37,400 | | |
| 495 | × 40% (savings) | 198 |
| —— | | |
| 37,895 | | |
| —— | | |
| Income tax liability | | 7,678 |
| Less Tax credits | | |
| Interest (20% × (£650 + £1,115)) | | (353) |
| | | —— |
| Income tax payable | | 7,325 |
| | | —— |

**Notes:**

(1) The property income, being joint income, is divided between Norman and Kate on a 50:50 basis (£4,100 ÷ 2 = £2,050).

(2) The War Loan interest is assessed on Kate because her daughter is under 18 and unmarried and the income is derived from capital provided by the parent, and the income is more than £100.

KAPLAN PUBLISHING

# Employment income and related NIC

## Chapter learning objectives

Upon completion of this chapter you will be able to:

- recognise the factors that determine whether an engagement is treated as employment or self-employment and state the differences in the tax treatment

- given details of a remuneration package calculate the employment income assessable taking into account any allowable deductions

- explain the basis of determining whether an individual is a P11D employee

- explain the purpose of a dispensation

- distinguish between the structure of a share option scheme and other share awards to employees

- differentiate between the taxation consequences of unapproved and approved share option schemes

- describe the operation of the various share incentive schemes and identify the key requirements for approval

- identify how an employer would choose which approved scheme to offer

- identify the income tax and NIC treatment of lump sum receipts from employment

- summarise the different classes of national insurance relevant to employers and employees and calculate amounts due.

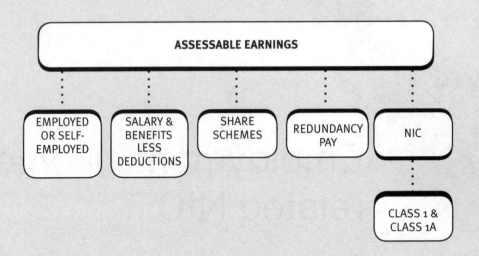

## 1 Introduction

This chapter is mainly a revision of the income tax implications of being employed covered in F6.

A brief reminder of F6 content is given in expandable text and revision examples are provided to check your retention of the required F6 knowledge.

The main new topics introduced are the tax implications of shares schemes and the treatment of termination payments. Recommendation of a suitable approved share scheme based on the facts in a particular situation is a common requirement in the examination.

### Employment status

The distinction between employment and self-employment is fundamental:

*   an employee is taxable under the employment income provisions
*   a self-employed person is assessed on the profits derived from his trade, profession or vocation under the rules governing trading income.

HMRC look at various factors, laid down by statute and case law decisions, to decide whether an individual is employed or self-employed.

The factors considered to determine employment of self-employment status are frequently examined.

## Factors of employment or self-employment

The primary test to consider is the nature of the contract that exists:

- Employment contract of service
- Self employment contract for services

However, even in the absence of a contract of service the following factors would be taken into account when deciding whether an employment exists:

- Obligation – by the 'employer' to offer work and the 'employee' to undertake the work offered. An 'employee' would not normally be in a position to decline work when offered.

- Control – the manner and method of the work being controlled by the 'employer'.

- Fixed hours – the 'employee' being committed to work a specified number of hours at certain fixed times.

- Integration – the work performed by the 'employee' is an integral part of the business of the 'employer' and not merely an accessory to it.

- Risk – the economic reality of self-employment is missing – namely the financial risk arising from not being paid an agreed, regular remuneration.

- Equipment – the use of equipment can be a useful factor in determining 'employee' status.

- Rights – if the person has rights under employment legislation, or has the right to receive regular remuneration, holiday pay, redundancy pay or benefits.

- Source of work – how many different sources of income does the individual have.

The tax status of an individual is very important in determining how earnings are taxed. A summary of the key differences is set out below.

|  | **Self-employed** | **Employee** |
|---|---|---|
| **Income tax** | • Trading profits: current year basis<br>• Expenses: 'wholly and exclusively' | • Employment income: receipts basis<br>• Expenses. 'wholly exclusively and necessarily' |
| **Payment of income tax** | • Self assessment | • Monthly – PAYE |
| **NICs** | • Class 2 – flat weekly rate<br>• Class 4 based on profits | • Class 1 primary |
| **Payment of NICs** | • Class 2 – monthly, direct debit<br>• Class 4 – with income tax | • Monthly – PAYE |
| **Pensions** | • Personal pension scheme | • Occupational pension scheme or<br>• Personal pension scheme |
| **VAT** | • Register<br>• Reclaim input VAT | • Suffer input VAT |

KAPLAN PUBLISHING

## 2 Calculation of employment income

### Proforma – Employment income computation

| | £ | £ |
|---|---|---|
| Salary | | X |
| Bonus/Commission | | X |
| Benefits | | X |
| Reimbursed expenses | | X |
| Cash vouchers | | X |
| | | ___ |
| | | X |
| | | |
| Less: Allowable deductions | | |
|     – Expenses incurred wholly, exclusively, necessarily | | (X) |
|     – Contributions to employer's pension plan | | (X) |
|     – Subscriptions to professional bodies | | (X) |
|     – Travel and subsistence expenses | | (X) |
|     – Deficit on mileage allowance | | (X) |
|     – Cost of any shares acquired in a SIP | | (X) |
| | | ___ |
| | | X |
| | | |
| Add: Redundancy payment | X | |
| Less: Exemption | (X) | |
| | ___ | |
| Employment income | | X |
| | | ___ |

### Basis of assessment

Directors and employees are assessed on the amount of earnings received in the tax year (the **receipts basis**).

### Earnings

The term 'earnings' includes cash wages or salary, bonuses, commission and benefits made available by the employer.

---

**Earnings**

The following state benefits are also subject to income tax:

- Statutory sick pay (SSP).

- Statutory maternity pay (SMP).

- Retirement pension and bereavement benefits.

- The jobseeker's allowance which is paid to the unemployed.

Earnings can include amounts paid for services rendered in the past or to be rendered in the future.

**'Golden hellos':**

- A payment made to induce an individual to enter into employment will be taxable unless it represents compensation paid for giving up something received under their previous employment in order to enter into the current employment.

**Third party payments:**

- Payments made by persons other than the employer if they relate to the provision of services. This would include, for example, tips received by a taxi-driver or waiter.

**'Golden handshakes' and restrictive covenant payments:**

- A payment made to an employee in return for an undertaking to restrict his activities. An example would be where the employee agrees not to work for a competitor within a set period of time after leaving his current employment.

### The receipts basis

The date of receipt is the **earlier** of:

- the actual date of payment, or
- the date the individual becomes entitled to the payment.

In the case of directors who are in a position to manipulate the timings of payments there are extra rules. They are deemed to receive earnings on the **earlier** of:

- the actual date of payment
- the date the individual becomes entitled to the payment
- when sums on account of earnings are credited in the accounts
- at the end of a period of account, where earnings are determined before the end of that period
- when the amount of earnings for a period are determined, if that is after the end of that period.

## Test your understanding 1

Broadfoot, a director of RIK Ltd, received a bonus of £25,000 on 1 September 2009.

The bonus related to the results of the company for the year ended 31 March 2009. It was credited to Broadfoot in the accounts on 15 July 2009 following a board meeting on 30 June 2009.

**Advise when the bonus is assessable as employment income.**

## Allowable deductions

The general rule is that expenditure will only be deductible if it is incurred **wholly, exclusively** and **necessarily in the performance** of the duties.

The other types of allowable expenditure shown in the proforma computation are specifically permitted by statute law.

A reminder of the rules for travel expenses and the mileage allowance deduction is given in expandable text and is summarised in the diagram below.

## Travel expenditure

Travelling expenses may be deducted only where they:

- are incurred necessarily in the performance of the duties of the employment, or
- are attributable to the necessary attendance at any place by the employee in the performance of their duties.

Relief is not given for the cost of journeys that are ordinary commuting or for the cost of private travel.

- Ordinary commuting is the journey made each day between home and a permanent workplace.
- Private travel is a journey between home and any other place that an employee does not have to attend for the purposes of their employment.

Relief is given where an employee travels directly from home to a **temporary** place of work.

- A temporary workplace is defined as one where an employee goes to perform a task of limited duration, or for a temporary purpose.

- However, a place of work will not be classed as a temporary workplace where an employee works there continuously for a period that lasts, or is expected to last, more than 24 months.

Where an employee passes their normal permanent workplace on the way to a temporary workplace, relief will still be available provided the employee does not stop at the normal workplace, or any stop is incidental e.g. to pick up some papers.

Where an employee's business journey qualifies for relief, then the amount of relief is the full cost of that journey. There is no need to take account of any savings the employee makes by not having to make his or her normal commuting journey to work.

## Approved Mileage Allowance Payments

Employees who use their own vehicles for work will normally be paid a mileage allowance.

There are approved mileage allowance payment (AMAP) rates set by HMRC as follows:

| Cars and vans (these rates given in the examination): | |
| --- | --- |
| First 10,000 miles p.a. | 40p |
| Over 10,000 miles p.a. | 25p |
| Passenger rate | 5p |
| Motorcycles | 24p |
| Bicycles | 20p |

- Provided the mileage allowance received is within these rates; no assessable benefit arises.

- Where the mileage allowance received is:

| | Effect on employment income: |
| --- | --- |
| > AMAP rates | Excess = assessable benefit |
| < AMAP rates, or no allowance received | Difference = allowable deduction |

- However, no deduction claim is allowed for any shortfall on the passenger rate where less than 5p a mile is paid.

KAPLAN PUBLISHING

## Summary

```
                    ┌──────────────────────┐
                    │  Employment income   │
                    └──────────────────────┘
```

**Allowable deductions**

- Expenses incurred wholly, exclusively and necessarily
- Contributions to employer's pension plan
- Subscriptions to professional bodies
- Travel expenditure
- AMAPs

**AMAPs**

- Tax free mileage allowance for use of own vehicle for work
- If mileage allowance received > AMAP:
  - Excess = benefit
- If mileage allowance received < AMAP:
  - Difference = allowable deduction

**Travel expenditure**

- Must be necessarily incurred in performance of duties
- Relief available for travel to temporary workplace
- No relief for
  - Ordinary commuting
  - Private travel
- Do not reduce travel to temporary workplace for travel from home to normal place of work

### Test your understanding 2

Bernard uses his own car for business purposes for which his employer pays an agreed allowance. Bernard drives 12,000 business miles in 2009/10.

**Calculate the assessable benefit on Bernard or the mileage expenses claim for 2009/10 assuming Bernard's employer pays (a) 20p per mile or (b) 45p per mile.**

## 3 Employment benefits

### Introduction

The benefit rules were covered in detail at F6 and the rules have not changed in FA2009. This section provides a reminder of the key rules that need to be retained for P6.

There are three main types of employment benefits:

- Exempt benefits

- Benefits assessable on all employees

- Benefits assessable only on directors and employees earning at a rate of £8,500 p.a. or more (known as P11D employees or 'higher paid employees').

Note that a benefit is taxable if

- it arises 'by reason of employment', and
- is provided either to the employee or to a member of his family or household
- either directly by the employer or by a third party.

The following table summarises the key assessable benefits:

| **Assessable on all employees** | **Assessable on P11D employees only** |
|---|---|
| General rule = Assessed on:<br><br>• Cash equivalent value of the benefits | General rule = Assessed on:<br><br>• Cost to the employer<br>• Marginal cost to the employer if an 'in house' benefit |
| Specific valuation rules for some benefits:<br><br>• Non-cash vouchers<br>• Credit cards<br>• Living accommodation | Specific valuation rules for some benefits:<br><br>• Expenses relating to living accommodation<br>• Use and gift of assets<br>• Cars, fuel and vans<br>• Beneficial loans<br>• Scholarships<br>• Payment of a director's liability |

Remember that:

- Where a benefit is only available for part of the year; the assessable amount is time apportioned.
- Where an employee contributes towards the benefit; the employee contribution is an allowable deduction (exception = the provision of private fuel).
- Where employers provide in-house benefits (such as free air tickets for employees of an airline) the measure of the benefit is the additional or marginal cost incurred by the employer, not a proportion of the total cost.

## PIID employees

- To determine whether an individual is a P11D employee, 'total earnings' are compared to £8,500 as follows:

|  | £ |
|---|---|
| Cash earnings (e.g. salary, bonuses and other cash remuneration, including reimbursed expenses) | X |
| Plus Benefits assessable on all employees | X |
| Plus Benefits assessable only on P11D employees | X |
|  | X |
| Less: Contributions to employer's pension plan | (X) |
| Less: Donations to charity under payroll giving scheme | (X) |
| Total earnings (for £8,500 test purposes) | X |

    Note that for the purposes of this test, the calculation includes all potential benefits.

- If the total earnings for the test is £8,500 or more, the individual is a P11D employee and is assessed on all of the benefits.

- If the total for the test is less than £8,500, the individual is only assessed on those benefits relating to all employees.

- Directors are automatically subject to the P11D benefit rules unless:
  - they are a full time working director
  - earn less than £8,500, and
  - do not have a material interest in the company (i.e. they own less than 5% of the ordinary share capital).

## Exempt benefits

A reminder of the rules relating to the types of exempt benefits is given in expandable text and the examples include some exempt benefits to check your retention of the required F6 knowledge.

## Exempt benefits

- Employer's contribution to a registered pension scheme
- Pensions advice up to £150 per employee per year
- Subsidised canteen facilities
- Luncheon vouchers up to 15p per day
- Car parking space
- Provision of work buses, bicycles, subsidies for public transport
- One mobile phone per employee
- Work related training provided by employer
- In-house sports and recreational facilities
- Staff parties of up to £150 p.a. per employee
- Entertainment from a third party to generate goodwill and gifts from a third party up to £250 from any one source in a tax year
- Welfare counselling
- Workplace nurseries
- Child care costs up to £55 per week
- Contribution towards home worker expenses up to £3 per week without documentation, more with documentation
- Job related accommodation
- Relocation and removal expenses up to £8,000
- Overnight expenses up to £5 per night in UK and £10 per night overseas
- Employer liability insurance, death in service benefits and permanent health insurance
- Medical insurance and treatment while working abroad
- Eye care tests
- Long service awards up to £50 per year of service

## Specific benefits assessable on all employees

| Benefit | Valuation rule |
|---|---|
| • Non-cash vouchers | • Cost to employer of providing voucher |
| • Credit cards | • Cost charged to card for personal use |
| • Living accommodation | • Two key benefits to assess |

A reminder of the rules relating to the living accommodation benefits assessed on all employees is given in expandable text and the rules are summarised in the diagram in section 4.

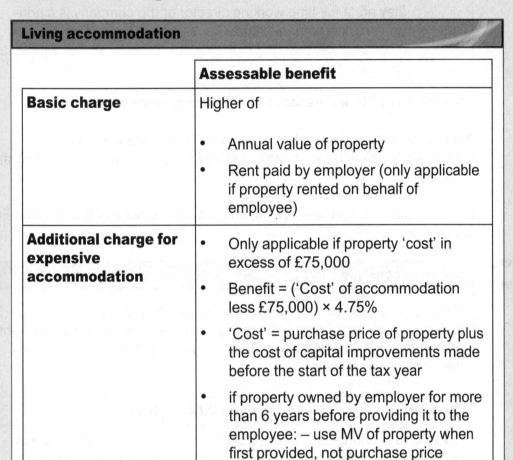

**Living accommodation**

| | Assessable benefit |
|---|---|
| **Basic charge** | Higher of<br><br>• Annual value of property<br><br>• Rent paid by employer (only applicable if property rented on behalf of employee) |
| **Additional charge for expensive accommodation** | • Only applicable if property 'cost' in excess of £75,000<br><br>• Benefit = ('Cost' of accommodation less £75,000) × 4.75%<br><br>• 'Cost' = purchase price of property plus the cost of capital improvements made before the start of the tax year<br><br>• if property owned by employer for more than 6 years before providing it to the employee: – use MV of property when first provided, not purchase price |

**Job related accommodation (JRA)**
No benefit arises where the property is job-related accommodation.

• To qualify as JRA, the property must be provided:
  – where it is necessary for the proper performance of the employee's duties (e.g. a caretaker)
  – for the better performance of the employee's duties and, for that type of employment, it is customary for employers to provide living accommodation (e.g. hotel-worker)
  – where there is a special threat to the employee's security and he resides in the accommodation as part of special security arrangements. (e.g. prime minister).

- A director can only claim one of the first two exemptions if:
  - they have no material interest in the company (i.e. holds no more than 5% in the company's ordinary share capital)
  - they are a full-time working director or the company is a non-profit making organisation.

## Specific benefits assessable on P11D employees only

A reminder of the rules relating to the benefits assessable on P11D employees is given in expandable text and are summarised in the diagram in section 4.

Revision examples are provided to check your retention of the required F6 knowledge.

### Living accommodation

Expenses connected with living accommodation (i.e. ancillary benefits), such as lighting and heating, and use of assets provided in the accommodation are taxable on an employee where the cost is met by the employer as follows:

| Benefit | If not JRA | If JRA |
|---|---|---|
| Expenses in connection with living accommodation | Cost to employer | Total benefits = limited to 10% rule (see note below) |
| Use of assets | 20% rule (see below) | |

**Notes**

- Ancillary benefits are only taxable on P11D employees (with the exception of council tax which is assessed on all employees).

- The 10% JRA limit applies to the following types of expense:
  - heating, lighting and cleaning
  - repairing, maintaining or decorating the premises, and
  - the use of furniture and other goods normal for domestic occupation.

- The total accommodation benefits assessed on a P11D employee for JRA is limited to 10% of 'net earnings'
  - 'net earnings' = employment income (including all assessable benefits other than the living accommodation ancillary benefits).

## Use of assets

Where the ownership of the asset is retained by employer, but the employee has private use of the asset, the assessable benefit is:

- 20% × open market value when first made available (usually cost).

- Where the employer rents the asset made available to the employee instead of buying it, the employee is taxed on the higher of:
  - the rent paid by employer
  - 20% rule.

- The provision of one mobile phone to an employee is an exempt benefit. However, the 20% rule will apply to any additional mobile phones provided.

## Example 1 – Living accommodation

Mr X, a director of X Ltd, lives in a furnished company flat that cost the company £105,000 in June 2006. The accommodation is not job related.

The annual value of the flat is £2,500 and Mr X pays X Ltd rent of £150 a month. Furniture was worth £6,000 in June 2006. The company pays £2,000 for the running costs of the flat and £1,500 in council tax. The official rate of interest is 4.75% for 2009/10.

**Calculate Mr X's total assessable benefits for 2009/10.**

**Solution**

| Total assessable benefits – 2009/10 | £ |
|---|---|
| Basic charge (annual value) | 2,500 |
| Further charge (£105,000 – £75,000) × 4.75% | 1,425 |
| Council tax | 1,500 |
| | ––––– |
| | 5,425 |
| Less Contribution (£150 × 12) | (1,800) |
| | ––––– |
| Accommodation Benefit | 3,625 |
| Use of furniture (20% × £6,000) | 1,200 |
| Living expenses benefit | 2,000 |
| | ––––– |
| Total assessable benefits | 6,825 |
| | ––––– |

## Gift of assets

- If an employer purchases a new asset and gives it to an employee immediately, the employee is taxed on the cost to the employer.

- Where an employee has had the private use of an asset which is then given to him, the employee is taxed on the higher of:

|  | £ | £ |
|---|---|---|
| (i) MV of asset when gifted | | X |
| (ii) MV of asset when first made available to the employee | X | |
| Less Benefits already assessed on employee for private use | (X) | |
| | | —X |

- Any employee contribution can be deducted from the assessable amounts computed according to the rules above

- Where the asset being given to an employee is a used car or van:
  - Benefit = MV at the date of transfer less any payment made by the employee for the asset.

## Example 2 – Use and gift of asset

Rooney was provided with a new video camera by his employer on 6 October 2007 costing £2,000. He was allowed to keep the camera on 5 January 2010 when its value was £500.

**Show the benefit assessable on Rooney for all years.**

**Solution**

**Assessable benefits**

|  |  | £ |
|---|---|---|
| 2007/08 | Use of asset: £2,000 × 20% × 6/12 | 200 |
| 2008/09 | Use of asset: £2,000 × 20% | 400 |
| 2009/10 | Use of asset: £2,000 × 20% × 9/12 | 300 |
| | Plus | |
| | Gift of asset: (working) | 1,100 |

**Working: Gift of asset**

| 2009/10 | Further benefit on gift of asset – higher of | £ | £ |
|---|---|---|---|
| | (i) MV at date of gift | | 500 |
| | (ii) Original MV | 2,000 | |
| | less: Assessed to date | (900) | |
| | (£200 + £400 + £300) | | 1,100 |
| | | | |
| | Thus total amount assessable in 2009/10 | | |
| | (£300 + £1,100) | | 1,400 |

## Company car benefit

- Where a car is made available for private use, the assessable benefit is:

| | £ |
|---|---|
| Appropriate % × List price of car when first registered | X |
| Less Employee contributions for private use of car | (X) |
| Assessable benefit | X |

- The list price of the car is the price when first registered
  - includes the cost of extras, both those provided with the car and any made available subsequently
  - can be reduced by any capital contribution made by the employee, subject to a maximum of £5,000
  - is subject to a maximum amount (after deducting capital contributions) of £80,000.

- The appropriate percentage:
  - depends on the rate at which the car emits carbon dioxide

- The rules can be summarised as follows:

| $CO_2$ emissions per km | Petrol car % | Diesel car |
|---|---|---|
| 120 grams or less | 10 | 13 |
| 121 – 135 grams | 15 | 18 |
| Each complete additional 5% emission above 135 grams | An additional 1% is added to the 15% or 18% up to a maximum % of 35 % | |

- The benefit charge is reduced by periods for which the car was unavailable for more than 30 days.

- The benefit is reduced if the employee makes contributions towards the running costs.

- The benefit takes into account all running expenses of the vehicle. Therefore there is no additional charge for insurance, repairs, car tax etc.

- A separate benefit applies if private fuel is provided.

- If more than one car is provided to employee/relative, then separate benefits for the car and private fuel are calculated for each car.

- No benefit on pool cars.

- The maximum % that can be applied to any car is 35%.

## Fuel Benefit

- Where an employer provides private fuel the benefit is:
  - same percentage used for car benefit × £16,900.

- The £16,900 is given in the tax rates and allowances in the examination.

- Contributions made by the employee towards the private fuel are ignored unless **all** private fuel is reimbursed in full (in which case no benefit arises).

- The benefit charge is reduced for periods of non-availability.

## Test your understanding 3

Charles took up employment with Weavers Ltd on 1 July 2009.

His remuneration package included a two-year old 2,500 cc petrol-driven car, list price £24,000. He took delivery of the car on 1 July 2009. The $CO_2$ emission rating is 257 gms/km.

As a condition of the car being made available to him for private motoring, Charles paid £100 per month for the car and £50 per month for petrol. Weavers Ltd incurred the following expenses in connection with Charles' car:

**Calculate Charles' assessable car and fuel benefits for 2009/10.**

|  | £ |
|---|---|
| Servicing | 450 |
| Insurance | 780 |
| Fuel (of which £1,150 was for business purposes) | 2,500 |
| Maintenance | 240 |

## Van benefit

Where a van is made available for private use to an employee the assessable benefit is:

- £3,000 pa for unrestricted private use of the van

- £500 pa if private fuel is provided by the employer.

- Both benefits are time apportioned if the van is unavailable to the employee for 30 days or more during any part of the tax year.

- Taking the van home at night is not treated as private use and incidental private use is also ignored.

- Contributions by the employee towards the van (not the fuel) reduce the benefit chargeable.

## Example 3 – Company Car vs Van

A plc is offering Tom two possible new vehicles for his private use. The first vehicle on offer is a petrol engined 1,500cc car with a list price of £15,000 including VAT and $CO_2$ emission of 117g/km.

The second vehicle is a petrol engined 1,500cc van with the same list price and $CO_2$ emission.

A plc will pay for all running costs including fuel for both vehicles.

**Compute the benefit assessable on Tom in 2009/10 for the two vehicles and advise him which one he should select. Tom is a higher rate taxpayer.**

## Solution

| | £ |
|---|---|
| **Option 1 – Provision of a company car** | |
| Car benefit (£15,000 × 10%) (W) | 1,500 |
| Fuel benefit (£16,900 × 10%) | 1,690 |
| | ———— |
| Total Benefits | 3,190 |
| | ———— |
| IT payable (40% × £3,190) | 1,276 |
| | ———— |

| | |
|---|---|
| **Option 2 – Provision of company van** | |
| Van benefit | 3,000 |
| Fuel benefit | 500 |
| | ———— |
| Total benefits | 3,500 |
| | ———— |
| IT payable (40% × £3,500) | 1,400 |
| | ———— |

### Conclusion

The company car would be more tax efficient for Tom

### Working: Appropriate percentage

$CO_2$ emissions are ≤ 120g/km, the appropriate percentage is 10%.

## Beneficial loan

- Beneficial loans are loans made to an employee with an interest rate below the official rate of interest (4.75% for 2009/10).

- The benefit is calculated as follows:

| | £ |
|---|---|
| Interest at the official rate (using either the average or precise method) | X |
| Less Interest actually paid in the tax year | (X) |
| | — |
| Assessable benefit | X |
| | — |

- A small loan exemption applies where the total of an employee's beneficial loans is ≤ £5,000.

KAPLAN PUBLISHING

- Two methods of calculating the interest at the official rate:
  - Average method = charge is based on the average capital

    (Opening balance + Closing balance) / 2 = average capital

  - Precise method = calculate interest on a day to day basis on the balance of the loan outstanding
- Either the taxpayer or HMRC can elect for the precise method.
- HMRC will only elect where it appears that the average method is being exploited or the precise method gives a materially higher figure.

## Example 4 – Beneficial loan

Daniel was granted a loan of £35,000 by his employer on 31 March 2009 to help finance the purchase of a yacht. Interest is payable on the loan at 3% per annum.

On 1 June 2009 Daniel repaid £5,000 and on 1 December 2009 he repaid a further £14,000. The remaining £16,000 was still outstanding on 5 April 2010. Daniel earns £30,000 per annum.

**Assuming that the official rate of interest is 4.75% p.a., calculate the assessable benefit for 2009/10 using both the average method and the precise method.**

### Solution

| Average method | | £ | £ |
|---|---|---|---|
| (£35,000 + £16,000) / 2 × 4.75% | | | 1,211 |
| Less: Interest paid | | | |
| 06.04.09 – 31.05.09 | £35,000 × 3% × 2/12 | 175 | |
| 01.06.09 – 30.11.09 | £30,000 × 3% × 6/12 | 450 | |
| 01.12.09 – 05.04.10 | £16,000 × 3% × 4/12 | 160 | |
| | | | (785) |
| | | | |
| Assessable benefit | | | 426 |

**Precise method**

|  |  | £ |
|---|---|---|
| 06.04.09 – 31.05.09 | £35,000 × 4.75% × 2/12 | 277 |
| 01.06.09 – 30.11.09 | £30,000 × 4.75% × 6/12 | 712 |
| 01.12.09 – 05.04.10 | £16,000 × 4.75% × 4/12 | 253 |
|  |  | 1,242 |
| Less: Interest paid – as above |  | (785) |
| Assessable benefit |  | 457 |

## Scholarships

If a scholarship is provided to a member of an individual's family or household, the cost of it is taxable as a benefit.

No taxable benefit arises where:

- the scholarship is awarded from a separate trust scheme

- the person receiving it is in full-time education at a school, college or university

- not more than 25% of payments made in the tax year from the scheme are made by reason of a person's employment.

Scholarship income is exempt in the hands of the recipient.

## Payment of director's tax liability

- Where tax should have been deducted from a director's earnings under the PAYE system, but was not, and the tax is paid over to HMRC by the employer, the director is treated as receiving a benefit.

- The benefit is the amount of tax accounted for, less any reimbursement by the director (if any).

- Note that this rule applies only to directors.

KAPLAN PUBLISHING

## Comprehensive example

### Test your understanding 4

Vigorous plc runs a health club. The company has three employees who received benefits during 2009/10 and it therefore needs to prepare forms P11D for them. Each of the three employees is paid an annual salary of £35,000. The following information is relevant:

**Andrea Lean**

(1) Andrea was employed by Vigorous plc throughout 2009/10.

(2) Throughout 2009/10 Vigorous plc provided Andrea with a 2200 cc petrol powered company motor car with a list price of £19,400. The official $CO_2$ emission rate for the motor car is 275 g/km. Vigorous plc paid for all of the motor car's running costs of £6,200 during 2009/10, including petrol used for private journeys. Andrea pays £150 per month to Vigorous plc for the use of the motor car.

(3) Vigorous plc has provided Andrea with living accommodation since 1 November 2007. The property was purchased on 1 January 2005 for £130,000. The company spent £14,000 improving the property during March 2006, and a further £8,000 was spent on improvements during May 2009. The value of the property on 1 November 2007 was £170,000, and it has a rateable value of £7,000. The furniture in the property cost £6,000 during November 2007. Andrea personally pays for the annual running costs of the property amounting to £4,000.

(4) Throughout 2009/10 Vigorous plc provided Andrea with a mobile telephone costing £500. The company paid for all business and private telephone calls.

**Ben Slim**

(1) Ben commenced employment with Vigorous plc on 1 July 2009.

(2) On 1 July 2009 Vigorous plc provided Ben with an interest free loan of £120,000 so that he could purchase a new main residence. He repaid £20,000 of the loan on 1 October 2009.

(3) During 2009/10 Vigorous plc paid £9,300 towards the cost of Ben's relocation. His previous main residence was 125 miles from his place of employment with the company. The £9,300 covered the cost of disposing of Ben's old property and of acquiring his new property.

(4) During the period from 1 October 2009 until 5 April 2010 Vigorous plc provided Ben with a new diesel powered company motor car which has a list price of £11,200. The official $CO_2$ emission rate for the motor car is 134 g/km. Ben reimburses Vigorous plc for all the diesel used for private journeys.

**Chai Trim**

(1) Chai was employed by Vigorous plc throughout 2009/10.

(2) During 2009/10 Vigorous plc provided Chai with a two-year old company van, which was available for private use. The van was unavailable during the period 1 August to 30 September 2009. Chai was also provided with private fuel for the van.

(3) Vigorous plc has provided Chai with a television for her personal use since 6 April 2007. The television cost Vigorous plc £800 in April 2007. On 6 April 2009 the company sold the television to Chai for £150, although its market value on that date was £250.

(4) Throughout 2009/10 Vigorous plc provided Chai with free membership of its health club. The normal annual cost of membership is £800. This figure is made up of direct costs of £150, fixed overhead costs of £400 and profit of £250. The budgeted membership for the year has been exceeded, but the health club has surplus capacity.

(5) On 1 January 2010 Vigorous plc provided Chai with a new computer costing £1,900. She uses the computer at home for personal study purposes.

**Calculate the benefit figures that Vigorous plc will have to include on the forms P11D for Andrea, Ben and Chai for 2009/10.**

## 4 Summary

Employment benefits

### Exempt benefits

- Employer's contribution to pension
- Pensions advice (up to £150)
- Subsidised canteen
- Car parking space
- Work buses, bicycles, subsidies for public transport
- One mobile phone per employee
- Work related training
- Sports and recreational facilities
- Staff parties (up to £150 p.a)
- Welfare counselling
- Workplace nurseries
- Child care costs up to £55 per week
- Home worker expenses (up to £3 per week)
- Job related accommodation
- Relocation expenses (up to £8,000)
- Overnight expenses (up to £5 per night in UK and £10 per night overseas)
- Employer liability insurance, death in service benefits and PHI

### Assessable on all employees

- **Non-cash vouchers:**
  - cost to employer
- **Credit card:**
  - cost charged to card for personal use
- **Living accommodation:**
  Basic charge = higher of
  (i)   annual value
  (ii)  rent paid by employer

  Expensive accommodation charge = (Cost less £75,000) x 4.75%

  Cost = purchase price

  Include improvements up to start of tax year

  If owned by employer for 6 years before first occupation:
  - Use MV when first provided, not purchase price

**Assessable on P11D employees**

General rule = Cost to employer ('in house' benefits = marginal cost)
- Deduct employee contributions
- Time apportion if not available all year

**Accommodation related benefits**

**Other benefits**

**Vehicle related benefits**

**Expenses for accommodation**
- Cost to employer

**Use of assets**
- 20% x MV when first available

**Job related accommodation**
- No basic charge
- No additional charge for expensive accommodation
- Expenses benefit and use of assets
  - If not P11D employee = no benefit
  - If P11D employee = restricted to (10% x employment income)

**Gift of assets**
- New asset gifted = cost to employer
- Use of asset followed by gift
  = Higher of
  (i) MV when gifted
  (ii) MV when first available less benefits already assessed

**Beneficial loan**
= interest at 4.75% less interest paid
- Average method = (op.balance + cl.balance) x 1/2 x 4.75%
- Precise method = daily rate applied to outstanding balance
- HMRC and taxpayers can elect for precise method
- No benefit if total loans < £5,000

**Cars**
= (Appropriate % x list price)
- Appropriate %
  - min 15% (petrol), 18% (diesel)
  - Add 1% for each 5 g/km over 135g
  - Max 35%
- Low emission cars < 120g
  - 10% petrol
  - 13% diesel
- List price (max £80,000)
  - Includes cost of extras
  - Deduct capital contribution (max £5,000)
- Unavailable > 30 days: time apportion
- No benefit on pool cars

**Fuel**
= (Appropriate % x £16,900)
- Appropriate %
  - Same as for car benefit
- Ignore employee contributions

**Company van**
- Private use = £3,000
- Private fuel = £500
- Unavailable > 30 days: time apportion

## 5 Dispensations

A dispensation is an agreement between an employer and HMRC not to report certain benefits provided to employees.

Full detail of the rules for dispensations is covered in expandable text.

### Dispensations

A dispensation usually applies:

- where all expenses paid to an employee are 'wholly, exclusively and necessarily' incurred in the duties of the employment.
- the employer has arranged to pay any tax due on assessable benefits by way of a PAYE settlement agreement (PSA).

If a dispensation has been granted:

- No report is required of any benefits covered by the dispensation.

Employers may make a PAYE settlement agreement with HMRC so that the employer pays the income tax and NIC arising on an employee's assessable benefits.

Employers pay NICs on the employee's tax paid under the PSA at 12.8%.

## 6 Share schemes

It has long been recognised by employers that there are commercial benefits in schemes to motivate employees that are linked to a company's profitability.

These may take the form of:

- Share incentives    - the allocation of company shares to the employee.

- Share options    - the grant of options to buy company shares in the future.

Successive governments have encouraged these incentives by giving tax privileges to schemes, provided that they meet the relevant requirements.

Schemes that satisfy conditions are known as **approved** schemes and those that do not are known as **unapproved** schemes.

### Share options

A share option is an offer to an employee of a right to purchase shares at a future date at a predetermined fixed price set at the time the offer is made.

The taxation consequences of share options depends on whether or not they are approved by HMRC as follows:

| Event | Unapproved | | Approved | |
|---|---|---|---|---|
| Granting of option. | No tax. | | No tax. | |
| Exercise of option. | **Income tax charge:** | £ | No tax. | |
| | MV @ exercise date | X | | |
| | Cost of option | (X) | | |
| | Cost of shares | (X) | | |
| | | — | | |
| | Employment income | X | | |
| | | — | | |
| | NIC charge if shares readily convertible into cash. (Note 1) | | | |
| Disposal of shares. | **Capital gain arises:** | £ | **Capital gain arises:** | £ |
| | Sale proceeds | X | Sale proceeds | X |
| | MV @ exercise date | (X) | Cost of option | (X) |
| | | — | Cost of shares | (X) |
| | Gain (Note 2) | X | | — |
| | | — | Gain (Note 2) | X |
| | | | | — |

**Notes:**

(1) Class 1A NIC will be payable by the employer unless the shares are quoted, in which case Class 1 will apply, which means the employee will also be liable.

(2) Entrepreneurs' relief will be available if the employee owns $\geq$ 5% shareholding in the company.

> ## Test your understanding 5
>
> Alan is employed by Sugar Ltd. On 1 July 2006 he was granted the option to buy 1,000 shares in Sugar Ltd for £2, their market value at that time.
>
> He exercises the option on 17 October 2009 when the shares are worth £4.50. On 20 October 2009 he sells them for £5 each.
>
> **Explain the tax implications of the above events assuming the scheme is approved or unapproved. The shareholding represents less than a 5% interest in the company.**

### Share incentives

An employer may gift shares in the employing company to an employee or allow the employee to buy them at a discounted price.

Where this happens the employee will include in their earnings the difference between the value of the shares and the price paid (if any) for the shares.

If the shares are quoted they are 'readily convertible' and so this amount will also be liable to Class 1 NIC.

Where they are unquoted, and not 'readily convertible' Class 1A NIC will apply.

### 7 Approved share option and incentive schemes

There are four types of scheme that receive favourable tax treatment:

- Savings-related share option schemes (SAYE)
- Company share option plans (CSOP)
- Enterprise management incentive scheme (EMI)
- Share incentive plans (SIP)

The detail of how each scheme operates and the conditions which must be satisfied is given in expandable text.

The conditions and key rules are summarised in the tables below.

| | CSOP | EMI | SAYE |
|---|---|---|---|
| **Participation** | Employer chooses | Employer chooses | All employees |
| **Maximum value** | £30,000 per employee | £120,000 per employee. Scheme max £3m | £250 per month |
| **Exercise period** | 3 – 10 years | Up to 10 years | 3,5 or 7 years |
| **Issue price** | MV | Issue at MV to avoid IT charge | Not < 80% of MV |
| **Other** | | Gross assets ≤ £30m Employees < 250 | |

| Share incentive plan (SIP) | |
|---|---|
| **Participation** | **All employees** |
| Awarded free shares | Max £3,000 per year |
| Purchase partnership shares | Max = lower of:<br><br>• £1,500, and<br>• 10% salary |
| Awarded matching shares | Max 2 per partnership share |
| Dividends | Tax free if invested in further shares. Max £1,500 p.a. |
| Holding period | 5 years for full benefit |
| Base cost of shares | MV when removed from plan |

## SAYE

There is favourable tax treatment for share option schemes that are linked to a SAYE (Save As You Earn) contract.

### How the scheme operates

- The employees pay a maximum of £250 per month into a SAYE scheme, for a period of 3, 5 or 7 years.
- Interest on the scheme is exempt from income tax.

- At the end of the scheme the money can be used to exercise the share options or the employee may just withdraw the money for their own use.

As an approved scheme:

- No income tax will be charged on the grant or exercise of the option.
- On the subsequent disposal of the shares, a capital gain may arise.

**Conditions for the SAYE scheme**

- All employees must be able to participate in the scheme on similar terms although there may be variations in respect of a minimum period of employment.
- The purchase price of the shares is usually met by the employee out of the SAYE accumulated savings.
- The price at which options are offered is not less than 80% of market value of the shares when the option was granted.
- Employees owning more than 25% of the company are ineligible to participate.
- The costs of setting up such a scheme are allowable as a trading expense for the company.

**Company share option plan (CSOP)**

- This type of approved share option scheme differs from the SAYE schemes described above in that:
  - the aggregate value of options granted is potentially much higher
  - the company has much greater discretion in allocating options to employees.

**How the scheme operates**

- The company grants the employee the right to buy shares at some time in the future, at a price fixed at the time of the grant of the option.
- Some time later the employee will pay the required amount and the shares are issued to them.
- As an approved scheme:
  - No income tax or NIC on the grant of the option.

On the exercise of an option there is no charge to tax.

On the final disposal of scheme shares, CGT will be charged on any gain arising.

### Conditions for the CSOP scheme

- Eligible employees must be either full-time directors (i.e. working at least 25 hours per week) or full-time or part time employees.

- Close company directors with a material interest (> 25%) are ineligible. Subject to the above, the company has complete discretion as to participants.

- The option must be exercised between 3 and 10 years of the grant.

- The price payable for the shares on exercise of the option must not be materially less than their market value at the time.

- There is a £30,000 limit to the value of shares for which a participant may hold unexercised options at the time.

- Employees owning more than 25% of the company are ineligible to participate.

- The costs of setting up such a scheme are allowable as trading expenses.

- Participation in the scheme need not be extended to all employees nor be on equal terms to all participants.

## Enterprise Management Incentive Scheme (EMI)

The EMI scheme was introduced to enable options to be granted to selected employees in smaller companies. The rules are more generous than for CSOPs.

### How the scheme operates

- Enterprise management incentive schemes enable options worth up to £120,000 to be granted to **selected** employees.

- As an approved scheme:
  - There is no income tax or NIC on the grant of the option.

  - No income tax or NIC is charged on the exercise of the option if the option price at the time of grant was at least MV at that time.

  - If the exercise price was granted at a discount, the charge is based on the difference between the market value at the date of the grant and the exercise price (if any).

## Conditions for the EMI scheme

- There is no limit on the number of employees who may benefit, although the total value of options granted by the company may not exceed £3 million.

- Qualifying companies must have < 250 full time employees.

- An employee must work for the company for at least 25 hours per week, or for at least 75% of his working time if less, and must not have a material interest in the company (i.e. > 30%).

- The company must be a qualifying trading company. Certain trades, such as property development, are excluded. The company's gross assets must not exceed £30 million.

- An employee may not be granted options over shares worth more than £120,000 at the time of grant. Options granted under a company share option plan must also be taken into account.

- Options must be capable of being exercised within ten years of grant, and may be granted at a discount, or at a premium.

- The company must not be a 51% subsidiary or otherwise controlled by another company and persons connected with that company.

## Share Incentive Plans (SIPs)

A SIP is a scheme that allows the employer to give shares to their employees, and for the employees to buy further shares, without an income tax charge.

On disposal CGT will apply to any profit made.

### How the scheme operates

A SIP can involve the employees acquiring shares in 3 different ways.

- The employer may gift up to £3,000 shares to the employee each year. The amount received is usually dependent on the financial performance of the company. These are referred to as free shares.

- An employee may be allowed to buy partnership shares on a 1: 2 basis (e.g. if they receive £3,000 of free shares they can buy £1,500 of partnership shares). The cost is deducted from their pre-tax salary (up to a maximum of 10% of salary).

- The employer may chose to issue further free shares on a 2:1 basis to the partnership shares, so if the employee buys £1,500 the employer may issue a further £3,000 of shares at no cost to the employee. These are referred to as matching shares.

- Not all schemes offer partnership or matching shares.

- Up to £1,500 of dividends paid on employee's shares held under the plan can be reinvested tax free in further shares.

- As an approved scheme:

  - There is no income tax or NIC on the acquisition of the shares.

  - On the final disposal of scheme shares, CGT will be charged on any gain arising.

### Conditions for the SIP

- The plan must be available to all employees of the company or a group company.

- The employee must not have a material interest in the company.

- The plan must have no arrangements for loans to employees.

- For the tax free advantages, the plan shares must be held for at least 5 years.

### Taxation consequences of the value received

The taxation consequences of the value received from an approved SIP are as follows:

### Income tax

- Shares held in the plan for 5 years

  If free, partnership or matching shares are held in a plan for five years, there is no income tax or NIC at the time the plan shares are awarded.

- Shares held in the plan for 3 to 5 years

  If the shares have been held for between 3 and 5 years, income tax and NIC will be charged on the lower of:

  (i)  the initial value of the shares, or

  (ii)  the value at the date of withdrawal.

- Shares held in the plan for less than 3 years

  Tax and NIC will be payable on their value at the time when they cease to be held in the plan.

## Capital gains

- If employees take the shares out of the plan and sell them later, there is a capital gain arising on the increase in value after the shares were withdrawn.

- The cost of the shares is their value when taken out of the plan.

### Choice of approved scheme

In order to decide which scheme is most appropriate, the conditions of each scheme should be compared to the employer's requirements.

Key factors to consider are:

- Does the employer want to reward all employees, or just key employees?

- What size is the employer's business? EMI is only available to smaller companies.

- Does the employer want to award shares or offer share options?

- How much does the employer want to offer?

- What holding period for the shares/options does the employer want to impose?

### Example 5 – Unapproved vs Approved share option schemes

Claire is granted share options in her employing company, a fully listed plc. Claire has an annual salary of £50,000.

The planned arrangements are as follows:

(1) The cost of the option is 5p per share.

(2) 10,000 shares can be acquired for £1.60 per share (= market value at grant of option).

(3) The share option can be exercised at any point after 3 years but before 10 years has expired. Claire will exercise her options in November 2009.

(4) The MV of shares at the exercise date in November 2009 will be £3.80.

(5) The shares are sold in January 2010 for £4.20 per share.

Other capital transactions by Claire during 2009/10 have utilised her annual exemption.

**Assuming the share option scheme is either an unapproved scheme or an approved company share ownership plan:**

(i) **Prepare a table of the tax charges for Claire arising on the above events.**

(ii) **State the overall net cash position of the transaction, including the preferred option.**

**Solution**

**(a) Tax charges**

| | Unapproved | Approved |
|---|---|---|
| | £ | £ |
| IT (W1) | 8,600 | Nil |
| NIC (W1) | 215 | Nil |
| CGT (W1) (W2) | 720 | 4,590 |
| Total | 9,535 | 4,590 |

**(b) The net cash position:**

| | £ | £ |
|---|---|---|
| Receipt on disposal | 42,000 | 42,000 |
| Less: | | |
| Costs to acquire shares | (16,500) | (16,500) |
| Tax charges | (9,535) | (4,590) |
| Net cash flow | 15,965 | 20,910 |

**Conclusion**

Claire will be in a better overall position if the share options are organised through an approved CSOP.

## Workings

### (W1) Unapproved scheme

- No tax charge @ grant

| | £ |
|---|---|
| Exercise | |
| MV at date of exercise (10,000 × £3.80) | 38,000 |
| Less: | |
| Cost of option (10,000 × 5p) | (500) |
| Cost of shares (10,000 × £1.60) | (16,000) |
| Employment Income | 21,500 |

| | £ |
|---|---|
| Income tax charged (£21,500 @ 40%) | 8,600 |
| Employee's NIC (1% × £21,500) | 215 |

- Sale of shares

| | £ |
|---|---|
| Sale proceeds (10,000 × £4.20) | 42,000 |
| Less: MV at date of exercise | (38,000) |
| Capital gain | 4,000 |
| CGT (£4,000 × 18%) | 720 |

### (W2) Approved scheme

- No tax charge @ grant.
- No tax charge @ exercise.
- With an approved scheme the whole profit is charged to CGT on the ultimate disposal of the shares.

| | £ |
|---|---|
| Sale proceeds | 42,000 |
| Less: | |
| Cost of option | (500) |
| Cost of shares | (16,000) |
| Capital gain | 25,500 |
| CGT (£25,500 × 18%) | 4,590 |

## 8 Lump sum payments on termination or variation of employment

Lump sum payments from employment may be:

- partially exempt
- wholly exempt, or
- wholly chargeable.

The tax treatment of a lump sum payment made to an employee on the cessation of employment depends on whether or not the payment is a genuine redundancy payment on the cessation of employment.

### Taxation treatment

The position is summarised in the table below:

| Wholly exempt | Partially exempt | Wholly chargeable |
|---|---|---|
| • Statutory redundancy payments <br> • Payments for injury, disability or death <br> • Lump sum payments from an approved pension scheme | • Genuine ex gratia termination payments (see below) <br>  – first £30,000 exempt <br>  – limit reduced if statutory redundancy payments received | • Any other payment received which is expected, usual employer practise (e.g. gardening leave, customary payments in lieu of notice) <br> • Any payment which is contractual <br> • Restrictive covenants |

Genuine ex gratia termination payments include:

- redundancy payments
- compensation for loss of office
- some payments made in lieu of notice
- damages for breach of contract or wrongful dismissal

Note the first £30,000 exempt rule also applies to any benefits received as part of the termination package (e.g. the company car).

Taxable amounts are:

- Assessed in the year of receipt
- Paid net of PAYE if paid before leaving and P45 issued
- Paid net of 20% income tax if paid after leaving and P45 issued
- Taxed as the top slice of the individual's taxable income (after dividend income) at the individual's highest marginal rate of income tax. This will preserve the preferential dividend tax rates.

### Test your understanding 6

Albert, age 40 years, received an ex gratia lump sum of £80,000 from his employers following his redundancy in December 2009.

He has other remuneration of £35,000 and income from furnished accommodation of £4,745 for 2009/10.

Albert also received £5,000 statutory redundancy pay.

**Calculate Albert's taxable income for 2009/10.**

### Unapproved retirement benefits

- Where an ex-gratia payment is made to an employee approaching retirement age, HMRC can deem it to be made under an unapproved retirement benefit arrangement and thereby assessable in full (i.e. without the £30,000 exemption).
- Retrospective approval can be given for the sum to be fully exempt.

## 9 National Insurance Contributions (NIC)

The main classes of NIC paid in respect of an employed individual and the persons who are liable to pay are summarised as follows:

| Class of contribution | Basis of assessment | Person liable |
|---|---|---|
| Class 1 primary | A percentage-based contribution based on employee earnings in excess of £5,715 per year for 2009/10. | Employee |
| Class 1 secondary | | Employer |
| Class 1A | A percentage-based contribution based on assessable benefits provided to employees. | Employer |

The rules for NICs payable in respect of a self employed individual are covered in Chapter 17.

A reminder of the rules for Class 1 and Class 1A contributions covered at F6 is given in expandable text and are summarised in the diagram below.

### Class 1 NICs

#### Class 1 contributions – Employed persons

A liability for Class 1 contributions arises where an individual:

- is employed in the UK; and
- is aged 16 or over; and
- has earnings in excess of the earnings threshold of £5,715 p.a.

#### Primary contributions

- Employee's Class 1 NIC is paid at 11% and 1%.
- Contributions are calculated as a percentage of **gross earnings** with **no allowable deductions**.
- There is no liability where gross earnings do not exceed the earnings threshold of £5,715 per year.
- Employee primary contributions, at the rate of 11%, are paid on earnings in excess of the threshold but below the upper earnings limit of £43,875.
- Earnings in excess of the upper earnings limit are subject to a rate of 1%.
- Class 1 NICs are calculated on an 'earnings period' basis (i.e. if paid weekly, 1/52 of the limits are used, and if paid monthly, 1/12 of the limits are used).
- However, in the examination, the annual limits are supplied and it is acceptable to calculate the liabilities on an annual basis.
- Primary contributions cease when the employee reaches pensionable age (65 for a man, 60 for a woman).
- Where the employer provides an occupational pension scheme, then those employees who are members of such schemes can be 'contracted-out' of the Second State Pension Scheme (S2P). Contracted out employees pay a lower rate of National Insurance contributions.
- The employer is responsible for calculating and accounting for the primary contributions to HMRC under the PAYE system.

- The gross earnings on which Class 1 contributions are calculated comprise any remuneration derived from employment paid in cash or assets which are readily convertible into cash.

- Gross earnings includes:
  - Wages, salary, overtime pay, commission or bonus.
  - Sick pay, including statutory sick pay.
  - Tips and gratuities paid or allocated by the employer.
  - Payment of the cost of travel between home and work, or on any profit element where business travel is reimbursed (for example, the payment of mileage allowances in excess of HMRC authorised rates).
  - Remuneration, such as bonuses, made by using financial instruments such as shares, unit-trusts, options, gilts, gold, precious stones, fine wines and 'readily convertible' assets. An asset is 'readily convertible' if arrangements exist for its purchase.
  - Remuneration in the form of non-cash vouchers (e.g. M&S vouchers but not tax exempt vouchers such as vouchers for child care of no more than £55 per week).

- The following are disregarded in calculating gross earnings for primary contributions:
  - Most benefits (see above regarding use of financial instruments and vouchers).
  - Redundancy payments.
  - Payments of any pension.

## Employers' secondary contributions

- The rate of employer's Class 1 NIC is 12.8% on gross earnings above £5,715.

- The contributions are a deductible expense for the employer when calculating taxable profits.

- There is no liability where gross earnings do not exceed the earnings threshold of £5,715 p.a.

- Where earnings exceed the threshold then contributions are paid on earnings in excess of the threshold. There is no reduced rate when earnings exceed the upper earnings limit.

- As for primary contributions, reduced rates apply where the employee is contracted out of S2P.

- Secondary contributions cease when the employee leaves the employment. There is no upper age limit, the employer is liable in full even if the employee is above pensionable age.

## Class 1A contributions

- Employers are required to pay Class 1A contributions on taxable benefits provided to P11D employees.

- There is no Class 1A charge in respect of any benefits that are already treated as earnings for Class 1 contribution purposes (e.g. cash vouchers).

- No contributions are levied where employee's earnings are less than £8,500 a year.

- The rate of Class 1A NIC is 12.8%.

- The contributions are a deductible expense for the employer when calculating taxable profits.

## Employees reaching pensionable age

- An employee who continues to work after attaining pensionable age (65 for a man, 60 for a woman) has no liability for primary Class 1 contributions.

- The employer is still liable for full secondary contributions.

## Deduction and payment by the employer

- The employer calculates the primary and secondary Class 1 contributions at each weekly or monthly pay date.

- At the end of each PAYE month (5th) the total primary and secondary contributions become payable to HMRC's Accounts Office, along with income tax deducted under PAYE, not later than 14 days thereafter (i.e. by 19th).

- The Class 1A contributions are payable annually in arrears to HMRC by 19th July following the end of the tax year.

## Persons with more than one job

- A person with more than one job is separately liable for primary contributions in respect of each job falling within the scope of Class 1 contributions (where earnings are over the earnings threshold of £5,715 pa).

- Each employer is also separately liable for secondary contributions.

- The total Class 1 Primary contributions from all employments is subject to an overall annual maximum.

- Employees with more than one job can prevent overpayment of contributions by applying for deferment of contributions, or claiming a refund after the end of the tax year.

## Company directors

- Where a person is a company director he or she is deemed to have an annual earnings' period.

- The annual earnings thresholds and the annual upper earnings limit therefore apply.

- The rules prevent directors avoiding NIC by paying themselves a low monthly salary, and then taking a large bonus.

## Summary

```
                    NICS PAYABLE IN RESPECT
                      OF AN EMPLOYED PERSON


        PAID BY EMPLOYEE                      PAID BY EMPLOYER


      CLASS 1              CLASS 1                  CLASS 1A
      PRIMARY             SECONDARY
```

**Payable on:**
- gross cash earnings
  - no allowable deductions
  - includes vouchers

**Payable when:**
- aged 16–60/65 years' old

**Rate:**
- 11% on earnings between £5,715 and £43,875
- 1% thereafter

**Due date:**
- payable under PAYE by 19th of each month

**Payable on:**
- gross cash earnings
  - no allowable deductions
  - includes vouchers

**Payable when:**
- aged 16 or over

**Rate:**
- 12.8% on earnings above £5,715

**Due date:**
- payable under PAYE by 19th of each month

**Payable on:**
- taxable benefits of a higher paid employee
  - excludes exempt benefits and vouchers

**Payable when:**
- aged 16 or over

**Rate:**
- 12.8% on the value of taxable benefits

**Due date:**
- payable by 19th July following the end of the tax year

---

### Example 6 – NICs

Janet is paid a salary of £18,000 pa. She was also paid a bonus of £10,000 in the first week of March 2010.

**Calculate Janet's Class 1 NIC for 2009/10 if she is an employee or a director.**

| | Annual £ | Monthly £ |
|---|---|---|
| Limits are: | | |
| Primary threshold | 5,715 | 476 |
| Upper threshold | 43,875 | 3,656 |

## Solution

### (i)  An employee

If Janet is an employee she will pay NIC on earnings of £1,500 per month for 11 months and earnings of £11,500 for the month in which the bonus was paid as follows:

|  | £ |
|---|---|
| (£1,500 – £476) × 11% × 11 months | 1,239 |
| (£3,656 – £476) × 11% × 1 month | 350 |
| (£11,500 – £3,656) × 1% × 1 month | 78 |
|  | —— |
|  | 1,667 |
|  | —— |

### (ii)  A director

If Janet is a director, she will pay NIC by reference to her total earnings in the year as follows.

Annual remuneration = (£18,000 + £10,000) = £28,000.

|  | £ |
|---|---|
| Class 1 primary NICs (£28,000 – £5,715) × 11% | 2,451 |
|  | —— |

### Test your understanding 7

Alex is paid £7,990 and Betty £46,400 in 2009/10.

Betty also receives £9,600 assessable benefits of employment.

**Calculate the employee's and the employer's Class 1 and Class 1A NIC liability for the year.**

## 10 Chapter summary

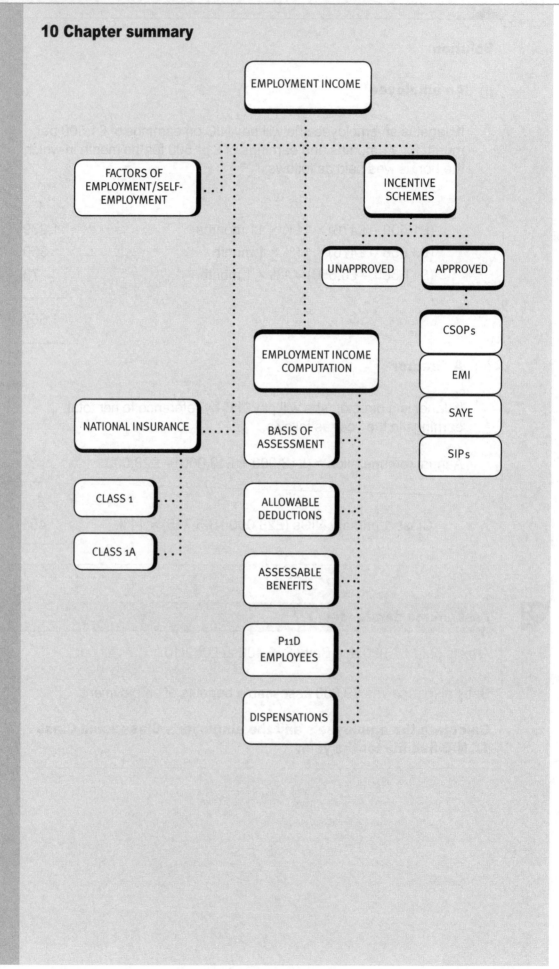

# Test your understanding answers

## Test your understanding 1

### Broadfoot

As a director of the company, Broadfoot is regarded as receiving the bonus on the earliest of the following dates:

| | |
|---|---|
| 1 September 2009 | Actual payment |
| 15 July 2009 | Credited in the accounts |
| 30 June 2009 | Bonus determined (after 31 March 2009) |

Accordingly, the bonus is taxable on 30 June 2009.

## Test your understanding 2

### Bernard

**(a) If Bernard receives 20p per mile**

| | | £ |
|---|---|---|
| Mileage allowance claimed | 12,000 × 20p | 2,400 |
| AMAP First 10,000 miles | 10,000 × 40p | (4,000) |
| Remaining 2,000 miles | 2,000 × 25p | (500) |
| | | ——— |
| Mileage expense claim = allowable deduction | | (2,100) |
| | | ——— |

**(b) If Bernard receives 45p per mile**

| | | £ |
|---|---|---|
| Mileage allowance claimed | 12,000 × 45p | 5,400 |
| AMAP First 10,000 miles | 10,000 × 40p | (4,000) |
| Remaining 2,000 miles | 2,000 × 25p | (500) |
| | | ——— |
| Mileage allowance assessable benefit | | 900 |
| | | ——— |

## Test your understanding 3

### Charles

Charles has the use of the car and fuel for 9 months of 2009/10 (1 July 2009 to 5 April 2010).

|  | £ |
|---|---|
| Car benefit (£24,000 × 35% (W) × 9/12) | 6,300 |
| Less: Payment for use (£100 × 9 months) | (900) |
|  | 5,400 |
| Fuel benefit (£16,900 × 35% × 9/12) | 4,436 |
| Assessable benefit | 9,836 |

**Note:** No reduction for contributions towards private fuel.

There is no additional charge for any running costs of the car with the exception of the fuel provision.

**Working:** Appropriate % = 15% + (255 – 135) × 1/5 = 39%, but restricted to 35% maximum.

## Test your understanding 4

### Vigorous plc

### Andrea Lean

|  |  | £ |
|---|---|---|
| Car benefit (£19,400 × 35%) |  | 6,790 |
| Less contribution by Andrea |  | (1,800) |
|  |  | 4,990 |
| Fuel benefit (£16,900 × 35%) |  | 5,915 |
| Living accommodation | – Rateable value | 7,000 |
|  | – Additional benefit | 3,277 |
|  | – Furniture (£6,000 at 20%) | 1,200 |
| Mobile telephone |  | Nil |

Notes:

(1) The relevant percentage for the car benefit is 43% (15% + 28% (275 – 135 = 140/5)), but this is restricted to the maximum of 35%.

(2) The contributions by Andrea towards the use of the motor car of £1,800 (£150 × 12) will reduce the benefit.

(3) The motor car was available throughout 2009/10 so the benefit is therefore £4,990 (£19,400 × 35% = £6,790 – £1,800 contribution).

(4) The living accommodation cost in excess of £75,000 so there will be an additional benefit.

(5) Since the property was purchased within six years of first being provided, the benefit is based on the purchase price of the property plus improvements prior to 6 April 2009.

(6) The additional benefit is therefore £3,277 ((£130,000 + £14,000) – £75,000 = £69,000 at 4.75%).

(7) The provision of one mobile telephone does not give rise to a taxable benefit, even if there is private use.

**Ben Slim**

|                  | £     |
|------------------|-------|
| Beneficial loan  | 3,800 |
| Relocation costs | 1,300 |
| Car benefit      | 1,008 |

**Notes:**

(1) The benefit of the beneficial loan using the average method is £3,919 ((£120,000 + £100,000)/2 = £110,000 at 4.75% × 9/12).

(2) Using the precise method the benefit is £3,800 ((£120,000 at 4.75% × 3/12) + (£100,000 at 4.75% × 6/12)).

(3) Ben will therefore elect to have the taxable benefit calculated according to the precise method.

(4) Only £8,000 of relocation costs are exempt, and so the taxable benefit is £1,300 (£9,300 – £8,000).

(5) The relevant percentage for the car benefit is 18% (15% + 3% charge for a diesel motor car), since the $CO_2$ emissions are below the base figure of 135 grams per kilometre.

(6) The motor car was only available for six months of 2009/10 so the benefit is £1,008 (£11,200 × 18% × 6/12).

(7) There is no fuel benefit as Ben reimburses the company for the full cost of private diesel.

**Chai Trim**

|                          | £     |
|--------------------------|------:|
| Van benefit              | 2,500 |
| Fuel benefit             | 417   |
| Television               | 330   |
| Health club membership   | 150   |
| Computer                 | 95    |

**Notes:**

(1) The van was only available for ten months of 2009/10 so the benefit is £2,500 (£3,000 × 10/12).

(2) Private fuel for the van was provided for ten months of 2009/10 so the benefit is £417 (£500 x 10/12).

(3) Chai will have been assessed to a benefit of £160 (800 at 20%) in respect of the television for both 2007/08 and 2008/09.

(4) The benefit on the sale of the television is £330 (£800 − £160 − £160 − £150), as this is greater than £100 (£250 − £150).

(5) In-house benefits are valued according to the marginal cost. The taxable benefit in relation to the health club membership is therefore the direct costs of £150.

(6) The computer was only available for 3 months so the benefit is £95 (£1,900 × 20% × 3/12)

**Test your understanding 5**

**Alan**

(i) **Approved share options**

| 1 July 2006 | Grant of option = No tax |
| 17 October 2009 | Exercise of option = No tax |
| 20 October 2009 | CGT on disposal: |

|  | £ |
| --- | --- |
| Sale proceeds | 5,000 |
| Less: Cost | (2,000) |
| Capital gain – 2009/10 | 3,000 |

(ii) **Unapproved share options**

| 1 July 2006 | Grant option = No tax |
| 17 October 2009 | Exercise of option: |
|  | Income Tax – earnings |
|  | 1,000 × (£4.50 – £2)  £2,500 |

| 20 October 2009 | CGT on disposal: |

|  | £ |
| --- | --- |
| Sale proceeds | 5,000 |
| Less: MV @ exercise | (4,500) |
| Capital gain – 2009/10 | 500 |

## Test your understanding 6

### Albert

**Income tax computation – 2009/10**

|  | £ | £ | £ |
|---|---|---|---|
| Remuneration |  |  | 35,000 |
| Lump sum |  | 80,000 |  |
| Less: Exempt amount | 30,000 |  |  |
| Less: Statutory redundancy pay | (5,000) |  |  |
|  |  | (25,000) |  |
| Taxable amount |  |  | 55,000 |
| Employment income |  |  | 90,000 |
| Property business income |  |  | 4,745 |
| Taxable income |  |  | 94,745 |
| Less: Personal allowance |  |  | (6,475) |
| Taxable income |  |  | 88,270 |

## Test your understanding 7

**Alex**

| | | £ |
|---|---|---|
| Employee's Class 1 NIC = (£7,990 – £5,715) | @ 11% | 250 |
| Employer's Class 1 NIC = (£7,990 – £5,715) | @ 12.8% | 291 |

**Betty**

| Employee's Class 1 NIC | | £ |
|---|---|---|
| (£43,875 – £5,715) | @ 11% | 4,198 |
| (£46,400 – £43,875) | @ 1% | 25 |
| | | 4,223 |
| Employer's Class 1 NIC = (£46,400 – £5,715) | @ 12.8% | 5,208 |
| Employer's Class 1A NIC = (£9,600 × 12.8%) | | 1,229 |

# Property and investment income

## Chapter learning objectives

Upon completion of this chapter you will be able to:

- calculate the assessable income arising from the letting of property

- define when a letting qualifies as Furnished Holiday Letting and explain the differences compared to normal lettings

- explain when rent a room relief will apply

- compute the amount assessable when a premium is received for the grant of a short lease

- demonstrate the reliefs available for a property business loss

- recognise the tax free income products

- explain the key features of an ISA

- identify the circumstances when accrued income provisions apply and calculate taxable amounts

- list the key conditions and purpose of an EIS scheme and recognise what IT relief is available to an investor and how it is given

- list the key conditions and purpose of a VCT scheme and recognise what IT relief is available to an investor and how it is given

- identify the circumstances for withdrawal of relief for both schemes and how this is affected.

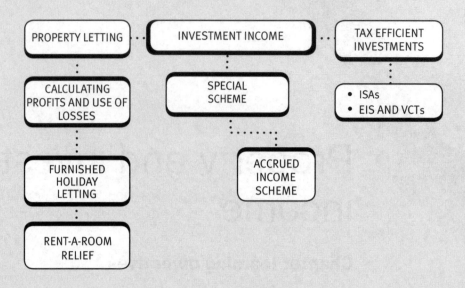

## 1 Introduction

This chapter is mainly a revision of the main types of exempt income and the income tax implications of letting property covered at F6.

A brief reminder of the F6 content is given in expandable text and revision examples are provided to check your retention of the required F6 knowledge.

The new topics introduced at P6 are the accrued income scheme, real estate investment trust income and tax efficient investments such as EIS and VCT investments.

## 2 Property income

### Introduction

All income from land and buildings is taxed on individuals as property income.

Property income includes:

- rental income under any lease or tenancy agreement less allowable expenses

- the premium received on the grant of a short lease

- profits arising from the commercial letting of furnished holiday accommodation

- rental income received under the rent-a-room scheme.

## Rental income

A reminder of the rules for computing assessable rental income under a lease or tenancy agreement covered at F6 is given in expandable text and is summarised in the diagram in section 6.

### Rental income

#### Basis of assessment

If an individual lets out a property or several properties, the profits from renting the properties is calculated as if the individual had a single trade as follows:

|  | £ |
|---|---|
| Rental income from all properties | X |
| Less Related expenses (see below) | (X) |
|  | ___ |
| Assessable income | X |
|  | ___ |

- the rental income is assessable on an accruals basis
- the related expenses are deductible on an accruals basis
- although treated as a trade, the income is investment income and taxed at 20%/40% as 'other income'.

#### Allowable deductions

The expenses allowable against the rental income are computed under the normal rules for a business.

- To be allowable, the expenses must have been incurred wholly and exclusively in connection with the business. This covers items such as:
  - insurance
  - utility costs
  - agents fees and other management expenses
  - repairs
  - interest on a loan to acquire or improve the property
  - irrecoverable debts.
- Any expenditure incurred before letting commences is allowable under the normal pre-trading expenditure rules.
- **Where property is not let at a full rent** (e.g. to an aged relative) a portion of the expenses incurred will be disallowed as not being wholly and exclusively incurred for the business.

For example, if rent charged is £250 per annum but a commercial rent would be £1,000 per annum, only 25% of expenses will be allowed.

In practice HMRC would allow the expenses but only up to the amount of the rent on that property.

- **If property is occupied for part of the year by the owner**, any expenses relating to the private use will not be allowed as a deduction.
- There is no deduction allowed for capital expenditure on the property or its furnishings.
- Repairs are allowed when incurred, providing they relate to the letting.
- Depreciation may be charged in the accounts but is not an allowable deduction for tax purposes.
- Normal capital allowances are not available for plant and machinery in a dwelling house
- No relief is available for the cost of furniture and fittings, a deduction for **'wear and tear' allowance** is given instead.
- Wear and tear allowance is calculated as follows:

  **(Rents received – council tax – water rates) × 10%.**

- A form of capital allowances known as the 'renewals basis' can be claimed for furnished accommodation. This allows the relief for the expense of renewing furniture to the same standard. The original cost and improvement element of any replacement is not allowable.

### Test your understanding 1

Giles owns a cottage which he lets out furnished at an annual rate of £3,600, payable monthly in advance. During 2009/10 he incurs the following expenditure:

|  |  | £ |
|---|---|---:|
| May 2009 | Cost of new garage | 2,000 |
| June 2009 | Insurance for year from 5 July (previous year = £420) | 480 |
| Nov 2009 | Drain clearance | 380 |
| May 2010 | Redecoration (work completed in March 2010) | 750 |

KAPLAN PUBLISHING

The tenant had vacated the property during June 2009 without having paid the rent due for June. Giles was unable to trace the defaulting tenant, but managed to let the property to new tenants from 1 July 2009.

**Calculate the property business profit for 2009/10.**

## 3 Furnished holiday lettings

Profits arising from the commercial letting of furnished holiday letting accommodation (FHLA) are:

- assessable as property business income, but
- treated as though the profits arose from a seperate trade, and
- treated as earned income, not investment income.

A reminder of the conditions for FHLA covered at F6 is given in expandable text and is summarised in the diagram in section 6.

### Qualifying conditions

In order to qualify as a FHLA, the accommodation must satisfy all of the following conditions:

- the property is situated in the UK or the EEA, furnished and let on a commercial basis

- it is available for commercial letting, to the public generally, as holiday accommodation for not less than 140 days a year

- the accommodation is actually let for at least 70 days a year (excluding periods of long term occupation)

- the accommodation is normally not let for > 31 consecutive days to the same person. However, if during a 12 month period there are periods of letting to the same person in excess of 31 consecutive days, the aggregate of these long periods must not exceed 155 days in total.

**Note:** Where there is more than one property, the 70 day test is satisfied if the average number of days let in the year is at least 70.

### The advantages of FHLA treatment

The profits will be treated as earned income arising from a single trade carried on by the landlord.

The advantages to being treated as earned income include:

- relief may be claimed for any losses as if they were trading losses, not property losses (see chapters 17 and 18)

- profits treated as earnings for personal pension relief (see chapter 4)

- normal capital allowances and the Annual Investment Allowance are available on all plant and machinery including furniture provided, instead of the wear and tear allowance (see chapters 17 and 18)

- property treated as business asset for CGT Entrepreneurs' relief (see chapter 9)

- capital gains tax roll-over relief is available on the disposal of FHLA (see chapter 9).

Note that it has been announced in FA2009 that these special furnished holiday lettings rules will be repealed in 2010/11.

## 4 Rent a room relief

When an individual lets furnished accommodation in their main residence, a special exemption applies.

- If the gross annual receipts (before expenses or capital allowances) are £4,250 or below:
    - the income will be exempt from tax
    - can elect to ignore the exemption for that year if a loss is incurred.
- If the gross annual receipts are more than £4,250:
    - the individual may choose between

    (i) paying tax on the excess of the gross rent over £4,250; and

    (ii) being taxed in the ordinary way on the profit from letting (rent less expenses).

### Married couples

A married couple who take in lodgers can either have:

- all the rent paid to one spouse (who will then have the full limit of £4,250), or

- have the rent divided between them (and each spouse will then have a limit of £2,125).

## 5 Property business losses

Profits and losses on all the properties are aggregated.

- If there is an overall loss, the property income assessment for the year will be £nil.
- The loss is carried forward and set against the first available future property business profits.

### Example 1 – Property losses

Sheila owns three properties which were rented out. Her assessable income and allowable expenses for the two years to 5 April 2010 were:

| Property | 1 | 2 | 3 |
|---|---|---|---|
| Income | £ | £ | £ |
| 2008/09 | 1,200 | 450 | 3,150 |
| 2009/10 | 800 | 1,750 | 2,550 |
| Expenses | | | |
| 2008/09 | 1,850 | 600 | 2,800 |
| 2009/10 | 900 | 950 | 2,700 |

**Calculate Sheila's property business profits or losses for 2008/09 and 2009/10.**

**Solution**

| Property business profits/losses | 2008/09 | 2009/10 |
|---|---|---|
| | £ | £ |
| Income | | |
| (£1,200 + £450 + £3,150) | 4,800 | |
| (£800 + £1,750 + £2,550) | | 5,100 |
| Less: Expenses | | |
| (£1,850 + £600 + £2,800) | (5,250) | |
| (£900 + £950 + £2,700) | | (4,550) |
| Profit/(loss) in year | (450) | 550 |
| Loss b/f | - | (450) |
| Property business profit | Nil | 100 |
| Loss c/f | 450 | Nil |

## 6 Summary

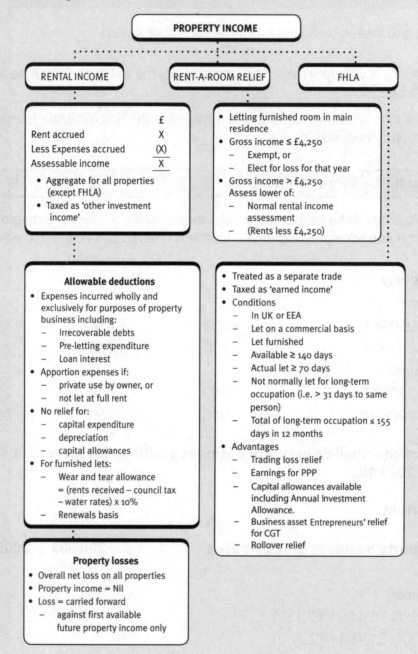

**PROPERTY INCOME**

- RENTAL INCOME
- RENT-A-ROOM RELIEF
- FHLA

|  | £ |
|---|---|
| Rent accrued | X |
| Less Expenses accrued | (X) |
| Assessable income | X |

- Aggregate for all properties (except FHLA)
- Taxed as 'other investment income'

**Allowable deductions**

- Expenses incurred wholly and exclusively for purposes of property business including:
  - Irrecoverable debts
  - Pre-letting expenditure
  - Loan interest
- Apportion expenses if:
  - private use by owner, or
  - not let at full rent
- No relief for:
  - capital expenditure
  - depreciation
  - capital allowances
- For furnished lets:
  - Wear and tear allowance
    = (rents received – council tax – water rates) x 10%
  - Renewals basis

**Property losses**

- Overall net loss on all properties
- Property income = Nil
- Loss = carried forward
  - against first available future property income only

- Letting furnished room in main residence
- Gross income ≤ £4,250
  - Exempt, or
  - Elect for loss for that year
- Gross income > £4,250
  Assess lower of:
  - Normal rental income assessment
  - (Rents less £4,250)

- Treated as a separate trade
- Taxed as 'earned income'
- Conditions
  - In UK or EEA
  - Let on a commercial basis
  - Let furnished
  - Available ≥ 140 days
  - Actual let ≥ 70 days
  - Not normally let for long-term occupation (i.e. > 31 days to same person)
  - Total of long-term occupation ≤ 155 days in 12 months
- Advantages
  - Trading loss relief
  - Earnings for PPP
  - Capital allowances available including Annual Investment Allowance.
  - Business asset Entrepreneurs' relief for CGT
  - Rollover relief

## 7 Premiums received on the grant of a lease

### Introduction

A lease premium is a lump sum payment made by the tenant to the landlord in consideration of the granting of a lease.

The receipt of a premium on the granting of:

- a short lease (≤ 50 years): has both income tax and CGT consequences

- a long lease (> 50 years): has no income tax consequences but is chargeable to CGT.

This chapter considers only the income tax consequences of granting leases, the CGT aspects are covered in Chapter 8.

## Short lease premiums

- A short lease is a lease for a period of 50 years or less
- Part of a premium received on the grant of a short lease is treated as rental income the tax year in which the lease is granted.
- The amount assessable to income tax as property business income is:

|  | £ |
| --- | --- |
| Premium | X |
| Less: Premium x 2% x (duration of lease - 1) | (X) |
| Property business income | X |

   Duration of the lease = number of **complete** years (ignore parts of a year).

- Alternatively, the amount assessable to income tax can be calculated using the following shortcut:

   $$\frac{51 - n}{50} \times \text{premium}$$

   where n = length of lease (in whole years)

### Length of lease

To avoid income tax it would be a simple matter to grant a lease for over 50 years, but to give the landlord the right to end the lease before the expiration of 50 years.

Anti-avoidance legislation provides that where the lease can be terminated at some date during the lease, the period of the lease is taken to the **earliest** date on which the lease **may** be terminated.

Rodney granted a 21-year lease of business premises to Charles on 1 July 2009 for a premium of £10,500.

He also granted a lease for another building with 14 years and 2 months left to run to Alice for a premium of £30,000.

**Calculate Rodney's property income assessment for 2009/10**

## Premiums for granting sublease

If a landlord grants a short lease on a property to a tenant (the head lease) and the tenant grants a short sublease to a subtenant:

- the premium received for the sublease is assessed on the tenant in the normal way.

- relief in respect of the premium paid on the head lease is available, calculated as:

$$\text{Taxable premium for head lease} \times \frac{\text{Duration of sublease}}{\text{Duration of head lease}}$$

**Example 2 – Grant of Lease**

Victor granted a lease to Alec on 1 August 2002 for a period of 20 years. Alec paid a premium of £20,000.

On 1 August 2009 Alec granted a sublease to Max for a period of five years. Max paid a premium of £24,000.

**Calculate the amount of property income assessable on Alec for 2009/10 in respect of the premium received from Max.**

**Solution**

|  | £ |
|---|---|
| Assessable premium on Alec (W) | 22,080 |
| Less Relief for head lease (£12,400 × 5/20) (W) | (3,100) |
| Assessable Premium | 18,980 |

> **Workings**
>
> | **Head lease:** | **Sub-lease:** |
> |---|---|
>
> $$\frac{51-20}{50} \times £20,000 = £12,400 \qquad \frac{51-5}{50} \times £24,000 = £22,080$$

## Reverse premiums

A reverse premium is a payment by a landlord to a prospective tenant as an inducement for the tenant to enter into the lease.

The detailed rules for reverse premiums are given in expandable text.

### Tax treatment of reverse premiums

- A reverse premium is subject to tax in the hands of the recipient, usually over the period of the lease, unless it has been taken into account in reducing expenditure qualifying for capital allowances.

- It is assessed as property business income unless the recipient has entered into the transaction for trading purposes, in which case it is assessed as trading income.

- Where the landlord is a dealer in land, the amount paid is deductible as a trading expense.

## Comprehensive example

### Test your understanding 3

John Wiles acquired two houses on 6 April 2009.

House 1 is let as furnished holiday accommodation. House 2 is let furnished.

House 1 was available for letting for 42 weeks during 2009/10 and was actually let for 14 weeks at £200 per week. During the 10 weeks that the house was not available for letting, it was occupied rent free by John's sister. Running costs for 2009/10 consisted of council tax £730, insurance £310 and advertising £545.

House 2 was unoccupied from 6 April 2009 until 31 December 2009 due to a serious flood in May 2009. As a result of the flood £7,250 was spent on repairs.

On 1 January 2010 the house was let on a four year lease for a premium of £4,000 and a rent of £8,600 per annum.

Immediately after the purchase, John furnished the two houses at a cost of £5,200 per house. During 2009/10 John also rented out one room of his main residence. He received rent of £4,600 and incurred allowable expenditure of £825

(i) **Briefly explain whether House 1 will qualify to be treated as a trade under the furnished holiday letting rules.**

   **State the tax advantages of the house being so treated.**

(ii) **Calculate John's property business loss for 2009/10 and advise him of the possible ways of relieving the loss.**

## 8 Real Estate Investment Trusts

A Real Estate Investment Trust (REIT) gives investors the opportunity to invest in a quoted property business set up as an investment trust.

Dividends received by an individual out of the profits of a REIT are not treated like other dividend income. Instead the income is:

(i) treated as property income

(ii) taxed as 'other' investment income (i.e. not savings and not dividend income)

(iii) received net of 20% tax.

### Illustration 1 – Real Estate Investment Trusts

An individual who receives dividends of £1,200 from a REIT will include gross property income in their tax return of £1,500 (£1,200 × 100/80).

The income will be taxed at the rates of 20% or 40%, depending on whether they pay tax at the basic or higher rate.

A tax credit of £300 (£1,500 × 20%) is available to reduce the actual tax payable, and can be repaid if relevant.

## 9 Tax free investments

The main types of investment giving tax free or exempt income are as follows:

- interest on National Savings Certificates
- income from Individual Savings Accounts (ISAs)
- dividends from shares held in a Venture Capital Trust (VCT)
- income tax repayment supplement
- Premium Bond, National Lottery and betting winnings.

### Individual Savings Accounts (ISAs)

An individual savings account (ISA) can be opened by any individual aged 18 (16 for cash ISAs) or over who is resident and ordinarily resident in the UK.

An ISA offers the following tax reliefs

- Income received is free of income tax.
- Disposals of investments within an ISA are exempt from CGT.
- There is no minimum holding period, so withdrawals can be made from the account at any time.

A reminder of the rules for the type of investment allowed through an ISA is given in expandable text.

### Types of investments

An ISA can be made up of either of the following components:

- Cash and cash-like equity products

  These include bank and building society accounts, as well as those National Savings products where the income is not exempt from tax.

  16 and 17 year olds may only invest cash ISAs.

- Stocks, shares and insurance products

  Investment is allowed in shares and securities listed on a stock exchange anywhere in the world.

The following stocks and shares qualify:

- ordinary shares

- fixed interest preference and convertible preference shares

- fixed interest corporate bonds and convertible bonds with at least five years to run until maturity

- Gilts with at least five years to run until maturity

- investments in unit trusts, investment trusts and open-ended investment companies.

Unlisted shares and shares traded on the Alternative Investment Market do not qualify.

## Subscription limits

For the tax year 2009/10 there is an annual subscription limit based on age and a stipulated maximum amount that can be invested in a cash ISA as follows:

| Age | Total limit | Maximum cash ISA limit |
|---|---|---|
| | £ | £ |
| 50 and over | 10,200 | 5,100 |
| Under 50 | 7,200 | 3,600 |

The balance of the annual total limit not invested in a cash ISA may be invested in a stocks ISA.

Note that husbands and wives each have their own limits.

## Account providers

Savers have a choice of account providers.

## 10 The accrued income scheme

### Introduction

The accrued income scheme was introduced to prevent the practice of 'bondwashing'.

Interest is normally paid on securities at regular intervals. As the interest payment date gets nearer, the capital value of the securities increases as any purchaser is buying the accrued income in addition to the underlying capital value.

When the securities are sold they are usually exempt from CGT so this element of growth relating to the interest escapes tax.

## Background – Bondwashing

This scheme applies to marketable securities such as gilts and debentures.

Interest is paid to the registered holder on a certain date. However, an individual who sells the security before that date will not receive the interest payment due on that date as by then it would be no longer owned.

However, the price the vendor receives for selling the security will be inflated to take account of the fact that the purchaser is due to receive the next interest payment.

By this time, the vendor has received a capital receipt in relation to the sale of the security, and as there is no income paid out, there is no charge to income tax in respect of the increased selling price.

As gilts and debentures are exempt from CGT, any gain arising on the disposal will also escape capital gains tax. Overall therefore, any interest due to be paid out and included in the selling price of the security will escape tax.

### How the scheme operates

- Under the scheme, interest is deemed to accrue on a daily basis.

- The purchase price (or disposal price) of the security is therefore apportioned between the income element and the capital element.

- The income element is assessed as interest income.

- The scheme does not apply unless the total nominal value of securities held by an individual exceeds £5,000 at some time during the year of assessment.

## 11 Enterprise Investment Scheme

The Enterprise Investment Scheme (EIS) is intended to encourage investors to subscribe for new shares in unquoted trading companies.

- Since the investor is committing the whole investment to one company, which may well not yet have a track record, this is a high risk investment.

- Furthermore, unless the shares become quoted, the investor may not be able to realise their investment. A successful company, however, may carry high returns.

### Qualifying conditions for EIS

- Amounts invested in ordinary shares in any unquoted company trading in the UK may qualify for relief.

- There is no requirement for the company to be resident in the UK.

- The company has no excluded activities.

- The investor must **not** be:

  (i)  an **employee** or director of the company; or

  (ii) have an **interest of 30% or more** in the company.

- Participation in the scheme is limited to those companies with:

  -  gross assets of **less than £7 million** before the share issue, and

  -  no more than **£8 million** after the issue.

- The company must be unquoted when shares are issued. Shares listed on the Alternative Investment Market count as unquoted for this purpose. Arrangements to obtain a quotation must not exist when the shares are issued.

- The company must carry on a qualifying trade, or research and development intended to lead to such a trade. It cannot carry on investment activities.

- There are a number of **investment activities** which are **excluded**, and therefore do not constitute a qualifying trade. These activities include:

  -  financial activities

  -  legal and accountancy services

  -  dealing in commodities, futures, shares, securities and other financial instruments

  -  property backed activities such as farming and market gardening and property development

  -  shipbuilding

  -  coal and steel production.

- The company must use all the funds raised within 2 years from issue or, if later, 2 years from commencing qualifying activities.

- There must be **50 or less full-time employees** in the investee company (or group of companies) at the time the investment is made.

- **A maximum investment of £2 million** can be raised by an EIS company in any 12 month period.

- An **effective 90% interest** trading subsidiary (i.e. through an indirect interest) will qualify for relief. Formerly only direct interest 90% trading subsidiaries qualified.

## Tax consequences

### Income tax

- Income tax relief = **(20% × amount subscribed for)**
  - Maximum amount that can be subscribed for each tax year = £500,000 p.a.
  - Deduct from the individual's income tax liability
  - Can reduce liability to £Nil, but can not create a tax repayment.

- An investor may elect to carry back the amount invested to the previous year, but cannot get relief on more than £500,000 in any one tax year.

- Note that dividends received from an EIS investment are taxable in the normal way.

### Test your understanding 4

Tom is not an employee of A Ltd (an unquoted company) and owns < 30% of shares in A Ltd. Tom subscribes for 10,000 new ordinary shares in A Ltd for £30,000 on 30 June 2009.

Tom's income tax liability in 2009/10 is £14,000.

**Show the amount of EIS relief allowable for 2009/10, assuming Tom does not wish to carry back the relief to 2008/09.**

### Capital gains tax

- Capital gains on the disposal of shares in qualifying companies are exempt provided the shares have been held for **three years**, but capital losses are allowable.

- It is also possible to obtain EIS deferral relief in respect of EIS shares, where the proceeds from the disposal of an asset are reinvested (see chapter 9).

- Although the CGT on the disposal is only deferred, the initial relief is effectively 38% (20% income tax on the EIS investment, and 18% CGT deferred).

### Inheritance tax

- Shares in an EIS scheme qualify for Business Property Relief as they are unquoted shares, provided they have been owned for two years.

## 12 Venture Capital Trusts

Relief for investment in venture capital trusts (VCTs) was introduced to encourage individuals to provide capital for unquoted trading companies.

The VCT buys shares in EIS companies and so an individual is able to invest in a **spread** of unquoted companies, thus reducing their risk.

### Qualifying conditions for a VCT

The qualifying conditions for a VCT are similar to the conditions for the EIS. The key rules are given in expandable text.

| Venture Capital Trust |
| --- |

- A VCT has to be quoted on the Stock Exchange.

- At least **70%** of the investments of a VCT have to be in unquoted trading companies, with not more than **15%** in any one company.

- At least **30%** of this investment must be in the form of new ordinary shares.

- The unquoted trading company must not be carrying on an excluded activity (as defined for EIS).

- Companies quoted on the Alternative Investment Market qualify as unquoted.

- At least **10%** of a VCT's total investment in any company must be held in the form of ordinary shares.

- The unquoted trading companies that are invested in must have gross assets of less than **£7 million** before the share issue, and no more than **£8 million** after the issue.

- A maximum of **£1 million** can be invested in any one company during the period:

  (i) six months ending on the date of investment; or

  (ii) the period from the start of the tax year to the date of investment whichever is the longer.

- There must be 50 or less full-time employees in the investee company (or group of companies) at the time the investment is made.

- A maximum investment of **£2 million** can be raised by a VCT in any 12 month period.

- An **effective 90% interest** trading subsidiary (i.e. through an indirect interest) will qualify for relief. Formerly only direct interest 90% trading subsidiaries qualified.

## Tax consequences

### Income tax

- Income tax relief **= (30% × the amount subscribed for)**
    - maximum amount that can be subscribed for each tax year = £200,000 p.a.
    - deduct from the individuals' income tax liability
    - can reduce liability to nil, but cannot create a tax repayment.
- No carry back facility
- Dividend income from a VCT = exempt from income tax.

### Capital gains tax

- Capital gains on the disposal of shares in a VCT are exempt for investments of up to £200,000 per annum.
- There is no relief for capital losses.

### Inheritance tax

- Shares in a VCT do not qualify for business property relief.

## Comparison of VCT and EIS

The key differences between EIS and VCT investments can be summarised as follows:

| | EIS | VCT |
|---|---|---|
| Level of risk | High as only one company invested in | Not as high risk as a number of investments made |
| Minimum retention period for income tax relief | 3 years | 5 years |
| Maximum amount invested | £500,000 | £200,000 |
| Rate of tax relief | 20% | 30% |
| Dividend income | Taxable | Exempt |
| Minimum retention period for CGT relief | 3 years | None |
| CGT deferral relief | Yes | No |
| CGT loss relief available | Yes | No |

### Withdrawal of income tax relief

- The income tax relief is withdrawn if the shares are not held for a minimum period of three years for EIS and five years for VCT.

- If the investor sells the shares within three years for EIS and five years for VCT they must repay the income tax relief given to HMRC.

## 13 Comprehensive example

### Test your understanding 5

Matthew has the following investment income in addition to a salary of £90,000:

- Dividends from VCT investment of £3,000

- Dividend from REIT of £4,992

- Dividend from IIP trust of £2,205

- Discretionary Trust income of £3,600

Both trusts comprised quoted shares only. He also invested £50,000 in a qualifying EIS scheme during the tax year.

He also sold 11% £10,000 Government stock on 13 May 2009 which he originally acquired on 1 July 2008. Interest is payable on 31 December and 30 June each year and the proceeds were £12,000.

He has paid private pension contributions during the period of £13,260.

**Calculate the income tax liability for 2009/10.**

## 14 Chapter summary

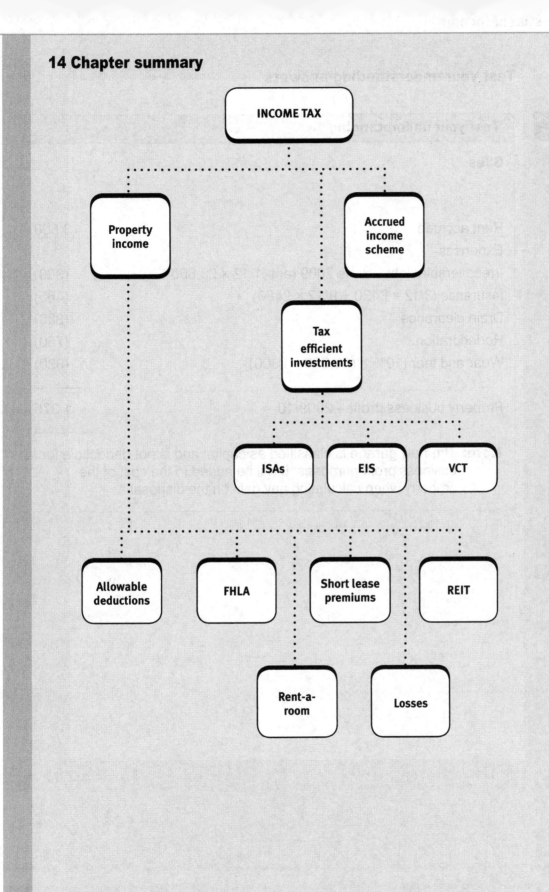

## Test your understanding answers

### Test your understanding 1

**Giles**

|  | £ |
|---|---|
| Rent accrued | 3,600 |
| Expenses |  |
| Irrecoverable debt – June 2009 rent (1/12 × £3,600) | (300) |
| Insurance (3/12 × £420 + 9/12 × £480) | (465) |
| Drain clearance | (380) |
| Redecoration | (750) |
| Wear and tear (10% × (£3,600 – £300)) | (330) |
| | |
| Property business profit – 2009/10 | 1,375 |

**Note:** The new garage is classified as capital and is not deductible for business profit purposes. It will be added to the cost of the property when calculating any gain on the disposal.

KAPLAN PUBLISHING

**Test your understanding 2**

**Rodney**

| | £ | £ |
|---|---|---|
| **21 year lease:** | | |
| Premium | 10,500 | |
| Less: £10,500 x 2% x (21 - 1) | (4,200) | |
| | | 6,300 |
| **14 year lease:** | | |
| Premium | 30,000 | |
| Less: £30,000 x 2% x (14 - 1) | (7,800) | |
| | | 22,200 |
| Property income assessment | | 28,500 |

**Alternative calculation**

| | £ |
|---|---|
| **21 year lease:** | |
| [(51 - 21)/50] x £10,500 | 6,300 |
| **14 year lease:** | |
| [(51 - 14)/50] x £30,000 | 22,200 |
| Property income assessment | 28,500 |

**Test your understanding 3**

**John Wiles**

(i) **House 1**

It is likely that House 1 will be regarded as a furnished holiday letting accommodation (FHLA) as it meets the following conditions:

- Situated in the UK or EEA, furnished and let on a commercial basis

- Available for letting to the public for not less than 140 days in 2009/10

- Actually let at least 70 days in that 140 day period

- It is not clear how long each person occupied the house for. However, in 2009/10, assuming there were no single lettings of > 31 days, the house will be a FHLA.

**Advantages of the house being FHLA**

- Capital allowances will be available on plant and machinery, such as furniture and kitchen equipment. The Annual Investment Allowance (AIA) of 100% is available (see chapters 17 and 18). This will be more beneficial than the wear and tear allowance.

- The property income profit will qualify as earnings for pension purposes

- Loss relief will be available against total income

- On disposal, the house will qualify for Entrepreneurs' relief if the conditions for the relief are met.

(ii) **UK property business profit/loss – 2009/10**

| **FHLA** | £ |
|---|---|
| Rent receivable (House 1) (14 x £200) | 2,800 |
| Less: Allowable expenses | |
| Council tax (£730 × 42/52) | (590) |
| Insurance (£310 × 42/52) | (250) |
| Advertising | (545) |
| AIA (£5,200 × 42/52) | (4,200) |
| | |
| FHLA loss (note 1) | (2,785) |

| **Other property income** | | £ |
|---|---|---|
| Rent receivable (House 2) (£8,600 × 3/12) | | 2,150 |
| Lease premium (W) | | 3,760 |
| Less: Allowable expenses | | |
| Repairs | | (7,250) |
| Wear and tear (10% x £2,150) | | (215) |
| | | |
| | | (1,555) |
| Rent from furnished room | 4,600 | |
| Rent a room relief | (4,250) | |
| | | 350 |
| | | |
| Property loss (note 2) | | (1,205) |

**Working: Lease premium**

$£4,000 \times [(51 - 4)/50] = £3,760$

**Notes:**

(1) The loss incurred in letting the FHLA is treated as a trading loss and can be relieved as follows:

– s64 ITA 2007 reduces total income of 2009/10 and/or 2008/09 with extended carry back against trading profit of 2008/09, 2007/08 and 2006/07

– s72 ITA 2007 reduces total income of 2006/07, 2007/08, 2008/09

– s83 ITA 2007 carry forward against first available future property income

(2) The net loss incurred in letting House 2 and the furnished room in John's main residence must be carried forward and offset against the first available future property income.

## Test your understanding 4

**Tom**

Tom can reduce his income tax in the tax year in which he buys the EIS shares by 20% of the amount invested.

|  | £ |
|---|---|
| Income tax liability | 14,000 |
| Less: EIS relief (20% × £30,000) | (6,000) |
|  | ———— |
|  | 8,000 |
|  | ———— |

Tom must repay the income tax saving to HMRC if he sells the shares within **three** years.

## Matthew

### Income tax computation – 2009/10

| | £ |
|---|---:|
| Employment income | 90,000 |
| Accrued income (W1) | 401 |
| Income from REIT (£4,992 × 100/80) | 6,240 |
| Discretionary trust income (£3,600 × 100/60) | 6,000 |
| IIP trust income (£2,205 ×100/90) (dividends) | 2,450 |
| | |
| Total income | 105,091 |
| Less PA | (6,475) |
| | |
| Taxable income | 98,616 |

### Analysis of income

| Dividends | Savings | Other income |
|---|---|---|
| £2,450 | £401 | (98,616 – 401 – 2,450) = £95,765 |

**Income Tax**

| £ | | £ |
|---:|---|---:|
| 53,975 | × 20% (other income) (W2) | 10,795 |
| 41,790 | × 40% (other income) | 16,716 |
| | | |
| 95,765 | | |
| 401 | × 40% (savings) | 160 |
| 2,450 | × 32.5% (dividends) | 796 |
| | | |
| 98,616 | | 28,467 |
| | | |
| Less Tax reducers: EIS (£50,000 × 20%) | | (10,000) |
| | | |
| Income tax liability | | 18,467 |

**Note:** Dividends from VCT shares are exempt

**Workings**

(W1) Accrued interest

The selling price includes interest accrued from 1/1/09-13/5/09 = 133 days

Accrued interest = (£10,000 x 11% x 133/365) = £401

(W2) Extended basic rate band

Matthew's basic rate band is extended by the gross pension contribution of £16,575 (£13,260 × 100/80)

Extended basic rate band is £53,975 (£37,400 + £16,575).

# Pensions

## Chapter learning objectives

Upon completion of this chapter you will be able to:

- explain the different types of pension schemes that can be registered with HM Revenue & Customs (HMRC)

- explain the basis for calculating the maximum annual contributions to a registered pension scheme for an individual

- calculate the tax relief available for pension contributions

- explain the concept of the lifetime allowance and the implications of the allowance being exceeded.

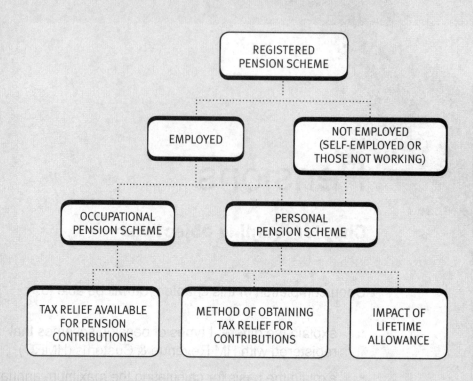

## 1 Introduction

This chapter is a revision of the tax consequences of investing in a registered pension scheme covered in F6.

A brief reminder of F6 content is given in expandable text and revision examples are provided to check your retention of the required F6 knowledge.

The main new topics introduced are the spreading of employer contributions, prohibited assets and benefits received on retirement and on death.

## 2 Registered pension schemes

### Introduction

An individual can set up an investment of funds to provide an income during their retirement in a tax efficient way by making payments into a registered pension scheme.

Investing in a registered pension scheme is a long-term investment. It is tax efficient for the following reasons:

- The individual obtains tax relief on the contributions made into the scheme.

- Where an employer contributes into the scheme, tax relief for the employer contributions is available with no taxable benefit for the employee.

- Registered pension schemes are exempt from income tax and capital gains tax.
- On retirement, part of the funds can be withdrawn as a tax-free lump sum.

## Types of registered pension schemes

To obtain the tax privileges, the pension scheme must satisfy certain conditions and be registered with HMRC.

The two main types of registered pension schemes available are:

- occupational pension schemes – applicable to employees only
- personal pension schemes – applicable to all individuals.

A reminder of the types of registered pension schemes is given in expandable text and is summarised in the diagram in section 4.

### Occupational pension schemes

An occupational pension scheme is a scheme set up by an employer for the benefit of their employees.

Contributions into occupational schemes may be made by:

- the employer, and
- the employee.

Registered occupational pension schemes may be 'defined benefit' or 'money purchase' schemes.

Under a defined benefit scheme the benefits obtained on retirement are linked to the level of earnings of the employee.

Under a money purchase scheme (also known as 'defined contribution' scheme) the benefits obtained depend upon the performance of the investments held by the pension fund.

### Personal pension schemes

Personal pension schemes can be established by **any** individual including those not working (including children).

Contributions into personal pension schemes may be made by:

- the individual, and
- any third party on behalf of the individual
- e.g. the employer, a spouse, parent or grandparents.

Personal pension schemes are usually 'money purchase' schemes administered by financial institutions on behalf of the individual.

### Overview of the tax relief rules for registered pension schemes

- The amount of tax relief available for pension contributions is the same regardless of whether the scheme is an occupational or personal pension scheme.
- The method of obtaining tax relief for the contributions is different.
- Once the funds are invested in the scheme, all registered pension schemes are governed by the same rules.

## 3 Tax relief for pension contributions

A reminder of the maximum annual contributions eligible for tax relief and the annual allowance tax charge is given in expandable text and is summarised in the diagram in section 4.

### Relief for contributions made by individuals

Tax relief is available for pension contributions if:

- the pension scheme is a registered scheme, and
- the individual is resident in the UK and aged under 75.

Regardless of the level of earnings, an individual may make pension contributions of **any amount** into:

- a pension scheme, or
- a number of different pension schemes.

However, tax relief is only available for a **maximum annual amount** each tax year.

The total maximum annual gross contribution for which an individual can obtain tax relief is the higher of

- £3,600, and

- 100% of the individual's 'relevant earnings', chargeable to income tax in the tax year.

Relevant earnings includes trading profits, employment income, and furnished holiday letting income but not investment income.

Note that:

- The maximum limit applies to the total gross contributions made into all schemes where:
  - An employee contributes to both an occupational and a personal pension scheme, or
  - An individual contributes into more than one personal pension scheme.

- An individual with no relevant earnings can obtain tax relief on gross contributions of up to £3,600 p.a.

## Contributions in excess of annual allowance

There is no limit on the amount of contributions that may be made into pension schemes by an individual, his employer or any other party.

However, a tax charge is levied on the individual if the total of all contributions on which relief has been obtained exceed an annual allowance of £245,000 for 2009/10.

The tax charge is a 40% income tax charge, which is:

- Added to the individual's income tax liability, and
- Paid through the self assessment system.

## 4 The method of obtaining relief for pension contributions

### Introduction

The method of obtaining relief for pension contributions is different depending on the type of pension scheme.

A reminder of the method of obtaining relief for pension contributions is given in expandable text and is summarised in the diagram in section 4.

### Relief for contributions made by an individual

#### Personal personal pension contributions

The method of obtaining tax relief for contributions into a personal pension scheme is the same whether they are made by an employee, a self-employed individual or an individual who is not working.

Relief is given as follows:

- For a basic rate taxpayer, tax relief at the basic rate is automatically obtained as payments are made to the pension fund net of 20% tax. The payment is ignored in the IT computation.

- For higher rate taxpayers, 40% tax relief is given as follows:
    - 20% at source.
    - 20% through the income tax computation, obtained by extending the basic rate band by the gross payment (so that more income is taxed at 20% and less at 40%).

#### Occupational pension scheme contributions

Where employees make pension contributions into an occupational pension scheme:

- payments are made gross, and

- tax relief is given through the PAYE system by reducing the earnings subject to tax, i.e. the payment is an allowable deduction from employment income.

## Test your understanding 1

The following individuals made gross pension contributions into a personal pension scheme in 2009/10 and had the following trading profits:

|  | Pension contributions(gross) | Trading profits |
|---|---|---|
|  | £ | £ |
| Cindy | 25,000 | 20,000 |
| Don | 40,000 | 85,000 |

**Explain how tax relief for the pension contributions will be given in 2009/10 for each individual and calculate the income tax liability of Don for 2009/10.**

## Test your understanding 2

Henry is employed by Lloyd Ltd on a salary of £80,000 pa. He is a member of the company's occupational pension scheme.

Henry pays 3% of his salary into the scheme each year. He has no other income.

**Calculate Henry's income tax liability for 2009/10, showing how tax relief is obtained for his pension contributions.**

## Relief for contributions by employers

Contributions paid by an employer into a registered pension scheme are:

- tax deductible in calculating the employer's taxable trading profits, provided the contributions are paid for the purposes of the trade

- an exempt employment benefit for the employee

- added to the pension contributions paid by the employee to determine whether the annual allowance has been exceeded and an income tax charge levied.

The deduction against the employer's trading profits is given in the accounting period in which the contribution is **paid**; the accounting treatment is not followed.

### Example 1 – Relief for contributions

Hugh is a self-employed builder who prepares accounts to September each year. His recent tax adjusted trading profits have been:

| | |
|---|---:|
| Year ended 30 September 2008 | £80,000 |
| Year ended 30 September 2009 | £90,000 |

Hugh's wife, Holly, has employment income from a part-time job of £3,500 pa.

They also have a joint bank account on which they earned interest of £5,000 (gross) in 2009/10.

During the year to 5 April 2010, Hugh paid £19,400 into his registered personal pension scheme. Holly paid £2,600 into her employer's registered occupational pension scheme and Holly's employer contributed a further £4,500.

**Calculate how much of the pension contributions made by Hugh, Holly and Holly's employer in 2009/10 will obtain tax relief and explain how the tax relief will be obtained.**

**Solution**

**Hugh**

- Hugh can obtain tax relief for a pension contribution of up to a maximum of 100% of his earnings in 2009/10.

- His earnings are his assessable trading profits for 2009/10, i.e. £90,000 (year ended 30 September 2009).

- Investment income such as bank interest is not included.

- Hugh will have paid the pension contribution net of basic rate tax of £4,850 (£19,400 × 20/80).

- The gross pension contribution is £24,250 (£19,400 × 100/80).

- Higher rate tax relief is obtained by extending the basic rate band by £24,250 from £37,400 to £61,650.

**Holly**

- Holly can obtain tax relief for a gross pension contribution of up to a maximum of the higher of £3,600 or 100% of her employment earnings in 2009/10 (i.e. £3,500).

- Her gross pension contribution of £2,600 is less than £3,600, therefore she can obtain tax relief for all £2,600 contributions paid.

- Holly's employer will deduct the gross contribution of £2,600 from her employment income before calculating her income tax liability under PAYE.

**Holly's employer**

- Holly's employer will obtain tax relief for all of the £4,500 contribution made into the occupational pension scheme.

- Relief is given as an allowable deduction in the calculation of the employer's taxable trading profits.

## Test your understanding 3

Marcus has been employed for many years.

In 2009/10 Marcus earned £280,000 and made his usual gross contribution of £136,000 into his personal pension scheme in 2009/10.

His employer contributed a further £120,000 into his personal pension scheme.

**Calculate Marcus' income tax liability for 2009/10.**

## Spreading of employer contributions

Where there is an increase in the level of employer contributions from one period to the next of over 210%, HMRC require the tax relief to be spread evenly over a number of years.

### Spreading provisions

The first 110% is relievable in the current year.

The excess is dealt with as follows:

| Excess (over 110% of previous year) | Tax relief obtained |
| --- | --- |
| Less than £500,000 | All in current year |
| Between £500,000 and £1,000,000 | Spread evenly over 2 years |
| Between £1,000,000 and £2,000,000 | Spread evenly over 3 years |
| £2,000,000 or more | Spread evenly over 4 years |

Additional contributions for existing pensioners are deductible when made.

## Prohibited assets

To be registered, a pension scheme must not invest in prohibited assets such as residential property and personal investments.

### Prohibited assets

Self invested personal pension schemes (SIPPs) and small self administered schemes (SSASs) are not allowed to invest in:

*   residential property, and
*   other personal chattels or private investment assets (e.g. fine wine, paintings, classic cars, antiques, art, race horses).

If a pension scheme purchases a 'prohibited' asset the individual member will be charged 40% tax on the value of the asset and the scheme administrator will be charged a further 15% tax.

In some cases there could be an additional 'unauthorised payment surcharge' and sanctions which could lead to the compulsory deregistration of the scheme.

Deregistration could result in further tax charges levied on the administrator at 40% on all the assets in the scheme.

## Summary

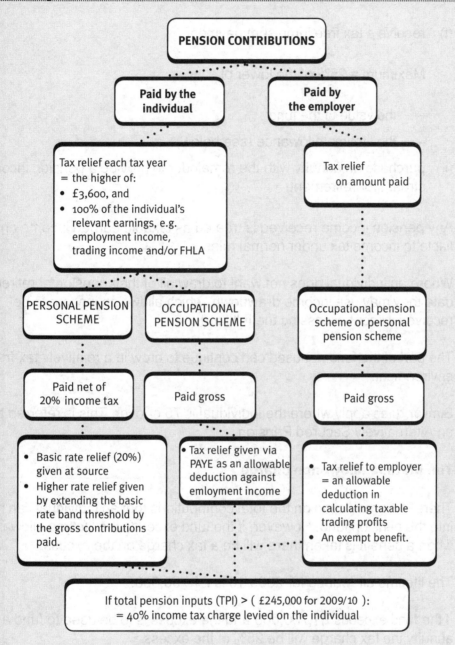

## 5 The lifetime allowance

### Benefits on retirement

Pensions will not normally be paid out of a pension scheme until the individual reaches the age of 55.

All or part of the pension fund can be taken to provide a pension at any time between the minimum age (above) and the age of 75.

It is therefore possible to receive a pension and still continue to work.

On retirement, the individual may:

(i) receive a tax free lump sum payment

Maximum = 25% of the lower of

– the value of the fund
– the lifetime allowance (see below)

(ii) purchase an annuity with the remainder to provide a pension income stream for retirement.

Any pension income received is treated as taxable earned income and is liable to income tax under normal rules.

Where an individual does not want to draw all of their pension at retirement date they may use income drawdown, which allows an income to be received without accessing the full fund.

The part of the fund not used can continue to grow in a relatively tax-free environment.

Similar rules apply where the individual is 75 or over. This is referred to as an Alternatively Secured Pension.

## The lifetime allowance charge

There is no restriction on the total contributions that an individual can make into the pension fund. However, if the fund exceeds the lifetime allowance when a benefit is taken there will be a tax charge on the excess.

The lifetime allowance for 2009/10 is £1,750,000.

If the fund exceeds £1,750,000 and the excess is to be used to fund a larger annuity the tax charge will be 25% of the excess.

Where the taxpayer chooses to take the excess in cash the tax charge will be 55% of the excess.

## Benefits on death

On the death of the individual, the pension scheme may provide:

- a pension income, and/or
- lump sums for dependants (e.g. spouse, civil partner, child under the age of 23 or other dependant).

Further tax charges may arise depending on:

- the individual's age
- whether the scheme is a money purchase or a defined benefit scheme, and
- whether any of the fund has already been utilised to provide benefits.

## Summary

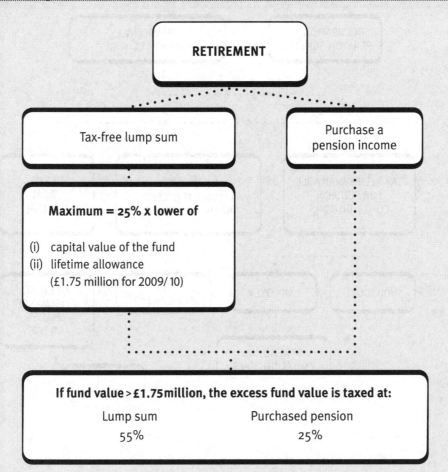

## 6 Chapter summary

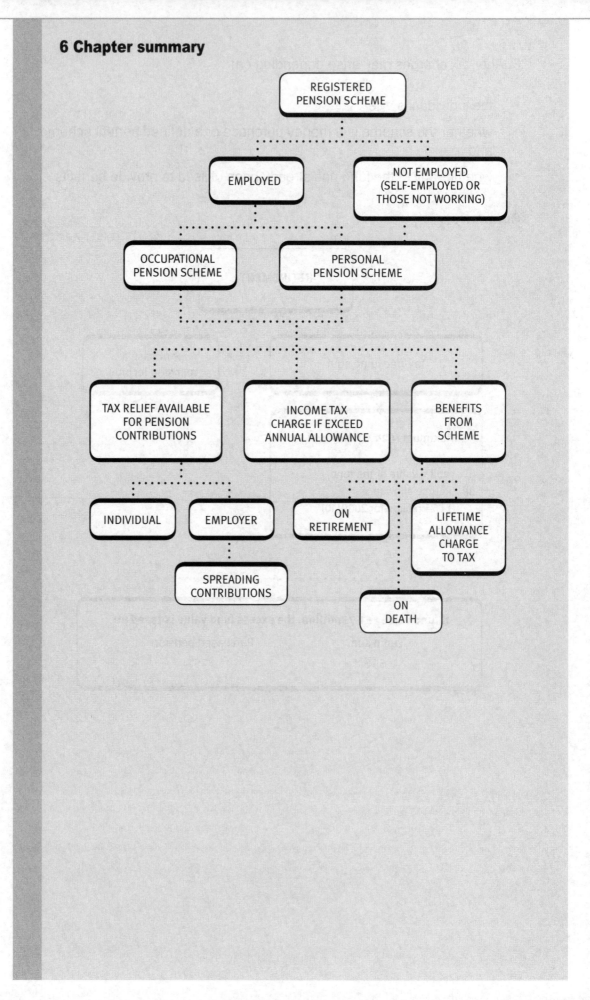

## Test your understanding answers

### Test your understanding 1

**Cindy**

- The tax relief available on Cindy's pension contributions is restricted to 100% of her earnings, i.e. £20,000.

- She will obtain basic rate tax relief at source of £4,000 (£20,000 × 20%) and pay £21,000 (£25,000 – £4,000) to the pension scheme.

**Don**

- Don's pension contributions are less than his earnings for the year and he will therefore receive tax relief on the full amount of the contribution.

- He will obtain basic rate tax relief at source of £8,000 ( £40,000 × 20%) and pay £32,000 (£40,000 – £8,000) to the pension scheme.

- Higher rate tax relief will be given by extending the basic rate band by £40,000 from £37,400 to £77,400.

- Don's income tax computation for 2009/10 will be:

|  | £ |
|---|---|
| Trading income | 85,000 |
| Less: Personal allowance | (6,475) |
| | ——— |
| Taxable income (all 'other income') | 78,525 |
| | ——— |

Income tax liability

| £ | | £ |
|---|---|---|
| 77,400 | @ 20% | 15,480 |
| 1,125 | @ 40% | 450 |
| ——— | | ——— |
| 78,525 | | 15,930 |
| ——— | | ——— |

**Henry**

**Income tax computation – 2009/10**

|  | £ |
|---|---|
| Salary | 80,000 |
| Less: Employee's pension contributions (3%) | (2,400) |
|  |  |
| Employment income | 77,600 |
| Less: Personal allowance | (6,475) |
|  |  |
| Taxable income | 71,125 |
|  |  |
| Income tax liability |  |

| £ |  |  |
|---|---|---|
| 37,400 | @ 20% | 7,480 |
| 33,725 | @ 40% | 13,490 |
|  |  |  |
| 71,125 |  | 20,970 |

## Test your understanding 3

### Marcus

- Marcus can obtain tax relief for a gross pension contribution of up to a maximum of 100% of his earnings, i.e. £280,000 in 2009/10, so relief will be available for the £136,000 paid.

- Marcus will have paid the pension contributions net of basic rate tax of £27,200 (£136,000 × 20%) and paid £108,800 (£136,000 × 80%) into the pension scheme.

- Higher rate relief is obtained by extending the basic rate band threshold by £136,000 from £37,400 to £173,400.

- Relief on £120,000 is given as an allowable deduction in computing the employer's taxable trading profits.

- The total gross contributions paid into the scheme in 2009/10 will be £256,000 (£136,000 + £120,000) which exceeds the annual allowance of £245,000.

- Marcus will therefore have an additional income tax liability in 2009/10 of £4,400 (£256,000 − £245,000 = £11,000 × 40%).

- Marcus' income tax computation for 2009/10 will be:

|  | £ |
|---|---|
| Employment income | 280,000 |
| Less: Personal allowance | (6,475) |
|  | |
| Taxable income | 273,525 |
|  | |

Income tax

| £ |  | £ |
|---|---|---|
| 173,400 | @ 20% | 34,680 |
| 100,125 | @ 40% | 40,050 |
|  | | |
| 273,525 | | 74,730 |
|  | | |
| Annual contributions charge (£11,000 × 40%) | | 4,400 |
|  | | |
| Income tax liability | | 79,130 |

# 5

# Income tax planning

## Chapter learning objectives

Upon completion of this chapter you will be able to:

- identify and advise on the types of tax efficient investments and other expenditure that will result in a reduction in income tax liabilities for an individual

- identify suitable tax planning measures in a given scenario to mitigate tax liabilities for an individual.

## 1 Mitigating income tax liabilities

### Introduction

This chapter is the first of a number of chapters contained in the workbook aimed at introducing tax planning measures to minimise tax liabilities.

This chapter only considers personal income tax aspects but later you will be expected to consider multi-taxation scenarios from both a personal and business tax aspect.

The main areas to consider for income tax planning are:

- tax efficient types of income and expenditure
- allowances available
- tax efficient remuneration.

### Tax efficient income

As there are different forms of income the areas of consideration will vary, however some of the key aspects to consider are:

- the range of exempt sources of income, as outlined in Chapter 3
- the range of tax exempt benefits, as covered in Chapter 2
- the different tax rates on alternative sources of taxable income, as revised in Chapter 1.

### Example 1 - Income and expenditure

Danka is a higher rate tax payer. She is 47 years old.

She has recently inherited various investment assets with a projected annual income comprising:

£10,000 gross UK dividends from quoted and unquoted shares.

£5,000 gross building society interest.

She wishes to minimise her income tax liability through a consideration of alternative forms of similar investments.

**Identify two suitable investments that will reduce Danka's future income tax liability.**

## Solution

An individual has the opportunity each tax year to invest in an ISA account. The maximum annual investment is £7,200 in stocks and shares or alternatively £3,600 can be in a cash component.

All income, both dividend and interest, is tax free. Therefore use of this facility each tax year could be recommended as it means the income will become tax free.

She could also consider using the Venture Capital Trust scheme. This quoted investment provides both tax free dividends and income tax relief at a rate of 30% on investments up to £200,000 p.a.

## Example 2 - Income and expenditure

Nilum, a non tax payer, has also inherited £10,000 and wants to maximise her immediate income.

**Identify the income tax factors that Nilum should consider before investing.**

## Solution

Dividend income is not suitable for Nilum as the tax credit is notional and not refundable whereas an interest bearing investment will generate a 20% real tax credit if received net of tax.

Ideally Nilum should make an appropriate election for the interest to be received gross or invest in gross paying investments (e.g. NSB accounts, gilt-edged securities).

## Tax efficient expenditure

An individual can obtain tax relief on certain types of expenditure. The rate of the relief and the precise treatment of each varies in the income tax computation, but the key types are summarised below:

| Type | Maximum tax relief | Treatment in I.T. computation | Details in: |
|---|---|---|---|
| PPP contributions | 40% | For higher rate payers only – extend BR band | Chapter 4 |
| Occupational pension contributions | 40% | Relief through PAYE | Chapter 4 |
| Qualifying loan interest | 40% | Deduct from total income | Chapter 1 |
| EIS | 20% on up to £500,000 investment | Tax reducer – deduct from IT liability | Chapter 1 and 3 |
| VCT | 30% on up to £200,000 investment | Tax reducer – deduct from IT liability | Chapter 1 and 3 |

## 2 Income tax planning scenarios

Earlier chapters have established the technical rules for computing income tax liabilities for an individual. This section considers some possible examination scenarios where you should consider basic income tax planning techniques.

## Husband and wife and registered civil partners

A couple should consider the following techniques:

* equalising income
* use tax-free investments
* maximising pension contributions
* maximising available allowances.

## Equalisation of income

Spouses and civil partners are taxed separately. They may choose to own assets in sole ownership or jointly.

The income from jointly owned assets is taxed in equal shares. Where the underlying ownership of the asset is not equal an election can be made to apportion the income using the proportion in which the investment is owned.

Transferring income can save tax where one spouse is a higher rate taxpayer and the other is not, or where one spouse does not have enough income to utilise their personal allowance and basic rate tax band.

It is important to recognise that the transfer of the interest in the asset to the spouse must be a genuine gift to be effective for income tax purposes. There is no immediate CGT/ IHT implication.

### Example 3 - Equalisation of income

Kyria and Spence, a married couple, both aged 42, have the following income details for 2009/10:

|  | Kyria | Spence |
| --- | --- | --- |
|  | £ | £ |
| Earned income | 2,000 | 41,000 |

They own a property in joint names but the cost was provided as follows:

*   Spence – 80%
*   Kyria – 20%

A declaration is in force to support the ownership percentage. The annual income from the property is £10,000.

In addition, they also have a joint investment bank account with a cash balance of £6,000 that earns interest of £800 gross per annum.

**Calculate the taxable income for Kyria and Spence respectively and advise them of any income tax planning measures they should consider to reduce their liabilities for the future.**

### Solution

|  | Kyria | Spence |
|---|---|---|
|  | £ | £ |
| Earned income | 2,000 | 41,000 |
| Investment income | 400 | 400 |
| Property (20:80) | 2,000 | 8,000 |
| Total income | 4,400 | 49,400 |
| Less: PA (restricted) | (4,400) | (6,475) |
| Taxable income | Nil | 42,925 |

### Tax planning

The problem

Kyria has unused PA, and basic rate band, whilst Spence is a higher rate tax payer with £5,525 (£42,925 – £37,400) taxed at 40%, so the couple should consider the transfer of income-producing assets to Kyria.

### Alternatives

The following could be considered:

- Transfer of a larger percentage ownership of the property to Kyria.

- The couple could each open an ISA for investment purposes instead of using the bank account. This would utilise their tax-free cash investment limits.

- Neither appear to making any payments into a pension.

### Effect

- A transfer of a larger percentage of the property to Kyria would save Spence tax at 40% and enable Kyria's surplus personal allowance and 20% basic rate tax band to be utilised.

- If Kyria's taxable non savings income remained below £2,440, the investment income would be taxed at 10% up to the £2,440 limit (assuming the bank balance was not transferred to an ISA).

- £3,600 cash each invested in a cash ISA (the maximum contribution per year) would result in tax-free earnings. Up to a further £3,600 could be invested in a stocks and shares ISA.

- In Spence's case, any pension contributions would provide tax relief at 40%.

## Effective use of allowances

Every individual is entitled to a personal allowance (PA), including children, provided they:

- are UK resident, or
- are a EU citizen, or
- in some circumstances where they are resident outside the EU (see Chapter 10).

The age allowance is restricted if the individual's income exceeds the limit. Therefore, transferring income to a spouse may reduce the restriction of the allowance.

### Example 4 - Use of allowances

Wilson, aged 71, and Marietta, aged 60, are married and have the following income:

|  | Wilson | Marietta |
|---|---|---|
| Pension income | £22,400 | £18,000 |
| Government stock interest | £2,000 | – |

**Advise Wilson on the availability of the personal age allowance and consider any income tax planning advice.**

### Solution

The age allowance will be restricted as Wilson's total income is in excess of £22,900 as follows:

Age allowance restriction (£24,400 – £22,900) × ½ = £750

Revised personal age allowance (£9,490 – £750) = £8,740

If the government stock were transferred to Marietta then a reduced restriction would apply as Wilson's total income would be £22,400.

There would be no age allowance restriction.

This would result in a saving to the couple of £150 (£750 × 20%)

## Pension contributions

Both husband and wife should be looking to make pension contributions. If the contributions are not to be made equally, the higher rate taxpayer should make the contributions.

Note that pension contributions made by a higher rate taxpayer with dividend income can achieve a saving in excess of 40%.

### Example 5 - Pensions

Julie is self-employed and made profits of £40,000 in the year ended 31 March 2010.

Her only other income is dividends received of £9,000.

**Calculate the tax saving that will be achieved if Julie pays £4,680 into her personal pension in 2009/10.**

**Solution**

|  | £ |
|---|---|
| Trading income | 40,000 |
| Dividend income (£9,000 × 100/90) | 10,000 |
| Total income | 50,000 |
| Less: Personal Allowance | (6,475) |
| Taxable income | 43,525 |

Analysis of income:

| Dividends | Other income |
|---|---|
| £10,000 | £33,525 |

**Income tax – with no pension contributions**

| £ | | | £ |
|---|---|---|---|
| 33,525 | x 20% | (other income) | 6,705 |
| 3,875 | x 10% | (dividend income) | 387 |
| 37,400 | | | |
| 6,125 | x 32.5% | (dividends) | 1,991 |
| 43,525 | | | |
| Income tax liability | | | 9,083 |

**Income tax – with pension contributions**

Gross pension contribution = (£4,680 × 100/80) = £5,850

Higher rate threshold = (£37,400 + £5,850) = £43,250.

| £ | | | £ |
|---|---|---|---|
| 33,525 | × 20% | (other income) | 6,705 |
| 9,725 | × 10% | (dividend income) | 972 |
| 43,250 | | | |
| 275 | × 32.5% | (dividends) | 89 |
| 43,525 | | | |

| Income tax liability | 7,766 |
|---|---|

**Tax saving**

| Tax saved in computation (£9,083 – £7,766) | 1,317 |
|---|---|
| Tax saved at source (£5,850 – £4,680) | 1,170 |
| | 2,487 |

## Tax efficient remuneration

The technical details on employment income were covered in Chapter 2. This is another possible scenario for income tax planning through the comparison of different remuneration packages.

A selection of areas to consider are:

- the provision of a company car compared to using the individual's own car and claiming mileage allowance
- comparison of approved and unapproved share schemes
- using a range of exempt benefits.

Workout plc runs a nation-wide chain of health clubs, with each club being run by a manager who is paid an annual salary of £42,500. The company has a flexible remuneration policy in that it allows managers to enhance their salary by choosing from a package of benefits.

Gareth Step is to be appointed as a manager of Workout plc on 6 April 2009 and he has asked for your advice regarding the tax implications arising from each aspect of the benefits package.

The package is as follows:

**Motor car**

Option 1:

Workout plc will provide a new 2198cc petrol car with a list price of £19,200 and $CO_2$ emissions of 182 g/km, and will pay for all running costs, including private fuel. Gareth will make a capital contribution of £3,000 towards the cost of the car, and will also be required to contribute a further £50 per month towards its private use. He will drive a total of 1,750 miles per month, of which 60% will be in respect of journeys in the performance of his duties for Workout plc.

Option 2:

Alternatively, Workout plc will pay Gareth additional salary of £500 per month, and he will lease a private motor car. Workout plc will then pay an allowance of 30 pence per mile for business mileage. The statutory rates allowed are 40 pence per mile for the first 10,000 miles, and 25 pence per mile thereafter.

**Accommodation**

Option 1:

Gareth currently lives 140 miles from where he is to be employed by Workout plc. The company will pay £7,500 towards the cost of relocation, and will also provide an interest free loan of £90,000 in order for Gareth to purchase a property. The loan will be repaid in monthly instalments of £1,000 commencing on 15 April 2009.

Option 2:

Alternatively, Workout plc will provide living accommodation for Gareth. This will be in a house that the company purchased in 1996 for £86,500. The house has a rateable value of £7,700 and is currently valued at £135,000. The furniture in the house cost £12,400. Workout plc will pay for the annual running costs of £3,900.

**Telephone**

Option 1:

Workout plc will provide Gareth with a mobile telephone costing £500, and will pay for all business and private telephone calls.

Option 2:

Alternatively, Workout plc will pay Gareth £75 per month towards the cost of his fixed telephone at home. The total annual cost will be £1,400, of which £300 is for line rental, £650 for business telephone calls and £450 for private telephone calls.

**Explain the tax implications for Gareth arising from each aspect of the benefits package.**

You should assume that benefits are provided on 6 April 2009.

NIC, VAT and the tax implications for Workout plc should be ignored.

## 3 Chapter summary

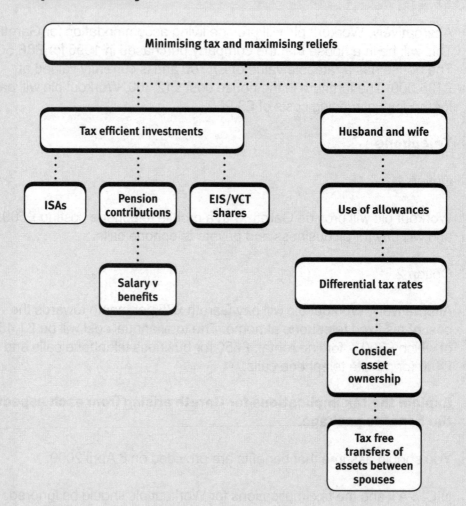

## Test your understanding answers

### Test your understanding 1

**Workout plc**

**Tutorial note:** You are required to explain the tax implications for Gareth only, but not required to advise him which options to choose.

**Company car**

Gareth will be assessed on employment income on a car benefit of £3,288 (W1) and a fuel benefit of £4,056 (W1).

The additional income tax liability is £2,938 (£3,288 + £4,056 = £7,344 at 40%).

**Cash alternative**

The additional salary of £500 per month will be taxed as employment income, with 40% income tax and 1% NIC.

This will leave cash of £3,540 (£500 × 12 = £6,000 × 59%) after tax and NIC.

Gareth will be paid an allowance of 30p per mile for 12,600 (1,750 × 12 × 60%) business miles.

The mileage allowance received will be tax free, and Gareth can make the following expense claim:

|  | £ |
|---|---:|
| 10,000 miles at 40p | 4,000 |
| 2,600 miles at 25p | 650 |
| | |
| AMAP | 4,650 |
| Mileage allowance received (12,600 at 30p) | (3,780) |
| | |
| Expense claim against employment income | 870 |

Gareth needs to consider whether the cash salary is preferable to the company car. If he accepts the cash he will receive:

|  | £ |
|---|---:|
| Cash – additional salary | 3,540 |
| Mileage allowance | 3,780 |
| Tax relief on shortfall (40% × £870) | 348 |
|  | 7,668 |
| Tax no longer payable on benefit | 2,938 |
| Increase in cash | 10,606 |

He needs to consider whether this is enough to buy and run his car personally. If it is, the cash alternative would appear to be better.

**Relocation costs**

As the £8,000 limit is not exceeded, there should not be a taxable benefit in respect of the relocation costs paid for by Workout plc. This is because Gareth does not live within a reasonable daily travelling distance of where he is to be employed.

The exemption covers such items as legal and estate agents' fees, stamp duty, removal costs, and the cost of new domestic goods where existing goods are not available in the new residence.

**Beneficial loan**

Gareth will be assessed on the difference between the interest paid on the loan and the official rate of interest as earnings. The 'average' method of calculation gives a taxable benefit for 2009/10 of £3,990 (W2).

The additional income tax liability is therefore £1,596 (£3,990 at 40%).

The balance at 5 April 2010 is after taking account of 12 monthly repayments of £1,000.

### Living accommodation

Gareth will be assessed on the provision of the living accommodation provided to him. There will be an additional benefit based on the market value of £135,000, since the house cost in excess of £75,000 and it was purchased more than six years before first being provided.

The taxable benefit will be:

|  | £ |
|---|---|
| Rateable value | 7,700 |
| Additional benefit (£135,000 – £75,000) × 4.75% | 2,850 |
| Furniture (£12,400 × 20%) | 2,480 |
| Running costs | 3,900 |
|  | ——— |
| Total accommodation benefits | 16,930 |
|  | ——— |

The income tax liability is £6,772 (£16,930 at 40%).

### Mobile telephone

The provision of one mobile telephone per employee does not give rise to a taxable benefit, even if there is private use.

### Fixed telephone

If Gareth receives £75 per month towards his home telephone, he will assessed on a taxable employment benefit of £900 (12 × £75). However he will be able to make an expense claim of £650 in respect of the expenditure on business calls.

The additional income tax liability is therefore £100 (£900 – £650 = £250 × 40%).

**Workings**

(W1)     **Car and fuel benefit**

$CO_2$ emissions = 182 g/km, available all year

Appropriate % = 15% + (180 − 135) × 1/5 = 24%

Cost = (£19,200 − £3,000 Capital contribution) = £16,200

|  | £ |
|---|---:|
| Car benefit (£16,200 × 24%) | 3,888 |
| Less Monthly contribution (£50 × 12) | (600) |
| Car benefit | 3,288 |
| Fuel benefit (£16,900 × 24%) | 4,056 |

(W2)     **Beneficial loan**

|  | £ |
|---|---:|
| Loan at start of year | 90,000 |
| Loan at end of year | 78,000 |
|  | 168,000 |
| Average loan = (168,000 ÷ 2) = £84,000 | |
| Assessable benefit (£84,000 × 4.75%) | 3,990 |

# 6

# CGT: Computations and stamp duty land tax

## Chapter learning objectives

Upon completion of this chapter you will be able to:

- compute the capital gains tax payable, given a variety of basic transactions for an individual including the treatment of losses

- recognise when a disposal is effective for capital gains tax purposes

- recognise when a negligible value claim can be made and the effect thereof

- determine when capital gains tax can be paid by instalments and evaluate when this would be advantageous to taxpayers

- identify the capital gains tax position for an individual at death and the additional relief available for capital losses

- advise on the capital gains tax implications of transfers of property into a trust

- explain the different types of stamp duty, identify when stamp duty land tax is payable on the transfer of land and calculate the amount of stamp duty payable.

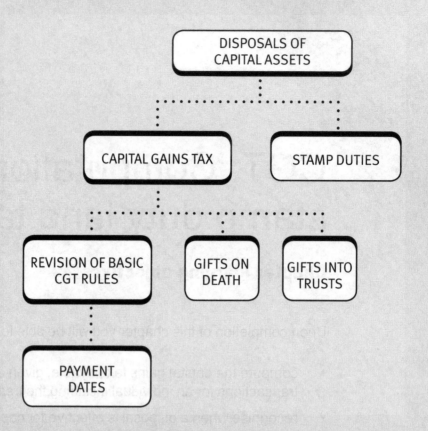

## 1 A revision of basic capital gains tax rules

### Introduction

This and the following three chapters deal with the way in which individuals are subject to capital gains tax on their chargeable gains.

Much of this chapter is a revision of the rules covered in F6. A brief reminder of F6 content is given, and revision examples are provided to check your retention of the required F6 knowledge.

The main new topics introduced include the implications of putting assets into a trust and stamp duty land tax.

### The scope of capital gains tax

Capital gains tax (CGT) is charged on gains arising from **chargeable disposals** of **chargeable assets** by **chargeable persons**.

A reminder of these important terms is given below.

| Chargeable disposal | Exempt disposal |
|---|---|
| The following are treated as chargeable disposals:<br><br>(i) sale or gift of the whole or part of an asset<br><br>(ii) exchange of an asset<br><br>(iii) loss or total destruction of an asset<br><br>(iv) receipts of a capital sum derived from an asset, for example:<br><br>    • compensation received for damage to an asset<br><br>    • receipts for the surrender of rights to an asset. | Exempt disposals include:<br><br>(i) disposals as a result of the death of an individual<br><br>(ii) gifts to charities. |

| Chargeable assets | Exempt assets |
|---|---|
| All forms of capital assets, wherever situated, are chargeable assets.<br><br>Common examples include:<br><br>• Freehold land and buildings<br><br>• Goodwill<br><br>• Short lease<br><br>• Long lease<br><br>• Unquoted shares<br><br>• Quoted shares<br><br>• Unit trusts<br><br>• Chattels bought and sold > £6,000.<br><br>(Chattels are tangible moveable assets e.g. furniture, plant and machinery) | Exempt assets include:<br><br>• Motor vehicles (including vintage cars)<br><br>• Main residence<br><br>• Cash<br><br>• Wasting chattels (e.g. racehorses and greyhounds)<br><br>• Chattels bought and sold < £6,000<br><br>• Investments held within an ISA<br><br>• Qualifying corporate bonds (QCBs)<br><br>• Gilt-edged securities<br><br>• National Savings Certificates<br><br>• Shares in a VCT<br><br>• Endowment policy proceeds<br><br>• Foreign currency for private use<br><br>• Debtors<br><br>• Trading stock<br><br>• Prizes and betting winnings. |

A chargeable person includes individuals, companies and partners in a partnership.

This chapter concentrates on the CGT implications of disposals by individuals.

## The basis of assessment

Individuals are assessed to CGT:

*   under self assessment

*   based on actual disposals of capital assets made between 6 April and 5 April.

## The date of disposal

Determining the date of disposal is very important as it determines the tax year in which a chargeable gain is assessed or an allowable loss arises.

| Event | Date of disposal |
|---|---|
| Lifetime transfer:<br><br>• normally | • Date of the contract/agreement to transfer the asset (not necessarily the same date as the actual date of transfer) |
| • conditional contract | • Date when all of the conditions are satisfied and the contract becomes legally binding |
| Transfers on death: | • Date of death of the individual (although no CGT payable on death) - see section 3 |

### Example 1 - Date of disposal

Emily decided to sell an investment property to Joe. Contracts were exchanged on 13 February 2010 with an intended completion date of 25 March 2010, but the contract was conditional on planning permission being obtained.

Planning permission was granted on 29 March 2010 and completion took place on 8 April 2010.

**State, with reasons, the tax year in which the gain on the investment property will be taxed.**

**Solution**

Emily will be taxed on the gain in 2009/10.

The completion date is not relevant. The sale agreement was a conditional contract and the disposal takes place when the condition is satisfied (i.e. 29 March 2010).

## The capital gains tax computation

The following steps should be carried out to compute the capital gains tax payable by an individual for a tax year:

**Step 1** Calculate the chargeable gains/allowable loss arising on the disposal of each chargeable asset separately

**Step 2** Consider the availability of any CGT reliefs (Chapter 9).

**Step 3** Calculate the net chargeable gains arising in the tax year = (capital gains less allowable losses)

**Step 4** Deduct capital losses brought forward

**Step 5** Deduct the annual exemption = taxable gains

**Step 6** Calculate the CGT payable at a flat rate of 18%.

### Proforma capital gains tax payable computation – 2009/10

|                                               | £        |
|-----------------------------------------------|----------|
| Net chargeable gains for the tax year         | X        |
| Less: Capital losses brought forward (see Note) | (X)     |
|                                               | X        |
| Less: Annual exemption (AE)                    | (10,100) |
| Taxable gains                                  | X        |
| CGT payable (18% × taxable gains)              | X        |

### The calculation of the individual chargeable gains/allowable losses

The calculation of the individual chargeable gains/allowable losses on each capital transaction should be presented using the following proforma:

|  | Notes | £ |
|---|---|---|
| Consideration | 1 | X |
| Less Incidental costs of sale | 2 | (X) |
|  |  |  |
| Net sale proceeds |  | NSP |
| Less Allowable expenditure |  |  |
| – Acquisition cost | 3 | (X) |
| – Incidental costs of acquisition | 2 | (X) |
| – Enhancement expenditure |  | (X) |
|  |  |  |
| Chargeable gain/(allowable loss) |  | X/(X) |

### Notes

(1) The consideration is normally:

- **disposal proceeds actually received** for a sale to an unconnected person

- **market value** for gifts and sale to connected persons.

(2) Allowable incidental costs of sale and acquisition include:

- legal expenses

- valuation fees, estate agent fees, auctioneer's fees

- advertising costs

- stamp duty (on shares) and stamp duty land tax (on land and buildings).

(3) The acquisition cost is normally:

- **actual cost** if the asset was purchased

- **market value** when acquired if the asset was gifted

- **probate value** at the date of the donor's death if the asset was inherited.

## Capital losses

### Current year capital losses

Capital losses arising on assets in the current tax year are set off against chargeable gains, arising in the same tax year;

- to the maximum possible extent
- they cannot be restricted to avoid wasting all or part of the AE.

Any unrelieved capital losses are carried forward to offset against gains in future years.

### Brought forward capital losses

Brought forward losses:

- are set against gains **after** any current year losses have been deducted
- will be restricted to preserve the AE of £10,100
- any unused loss is then carried forward for use in the future.

### Negligible value claims

If the value of an asset becomes negligible for whatever reason, the owner may claim relief.

They are then treated as having disposed of, and immediately reacquired, the asset at its negligible value. This treatment crystallises a capital loss.

The deemed disposal is treated as occurring:

- at the date of the claim, or
- up to two years before the start of the tax year in which the claim was made.

The back dating of the capital loss applies only if the asset was actually of negligible value at both the date of the claim and the earlier date.

## Annual exemption

Every individual is entitled to an annual exemption (AE) for each tax year.

- For 2009/10 the AE is £10,100.
- If the AE is not utilised in any particular tax year, then it is wasted.

## Test your understanding 1

Julie sold an investment property on 1 May 2009 for £650,000. She had acquired the building for £80,000 in June 1996 and had extended it at a cost of £30,000 in June 1998.

Julie also disposed of a painting on 1 June 2009 for £20,000, incurring auctioneer's fees of 1%. She had acquired the painting for £35,000 in April 1998.

Jade had capital losses brought forward of £16,000. Julie's taxable income in 2009/10 was £31,000.

**Calculate Julie's capital gains tax payable for 2009/10 and state the due date for payment.**

## A summary of the revision of basic CGT rules

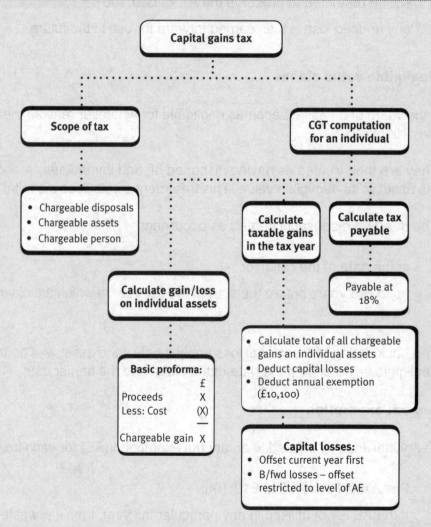

## 2 The payment of capital gains tax

### Payment under self assessment

CGT is normally payable:

*   under self assessment
*   in one payment along with the balancing payment of income tax
*   31 January 2011 for 2009/10.

### Payment by instalments

CGT may be paid by instalments:

*   where consideration is received in instalments, and
*   on certain lifetime gifts.

| Payment by instalments | |
| --- | --- |
| **Event** | **Payment details** |
| If the consideration is received in instalments over a period of more than 18 months. | Instalments may be spread over the shorter of: <br><br> • eight years <br> • the period over which payment of the disposal proceeds is spread. <br><br> Interest on overdue tax is only charged if an instalment is paid late. |
| Gifts: <br><br> • of land, or an interest in land; <br> • out of a controlling interest in shares or securities (quoted or unquoted) <br> • out of a minority interest in shares or securities of an unquoted company <br> • where the donor is not entitled to gift relief (see Chapter 9). | Instalments may be paid: <br><br> • in ten equal annual instalments <br> • starting on the normal due date. <br><br> The tax not paid on the normal due date (i.e. 90%) will attract interest on overdue tax calculated in the normal way. <br><br> The interest is payable with the remaining instalments. |

## 3 Capital gains tax on the death of an individual

### The CGT consequences of the event of death

CGT is a 'lifetime tax'. Transfers on the death of an individual are therefore exempt disposals.

The CGT consequences of death are as follows:

- no capital gain or allowable loss arises as a result of the death
- the beneficiaries inherit the assets of the deceased and are deemed to acquire the assets:
  - with a base cost equivalent to the market value of the asset at the date of death (i.e. at probate value)
  - on the date of death, regardless of the date they actually receive the asset.

However, note that whilst the increase in the capital value of the asset is not liable to CGT, there are inheritance tax implications arising from the death of an individual (see later chapters).

### Example 2 - Death of an individual

John bought an asset on 16 August 1987 for £300 and died on 10 December 2009 when the asset was worth £1,000,000. The asset is left to Malcolm, his son. The executors gave the asset to Malcolm on 24 March 2010.

Malcolm sold the asset for £1,200,000 on 16 March 2011.

**Explain the capital gains tax consequences arising from the above events.**

**Solution**

**John's death**

On John's death the following consequences arise:

- the increase in the value of the asset of £999,700 (£1,000,000 – £300) is exempt from capital gains tax
- Malcolm is deemed to acquire the asset at a base cost of £1,000,000 on 10 December 2009
- the fact that Malcolm actually received the asset on 24 March 2010 is not relevant.

**Sale of asset by Malcolm**

On the disposal of the asset by Malcolm:

- a capital gain of £200,000 (£1,200,000 - £1,000,000) will arise

## Capital losses in the year of death

Losses in excess of gains arising in the tax year of death can be:

- carried back three tax years
- on a LIFO basis
- and set against the remaining net gains in those years.

Note that the set off must be restricted to preserve the annual exemption, as for brought forward losses.

As a result of carrying back losses, a repayment of capital gains tax will be obtained from HMRC. This repayment will be an asset at the date of the individual's death, to be included in his estate (see Chapter 13).

## 4 Transfers of assets into a trust

An individual may gift assets into a trust fund during their lifetime or on their death under the provisions of their will.

The following CGT consequences will arise in respect of a gift into a trust:

| Lifetime gift by the donor | Gift on death of the donor |
|---|---|
| • Chargeable disposal at full market value <br> • Gift relief is available on any asset (Chapter 9) as there is an immediate charge to IHT | • No chargeable gain or allowable loss arises as a result of the death <br> • The trustees acquire the assets at probate value on the date of death |

Trusts are covered in more detail in Chapter 14.

## 5 Stamp duty land tax

### Introduction

There are two types of stamp duties:

| | Transactions |
|---|---|
| Stamp duty | Transfers of shares and other marketable securities |
| Stamp duty land tax | Transfers of UK land and property |

Stamp duty is covered in detail in Chapter 8. This section covers stamp duty land tax.

Stamp duty land tax (SDLT) is payable on transactions involving land, unless the transaction is specifically exempt.

SDLT is payable:

* by the purchaser
* on the transfer of UK land and property, lease premiums and rent paid under leases
* based on the value of the property transferred.

### Leases of UK land and property

SDLT is charged on premiums paid in respect of a lease and the rent paid on leases. However, this aspect of SDLT is not examinable.

### Purchases of UK land and property

SDLT is charged at a rate of up to 4% but depends upon the:

* consideration paid
* nature of the property.

The rates payable are given in the tax rates and allowances in the examination (see the front of this workbook for a copy of the rates).

Note that if the consideration exceeds a particular threshold, the whole of the consideration is charged at the corresponding rate.

## Consideration paid

The consideration subject to duty is any money or money's worth provided by the purchaser.

Where the payment of the consideration is subject to a contingency, it is assumed that the contingency is satisfied. On the other hand, any contingency that would result in a reduction of the consideration is assumed not to occur.

Where the consideration is unascertainable at the time of the transaction it must be estimated.

Any changes to the consideration caused by future events must be notified to HMRC and duty will be paid or repaid as appropriate.

## Example 3 - Stamp duty land tax

Peter Robinson purchased the following in September 2009

(a) A terraced house costing £110,000.

(b) A town house costing £300,000. Peter will use this house as his main residence.

(c) A retail shop costing £140,000.

(d) A office building costing £200,000.

**Calculate the amount of stamp duty land tax payable.**

**Solution**

(a) SDLT on the purchase of a terraced house:
£Nil, as the price paid is ≤ £175,000

(b) SDLT on the purchase of town house:
£300,000 × 3% = £9,000

(c) SDLT on the purchase of a shop (commercial property):
£140,000 × 0% = Nil, as the price is ≤ £150,000

(d) SDLT on the purchase of a freehold office (commercial property):
£200,000 × 1% = £2,000.

### Test your understanding 2

Wayne purchased a non-residential property for £420,000.

Ray sold some residential land to Margaret for £185,000. Margaret then sold some non-residential land to Beth for £145,000.

**Calculate the amount of SDLT payable by Wayne, Margaret and Beth assuming all transactions took place in 2009/10.**

### Exemptions from stamp duty land tax

There is no SDLT payable if the transfer is exempt.

The main exempt transfers are as follows:

- gifts, provided no consideration is given
- divorce arrangements
- variation of a will
- transfers of assets between members of a 75% group of companies.

### Transfers between 75% companies

There is no charge to stamp duty or SDLT where assets are transferred between two group companies.

Two companies are in a group where one is a 75% subsidiary of the other or they are both 75% subsidiaries of a third company. This definition may be regarded as the same as that for chargeable gains.

This relief is not available where, at the time the assets are transferred, arrangements exist for the purchasing company to leave the group.

Any relief given in respect of SDLT is withdrawn, with duty becoming payable, if the transferee company leaves the group within three years of the transfer whilst still owning the land transferred.

## Administration of stamp duty land tax

SDLT is payable:

- by the purchaser
- with the return which should be submitted within 30 days of the completion date (i.e. the date on which the contract for the land transaction is legally completed).

Interest is charged on late paid tax.

Penalties may be charged.

### Administration of SDLT

The purchaser will receive a certificate from HMRC which must be submitted to the Land Registry in order to register ownership of land.

In a manner similar to self assessment, HMRC will issue the certificate immediately but will then have nine months in order to make an enquiry into the return.

Penalties may be charged in respect of:

- incorrect returns (this follows the penalty regime for all other taxes, see Chapter 16)
- failure to provide information requested by HMRC
- assisting in the preparation of an incorrect return.

The fraudulent evasion of SDLT is an offence which may result in a fine and/or prison.

## Summary

```
                    ┌─────────────────────────┐
                    │   Stamp duty land tax   │
                    └─────────────────────────┘
```

```
┌──────────────────┐   ┌──────────────────┐   ┌──────────────────┐
│    Basic rules   │   │    Exemptions    │   │  Administration  │
└──────────────────┘   └──────────────────┘   └──────────────────┘
```

**Payable:**
- by the purchaser
- on the transfer of UK land and property
- based on the value of the property transferred

**Exempt transfers:**
- Gifts
- Divorce arrangements
- Variation of a will
- Transfers between 75% companies

- Payable within 30 days of the completion date
- Interest is charged on duty paid late
- Penalties may be charged in respect of:
  - incorrect returns
  - failure to provide information to HMRC
  - assisting in the preparation of an incorrect return

- charged at a rate of up to 4%
- depends upon the:
  - consideration paid, and
  - nature and location of the property (i.e. residential or non-residential)

## 6 Chapter summary

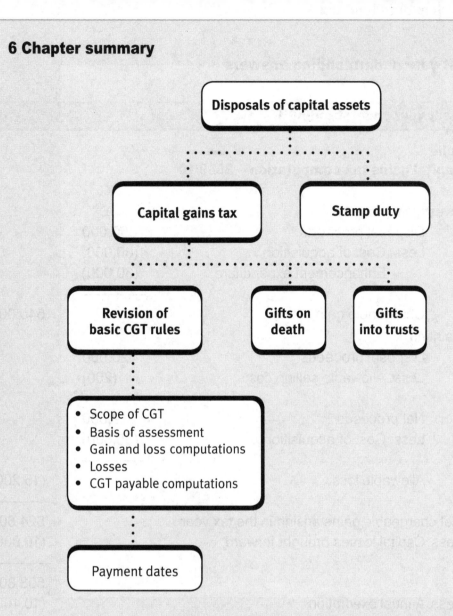

## Test your understanding answers

### Test your understanding 1

**Julie**
**Capital gains tax computation – 2009/10**

| | £ | £ |
|---|---:|---:|
| Investment property | | |
| Disposal proceeds | 650,000 | |
| Less: Cost of acquisition | (80,000) | |
| Enhancement expenditure | (30,000) | |
| Chargeable gain | | 540,000 |
| Painting | | |
| Disposal proceeds | 20,000 | |
| Less: Allowable selling costs | (200) | |
| Net proceeds | 19,800 | |
| Less: Cost of acquisition | (35,000) | |
| Allowable loss | | (15,200) |
| Net chargeable gains arising in the tax year | | 524,800 |
| Less: Capital losses brought forward | | (16,000) |
| | | 508,800 |
| Less: Annual exemption | | (10,100) |
| Taxable gains | | 498,700 |
| Capital gains tax payable (£498,700 × 18%) | | 89,766 |
| Due date | | 31.1.2011 |

### Test your understanding 2

| **Wayne** | | £ |
|---|---|---:|
| Wayne | (3% × £420,000) - commercial | 12,600 |
| Margaret | (1% × £185,000) - residential | 1,850 |
| Beth | (under £150,000) - commercial | Nil |

KAPLAN PUBLISHING

# CGT: Variations to computations

## Chapter learning objectives

Upon completion of this chapter you will be able to:

- identify connected persons for CGT purposes and advise on the implications of transfers between them

- recognise how capital transactions are treated for transfers between spouses and registered civil partners and identify tax planning opportunities for spouses and civil partners

- compute the CGT payable, given a variety of transactions including part disposals, chattels and plant and machinery

- state the effect for capital gains on the disposal of a wasting asset including those used in a trade

- identify the appropriate capital gains treatment of a small part disposal of land

- calculate the gain on the disposal of both long and short leases

- establish the tax effect of appropriations to and from trading stock

- explain the capital gains treatment where an asset is lost or destroyed and the effect of capital sums received

- explain the capital gains treatment where an asset is damaged and the effect of capital sums received.

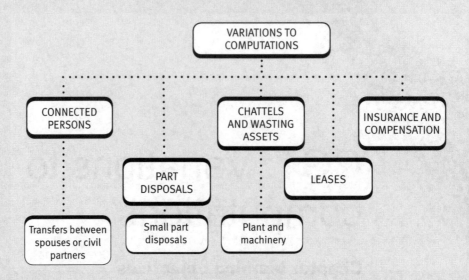

# 1 Introduction

The basic proforma for calculating chargeable gains/(allowable losses) can be used for all disposals of any assets. However, in certain circumstances there are additional special rules which need to be applied.

This chapter is mainly revision of topics covered at F6. A brief reminder of F6 content is given and revision examples are provided to check your retention of the required F6 knowledge.

The main new topics introduced at P6 include tax planning aspects, the assignment of leases and appropriations to and from trading stock.

# 2 The treatment of disposals between connected persons

## The definition of connected persons

An individual is essentially connected with their spouse or civil partner and relatives (and their spouses).

An individual is connected with their:

- spouse or civil partner

- relatives (and their spouses or civil partners)

- spouse's or civil partner's relatives (and their spouses or civil partners)

- their business associates

- a company they control.

The term '**relative**' means:

- brothers and sisters

- parents, grandparents and other ancestors

- children, grandchildren and other descendants.

The term '**business associate**' means:

- partners in business
- a business partner's spouse or civil partner
- relatives of the business partner.

## The implications of disposals to a connected person

The CGT implications of making a disposal to a connected person **other than to the spouse or civil partner** are as follows:

| Consideration used in the gain computation | • **Market value** at the date of the disposal (regardless of any consideration actually received). |
|---|---|
| Capital loss on a disposal to a connected person | • Can **only** be set off against current or future gains arising from disposals to the same connected person. |

## The implications of transfers between spouses or civil partners

Inter spouse transfers and transfers between civil partners are treated as 'nil gain/nil loss' (NGNL) transfers.

Inter spouse transfers and transfers between civil partners are treated as follows:

- the transfer is deemed to take place for a consideration which will give rise to neither a gain nor a loss, regardless of any actual consideration which may have been received
- if the transfer is on/after 6 April 2008, the transferor is deemed to have disposed of the asset at its acquisition cost
- if the transfer is before 6 April 2008, the transferor is deemed to have disposed of the asset at a 'base cost' which ensured that there was no gain or loss on the transfer under the 'pre 6 April 2008' capital gains tax rules.

  If applicable, the examiner will give you the appropriate 'base cost' to use in the examination question.

Note that these rules only apply whilst the couple are living together (i.e. not separated).

---

### Test your understanding 1

Charlie bought a seaside flat in Cornwall in December 1987 for £23,600 to use when he was on holiday from work. The flat has never been used as Charlie's main residence.

In November 2009 Charlie decided to gift the flat which was worth £175,000.

(a) **Calculate the chargeable gain arising on the gift of the flat assuming Charlie gifted the flat to:**

    (i) **his sister**

    (ii) **his wife.**

(b) **Calculate the chargeable gain arising if the sister sells the flat in May 2010 for £200,000.**

(c) **Calculate the chargeable gain arising if the wife sells the flat in May 2010 for £200,000.**

---

## Tax planning opportunities for spouses and civil partners

A couple can use the nil gain/nil loss (NGNL) transfer rule to their advantage to save tax in some situations.

For the purposes of this section reference is made to spouses, husbands and wives. However, note that the same tax planning opportunities apply to couples in a civil partnership.

### Utilising capital losses

Capital losses cannot be transferred between spouses.

Where one spouse will make a gain and the other a capital loss, it is possible to transfer the asset before the disposal on a nil gain/nil loss basis, so one spouse makes both disposals and the loss can be used to reduce the gain.

### Utilising annual exemptions

Each spouse is entitled to an annual exemption.

The couple can also utilise the nil gain/nil loss transfer rule to ensure each spouse fully utilises:

- any capital losses they may have from earlier years

- their annual exemption (£10,100 for 2009/10).

## Timing the disposals

Delaying disposals to the following tax year can give the individual taxpayer a cash flow advantage.

Any gains realised on disposals up to and including disposals on 5 April 2010 are assessable in 2009/10 and the associated CGT is payable on 31 January 2011.

Disposals later in the tax year should be delayed until 6 April 2010 or later. As a result, the gain is realised in 2010/11 and any CGT is payable on 31 January 2012.

## Impact on income tax

Inter spouse transfers of capital assets do not give rise to a CGT liability. However, care should be taken in advising which assets are transferred between spouses.

A transfer of:

- non-income generating assets (e.g. a painting, antiques) will have no impact on the couple's income tax position

- income generating assets (e.g. shares, letting property) will result in the income being taxed on the recipient spouse in the future.

- The couple should ensure that assets generating income are owned by the spouse paying income tax at the lowest rate.

  The couple can jointly own assets in equal or unequal proportions.

  However, it is important when giving advice to remember that:

  - even if owned in unequal proportions, any income generated from jointly owned assets will normally be split 50:50 between the spouses (unless the asset is shares in a close company)

  - unless the couple make a joint election to split the income according to beneficial ownership.

### Test your understanding 2

Alex owns an investment property that would realise a chargeable gain of £28,000 if sold in 2009/10.

His wife, Vanessa, has capital losses brought forward of £6,200.

**Explain the tax planning measures you would recommend and the taxation effect with supporting calculations as necessary.**

## 3 Part disposals

### The allowable expenditure calculation

The problem with part disposals is identifying how much of the original cost of the asset relates to the part disposed of.

The appropriate proportion is calculated as follows:

$$\text{Cost} \times \frac{A}{(A + B)}$$

where:

A = gross consideration of the part disposed of
B = market value of the remainder (at the time of the part disposal)

The appropriate proportion formula is applied to:

* the original cost (including any incidental acquisition costs)

* enhancement expenditure where the enhancement applies equally to the whole asset.

Note that if the enhancement relates:

| wholly to the part disposed of: | • deduct in full in the part disposal computation. |
|---|---|
| wholly to the part retained: | • do not deduct any in the part disposal computation. |

### Small part disposals of land and buildings

Where the proceeds received on the part disposal of land and buildings are 'small', a part disposal gain arises unless an election is made.

The effect of making an election is that:

* there will be no part disposal at the time

* the gain is deferred until the disposal of the remainder

* the gain is deferred by deducting the proceeds received on the small part disposal from the original cost of the asset

* the base cost of the part retained is therefore reduced and the gain arising on the subsequent disposal of the remainder will be higher.

## Definition of 'small'

> Proceeds are small if:
>
> :
>
> **Proceeds of the part disposal:**
> (i)  ≤ 20% of the value of land and building before the part disposal; and
> (ii)  Total of all land sales in the year ≤ £20,000.

### Test your understanding 3

Edward bought a 12 acre plot of land for £30,000 in March 2001 for investment purposes.

In June 2009, Edward sold two acres of the land for £9,500. The remaining 10 acres were worth £80,000.

In September 2010 Edward sold the remaining 10 acres for £135,000.

**Calculate the chargeable gains arising from the disposals of the land assuming:**

(i)  **an election is made to defer the gain on the part disposal.**

(ii)  **an election is not made.**

## 4 Chattels and wasting assets

### Chattels

A chattel is defined as tangible moveable property.

Chattels may be wasting assets (i.e. with a predictable life not exceeding 50 years) or non-wasting.

The CGT consequences of chattels can be summarised as follows:

| Wasting chattels | Non-wasting chattels |
|---|---|
| Expected life 50 years or less. | Expected life more than 50 years. |
| Examples: racehorse<br>     greyhound<br>     boat, caravan | Examples: antiques<br>     jewellery<br>     paintings |
| • Exempt.<br><br>• Exception: plant and machinery (see below). | • If bought and sold for under £6,000: – exempt.<br><br>• If bought and sold for more than £6,000:<br> – chargeable in the normal way<br><br>• Otherwise: Special rules apply – but not examinable at P6. |

## Wasting assets

Wasting assets have a predictable life of 50 years or less.

For CGT purposes, wasting assets can be split into three key categories.

- Chattels not eligible for capital allowances = exempt from CGT.
- Chattels eligible for capital allowances (e.g. plant and machinery).
- Other wasting assets.

## Plant and machinery

Plant and machinery is **always** deemed to be a wasting asset.

- Sold at a gain – normal calculations apply
- Sold at a loss – no gain/no loss as relief for loss given in capital allowances computation.

## Other wasting assets

This category covers wasting assets which are not chattels (for example, immoveable plant and machinery, copyrights and licences).

The special point about wasting assets that are not chattels is that the allowable expenditure is deemed to waste over the life of the asset.

Accordingly, when a disposal is made:

- the allowable expenditure is restricted to take account of the asset's natural fall in value

- the asset's fall in value is deemed to occur on a straight line basis over its predictable useful life

- the allowable cost is calculated as:

  C less [P/L × (C – R)]

  where:

  P is the disposer's period of ownership.
  L is the asset's predictable life.
  C is the cost of the asset.
  R is the residual value of the asset.

## Example 1 - Wasting assets

On 16 March 2002 Nicholas bought an asset at a cost of £45,000. It had an estimated useful life of 25 years and an estimated scrap value of £6,000. He sold the asset on 17 March 2010.

**Calculate the chargeable gain or allowable loss arising from the sale in March 2010 assuming:**

(i) **the asset is a wasting asset and was sold for £34,000**

(ii) **the asset is plant and machinery eligible for capital allowances and was sold for £34,000**

(iii) **the asset is plant and machinery eligible for capital allowances and was sold for £63,000.**

**Solution**

| (i) **Wasting asset – sold for £34,000** | £ | £ |
|---|---|---|
| Sale proceeds | | 34,000 |
| Less: Cost | 45,000 | |
| Less: Wasted cost | | |
| 8/ 25 × (£45,000 – £6,000) | (12,480) | |
| Allowable element of acquisition cost | | (32,520) |
| Chargeable gain | | 1,480 |

### (ii) P&M eligible for capital allowances – sold for £34,000

Nicholas has sold the machinery for a loss of £11,000 (£45,000 – £34,000).

He is compensated for this loss through the capital allowances system as he receives net capital allowances of £11,000 during his period of ownership of the machinery.

The allowable capital loss computation is therefore adjusted to reflect the relief for the loss already given through the capital allowances system and results in an NGNL situation as follows:

|  | £ | £ |
|---|---|---|
| Sale proceeds |  | 34,000 |
| Less: Cost | 45,000 |  |
| Less: Net capital allowances | (11,000) |  |
|  |  | (34,000) |
| Allowable loss |  | Nil |

### (iii) P&M eligible for capital allowances – sold for £63,000

Normal chargeable gain computation required as any capital allowances given will be claimed back with a balancing charge in the capital allowances system.

|  | £ |
|---|---|
| Sale proceeds | 63,000 |
| Less: Cost | (45,000) |
| Chargeable gain | 18,000 |

## 5 Leases

There are two situations relating to leases that are examinable:

- the assignment of a long lease
- the assignment of a short lease.

The assignment of a lease means the complete disposal of the leasehold interest in the property and is usually by way of a sale or a gift.

## The calculation of the chargeable gain

The CGT treatment on the assignment of a lease is as follows:

| Long lease | Short lease |
|---|---|
| (i.e. a lease with > 50 years to run at the date of disposal) | (i.e. a lease with 50 years or less to run at the date of disposal) |
| • Normal gain computation applies. | • Disposal of a wasting asset <br><br> • The allowable expenditure is adjusted to take account of the depreciating nature of the asset <br><br> • The cost is multiplied by the following fraction: <br><br> $$\frac{\% \text{ for life of the lease left on disposal date}}{\% \text{ for life of the lease left on acquisition}}$$ <br><br> • HMRC's lease depreciation percentages are given in the examination. |

HMRC's lease depreciation percentages for use in the questions in this workbook are given in the tax rates and allowances at the front of the workbook.

From the tables it can be seen that leases depreciate on a curvilinear basis: the lease loses value gradually at first, however at a much quicker rate nearer to the end of the life of the lease.

### Example 2 - Leases

Frank sold a leasehold shop for £90,000 on 30 September 2009. He had acquired the lease for £50,000 on 1 October 2008 when the lease had 40 years to run.

**Compute the chargeable gain arising on the assignment of the short lease in 2009/10.**

## Solution

|  | £ |
|---|---|
| Sale proceeds (September 2009) | 90,000 |

Less:

$$\text{Cost} \times \frac{\text{\% for life of the lease left on disposal date}}{\text{\% for life of the lease left on acquisition date}}$$

|  |  |
|---|---|
| £50,000 × $\dfrac{94.842 \,(\text{\% for 39 years})}{95.457 \,(\text{\% for 40 years})}$ | (49,678) |
| Chargeable gain | 40,322 |

### The lease percentage calculation

The length of time remaining on a lease at the time of disposal and acquisition is normally straightforward to calculate.

However, there are two situations to look out for:

- Where there are options within the lease to terminate the lease before expiry. The end of the lease is taken to be:

  - the earliest date when either the landlord or the tenant has the option to terminate the lease.

- The length of time remaining on the lease may not always be a whole number of years. Where this is the case:

  - calculations are performed to the nearest month

  - depreciation in between each year is deemed to occur on a straight line basis

  - $1/12^{\text{th}}$ of the difference between the percentages for the years either side of the actual duration is added for each extra month.

### Test your understanding 4

Geoffrey purchased a lease with 48 years to run on 1 September 2004 for £62,000. On 28 January 2010 he sold the lease for £75,000.

**Calculate the chargeable gain or allowable loss arising on the sale.**

## 6 Summary of variations to the basic computations

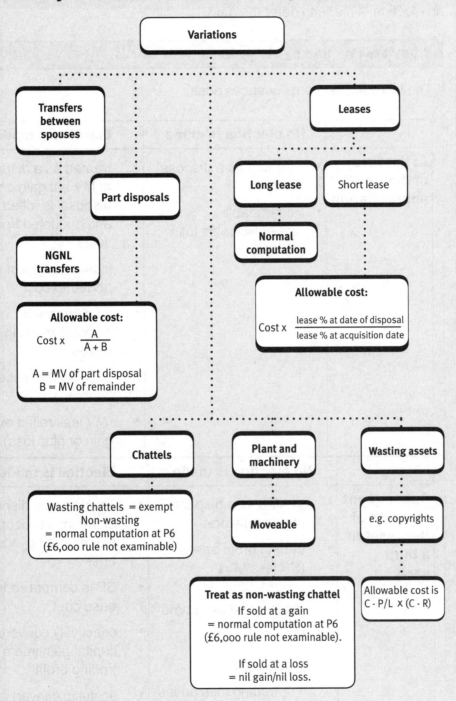

## 7 Transfers into and out of stock

### Transfers into trading stock

Where an asset is:

- acquired by an individual, then
- appropriated for the purposes of their trade,
- either on the commencement of trade or at a later date,

the transfer is treated as a disposal of the asset at full market value unless an election is made to defer the gain.

### Transfers into trading stock

The following tax consequences arise:

| | No election is made | Election is made |
|---|---|---|
| **At the time of the appropriation** | • treated as a disposal at MV <br><br> • chargeable gain/allowable loss arises | • treated as a disposal at MV but gain on disposal is rolled over and deducted from costs, or <br><br> • loss on disposal is added to cost <br><br> • no chargeable gain/allowable loss arises <br><br> • base cost of asset becomes: <br><br> • (MV less rolled over gain or plus loss). |
| | **No election is made** | **Election is made** |
| **Subsequent disposal of the asset to a third party** | • treated as a disposal of trading stock <br><br> • trading profit arises (SP less MV) <br><br> = assessed to income tax <br><br> • if sold < MV: <br> – trading loss arises <br> – relief per income tax rules | • Treated as a disposal of trading stock but higher trading income arises <br><br> • SP is compared to base cost <br><br> • effectively converts a capital gain into a trading profit <br><br> • useful to convert a potential capital loss into a trading loss |

### Transfers out of trading stock

Where an asset which is part of the trading stock of an individual's trade is:

- appropriated for another purpose, or
- retained by the individual on the cessation of trade

the transfer is treated as a disposal of a stock item at full market value.

A trading profit or loss will arise and there is no election available to change this treatment.

Similar rules apply to transfers to and from stock by a company.

## 8 Compensation and insurance

### Introduction

In most circumstances a capital transaction has two parties, a buyer and a seller.

However, when an asset is damaged, destroyed or lost and the asset's owner receives compensation (usually from an insurance company):

- the owner has received a capital sum without disposing of the asset
- the payer has received nothing in return.

Consequently a special set of rules is required.

The rules vary according to whether the asset has been:

- completely lost/destroyed or merely damaged
- whether the owner has replaced or restored the asset.

These rules were covered at F6 and are summarised in the following sections with diagrams and examples.

## Asset is totally destroyed or lost

Where an asset is lost or destroyed the CGT consequences are as follows:

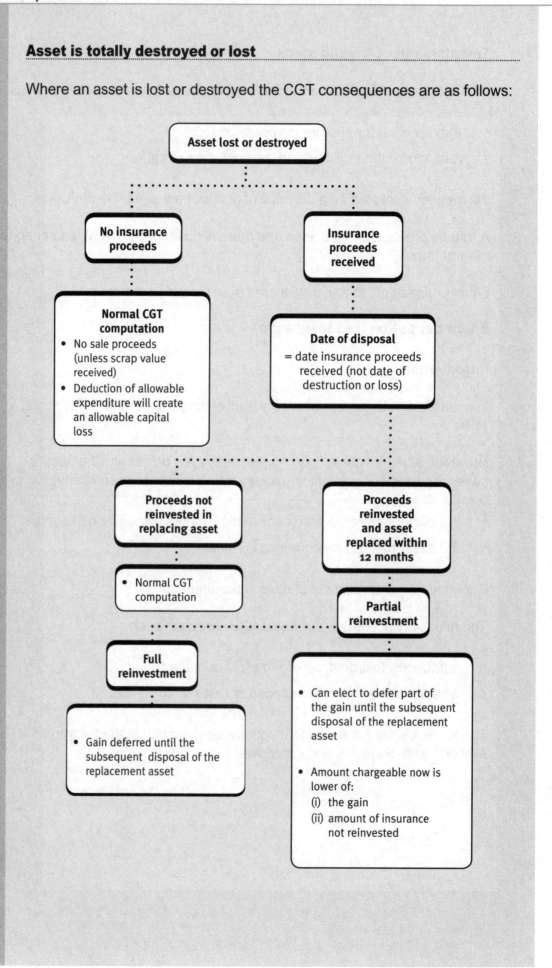

### Example 3 - Asset destroyed

Nadir purchased an asset for £15,000 on 1 April 1991 which was destroyed by fire on 31 July 2009. She received scrap proceeds of £1,000. The asset was not insured.

**Calculate the capital loss arising from the destruction of the asset.**

**Solution**

|  | £ |
|---|---|
| Proceeds – scrap proceeds | 1,000 |
| Cost | (15,000) |
|  | ———— |
| Allowable loss | (14,000) |
|  | ———— |

### Example 4 - Asset destroyed

Bill purchased an asset for £25,000 on 1 October 1992 which was destroyed by fire on 30 September 2009. He received scrap proceeds of £1,000 and compensation of £35,000 from his insurance company on 1 January 2010.

He purchased a replacement asset for £40,000 on 1 February 2010.

**Assuming that Bill claims the loss by fire to be a no gain/no loss disposal, calculate the allowable expenditure (base cost) of the replacement asset.**

**Solution**

|  |  | £ | £ |
|---|---|---|---|
| Cost of replacement asset |  |  | 40,000 |
| Less: | Compensation | 35,000 |  |
|  | Scrap proceeds | 1,000 |  |
|  |  | ———— |  |
|  |  | 36,000 |  |
| Less: | Cost of old asset | (25,000) |  |
|  |  | ———— | (11,000) |
|  |  |  | ———— |
| Replacement asset base cost |  |  | 29,000 |
|  |  |  | ———— |

### Test your understanding 5

Belinda purchased an antique necklace for £20,000 on 1 October 1998 which she lost on 30 June 2009. She received compensation of £45,000 from her insurance company on 1 October 2009 and purchased a replacement necklace for £50,000 on 1 November 2009.

She sold the replacement necklace for £65,000 on 1 March 2010.

**Assuming that Belinda claims the loss to be a no gain/no loss disposal, calculate the chargeable gain arising on the sale of the replacement necklace on 1 March 2010.**

### Asset is damaged but not totally destroyed or lost

Where an asset is damaged there are no implications for CGT purposes unless compensation, e.g. insurance proceeds, is received.

Where an asset is damaged and compensation is received there is a part disposal for CGT purposes. However, the computation is varied depending on whether or not the insurance proceeds are used to restore the asset.

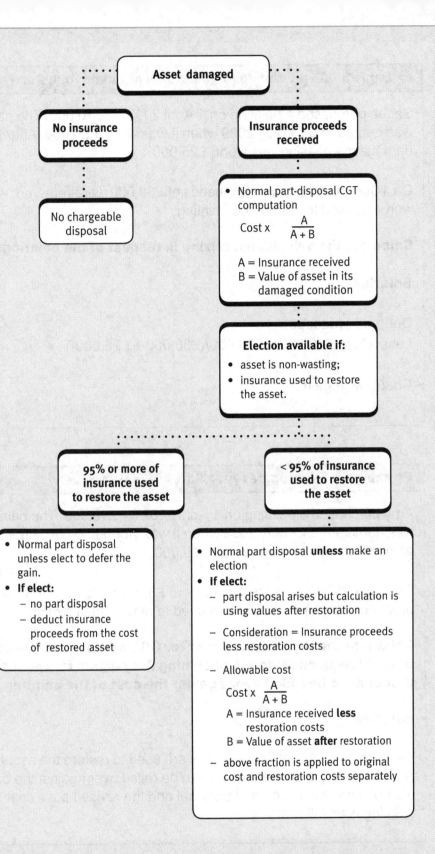

## Example 5 - Asset damaged, insurance not used to restore asset

Sasha purchased a painting on 1 April 2002 for £10,000. The painting was damaged on 1 May 2009 when it was worth £50,000. After the damage the painting was worth £25,000.

On 1 July 2009 insurance proceeds of £30,000 were received, which were not used to restore the painting.

**Calculate the gain, if any, arising in respect of the painting.**

**Solution**

|  | £ |
|---|---|
| Deemed proceeds | 30,000 |
| Less: Cost (£10,000 × £30,000/(£30,000 + £25,000)) | (5,455) |
| Chargeable gain | 24,545 |

## Example 6 - Asset damaged, > 95% of insurance used to restore

Amy purchased a painting on 1 April 2002 for £10,000. The painting was damaged on 1 May 2008 when it was worth £50,000. After the damage the painting was worth £40,000.

On 1 July 2009 insurance proceeds of £8,000 were received. All of the proceeds apart from £300 were used to restore the painting.

**Calculate the revised base cost for CGT purposes of the painting after it has been restored, assuming Amy elects for the insurance proceeds to be rolled over against the cost of the painting.**

**Solution**

As more than 95% of the proceeds are used to restore the asset and Amy has elected for the proceeds to be rolled over against the cost of the painting, there is no part disposal and the revised base cost of the painting is as follows:

| | £ |
|---|---|
| Original cost | 10,000 |
| Less: Insurance proceeds | (8,000) |
| | 2,000 |
| Cost of enhancement | 7,700 |
| Revised cost | 9,700 |

## Example 7 - Asset damaged, < 95% of insurance used to restore

Simone purchased an office block as an investment for £300,000 in April 2002. In May 2009 it was damaged by fire.

Restoration expenditure of £65,000 was incurred in July 2009 and Simone's insurance company eventually paid compensation of £160,000 in January 2010. After restoration, the office block had a market value of £1,500,000.

**Calculate the chargeable gain arising in 2009/10 assuming any election available is made.**

### Solution

| | £ | £ |
|---|---|---|
| Disposal proceeds (£160,000 – £65,000) | | |
| (compensation not used for restoration) | | 95,000 |
| Less: Proportion of original cost | | |
| (£95,000 / (£95,000 + £1,500,000)) × £300,000 | 17,868 | |
| Proportion of restoration cost | | |
| (£95,000 / (£95,000 + £1,500,000)) × £65,000 | 3,871 | |
| | | (21,739) |
| Chargeable gain | | 73,261 |

### Test your understanding 6

Shoesmith purchased an office block as an investment for £500,000 in April 2002. In September 2009 it was damaged by fire.

Restoration expenditure of £70,000 was incurred in February 2010 and Shoesmith's insurance company eventually paid compensation of £150,000 in June 2010. After restoration, the office block had a market value of £1,075,000.

**Calculate the chargeable gain arising in 2009/10 assuming Shoesmith makes any available election.**

KAPLAN PUBLISHING

# 9 Chapter summary

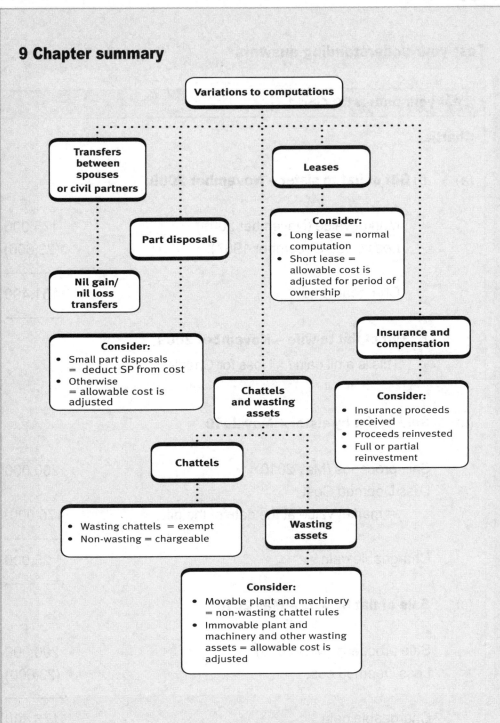

**Variations to computations**

**Transfers between spouses or civil partners**

**Leases**

**Part disposals**

**Consider:**
- Long lease = normal computation
- Short lease = allowable cost is adjusted for period of ownership

**Nil gain/ nil loss transfers**

**Consider:**
- Small part disposals = deduct SP from cost
- Otherwise = allowable cost is adjusted

**Chattels and wasting assets**

**Insurance and compensation**

**Consider:**
- Insurance proceeds received
- Proceeds reinvested
- Full or partial reinvestment

**Chattels**

- Wasting chattels = exempt
- Non-wasting = chargeable

**Wasting assets**

**Consider:**
- Movable plant and machinery = non-wasting chattel rules
- Immovable plant and machinery and other wasting assets = allowable cost is adjusted

## Test your understanding answers

### Test your understanding 1

**Charlie**

(a)    (i) **Gift of flat to sister – November 2009**

|  | £ |
|---|---|
| Market value (November 2009) | 175,000 |
| Less Cost (December 1987) | (23,600) |
| Chargeable gain | 151,400 |

    (ii) **Gift of flat to wife – November 2009**

This is a nil gain / nil loss for Charlie

(b)    **Sale of flat by sister – May 2010**

|  | £ |
|---|---|
| Sale proceeds (May 2010) | 200,000 |
| Less Deemed Cost | |
| = market value at the date of the gift | (175,000) |
| Chargeable gain | 25,000 |

(c)    **Sale of flat by wife – May 2010**

|  | £ |
|---|---|
| Sale proceeds (May 2010) | 200,000 |
| Less Deemed cost | (23,600) |
| Chargeable gain | 176,400 |

## Recommendations

Both husband and wife should consider making use of the CGT annual exemption. This can be achieved if Alex transfers part of the ownership of the property to Vanessa prior to the disposal to a third party. The transfer between spouses is treated as a nil gain/nil loss transaction.

As Vanessa has capital losses brought forward these could be used to offset any gain arising that belongs to her.

## The taxation effect

The % which needs to be transferred to obtain the optimum position on a disposal is calculated as follows:

Vanessa requires a gain of £nil after deducting the annual exemption of £10,100 and the £6,200 capital losses, a total of £16,300.

A gain of £16,300 for Vanessa out of a total of £28,000 is 58%. This leaves a gain of £11,700 for Alex.

CGT payable by Alex would be £288 ((£11,700 – £10,100) × 18%).

If no action is taken, Alex would have to pay CGT of £3,222 ((£28,000 – £10,100) × 18%).

The CGT saving would be £2,934 (£3,222– £288) if the transfer took place.

## Test your understanding 3

### Edward

(i) **An election to defer the gain on the part disposal is made**

**Disposal in June 2009**

In June 2009, the whole 12 acres are worth £89,500 (£9,500 + £80,000)

This is the only sale of land in the tax year, and the sale proceeds received of £9,500 are

– < £17,900 (20% × £89,500), and
– < £20,000.

Therefore an election can be made to defer the gain.

No gain arises on the part disposal, the base cost of the remaining 10 acres becomes £20,500 (£30,000 – £9,500).

| **Disposal in September 2010** | £ |
|---|---|
| Sale proceeds | 135,000 |
| Less: Base cost | (20,500) |
| | |
| Chargeable gain | 114,500 |

(ii) **No election is made**

| **Disposal in June 2009** | £ |
|---|---|
| Sale proceeds (2 acres) | 9,500 |
| Less: Cost (2 acres) | |
| = £30,000 × £9,500 / (£9,500 + £80,000) | (3,184) |
| | |
| Chargeable gain | 6,316 |

| **Disposal in September 2010** | £ |
|---|---|
| Sale proceeds | 135,000 |
| Less: Remaining cost (£30,000 – £3,184) | (26,816) |
| | |
| Chargeable gain | 108,184 |

### Test your understanding 4

**Geoffrey**

|                                   | £        |
|-----------------------------------|----------|
| Disposal proceeds (January 2010)  | 75,000   |
| Less: Deemed cost (W)             | (60,504) |
|                                   | ———      |
| Chargeable gain                   | 14,496   |
|                                   | ———      |

**Working: Deductible lease cost**

Years left to run at acquisition:  48 years
Years left to run at disposal:     42 years 7 months

The percentage for 42 years 7 months is:

96.593 + 7/12 × (97.107 - 96.593) = 96.893

The allowable cost to deduct in the computation is therefore:

$$\text{Cost} \times \frac{\text{\% for life of the lease left on disposal date}}{\text{\% for life of the lease left on acquistion date}}$$

$$= £62,000 \times \frac{96.893 \text{ (\% for 42 years 7 months)}}{99.289 \text{ (\% for 48 years)}}$$

$$= £60,504$$

### Test your understanding 5

**Belinda**

|  | £ |
|---|---|
| Proceeds | 65,000 |
| Less: Cost (W) | (25,000) |
| Chargeable gain | 40,000 |

**Working: Replacement asset base cost**

|  | £ | £ |
|---|---|---|
| Cost of replacement necklace |  | 50,000 |
| Insurance proceeds | 45,000 |  |
| Less: Cost | (20,000) |  |
|  |  | (25,000) |
| Replacement asset base cost |  | 25,000 |

### Test your understanding 6

**Shoesmith**

|  | £ | £ |
|---|---|---|
| Disposal proceeds (£150,000 – £70,000) |  |  |
| (compensation not used for restoration) |  | 80,000 |
| Less: Proportion of original cost |  |  |
| £80,000 / (£80,000 + £1,075,000) × £500,000 | 34,632 |  |
| Proportion of restoration cost |  |  |
| £80,000 / (£80,000 + £1,075,000) × £70,000 | 4,848 |  |
|  |  | (39,480) |
| Chargeable gain |  | 40,520 |

Note that the date of disposal is June 2010 (when the insurance compensation was received, **not** September 2009 when the damage took place).

# CGT: Shares and securities for individuals and stamp duty

## Chapter learning objectives

Upon completion of this chapter you will be able to:

- calculate the gain on the disposal of shares by an individual including situations which involve bonus and rights issues

- define a qualifying corporate bond (QCB), understand what makes a corporate bond non-qualifying and identify the capital gains tax implications of the disposal of QCB's

- identify the alternative capital gains tax treatment of the sale of rights issues

- identify the capital gains tax implications for an individual of a takeover or reorganisation of a shareholding in exchange for other shares, and where there is cash consideration received

- identify the capital gains tax implications for an individual of a takeover involving an exchange of shares for shares, cash and/or QCBs

- explain the capital gains tax implications arising from the liquidation of a company

- recognise the relief available for a capital loss on unquoted trading company shares

- identify when stamp duty is payable on the transfer of shares and securities and calculate the amount of stamp duty payable.

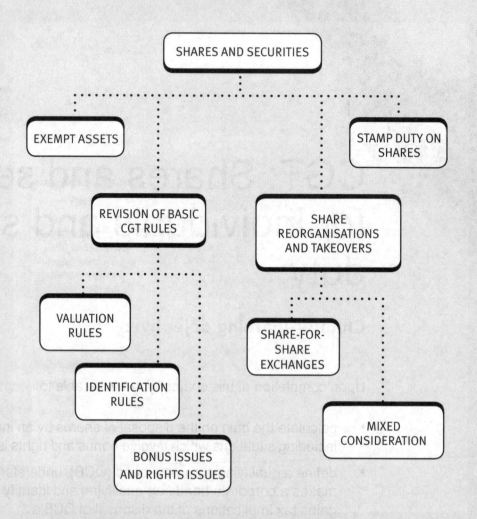

## 1 A revision of basic shares and securities rules

### Introduction

This chapter revises the CGT rules as they apply to shares and securities, which were covered at F6.

A brief reminder of F6 content is given, with the new rules introduced in the FA2008, and revision examples are provided to check your retention of the required F6 knowledge.

New topics introduced at P6 include the treatment of the sale of rights nil paid, share reorganisations with mixed consideration, the liquidation of a company and stamp duty which is levied on transactions in shares.

### Exempt shares and securities

All shares and securities in quoted and unquoted companies are chargeable assets for CGT purposes with the exception of:

- gilt-edged securities (for example, Treasury Stock, Exchequer stock)

- qualifying corporate bonds (QCB).

Note that gilt-edged securities and QCBs are exempt assets only when disposed of by an individual.

Gains and losses arising from the disposals of gilt-edged securities and QCBs by a company are taxable. The rules for companies are covered in Chapter 22.

**Definition of a QCB**

A QCB is a security which:

(a) represents a normal commercial loan

(b) is expressed in sterling and has no provision for either conversion into, or redemption in, any other currency; and

(c) was issued after 13 March 1984 or was acquired by the disposer after that date (whenever it was issued)

(d) it cannot be converted into shares.

The term 'corporate bond' includes permanent interest-bearing shares in building societies, provided they meet the condition set out in (b) above.

<u>**Valuation rules for shares**</u>

For the purposes of the rest of this chapter, the rules described apply to both shares and securities which are not exempt. However, for simplicity the term 'shares' will be used to denote both shares and securities.

On the sale of shares to an unconnected person, the actual sale proceeds are used in the capital gains computation.

On the gift of shares, or the transfer to a connected person, the market value must be used.

The market value of shares for CGT purposes is calculated as follows:

| **Quoted Shares** | Value = Lower of: <br><br> (1) 'Quarter Up' method <br>     = lower price + ¼ × (higher price − lower price). <br><br> (2) Average of the highest and lowest recorded bargains. |
|---|---|
| **Unquoted Shares** | In the examination the appropriate value will usually be given. |

**Test your understanding 1**

Shares in ABC plc are quoted in the Stock Exchange Daily Official List at 230p-270p. On the same day the highest and lowest recorded bargains were 224p and 276p.

**Calculate the value of ABC plc shares for capital gains tax purposes, assuming that they are gifted to another person.**

### Identification rules for individuals

Disposals of shares are matched in the following order with:

(1) acquisitions on the same day as the date of disposal

(2) acquisitions within the **following** 30 days on a first in, first out (FIFO basis)

(3) the share pool (i.e. shares acquired before the date of disposal are pooled together).

The share pool simply keeps a record of the number of shares in the same company acquired and sold, and the cost of those shares.

When shares are disposed out of the share pool the appropriate proportion of the cost that relates to the shares disposed of is calculated. The shares are disposed of at their average cost.

### Bonus issues and rights issues

The treatment of bonus and rights issues for CGT purposes can be summarised as follows:

| | Bonus issue | Rights issue |
|---|---|---|
| **Explanation** | A bonus issue is:<br><br>• the distribution of free shares<br>• to existing shareholders only<br>• in proportion to their existing shareholding. | A rights issue is:<br><br>• the offer of new shares<br>• to existing shareholders only<br>• in proportion to their existing shareholding<br>• usually at a discount on the current market value. |
| **For identification purposes** | Bonus and rights shares are included in the share pool. | |
| **For the purposes of calculating the gain on the shares** | As bonus shares are free.<br><br>• the number of shares are included in the pool, but no cost<br>• the total cost of the shares purchased is shared between all of the shares in issue after the bonus issue. | As there is cost involved in purchasing the rights shares:<br><br>• the number of shares are included in the pool, and the cost is added in the same way as a normal purchase<br>• the total cost is shared between all of the shares in issue after the rights issue. |

### Example 1 - Bonus and rights issues

Carmichael had the following transactions in Rudderham Ltd shares.

| | |
|---|---|
| January 2008 | purchased 1,800 shares for £5,400 |
| March 2009 | bonus issue of 1 for 2 |
| May 2009 | purchased 600 shares for £1,500 |
| June 2009 | took up 1-for-3 rights issue at £2.30 per share |
| August 2009 | sold 4,000 shares for £14,000 |

Assume that Rudderham Ltd is not Carmichael's personal trading company.

**Calculate the chargeable gains or allowable loss on the disposal in August 2009.**

**Solution**

|  |  | Number | Cost £ |
|---|---|---|---|
| January 2008 | Purchase | 1,800 | 5,400 |
| March 2009 | Bonus issue (1:2) | 900 | Nil |
| May 2009 | Purchase | 600 | 1,500 |
|  |  | 3,300 | 6,900 |
| June 2009 | Rights issue (1:3) × £2.30 | 1,100 | 2,530 |
|  |  | 4,400 | 9,430 |
| August 2009 | Sale | (4,000) | (8,573) |
| Balance c/f |  | 400 | 857 |

|  | £ |
|---|---|
| Sale proceeds | 14,000 |
| Less: Cost | (8,573) |
| Chargeable gain | 5,427 |

### Test your understanding 2

| Tom Chalk purchased the following shares in A plc: | Number | Cost £ |
|---|---|---|
| 18.04.88 | 1,500 | 900 |
| 14.06.91 Rights issue (70p each) | 1:3 |  |
| 31.05.00 | 1,000 | 2,000 |
| 31.07.00 Bonus issue | 1:4 |  |
| 31.08.04 | 900 | 1,500 |
| 28.01.10 | 1,500 | 3,000 |

Tom disposed of 4,500 shares in A plc on 31 December 2009 for £22,500. Assume A plc is not Tom's personal trading company.

**Identify which shares are sold and calculate the total taxable gains arising in 2009/10.**

## Sale of rights nil paid

If the shareholder who is offered the rights issue does not wish to purchase more shares in the company they can sell the right to buy the new shares to another person. This is known as a 'sale of rights nil paid'.

The treatment of a 'sale of rights nil paid' for CGT purposes depends on the amount of sale proceeds (SP) received as follows:

| If SP received are: | (i) > 5% of the value of the shares on which the rights are offered; **and**<br><br>(ii) > £3,000. | (i) ≤ 5% of the value of the shares on which the rights are offered; **or**<br><br>(ii) ≤ £3,000 if higher. |
|---|---|---|
| CGT treatment: | • deemed part disposal of original shares held.<br><br>• normal part disposal computation required. | • no chargeable disposal at the time of the sale of rights nil paid.<br><br>• SP received are deducted from the cost of the original shares. |

### Test your understanding 3

Ernest acquired 12,000 shares in Pickford plc on 22 July 1990 for £24,000.

On 13 August 2009 there was a 1 for 5 rights issue at £2.30 per share. The market value of the shares after the issue was £2.65 per share.

Ernest did not take up the issue, but sold his rights nil paid on 25 August 2009.

He sold 10,000 of his shares in Pickford plc for £37,000 on 23 June 2010.

Assume that Pickford plc is not Ernest's personal trading company.

**Calculate the chargeable gains arising assuming the rights are sold nil paid for:**

(a) **£6,000**

(b) **£1,500**

## Summary

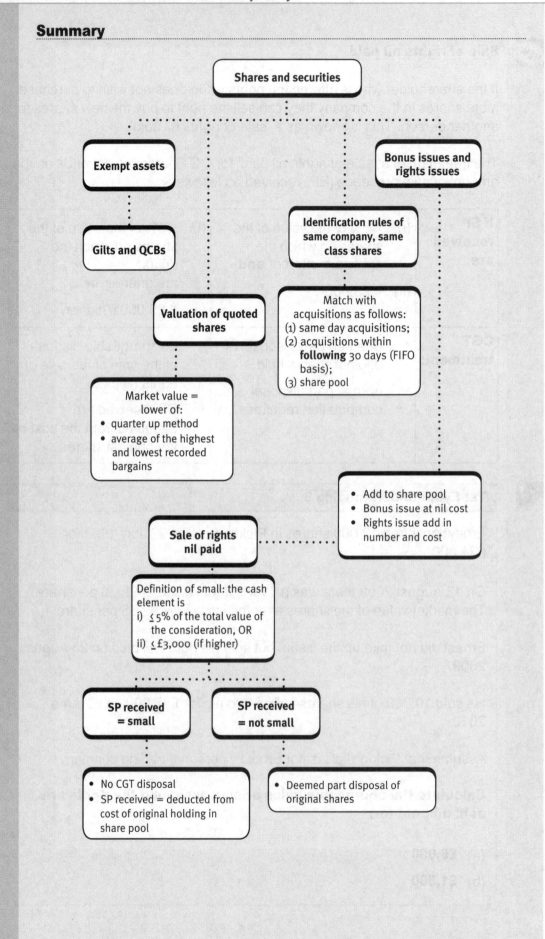

## 2 Reorganisations and takeovers

### Introduction

A reorganisation involves the exchange of existing shares in a company for other shares of another class in the same company.

A takeover occurs when a company acquires shares in another by issuing:

- shares
- debentures or loan stock
- cash.

### Share for share exchanges

Where the consideration for a reorganisation or takeover only involves the issue of shares in the acquiring company, the transaction is referred to as a 'paper for paper' transaction.

A reminder of the share for share exchange rules covered at F6 is given in expandable text and is summarised in the diagram below.

### Share for share exchange

The tax consequences are as follows:

- No CGT is charged at the time of the reorganisation/ takeover.
- The new shares acquired are treated as if they were acquired at the same time and at the same cost as the original shares.
- The new shares 'stand in the shoes' of the old shares (i.e. the date of purchase and the cost of the original shares become the deemed date of purchase and cost of the new shares acquired).
- Where the shareholder receives more than one type of share in exchange for the original shares, the cost of the original shares is apportioned to the new shares by reference to the **market values** of the replacement shares and securities as follows:
  - quoted shares:**on the first day of quotation**
  - unquoted shares: **at the time of the first disposal** of those shares.

For this treatment to apply where Company A is taking over Company B, the following qualifying conditions must be satisfied:

- Company A obtains more than 25% of Company B's ordinary share capital as a result of the offer; or

- there is a general offer to members of Company B which would give control to Company A if accepted; or

- Company A can exercise more than 50% of the voting power in Company B.

- The exchange is for a bona fide commercial reason.

- The exchange is not part of a scheme or arrangement which has as its main purpose the avoidance of CGT or corporation tax.

The acquiring company can obtain advance clearance from HMRC that the transaction comes within these rules and that the qualifying conditions have been met.

### Test your understanding 4

Major purchased 2,000 ordinary shares in Blue plc for £5,000 in June 2007.

In July 2009 Blue plc underwent a reorganisation and Major received two 'A' ordinary shares and one preference share for each ordinary share. Immediately after the reorganisation 'A' ordinary shares were quoted at £2 and preference shares at £1.

In December 2009 Major sold all his holding of 'A' ordinary shares for £8,000.

Assume that Blue plc is not Majors' personal trading company.

**Calculate the chargeable gain or allowable loss arising on the disposal in December 2009.**

### Interaction with Entrepreneurs' relief

- Entrepreneurs' relief will only be available on a future disposal of the replacement shares if the replacement shares meet the necessary conditions (see Chapter 9).

- It therefore may be more beneficial to choose to disapply the normal share for share exchange rules, so that any gain on disposal of ordinary shares is chargeable to CGT immediately to take advantage of Entrepeneurs' relief available now.

## Takeovers: Consideration in cash and shares

If the consideration for the takeover consists of a mixture of cash and shares, the tax consequences depend on whether the cash element of the transaction is small.

The tax consequences can be summarised as follows:

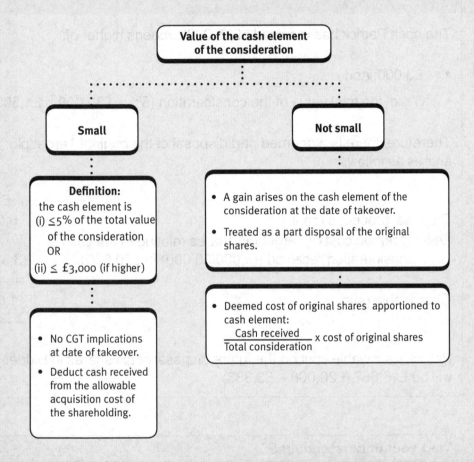

---

### Example 2 - Takeovers

Patrick bought 10,000 shares in Target plc in May 2005 for £20,000.

On 3 November 2009 the entire share capital of Target plc was acquired by Bidder plc. Target plc shareholders received 2 Bidder plc shares and £0.50 cash for each share held. Bidder plc shares were quoted at £1.25.

**Calculate the chargeable gain accruing to Patrick as a result of the takeover in November 2009.**

### Solution

|  | £ |
|---|---|
| Shares (20,000 × 1.25) | 25,000 |
| Cash (10,000 × £0.50) | 5,000 |
| Total consideration from Bidder plc | 30,000 |

The cash Patrick has received of £5,000 exceeds higher of:

* £3,000; and
* 5% of the total value of the consideration (5% × £30,000 = £1,500).

Therefore, there is a deemed part disposal of the original Target plc shares as follows:

|  | £ |
|---|---|
| Disposal proceeds (cash) | 5,000 |
| Less: Deemed cost of Target plc shares relating to the cash consideration received ((5,000/30,000) × £20,000) | (3,333) |
| Chargeable gain | 1,667 |

Patrick's allowable cost on the future disposal of his shares in Bidder plc will be £16,667 (£20,000 – £3,333).

### Test your understanding 5

Victoria held 20,000 shares in Forum Follies Ltd, an unquoted trading company, which she purchased in May 2000 for £15,000.

In January 2010 Exciting Enterprises plc acquired all the share capital of Forum Follies Ltd.

Under the terms of the takeover, shareholders in Forum Follies Ltd received three ordinary shares and one preference share in Exciting Enterprises plc, plus £1 cash for every two shares previously held in Forum Follies Ltd.

Immediately after the takeover, the shares in Exciting Enterprises plc are quoted at £3 each (ordinary shares) and £1.50 each (preference shares).

Victoria has never worked for Forum Follies Ltd.

**Calculate Victoria's capital gains tax liability for 2009/10.**

## Takeovers: Mixed consideration, including QCBs

If the consideration for the takeover consists of a mixture of shares, cash and QCBs, there are CGT consequences relating to:

- the cash element of the consideration
- the QCBs received.

### At the time of the takeover

The tax consequences relating to the cash element of the consideration are the same as summarised in the previous section above.

The tax consequences of receiving QCBs in exchange for shares as part of the takeover consideration are as follows:

- a capital gain is computed at the time of the takeover, as if the corporate bond were cash
- the gain is not taxed at that time
- the gain is 'frozen' and is not charged until the corporate bond is disposed of at a later date.

### Subsequent disposal of corporate bond

When the corporate bond is disposed of:

- no gain arises on the bond itself as QCBs are exempt assets
- the 'frozen' gain becomes chargeable.

When the frozen gain becomes chargeable, Entrepreneurs' relief may be available, provided the relief was available at the time of the disposal when the gain was deferred (Chapter 9).

## Tax planning

These rules provide a tax planning opportunity as the individual:

- can choose when they will dispose of the QCBs
- can dispose of the QCBs in small amounts on a piecemeal basis.

They can plan to ensure that, as far as possible, the deferred gain is crystallised and matched against:

- any unused annual exemption each year
- any available capital losses

so that no CGT arises on the disposal of the QCBs.

### Example 3 - Mixed consideration

On 26 May 2009, Mike sold 200 £1 ordinary shares in Café plc for £5,500 and all of his debentures in Café plc for £9,600.

Mike originally bought 1,500 shares in Joe's Café Ltd in July 2005 for £1,215 when he started to work for the business.

Joe's Café Ltd was taken over by Café plc in August 2006.

For every 20 ordinary shares held in Joe's Café Ltd a shareholder received:

- £100 in cash
- 10 ordinary shares in Café plc
- £1 Debenture stock in Café plc.

Immediately after the takeover the value of Café plc's shares and securities were as follows:

| | |
|---|---|
| £1 ordinary shares | £12 |
| Debenture stock | £55 |

Assume Joe's Cafe Ltd is not Mikes' personal trading company.

### Calculate the capital gains arising in 2006/07 and 2009/10.

### Solution

Apportionment of cost of Joe's Café Ltd 1,500 ordinary shares to the consideration received August 2006.

| | Purchase consideration | Cost allocation |
|---|---|---|
| | £ | £ |
| Cash | | |
| (£100 × 1,500/20) | 7,500 | |
| (£1,215 × £7,500/£20,625) | | 442 |
| 750 ordinary shares in Café plc | | |
| (10 × £12 × 1,500/20) | 9,000 | |
| (£1,215 × £9,000/£20,625) | | 530 |
| Debenture stock | | |
| (£55 × 1,500/20) | 4,125 | |
| (£1,215 × £4,125/£20,625) | | 243 |
| | ——— | ——— |
| | 20,625 | 1,215 |
| | ——— | ——— |

Cash consideration of £7,500 exceeds £3,000 and exceeds £1,031 (5% of £20,625).

Therefore cash consideration is not small. A part disposal would have arisen in 2006/07 on the cash consideration as follows:

**Disposal of Joe's Café Ltd shares for cash – August 2006**

| | £ |
|---|---|
| Cash received | 7,500 |
| Less: Deemed cost | (442) |
| | ——— |
| Chargeable gain | 7,058 |
| | ——— |

**Disposal of Joe's Café Ltd shares for QCBs – August 2006**

| | £ |
|---|---|
| Value of debentures received | 4,125 |
| Less: Deemed cost | (243) |
| | ——— |
| 'Frozen' gain | 3,882 |
| | ——— |
| Taxable at time of takeover in 2006/07 | Nil |
| | ——— |
| Total chargeable gains in 2006/07 (£7,058 + Nil) | 7,058 |
| | ——— |

**Disposal of 200 Café plc shares – 26 May 2009**

| | £ |
|---|---|
| Proceeds | 5,500 |
| Deemed cost (£530 × 200/750) | (141) |
| | ——— |
| Chargeable gain | 5,359 |
| | ——— |

### Disposal of Café plc debentures – 26 May 2009

The gain on the disposal of the debentures is exempt from CGT, as the debentures are QCBs.

However, the frozen gain that crystallised at the time of the takeover in 2006/07 becomes chargeable in 2009/10 on the disposal of the debentures.

|  | £ |
|---|---|
| Chargeable gain in 2009/10 when the debentures are sold | 3,882 |
| Total chargeable gains in 2009/10 (£5,359 + £3,882) | 9,241 |

### Test your understanding 6

On 31 March 2010, Jasper sold 400 £1 ordinary shares in Grasp plc for £3,600.

Jasper had acquired the Grasp plc shares as a result of a successful takeover bid by Grasp plc of Cawte plc on 5 December 2009.

Prior to the takeover Jasper had owned 12,000 £1 ordinary shares in Cawte plc (not his personal trading company), which he had acquired for £15,700 on 3 May 2008.

The terms of the take-over bid were:

- one £1 ordinary share in Grasp plc, plus
- two 10% debentures in Grasp plc, plus
- 40p in cash

for every £1 ordinary share in Cawte plc.

The following are the quoted prices for the shares and debentures of Grasp plc at 5 December 2009:

| | |
|---|---|
| £1 ordinary shares | 350p |
| 10% debentures | 110p |

(a) **Calculate the chargeable gains arising in 2009/10.**

(b) **Explain the CGT consequences that would arise if Jasper were to sell all of his debentures in Grasp plc in June 2011 for £32,000.**

## Summary

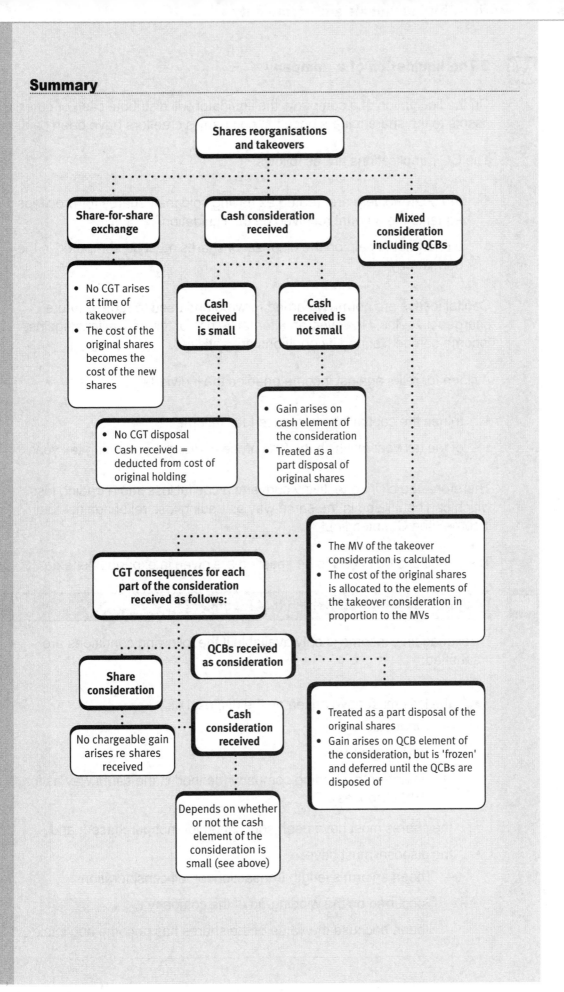

## 3 The liquidation of a company

On the liquidation of a company, the liquidator will distribute cash or other assets to the shareholders once the company's creditors have been paid.

The CGT implications are as follows:

*   the shareholders are treated as having sold their shares for proceeds equal to the amount received on the liquidation

*   a chargeable gain on the disposal of shares must be computed in the normal way.

Capital losses are normally carried forward and used to reduce future chargeable gains. However, an alternative use of the capital loss against income can be claimed if conditions are satisfied.

A claim for relief against income enables the individual:

*   to use the capital loss to reduce total income

*   of the tax year in which the loss arose and/or the preceding tax year.

Therefore, the claim effectively converts a capital loss into a trading loss which can be utilised in the same way as trading loss relief against total income (see Chapter 17).

The conditions that need to be satisfied are given in expandable text.

### Conditions for loss relief against income

Relief against income is only available if the following conditions are satisfied:

*   the loss must have arisen on the disposal of:
    *   unquoted
    *   ordinary shares
    *   in an eligible trading company (defined in the same way as for EIS purposes).

*   the shares must have been subscribed for, not purchased; and

*   the disposal must have:
    *   been an arm's length transaction for full consideration
    *   occurred on the winding-up of the company
    *   been because the value of the shares has become negligible.

### Test your understanding 7

Bob subscribed for 5,000 shares in W Ltd, an unquoted trading company, in August 2003 for £3 per share.

On 1 December 2009, Bob received a letter informing him that the company had gone into receivership. As a result, the shares are almost worthless.

The receivers dealing with the company estimate that on the liquidation, he will receive 10p per share.

Bob has other income £45,000 in 2009/10.

**State any reliefs Bob can claim regarding the fall in value of his shares in W Ltd and describe the operation of any reliefs which could reduce Bob's taxable income.**

## 4 Stamp Duty

### Introduction

Stamp duty land tax is covered in detail in Chapter 6. This section covers stamp duty.

Stamp duty is payable on the transfer of shares and other marketable securities unless the transfer is specifically exempt.

Stamp duty is payable:

- normally by the purchaser
- on the transfer of shares and securities when transferred by a formal instrument (e.g. a written document known as a stock transfer form)
- based on the consideration payable for the shares/securities.

Where shares and securities are transferred without a written document, for example where shares are transferred electronically. Stamp Duty Reserve Tax (SDRT) applies.

### Consideration for shares/securities

Where shares are purchased through the Stock Exchange the consideration will be the amount payable for the shares. This will also be true in most cases where unlisted shares are purchased.

In some cases however, particularly on the sale of a private company, the consideration may not be ascertainable at the time of sale.

The rules for determining the consideration are:

- if there is a stated amount which may vary (up or down), the consideration is that stated amount

- if there is a minimum amount (whether stated explicitly or able to be calculated), the consideration is that minimum amount

- if there is a maximum amount (whether stated explicitly or able to be calculated), the consideration is that maximum amount

- if there is both a minimum and a maximum amount, the consideration is that maximum amount

- if the amount cannot be determined, the market value at the date of the transfer is used.

## The rate of duty payable

Stamp duty is normally:

- charged at a rate of ½% of the consideration payable for the shares/securities

- rounded up to the nearest £5

- levied on the date of the transfer document.

However, a £5 fixed rate duty is charged on some types of documents, unless they are specifically exempt.

Stamp Duty Reserve Tax (SDRT) is normally:

- charged at a rate of ½% of the consideration payable for the shares/securities

- levied on the date of the agreement.

## The £5 fixed rate stamp duty

A £5 fixed rate of stamp duty is charged on certain types of documents, unless they are exempted from the charge to stamp duty.

The types of documents liable to the fixed rate of stamp duty are:

(a) **Transfers otherwise than on sale**

This covers any transfer of property to another person, apart from transfers on sale which are liable to ad valorem stamp duty.

This category is extremely wide, but in practice many documents which would otherwise be caught are specifically exempted, such as gifts. An example of a document which would be caught would be the transfer to a nominee.

(b) **Declaration of trust**

A formal trust deed would be liable to a £5 fixed duty as a declaration of trust.

A declaration of trust may also be used to make gifts of shares to minors. Since minors cannot hold shares in their own name, the shares will be registered in the name of a parent, or perhaps the grandparent making the gift.

The parent or grandparent may then make a declaration of trust declaring that the shares belong to the minor.

(c) **Duplicate or counterpart**

Sometimes when a document is executed a second document will also be executed so that each party to the transaction holds a formal document.

Although ad valorem stamp duty will be payable on the main document, the duplicate is liable only to the fixed £5 duty.

## Paperless transaction followed by stamping

Where shares are transferred via a paperless transaction, SDRT is paid. If at a later date a subsequent stock transfer form is raised for the transaction which is liable to stamp duty, the SDRT is refunded.

## Exemptions from stamp duty

The main exemptions from stamp duty relate to either the type of transfer or the type of security being transferred as follows:

- exempt transfers:
    - gifts, provided no consideration is given
    - divorce arrangements
    - variation of a will
    - change in composition of trustees
    - takeovers and reconstructions where the new shareholdings mirror the old shareholdings
    - transfers between 75% group companies
    - investment transfers.

- exempt securities:
    - government stocks
    - most company loan stock (but not convertible loan stock)
    - unit trusts.

To qualify for exemption, the transfer document must state which exemption is being claimed.

## Transfers between 75% companies

There is no charge to stamp duty or stamp duty land tax where assets are transferred between two group companies.

Two companies are in a group where one is a 75% subsidiary of the other or they are both 75% subsidiaries of a third company. This definition may be regarded as the same as that for chargeable gains.

This relief is not available where, at the time the assets are transferred, arrangements exist for the purchasing company to leave the group.

## Company loan stock exempt from stamp duty

Most company loan stock is exempt stamp duty provided the loan stock:

(a) cannot be converted into shares or other securities; and

(b) does not carry interest at more than a commercial rate or at a rate linked to the company results; and

(c) does not carry the right to the repayment of more than the nominal amount of the capital, unless the premium is reasonable in relation to other loan stock listed in the Stock Exchange Daily Official List.

## Example 4 - Stamp duty

Harry made the following purchases in 2009/10:

(a) 5,000 shares in a quoted company for £10,000

(b) £8,000 8% convertible loan stock of a quoted company for £12,000

(c) £10,000 5% Treasury Stock 2013 for £9,000

(d) 5,000 units in Growbig unit trust for £6,250

(e) 10,000 £1 ordinary shares in an unquoted company for £75,000. The shares had a market value of £250,000 at that time.

**Show how much stamp duty is payable by Harry on each of these transactions.**

**Solution**

(a) 0.5% x £10,000 = £50

(b) 0.5% × £12,000 = £60

(c) Nil – there is no stamp duty on the purchase of government securities

(d) Nil – there is no stamp duty on the purchase of units in a unit trust

(e) 0.5% × £75,000 = £375 – the market value of the shares is not relevant

### Test your understanding 8

In February 2009, Hooker purchased the following:

(a)  5,000 shares in Summit plc for £10,000.

(b)  the whole of the issued share capital of Harcourts Ltd for £125,000 plus an additional payment of £35,000 if the company's profits for the year ending 31 December 2009 exceed £80,000.

(c)  £10,000 5% Treasury Stock 2013 for £9,500.

**Calculate the amount of stamp duty payable.**

### Administration of stamp duty

The legislation does not specify who is responsible for paying stamp duty but it is normally paid by the purchaser.

The failure to stamp a document is not an offence.

However, a document which is not stamped, or not properly stamped, may not (except in criminal cases) be given in evidence. This rule ensures the payment of stamp duty.

A penalty may be imposed if a document is not stamped within 30 days:

- of its execution; or

- being brought into the UK if it was executed outside the UK (and does not relate to UK).

Interest is charged from 30 days after the date of execution, whether the document was executed in the UK or not.

A penalty for an incorrect return may be imposed in line with the penalty regime for all taxes (see Chapter 16).

## Summary

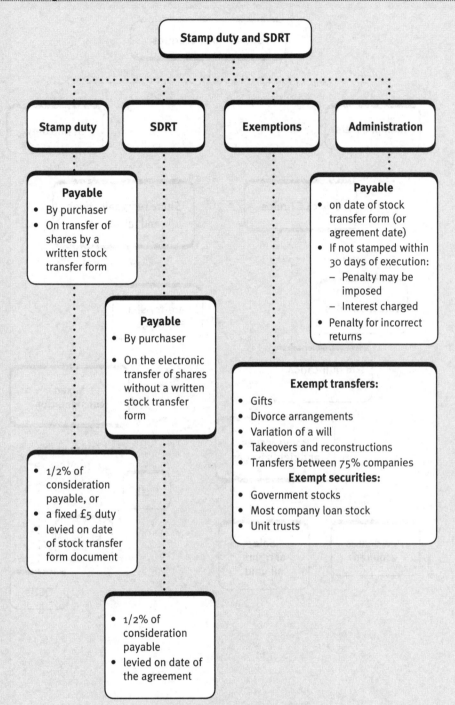

**Stamp duty and SDRT**

**Stamp duty**

**SDRT**

**Exemptions**

**Administration**

**Payable**
- By purchaser
- On transfer of shares by a written stock transfer form

**Payable**
- By purchaser
- On the electronic transfer of shares without a written stock transfer form

**Payable**
- on date of stock transfer form (or agreement date)
- If not stamped within 30 days of execution:
  - Penalty may be imposed
  - Interest charged
- Penalty for incorrect returns

**Exempt transfers:**
- Gifts
- Divorce arrangements
- Variation of a will
- Takeovers and reconstructions
- Transfers between 75% companies

**Exempt securities:**
- Government stocks
- Most company loan stock
- Unit trusts

- 1/2% of consideration payable, or
- a fixed £5 duty
- levied on date of stock transfer form document

- 1/2% of consideration payable
- levied on date of the agreement

## 5 Chapter summary

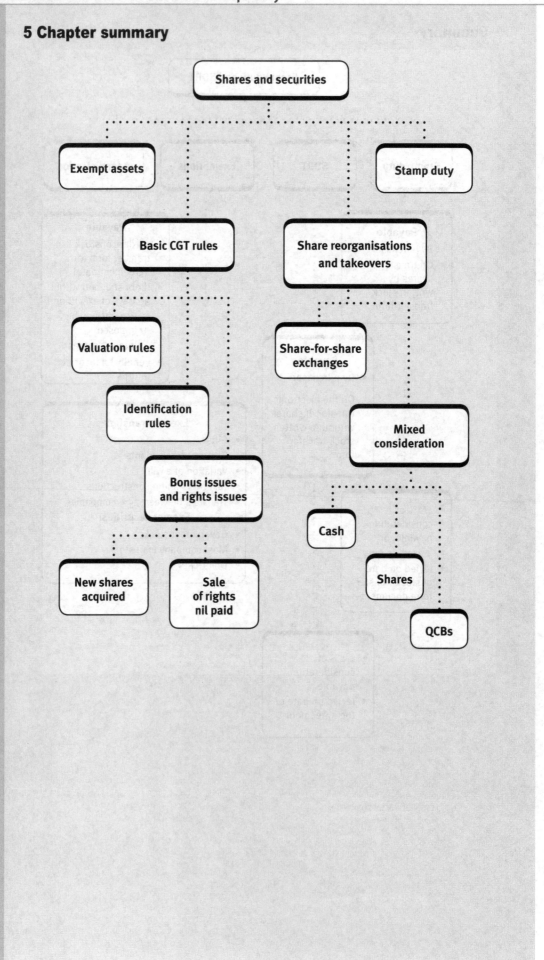

## Test your understanding answers

### Test your understanding 1

**ABC plc**

The Value of ABC plc shares is the lower of:

| | | |
|---|---|---:|
| (a) | Quarter up rule: | |
| | Lower price | 230p |
| | Add (270p – 230p) × ¼ | 10p |
| | | ───── |
| | | 240p |
| (b) | Average of the lowest and highest marked bargains | ───── |
| | (224p + 276p) × ½ | 250p |
| | | ───── |

Their value is therefore 240p per share.

### Test your understanding 2

**Tom Chalk**

| Shares sold matched with: | Number |
|---|---:|
| (a)   Shares acquired on the same day | Nil |
| (b)   Shares acquired in the next 30 days | 1,500 |
| (c)   Share pool 3,000 out of 4,650 (W) | 3,000 |
| | ───── |
| | 4,500 |
| | ───── |

**Capital gains computation**

| | | £ | £ |
|---|---|---|---|
| (1) | **Share acquired 28.01.10** | | |
| | Proceeds (1,500/4,500) × £22,500 | 7,500 | |
| | Less: Cost | (3,000) | |
| | | ——— | 4,500 |
| | | | |
| (2) | **Shares in share pool** | | |
| | Proceed (3,000/4,500) × £22,500 | 15,000 | |
| | Less: Cost (W) | (3,064) | |
| | | ——— | 11,936 |
| | | | |
| | Total chargeable gains | | 16,436 |
| | Less: Annual exemption | | (10,100) |
| | | | |
| | Taxable gains | | 6,336 |

| **Working: Share pool** | | Number | Cost £ |
|---|---|---|---|
| April 1988 | Purchase | 1,500 | 900 |
| June 1991 | Rights issue (1:3) × 70p | 500 | 350 |
| | | 2,000 | 1,250 |
| May 2000 | Purchase | 1,000 | 2,000 |
| | | 3,000 | 3,250 |
| July 2000 | Bonus issue (1:4) | 750 | Nil |
| | | 3,750 | 3,250 |
| August 2004 | Purchase | 900 | 1,500 |
| | | 4,650 | 4,750 |
| December 2009 | Sale | (3,000) | (3,064) |
| Balance c/f | | 1,650 | 1,686 |

## Test your understanding 3

**Ernest**

(a) **Gain on the sale of rights nil paid – 25 August 2009**

Sale proceeds received = £6,000

Value of shares after rights issue = (£2.65 × 12,000) = £31,800
5% × £31,800 = £1,590

The sale proceeds are > £3,000 **and** > 5% of the value of the shares on which the rights are offered, therefore there is a part disposal of the original shares held:

|  | £ |
|---|---|
| Sale proceeds | 6,000 |
| Less Allowable cost (6,000/37,800 × £24,000) | (3,810) |
| Chargeable gain | 2,190 |

**Gain on the sale of the original shares – 23 June 2010**

|  | £ |
|---|---|
| Sale proceeds | 37,000 |
| Less Allowable cost | |
| (10,000/ 12,000 × (£24,000 – £3,810)) | (16,825) |
| Chargeable gain | 20,175 |

(b) **Gain on the sale of rights nil paid – 25 August 2009**

Sale proceeds received = £1,500

The sale proceeds are < £3,000 therefore no gain arises on the sale of rights nil paid.

The sale proceeds are deducted from the cost of the original shares.

**Note:** There is no need to consider the 5% rule if the sale proceeds are < £3,000. Only one of the conditions need to be satisfied.

### Gain on the sale of the original shares – 23 June 2010

| | £ |
|---|---|
| Sale proceeds | 37,000 |
| Less Allowable cost (W) | (18,750) |
| | |
| Capital gain | 18,250 |

**Working: Share pool**

| | | Number | Cost £ |
|---|---|---|---|
| 22.07.1990 | Purchase | 12,000 | 24,000 |
| 25.08.2009 | Sale of rights nil paid | | (1,500) |
| | | 12,000 | 22,500 |
| 23.06.2010 | Sale of shares | (10,000) | (18,750) |
| | | | |
| Balance c/f | | 2,000 | 3,750 |

## Test your understanding 4

**Major**

| | £ |
|---|---|
| Disposal proceeds | 8,000 |
| Less: Cost (W) | (4,000) |
| | |
| Chargeable gain | 4,000 |

**Working – cost of 'A' ordinary shares**

July 2009 Major received:

| | £ |
|---|---|
| 4,000 'A' ordinary shares, valued at (4,000 × £2) | £8,000 |
| 2,000 preference shares, valued at (2,000 × £1) | £2,000 |

Cost attributable to the 'A' ordinary shares is therefore:

$£5,000 × (£8,000/£10,000) = £4,000$

**Test your understanding 5**

| Victoria | MV Jan 2010 | Cost |
|---|---|---|
| Exchanged Assets: | £ | £ |
| 30,000 ordinary shares (£15,000 × 90/115) | 90,000 | 11,739 |
| 10,000 preference shares (£15,000 × 15/115) | 15,000 | 1,957 |
| £10,000 cash (£15,000 × 10/115) | 10,000 | 1,304 |
| | 115,000 | 15,000 |

Is the cash element material? = Yes

- The cash received is £10,000 which is > £3,000.

- The cash element also represents > 5% of the total value of exchanged assets (£115,000 x 5% = £5,750).

A chargeable gain is assessable in 2009/10 based on the part disposal of the shares as follows:

| | £ |
|---|---|
| Sale poceeds | 10,000 |
| Less:Cost | (1,304) |
| Chargeable gain | 8,696 |

Victoria will have no CGT liability in 2009/10 as her chargeable gain is covered by her annual exemption of £10,100.

**Test your understanding 6**

(a) **Chargeable gains in 2009/10**

Apportionment of cost of Cawte plc shares to the new securities and cash on 5 December 2009

| For 12,000 Cawte plc ord shares: | Purchase consideration £ | Cost allocation £ |
|---|---|---|
| 12,000 Grasp £1 ord shs @ 350p | 42,000 | |
| £15,700 × (£42,000/£73,200) | | 9,008 |
| 24,000 Grasp 10% debs @ 110p | 26,400 | |
| £15,700 × (£26,400/£73,200) | | 5,662 |
| Cash (12,000 × 40p) | 4,800 | |
| £15,700 × (£4,800/£73,200) | | 1,030 |
| | 73,200 | 15,700 |

Cash consideration of £4,800 exceeds £3,000 and exceeds £3,660 (5% of £73,200). Therefore cash consideration is not small and the part disposal rules apply.

| | £ | £ |
|---|---|---|
| **Disposal for cash – 5 December 2009** | | |
| Cash received | | 4,800 |
| Less: Deemed cost | | (1,030) |
| Chargeable gain | | 3,770 |
| **Disposal for QCBs – 5 December 2009** | | |
| Value of debentures received | 26,400 | |
| Less: Deemed cost | (5,662) | |
| 'Frozen' gain | 20,738 | |
| Taxable at time of takeover | | Nil |

**Disposal of Grasp plc shares – 31 March 2010**

| | | |
|---|---:|---:|
| Proceeds | 3,600 | |
| Deemed cost (£9,008 × 400/12,000) | (300) | |
| | —— | 3,300 |
| | | —— |
| Total chargeable gains for 2009/10 | | 7,070 |
| | | —— |

(b) **CGT consequences – selling the debentures in June 2011**

If Jasper were to sell the debentures in June 2011 for £32,000, the increase in value of the debentures from £26,400 to £32,000 is exempt from CGT as QCBs are exempt assets.

However, the disposal of the debentures will crystallise the 'frozen' deferred gain of £20,738 in 2011/12.

---

### Test your understanding 7

**Bob**

On the liquidation of the company, the shareholders are treated as having sold their shares for proceeds equal to the amount received on the liquidation and a normal capital gain/loss computation is required.

In this case, Bob will make a capital loss on the disposal of his shares.

Bob can make a negligible value claim as at 1 December 2009. This will give rise to a capital loss of £14,500 (£500 – £15,000) which will be deemed to arise in the year 2009/10.

As the capital loss arises on the disposal of unquoted trading company shares and Bob subscribed for the shares, relief against income is available.

Bob can relieve the loss against his total income for

- 2009/10 (i.e. the year in which the loss arose); and/or
- 2008/09 (i.e. the previous tax year).

If losses are first relieved against current year income, any excess is available for offset against the prior year's income.

By making the claim, Bob's total income in 2009/10 will be reduced to £30,500 (£45,000 – £14,500).

### Test your understanding 8

**Hooker**

|  |  | £ |
|---|---|---:|
| (a) | Summit plc (½% × £10,000) | 50 |
| (b) | Harcourts Ltd (½% × (£125,000 + £35,000)) | 800 |
| (c) | Treasury stock – Exempt | – |
|  | Total stamp duty payable | 850 |

# CGT: Reliefs for individuals

## Chapter learning objectives

Upon completion of this chapter you will be able to:

- explain and calculate Entrepreneurs' relief

- identify the principal private residence exemption and letting relief available in a variety of circumstances on the disposal of an individual's main residence.

- explain and apply rollover relief as it applies to individuals

- identify from a scenario when gift relief will be available, explain the conditions and show the application of gift relief in computations

- recognise and state the conditions for the availability of CGT deferral relief on the transfer of a business to a company

- calculate the relief where the consideration is wholly or partly in shares

- understand and apply Enterprise Investment Scheme reinvestment relief ensuring that other available reliefs are maximised

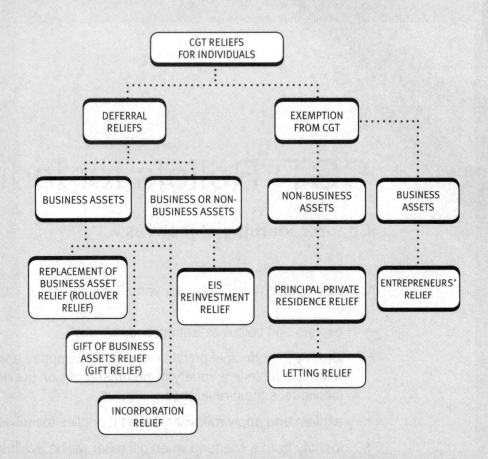

## 1 Introduction

After calculating the gains on disposals of individual assets, consideration must be given to the availability of CGT reliefs.

Some reliefs completely exempt all or part of a gain from CGT, other reliefs defer the gain to a later period. This chapter covers the detailed rules relating to the CGT reliefs that are available to an individual.

The main reliefs available are:

| Deferral reliefs | Exemptions |
|---|---|
| • Replacement of business asset relief (Rollover relief) | • Entrepreneurs' relief |
| • Gift of business asset relief (Gift relief) | • Principal private residence (PPR) relief |
| • Incorporation relief | • Letting relief |
| • EIS reinvestment relief | |

Much of this chapter is a revision of F6 knowledge with examples to check your retention of the required F6 knowledge. However, note that a greater depth of understanding is required at P6. The main new relief introduced at P6 is EIS reinvestment relief.

The reliefs feature regularly in the examinations. It is important to be able to calculate the amount of relief, to state the conditions that have to be satisfied and to explain the tax implications of claiming each relief.

## 2 Entrepreneurs' relief

Entrepreneurs' relief reduces the capital gains tax payable on certain qualifying business disposals.

A reminder of how the relief operates is given in expandable text and is summarised in the diagram below.

### Operation of the relief

- The first £1 million of gains on 'qualifying business disposals' on or after 6 April 2008 will be reduced by 4/9ths.

- The remaining 5/9ths of the first £1 million of gains are taxed at the new flat rate of 18%, resulting in an effective rate of 10% on the first £1 million of gains (18% x 5/9 = 10%).

- Any gains above the £1 million limit are taxed in full at the 18% rate.

The relief is given before the deduction of:

- allowable losses (other than any losses on assets that are part of the disposal of the business), and

- the annual exemption.

The relief must be claimed within 12 months of the 31 January following the end of the tax year in which the disposal is made.

For 2009/10 disposals, the relief must be claimed by 31 January 2012.

The £1 million limit is a lifetime limit which is diminished each time a claim for the relief is made.

### Qualifying business disposals

The relief applies to the disposal of:

- the whole or part of a business carried on by the individual either alone or in partnership

- assets of the individual's or partnership's trading business that has now ceased

- shares provided:

    - the shares are in the individual's 'personal trading company', and

    - the individual is an employee of the company (part time or full time).

An individual's 'personal trading company' is one in which the individual:

- owns at least 5% of the ordinary shares

- which carry at least 5% of the voting rights.

Note in particular that:

- the disposal of an individual business asset used for the purposes of a continuing trade does not qualify. There must be a disposal of the whole or part of the trading business. The sale of an asset in isolation will not qualify.

- "Part of a business" is likely to be interpreted as meaning a "substantial part" which is "capable of independent operation".

- Where the disposal is a disposal of assets (i.e. not shares), relief is not available on gains arising from the disposal of those assets held for investment purposes.

- There is no requirement to restrict the gains qualifying for relief on shares by reference to any non-trading assets held by the company.

- There are no rules about the minimum working hours of officers or employees; they just need to be an officer or employee throughout the one year qualifying period. Further non-executive directors and company secretaries will qualify as employees.

## Qualifying ownership period

The asset(s) being disposed of must have been owned by the individual making the disposal in the 12 months prior to the disposal.

Where the disposal is an asset of the individual's or partnership's trading business that has now ceased the disposal must also take place within three years of the cessation of trade.

## Example 1 – Entrepreneurs' relief

In 2009/10, Kim sold her trading business which she set up in 1991 and realised the following gains/losses:

| | £ |
|---|---|
| Factory | 275,000 |
| Goodwill | 330,000 |
| Warehouse | (100,000) |
| Investment property | 200,000 |

All of the assets have been owned for many years.

Kim also sold her shares in an unquoted trading company and realised a gain of £600,000. She owned 25% of the ordinary shares of the company which she purchased ten years ago. She has worked for the company on a part time basis for the last three years.

Kim has not made any other capital disposals in 2009/10.

**Calculate Kim's capital gains tax payable for 2009/10**

### Solution

| | £ | £ | £ |
|---|---|---|---|
| *Sale of trading business* | | | |
| Factory | | 275,000 | |
| Goodwill | | 330,000 | |
| Warehouse | | (100,000) | |
| | | ———— | |
| | | 505,000 | |
| Less: Entrepreneurs' relief | 505,000 × 4/9 | (224,444) | |
| | | ———— | 280,556 |
| *Sale of shares* | | | |
| Gain on shares | | 600,000 | |
| Less: Entrepreneurs' relief | 495,000 × 4/9 | (220,000) | |
| | ———— | ———— | 380,000 |
| | 1,000,000 | | |
| | | | ———— |
| | | | 660,556 |
| *Sale of investment property* | | | 200,000 |
| | | | ———— |
| Net chargeable gains | | | 860,556 |
| Less: Annual exemption | | | (10,100) |
| | | | ———— |
| Taxable gains | | | 850,456 |
| | | | ———— |

| | |
|---|---|
| Capital gains tax payable (£850,456 × 18%) | 153,082 |

---

### Test your understanding 1

In 2009/10 Paul sold shares in Dual Ltd, an unquoted trading company, and realised a gain of £430,000. Paul has worked for Dual Ltd for many years and has owned 10% of the ordinary shares of the company for the last five years.

Paul set up a trading business in 2004 and in 2009/10 he sold a warehouse used in the business, realising a gain of £245,000.

In 2010/11 Paul sold the rest of the business and realised the following gains:

| | £ |
|---|---|
| Factory | 495,000 |
| Goodwill | 130,000 |

All of the assets in the business have been owned for many years.

Paul also sold an antique clock and realised a gain of £5,325.

**Calculate Paul's capital gains tax payable for 2009/10 and 2010/11.**

Assume that the annual exemption for 2009/10 continues in the future.

### Associated disposals

The relief also applies to assets owned by the individual and used in their personal trading company or trading partnership **provided:**

- the individual also disposes of all or part of their partnership interest/shares

- as part of their withdrawal of involvement in the partnership/company business.

These disposals are referred to as associated disposals.

In order for full relief to be available for associated disposals, the individual must not have charged rent to the business for the use of the assets.

## Interaction with other reliefs

Note that other specific capital gains tax reliefs (e.g. gift relief, roll-over relief and incorporation relief) are given before Entrepreneurs' relief.

This means that if Entrepreneurs' relief is applicable it is applied to the remaining gain:

- after other reliefs have been considered, but
- before deducting capital losses and the annual exemption.

More detail on how the interaction between reliefs works is given later with the detail on the specific reliefs.

## Interaction with takeovers

With a share for share exchange, it is possible that:

- the old shares would qualify for Entrepreneurs' relief if it were treated as a disposal
- but the new company is not the shareholder's personal trading company and so the later disposal of its shares would not qualify for relief.

However, where the share exchange takes place after 5 April 2008, the individual shareholder can:

- elect for the event to be treated as a disposal for CGT purposes, and
- claim Entrepreneurs' relief.

## Summary

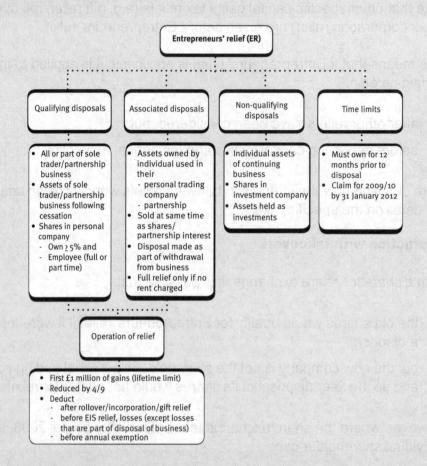

### 3 Principal private residence relief and letting relief

Principal private residence relief (PPR) applies when an individual disposes of:

- a dwelling house (including normally up to half a hectare of land)
- that has at some time during their ownership been their only or main private residence.

There are four possible scenarios to consider:

| Occupation of the house | Consequence for CGT |
|---|---|
| 1 The owner occupies the residence throughout the whole period of ownership | • Gain is exempt |
| 2 The owner is absent from the residence for certain periods and house is not let | • Calculate gain<br>• PPR relief available |
| 3 The owner is absent for certain periods and house is let out | • Calculate gain<br>• PPR relief available |
| 4 Part of the main residence is let out (with or without absence by owner) | • Letting relief |

## The meaning of 'dwelling house'

The meaning of 'dwelling house' is not defined in the legislation and so it has been left to the courts to determine the limits of the expression. A number of principles have emerged from decided cases.

- Caravans connected to mains services such as electricity and water qualify as dwellings.

- A taxpayer sold a bungalow and a small amount of land that was within the grounds of his house and which had been occupied by a part-time caretaker. It was held that the bungalow provided services for the benefit of the main house, was occupied by the taxpayer through his employee, and so qualified as part of the taxpayer's residence.

  A test resulting from this case is that buildings must together form an entity that can be regarded as a dwelling house, albeit divided into different buildings performing different functions.

- Where a taxpayer owns a large property which is divided into several self contained units, only those parts that the taxpayer actually occupies qualify for exemption.

- A taxpayer first sold his house and part of his garden and then, about a year later, sold the remainder of the garden at a substantial profit. It was held that the principal private residence exemption applied only to the first disposal, because when the remainder of the land was sold, it no longer formed part of the individual's principal private residence. It is likely that even if the order of sales were reversed, the land sold independently of the buildings would still not qualify for relief.

### Ownership of more than one residence

Where an individual has more than one residence he is entitled to nominate which of them is to be treated as his principal residence for capital gains purposes by notifying HMRC in writing.

The election must be made within two years of acquiring an additional residence otherwise it is open to HMRC, as a question of fact, to decide which residence is the main residence.

### Married couples/civil partners

Provided that they are not treated as being separated or divorced, a married couple (or civil partnership) are entitled to only one residence between them for the purposes of the private residence exemption.

### The operation of the relief

Where there has been a period of absence the procedure is as follows:

(i)   Calculate the gain on the property.

(ii)  Compute the total period of ownership.

(iii) Calculate periods of occupation (see below).

(iv)  Calculate the amount of PPR relief as follows:

$$\text{PPR relief} = \text{Gain} \times \frac{\text{Periods of occupation}}{\text{Total period of ownership}}$$

(v)   If applicable, calculate the amount of letting relief available.

### Periods of occupation

The 'periods of occupation' include:

*   **any** period of **actual** occupation

*   the **last three years** of ownership

*   the following periods of **deemed occupation:**

    (i)   up to **three years** of absence for any **reason**

    (ii)  **any** period spent **working abroad**

    (iii) up to **four years** of absence while **working elsewhere in the UK**.

Note that

- The periods of deemed occupation above must be preceded and followed by a period of actual occupation.

- The condition to reoccupy after the period of absence does not need to be satisfied for periods (ii) and (iii) above where an employer requires the individual to work elsewhere immediately, thus making it impossible to resume occupation.

### Example 2 - PPR relief

On 1 May 1985 Mr Flint purchased a house in Southampton for £25,000, which he lived in until he moved to a rented flat on 1 July 1986.

He remained in the flat until 1 October 1988 when he accepted a year's secondment to his firm's New York office. On coming back on 1 October 1989 he moved into a relative's house, where he stayed until he returned to his own home on 31 January 1990.

On 1 July 2000 he changed jobs and rented a flat near his new employer's offices in Newcastle. Here he remained until he sold his Southampton house on 1 February 2010 for £95,000.

**Calculate the chargeable gain, if any, arising on the disposal of the house on 1 February 2010.**

**Solution**

|  | £ |
|---|---|
| Disposal proceeds | 95,000 |
| Less: Cost | (25,000) |
|  | ───── |
|  | 70,000 |
| Less: PPR relief (W) | (51,380) |
|  | ───── |
| Chargeable gain | 18,620 |
|  | ───── |

**Working – Chargeable and exempt periods of ownership**

| | | Chargeable months | Exempt months |
|---|---|---|---|
| 1.5.85 – 30.6.86 | (actual occupation) | – | 14 |
| 1.7.86 – 30.9.88 | (absent – any reason) | – | 27 |
| 1.10.88 – 30.9.89 | (absent – employed abroad) | – | 12 |
| 1.10.89 – 31.1.90 | (absent – any reason) | – | 4 |
| 1.2.90 – 30.6.00 | (actual occupation) | – | 125 |
| 1.7.00 – 31.1.07 | (absent – see note) | 79 | – |
| 1.2.07 – 31.1.10 | (final 36 months) | – | 36 |
| | | 79 | 218 |

Total period of ownership = (79 + 218) = 297 months.

Exempt element of gain = (218/297) × £70,000 = £51,380

**Notes:**

(1) After Mr Flint left his residence to work in Newcastle he never returned. Consequently the exemption for working away from home is not available as there is not actual occupation both before and after the period of absence.

(2) The remaining 5 months (3 years – 27 months – 4 months) for any reason is also not available for exemption as Mr Flint never reoccupied the property after leaving for Newcastle.

(3) In contrast the exemption for the final 36 months of ownership has no such restriction and is therefore still available.

## Letting relief

Letting relief is available where an individual's principal private residence is let out for residential use.

It applies when:

- the owner is absent from the property and lets the house out or
- the owner lets part of the property whilst still occupying the remainder.

It does not apply to let property that is not the owner's PPR (e.g. buy to let properties).

Letting relief is the lower of:

(i)   £40,000

(ii)  the amount of the gain exempted by the normal principal private residence rules

(iii) the part of the gain **after PPR** relief attributable to the letting period.

### Test your understanding 2

Mr Dearden bought a house on 1 April 1986. Occupation of the house has been as follows:

01.04.86 – 31.03.88    lived in the house as his PPR.

01.04.88 – 30.09.93    travels the world and lets the house.

01.10.93 – 31.03.02    lived in the house as his PPR.

01.04.02 – 31.03.10    house was left empty.

On 31 March 2010, Mr Dearden sells the house realising a gain before relief of £194,800.

**Calculate the chargeable gain arising on the disposal of the house in 2009/10.**

## Business use

Where a house, or part of it, is used wholly and exclusively for business purposes, the part used for business purposes is not eligible for PPR relief.

Note that:

- the taxpayer cannot benefit from the rules of deemed occupation for any part of the property used for business purposes

- there is one exception:
    - if that part of the property used for business purposes was at any time used as the taxpayer's main residence, the exemption for the last 36 months still applies to that part

    - it does not apply to any part of the property used for business purposes throughout the ownership.

### Test your understanding 3

On 30 June 2009 Alex sold his house for £125,000, resulting in a capital gain of £70,000. The house had been purchased on 1 July 1998, and one of the five rooms had been used for business purposes from 1 January 2001 to the date of sale.

**Calculate the chargeable gain arising on the sale of the house.**

### Tax planning points

#### General advice

CGT planning concerning an individual's private residence focuses on two main areas:

- If the taxpayer's circumstances are such that any gain realised will be exempt he should ensure that this is maximised.

- Where he is absent from the property he should attempt to structure his absences in such a way that he benefits as much as possible from the deemed occupation rules and the letting exemption.

For example:

- ensure taxpayer reoccupies the property after the period of absence

- ensure property let during periods of absence not covered by PPR relief.

#### Specific tax advice

#### More than one residence

Where the taxpayer has more than one residence he should ensure that he nominates the property with the greatest potential for gain as his main residence.

It should be noted, however, that any property subject to an election must be used by the taxpayer at some time as his residence. It is not acceptable to purchase a property as a financial investment, nominate it as the main residence of the taxpayer, and never set foot in it.

If an individual's finances permit, he should purchase a new residence before disposing of the old one. He can elect for the new residence to be treated as his main residence for the CGT exemption but this does not prevent him gaining exemption on the old residence for the final 36 months of his ownership.

In this way he can effectively gain exemption on two residences at once for a maximum of three years.

## Business use of property

Subject to tax and other financial considerations, exclusive business use of the property should be avoided.

Where business use is necessary thought should be given to the proportion of household expenses claimed under the income tax rules because these will be a material factor in determining the extent to which the principal private residence exemption is lost.

## Letting the property

When the taxpayer is absent in circumstances that make him ineligible for exemption under the deemed occupation rules, he should give serious thought to letting his property.

Whether this constitutes good tax planning will depend, on the one hand, at the rate his property is rising in value, and on the other hand, on the income and expenditure connected with the letting.

## Summary

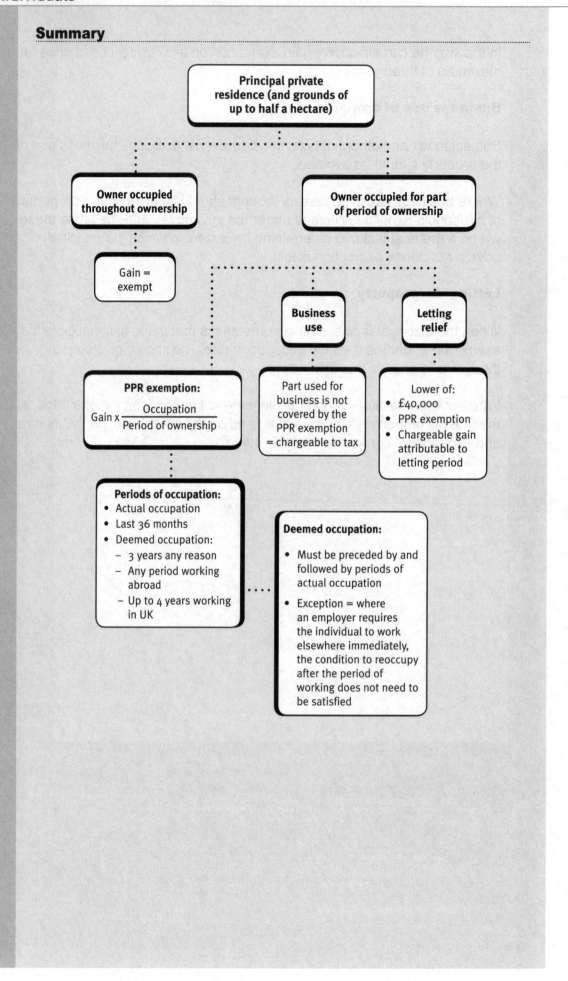

## 4 Comprehensive example

### Test your understanding 4

Paul Opus disposed of the following assets during the tax year 2009/10

(1) On 10 April 2009 Paul sold 5,000 £1 ordinary shares in Symphony Ltd, an unquoted trading company, for £23,600.  He had originally purchased 40,000 shares in the company on 23 June 2006 for £110,400.

(2) On 15 June 2009 Paul made a gift of his entire shareholding of 10,000 £1 ordinary shares in Concerto plc to his daughter.  On that date the shares were quoted on the Stock Exchange at £5.10 – £5.18, with recorded bargains of £5.00, £5.15 and £5.22. Paul's shareholding had been purchased on 29 April 1993 for £14,000.  The shareholding is less than 1% of Concerto plc's issued share capital, and Paul has never been employed by Concerto plc.

(3) On 9 August 2009 Paul sold a motor car for £16,400.  The motor car had been purchased on 21 January 2005 for £12,800.

(4) On 4 October 2009 Paul sold an antique vase for £12,400.  The antique vase had been purchased on 19 January 2008 for £8,400.

(5) On 31 December 2009 Paul sold a house for £220,000.  The house had been purchased on 1 April 2003 for £114,700.  Paul occupied the house as his main residence from the date of purchase until 30 June 2006.  The house was then unoccupied until it was sold on 31 December 2009.

(6) On 16 February 2010 Paul sold three acres of land for £285,000.  He had originally purchased four acres of land on 17 July 2008 for £220,000.  The market value of the unsold acre of land as at 16 February 2010 was £90,000.  The land has never been used for business purposes.

(7) On 5 March 2010 Paul sold a freehold holiday cottage for £125,000.  The cottage had originally been purchased on 28 July 2007 for £101,600 by Paul's wife.  She transferred the cottage to Paul on 16 November 2009 when it was valued at £114,800.

**Compute Paul's capital gains tax liability for the tax year 2009/10, and advise him by when this should be paid.**

## 5 Replacement of business asset relief (Rollover relief)

Rollover relief is available to both individuals and companies.

This section deals with the rules as they apply to an unincorporated business. The rules for companies are very similar but the differences are explained in Chapter 23.

### The operation of the relief

Where an individual:

- sells a qualifying business asset at a gain; and
- reinvests the sale proceeds in a replacement qualifying business asset;
- within a qualifying time period

The individual may **make a claim** to defer the gain until the subsequent disposal of the replacement asset.

A reminder of how the relief operates and the conditions for the relief covered at F6 is given in expandable text, and is summarised in the diagram below.

### Operation of the relief

The relief operates as follows:

- on the disposal of a business asset, the gain is 'rolled over' against (i.e. deducted from) the acquisition cost of the replacement asset
- provided the proceeds are fully reinvested, no tax is payable at the time of the disposal as the gain is deferred
- the relief effectively increases the gain arising on the disposal of the replacement asset, as its base cost has been reduced by rollover relief
- rollover relief is not automatic, it must be claimed.

Note that:

- gains may be 'rolled over' a number of times provided a qualifying replacement business asset is purchased, therefore a tax liability will only arise when there is a disposal without replacement
- the relief is very flexible, where several assets are sold and several more acquired, the gains can be rolled over against the new assets in whatever order or proportion the individual chooses

- making a rollover relief claim is optional. An individual may prefer to crystallise a gain in the current year if it is covered by their capital losses and annual exemption

- the base cost of the replacement asset is reduced for CGT purposes only. For income tax purposes, capital allowances (if applicable) are still available on the full cost in the normal way.

**Gains deferred before 6 April 2008**

If the disposal of a qualifying asset was made prior to 6 April 2008 and a roll-over relief claim is made, the examiner will either:

- give the amount of the deferred gain, or
- the calculation will be the same as the current rules (i.e. sale proceeds less cost).

Note, however, that regardless of how the gain is calculated, the deferred gain arising would have been deducted from the base cost of the replacement asset and deferred until the subsequent disposal of the replacement asset in the same way as before.

Pre 6 April 2008 an individual was entitled to an indexation allowance on purchases from March 1982 to April 1998. The indexed gain was deferred when a roll-over relief claim was made.

## Conditions for the relief

**Qualifying business assets**

There are many categories of qualifying business assets (QBAs), however for examination purposes, the main assets which qualify for rollover relief are:

- goodwill (for unincorporated businesses only)
- land and buildings (freehold and leasehold) occupied and used for trading purposes
- fixed plant and machinery.

Note that:

- shares are not qualifying assets for rollover relief purposes
- both the old and the replacement assets:
  - must be qualifying business assets, however they do not have to be the same category of qualifying asset
  - they do not have to be used in the same trade if the vendor has more than one trade.

### Qualifying time period

The replacement assets must be acquired within a four year period:

- beginning one year before and
- ending three years after

the date of sale of the old asset.

### Claim time period

For 2009/10 disposals, individuals must claim rollover relief by 5 April 2014.

## Partial reinvestment

If **all** of the proceeds from the sale of the old asset are reinvested, full rollover relief is available (i.e. **all** of the gain is deferred).

However, where there is partial reinvestment of the proceeds:

- part of the gain will be chargeable at the time of the disposal
- the rest of the gain can be deferred with a rollover relief claim.

The gain which is taxable at the time of the disposal is the lower of:

- the full gain
- the amount of the proceeds not reinvested.

**Test your understanding 5**

In May 1985, Keith sold a freehold commercial building for £100,000 and realised a capital gain of £58,240.

In August 1985 Keith bought another freehold commercial building for £80,000 which he sold in April 2009 for £300,000. He did not replace this building with any other business assets.

**Calculate the chargeable gain arising in 2009/10.**

## Non-business use

Adjustments need to be made to the calculation of the amount of rollover/holdover relief available if there is an element of non-business use. This may occur because:

- an asset may be used partly for business purposes and partly for private use

- an asset is not used for business purposes for the whole of the period of ownership.

### Interaction with Entrepreneurs' relief

If the entire business is being sold and the proceeds are reinvested into new qualifying assets, both rollover and Entrepreneurs' relief are available.

- Rollover relief is given before Entrepreneurs' relief (i.e. the capital gains **before** Entrepreneurs' relief are deferred).

- On a subsequent disposal of the replacement assets (as part of the sale of new business as a whole) Entrepreneurs' relief will be available if the retention period of 12 months is met.

Effectively, the use of the lifetime relief is also deferred.

However, rollover relief is optional and the taxpayer can choose **not to claim** rollover relief and utilise the availble Entrepreneurs' relief earlier if they want to.

### Reinvestment in depreciating assets

Where the new asset purchased is a depreciating asset, relief to defer the gain is still available however the operation of the relief is modified. This form of relief is sometimes referred to as 'hold over relief', and affects:

- the way in which the deferral is obtained
- the length of time for which the deferral can be achieved.

A reminder of the definition of a depreciating asset and the way in which the relief operates is given in expandable text, and is included in the summary diagram.

## Holdover relief

A depreciating asset is defined as:

- a wasting asset (i.e. with a predictable life of 50 years or less)
- an asset that will become a wasting asset within ten years.

The most common examples of qualifying depreciating assets are:

- leasehold land and buildings with 60 years or less to run on the lease
- fixed plant and machinery.

### The operation of the relief

The relief for depreciating assets operates in the following way.

- The capital gain is not 'rolled over' and deducted from the base cost of the replacement asset, instead it is deferred i.e. 'frozen' and becomes chargeable on the **earliest** of the following three events:

  (1) the **disposal** of replacement depreciating asset

  (2) the depreciating asset **ceases to be used** for the purposes of the trade

  (3) **ten years** from the date of acquisition of the replacement depreciating asset.

- However, if before the deferred gain crystallises, a non-depreciating asset is purchased, then the original deferred gain can then be rolled over.

  This means that the deferred gain can be matched with the later purchase of a non-depreciating asset and the deferred gain will be deducted from the cost of the new asset.

Note that the partial reinvestment and non-business use rules apply in calculating the amount of the held over gain that can be deferred, in the same way as for rollover relief.

### Example 3 - Rollover relief

Smith purchased a factory in February 1989 for £195,000.

In May 2009 he sold it for £380,000 and acquired a lease of commercial property (with 55 years to expiry) in June 2009 for £385,000.

In April 2010 he purchased a new factory for £390,000 and he sold the lease for £430,000 in December 2010. In May 2012 he sold the second factory for £425,000.

**Calculate the chargeable gain on:**

(a) **the disposal of the first factory;**

(b) **the disposal of the lease; and**

(c) **the disposal of the second factory.**

**Solution**

**(a) Gain on first factory – May 2009**

|  | £ |
|---|---|
| Disposal proceeds | 380,000 |
| Less: Cost | (195,000) |
|  |  |
| Chargeable gain | 185,000 |

**(b) Disposal of the lease – December 2010**

|  | £ |
|---|---|
| Disposal proceeds | 430,000 |
| Less: Allowable expenditure (see note) | (385,000) |
|  |  |
| Chargeable gain | 45,000 |

**(c) Disposal of second factory – May 2012**

|  | £ | £ |
|---|---|---|
| Disposal proceeds |  | 425,000 |
| Less: Cost | 390,000 |  |
| Rolled over gain | (185,000) |  |
|  |  | (205,000) |
|  |  |  |
| Chargeable gain |  | 220,000 |

**Notes:**

(1) The lease, although a depreciating asset for rollover relief purposes, is not a wasting asset because it had more than 50 years to expiry when it was sold. Its cost is therefore not wasted when computing the gain or loss on disposal.

(2) As Smith reinvested the proceeds of the first factory in a depreciating asset (i.e. the lease), the gain on the first factory is held over. Smith then purchased another non-depreciating asset (i.e. the second factory) before the depreciating asset was sold. He could therefore rollover the gain on the first factory into the second.

(3) Entrepreneurs' relief is not available as this is the disposal of an individual asset used for the purposes of a continuing trade.

### Test your understanding 6

Sophie operates a business as a sole trader. The business has a 31 March year end.

Sophie purchased an office block in October 1999 for £70,000 and sold it in August 2005 for £120,000. She acquired fixed plant and machinery at a cost of £100,000 in April 2006. The maximum possible rollover relief was claimed, in respect of the gain arising on the office block, against the purchase of the fixed plant and machinery.

In November 2009 Sophie sold the fixed plant and machinery for £60,000.

**Calculate the Sophie's chargeable gain in 2009/10.**

### Tax planning points

Much of tax planning for replacement of business assets involves taking care to ensure that the various conditions are met.

- Disposals and acquisitions need to be planned well in advance to ensure that the time limit for reinvestment is adhered to. It may be necessary to advance or delay capital expenditure (where commercially possible).

- It is not possible to choose to roll over only part of a gain leaving sufficient to cover the annual exemption. However, it may be possible to reinvest all but £10,100 of proceeds in replacement assets.

- The interaction between rollover relief and Entrepreneurs' relief should also be considered carefully. It might not be advisable to rollover gains on asset qualifying for Entrepreneurs' relief, if the new business may be held for a period of less than twelve months.

### Test your understanding 7

Your client, Medway, has been offered £160,000 for a freehold factory he owns and is considering disposing of it in early October 2009. He acquired the factory for £40,000 on 31 March 1983. The sale of the factory is part of a disposal of the entire business.

(a) **Compute the capital gains tax that will arise if Medway disposes of the factory, and does not claim rollover relief.**

(b) **Indicate to Medway the capital gains consequences of each of the following alternative courses of action he is considering taking, following the sale, and give any advice you consider to be relevant.**

    (i) **acquiring a new freehold factory as part of a new business in 2010 for £172,000.**

    (ii) **acquiring a new freehold factory as part of a new business in 2010 for £150,000 and using the remainder of the proceeds as working capital.**

## Summary

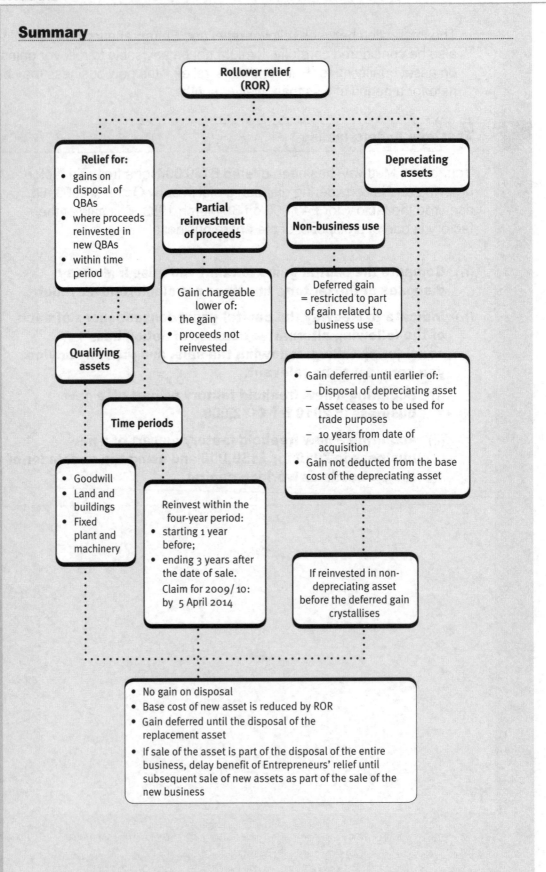

**Rollover relief (ROR)**

**Relief for:**
- gains on disposal of QBAs
- where proceeds reinvested in new QBAs
- within time period

**Partial reinvestment of proceeds**

Gain chargeable lower of:
- the gain
- proceeds not reinvested

**Non-business use**

Deferred gain = restricted to part of gain related to business use

**Depreciating assets**

- Gain deferred until earlier of:
  - Disposal of depreciating asset
  - Asset ceases to be used for trade purposes
  - 10 years from date of acquisition
- Gain not deducted from the base cost of the depreciating asset

**Qualifying assets**

**Time periods**

- Goodwill
- Land and buildings
- Fixed plant and machinery

Reinvest within the four-year period:
- starting 1 year before;
- ending 3 years after the date of sale.

Claim for 2009/10: by 5 April 2014

If reinvested in non-depreciating asset before the deferred gain crystallises

- No gain on disposal
- Base cost of new asset is reduced by ROR
- Gain deferred until the disposal of the replacement asset
- If sale of the asset is part of the disposal of the entire business, delay benefit of Entrepreneurs' relief until subsequent sale of new assets as part of the sale of the new business

## 6 Gift of qualifying assets

Gift of qualifying assets relief applies to:

- lifetime gifts
- sales at undervaluation.

The relief allows the gain on some lifetime gifts and some transactions that have an element of a gift (i.e. sales at undervaluation) to be deferred until the asset is subsequently disposed of by the recipient of the gift (i.e. the donee).

### The operation of the relief

A reminder of the operation of the relief covered at F6 is given in expandable text and is summarised in the diagram below.

### Operation of the relief

The relief is only available for gifts or sales at undervaluation:

- of qualifying assets
- by individuals to other individuals, trustees or a company
- if the recipient is resident or ordinarily resident in the UK at the time of the gift, and
- a claim is made.

The relief operates as follows:

| Donor | Donee |
| --- | --- |
| • the gain is calculated as normal using market value of the asset as consideration. | • the gift relief (i.e. the deferred gain) is deducted from the acquisition cost of the asset to the donee. |
| • if an outright gift:<br>  – no tax is payable at the time of the gift by the donor as the gain is deferred. | • the base cost of the asset to the donee = (Market value less gift relief) |

| | |
|---|---|
| • if a sale at undervaluation:<br><br>– a chargeable gain arises at the time of the sale if the actual sale proceeds received exceed the original cost of the asset<br><br>– the balance of the gain is eligible for gift relief.<br><br>– if sale is part of a disposal of the entire business or shareholding, Entrepreneurs' relief will be available on any gains not deferred | • on a subsequent disposal of the entire business or shareholding Entrepreneurs' relief will be available if the donee has owned the asset for twelve months. |

Note that:

- Gift relief is not automatic, it must be claimed:
  - by both the donor and the donee
  - by 5 April 2014 for gifts in 2009/10.

### Gift before 6 April 2008

If the gift was made prior to 6 April 2008 and a gift relief claim is made, the examiner will either:

- give the amount of the deferred gain, or

- the calculation will be the same as the current rules (i.e. sale proceeds less cost).

Note however that regardless of how the gain is calculated, the deferred gain arising would have been deducted from the base cost of the donee and deferred until the subsequent disposal of the asset by the donee.

### Qualifying assets

The main categories of qualifying assets for gift relief purposes are as follows:

(1) Assets used in the trade of:

- the donor (sole trader or partnership)

- the donor's personal company.

(2) Shares and securities in any unquoted trading company.

(3) Shares and securities in the individual donor's personal trading company (quoted or unquoted).

(4) Any asset where there is an immediate charge to inheritance tax (see Chapter 11).

(5) Any asset where APR is available (See Chapter 12).

Note that:

- a company qualifies as an individual's personal company if they own at least 5% of the voting rights

- no relief is available for business assets used in an investment business or shares in an investment company.

**Interaction with Entrepreneurs' relief**

Gift relief is given **before** Entrepreneurs' relief.

If Entrepreneurs' relief is applicable:

- the deferred gain is not reduced by Entrepreneurs' relief

- the donee may be able to make his or her own claim to Entrepreneurs' relief on a subsequent disposal if the conditions are satisfied

- the donor may choose not to claim gift relief in order to crystallise a gain and claim Entrepreneurs' relief instead if this is advantageous (i.e. if the donee will not qualify for the relief, for example if they would not satisfy the one-year ownership rule).

- if gift relief is claimed, the full amount of relief available must be deferred, it is not possible to make a partial claim to defer only some of the gain.

    However, the individual could sell the asset at an undervaluation rather than making an outright gift to ensure that a gift relief claim will leave a gain to be taxed which utilises his capital losses, the annual exemption, and if relevant, Entrepreneurs' relief.

**Restrictions to gift relief**

**Non-business use**

Adjustments need to be made to the calculation of the amount of gift relief available if there is an element of non-business use because the asset was:

- used partly for business purposes and partly for private use

- not used for business purposes for the whole of the period of ownership by the donor.

Where the asset has not been used entirely for business purposes, only the business portion of the gain is eligible for relief.

### Shares in the donor's personal trading company

Gift relief is also restricted if:

- shares in the donor's personal company are gifted

- the company holds chargeable non-business assets (for example, investments in property or shares).

The portion of the gain that is eligible for gift relief is calculated as follows:

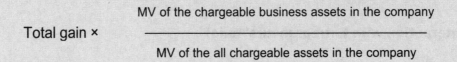

$$\text{Total gain} \times \frac{\text{MV of the chargeable business assets in the company}}{\text{MV of the all chargeable assets in the company}}$$

Note that

- where the donor holds less than 5% of the voting rights in the company there is no restriction to the relief when shares are gifted

- a chargeable asset is one that, if sold, would give rise to a chargeable gain (or an allowable loss)

- chargeable business assets are defined as chargeable assets used for the purposes of a trade and are specifically to exclude shares, securities or other assets held for investment.

These definitions can be applied to most businesses to mean the following:

| | Chargeable assets (CA) | Chargeable business assets (CBA) |
|---|---|---|
| Freehold/leasehold property | √ | √ |
| Goodwill acquired pre 1 April 2002 | √ | √ |
| Motor cars | x | x |
| Plant and machinery (Cost £6,000 or less, proceeds £6,000 or less) | x | x |
| Investments | √ | x |
| Net current assets | x | x |

Note that if the individual disposes of shares in a personal trading company:

- gift relief is available:
  - subject to the (CBA / CA) restriction above
  - regardless of whether the individual works for the company

- Entrepreneurs' relief is also available provided:
  - the individual works for the company, and
  - it has been the individual's personal trading company
  - for the 12 months prior to the disposal.

Remember that gift relief is given **before** Entrepreneurs' relief.

### Test your understanding 8

Fred is a sole trader. He gave his son, Ashley, a business asset on 1 June 2009 when its market value was £75,000. Fred paid £20,000 for the asset on 1 May 1989. Ashley sells the asset for £95,000 on 1 October 2010.

(a) **Compute the taxable gains arising on these disposals if gift relief is not claimed.**

(b) **Compute the taxable gains arising on these disposals if gift relief is claimed.**

(c) **If Ashley paid his father £53,000, what impact would this have.**

### Test your understanding 9

Jack Jones gave 30,000 ordinary shares (representing his entire 30% holding) in Cross Ltd, an unquoted trading company, to his son Tom on 16 June 2009. The shares were valued at £450,000 on that date.

Jack purchased the shares on 16 October 2000, the day he became a full time director in the company. The shares cost Jack £200,000.

The company's issued share capital is 100,000 ordinary shares, and its net assets had the following market value on 16 June 2009:

|  | £ |
|---|---|
| Freehold factory | 1,140,000 |
| Investments | 60,000 |
| Net current assets | 370,000 |
|  | 1,570,000 |

**Calculate the chargeable gain for Jack and show the base cost for Tom, assuming all reliefs are claimed.**

### The emigration of the donee

To qualify for gift relief, the recipient must be resident or ordinarily resident in the UK at the time of the gift (definition of these terms is considered in Chapter 10).

If the recipient of a gift on which gift relief is given:

- emigrates from the UK within six years of the date of the gift
- the held over gain from the time of the gift crystallises and is chargeable on the donee the day before emigration.

### Exception to the rule

Where the donee goes overseas to take up full time employment abroad a chargeable gain will not crystallise on his departure from the UK provided:

(i) they resume their status as UK resident or ordinarily resident within three years; and

(ii) they have not disposed of the asset whilst abroad.

### Reasoning behind emigration rules

The overseas rules covered in Chapter 10 states that if an individual is not UK resident and not ordinarily resident in the UK, capital disposals are exempt from CGT if the individual leaves the UK for at least 5 years.

Gift relief is not available in respect of gifts to a non-UK resident person as the non-UK resident could dispose of the asset whilst abroad and avoid CGT on the donor's original gain and any increase in value since the donee received the asset.

Therefore, to qualify for gift relief, the recipient must be resident or ordinarily resident in the UK at the time of the gift.

In addition, anti-avoidance legislation has been introduced to prevent individuals getting around the rules by:

- gifting assets to a UK resident person, and
- then the donee emigrates and disposes of the asset;
- to try and take advantage and avoid CGT on the donor's original gain and any increase in value since the donee received the asset.

## Tax planning points

Much of tax planning for gift relief involves taking care to ensure that annual exemptions are utilised and Entrepreneurs' relief is not lost.

- It is not possible to choose to defer only part of a gain under the gift relief provisions. However, it may be possible to arrange for the donee to pay some actual proceeds to crystallise a gain of £10,100 which is covered by the annual exemption.

- The interaction between gift relief and Entrepreneurs' relief should be considered carefully. It might not be advisable to defer a gain on an asset qualifying for the maximum Entrepreneurs' relief, if the donee plans to hold the asset for less than twelve months or not fulfil the qualifying conditions, such as being an employee of a company in which $\geq 5\%$ shares have been gifted.

Lifetime gifts have both CGT and inheritance tax consequences. Therefore, the impact of inheritance tax must also be considered before giving advice. The interaction of CGT and IHT is covered in Chapter 13.

## Summary

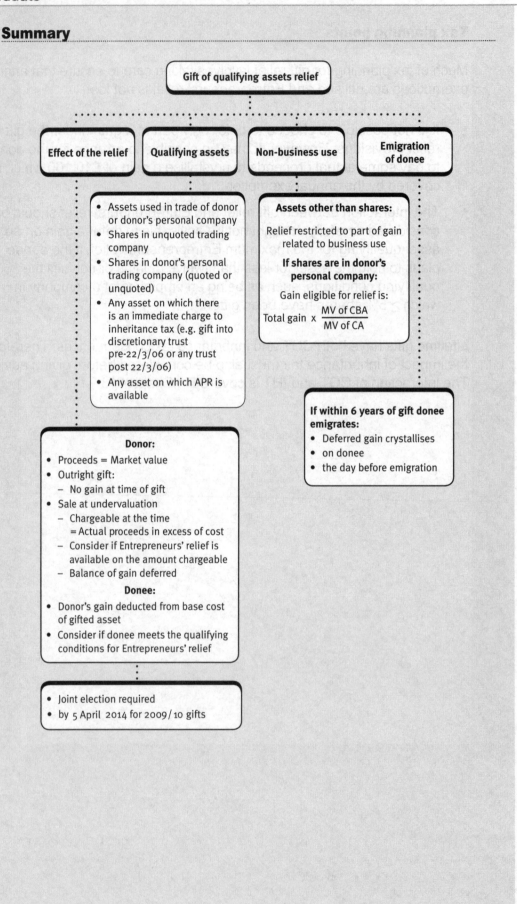

**Gift of qualifying assets relief**

**Effect of the relief**    **Qualifying assets**    **Non-business use**    **Emigration of donee**

**Qualifying assets**
- Assets used in trade of donor or donor's personal company
- Shares in unquoted trading company
- Shares in donor's personal trading company (quoted or unquoted)
- Any asset on which there is an immediate charge to inheritance tax (e.g. gift into discretionary trust pre-22/3/06 or any trust post 22/3/06)
- Any asset on which APR is available

**Non-business use**

**Assets other than shares:**

Relief restricted to part of gain related to business use

**If shares are in donor's personal company:**

Gain eligible for relief is:

$$\text{Total gain} \times \frac{\text{MV of CBA}}{\text{MV of CA}}$$

**Emigration of donee**

**If within 6 years of gift donee emigrates:**
- Deferred gain crystallises
- on donee
- the day before emigration

**Donor:**
- Proceeds = Market value
- Outright gift:
  - No gain at time of gift
- Sale at undervaluation
  - Chargeable at the time = Actual proceeds in excess of cost
  - Consider if Entrepreneurs' relief is available on the amount chargeable
  - Balance of gain deferred

**Donee:**
- Donor's gain deducted from base cost of gifted asset
- Consider if donee meets the qualifying conditions for Entrepreneurs' relief

- Joint election required
- by 5 April 2014 for 2009/10 gifts

## 7 Incorporation relief

Where an individual transfers their unincorporated business (i.e. a sole trader business or a partnership) to a company, the individual assets of the business are deemed to have been disposed of at market value to the company.

Incorporation relief is available to allow the gains arising on incorporation to be deferred until the shares in the company are disposed of.

### The operation of the relief

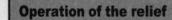

A reminder of the operation of the relief, the conditions and how the amount of relief is calculated covered at F6 is given in expandable text and is summarised on the diagram below.

### Operation of the relief

Incorporation relief operates as follows:

- The gains before Entrepreneurs' relief arising on the deemed disposal of the individual assets are aggregated.

- The total gains are 'rolled over' against the deemed acquisition cost of the shares in the new company (i.e. deducted from the base cost of the shares).

- Entrepreneurs' relief on the subsequent disposal of shares is based on the qualifying conditions.

- The relief is automatic provided certain conditions are met.

### Conditions for the relief

All of the following conditions must be satisfied:

- The unincorporated business is transferred as a going concern.

- All of the assets of the business (other than cash) are transferred to the company.

- The consideration received for the transfer of the business must be received wholly or partly in the form of shares in the company.

Where all of these conditions are met the relief is **automatic** and **mandatory.**

## The calculation of the incorporation relief

The amount of the 'total gains' arising on incorporation that can be deferred depends on whether the transfer is wholly or partly for shares.

### Transfer wholly for shares

Where the consideration for the transfer of the business to the company is wholly shares:

- the total net gains on the individual chargeable assets transferred to the company are rolled over
- no chargeable gain arises at the time of the incorporation
- the market value of the shares acquired = the market value of the unincorporated business less the rolled over gains.

### Transfer partly for shares

Where part of the consideration for the transfer of the business is not in the form of shares (for example, cash, loan stock and/or debentures):

- incorporation relief

$$= \text{Total gains} \times \frac{\text{Market value of share consideration}}{\text{Market value of total consideration}}$$

- gain becomes chargeable at the time of incorporation

$$= \text{Total gains} \times \frac{\text{Market value of share consideration}}{\text{Market value of total consideration}}$$

Note that:

- can not make a partial claim to defer only some of the gain
- however, the individual could choose to accept some cash or other non-share consideration to ensure that incorporation relief will leave a gain to be taxed which utilises their capital losses, Entrepreneurs' relief and annual exemption.

### Disapplying incorporation relief

- An individual can elect for incorporation relief not to apply (i.e. disapply the relief).
- The election to disapply the incorporation relief rules must be made by 31 January 2013 for an incorporation that takes place in 2009/10.

- However, if the shares received are sold by the end of the tax year following the tax year of incorporation, this deadline is brought forward by one year (i.e. to 31 January 2012 for incorporation in 2009/10 with sale of shares during 2010/11).

**Interaction with Entrepreneurs' relief**

If applicable, incorporation relief is given **before** Entrepreneurs' relief.

This means that if Entrepreneurs' relief is available:

- the deferred gain is not reduced by Entrepreneurs' relief
- but where part of the consideration is in the form of cash, the remaining gain can be reduced by Entrepreneurs' relief
- the subsequent disposal of the shares should normally qualify for Entrepreneurs' relief provided the conditions are satisfied
- however if this in unlikely, the individual may **disapply** incorporation relief in order to crystallise a gain and claim Entrepreneurs' relief instead if this is advantageous (i.e. if the individual plans to dispose of the shares within one year and fails the one-year ownership rule).

**Test your understanding 10**

On 31 January 2010, Stuart sold his business to a limited company for an agreed value of £1,100,000. He set up the business in August 2000.

All of the assets were transferred to the company with the exception of the cash. The assets transferred were as follows

|  | Date of Purchase | Market value 31 January 2010 | Cost |
|---|---|---|---|
|  |  | £ | £ |
| Freehold premises | August 2000 | 700,000 | 240,000 |
| Goodwill | – | 250,000 | – |
| Stock & debtors | – | 150,000 | – |
|  |  | 1,100,000 |  |

(a) Calculate the gain immediately chargeable and the base cost of these shares assuming Stuart received:
 (i) 100,000 £1 ordinary shares in the company.
 (ii) 80,000 £1 ordinary shares plus £220,000 in cash.

(b) State the tax planning advice you would give to Stuart.

## Alternative deferral using the gift relief provisions

One of the disadvantages of incorporation relief is that all of the assets (except cash) must be transferred to the company. If the trader wishes to retain any assets of the business other than cash, incorporation relief is denied and significant gains may crystallise on incorporation.

As an alternative, the individual may use the gift relief provisions to defer gains as follows:

(i)   the individual sets up a company with a nominal value cash (say £100)

(ii)  non-chargeable assets (for example, stocks and debtors) are sold to the company and no gains arise

(iii) the chargeable business assets which the individual wants to transfer in to the company are gifted to the company or sold at their capital gains base cost

(iv)  gains arise but gift relief is then claimed on the transfer of those business assets to defer the gains against the base cost of the asset in the company.

The effects of deferring the gains under gift relief are as follows:

*   The assets have a low base cost in the company, which will give rise to higher gains taxed on the company to corporation tax when the assets are disposed of.

*   The individual has a low base cost of shares held in the company (£100), which will give rise to higher gains taxed on the individual when the shares are later sold.

However, this route enables the trader to defer gains whilst retaining personal ownership of some assets of their business.

Assets the trader may wish to retain on incorporation are those with large growth potential (i.e. those expected to increase in value significantly).

It is common for the trader to retain ownership of the freehold premises and to rent it to the company for use in the trade.

This is because transferring assets to the company potentially gives rise to a double charge to capital gains:

*   on sale of asset by company

*   on sale of company shares
    *   part of the value of the shares relates to the gain realised on the sale of the capital assets by the company.

Retaining property outside the company also saves the company paying Stamp Duty Land Tax on the transfer.

However, retaining ownership of assets and renting to the company will deny the individual Entrepreneurs' relief on a future sale of the building, even if associated to the sale of the company shares.

The building would have to be used in the company rent free to preserve Entrepreneurs' relief.

## Sale of goodwill to the company

Another possibility would be for the individual to sell the goodwill to the company and pay tax on the gain at a maximum of 18%, rather than extracting funds from the company as, say, salary and paying up to 40% income tax plus national insurance.

For this approach to succeed, the goodwill must be properly valued and cannot be sold to the company for more than its market value.

The way this would normally be achieved is as follows:

(i) the goodwill is sold to the company, with proceeds left in a loan account within the company to be repaid later

(ii) a gain will arise based on full market value. This gain will be subject to tax at only 10% (if Entrepreneurs' relief is available) or 18% (if no Entrepreneurs' relief available), or even less if the annual exemption has not already been used.

(iii) the payment for the goodwill can then be withdrawn from the company when funds become available, at no extra tax cost.

(iv) this may be much more tax efficient than later extracting funds from the company in the form of:

    (i) salary (subject to income tax at 20% or 40%, and national insurance at 11% or 1%, plus employers' national insurance for the company)

    (ii) dividends (subject to income tax at 10% or 32.5% with a 10% tax credit). However, if the individual has no other income, there would be no extra tax on dividends falling into the basic rate band in any case, as the 10% tax would be covered by the tax credit.

## Treatment of goodwill in the company

Where the individual's business commenced on or after 1 April 2002, or was purchased from a third party on or after this date, the goodwill purchased by the company will qualify as a "new" intangible. This means that the company will be able to claim a deduction for amounts written off in the accounts, or elect to claim a 4% writing down allowance based on the value of the goodwill acquired (see Chapter 23).

### Example 4 - Incorporation relief

Tristan, bought a travel agency in Cornwall in April 2002 paying £11,500 for goodwill.

On 15 July 2009 he sold the business as a going concern to Kareol Travel Ltd, an existing company, which took over all of the assets, except for cash, at the following agreed values:

|  | £ |
|---|---|
| Freehold premises | 284,000 |
| Goodwill | 44,000 |
| Estate car | 6,000 |
| Stock and debtors | 6,000 |
|  | 340,000 |

The freehold premises cost £66,000 in May 2003.

The consideration for the sale was settled by Kareol Ltd allotting to Tristan 70,000 ordinary shares of 20p each, valued at 350p per share, and paying him cash of £95,000. The shares are not quoted.

On 25 March 2010 Tristan sold 10,000 ordinary shares in Kareol Ltd for £22,664 to an unconnected person. On the same day Tristan gave a further 10,000 shares in Kareol Ltd to his daughter.

**Calculate the CGT payable by Tristan as a result of the above disposals, assuming that incorporation relief and any other available reliefs are claimed.**

**Solution**

**Capital gains tax computation – 2009/10**

|  | £ |
|---|---|
| Incorporation of Kareol Ltd (W1) | 38,885 |
| Sale of Kareol Ltd shares (W2) | 13,451 |
| Gift of Kareol Ltd shares (W3) | Nil |
|  |  |
| Total chargeable gains | 52,336 |
| Less Annual exemption | (10,100) |
|  |  |
| Taxable gain | 42,236 |
|  |  |
| Capital gains tax (£42,236 × 18%) | 7,602 |

## Workings

### (W1) Incorporation of Kareol Travel Ltd – July 2009

| | £ | £ |
|---|---:|---:|
| **Freehold premises** | | |
| Deemed proceeds (MV) | 284,000 | |
| Less: Cost | (66,000) | |
| | | 218,000 |
| **Goodwill** | | |
| Deemed proceeds (MV) | 44,000 | |
| Less: Cost | (11,500) | |
| | | 32,500 |
| **Estate car/stock and debtors** (Exempt assets) | | Nil |
| Total gains before reliefs | | 250,500 |
| Less: Incorporation relief | | |
| £250,000 × £245,000/£340,000 | | (180,507) |
| | | 69,993 |
| Less: Entrepreneurs' relief (£69,993 × 4/9) | | (31,108) |
| Chargeable gain | | 38,885 |

### (W2) Sale of 10,000 Kareol Ltd shares

| | £ | £ |
|---|---:|---:|
| Sale proceeds | | 22,664 |
| Shares acquired (July 2009) | | |
| (70,000 × £3.50) | 245,000 | |
| Less: Rolled-over gain | (180,507) | |
| Base cost of total shareholding | 64,493 | |
| Deemed cost of sale of 10,000 shares: | | |
| (£64,493 × 10,000/70,000) | (9,213) | (9,213) |
| Deemed base cost of remaining shares | 55,280 | |
| Chargeable gain | | 13,451 |

**Note:** As Tristan owned the shares for less than 12 months, Entrepreneurs' relief is not available.

Note that even if he had owned them for > 12 months, if he is not an employee of the company and owned ≤ 5%, Entrepreneurs' relief would be denied.

### (W3) Gift of 10,000 Kareol Ltd shares

|                                               | £        |
| --------------------------------------------- | -------- |
| Capital gain (computed as above)              | 13,451   |
| Less: Relief for gift of business assets (Note) | (13,451) |
| Chargeable gain                               | Nil      |

**Note**: The gift of unquoted trading company shares is an outright gift of qualifying shares for gift relief purposes. The base cost of the daughter's shares will be £9,213 (£22,664 − £13,451).

# Summary

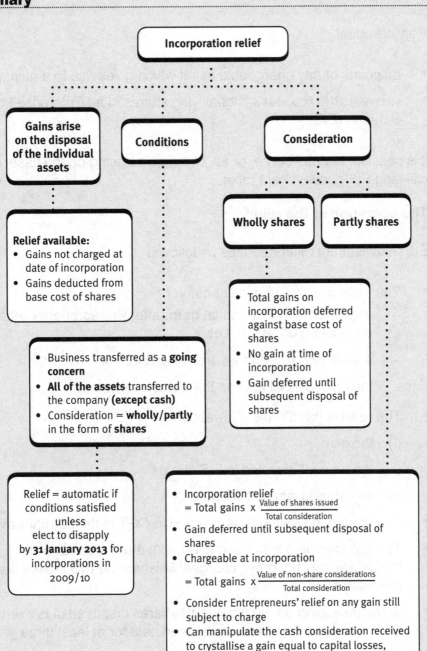

**Incorporation relief**

**Gains arise on the disposal of the individual assets**

**Conditions**

**Consideration**

**Relief available:**
- Gains not charged at date of incorporation
- Gains deducted from base cost of shares

- Business transferred as a **going concern**
- **All of the assets** transferred to the company **(except cash)**
- Consideration = **wholly/partly** in the form of **shares**

Relief = automatic if conditions satisfied unless elect to disapply by **31 January 2013** for incorporations in 2009/10

**Wholly shares**     **Partly shares**

- Total gains on incorporation deferred against base cost of shares
- No gain at time of incorporation
- Gain deferred until subsequent disposal of shares

- Incorporation relief
  = Total gains $\times \dfrac{\text{Value of shares issued}}{\text{Total consideration}}$
- Gain deferred until subsequent disposal of shares
- Chargeable at incorporation
  = Total gains $\times \dfrac{\text{Value of non-share considerations}}{\text{Total consideration}}$
- Consider Entrepreneurs' relief on any gain still subject to charge
- Can manipulate the cash consideration received to crystallise a gain equal to capital losses, Entrepreneurs' relief and annual exemption
- Alternative claim for gift relief possible

## 8 EIS reinvestment relief

If an individual:

- disposes of any chargeable asset which gives rise to a gain; and
- reinvests the proceeds in qualifying shares in an Enterprise Investment Scheme (EIS);

it is possible to defer some, or all, of the gain arising on the asset by claiming EIS reinvestment relief.

### The operation of the relief

EIS reinvestment relief operates as follows:

- The individual can choose to defer:
  - **any** amount of any capital **gain** (after Entrepreneurs' relief if applicable) on **any** asset
  - if qualifying EIS shares are subscribed for
  - the relief cannot exceed the amount invested.

- The relief is therefore the lowest of:

  (i) the gain

  (ii) the amount invested in EIS shares

  (iii) any smaller amount chosen.

- Any amount not deferred is charged to CGT in the normal way.

- The deferred gain is not deducted from the base cost of the EIS shares, the gain simply becomes chargeable when the EIS shares are disposed of.

- Any gain arising on the actual EIS shares disposed of is exempt from CGT, provided the shares have been held for at least three years.

- EIS reinvestment relief must be claimed.

- If the original asset on which the gain arose was disposed of prior to 6 April 2008:
  - Entrepreneurs' relief will be available in respect of the deferred gain that comes into charge on the sale of the EIS shares
  - if the sale of the original asset would have qualified for Entrepreneurs' relief had it been available at the time of disposal.

## Conditions for EIS relief

To qualify for EIS relief:

*   The individual must be UK resident or ordinarily resident in the UK when the gain arises and when the reinvestment is made (definitions of these terms are considered in Chapter 10).

*   The reinvestment must be:
    *   subscribing for new shares
    *   wholly for cash
    *   in an unquoted trading company trading wholly or mainly in the UK.

*   The reinvestment must be made within a four year qualifying time period which runs from 12 months before to 36 months after the date the gain arose.

*   The claim must be made by 31 January 2016 for 2009/10 disposals.

Note that:

*   for EIS income tax relief there is a maximum investment of £500,000. However, there is no maximum amount for the purposes of this CGT reinvestment relief. The relief is effectively unlimited

*   any amount of reinvestment relief can be claimed, therefore the individual should choose an amount of relief so that the remaining gain (after Entrepreneurs' relief, if applicable) is equal to any capital losses and annual exemption available.

### Test your understanding 11

Alex sold a painting in November 2009 for £275,000 realising a capital gain of £150,000.

Alex subscribes for qualifying EIS shares in Milan Ltd, a trading company, the following month at a cost of £268,000. She has no other capital transactions for 2009/10.

Three years later in 2012/13 Alex sells the EIS shares making a profit of £175,000.

(a)  **Calculate the amount of reinvestment relief that Alex should claim.**

(b)  **Explain the capital gains tax consequences of the sale of the EIS shares in 2012/13.**

### Test your understanding 12

Chris sold his 10% holding in Cracker Ltd in September 2009 for £750,000, realising a capital gain of £250,000.

He acquired the shares in July 2007 and has been a director of Cracker Ltd throughout his period of ownership.

In November 2009 he subscribed for qualifying EIS shares in Cream Ltd, a trading company, at a cost of £375,000.

Chris had no other capital transactions in 2009/10 but has capital losses brought forward of £50,000.

**Calculate the amount of EIS reinvestment relief Chris should claim in 2009/10.**

# Summary

```
                        ┌─────────────────────────┐
                        │  EIS  reinvestment relief │
                        └─────────────────────────┘
```

**EIS reinvestment relief**

**Relief for:**
- gains on disposal of any asset
- where proceeds reinvested in qualifying EIS shares
- within time period

**Amount of relief**

**Lowest of:**
- the capital gain
- the amount invested
- any smaller amount chosen

**Operation of relief**
- the gain is deferred until the EIS shares are disposed of
- any amount not deferred = charged in the normal way
- the deferred gain is frozen until the disposal of EIS shares, then taxed in the normal way
- the gain on the EIS shares is exempt provided owned for at least three years
- The gain deferred is after Entrepreneurs' relief, if applicable

**Time period**

**Reinvest:**
Within the four year period:
– starting 1 year before
– ending 3 years after the date of sale

Claim for 2009/10:
By 31 January 2016

**Conditions**

**Individual:**
- UK resident or ordinarily resident in the UK when the gain arises and when the reinvestment is made

**Investment:**
- subscribing for new shares
- wholly for cash

## 9 Chapter summary

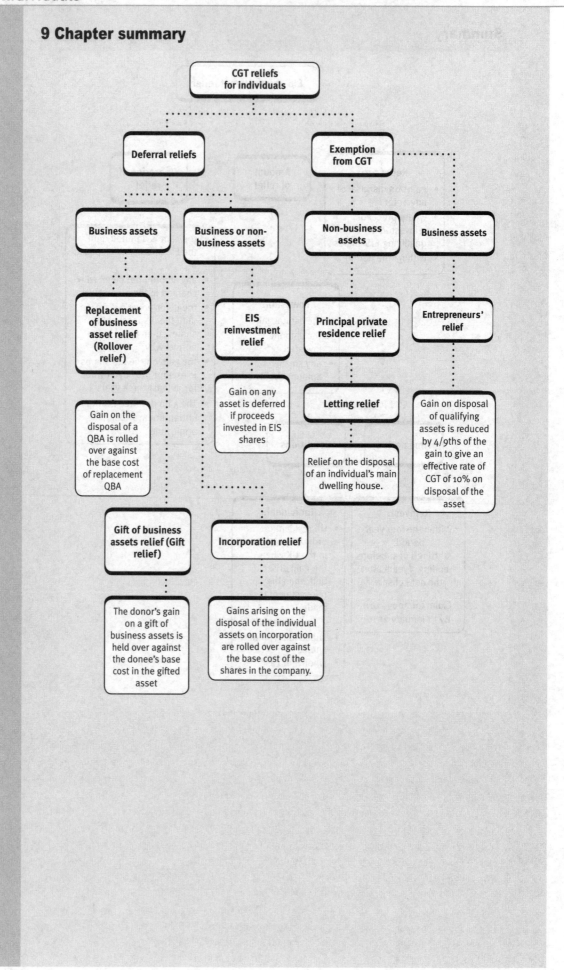

# Test your understanding answers

**Test your understanding 1**

**Paul**

| 2009/10 | | £ | £ |
|---|---|---:|---:|
| *Sale of shares* | | | |
| Gain on shares | | 430,000 | |
| Less: Entrepreneurs' relief | £430,000 × 4/9 | (191,111) | |
| | | | 238,889 |
| *Sale of Warehouse (Note)* | | | 245,000 |
| | | | |
| Net chargeable gains | | | 483,889 |
| Less: Annual exemption | | | (10,100) |
| | | | |
| Taxable gains | | | 473,789 |
| | | | |
| Capital gains tax payable (£473,789 × 18%) | | | 85,282 |

**Note:** The disposal of the warehouse in 2009/10 is the disposal of an individual business asset used for the purposes of a continuing trade. It is not associated with the disposal of the whole business and therefore does not qualify. To qualify there must be a disposal of the whole or part of the trading business. The sale of an asset in isolation will not qualify.

| 2010/11 | | £ | £ |
|---|---|---:|---:|
| *Sale of trading business* | | | |
| Factory | | 495,000 | |
| Goodwill | | 130,000 | |
| | | | |
| | | 625,000 | |
| Less: Entrepreneurs' relief (W) | £570,000 × 4/9 | (253,333) | |
| | | | 371,667 |
| *Sale of Grandfather clock* | | | 5,325 |
| | | | |
| Net chargeable gains | | | 376,992 |
| Less: Annual exemption | | | (10,100) |
| | | | |
| Taxable gains | | | 366,892 |
| | | | |
| Capital gains tax payable (£366,892 × 18%) | | | 66,041 |

**(W)** Rest of the lifetime allowance (£1,000,000 – £430,000)

## Test your understanding 2

**Mr Dearden**

|  | £ |
|---|---|
| Capital gain before reliefs | 194,800 |
| Less: PPR relief (W1) (£194,800 × 198/288) | (133,925) |
|  | 60,875 |
| Less: Letting relief (W2) | (20,292) |
| Chargeable gain | 40,583 |

### Workings

(1) **Compute and analyse total period of ownership**

01.04.86 – 31.03.10 = 24 years (or 288 months)

|  | Exempt months | Chargeable months | Total months |
|---|---|---|---|
| 01.04.86 – 31.03.88 | 24 |  | 24 |
| 01.04.88 – 30.09.93 | 36 | 30 | 66 |
| (3 years any reason) |  |  |  |
| 01.10.93 – 31.03.02 | 102 |  | 102 |
| 01.04.02 – 31.03.07 (Balance) |  | 60 | 60 |
| 01.04.07 – 31.03.10 | 36 |  | 36 |
| (last 3 years of ownership) |  |  |  |
|  | 198 | 90 | 288 |

(2) **Letting relief:**

The house was let for 66 months, from 01.04.88 – 30.09.93, but 36 months of that was exempted under the PPR rules therefore only 30 months is considered.

Letting relief is the lower of:

(1) £40,000

(2) PPR = £133,925

(3) Gain on letting = £194,800 × 30/288 = £20,292

### Test your understanding 3

**Alex**

Alex owned the house for 132 months and used 1/5th of the house (one of the five rooms) for business purposes for 102 months.

The last 36 months of ownership are exempt (the room had been used as part of the residence at some time).

The gain is therefore: £70,000 × 1/5 × (102 – 36)/132 = £7,000

| Alternative approach: | £ | £ |
|---|---|---|
| Capital gain before reliefs | | 70,000 |
| Less: PPR relief | | |
| £70,000 × 4/5 | 56,000 | |
| £70,000 × 1/5 × (132 – (102 – 36))/132 | 7,000 | |
| | | (63,000) |
| Chargeable gain | | 7,000 |

**Paul Opus**

**Capital gains tax liability – 2009/10**

| | £ | £ |
|---|---|---|
| *Ordinary shares in Symphony Ltd* | | |
| Disposal proceeds | 23,600 | |
| Less: Cost (£110,400 × 5,000/40,000) (Note 1) | (13,800) | |
| | | 9,800 |
| *Ordinary shares Concerto plc* | | |
| Deemed proceeds (10,000 × £5.11) (Note 2) | 51,100 | |
| Less: Cost (Note 1) | (14,000) | |
| | | 37,100 |
| *Antique vase* (Note 5) | | 4,000 |
| *House* | | |
| Disposal proceeds | 220,000 | |
| Less: Cost | (114,700) | |
| | | |
| | 105,300 | |
| Less: PPR relief (Note 6) | (97,500) | |
| | | 7,800 |
| *Land* | | |
| Disposal proceeds | 285,000 | |
| Less: Cost (Note 7) | (167,200) | |
| | | 117,800 |
| | | |
| *Holiday cottage* | | |
| Disposal proceeds | 125,000 | |
| Less: Cost (Note 8) | (101,600) | |
| | | 23,400 |
| | | |
| Total chargeable gains | | 199,900 |
| Less: Annual exemption | | (10,100) |
| | | |
| Taxable gains | | 189,800 |
| | | |
| Capital gains tax (£189,800 × 18%) | | 34,164 |
| | | |
| Due date | | 31 January 2011 |

**Notes:**

(1)  The shares are disposed of from the share pool

(2) The shares in Concerto plc are valued at the lower of £5.12 (£5.10 + ¼ (£5.18 – £5.10)) and £5.11 ((£5.00 + £5.22)/2).

(3) Entrepreneurs' relief is not available on the disposal of the Concerto plc shares as the disposal is not from a personal trading company. Gift relief is not available either as Paul's holding is ≤ 5%.

(4) Motor cars are exempt from CGT.

(5) The antique vase is a non-wasting chattel. The gain is (£12,400 – £8,400) = £4,000.

(6) The total period of ownership of the house is 81 months, of which a total of 75 months (period of occupation plus final 36 months) qualify for exemption. The exemption is therefore £97,500 (£105,300 × 75/81).

(7) The cost relating to the three acres of land sold is £167,200 (£220,000 × £285,000/£375,000).

(8) The transfer of the holiday cottage between Paul and his wife is effectively ignored for CGT purposes, so the wife's original cost is used in calculating Paul's capital gain.

## Test your understanding 5

### Keith

Not all of the sale proceeds have been reinvested therefore some of the gain will be taxable at the time of the disposal.

### May 1985

The gain taxable in May 1985 was the lower of:

| | |
|---|---|
| • the full gain | £58,240 |
| • the amount of the proceeds not reinvested (£100,000 – £80,000) | £20,000 |
| The gain rolled over was therefore (£58,240 – £20,000) | £38,240 |

### April 2009

|  | £ | £ |
|---|---|---|
| Proceeds on sale of building 2 |  | 300,000 |
| Less Cost | 80,000 |  |
| Gain rolled over | (38,240) |  |
|  |  | (41,760) |
| Chargeable gain |  | 258,240 |

**Note:** Entrepreneurs' relief is not available as this is the disposal of an individual asset used for the purposes of a continuing trade.

### Test your understanding 6

**Sophie**

| Disposal of office block – August 2005 | £ |
|---|---|
| Sale proceeds | 120,000 |
| Less Cost | (70,000) |
|  | 50,000 |
| Cash retained (£120,000 – £100,000) = £20,000 |  |
| Deferred gains (£50,000 – £20,000) | (30,000) |
| Chargeable gain in 2005/06 | 20,000 |

The £30,000 gain is deferred until the earliest of:

(1) the disposal of replacement depreciating asset (November 2009)

(2) the depreciating asset ceases to be used for the purposes of the trade (November 2009)

(3) ten years from the date of acquisition of the replacement depreciating asset (April 2016).

Therefore, the deferred gain of £30,000 becomes chargeable in 2009/10.

**Note:** No Entrepreneurs' relief is available as this is a disposal of an individual asset used for the purposes of a continuing trade.

**Disposal of fixed plant and machinery – November 2009**

Sophie has sold the machinery for a real loss of £40,000 (£100,000 – £60,000).

No capital loss arises as capital allowances will have been given to cover the loss.

**Test your understanding 7**

**Medway**

(a)  **Capital gain on the disposal of the factory**

|  |  | £ |
|---|---|---:|
| Proceeds | | 160,000 |
| Less: Cost | | (40,000) |
| | | |
| | | 120,000 |
| Less: Entrepreneurs' relief (£120,000 × 4/9) | | (53,333) |
| | | |
| Chargeable gain | | 66,667 |
| Less: Annual exemption | | (10,100) |
| | | |
| Taxable gain | | 56,567 |
| | | |
| Capital gains tax @ 18% | | 10,182 |

(b) (i)  **New factory cost £172,000**

All of the gain will be rolled over against the base cost of the new factory as all of the proceeds are reinvested

|  | £ |
|---|---:|
| Capital gain on factory (1) | 120,000 |
| Less: Rollover relief | (120,000) |
| | |
| Chargeable gain | Nil |

**Base cost of new factory**

| | £ |
|---|---|
| Cost of new factory | 172,000 |
| Less: Gain deferred | (120,000) |
| Base cost of new factory | 52,000 |

When Medway subsequently sells the replacement factory, as part of the sale of the whole of the new business, Enterpreneurs' relief will be available if the conditions are satisfied.

## (ii) New factory cost £150,000

As only part of the proceeds are reinvested, the gain that cannot be rolled over will be £10,000 (£160,000 – £150,000). The rest of the gain £110,000 (£120,000 – £10,000) can be deferred

| | £ |
|---|---|
| Capital gain before reliefs | 120,000 |
| Less: Rollover relief | (110,000) |
| | 10,000 |
| Less: Entrepreneurs' relief (4/9 × £10,000) | (4,444) |
| Chargeable gains | 5,556 |
| Less: Annual exemption | (5,556) |
| Taxable gain | Nil |

**Base cost of new factory**

| | £ |
|---|---|
| Cost of new factory | 150,000 |
| Less: Gain deferred | (110,000) |
| Base cost of new factory | 40,000 |

When Medway subsequently sells the replacement factory, as part of the sale of the whole of the new business, Entrepreneurs' relief will be available if the conditions are satisfied. The remaining relief available is £990,000 (£1,000,000 – £10,000).

**Test your understanding 8**

**Fred's taxable gains**

| 2009/10 | (a) £ | (b) £ | (c) £ |
|---|---|---|---|
| Deemed proceeds (1 June 2009) | 75,000 | 75,000 | 75,000 |
| Less Cost | (20,000) | (20,000) | (20,000) |
| | 55,000 | 55,000 | 55,000 |
| Less Gift relief | Nil | (55,000) | (22,000) |
| Chargeable gain | 55,000 | Nil | 33,000 |
| Less: Annual exemption | (10,100) | | (10,100) |
| Taxable gain | 44,900 | Nil | 22,900 |

**Note**: Under (c) Fred realises an actual profit of £33,000 (£53,000 – £20,000) and so this amount becomes chargeable leaving the balance to be deferred. Entrepreneurs' relief is not available as this is the disposal of an individual asset not the whole or substantial part of the business.

| Base cost for Ashley | £ | £ | £ |
|---|---|---|---|
| Deemed cost | 75,000 | 75,000 | 75,000 |
| Less Gift relief | (Nil) | (55,000) | (22,000) |
| Base cost for future CGT disposal | 75,000 | 20,000 | 53,000 |

| Ashley's taxable gains 2010/11 | (a) £ | (b) £ | (c) £ |
|---|---|---|---|
| Proceeds (1 October 2010) | 95,000 | 95,000 | 95,000 |
| Less Base cost | (75,000) | (20,000) | (53,000) |
| Chargeable gain | 20,000 | 75,000 | 42,000 |
| Less: Annual exemption | (10,100) | (10,100) | (10,100) |
| Taxable gain | 9,900 | 64,900 | 31,900 |

**Test your understanding 9**

**Jack Jones**

| Gift of shares – June 2009 | £ |
|---|---:|
| Market value | 450,000 |
| Less: Cost | (200,000) |
| | |
| Capital gain before reliefs | 250,000 |

As the gain is on shares in Tom's personal trading company, and the company holds investments, the amount eligible for gift relief is restricted as follows:

$$\text{Gift relief} = £250,000 \times \frac{£1,140,000}{£1,140,000 + £60,000} = £237,500$$

**Note**: Market values must be used in the CBA/CA fraction.

The chargeable gain at the time of the gift is therefore:

| | £ |
|---|---:|
| Capital gain (as above) | 250,000 |
| Less Gift relief (or 'held over' gain) | (237,500) |
| | |
| | 12,500 |
| Less: Entrepreneurs' relief (£12,500 × 4/9) | (5,555) |
| | |
| Chargeable gain | 6,945 |

| Base cost of shares to Tom | |
|---|---:|
| Market value | 450,000 |
| Less Gift relief | (237,500) |
| | |
| Cost of shares | 212,500 |

When Tom sells his entire holding, assuming he works for the company and owns the shares for 12 months, Entrepreneurs' relief will be available.

**Test your understanding 10**

**Stuart**

**(a) (i) Chargeable gain on disposal of business – 2009/10**

|  | £ | £ |
|---|---|---|
| Premises: Proceeds | 700,000 | |
| Less: Cost | (240,000) | |
| | | 460,000 |
| Goodwill: Proceeds | 250,000 | |
| Less: Cost | – | |
| | | 250,000 |
| Total capital gains before reliefs | | 710,000 |
| Less Incorporation relief | | (710,000) |
| Chargeable gain – 2009/10 | | Nil |

**Base cost of shares**

| | |
|---|---|
| Market value of assets transferred | 1,100,000 |
| Less Incorporation relief | (710,000) |
| Base cost | 390,000 |

Entrepreneurs' relief is delayed until a subsequent disposal of the shareholding provided the conditions are satisfied.

### (a) (ii) Chargeable gain on disposal of business – 2009/10

|  | £ | £ |
|---|---:|---:|
| Total capital gains before reliefs (as above) |  | 710,000 |
| Total consideration |  |  |
| Cash | 220,000 |  |
| Shares (balance) | 880,000 |  |
|  | 1,100,000 |  |
| Less: Incorporation relief (deferred gain) (£710,000 x 880,000/1,100,000) |  | (568,000) |
|  |  | 142,000 |
| Less: Entrepreneurs' relief (£142,000 x 4/9) |  | (63,111) |
| Chargeable gain |  | 78,889 |

**Base cost of shares**

|  |  | £ |
|---|---|---:|
| MV of share consideration |  | 880,000 |
|  |  | (568,000) |
| Base cost of shares |  | 312,000 |

Entrpreneurs' relief will be available on a subsequent disposal of the shares if the conditions are satisfied

### (b) Tax advice for Stuart

Assuming Stuart has no other capital gains in the year, Stuart should consider accepting non-share consideration to the value that would give rise to a chargeable gain (after Entrepreneur's relief) which is covered by his annual exemption.

| | |
|---|---:|
| = £10,100 × 9/5 | £18,180 |
| The deferred gains should be (£710,000 − £18,180) = | £691,820 |
| Therefore the market value of the shares should be: | |
| £691,820 = MV of shares × (£710,000/£1,100,000) | |
| MV of shares = | £1,071,834 |
| Therefore the market value of cash should be: | |
| (£1,100,000 − £1,071,834) = | £28,166 |

| Proof: | £ |
|---|---|
| Capital gain before reliefs | 710,000 |
| Less: Incorporation relief | (691,820) |
| | 18,180 |
| Less: Entrepreneurs' relief (£18,180 × 4//9) | (8,080) |
| Chargeable gain | 10,100 |
| Less: Annual exemption | (10,100) |
| Taxable gain | Nil |

### Test your understanding 11

**Alex**

(a) **Amount of reinvestment relief**

Alex can claim relief for any amount up to £150,000.

However, to claim this full amount will mean that she does not make full use of her annual exemption for 2009/10.

The EIS relief claim should therefore be calculated as follows:

| | £ | |
|---|---|---|
| Capital gain | 150,000 | |
| Less: EIS Reinvestment Relief | (139,900) | Balancing figure |
| Chargeable gain | 10,100 | |
| Less: Annual Exemption | (10,100) | |
| Taxable gain | Nil | |

(b) **Sale of EIS shares**

When Alex disposes of the EIS shares in 2012/13, the gain of £139,900 will become chargeable.

The gain on the EIS shares will be exempt from CGT as they have been held for more than 3 years.

## Test your understanding 12

**Chris**

|  | £ |  |
|---|---|---|
| Capital gain before reliefs | 250,000 | |
| Less: Entrepreneurs' relief | | |
| (£250,000 × 4/9) | (111,111) | |
| | | |
| Chargeable gain | 138,889 | |
| Less: Capital loss b/f | (50,000) | |
| Less: EIS reinvestment relief | (78,789) | Balancing figure |
| | | |
| Total chargeable gain | 10,100 | |
| Less: Annual exemption | (10,100) | |
| | | |
| Taxable gain | Nil | |

The deferred gain of £78,789 will become chargeable when the EIS shares are disposed of. If the EIS shares are held for 3 years, any rise in value of the EIS shares will be exempt, any losses are always allowable.

KAPLAN PUBLISHING

# Overseas aspects of income tax and capital gains tax

## Chapter learning objectives

Upon completion of this chapter you will be able to:

- Explain and apply the concepts of residence, ordinary residence and domicile

- Advise on the tax position of individuals coming to and leaving the UK

- Advise on the relevance of an individual's tax status to income tax and capital gains tax

- Advise on the availability of the remittance basis to UK resident individuals and non-UK domiciled individuals

- Determine the income tax treatment of overseas income

- Advise on the overseas aspects of income from employment, including travel and subsistence expenses

- Recognise the tax treatment of overseas trade travelling expenses

- Determine the UK taxation treatment of foreign gains

- Understand the relevance of the OECD model double tax treaty to given situations

- Calculate and advise on the double taxation relief available to individuals for income tax and capital gains tax

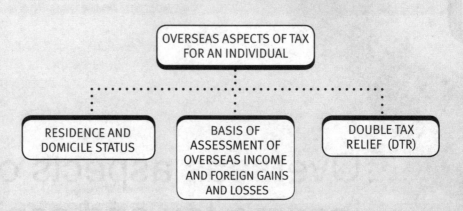

## 1 Introduction

This chapter explains the rules for determining the tax status of an individual and covers the overseas aspects of income tax and capital gains tax.

Much of the content in this chapter is new at P6.

## 2 The tax status of an individual

The tax status of an individual is fundamental in determining their basis of assessment to both income tax and capital gains tax.

Determining whether or not an individual has UK residence, ordinary residence and domicile is therefore vital.

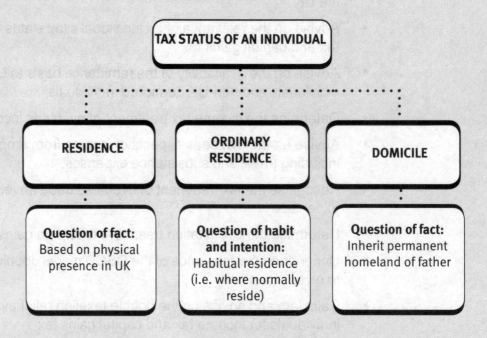

## Residence

The residence status of an individual coming into the UK depends on the length of their stay in the UK:

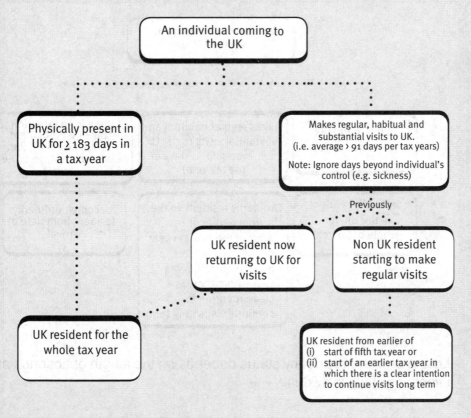

**Note:** An individual is present in the UK on any day when he is here at midnight at the end of the day.

Losing residence status depends on the length of absence and intentions of the individual:

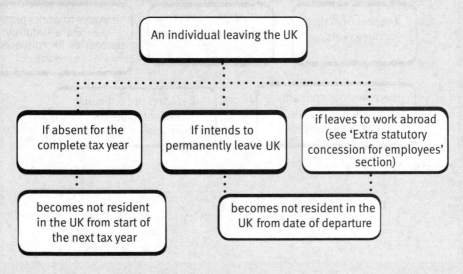

### Ordinary Residence

The ordinary residence status of an individual depends on where the individual normally resides, and their intentions:

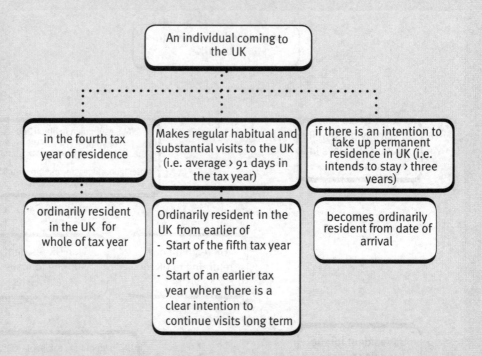

Losing ordinary residency status depends on the length of absence and intentions of the individual:

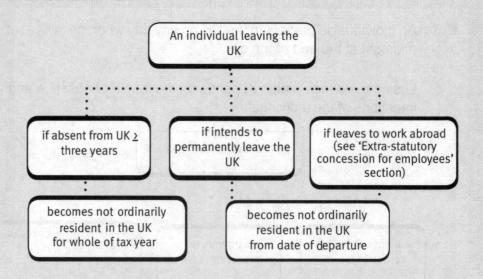

## Domicile

The domicile status of an individual differs from the concepts of nationality and residence, it is based on the individual's permanent home. A person can only have one domicile at any one time.

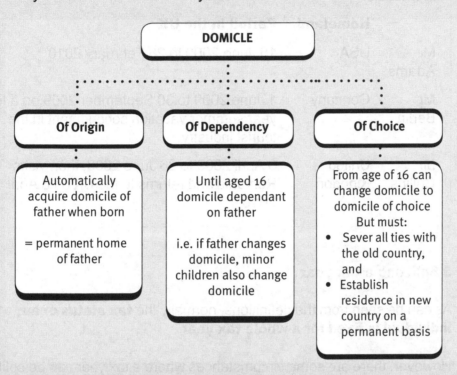

### Example 1 – Residence status

George is resident, ordinarily resident and domiciled in the US.

He came to the UK on 1 June 2009 and then returns home to the US on 31 July 2010.

**Explain George's resident status in 2009/10 and 2010/11.**

**Solution**

George will be treated as UK resident in a particular tax year if he spends at least 183 days in the UK.

|  | **UK days** |  | **Tax status** |
|---|---|---|---|
| 2009/10 | 01.06.09 – 05.04.10 | 309 days in the UK (≥ 183 days) | Resident in UK but not ordinarily resident and not domiciled in the UK |
| 2010/11 | 06.04.10 – 31.07.10 | 116 days in the UK (< 183 days) | Not resident, not ordinarily resident and not domiciled in UK. |

**Test your understanding 1**

State the residence and ordinary residence status of the following individuals:

| | Homeland | Period in the UK |
|---|---|---|
| Mr Adams | USA | 16 June 2009 to 26 February 2010 |
| Mr Berlin | Germany | 1 June 2009 to 30 September 2009 on a four year summer vacation secondment in the tourist industry |
| Mr Collins | United Kingdon | 6 April 2009 to 26 June 2009, then visits Romania and returns to the UK on 8 April 2010 |

## 3 Splitting a tax year

As can be seen from the definitions, normally the **tax status of an individual is fixed for a whole tax year**.

However, there are some circumstances where a tax year can be split and an individual is deemed to have a different tax status for part of a tax year.

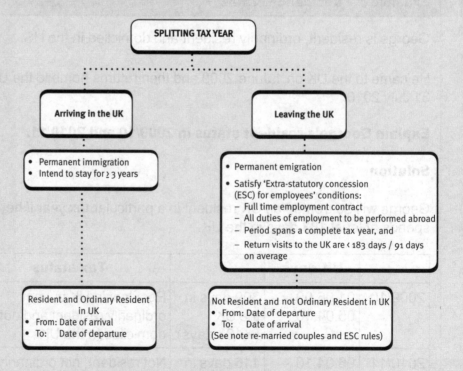

**Note:** Where an individual is married:

- The tax status of the individual and his spouse is normally determined independently.

- Therefore, a husband working full-time overseas may be non-UK resident but his wife may be UK resident.

- However, if the ESC conditions are satisfied, the spouse will automatically be treated as having the same tax status as the employee working under the full-time contract (i.e. not resident and not ordinarily resident in UK from the date of departure to the date of return).

### Test your understanding 2

Sally is resident, ordinarily resident and domiciled in the UK.

She left to go to Australia on 1 September 2009 until 30 April 2011.

**Explain Sally's tax status for the tax years 2009/10 through to 2011/12, assuming Sally went to Australia to:**

(a) **visit her sister**

(b) **take up a full-time contract of employment**

## 4 Overseas income – basis of assessment for income tax

### Introduction

The tax status of an individual determines:

- the liability of income to UK income tax, and
- the availability of personal allowances

## Basis of assessment

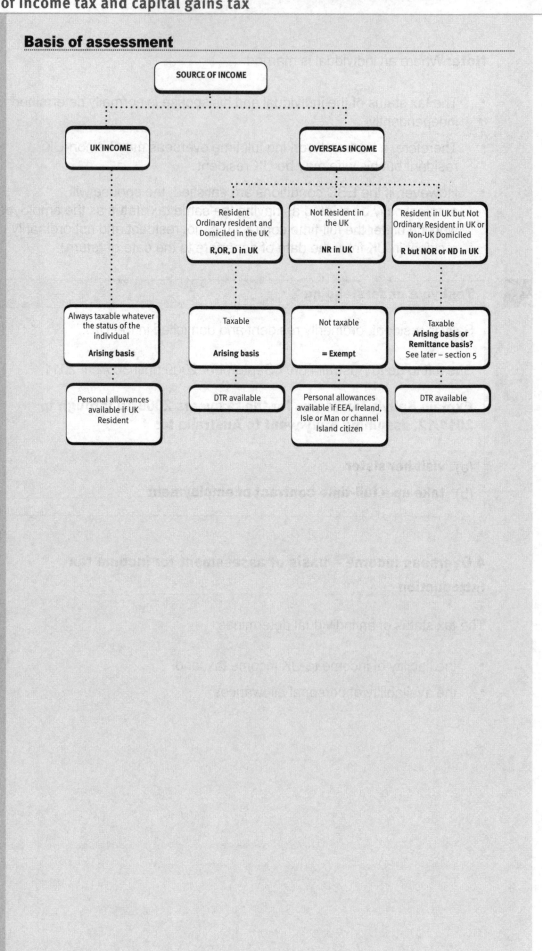

## Types of overseas income

The following sources of overseas income may be included in an individual's UK income tax computation:

| Source of overseas income | Basis of assessment |
|---|---|
| Dividends, rental income and interest | • Income grossed up for overseas tax suffered<br>• UK residents owning shares in an overseas company will treat the grossed up overseas dividends like UK dividends i.e. the dividends are further grossed up at 100/90 and are entitled to a deemed 10% tax credit<br>• If overseas dividends are assessed on a remittance basis (see later),for higher rate tax payers, they are taxed at 40% (not 32.5%)<br>• DTR may be available |
| Trading income from business wholly abroad | • Calculate trading income as in the UK<br>• Special rules apply for travelling expenses (see below)<br>• Income grossed up for overseas tax suffered<br>• DTR may be available |
| Pensions | • If assessed on an arising basis = 90% of pension is taxable<br>• If assessed on a remittance basis = 100% of pension remitted<br>• Income grossed up for overseas tax suffered<br>• DTR may be available |
| Employment income | • Assessment rules are basically the same as for other overseas income<br>• Exception to the rule (see later):<br>  – if the individual is resident and ordinarily resident in the UK, but non-UK domiciled<br>  – works for an overseas employer, and<br>  – performs all of his duties of employment abroad. |

### Example 2 - Tax planning re: overseas income

Sandip, until recently a UK domicile, resident and ordinarily resident individual, has left the UK for a 2 year overseas employment contract.

He has just won £50,000 on the premium bond prize draw and is considering whether to invest it in a UK bank account or an overseas account for the next 2 years until he returns.

The rate of return in the UK/Overseas is 6%. The overseas tax rate is 10%

**Advise Sandip of the most tax efficient option for investment.**

**Solution**

As Sandip is in employment outside the UK for at least one complete tax year he will be treated as not resident nor ordinarily resident from the date of departure until his return.

This means that any overseas income is exempt from UK income tax. However, as a UK/EU citizen he is entitled to use his personal allowance against any income arising in the UK.

Therefore, if he places the cash on deposit in the UK, any earnings of up to £6,475 will be covered by his personal allowance.

If he places it overseas it will be subject to overseas tax of 10% with no relief in the UK as he has no UK liability. He should therefore use the UK account.

## Overseas travelling expenses relating to a trade

The following travelling and subsistence expenses will be allowable deductions when computing the adjusted trading profits:

- travelling to and from any place in the UK to the place where the trade is carried on overseas

- board and lodging at that overseas place

- the costs for the spouse and children (under age 18) visiting the overseas place of work up to two return trips in any year of assessment, once the individual has been absent from the UK for 60 or more continuous days.

The relief is only available to individuals who:

- carry on a trade, profession or vocation wholly overseas, and do not qualify for the remittance basis of assessment.

## Overseas employment income

The basis of assessment for employment income basically follows the normal overseas income rules. However, technically the basis of assessment depends not only on the tax status of the individual, but also where the duties of the employment are performed.

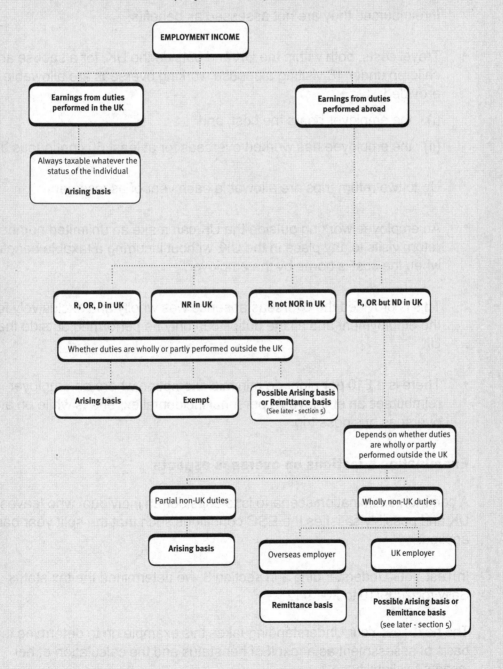

### Overseas travelling and subsistence expenses relating to employment

The rules regarding allowable travelling and subsistence expenses in relation to work performed overseas are as follows:

- Travelling costs to or from the UK at the beginning and end of the employment, and overseas board and lodging expenses borne by the employer are allowable as a deduction from eligible earnings if included as part of the earnings.

  If reimbursed they are not assessed as benefits.

- Travel costs, both within the UK and outside the UK, for a spouse and children under 18 visiting a spouse working overseas are allowable provided:

  (i)  the employer bears the cost; and

  (ii)  the employee has worked overseas for at least 60 continuous days.

  Up to two return trips are allowable each year of assessment.

- An employee working outside the UK can make an unlimited number of return visits to any place in the UK, without incurring a taxable benefit when the cost is borne by the employer.

  This is provided the overseas absence was wholly and exclusively for the employment and all the duties can only be performed outside the UK.

- There is a £10 per night de minimis exemption where an employer reimburses an employee's personal incidental expenses while on an overseas business trip.

### Examination questions on overseas aspects

A common examination scenario is to consider an individual who leaves the UK and possibly satisfies the ESC conditions such that the split year basis applies.

In Test Your Understanding 2 in section 3, we determined the tax status of Sally for 2009/10 to 2011/12.

The next Test Your Understanding takes this example on to determine the basis of assessment as a result of her status and the calculation of her income tax liability.

### Test your understanding 3

Sally is resident, ordinarily resident and domiciled in the UK. She left the UK to go to Australia on 1 September 2009 until 30 April 2011 to visit her sister.

Sally has a villa in Spain which generates income of £12,000 per annum and during her time in Australia Sally lets her main residence for £15,000 per annum.

(i)   **Explain how Sally will be assessed to income tax during the period she spends in Australia.**

(ii)  **Compute Sally's taxable income for all years she is in Australia.**

(iii) **Explain how Sally will be assessed to income tax if Sally's employer had sent her to Australia on a contract of employment and pays her a salary of £36,000 pa.**

(iv)  **Compute Sally's taxable income for all years she is in Australia.**

**Assume the 2009/10 tax rates and allowances apply throughout.**

## 5 The remittance basis of assessment overseas income

### Introduction

In section 4 we see that if an individual is resident in the UK but is

- Not ordinarily resident in UK, and/or
- Not UK Domiciled

they are assessed to tax on either an arising or remittance basis.

In some circumstances the individual will have no choice, however, in other circumstances he may be able to choose the basis on which he will be assessed to income tax and capital gains tax.

## Consequences of being NOR in the UK and/or Non-UK domiciled

The rules depend on the level of unremitted income and gains in the tax year and the consequences are summarised as follows:

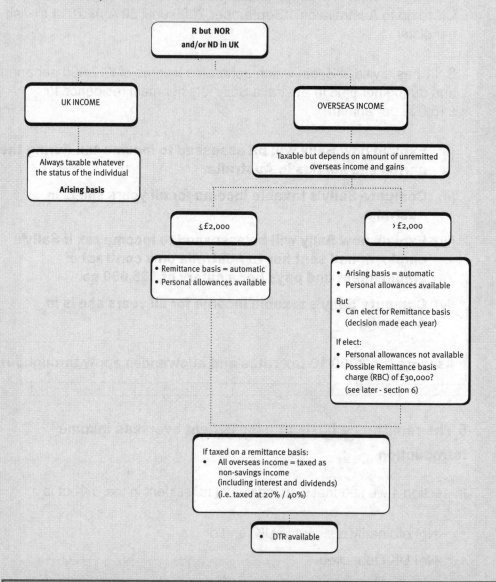

### Test your understanding 4

Ewa Scott, a Polish national, has been resident in the UK for the last two years. She has her own self-employed hairdressing business and earns £25,000 in the UK. She also has £3,000 (gross) interest from Polish investments that she does not remit to the UK.

**Calculate Ewa's income tax liability assuming that the election for the remittance basis**

(a) is not made

(b) is made.

## Definition of remittance

The term remittance includes

(1) Bringing overseas income directly into the UK

(2) Using overseas income to settle debts in the UK

(3) Using overseas income to purchase goods and services which are subsequently brought into the UK with the exception of

  – personal items (e.g. clothes, shoes, jewellery, watches)

  – items brought into the UK for repair

  – items costing ≤ £1,000

  – temporary importation rule (i.e. in UK for < 275 days) (e.g. works of art brought into the UK to exhibit).

## 6 The Remittance Basis Charge (RBC)

### Introduction

The RBC was introduced to prevent long term residents deliberately using the old remittance basis rules to avoid paying UK income tax and capital gains tax by not remitting income and gains each year.

The RBC is an additional tax charge of £30,000 p.a. that is added to the individual's income tax liability and is paid under self-assessment.

However, note that the RBC aims to penalise **long t erm UK residents** who are **not ordinarily resident** in the UK and/or are **not-UK domiciled.**

It is therefore only levied if the individual:

• is aged ≥ 18 years old in the tax year

• is not ordinarily resident in the UK and/or not-UK domiciled.

• is UK resident in the current year, and

• has been UK resident for 7 out of the last 9 tax years

• has unremitted income and gains > £2,000, and

• elects for the remittance basis to apply.

Note that for this purpose a 'split year' (see section 3) counts as a tax year of UK Residence.

## Example 3 – The remittance basis charge

Mr and Mrs Rich are domiciled in the USA but have been resident in the UK for the last 10 years. Their income for 2009/10 is as follows:

|  | Mr Rich | Mrs Rich |
|---|---|---|
|  | £ | £ |
| Overseas income | 300,000 | 40,000 |
| Remitted to the UK | 55,000 | 18,000 |

**Decide whether or not Mr and Mrs Rich should elect for the remittance basis to apply.**

### Solution

Mr Rich will be better off if he claims the remittance basis and pays tax on £55,000 as well as paying the £30,000 charge:

|  |  |  | Arising basis | Remittance basis |
|---|---|---|---|---|
|  |  |  | £ | £ |
| Income |  |  | 300,000 | 55,000 |
| Less: Personal allowance |  |  | (6,475) | Nil |
| Taxable income |  |  | 293,525 | 55,000 |

Income tax

| £ | £ |  | £ | £ |
|---|---|---|---|---|
| 37,400 | 37,400 | at 20% | 7,480 | 7,480 |
| 256,125 | 17,600 | at 40% | 102,450 | 7,040 |
| 293,525 | 55,000 |  |  |  |
| Additional charge |  |  |  | 30,000 |
| Total liability |  |  | 109,930 | 44,520 |

Mrs Rich will be better off if she pays tax on the arising basis:

|  | Arising basis | Remittance basis |
|---|---|---|
|  | £ | £ |
| Income | 40,000 | 18,000 |
| Less: Personal allowance | (6,475) | Nil |
| Taxable income | 33,525 | 18,000 |

| Income tax | | |
|---|---|---|
| £33,525 / £18,000 at 20% | 6,705 | 3,600 |
| Additional charge | | 30,000 |
| Total liability | 6,705 | 33,600 |

## Test your understanding 5

Gita Hoffheim, who is domiciled in Germany, has been resident in the UK since 1996.

In 2009/10 she earned a salary of £78,000 for which all duties were carried out in the UK. She also has significant overseas investments which generated gross interest of £43,000 and gross dividends of £85,000.

Gita remits £10,000 of overseas interest into the UK each year.

**Calculate Gita's income tax liability for 2009./10 assuming:**

(a) **she does not claim the remittance basis**

(b) **she does claim the remittance basis**

Ignore DTR.

## Nominating income and gains

The RBC represents tax paid in advance on income/gains arising abroad but not yet remitted into the UK. The individual can choose which overseas income or gains the charge relates to.

Therefore, when the RBC is paid, the individual must nominate the unremitted income/gains to which the charge applies.

In the future, when the individual remits funds into the UK, the remittances are treated as being a remittance of:

- un-nominated sources first
  = therefore taxed when remitted, as not yet taxed

- then nominated sources
  = not taxed again when remitted, as already taxed in the £30,000 in a previous year.

It is not possible to claim that overseas income and gains have been remitted from nominated sources until all other untaxed overseas income and gains have been remitted and tax paid on those remittances first.

Note that if the individual is taxed on a remittance basis in the year the income / gains arose, when the unremitted un-nominated income / gains are remitted in a subsequent year it will be taxed even if the individual is being taxed on an arising basis in the year of the remittance.

## 7 Double taxation relief - income tax

### Introduction

As seen in section 4, an individual who is:

- R, OR and D in the UK
  = taxed in the UK on their worldwide income

- R in the UK, but NOR in the UK and/or non-UK domiciled
  = taxed in the UK on their overseas income on either an arising or remittance basis

However, in addition, the overseas income may also be taxed to income tax overseas. To avoid a double charge to tax, double taxation relief (DTR) is available.

DTR is given in one of three ways:

- Under a DTR treaty agreement

- As a tax credit relief (known as 'unilateral relief')

- As an expense relief (only applicable where the individual has losses and unilateral relief is not available).

However, in computational **examination questions**, **unilateral relief** is to be applied. This is because expense relief is not examinable, and detailed knowledge of specific DTR agreements will not be examined.

You should have an awareness of standard treaty clauses and the importance of bilateral DTR agreements in practice, but you will not be expected to apply treaty provisions in the exam.

Further details of the principles behind DTR treaty agreements are given in expandable text. In addition, as DTR treaties are more relevant in the examination in a corporate scenario, more detail concerning standard treaty clauses is given in Chapter 27.

### DTR treaties

Under DTR treaty agreements:

- The two countries usually agree reciprocal arrangements to exempt certain types of income from tax in the overseas country so that there is no double taxation, and

- Allow 'unilateral relief' as a tax credit from the UK income tax liability for any overseas income that is still taxed twice.

Relief under the terms of a treaty is the usual method of obtaining relief in practice. The UK has over a hundred DTR treaties with different countries.

## Unilateral relief

Where there is no DTR treaty agreement, and the income is taxed overseas, DTR is normally allowed as a tax credit deduction against the UK income tax liability.

---

**DOUBLE TAXATION RELIEF**

Deduct from the individual's income tax liability
Lower of:
- Overseas tax withholding tax suffered
- UK income tax on that source of overseas income

---

Uk income tax attributable to a source of overseas income
= the reduction in the total income tax liability that would arise if that source of overseas income is excluded from taxable income

---

To calculate UK income tax on overseas income:
- Alway treat overseas income as the 'top slice' of income type
- Calculate total income tax **including** that source of overseas income
- Calculate total income tax **without** that source of overseas income
- Difference = UK income tax on that source income

---

If more than one source of overseas income:
- Need separate DTR calculation for each source of overseas income
- Take out the source with the **highest rate of overseas tax** first

### Example 4 – Double tax relief

Dean is resident, ordinarily resident and domiciled in the UK.

In 2009/10 his only taxable income is an overseas dividend of £42,750. The dividend is received after a 5% foreign tax withheld in the country of origin.

**Calculate Dean's UK income tax payable in 2009/10**

**Solution**

| Income Tax computation – 2009/10 | £ |
|---|---|
| Overseas dividend | |
| (£42,750 × 100/95) = £45,000 × 100/90 | 50,000 |
| Less PA | (6,475) |
| | |
| Taxable income | 43,525 |
| | |
| Income tax: | |
| £37,400 × 10% (dividend income) | 3,740 |
| £6,125 × 32.5% (Note) | 1,991 |
| | |
| | 5,731 |
| Less DTR | |
| Lower of | |
| (i)  Overseas tax (£45,000 × 5%) = £2,250 | (2,250) |
| (ii) UK tax = £5,731 (above) | |
| | |
| Income Tax liability | 3,481 |
| Less Tax credits: | |
| Overseas dividends (restricted) | (3,481) |
| | |
| Income tax payable | Nil |

**Note:** Dividends falling into the higher rate are taxed at 32.5% (not 40%) as Dean is assessed on an arising basis.

The dividend tax credit is £5,000 (£50,000 x 10%) , but as this is greater than the tax liability it is restricted as it is non refundable.

## Test your understanding 6

Herbert, aged 86, who is resident, ordinarily resident and domiciled in the UK, received income in 2009/10 from various sources as follows:

|  | £ |  |
|---|---|---|
| State pension | 4,380 | gross |
| Pension from former employer | 16,100 | PAYE £1,925 |
| NSB investment account interest | 103 | |
| Bank deposit account interest | 557 | |
| Building society interest | 285 | |
| UK dividends | 2,700 | |
| Foreign interest (15% foreign tax paid) | 240 | gross |

**Calculate the income tax payable for 2009/10.**

## Example 5 – Double tax relief

Jeffrey has the following income:

|  | £ | Overseas tax suffered |
|---|---|---|
| Employment income – UK | 40,000 | |
| Overseas bank interest (1) (gross) | 1,500 | 26% |
| Overseas bank interest (2) (gross) | 3,000 | 23% |
| | ——— | |
| Total income | 44,500 | |
| Less: Personal allowance | (6,475) | |
| | ——— | |
| Taxable income | 38,025 | |
| | ——— | |

Analysis of income:

| Savings | Other income |
|---|---|
| £4,500 | (£38,025 – £4,500) = £33,525 |

Income tax liability (before DTR) is:

| £ | | £ |
|---|---|---|
| 33,525 × 20% (other income) | | 6,705 |
| 3,875 × 20% (savings) | | 775 |
| ——— | | |
| 37,400 | | |
| 625 × 40% (savings) | | 250 |
| ——— | | |
| 38,025 | | |
| ——— | | |
| Income tax liability (before DTR) | | 7,730 |

**Advise how much DTR is available on each source of income.**

**Solution**

The overseas bank interest is charged in the UK partly at 40% and partly at 20%.

To obtain the maximum DTR, the interest suffering the highest overseas rate of tax is considered first.

Overseas source (1) has the highest overseas tax rate, so the DTR on that source of income will be:

| | | | £ | £ |
|---|---|---|---|---|
| (i) | Overseas tax paid (£1,500 × 26%) | | | 390 |
| (ii) | UK tax on the overseas income | | | |
| | £ | | | |
| | 625 (top slice) | @ 40% | | 250 |
| | 875 | @ 20% | | 175 |
| | ——— | | | |
| | 1,500 | | | 425 |
| | | | | ——— |

DTR = lower amount = £390 (i.e. full credit for overseas tax paid)

The DTR on overseas source (2) will then be:

|  | £ |
|---|---|
| (i) Overseas tax paid (£3,000 × 23%) | 690 |
| (ii) UK tax on overseas income (£3,000 × 20%) | 600 |

DTR = lower amount = £600

**Note:** The unrelieved overseas tax of £90 on overseas source (2) is lost.

### Test your understanding 7

Benny, a UK domicile, resident and ordinarily resident individual, has the following income assessable in 2009/10.

|  | £ |
|---|---|
| Salary from UK employment (gross) | 39,650 (PAYE £6,635) |
| Bank interest received from UK bank | 2,468 |
| Utopian bank interest (50% Utopian tax paid) | 1,100 (gross) |
| Ruritanian rent (15% Ruritanian tax paid) | 600 (gross) |

**Calculate the income tax payable considering all available reliefs.**

## 8 Overseas aspects of capital gains tax

### Introduction

As for income tax, the tax status of an individual is important in determining the gains on which they are assessed.

The consequences of an individual's status is as follows:

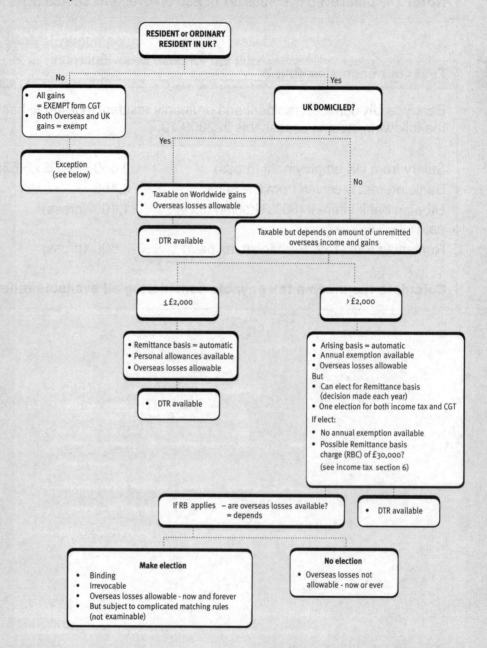

## Notes:

- The individual will need to consider the remittance basis each year separately as a large overseas gain in a year may make the remittance basis claim worthwhile in that year but not in others

- There appears to be no major reason for not making the election to allow capital losses if the remittance basis is claimed, other than the requirement of having to disclose all overseas gains and losses.

- Where proceeds from the sale of an overseas capital asset are remitted to the UK, the amount of the capital gain is deemed to be remitted first (not a proportion of the gain).

### Example 6 - overseas aspects of capital gains tax

Jason sold an investment property in Spain for £500,000 on 16 February 2010. Half of the proceeds were paid into his Spanish bank account and the other half into his UK bank account.

The gain on the disposal is £278,850. Jason purchased the property in August 1993.

**Explain the CGT position assuming Jason is:**

(a) **UK resident, ordinarily resident and domiciled in the UK**

(b) **UK resident and ordinarily resident for the previous 5 tax years but not UK domiciled and elected for the remittance basis**

(c) **UK resident and ordinarily resident for the previous 10 years but not UK domiciled and elected for the remittance basis**

(d) **not UK resident or ordinarily resident but UK domiciled.**

**Solution**

(a) **UK resident, ordinarily resident and domiciled in the UK**

Jason is liable to CGT on gains arising on his worldwide assets, regardless of whether or not the proceeds are remitted to the UK.

| | |
|---|---|
| Chargeable gain | £278,850 |

The annual exemption is fully available.

(b) **UK resident and ordinarily resident for 5 tax years but not UK domiciled**

Jason is liable to CGT on gains arising on his overseas assets only to the extent that the proceeds are remitted to the UK as he has elected for the remittance basis.

As £250,000 (£500,000 ÷ 2) of the proceeds are remitted to the UK, this is deemed to be £250,000 worth of chargeable gain and will be assessed on Jason in 2009/10.

Chargeable gain                                                 £250,000

No annual exemption is available.

The remaining gain of £28,850 (£278,850 – £250,000) will be taxed when more of the proceeds are remitted.

(c) **UK resident and ordinarily resident for 10 tax years but not UK domiciled**

Jason is liable to CGT on gains arising on his overseas assets only to the extent they are remitted to the UK as he has elected for the remittance basis.

However, as he has been resident for 7 out of the last 9 tax years immediately preceding the current tax year, a £30,000 tax charge is payable for this benefit.

In addition as half of the proceeds are remitted to the UK, £250,000 of the gain will be taxed in 2009/10.

No annual exemption is available.

(d) **Not UK resident or ordinarily resident but UK domiciled**

Jason is only assessed to CGT if he disposes of an asset which is used in carrying on a trade, profession or vocation, through a permanent establishment in the UK

He is not liable to CGT on any overseas asset.

---

### Test your understanding 8

Cecilia is domiciled in Austria, but has lived in the UK for the last 4 years.  For 2008/09 she elected for the remittance basis to apply to her income and gains.

In 2009/10, she sells the following assets:

(1) An investment property in Austria for £220,000 and realised a capital gain of £55,000. She remitted £40,000 of the proceeds into the UK.

> (2) An asset in Hungary for £80,000 and realised a capital loss of £35,000.
>
> (3) A UK asset for £49,500 and realised a capital gain of £25,350.
>
> (4) UK quoted shares for £30,100 and realised a capital loss of £18,000.
>
> **Calculate Cecilia's CGT liability for 2009/10, assuming:**
>
> (a) **She does not claim the remittance basis for 2009/10**
>
> (b) **She claims the remittance basis for 2009/10 but no election has been made in respect of capital losses in 2008/09**

## Exceptions to the exemption from CGT

All gains (both UK and overseas gains) of an individual that is NR and NOR in the UK are exempt, except in two key circumstances:

- in the rare situation where the individual operates a trade, profession or vocation through a permanent establishment in the UK and disposes of an asset from the business

- where the temporary absence abroad conditions are satisfied (see section 10).

## 9 Double taxation relief – capital gains tax

### Introduction

As seen in section 8, an individual who is:

- R or OR in the UK and is D in the UK
  = taxed in the UK on their worldwide gains

- R or OR in the UK, but is non-UK domiciled
  = taxed in the UK on their overseas gains on either an arising or remittance basis

However, in addition, the overseas gains may also be taxed to capital gains tax overseas.

Double taxation relief (DTR) is available as follows:

(a) under a bilateral double taxation treaty agreement between the UK and the overseas country, or

(b) unilaterally as a tax credit relief.

> **Double taxation relief**
>
> **Deduct from the individual's capital gains tax liability**
> lower of:
> - Overseas capital gains tax suffered
> - UK capital gains tax on the disposal of that overseas asset
>   (18% × chargeable gains less a proportion of the annual exemption)

**Note:** The annual exemption is allocated pro-rata to the amount of chargeable gains

### Example 7 – Double taxation relief

Julie is resident and domiciled in the UK. In 2009/10 she sells assets which give rise to the following chargeable gains:

| | |
|---|---:|
| UK asset | £22,000 |
| Overseas asset | £66,000 |

Overseas capital taxes of £14,000 are payable on the disposal of the overseas asset.

**Calculate Julie's CGT liability for 2009/10**

**Solution**

| | £ |
|---|---:|
| UK asset | 22,000 |
| Overseas asset | 66,000 |
| | |
| Total chargeable gain | 88,000 |
| Less Annual exemption | (10,100) |
| | |
| Taxable gain | 77,900 |

| | £ |
|---|---:|
| CGT liability (£77,900 × 18%) | 14,022 |
| Less DTR (W) | (10,517) |
| | |
| CGT payable | 3,505 |

KAPLAN PUBLISHING

**Working: DTR**

|  | £ | £ |
|---|---|---|
| Lower of | | |
| (i)  Overseas tax suffered (given) | | 14,000 |
| (ii) UK tax on overseas gain: | | |
| Overseas gain | 66,000 | |
| Less Propotion of annual exemption | | |
| £10,100 × (66,000/£88,000) | (7,575) | |
| | 58,425 × 18% | 10,517 |

### Test your understanding 9

Diane is UK resident and domiciled in the UK. She disposed of the following assets in 2009/10:

(a)  A UK asset was sold on 8 May 2009 giving rise to a gain of £22,000.

(b)  An overseas investment asset was sold on 14 September 2009 giving rise to a gain of £12,760. Overseas CGT payable was £3,850.

(c)  A UK asset was sold on 29 October 2009 giving rise to a gain of £29,000.

**Calculate Diane's capital gains tax payable for 2009/10.**

## 10 Splitting tax years

As for income tax, for capital gains tax, an individual normally retains his tax status for whole tax years.

However, the split year basis applies to capital gains tax in the same way as income tax (see diagram in section 3) where there is:

- permanent immigration

- permanent emigration

- intention to come into the UK for > 3 years, and

- where the ESC for employees conditions are satisfied.

As a result, an individual that satisfies the ESC for employee conditions:

- will be treated as not resident and not ordinarily resident in the UK from the date of departure to the date of return, and

- will not be liable to CGT on any disposals of capital assets whilst abroad, not even UK assets.

However, the **exemption** from CGT from the date of departure to the date of return only **applies** to periods of temporary absence abroad **if**:

- the individual was resident in the UK for four out of the seven years before leaving the UK, and

- the **period spent abroad exceeds five complete tax years**.

## Temporary absence abroad

If the individual takes up a full-time contract abroad or intends to leave permanently but **returns to the UK within five complete tax years**, the individual will remain liable to CGT.

However the way in which the gains are assessed are as follows:

```
┌─────────────────────────────────────┐
│ Individual leaving the UK under full │
│ time employment contract spanning    │
│ a complete tax year / or intends to  │
│ leave permanently                    │
└─────────────────────────────────────┘
                   ┆
┌─────────────────────────────────────┐
│ Year of departure:                   │
│  • Liable on all gains in that year  │
│ Years whilst abroad:                 │
│  • No CGT                            │
└─────────────────────────────────────┘
                   ┆
┌─────────────────────────────────────┐
│ Year of re-entry into the UK:        │
└─────────────────────────────────────┘
        ┆                    ┆
┌──────────────────────┐  ┌──────────────────────┐
│ Return within five   │  │ Return after five    │
│ complete tax years   │  │ complete tax years   │
│                      │  │                      │
│ Liable on            │  │ Liable on            │
│ • disposals of all   │  │ • disposals after    │
│   assets whilst      │  │   the date of        │
│   abroad, if the     │  │   return only        │
│   asset was owned    │  │                      │
│   before leaving     │  │ • No CGT on disposals│
│   the UK             │  │   whilst abroad      │
│ • disposals after    │  │                      │
│   the date of return │  │                      │
└──────────────────────┘  └──────────────────────┘
```

### Illustration

Assume an individual takes up a full-time contract abroad on 14 February 2008 and returns to the UK on 24 March 2013. He will be assessed to UK CGT as follows:

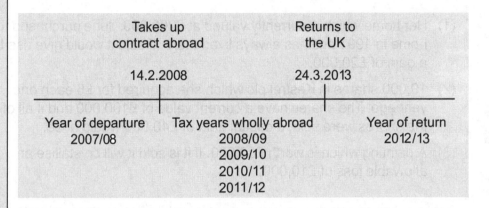

| Tax year of departure (2007/08) | Tax years wholly abroad (2008/09 to 2011/12) | Tax year of return (within 5 complete tax years) (2012/13) |
| --- | --- | --- |
| Liable on<br><br>• **all disposals in the tax year of departure**<br><br>• both before and after the date of departure | **No CGT on any disposals** whilst abroad | Liable on<br><br>• **all disposals of assets whilst abroad** if the assets were owned by the individual before leaving the UK (known as a 're-entry charge')<br><br>• **any disposals made in the tax year of return** |

Note that

• Assets that the individual **acquired after leaving the UK** which he then sells whilst abroad are not liable to UK capital gains tax.

• In this example, if the individual had stayed abroad for a further 14 days, he would be exempt from CGT on all disposals whilst abroad. This is because the period of absence from the UK would have spanned five complete tax years.

**Example 8 – Temporary absence abroad**

June is planning to emigrate to Australia on 31 December 2009.

She owns the following UK assets:

(1) Her home which is currently valued at £200,000. June purchased the home in 1991 and has always lived there. If sold it would give rise to a gain of £20,000.

(2) 10,000 shares in Kestrel plc which she acquired for £6 each one year ago. The shares have a current value of £100,000 and if all of the shares were sold, a capital gain of £40,000 would arise.

(3) A painting which is worth £80,000. If it is sold it will crystallise an allowable loss of £10,000.

June wishes to sell as many assets as possible before she emigrates, but does not want to pay any capital gains tax.

Assume today's date is 10 December 2009 and that June has asked you for some advice.

(a) **Advise June of the assets she should sell before leaving the UK.**

(b) **Explain the consequences of selling the shares in Kestrel plc while she is abroad if:**

   (i) **she returns to the UK on 31 December 2013 as she is homesick**

   (ii) **she returns to the UK on 31 December 2017 as she is sick.**

**Solution**

**(a) Disposal of assets before leaving the UK**

| Asset | Sell? | Reason |
|-------|-------|--------|
| Home | Yes | An individual's principal private residence is exempt from CGT |
| Painting | Yes | This is the disposal of a chargeable asset which generates an allowable capital loss of £10,000 |
| Kestrel plc shares | Yes, but only some of the shares | June should dispose of sufficient shares to realise a gain of £20,100 which is covered by the allowable capital loss and her annual exemption.<br><br>Therefore, June should dispose of 5,025 shares (see below) |

**Calculation of the optimum number of Kestrel plc shares to sell**

|  | £ |
|---|---|
| Sale proceeds for each share | 10 |
| Cost of each share | (6) |
|  | ___ |
| Chargeable gain realised on disposal of each share | 4 |
|  | ___ |

Therefore, to crystallise a chargeable gain of £20,100, June should dispose of 5,025 shares (£20,100 ÷ £4).

**(b) Consequences of selling the remaining shares whilst abroad**

|  | (i) | (ii) |
|---|-----|------|
| Tax year of departure | 2009/10 | 2009/10 |
| Tax year of return to UK | 2013/14<br>= 3 complete tax years | 2017/18<br>= 7 complete tax years |
| CGT on disposals of chargeable assets made while June is in Australia | As June is in Australia for less than 5 complete tax years, any gains made while in Australia will be subject to CGT in the tax year she returns to UK (2013/14) | As June is in Australia for 5 complete tax years, no CGT is payable on disposals made while she is in Australia. |

### Test your understanding 10

Yolanda, aged 45, is a UK national who has lived in the UK since birth. On 15 May 2006 she took up a full-time contract of employment in Columbia. She returned to the UK on 24 October 2009.

Her disposals during this period were as follows:

| Asset | Date of purchase | Date of sale | Gain |
|-------|------------------|--------------|------|
| | | | £ |
| 1 | 14 June 2002 | 31 March 2007 | 128,800 |
| 2 | 3 Sept 1986 | 17 July 2007 | 125,896 |
| 3 | 9 July 1992 | 18 Oct 2008 | 5,024 |
| 4 | 12 Aug 2006 | 27 Feb 2009 | 78,400 |

**Explain which disposals will be chargeable and when any gains arising as a result of the disposals will be assessed.**

## 11 Chapter summary

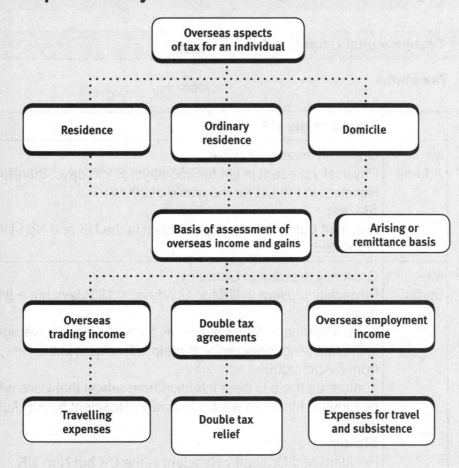

### Test your understanding answers

| | |
|---|---|
| **Test your understanding 1** | |

**Tax status**

| | **Period in the UK** |
|---|---|
| Mr Adams | Ordinarily resident in USA<br>Physically present in UK for 255 days, ≥ 183 days, therefore Resident in the UK for the whole of 2009/10<br>**Status:**<br>Resident but not Ordinarily Resident in the UK and Non-UK domiciled |
| Mr Berlin | Ordinarily resident in Germany<br>Physically present in UK for 121 days, < 183 days but > 91 days<br>Clear intention to return to the UK for > 91 days on average in the following three years, therefore Resident in the UK from 6 April 2009<br>Further, as there is clear intention from arrival that visits will be regular, Mr Berlin will be Ordinarily Resident from 6 April 2009<br>**Status:**<br>Resident and Ordinarily Resident in the UK but Non-UK domiciled |
| Mr Collins | Ordinarily resident in UK<br>Physically present in UK for 81 days, < 183 days and < 91 days<br>But normally resident in the UK and not absent for a complete tax year, therefore remains UK Resident for the whole of the tax year<br>**Status:**<br>Resident, Ordinarily Resident and Domiciled in the UK |

**Note:** As an individual is present in the UK on any day when he is here at midnight at the end of the day, the day of arrival has been counted, but not the day of departure.

**Test your understanding 2**

**Sally**

**(a) Sally went to Australia to visit her sister**

1 September 2009 to 30 April 2011 spans a complete tax year but Sally not working abroad.

| Tax year | Status |
|----------|--------|
| 2009/10 | • R, OR, D in UK for whole tax year |
| 2010/11 | • NR, but OR and D in UK for whole tax year |
| 2011/12 | • R, OR, D in UK for whole tax year |

**(b) Sally went to Australia under a full-time employment contract**

1 September 2009 to 30 April 2011 spans a complete tax year but Sally is working abroad.

| Tax year | Status |
|----------|--------|
| 2009/10 | Split year basis applies:<br><br>• R, OR, D in UK up to 31 August 2009<br>• NR, NOR but D in UK from 1 September to 5 April 2010 |
| 2010/11 | Status applies for whole tax year<br><br>• NR, NOR but D in UK for whole tax year |
| 2011/12 | Split year basis applies:<br><br>• NR, NOR but D in UK from 6 April 2011 to 30 April 2011<br>• R, OR, D in UK from 1 May 2011 |

**Test your understanding 3**

**Sally**

(i) **Sally went to Australia to visit sister**

1 September 2009 to 30 April 2011 spans a complete tax year but Sally not working abroad.

| Tax year | Status | Basis of assessment |
|---|---|---|
| 2009/10 | R, OR, D in UK for whole tax year | Worldwide income = taxable on an arising basis |
| 2010/11 | NR, but OR and D in UK for whole tax year | All UK income = taxable on an arising basis Overseas income = exempt |
| 2011/12 | R, OR, D in UK for whole tax year | Worldwide income = taxable on an arising basis |

(ii) **Sally's taxable income**

|  | 2009/10 £ | 2010/11 £ | 2011/12 £ |
|---|---|---|---|
| Property income (£1,250 pm) | 8,750 | 15,000 | 1,250 |
| Foreign rent | 12,000 | Nil | 12,000 |
| Total income | 20,750 | 15,000 | 13,250 |
| Less PA | (6,475) | (6,475) | (6,475) |
| Taxable income | 14,275 | 8,525 | 6,775 |

## (iii) **Sally went to Australia under a full-time employment contract**

1 September 2009 to 30 April 2011 spans a complete tax year but Sally is working abroad.

| Tax year | Status | Basis of assessment |
|---|---|---|
| 2009/10 | **Split year basis applies:** R, OR, D in UK up to 31 August 2009 | Worlwide income = taxable on an arising basis |
| | NR, NOR but D in UK from 1 September to 5 April 2010 | All UK income = taxable on an arising basis Overseas income = exempt |
| 2010/11 | NR, NOR but D in UK for whole tax year | All UK income = taxable on an arising basis Overseas income = exempt |
| 2011/12 | **Split year basis applies:** NR, NOR but D in UK from 6 April 2011 to 30 April 2011 | All UK income = taxable on an arising basis Overseas income = exempt |
| | R, OR, D in UK From 1 May 2011 | Worldwide income = taxable on an arising basis |

### Sally's taxable income

|  | 2009/10 £ | 2010/11 £ | 2011/12 £ |
|---|---|---|---|
| UK property income | 8,750 | 15,000 | 1,250 |
| Foreign property income (5/12 × £12,000)/(11/12 x £12,000) | 5,000 | Nil | 11,000 |
| Salary (5/12 × £36,000)/(11/12 x £36,000) | 15,000 | Nil | 33,000 |
| Total income | 28,750 | 15,000 | 45,250 |
| Less PA | (6,475) | (6,475) | (6,475) |
| Taxable income | 22,275 | 8,525 | 38,775 |

### Test your understanding 4

**Ewa Scott**

Unremitted income in 2009/10 is £3,000 which is > £2,000.

Therefore the arising basis will apply automatically and the personal allowance is available.

However, Ewa can elect for the remittance basis (RB) to apply. If the election is made, personal allowances will not be available.

**Income tax computation – 2009/10**

|  | No RB election £ | With RB election £ |
|---|---|---|
| Trading profits in UK | 25,000 | 25,000 |
| Overseas interest (gross) | 3,000 | Nil |
| Total income | 28,000 | 25,000 |
| Less Personal allowance | (6,475) | (Nil) |
| Taxable income | 21,525 | 25,000 |
| Income tax liability | 4,305 | 5,000 |

**Conclusion**: Ewa should not claim the remittance basis in 2009/10

**Test your understanding 5**

**Gita Hoffheim**

**Income tax computation – 2009/10**

|  | No RB election £ | With RB election £ |
|---|---|---|
| Salary | 78,000 | 78,000 |
| Overseas interest (gross) | 43,000 | 10,000 |
| Overseas dividends (gross) | 85,000 | Nil |
| | | |
| Total income | 206,000 | 88,000 |
| Less Personal allowance | (6,475) | (Nil) |
| | | |
| Taxable income | 199,525 | 88,000 |
| | | |
| Income tax | | |
| £37,400 / £37,400 × 20% (other income) | 7,480 | 7,480 |
| £34,125 / £40,600 × 40% (other income) | 13,650 | 16,240 |
| £43,000 / £10,000 × 40% (savings) | 17,200 | 4,000 |
| £85,000 × 32.5% (dividends) | 27,625 | Nil |
| | | |
| | 65,955 | 27,720 |
| Plus Remittance basis charge | Nil | 30,000 |
| | | |
| Income tax liability | 65,955 | 57,720 |

Gita would be better off if she elects for the remittance basis to apply

Notes:

- The decision re-the remittance basis is made each year

- The £85,000 overseas dividend given in the question is gross of both overseas tax and has been grossed up by 100/90. If assessed on an arising basis, it is then treated as if it were UK dividends (i.e. taxed at 32.5% with a deemed 10% tax credit)

- When assessed on a remittance basis, all overseas income is assessed as non-savings income and taxed at 20/40%. Therefore, if in this question Gita had remitted overseas dividends rather than overseas interest, the income tax liability would have been the same as the dividend income remitted would have been assessed at 40%, not 32.5%.

### Test your understanding 6

**Herbert**

**Income tax computation – 2009/10**

|  | £ | £ |
|---|---|---|
| State pension |  | 4,380 |
| Pension from former employer |  | 16,100 |
|  |  | 20,480 |
| NSB interest | 103 |  |
| Foreign interest | 240 |  |
| Bank interest (£557 × 100/80) | 696 |  |
| Building society interest (£285 × 100/80) | 356 |  |
|  |  | 1,395 |
| UK dividends (£2,700 × 100/90) |  | 3,000 |
| Total income |  | 24,875 |
| Less: PAA (W1) |  | (8,653) |
| Taxable income |  | 16,222 |
| Analysis of income: |  |  |
| Other income |  | 11,827 |
| Savings |  | 1,395 |
| Dividends |  | 3,000 |

Income tax

| £ | | £ |
|---|---|---|
| 11,827 | @ 20% (other income) | 2,365 |
| 1,395 | @ 20% (savings) | 279 |
| 3,000 | @ 10% (dividends) | 300 |
| 16,222 | | |
| | | 2,944 |

Less: DTR (W2)                (36)

| | |
|---|---|
| Income tax liability | 2,908 |
| Less: Tax credits | |
|     On dividends (10% × £3,000) | (300) |
|     On savings (20% × (£696 + £356) | (210) |
|      PAYE on pension from former employer | (1,925) |
| Income tax payable | 473 |

## Workings

### (1) Age allowance

| | £ |
|---|---|
| Age allowance | 9,640 |
| Less: Abatement: ½ × (£24,875 – £22,900) | (987) |
| | 8,653 |

### (2) DTR

| | | £ |
|---|---|---|
| Lower of | (i)  foreign tax suffered (£240 × 15%) | 36 |
| | (ii) UK tax attributable (£240 × 20%) | 48 |

### Test your understanding 7

**Benny**

**Income tax computation – 2009/10**

|  | £ |
|---|---:|
| Employment income | 39,650 |
| Ruritanian rent | 600 |
| Utopian bank interest | 1,100 |
| Bank interest (£2,468 ×100/80) | 3,085 |
|  | ——— |
| Total income | 44,435 |
| Less Personal allowance | (6,475) |
|  | ——— |
| Taxable income | 37,960 |
|  | ——— |

Analysis of income:

| Savings | Other income |
|---|---|
| £4,185 | (£37,960 – £4,185) = £33,775 |

Income tax:

| £ |  | £ |
|---:|---|---:|
| 33,775 | × 20% (other income) | 6,755 |
| 3,625 | × 20% (savings) | 725 |
| 560 | × 40% (savings) | 224 |
| ——— |  | ——— |
| 37,960 |  | 7,704 |
| ——— |  |  |

| Less DTR – Utopian tax (W1) | (332) |
|---|---:|
| – Ruritanian tax (W2) | (90) |
|  | ——— |
| Income tax liability | 7,282 |
| Less   Tax credits |  |
| UK bank interest (20% × £3,085) | (617) |
| PAYE | (6,635) |
|  | ——— |
| Income tax payable | 30 |
|  | ——— |

**Workings**

**(W1) DTR on Utopian income**

The Utopian income has suffered the higher rate of overseas tax and therefore relief is calculated in respect of this source of income first.

DTR = lower of

| | £ | £ |
|---|---|---|
| (a) UK tax on £1,100: | | |
| £560× 40% | 224 | |
| £540× 20% | 108 | |
| | —— | 332 |
| (b) Overseas tax = (50% × £1,100) | | 550 |

**(W2)    DTR on Ruritanian income**

| | £ |
|---|---|
| DTR = lower of | |
| (a) UK tax (20% × £600) | 120 |
| (b) Overseas tax (15% × £600) | 90 |

**Test your understanding 8**

**Cecilia**

**Capital gains tax computation – 2009/10**

| | No RB election £ | With RB election £ |
|---|---|---|
| Investment property in Austria | 55,000 | 40,000 |
| Asset in Hungary | (35,000) | Nil |
| UK asset | 25,350 | 25,350 |
| UK quoted shares | (18,000) | (18,000) |
| | | |
| Total chargeable gains | 27,350 | 47,350 |
| Less Annual exemption | (10,100) | (Nil) |
| | | |
| Taxable gains | 17,250 | 47,350 |
| | | |
| Capital gains tax £17,250/£47,350 × 18% | 3,105 | 8,523 |

Cecilia would be better off if she does not elect for remittance basis to apply in 2009/10.

**Notes:**

- The decision re-the remittance basis is made each year

- The decision re-the use of overseas losses must be made the first time the remittance basis is claimed and the decision is irrevocable and binding on subsequent years

- Had Cecilia made the election re-overseas capital losses in 2008/09, she would have been better off electing for the remittance basis in 2009/10

## Test your understanding 9

**Diane**
**Capital gains tax computation – 2009/10**

|  | £ |
|---|---|
| UK Asset | 22,000 |
| Overseas Asset | 12,760 |
| UK Asset | 29,000 |
| | |
| Total capital gains | 63,760 |
| Less Annual exemption | (10,100) |
| | |
| Taxable gains | 53,660 |
| | |
| Capital gains tax (£53,660 × 18%) | 9,659 |

Less DTR
   Lower of

| | | |
|---|---|---|
| (i)  Overseas CGT suffered | £3,850 | |
| (ii) UK CGT applicable to overseas asset (W) | £1,933 | (1,933) |

| | |
|---|---|
| CGT payable | 7,726 |

**Note:** As Diane is UK resident and domiciled in the UK, she is liable on her worldwide asset gains on an arising basis. Full AE is available. DTR is available.

### Working: UK CGT on overseas asset

| | £ |
|---|---|
| Overseas gain | 12,760 |
| Less Portion of AE | |
| (£10,100 × (12,760/63,760) | (2,021) |
| | ───── |
| | 10,739 × 18% = £1,933 |
| | ───── |

### Test your understanding 10

**Yolanda**

| | |
|---|---|
| Year of departure: | 2006/07 |
| Year of return: | 2009/10 |
| Complete tax years abroad: | 2007/08 and 2008/09 = 2 years |

**Chargeable in the year of departure: 2006/07**

**Asset 1:** Chargeable gain £128,800

**Chargeable whilst abroad:**

There is no CGT liability arising in the years whilst Yolanda is abroad.

However, the gains arising on the disposal of assets owned by Yolanda on 15 May 2006 become chargeable when she re-enters the UK in 2009/10.

**Chargeable in the year of return to the UK: 2009/10**

**Assets 2 and 3:** These assets were owned by Yolanda before she went abroad, therefore chargeable on return.

| | £ |
|---|---|
| Chargeable gain – Asset 2 | 125,896 |
| Chargeable gain – Asset 3 | 5,024 |
| | ───── |
| | 130,920 |
| | ───── |

**Asset 4:** There is no CGT liability arising on the disposal of asset 4 as the asset was not owned by Yolanda before she went abroad on 15 May 2006, and it was sold before she returned.

# An introduction to inheritance tax

## Chapter learning objectives

Upon completion of this chapter you will be able to:

- outline the principal events for IHT

- explain the concept of 'transfer of value'

- consider 'excluded property'

- state which persons are chargeable to IHT

- outline the effect for IHT of domicile status

- list the rules for identifying whether an asset is UK or overseas and determine whether an asset is chargeable to IHT

- recognise and explain the different types of lifetime gifts

- calculate the transfer of value for IHT

- explain the annual exemption and demonstrate how it reduces the transfer of value

- explain the procedure and calculate the charge to IHT on a chargeable lifetime transfer during lifetime

- demonstrate the seven year cumulation period

- explain the procedure and calculate the charge to IHT on all lifetime transfers within 7 years of death

- recognise when taper relief is available to reduce the IHT charge

- calculate the IHT on the death estate where the value of the chargeable estate is provided.

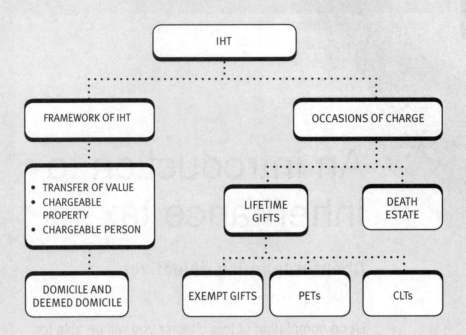

## 1 Introduction

This and the following three chapters deal with the way in which an individual is liable to inheritance tax (IHT).

Most IHT is collected on the death of an individual based on the value of their death estate. However, if IHT only applied on death, it would be an easy tax to avoid by giving away assets immediately before death. Therefore, there are IHT implications arising on some lifetime gifts as well as on death.

This chapter covers the principles that underpin IHT and considers the IHT payable calculations on lifetime gifts and on the death estate. Subsequent chapters cover more advanced aspects of the tax on lifetime gifts such as exemptions and reliefs and the detail of the computation of an individual's estate on death.

Lifetime gifts often feature in the examination as consideration of both the CGT and IHT implications of gifts is required. The two taxes are applicable where assets are gifted, but they work very differently. It is important to understand the distinction and interaction between the two taxes as the multi-tax aspects of capital transactions are frequently tested in the examination. Questions often require advice on how a transfer of assets could be organised more tax effectively.

The interaction of CGT and IHT is considered in Chapter 13, along with the tax implications and tax planning points to consider when planning to gift to the next generation either during your lifetime or on death in your will.

**2 The charge to Inheritance Tax (IHT)**

Inheritance tax is charged on:

*   a **transfer of value**
*   of **chargeable property**
*   by a **chargeable person**.

A charge to inheritance tax (IHT) arises:

*   on the death of an individual
*   on lifetime gifts where the donor dies within 7 years of date of gift
*   on some lifetime gifts which are taxed immediately.

**Transfer of value**

A transfer of value is **a gift of any capital asset** which results in a reduction in the value of the donor's estate.

To calculate the transfer of value for IHT purposes, the **loss to donor** principle is used (also referred to as the **diminution in value** concept).

The loss to the donor, is the difference between the value of the donor's estate before and after the gift. This is the starting point for IHT calculations.

In most cases, the value of the transfer is the **open market value** of the asset that is gifted.

However, special valuation rules apply to gifts of certain assets. Therefore in some circumstances, the transfer of value from the donor's point of view is not necessarily the same as the value of the asset received from the donee's point of view. These special valuation rules are covered in Chapter 12.

**Chargeable property**

Note that **all property to which a person is beneficially entitled** is deemed to form part of their estate.

Therefore, a gift of any asset to which the person is beneficially entitled is a transfer of value, unless it is **excluded property**.

Excluded property is not chargeable to IHT and includes:

*   property situated overseas where the owner is not UK domiciled

- reversionary interests in trust funds (see Chapter 14).

## Chargeable persons

A chargeable person includes:

- individuals
- trustees of certain trusts.

However, examination questions will focus on individuals.

## Individuals

All individuals are potentially liable to IHT on their transfers of value.

However, for IHT purposes, the domicile status of the individual is the key concept used to determine the extent of the individual's liability.

Note that a husband and wife and partners in a registered civil partnership are chargeable to IHT separately.

## Domicile and deemed domicile

For IHT purposes, the definition of domicile is the same as for income tax and capital gains tax. This definition is covered in Chapter 10.

The concept of deemed domicile only applies for IHT:

- A person who has been domiciled in the UK and moves abroad retains their UK domicile for three years.
- Individuals who have been resident in the UK for at least 17 out of the previous 20 tax years (ending with the tax year of the chargeable transfer) will be treated as UK domiciled.

## The effect of an individual's domicile status for IHT

Individuals are assessed to IHT as follows:

| Domicile status: | Charged to IHT on: |
| --- | --- |
| UK Domiciled or Deemed domiciled in the UK. | Transfers of worldwide assets. |
| Non-UK Domiciled | Transfers of UK assets only. |

## Test your understanding 1

Graham has been domiciled in the UK since birth.

On 1 June 2006, he emigrated to France with the intention of remaining there permanently and changed his domicile.

He died on 31 March 2009.

**Explain the extent to which Graham will be liable to IHT.**

## Test your understanding 2

Jack is domiciled in Germany. He became UK resident on 1 May 1991 and died on 1 March 2010.

**Explain the extent to which Jack will be liable to IHT.**

## Location of assets

UK domiciled individuals are charged to IHT regardless of the location of their assets. A non-UK domiciled individual is only liable to IHT on his UK assets.

It is therefore necessary to be able to identify where in the world an asset is deemed to be located for IHT purposes.

The following rules should be applied:

| Type of asset | Location of asset |
|---|---|
| Land and buildings | Physical location |
| Registered shares and securities | Place of registration |
| Chattels | Location at time of transfer |
| Debtors | Where the debtor resides at the time of the transfer |
| Bank accounts | Location of the branch which maintains the account |
| Life assurance policies | Where the proceeds are payable |
| Business | Where the business is carried on |

## Test your understanding 3

Sam has lived in the UK for the last six years, however he is not UK domiciled and is not deemed to be domiciled in the UK. He owns the following property.

(i)   Freehold property situated in the UK.

(ii)  Leasehold property situated in the USA.

(iii) Shares in USA Inc., a company quoted and registered on the US stock exchange.

(iv)  Antiques situated in Sam's US residence.

(v)   A loan due to Sam by his sister who is resident in the USA. The sister used the loan to buy property situated in the UK.

(vi)  A car that was bought in the USA, but is now situated in the UK.

(vii) Bank deposits in sterling with the UK Branch of a US Bank.

(viii)UK government stocks

(ix)  US government stocks.

**Explain whether Sam is liable to be charged to IHT if he transferred his property.**

## Summary

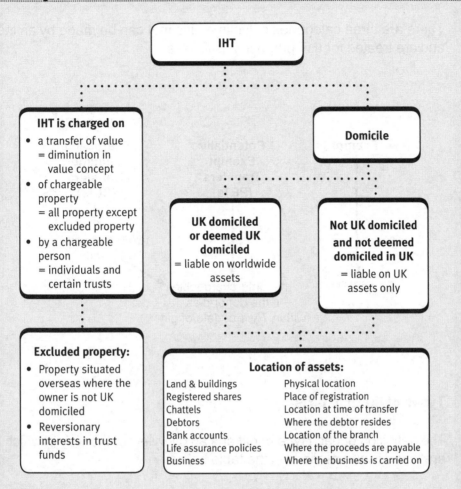

### 3 Occasions of charge

The main charge to IHT arises on the death of an individual as they become liable on the following:

*   the value of all of their net assets in their estate at the date of death
*   any lifetime gifts made in the seven years before their death, provided they are not exempt gifts.

The rest of this chapter and the next chapter cover the charges arising during an individual's lifetime and on their lifetime gifts as a result of death.

Chapter 13 deals with the charge to IHT arising on his death estate.

## 4 Lifetime gifts

There are three categories of lifetime gifts that can be made by an individual and are treated for IHT purposes as follows:

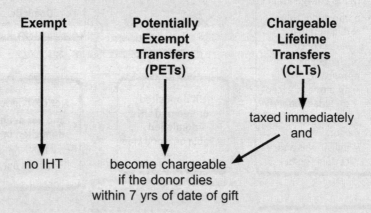

## Types of lifetime gifts

The definition of each type of gift and an overview of the way in which they are taxed is summarised in the table below:

KAPLAN PUBLISHING

| Exempt transfers | Potentially Exempt Transfers (PETs) | Chargeable lifetime transfers (CLTs) |
|---|---|---|
| **Definition**<br><br>A gift that is specifically deemed to be exempt from IHT<br><br>Main examples:<br><br>• Normal expenditure out of income<br>• Inter spouse gifts<br>• Gifts between civil partners<br>• Small gifts<br>• Wedding gifts<br>• Gifts to qualifying political parties<br>• Gifts to UK charities<br>• Gifts covered by the annual exemption | **Definition**<br><br>A gift by an individual<br><br>• to another individual<br>• an IIP trust before 22.3.06<br>• an A&M trust before 22.3.06<br>• a disabled trust | **Definition**<br><br>No definition = residual category (i.e. a gift which is not exempt nor a PET)<br><br>Main examples:<br><br>A gift into<br><br>• any trust on/after 22.3.06 (except a charitable or disabled trust)<br>• a discretionary trust before 22.3.06 |
| **During lifetime**<br><br>No IHT payable | **During lifetime**<br><br>No IHT payable | **During lifetime**<br><br>IHT to pay, calculated using the lifetime rates of tax |
| **If Donor lives 7 years**<br><br>No IHT payable | **If Donor lives 7 years**<br><br>No IHT payable | **If Donor lives 7 years**<br><br>No IHT payable |
| **If Donor dies within 7 years**<br><br>No IHT payable | **If Donor dies within 7 years**<br><br>The PET becomes chargeable on death for the first time | **If Donor dies within 7 years**<br><br>Possibly extra IHT, calculated using the death rates of tax |

It is important to note that in practice, the majority of lifetime transfers made by individuals are:

- exempt transfers, or
- transfers from one individual to another (i.e. a PET).

A CLT is a gift which is not exempt and not a PET. They are not common in practice, but appear in examination questions because they are chargeable to IHT at the time of the gift.

The main example of a CLT made by an individual during their lifetime is a gift into a trust. However, note that:

- Before 22 March 2006, lifetime gifts into a discretionary trust were the only example of a CLT made by an individual. Gifts into other types of trust were PETs.
- Since 22 March 2006, lifetime gifts into any trust (other than a charitable or disabled trust) are treated as CLTs.

## Potentially exempt transfers (PETs)

PETs have derived their name from the fact that if the donor lives for more than seven years after making the gift, then the transfer is free from IHT. Therefore, at the time of such transfer, it has the potential to be exempt.

However, if the donor dies within seven years of making the gift, then IHT may become chargeable on these gifts.

Note that transfers on death can never be PETs (see chapter 13).

## The amount of lifetime gifts chargeable to IHT

To calculate the IHT on:

- CLTs at the time of the gift, and
- CLTs and PETs within 7 years of the date of death

it is necessary to determine the amount which is chargeable to tax.

The chargeable amount is calculated as follows:

|  | £ |
|---|---|
| Value of estate before transfer | X |
| Value of estate after transfer | (X) |
| Transfer of value | X |
| Less   Business property relief and agricultural property relief | (X) |
|        Marriage exemption | (X) |
|        Annual exemptions | (X) |
| Chargeable amount | X |

Exemptions, reliefs and the marriage exemption are dealt with in more detail in chapter 12.

However, the annual exemption is important as it is available against most gifts (PETs and CLTs) and therefore it is considered in more detail in this chapter.

## The annual exemption

The annual exemption (AE) is an exemption available against **lifetime** transfers which operates as follows:

- The AE:
  - exempts the **first £3,000** of lifetime transfers in any one tax year
  - is applied chronologically to the first gift in the tax year, then (if there is any left) the second gift and so on
  - must be applied to the first gift each year, even if the first gift is a PET and never becomes chargeable.

- Any unused AE:
  - may be carried forward to the next year
  - however, it can be carried forward for one year only, and
  - can only be used after the current year's AE.

- If other exemptions or reliefs are available they are given before the AE.

## The annual exemption

The first £3,000 of value transferred in each tax year is exempt.

The AE is used up by PETs as well as by CLTs. This is despite the fact that a PET might become completely exempt.

Therefore, where more than one transfer is to be made during a tax year, CLTs should be made before PETs to ensure that the optimum use is made of the AE.

## Test your understanding 4

Julie made the following lifetime gifts:

(a) 31 August 2007, £600, to her son

(b) 31 October 2007, £800, to a discretionary trust

(c) 31 May 2008, £2,100, to an interest in possession (IIP) trust

(d) 30 November 2008, £1,100, to a discretionary trust

(e) 30 April 2009, £5,000, to her daughter.

**Calculate the chargeable amounts of each of the gifts.**

## 5 IHT payable during an individual's lifetime on CLTs

Lifetime IHT is payable when an individual makes a gift into a discretionary trust before 22.3.06 and into any trust (other than a trust for a charity or a disabled person) on/after 22.3.06.

## The procedure to calculate the lifetime IHT on a CLT

The procedure to calculate the lifetime IHT on a CLT is as follows:

(1) Calculate the chargeable amount of the gift (see above)

(2) Calculate the tax liability of each gift in chronological date order taking account of:
    – who has agreed to pay the tax; the donor or the donee
    – the nil rate band (see below)
    – the appropriate rate of tax (see below), and
    – the seven year cumulation period (see below).

(3) Calculate the gross amount of the gift to carry forward for future computations

(4) If required by the examination question, state the due date of payment of the IHT (see below).

## The normal due date of payment of lifetime IHT

The date of payment of lifetime IHT depends on the date of the gift:

| Date of CLT | Due date of payment |
| --- | --- |
| 6 April to 30 September | 30 April in the following year |
| 1 October to 5 April | Six months after the end of the month of the CLT |

## The nil rate band

All individuals are entitled to a nil rate band (NRB) and are taxed on the value of gifts in excess of the nil rate band at different rates depending on who has agreed to pay the lifetime tax.

The NRB identifies the maximum value of lifetime and death gifts, which can be gifted without incurring any IHT liability.

The NRB changes each tax year and in practice, the appropriate NRB at the time of the gift should be used.

For example, the most recent NRBs are as follows:

| | |
| --- | --- |
| 2008/09 | £312,000 |
| 2009/10 | £325,000 |

In the examination, the examiner has stated that the **NRB of £325,000** should be **used in all calculations**.

### The appropriate rate of tax

The appropriate rate of tax to apply to lifetime gifts depends on who has agreed to pay the tax due.

If the **trustees** of the trust (i.e. the donee) agree to **pay** the tax:

* the gift is referred to as a **gross gift**, and
* the appropriate rate of tax is 20%.

If the **donor** agrees to **pay** the tax:

* the gift is referred to as a **net gift**.
* their estate is being reduced by:
    – the value of the gift, **and**
    – the associated tax payable on the gift.
* therefore the amount of the gift needs to be 'grossed up' to include the amount of tax that the donor has to pay
* the appropriate rate of tax is therefore 25% (i.e. 20/80ths of the net gift).

Note that the tax due on a CLT is primarily the responsibility of the donor.

Therefore, where an examination question does not specify who has agreed to pay the tax, always assume that the donor will pay and that the gift is therefore a net gift.

The appropriate rate of tax on the value of CLTs in excess of the NRB is therefore:

| Payer: | | Appropriate rate |
|---|---|---|
| Trustees of the trust | Gross gift | 20% |
| Donor | Net gift | 25% |

### Test your understanding 5

Charlotte makes a gift into a trust on 13 June 2009 of £366,000. She has made no previous lifetime gifts. The trustees of the trust have agreed to pay any IHT due.

**Calculate the amount of lifetime IHT due on the gift into the trust and state the gross chargeable amount of the gift to carry forward for future computations.**

**Test your understanding 6**

Rosemarie made a CLT on 15 July 2009 of £366,000.

She has agreed to pay any tax due on the CLT. She has made no other lifetime gifts.

**Calculate the amount of lifetime IHT due on the gift into the trust and state the gross chargeable amount of the gift to carry forward for future computations.**

## The seven year cumulation period

Each time a CLT is made, in order to calculate the IHT liability, it is necessary to look back seven years and calculate how much NRB is available to match against that particular gift.

This is because, to calculate the NRB available at any point in time, it is necessary to take account of the total of the gross amounts of all other **CLTs** made within the **previous seven years**.

These CLTs in the seven year cumulation period are deemed to have utilised the NRB first.

There will therefore only be NRB available to match against this latest gift if the total of the CLTs in the previous seven years is less than £325,000.

**Test your understanding 7**

During his lifetime Alex had made the following gifts into discretionary trusts:

- 30 June 2001, £170,000
- 30 June 2007, £194,000
- 31 December 2009, £256,000

The trustees of the first two trusts paid the IHT liabilities. Alex paid the tax on the last gift.

**Calculate the IHT arising as a result of Alex's lifetime transfers.**

### Test your understanding 8

During his lifetime Sidney had made the following cash gifts into discretionary trusts:

*   21 April 2001, £123,000
*   19 March 2007, £227,000
*   9 May 2009, £395,000

Any IHT liability was paid by the trustees of the relevant trust.

**Calculate the IHT arising as a result of Sidney's lifetime transfers.**

### Summary of lifetime calculations

Remember to:

*   only calculate IHT on CLTs
*   consider the IHT position for each CLT separately and in chronological date order
*   use the valuation rules to calculate the chargeable amount
*   tax is due at 20% if the trustees pay, and 25% if the donor pays.

Also remember that PETs are not chargeable at this stage, but may use the annual exemptions.

### 6 IHT payable on lifetime gifts as a result of death

On the death of an individual, an inheritance tax charge could arise in relation to lifetime gifts (which are not exempt gifts) **within seven years of death** as follows:

*   PETs become chargeable for the first time.
*   Additional tax may be due on a CLT.

The IHT payable on lifetime gifts as a result of death is **always** paid by:

| Type of gift: | Paid by: |
| --- | --- |
| CLT | Trustees of the trust |
| PET | Donee (i.e. recipient of the gift) |

KAPLAN PUBLISHING

## Calculating the death IHT on lifetime gifts

The procedure to calculate the death IHT on lifetime gifts within seven years of death is as follows.

(1) Identify all gifts within seven years of death, calculate the chargeable amount of each gift and any lifetime tax paid.

(2) Calculate the tax liability on each gift in chronological date order taking account of:
   - the nil rate band
   - the death rate of tax (40%), and
   - the seven year cumulation period.

(3) Calculate and deduct any taper relief available.

(4) For CLTs, deduct any lifetime IHT paid.

(5) If required by the question, state who will pay the tax and the due date of payment.

On death calculations it is important to note the following differences in the calculations.

### Chargeable amount

The **gross** chargeable amount of each gift is taxed on death.

Note that:

- the gross amount of CLTs will have already been calculated in the lifetime IHT calculations

- remember to use the grossed up value of any CLTs where the tax is paid by the donor

- the chargeable amount of a PET is calculated using the values at the time of the gift and PETs may use up the annual exemptions, even though they only become chargeable if the donor dies within 7 years.

### The nil rate band

The NRB to be used in examination questions is always £325,000.

Note that:

- the nil rate band of £325,000 available to an individual is first used against the lifetime calculations as seen above

- it is then used again to calculate the death tax but this time it is matched against all chargeable gifts (i.e. CLTs and PETs) in chronological order.

## The death rate of tax

The death rate of IHT to apply is 40% on the excess over the NRB available.

## The seven year cumulation period

The seven year cumulation period applies in a similar way as for the lifetime calculations.

However, note that:

- it is necessary to take into account of the total of the gross amounts of all **chargeable gifts** made within the **previous seven years** (not just CLTs)
- therefore, to calculate the death IHT on each gift, it is necessary to look back seven years from the date of each gift and include the gross amount of:
  - all CLTs, **and**
  - PETs which have become chargeable due to the death of the individual.

However, ignore any PETs made more than 7 years ago as they are not taxable.

## The normal due date of payment of IHT on death

IHT as a result of death is due **six months** after the **end of the month of death**.

## Taper relief

Where IHT is chargeable on **any** lifetime transfer due to death, the amount of IHT payable on death will be reduced by taper relief:

- where more than 3 years have elapsed since date of gift
- by a percentage reduction according to the length of time between
  - the date of the gift and
  - the date of the donor's death.

Note that the relief applies to both CLTs and PETs.

The rates of taper relief are as follows:

*Years between date of gift and date of death:*

| More than | Not more than | Taper relief % | % of IHT chargeable |
|:---:|:---:|:---:|:---:|
| 0 | 3 | Nil | 100 |
| 3 | 4 | 20 | 80 |
| 4 | 5 | 40 | 60 |
| 5 | 6 | 60 | 40 |
| 6 | 7 | 80 | 20 |
| 7 | | 100 | Nil |

Note that these rates of taper relief are not given in the examination and therefore need to be learnt.

However, to help you remember, note that

- for the first 3 years no taper relief is given
- then for each year after that, 20% relief is available.

## Deduction of lifetime IHT paid

For CLTs, any lifetime IHT already paid can be deducted from the liability calculated on death.

However, no refund is made if the tax already paid is higher than the amount now due on death. At best, the deduction of lifetime tax paid will bring the liability on death down to £Nil.

### Example 1 – Death tax payable on lifetime gifts

Fred had made the following lifetime transfers:

- 31 July 2001, £80,000, to his son
- 30 November 2006 , £110,000, to his daughter
- 30 April 2007, £235,000, to his son.

**Calculate the IHT arising as a result of Fred's death on 30 June 2009. State who will pay the tax and the due date of payment.**

**Solution**

**PET – 31 July 2001**

- The PET made on 31 July 2001 to his son is more than seven years before 30 June 2009.

- It is therefore completely exempt. No IHT is payable during his lifetime and no IHT is due as a result of his death.

- The gift is ignored and is not accumulated for future calculations.

**PETs – 30 November 2006 and 30 April 2007**

The two gifts on 30 November 2006 and 30 April 2007 are PETs. Therefore no lifetime IHT is payable. However, both gifts will become chargeable as a result of Fred's death within seven years.

**IHT payable on death**

| **30 November 2006 – PET** | £ | £ |
|---|---|---|
| Transfer of value | | 110,000 |
| AE  – 2006/07 | | (3,000) |
|      – 2005/06 b/f | | (3,000) |
| | | |
| Gross chargeable amount | | 104,000 |
| NRB at death | 325,000 | |
| Gross chargeable transfers (GCTs) in seven years before this gift (30.11.99 to 30.11.06) (Ignore previous PET which is completely exempt) | (Nil) | |
| | | |
| NRB available | | (325,000) |
| | | |
| Taxable amount (gift is covered by NRB) | | Nil |
| | | £ |
| IHT payable on death | | Nil |

**30 April 2007 – PET**

| | | |
|---|---:|---:|
| Transfer of value | | 235,000 |
| AE  – 2007/08 | | (3,000) |
|      – 2006/07 (already used) | | (Nil) |
| | | |
| Gross chargeable amount | | 232,000 |
| NRB at death | 325,000 | |
| GCTs in 7 yrs pre-gift | | |
| (30.4.00 to 30.4.07) (Ignore previous PET | | |
| which is completely exempt) | (104,000) | |
| | | |
| NRB available | | (221,000) |
| | | |
| Taxable amount | | 11,000 |
| | | |
| IHT due on death (£11,000 × 40%) | | 4,400 |
| Less Taper relief (30.4.07 to 30.6.09) | | |
|       (< 3 years before death) | | (Nil) |
| Less IHT paid in lifetime (PET) | | (Nil) |
| | | |
| IHT payable on death | | 4,400 |
| | | |
| Payable by (always the donee) | | Son |
| Due date | | 31.12.09 |
| (six months from the end of the month of death) | | |

### Example 2 – Death tax payable on lifetime gifts

On 15 July 2004 Zoe made a transfer of £355,000 into a discretionary trust. She has made no other lifetime transfers.

The IHT due in respect of this gift was paid by Zoe.

Zoe died on 30 September 2009.

**Calculate the IHT arising on Zoe's lifetime gift, and the additional IHT arising as a result of her death.**

**State who will pay the tax and the due date of payment.**

**Solution**

**Lifetime IHT**

| **15 July 2004 – CLT** | £ | £ |
|---|---:|---:|
| Transfer of value | | 355,000 |
| AE  – 2004/05 | | (3,000) |
| – 2003/04 b/f | | (3,000) |
| Net chargeable amount | | 349,000 |
| NRB at date of gift | 325,000 | |
| GCTs in 7 yrs pre-gift (15.7.97 to 15.7.04) | | |
| (no previous gifts) | (Nil) | |
| NRB available | | (325,000) |
| Taxable amount | | 24,000 |

| | £ |
|---|---:|
| Lifetime IHT due (£24,000 × 25%) | 6,000 |
| (= net gift as Zoe paying the tax) | |
| Payable by | Zoe |
| Due date (gift in first half of tax year) | 30.4.05 |
| Gross amount to carry forward for future computations | |
| (£349,000 + £6,000) | 355,000 |

**IHT payable on death**

| **15 July 2004 – CLT** | £ | £ |
|---|---:|---:|
| Gross chargeable amount (above) | | 355,000 |
| NRB at death | 325,000 | |
| GrCTs in 7 yrs pre-gift (15.7.97 to 15.7.04) | | |
| (no previous gifts) | (Nil) | |
| NRB available | | (325,000) |
| Taxable amount | | 30,000 |

| IHT due on death (£30,000 × 40%) | 12,000 |
|---|---|
| Less Taper relief | |
| (15.07.04 to 30.09.09) (5 – 6 yrs) (60%) | (7,200) |
| Chargeable (40%) | 4,800 |
| Less IHT paid in lifetime (CLT) | (6,000) |
| IHT payable on death | Nil |

There is no repayment of lifetime HT.

### Example 3 – IHT payable on lifetime gifts as a result of death

Matthew has made the following lifetime gifts:

* 1 September 2001, £120,000, to a discretionary trust.
* 1 May 2005, £275,000, to his son Alexander.
* 1 June 2006, £236,000, to a discretionary trust.
* 1 July 2008, £21,000, to his daughter Jayne.
* 1 August 2009, £93,000, to an interest in possession trust.

Matthew has agreed to pay any IHT due on CLTs.

Matthew died on 1 December 2009.

**Calculate the IHT payable on the lifetime transfers during Matthew's lifetime and on his death.**

**State who will pay the tax and the due date of payment.**

**Solution**

| **1 September 2001 – CLT** | £ |
|---|---|
| Transfer of value | 120,000 |
| Less AE – 2001/2002 | (3,000) |
| – 2000/2001 b/f | (3,000) |
| Net chargeable amount | 114,000 |

This gift is covered by the nil rate band of £325,000, therefore no lifetime tax due.

| GCT c/f | 114,000 |
|---|---|

| **1 May 2005 – PET** | £ |
|---|---:|
| Transfer of value | 275,000 |
| AE – 2005/06 | (3,000) |
| – 2004/05 b/f | (3,000) |
| Gross chargeable amount | 269,000 |

Gift is a PET, therefore no lifetime IHT due.

| **1 June 2006 – CLT** | £ | £ |
|---|---:|---:|
| Transfer of value | | 236,000 |
| AE – 2006/07 | | (3,000) |
| – 2005/06 (already used) | | (Nil) |
| Net chargeable amount | | 233,000 |
| (as Matthew agreed to pay the tax due) | | |
| NRB at date of gift | 325,000 | |
| GCT in 7 yrs pre-gift (1.6.99 to 1.6.06) | | |
| (ignore PETs in lifetime but include CLTs) | (114,000) | |
| NRB available | | (211,000) |
| Taxable amount | | 22,000 |
| Lifetime IHT due (£22,000 × 25%) | | 5,500 |
| GCT c/f (£233,000 + £5,500) | | 238,500 |

| **1 July 2008– PET** | £ |
|---|---:|
| Transfer of value | 21,000 |
| AE – 2008/09 | (3,000) |
| – 2007/08 b/f | (3,000) |
| Gross chargeable amount | 15,000 |
| Gift is a PET, therefore no lifetime IHT due | Nil |

| 1 August 2009 – CLT | £ | £ |
|---|---|---|
| Transfer of value | | 93,000 |
| AE – 2009/10 | | (3,000) |
| – 2008/09 (already used) | | (Nil) |
| | | |
| Net chargeable amount | | 90,000 |
| NRB at date of gift | 325,000 | |
| GCTs in 7 yrs pre-gift (1.8.02 to 1.8.09) | | |
| (ignore PETs in lifetime calculations) | (238,500) | |
| | | |
| NRB available | | (86,500) |
| | | |
| Taxable amount | | 3,500 |
| | | |
| Lifetime IHT due (£3,500 × 25%) | | |
| (= net gift as Matthew paying the tax) | | 875 |
| | | |
| Payable by | | Matthew |
| Due date (gift in first half of tax year) | | 30.4.10 |
| | | |
| GCT c/f (£90,000 + £875) | | 90,875 |

**IHT payable on death**

| | | |
|---|---|---|
| Date of death: | 1.12.2009 | |
| Seven years before: | 1.12.2002 | |

All gifts within seven years of the date of death become chargeable on Matthew's death.

| 1 September 2001 – CLT | | £114,000 |
|---|---|---|

This is more than 7 years prior to death, so there is no additional IHT due on this gift.

| 1 May 2005 – PET | £ | £ |
|---|---|---|
| Gross chargeable amount (above) | | 269,000 |
| NRB at death | 325,000 | |
| GCTs in 7 yrs pre-gift | | |
| (1.5.98 to 1.5.05) (CLT) | (114,000) | |
| | | |
| NRB available | | (211,000) |
| | | |
| Taxable amount | | 58,000 |

| | £ |
|---|---|
| IHT due on death (£58,000 × 40%) | 23,200 |
| Less Taper relief (1.5.05 to 1.12.09) | |
| (4 – 5 years) (40%) | (9,280) |
| | |
| Chargeable (60%) | 13,920 |
| Less IHT paid in lifetime (PET) | (Nil) |
| | |
| IHT Payable on death | 13,920 |
| | |
| Payable by | Alexander |
| Due date (6m from the end of the month of death) | 30.6.10 |

**1 June 2006 – CLT**

| | £ | £ |
|---|---|---|
| Gross chargeable amount (above) | | 238,500 |
| NRB at death | 325,000 | |
| GCTs in 7 yrs pre-gift (1.6.99 to 1.6.06) | | |
| (Include PET as it has become chargeable on death) | (383,000) | |
| (£114,000 + £269,000) | | |
| | | |
| NRB available | | (Nil) |
| | | |
| Taxable amount | | 238,500 |

| | £ |
|---|---|
| IHT due on death (£238,500 × 40%) | 95,400 |
| Less Taper relief (1.6.06 to 1.12.09) | |
| (3 – 4 years) (20%) | (19,080) |
| | |
| Chargeable (80%) | 76,320 |
| Less IHT paid in lifetime | (5,500) |
| | |
| IHT payable on death | 70,820 |
| | |
| Payable by | Trustees |
| Due date (6m from the end of the month of death) | 30.6.10 |

| **1 July 2008 – PET** | £ | £ |
|---|---|---|
| Gross chargeable amount (above) | | 15,000 |
| NRB at death | 325,000 | |
| GCTs in 7 yrs pre-gift (1.7.01 to 1.7.08) | | |
| (£114,000 + £269,000 + £238,500) | | |
| (Include PET which became chargeable | (621,500) | |
| and CLT) | | |
| | ――――― | |
| NRB available | | (Nil) |
| | | ――――― |
| Taxable amount | | 15,000 |
| | | ――――― |
| IHT due on death (£15,000 × 40%) | | 6,000 |
| Less Taper relief (1.7.09 to 1.12.09) | | (Nil) |
| (< 3 years before death) | | |
| Less IHT paid in lifetime (PET) | | (Nil) |
| | | ――――― |
| IHT payable on death | | 6,000 |
| | | ――――― |
| Payable by | | Jayne |
| Due date (6m from the end of the month of death) | | 30.6.10 |

| **1 August 2009 – CLT** | £ | £ |
|---|---|---|
| Gross chargeable amount (above) | | 90,875 |
| NRB at death | 325,000 | |
| GCTs in 7 yrs pre-gift (1.8.02 to 1.8.09) | | |
| (£269,000 + £238,500 + £15,000) | | |
| (Include PETs which have become | | |
| chargeable on death and CLT) | (522,500) | |
| | ――――― | |
| NRB available | | (Nil) |
| | | ――――― |
| Taxable amount | | 90,875 |
| | | ――――― |
| IHT due on death (£90,875 × 40%) | | 36,350 |
| Less Taper relief | | |
| (1.8.09 to 1.12.09) (< 3 years) | | (Nil) |
| Less IHT paid in lifetime (CLT) | | (875) |
| | | ――――― |
| IHT payable on death | | 35,475 |
| | | ――――― |
| Payable by | | Trustees |
| Due date (6m from the end of the month of death) | | 30.6.10 |

### Test your understanding 9

Mr Ambrose makes the following lifetime gifts:

| | |
|---|---|
| 1 May 2001 | £205,000 to a discretionary trust, Ambrose is to pay the IHT. |
| 30 June 2002 | £60,000 to his niece on the occasion of her 21st birthday. |
| 11 June 2003 | £133,000 to his nephew. |
| 11 November 2005 | £136,000 to a discretionary trust, the trustees are to pay the IHT. |

Assume that the 2009/10 rates and allowances apply throughout.

(a) **Calculate the IHT liabilities arising as a result of the lifetime gifts.**

(b) **If Ambrose dies on 14 February 2010, calculate the additional IHT on the lifetime gifts as a result of Ambrose's death.**

(c) **Calculate the nil rate band left to set against the death estate.**

## 7 IHT payable on the death estate

On the death of an individual, an inheritance tax charge arises on the value of their estate at the date of death.

The detailed computation of a death estate is covered in Chapter 13. This section explains how the IHT charge is calculated once the estate value has been established.

### The procedure to calculate the IHT on the death estate

The procedure to calculate the IHT on the death estate is as follows.

(1) Deal with the IHT on lifetime gifts within seven years of the date of death **before** looking at the estate computations.

(2) Calculate the gross chargeable estate value.

(3) Calculate the tax liability taking account of:

 – the nil rate band

 – the appropriate rate of tax, and

 – the seven year cumulation period.

(4) Deduct quick succession relief and double taxation relief, if applicable (see Chapter 13).

(5) If required by the question, state who will pay the tax and the due date of payment.

## The nil rate band

The nil rate band of £325,000 available to an individual is first used against the lifetime calculations as seen above. It is then used to calculate the death tax on the estate after the lifetime gifts have been dealt with.

## The death rate of tax

The death rate of IHT to apply is 40% on the excess over the NRB available.

## The seven year cumulation period

The seven year accumulation period applies in a similar way to the death calculations on lifetime gifts as follows:

- it is necessary to take into account the total of the gross amounts of all **chargeable gifts** made within the **previous seven years**

- therefore, look back seven years from the date of death and accumulate the gross amounts of:
    - **all** CLTs, **and**
    - **all** PETs (because all PETs within 7 years of death will have become chargeable on death).

## The normal due date of payment of IHT on death

IHT as a result of death is due **six months** after the end of the month of death.

Note that who pays the tax on the estate value depends on the make-up of the estate. This is covered in detail in Chapter 13.

### Example 4 – IHT payable on the death estate

Sara died on 15 June 2009 leaving a gross chargeable estate valued at £427,000 which was bequeathed to her brother.

(a) **Calculate the IHT liability arising on Sara's estate assuming she made no lifetime transfers**

(b) **What if sara had gross chargeable transfers of £147,000 in the seven years prior to her death?**

## Solution

### (a) No lifetime transfers

| | £ | £ |
|---|---:|---:|
| Gross chargeable estate value | | 427,000 |
| NRB at death | 325,000 | |
| Gross chargeable transfers (GCTs) in seven years before death | (Nil) | |
| | ——— | |
| NRB available | | (325,000) |
| | | ——— |
| Taxable amount | | 102,000 |
| | | ——— |
| IHT due on death (£102,000 × 40%) | | 40,800 |
| | | ——— |

### (b) Lifetime transfers = £147,000

| | £ | £ |
|---|---:|---:|
| Gross chargeable estate value | | 427,000 |
| NRB at death | 325,000 | |
| GCTs in 7 yrs pre-death | (147,000) | |
| | ——— | |
| NRB available | | (178,000) |
| | | ——— |
| Taxable amount | | 249,000 |
| | | ——— |
| IHT due on death (£249,000 × 40%) | | 99,600 |
| | | ——— |

### Test your understanding 10

Timothy died on 23 April 2009 leaving a gross chargeable estate valued at £627,560 which was bequeathed to his girlfriend.

Timothy had made the following lifetime gifts:

- 1 June 2001, £180,000, to a discretionary trust
- 16 March 2006, £228,000, to his cousin

**Calculate the IHT liability arising on Timothy's estate and death the due date of payment.**

## Summary

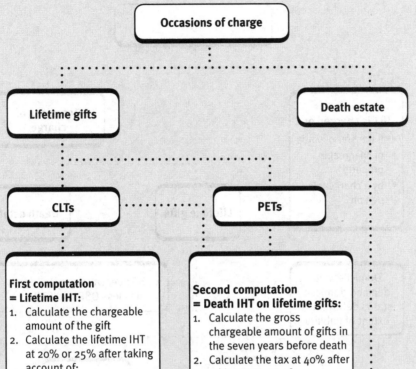

**First computation
= Lifetime IHT:**
1. Calculate the chargeable amount of the gift
2. Calculate the lifetime IHT at 20% or 25% after taking account of:
   – whether a gross or net gift
   – the NRB available
     gross CLTs in the 7-year-cumulation period
3. Calculate the gross amount to carry forward for future computations

**Second computation
= Death IHT on lifetime gifts:**
1. Calculate the gross chargeable amount of gifts in the seven years before death
2. Calculate the tax at 40% after taking account of
   – the NRB available
   – gross CLTs and PETs which have become chargeable in the 7-year cumulation period
3. Calculate and deduct taper relief
4. For CLTs, deduct lifetime IHT paid

**Last computation = Death IHT on estate value:**
1. Calculate the gross chargeable estate value
2. Calculate the tax at 40% after taking account of
   – the NRB available
   – gross CLTs and PETs in the 7 years before death
3. Calculate and deduct QSR and DTR, if applicable

## 8 Chapter summary

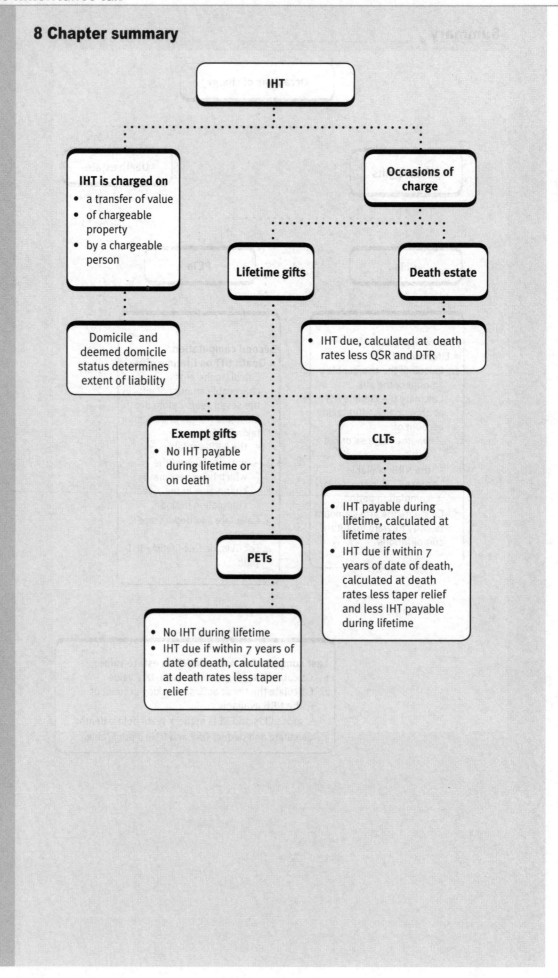

# Test your understanding answers

## Test your understanding 1

### Graham

Graham ceased to be domiciled in the UK on 1 June 2006. For IHT purposes, he is deemed to be UK domiciled for a further three years until 31 May 2009.

As his death occurred before this date, he will be liable to UK IHT on his worldwide assets.

## Test your understanding 2

### Jack

Jack was resident in the UK for 19 tax years (1991/92 to 2009/10 inclusive).

He is therefore deemed to be domiciled in the UK, and will be liable to UK IHT on his worldwide assets.

## Test your understanding 3

### Sam

Sam is a non UK domiciled individual and therefore he will only be chargeable to IHT on his assets located in the UK.

(i) The freehold property is situated in the UK and so is a chargeable asset for IHT.

(ii) The leasehold property situated in the USA is not in the UK and therefore not a chargeable asset.

(iii) The 20,000 shares in USA Inc. are registered in the US and therefore not a chargeable asset to Sam.

(iv) The antiques are in the US residence, so they are not chargeable to IHT at present. If Sam should bring them to the UK, then this would change their location for IHT to the UK.

(v) The sister used the loan to buy property situated in the UK. As the debtor (his sister) lives in the USA, this is not an asset located in the UK but the USA. Therefore it is not a chargeable asset.

(vi) The motor car is now a UK located asset and therefore a chargeable asset.

(vii) Bank deposits in sterling with the UK Branch of a US Bank – located in the UK therefore chargeable.

(viii) The place of registration of the UK government stocks would have been the UK which makes this also a chargeable asset.

(ix) The US government stocks would have been registered in the US, which makes them an overseas asset and therefore not chargeable.

### Test your understanding 4

**Julie**

| **31 August 2007 – PET** | £ |
|---|---|
| Transfer of value | 600 |
| AE – 2007/08 | (600) |
| | —— |
| Chargeable amount | Nil |
| | —— |

| **31 October 2007 – CLT** | |
|---|---|
| Transfer of value | 800 |
| AE – 2007/08 | (800) |
| | —— |
| Chargeable amount | Nil |
| | —— |

£1,600 (£3,000 – £600 – £800) of the AE for 2007/08 is carried forward.

| **31 May 2008 – CLT** | £ |
|---|---|
| Transfer of value | 2,100 |
| AE – 2008/09 | (2,100) |
| | —— |
| Chargeable amount | Nil |
| | —— |

| 30 November 2008 – CLT | £ | £ |
|---|---|---|
| Transfer of value | | 1,100 |
| AE – 2008/09 (£3,000 – £2,100) | 900 | |
| – 2007/08 b/f | 200 | |
| | ——— | (1,100) |
| Chargeable amount | | Nil |

The unused part of the 2007/08 AE of £1,400 (£1,600 – £200) is lost, and so the amount carried forward to 2009/10 is nil.

**30 April 2009 – PET**

| | £ |
|---|---|
| Transfer of value | 5,000 |
| AE – 2009/10 | (3,000) |
| – 2008/09 (already used) | Nil |
| | ——— |
| Chargeable amount | 2,000 |

## Test your understanding 5

### Charlotte

The gift is a gross gift as the trustees have agreed to pay the tax.

| | £ |
|---|---|
| CLT – Transfer value | 366,000 |
| Less AE: 2009/10 (current year first) | (3,000) |
| 2008/09 (previous year) | (3,000) |
| | ——— |
| Gross chargeable amount | 360,000 |
| Less NRB available | (325,000) |
| | ——— |
| Taxable amount | 35,000 |
| | ——— |
| Lifetime IHT due (£35,000 @ 20%) | £7,000 |
| | ——— |

The gross chargeable transfer carried forward (GCT c/f) is £360,000.

## Test your understanding 6

### Rosemarie

The gift is a net gift as Rosemarie has agreed to pay the tax.

| | £ |
|---|---:|
| CLT — Transfer of value | 366,000 |
| Less AE: 2009/10 (current year first) | (3,000) |
| 2008/09 (previous year) | (3,000) |
| | ——— |
| Net chargeable amount | 360,000 |
| Less NRB available | (325,000) |
| | ——— |
| Taxable amount | 35,000 |
| | ——— |
| Lifetime IHT due (£35,000 @ 25%) | £8,750 |
| | ——— |
| GCT c/f (£360,000 + £8,750) | £368,750 |
| | ——— |

## Test your understanding 7

### Alex

All of the gifts to the discretionary trusts are CLTs. The first two gifts are gross gifts as the trustees have agreed to pay the associated tax.

**30 June 2001 – CLT**

| | £ |
|---|---:|
| Transfer of value | 170,000 |
| Less AE: 2001/02 | (3,000) |
| 2000/01 b/f | (3,000) |
| | ——— |
| Gross chargeable amount | 164,000 |
| | ——— |

No IHT is due in respect of the gift on 30 June 2001 as it is covered by the NRB of £325,000.

GCT c/f £164,000.

**30 June 2007 – CLT**

|  | £ |
|---|---|
| Transfer of value | 194,000 |
| Less AE:  2007/08 | (3,000) |
|          2006/07 b/f | (3,000) |
| Gross chargeable amount | 188,000 |

IHT liability – payable by trustees
(£188,000 – £161,000 [Note below]) × 20%
= £27,000 × 20%    **5,400**

GCT c/f £188,000.

**Note:** The CLT made on 30 June 2001 is taken into account when calculating the IHT due in respect of the CLT made on 30 June 2007, as it is within the seven year cumulation period.

|  | £ |
|---|---|
| NRB | 325,000 |
| GCTs in 7 yrs pre-gift (30.6.00 – 30.6.07) | (164,000) |
| NRB available | 161,000 |

**31 December 2009 – CLT**

|  | £ |
|---|---|
| Transfer of value | 256,000 |
| Less AE:  2009/10 | (3,000) |
|          2008/09 b/f | (3,000) |
| Net chargeable amount | 250,000 |

IHT liability – Payable by Alex
(£250,000 – £137,000 [note below]) × 25%
= £113,000 × 25%    **28,250**

GCT c/f £278,250 (£250,000 + £28,250).

**Note:** This gift on 31 December 2009 is more than seven years after the gift on 30 June 2001. Therefore, only the CLT made on 30 June 2007 is taken into account when calculating the IHT due on the transfer.

The remaining NRB available is therefore:

|  | £ |
|---|---|
| NRB | 325,000 |
| GCTs in 7 yrs pre-gift (31.12.02 – 31.12.09) | (188,000) |
| NRB available | 137,000 |

### Test your understanding 8

**Sidney**

All of the gifts to the discretionary trusts are gross CLTs as the trustees have agreed to pay the associated tax.

The IHT will be calculated as follows:

**21 April 2001 – CLT**

|  | £ |
|---|---|
| Transfer of value | 123,000 |
| Less AE – 2001/02 | (3,000) |
| – 2000/01 b/f | (3,000) |
| Gross chargeable amount | 117,000 |

No IHT is due in respect of the gift on 21 April 2001 as it is covered by the NRB of £325,000.
GCT c/f £117,000.

**19 March 2007 – CLT**

|  | £ |
|---|---|
| Transfer of value | 227,000 |
| Less AE – 2006/07 | (3,000) |
| – 2005/06 b/f | (3,000) |
|  | |
| Gross chargeable amount | 221,000 |

IHT liability – payable by trustees
(£221,000 – £208,000 [Note below]) × 20%
= £13,000 × 20%         2,600

GCT c/f £221,000.

**Note:** The CLT made on 21 April 2001 is taken into account when calculating the IHT due in respect of the CLT made on 19 March 2007, as it is within the seven year cumulation period.

|  | £ |
|---|---|
| NRB | 325,000 |
| GCTs in 7 yrs pre-gift (19.3.00 – 19.3.07) | (117,000) |
|  | |
| NRB available | 208,000 |

**9 May 2009 – CLT**

|  | £ |
|---|---|
| Transfer of value | 395,000 |
| Less AE – 2009/10 | (3,000) |
| – 2008/09 b/f | (3,000) |
|  | |
| Gross chargeable amount | 389,000 |

IHT liability – payable by trustees
(£389,000 – £104,000 [Note below]) × 20%      57,000
= £285,000 × 20%

> **Note:** This gift on 9 May 2009 is more than seven years after the gift on 21 April 2001. Therefore, the NRB is re-calculated and the first gift falls out of the cumulative total.
>
> Only the chargeable lifetime transfer made on 19 March 2007 is taken into account when calculating the IHT due on the transfer.
>
> | | £ |
> |---|---:|
> | NRB | 325,000 |
> | GCTs in 7 yrs pre-gift (9.5.02 – 9.5.09) | (221,000) |
> | | |
> | NRB available | 104,000 |

### Test your understanding 9

**Mr Ambrose**

(a) **Lifetime IHT payable**

| 1 May 2001 - CLT | £ | £ |
|---|---:|---:|
| Transfer of value | | 205,000 |
| AE – 2001/02 | | (3,000) |
| – 2000/01 b/f | | (3,000) |
| | | |
| Net chargeable amount | | 199,000 |
| NRB at date of gift | 325,000 | |
| GCTs in 7 yrs pre-gift (1.5.94 – 1.5.01) | (Nil) | |
| | | |
| NRB available | | (325,000) |
| | | |
| Taxable amount | | Nil |
| | | |
| Lifetime IHT due | | Nil |
| | | |
| GCT c/f (£199,000 + £Nil) | | 199,000 |

| 30 June 2002 - PET | £ |
|---|---|
| Transfer of value | 60,000 |
| AE – 2002/03 | (3,000) |
| – 2001/02 (already used) | (Nil) |
| | |
| Gross chargeable amount | 57,000 |
| | |
| Lifetime IHT due | Nil |

| 11 June 2003 - PET | £ |
|---|---|
| Transfer of value | 133,000 |
| AE – 2003/04 | (3,000) |
| – 2002/03 (already used) | (Nil) |
| | |
| Gross chargeable amount | 130,000 |
| | |
| Lifetime IHT due | Nil |

| 11 November 2005 - CLT | £ | £ |
|---|---|---|
| Transfer of value | | 136,000 |
| AE – 2005/06 | | (3,000) |
| – 2004/05 b/f | | (3,000) |
| | | |
| Gross chargeable amount | | 130,000 |
| NRB at date of gift | 325,000 | |
| GCTs in 7 yrs pre-gift (11.11.98 – 11.11.05) | (199,000) | |
| | | |
| NRB available | | (126,000) |
| | | |
| Taxable amount | | 4,000 |
| | | |
| Lifetime IHT due (£4,000 x 20%) (gross gift) | | 800 |
| | | |
| Payable by | | Trustees |
| Due date | | 31.5.2006 |
| | | |
| GCT c/f | | 130,000 |

**(b) IHT payable on death**

| | |
|---|---|
| Date of death: | 14.2.2010 |
| Seven years before: | 14.2.2003 |

**Gifts on 1 May 2001 and 30 June 2002**

These gifts are more than seven years before death, therefore there is no IHT payable on death.

**11 June 2003 – PET**

| | £ | £ |
|---|---|---|
| Gross chargeable amount (above) | | 130,000 |
| NRB at death | 325,000 | |
| GCTs in 7 yrs pre-gift (11.6.96 – 11.6.03) | | |
| (ignore PET on 30.6.02 as not chargeable on death) | (199,000) | |
| | _____ | |
| NRB available | | (126,000) |
| | | _____ |
| Taxable amount | | 4,000 |
| | | _____ |

| | £ |
|---|---|
| IHT due on death (£4,000 x 40%) | 1,600 |
| Less Taper relief | |
| (11.6.03 to 14.2.10) (6 – 7 years) (80%) | (1,280) |
| | _____ |
| Chargeable (20%) | 320 |
| Less IHT paid in lifetime (PET) | (Nil) |
| | _____ |
| IHT payble on death | 320 |
| | _____ |
| Payable by | Nephew |
| Due date | 31.8.2010 |

| **11 November 2005 – CLT** | £ | £ |
|---|---|---|
| Gross chargeable amount | | 130,000 |
| NRB at death | 325,000 | |
| GCTs in 7 yrs pre-gift (11.11.98 to 11.11.05) | | |
| (£199,000 + £130,000) | (329,000) | |
| (ignore PET on 30.6.01 as not chargeable on death, but include PET on 11.6.02 as it became chargeable on death) | ——— | |
| NRB available | | (Nil) |
| Taxable amount | | 130,000 |

| | £ |
|---|---|
| IHT due on death (£130,000 x 40%) | 52,000 |
| Less Taper relief (11.11.05 to 14.2.10) | |
| (4 – 5 years) (40%) | (20,800) |
| Chargeable (60%) | 31,200 |
| Less IHT paid in lifetime | (800) |
| IHT payable on death | 30,400 |
| Payable by | Trustees |
| Due date | 31.8.2010 |

(c) **Nil rate band left to set against the death estate**

| | £ |
|---|---|
| NRB at death | 325,000 |
| GCTs in 7 yrs pre-death (14.2.03 to 14.2.10) (£130,000 + £130,000) (first two gifts = too old, include PET on 11.6.03 as it became chargeable on death) | (260,000) |
| NRB available against death estate | 65,000 |

## Test your understanding 10

**Timothy**

**Lifetime gifts**

|  | £ |
|---|---|
| **1 June 2001 – CLT** | |
| Transfer of vaue | 180,000 |
| Less AE – 2001/02 | (3,000) |
| – 2000/01 b/f | (3,000) |
| | ——— |
| Chargeable transfer | 174,000 |
| | ——— |

This gift is covered by the nil rate band of £325,000.

GCT c/f £174,000

| **16 March 2006 – PET** | |
|---|---|
| Transfer of value | 228,000 |
| Less AE – 2005/06 | (3,000) |
| – 2004/05 b/f | (3,000) |
| | ——— |
| Gross chargeable transfer | 222,000 |
| | ——— |

The gift is a PET so no lifetime tax is due.

**IHT Payable on death**

| Date of death | 23.04.2009 |
|---|---|
| Seven years before | 23.04.2002 |

| **1 June 2001 – CLT** | £174,000 |
|---|---|

This is more than 7 years prior to death so no additional IHT is due.

**16 March 2006 – PET**

| | £ | £ |
|---|---|---|
| Gross chargeable transfer | | 222,000 |
| NRB at death | 325,000 | |
| GCTs in 7 yrs pre-gift (16.3.99 – 16.3.06) | (174,000) | |
| NRB available | | (151,000) |
| Taxable amount | | 71,000 |

| | | £ |
|---|---|---|
| IHT due on death (£71,000 × 40%) | | 28,400 |
| Less Taper relief (16.03.06 – 23.4.09) (3 – 4 years) (20%) | | (5,680) |
| Chargeable (80%) | | 22,720 |
| Less IHT paid in lifetime | | (Nil) |
| IHT payable on death | | 22,720 |
| Payable by | | Cousin |
| Due date | | 31.10.09 |

**23 April 2009**

| | £ | £ |
|---|---|---|
| Gross chargeable estate value | | 627,560 |
| NRB at death | 325,000 | |
| GCTs in 7 yrs pre-death (23.4.02 to 23.4.09) (Note) | (222,000) | |
| NRB available | | (103,000) |
| Taxable amount | | 524,560 |
| IHT due on death (£524,560 × 40%) | | 209,824 |
| Due date (6m from the end of the month of death) | | 31.10.09 |

**Note:** The Gift on 1 June 2001 does not affect the NRB on death as it is more than 7 years prior to death. The Gift 'drops out' of the calculation.

# Further aspects of IHT affecting lifetime gifts

## Chapter learning objectives

Upon completion of this chapter you will be able to:

- identify the basis of valuation for different types of assets

- consider the related party valuation rule, consider when this rule must be used and calculate the effect on lifetime transfers

- identify when exemptions are available to reduce a lifetime transfer of value and apply them in the most beneficial way

- recognise the different types of reliefs available for lifetime transfers

- recognise when a claim for fall in value on a lifetime gift can be made and demonstrate the effect

- recognise the different types of business property for IHT and the rates of relief

- explain the conditions for Business Property Relief to apply and calculate any restrictions

- recognise the different types of Agricultural Property for IHT and the rates of relief

- explain the conditions for Agricultural Property Relief to apply

- define a gift with reservation

- explain the taxation implications arising and how they may be mitigated

- consider the rules for pre-owned assets and explain the taxation implications.

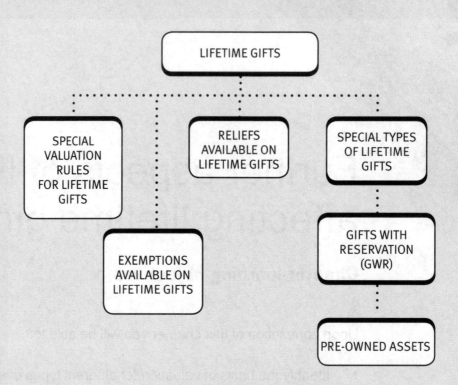

## 1 Introduction

The previous chapter covered the fundamental principles of IHT and the calculation of lifetime and death tax on lifetime gifts. This chapter covers further considerations which can affect the calculation of IHT on lifetime gifts.

To recap, the chargeable amount of lifetime gifts is calculated as follows:

|  | £ |
|---|---|
| Value of estate before transfer | X |
| Value of estate after transfer | (X) |
|  | — |
| Transfer of value  (diminution in value principle) | X |
| Less    Specific exemptions | |
| (i.e. spouse, charity, political party, small gift) | (X) |
| Business property relief and agricultural property relief | (X) |
| Marriage exemption | (X) |
| Annual exemptions | (X) |
|  | — |
| Chargeable amount | X |
|  | — |

## 2 Special valuation rules for lifetime gifts

As stated in the previous chapter, the transfer of value is normally the **open market value (OMV)** of the asset gifted.

However, there are special rules that apply to the valuation of **lifetime gifts** of some assets.

The lifetime gifts requiring special valuation rules which are frequently examined are gifts of shares and securities and related property.

### Open market value

Open market value is the price which property might reasonably be expected to fetch if sold in the open market at that time.

The following points must be considered when establishing a sale in the open market.

(1) The valuation assumes that there has been adequate publicity prior to the sale.

(2) The price is not reduced to take account of the fact that the whole property is placed on the market at once

(3) The opinion of a suitably qualified expert will normally suffice in order to establish what constitutes open market value (e.g. an estate agent will be able to value land and property).

(4) HMRC can set aside any valuation that they consider to be unreasonable.

### Quoted shares and securities

For IHT purposes, the valuation of quoted shares and securities is the same as for capital gains tax purposes as covered in Chapter 8.

The values are computed as follows:

Value = Lower of:

(1) 'Quarter Up'
= lower price + ¼ × (higher price – lower price).

(2) Average of the highest and lowest recorded bargains.

### Valuation of quoted shares and securities

These valuation rules apply to all quoted shares and securities, including those held in:

• investment trusts

• open ended investment companies (OEICs)

- gilt-edged securities
- venture capital trusts (VCTs)
- real estate investment trusts (REITs).

Further special rules apply if shares are quoted ex-dividend and securities are quoted ex-interest.

However, in the examination, these situations usually occur in the death estate computation rather than on lifetime gifts. These rules are therefore considered in more detail in Chapter 13.

## Unquoted shares and securities

Unquoted shares and securities are more difficult to value for IHT purposes, this is because:

- there is no ready market for the shares
- not all shares will be valued at the same amount.

A majority shareholding is likely to be worth considerably more than a small minority shareholding because the owner has control of the company.

The value to be used has to be agreed with the HMRC's Share Valuation Division. However, in an examination question, the value of unquoted shares and securities is given in the question.

### Test your understanding 1

Linda owns 6,000 shares which represents a 60% holding in Loot Ltd. On 31 December 2009 she gifted a 20% holding in the company to her friend, Bob.

The values of shareholdings in Loot Ltd on 31 December 2009 have been agreed for IHT purposes as follows:

| Holding | Value per share |
|---|---|
| Up to 25% | £9 |
| 26% to 50% | £15 |
| 51% to 74% | £26 |
| 75% or more | £45 |

**Calculate the transfer of value relating to the gift of unquoted shares for IHT purposes.**

## Related property

'Related property' is a concept unique to IHT.

Property is 'related' to the donor's property if it is **property of a similar kind owned by**:

- the **donor's spouse** (or civil partner)
- **an exempt body** as a result of a gift from that person or their spouse (or civil partner).

  An exempt body means a charity, qualifying political party, national body or housing association.

  Property held by the exempt body is deemed to be related:

  - for as long as that body owns the asset, and
  - for five years after they have disposed of it.

In the examination, the most common related property is **property owned by the donor's spouse**.

Note that property of a similar kind owned by the donor's children or other family members is **not** related property.

### The special valuation rules for related property

The related property valuation rules apply to the valuation of:

- unquoted shares
- collections of antiques and chattels
- adjacent plots of land.

However, in the examination, the related property rules normally apply to unquoted shares.

The related property valuation should be calculated as follows:

$$\frac{A}{A + B} \times (\text{Value of the total combined assets of a similar kind})$$

The meaning of A and B in the formula is slightly different depending on whether the asset is shares or assets other than shares, as follows:

| | Assets other than shares | Shares |
|---|---|---|
| A = | Value of the donor's asset | Number of shares held by the donor |
| B = | Value of the related parties' assets | Number of shares held by the related parties |

### Test your understanding 2

Sara owns two antique chairs which are part of a set of six. Her husband owns another three, and her daughter owns one.

Sara gifts one chair to her son on 23 April 2009.

The values of the chairs on that date are as follows:

| | |
|---|---|
| 1 chair | £5,000 |
| 2 chairs | £15,000 |
| 3 chairs | £25,000 |
| 4 chairs | £40,000 |
| 5 chairs | £60,000 |
| 6 chairs | £90,000 |

**Calculate the transfer of value relating to the gift of one chair for IHT purposes.**

### Example 1 – Special valuation rule for lifetime gifts

Ordinary shares in Monsoon Ltd, an unquoted trading company, with an issued share capital of 100 shares of £1 each, are held as follows.

| | % of shares (before the gift) |
|---|---|
| John | 40 |
| Geraldine – his wife | 35 |
| Jonathan – his son | 15 |
| Jennifer – his daughter | 10 |
| | 100 |

John gave 5% of his shares to his daughter on 30 June 2009.

The value of the shares on 30 June 2009 was as follows:

|  | £ |
|---|---|
| 100% | 150,000 |
| 75% | 105,000 |
| 70% | 80,000 |

**Compute the value of the gift to the daughter for IHT purposes before exemptions and reliefs.**

| **Solution** | Before the gift % holding | After the gift % holding |
|---|---|---|
| John | 40% | 35% |
| Geraldine – wife | 35% | 35% |
|  | 75% | 70% |
| Total value | £105,000 | £80,000 |

|  | £ |
|---|---|
| Value of John's shares before (45/75) × £105,000 | 56,000 |
| Value of John's shares after (35/70) × £80,000 | (40,000) |
| Transfer of value | 16,000 |

### Test your understanding 3

On 28 November 2009, James gave his son 6,000 ordinary shares in Simons Ltd, an unquoted trading company.

The company's share capital immediately before the transfer comprised 20,000 ordinary shares held as follows:

|  | Number |
|---|---|
| James | 8,000 |
| His wife | 2,000 |
| His brother | 5,000 |
| His sister | 3,000 |
| His father | 2,000 |
|  | 20,000 |

The agreed values for the shares are:

| Holding | £ |
|---|---|
| 75% or more | 10 |
| 50.01% – 74.99% | 8 |
| 50% exactly | 7 |
| 30% – 49.99% | 6 |
| 10% – 29.99% | 4 |
| Under 10% | 3 |

**Calculate the transfer of value relating to the gift of shares for IHT purposes.**

## The need for special related property rules

The special related property valuation rules prevent a husband and wife (or civil partnership) couple from deliberately splitting the ownership of similar assets to avoid IHT.

Consider the following scenario:

(i) On 1 July 2009 Joe owned 60% of the share capital of XYZ Ltd, an unquoted company. This shareholding was valued at £600,000.

(ii) On 2 July 2009 Joe gave 30% of the XYZ Ltd shareholding to his wife. This transfer, being to a spouse, is exempt from IHT.

A 30% shareholding in XYZ Ltd valued in isolation is worth £200,000.

Two 30% shareholdings are worth less than a 60% shareholding because a 60% holding gives control, whilst a 30% holding is only a minority interest.

(iii) On 3 July 2009 both Joe and his wife died in a car crash.

Without the related property rules, the estates of Joe and his wife would each include shares valued at £200,000 based on 30% shareholdings.

Without the special rules, the total value of the original 60% interest which will become subject to IHT is £400,000. However, the 60% interest has a value of £600,000. By splitting the interest between the couple, £200,000 of value would escape IHT without the special valuation rules.

KAPLAN PUBLISHING

## Summary of special valuation rules for lifetime gifts

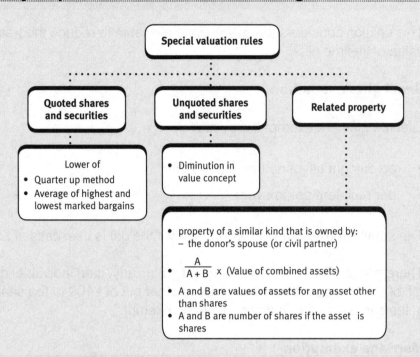

## 3 Exemptions and reliefs for IHT

| Exemptions and reliefs available against: | | |
|---|---|---|
| **Lifetime gifts only** | **Lifetime gifts and death estate** | **Death estate only** |
| • Annual exemption<br>• Small gifts exemption<br>• Marriage exemption<br>• Normal expenditure out of income<br>• Fall in value relief | • Inter spouse exemption<br>• Charity exemption<br>• Political party exemption<br>• Agricultural property relief (APR)<br>• Business property relief (BPR) | • Quick succession relief (QSR)<br>• Double taxation relief (DTR) |
| The annual exemption has already been covered in Chapter 11. The remaining exemptions and reliefs listed above are considered in detail in this chapter | | These reliefs are considered in more detail in Chapter 13 as they only affect the death estate |

## 4 Exemptions available to reduce a lifetime transfer of value

This section considers the exemptions available to reduce the transfer of value of lifetime gifts.

### Small gifts exemption

Lifetime gifts are exempt if they are:

- an outright gift of no more than £250

- per recipient per tax year.

The small gift exemption does not apply if the gift is in excess of £250.

Therefore, a gift of £300 will not qualify. Similarly, if an individual makes a gift of £240 to a person followed by another gift of £100 to the same person in the same tax year, neither gift will be exempt.

### Marriage exemption

A lifetime transfer made "in consideration of a marriage" is exempt up to the following maximum limits:

- £5,000 by a parent
- £2,500 by a grandparent or remoter ancestor
- £2,500 by a party to the marriage or civil partnership (e.g. from the groom to the bride)
- £1,000 by anyone else.

The exemption is conditional on the marriage taking place.

### Normal expenditure out of income

IHT is levied on transfers of capital wealth.

Therefore, a lifetime transfer will be exempt if it can be shown that the gift:

- is made as part of a person's normal expenditure out of income
- does not affect the donor's standard of living.

For example, birthday and Christmas presents.

### Inter spouse and civil partner exemption

Transfers between spouses, or partners in a civil partnership, are exempt whether they are made during the individual's lifetime or on death.

There is no maximum limit to this exemption **unless**

- the transferor is UK domiciled and
- the transferee spouse or civil partner is non-UK domiciled.

In this case, there is a maximum exemption limit of **£55,000** that can be deducted from the transfer of value.

## Political party exemption

Gifts to qualifying political parties are exempt whether they are made during the individual's lifetime or on death.

There is no maximum limit to this exemption.

A donation to a political party qualifies for exemption if, at the last General Election preceding the transfer of value, the following conditions are met:

- two members were elected to the House of Commons
- one member was so elected and at least 150,000 votes were cast for the party.

## Charity exemption

Gifts to recognised charities are exempt whether they are made during the individual's lifetime or on death.

There is no maximum limit to this exemption.

| Gifts to registered charities |
| --- |
| Gifts to the following charities are exempt: <br><br> • UK charities <br> • UK charitable trusts <br> • Registered community clubs <br> • Housing associations <br> • National Heritage Bodies (e.g. Museums). |

## Test your understanding 4

Maggie made the following lifetime transfers:

(i) Unquoted shares worth £525,000 in the family company to her husband on 1 June 2009.

(ii) £15,000 to her son on 6 July 2009 as a wedding present.

(iii) £20,000 to her nephew on 27 September 2009.

(iv) £270,000 into a discretionary trust on 24 December 2009.

(v) £90,000 to the International Red Cross, a registered charity, on 1 January 2010.

(vi) £20,000 to the Labour Party on 14 February 2010.

**Calculate the chargeable amount of each of Maggie's lifetime gifts.**

## Other exempt gifts

### Gifts for the public benefit or for national purposes

- Gifts to non-profit making institutions are, with Treasury approval, exempt.

- Examples could include land and buildings of outstanding beauty, or of historic interest.

- Undertakings are required concerning the use, preservation and public access of the property

### Gifts to a number of national institutions are also exempt

These include:

- the British Museum
- the National Gallery
- approved museums, libraries and art galleries
- the National Trust.

### Gifts to housing associations

Gifts of land to housing associations are exempt from IHT.

## 5 Reliefs available to reduce a lifetime transfer of value

There are three key reliefs that reduce the transfer of value of lifetime gifts.

- Fall in value relief.
- Business Property relief (BPR).
- Agricultural property relief (APR).

Fall in value relief only applies to lifetime gifts. BPR and APR apply to both lifetime and death transfers.

## 6 Fall in value relief

The chargeable amount of a lifetime gift (CLT or PET) is calculated and fixed **at the time of the gift**.

If the gift becomes chargeable on the death of the donor:

- any increase in value between the date of the gift and the date of the donor's death is ignored
- if the asset decreases in value between the date of the gift and the date of the donor's death, relief is available to reduce the chargeable amount of this gift on death.

To qualify for this relief, the asset must:

- either still be owned by the donee at the date of the donor's death, or
- it was sold in an arms length transaction before the donor died.

The relief operates by reducing the chargeable amount by the fall in value, calculated from **the donee's point of view**.

The fall in value is the difference between:

- the value of the asset at the date of the gift
- the value of the asset at
    - the date of the donor's death, or
    - the date of the sale (if earlier).

Note that this relief :

- applies to both PETs and CLTs
- only affects the calculation of the IHT on that one gift

- has no effect on lifetime IHT already paid

- has no effect on the IHT payable on any subsequent gifts or the death estate.

Therefore, the **original gross chargeable amount** is accumulated and carried forward to calculate the IHT on subsequent events.

Note that this relief is not available in respect of any property which is expected to fall in value over time. For example, assets such as plant and machinery and wasting chattels (i.e. tangible moveable property with a predictable useful life of less than 50 years).

### Test your understanding 5

Tim died on 30 June 2009.

On 30 April 2007 Tim had made a gift of 100,000 shares (a 1% holding) in ABC plc, a quoted company, into a discretionary trust. Tim paid the IHT arising on the gift.

ABC plc's shares were worth £3.65 each on 30 April 2007, and £3.35 each when Tim died on 30 June 2009.

(a) **Calculate the IHT liability arising in respect of Tim's lifetime transfer on 30 April 2007, stating when it is due for payment.**

(b) **Calculate the gross chargeable amount to carry forward for the IHT on the death estate computation.**

### 7 Business Property Relief

Business Property Relief (BPR) is a very important relief that significantly reduces the value of lifetime gifts and the value of an individual's death estate value if certain conditions are satisfied.

The relief:

- is given automatically if the conditions are satisfied, no claim is required

- reduces the transfer of value by either 50% or 100%, depending on the type of business property being transferred

- applies to worldwide relevant business property

- applies to both lifetime transfers and the death estate valuation

- on lifetime gifts, is deducted from the transfer of value **before** any other exemptions or reliefs.

## Conditions to be satisfied

To qualify for BPR, there are two key conditions which must be satisfied as follows:

- The property must be relevant business property.
- It must have been held for the minimum period of ownership.

## Relevant business property

BPR is given on the following property and at the following rates:

| Type of property | | % relief |
|---|---|---|
| Unincorporated business | • e.g. sole trader or partnership interest | 100% |
| Unquoted shares and securities | • including AIM listed shares and securities | 100% |
| | • relief on shares is available regardless of the number of shares held | |
| | • relief is also available for securities in an unquoted company, but only if the individual has voting control of the company immediately before the transfer based on share ownership | |
| Quoted shares and securities | • relief is only available if the individual has voting control of the company immediately before the transfer | 50% |
| Land, buildings, plant or machinery used in a business | • relief is only available if carried on by:<br>– a company of which the donor has control<br>– a partnership in which the donor is a partner | 50% |

Note that:

- to qualify, an unincorporated business must be a **trading** business and the companies in which the individual has shares must be **trading** companies.
- to determine control, **related property holdings** must be considered

- BPR is not available if the asset concerned is subject to a **binding contract for sale** at the date of transfer.

  The most common example of where this happens is where a partnership agreement provides for the interest of a partner to be sold to the other partners in the event of death. As a binding contract of sale, no BPR is available.

  However, if the agreement provides an option for the other partners to purchase the interest, but not a binding obligation to do so, BPR would be available.

### Test your understanding 6

David owns the following assets:

(1)  45% of the ordinary share capital of ABC plc, a quoted trading company.

(2)  15% of the ordinary share capital of DEF Ltd, an unquoted trading company.

(3)  A factory owned personally by David, but used in a partnership of which David is not a partner.

(4)  35% of the ordinary share capital of GHI plc, a quoted trading company. David's wife also owns 12% of the share capital, and David's daughter owns a further 6%.

(5)  A 25% shareholding in Green Ltd, an AIM listed trading company.

**State whether David's assets qualify as relevant business property, and if so state the amount of BPR that will be given.**

### Minimum period of ownership

To qualify for BPR, the relevant business property must have been held for a minimum period of **two years** immediately preceding the transfer.

If the asset was inherited on the death of a spouse (or civil partner), the couple's combined ownership period is taken into account.

### Example 2 – Business Property Relief

Peter inherited an unincorporated business from his wife on 1 January 2008. Peter died on 30 June 2009. Peter's wife had owned the property for one year.

**State whether BPR is available on the unincorporated business on Peter's death.**

### Solution

Although Peter has owned the property for only 18 months, BPR will be available since his wife's one year period of ownership can be included to make a total combined period of ownership exceeding two years.

### Exceptions to the two year qualifying rule

There are two key situations where the two year qualifying rule is not satisfied but BPR is still available. They are as follows:

- Replacement property.

  BPR is still available where

  - the relevant business property has not been held for two years because it **replaced** business property previously held, **and**

  - the individual owned some type of relevant business property for a combined period of ownership of at least **two out of the last five years**.

  BPR is given on the lower of the two property values (i.e. it cannot exceed the BPR that would have been given on the original property).

- Successive transfer.

  BPR is still available where

  - the relevant business property held was eligible for BPR **at the time it was acquired,** and

  - it was either acquired as a result of death, or is now chargeable as a result of death.

### Test your understanding 7

On 31 December 2008, an unquoted trading company JKL Ltd was taken over by MNO Ltd, another unquoted trading company. Marsha had owned ordinary shares in JKL Ltd for four years before the takeover. The consideration on the takeover consisted of ordinary shares in MNO Ltd.

On 30 June 2009, Marsha gifted her shares in MNO Ltd to her sister. The shares in MNO Ltd were worth £160,000. She had made no other lifetime gifts.

Her shares in JKL Ltd had been worth £110,000 on 31 December 2008.

**Calculate the gross chargeable amount of Marsha's lifetime gift to her sister.**

## Excepted assets

To qualify for BPR, an unincorporated business must be a **trading** business and the companies in which the individual has shares must be **trading** companies. There is no relief for interests in an investment business.

An individual may own an interest in a trading business but that business owns investment assets (known as "excepted assets"). Where this is the case, BPR is available but the amount of relief is restricted.

### Investment activities

The following investment activities prevent BPR from being available:

- dealing in securities, stocks and shares
- dealing in land and buildings
- making or holding investments, which includes the holding of land that is let.

## Definition of excepted assets

An 'excepted asset' is an asset that:

- has not been used wholly or mainly for business purposes during the preceding two years, and
- is not likely to be required for future use in the business.

The main examples of excepted assets are:

- large cash balances in excess of reasonable business requirements
- investments in shares and securities
- investments in land and buildings which are let.

## Restriction of BPR

On the transfer of an unincorporated business, BPR is only available on the business assets. No relief is available for excepted assets.

On the transfer of shares in a company that has excepted assets, BPR is only available on the business asset proportion of the total assets in the business, calculated as follows:

$$\text{Transfer of value} \times \frac{\text{Value of total assets less value of expected assets}}{\text{Value of total assets}}$$

### Test your understanding 8

On 31 May 2009, Wendy gifted 40,000 shares in STU Ltd, an unquoted trading company to her niece on the occasion of her marriage. Wendy had owned the shares since 1996 and on 31 May 2009 the shares were worth £180,000.

On that date, STU Ltd owned assets worth £500,000 which included an investment property valued at £50,000.

Wendy had made no other lifetime transfers.

**Calculate the gross chargeable amount of Wendy's lifetime gift.**

## Withdrawal of BPR on death

If conditions are not satisfied at the date of death, BPR is withdrawn when calculating the IHT payable on lifetime gifts due to the death of the donor.

The detailed rules for the withdrawal of BPR are covered in expandable text.

## Withdrawal of BPR on death

For lifetime gifts:

- The conditions for BPR are considered at the time of the gift and BPR is given at the appropriate rate when calculating the chargeable amount of a CLT or PET.

- If the gift becomes chargeable on death, BPR must be considered again at the time of death.

- BPR is available again on the death calculation provided:
    - the asset is still relevant business property at the date of death, and

    - the donee still owns the business property (or replacement business property) at the date of the donor's death (or the date of their death, if they predeceased the donor).

- If these two conditions are not satisfied, BPR is withdrawn and is not available in the death calculation.

## 8 Agricultural Property Relief

Agricultural Property Relief (APR) is very similar to BPR, but gives relief for transfers of agricultural property.

The relief:

- is given automatically if the conditions are satisfied, no claim is required

- reduces the transfer of value by 100%

- applies to both lifetime transfers and the death estate valuation

- on lifetime gifts, is deducted from the transfer of value first, **before** any other exemptions and before other reliefs (including BPR).

## Conditions to be satisfied

To qualify for APR, there are two key conditions which must be satisfied:

- the property must be relevant agricultural property

- it must have been held for the minimum period of ownership.

### Relevant agricultural property

APR is given at a rate of 100% on the **agricultural value** of **agricultural property**.

### Agricultural value

The agricultural value is the value of the land and buildings assuming there is a perpetual covenant on the land preventing any other use of the land other than agriculture.

It is likely that the commercial value of the farming land and business will be considerably higher due to its development potential.

The difference between the market value of the business and the agricultural value is often referred to as the development value.

### Agricultural property

Agricultural property is defined as the agricultural land and buildings.

Agricultural property therefore includes:

*   farm land and pasture
*   farm buildings, including the farmhouse, cottages, barns, pig sheds, milking parlours etc.

Unlike BPR, APR is **not available on worldwide agricultural property.** APR is only **available if** the property **is situated in the UK. the EEA, the Channel Islands or the Isle of Man.**

As with BPR, APR is not available if the asset concerned is subject to a **binding contract for sale** at the date of transfer.

| APR at 50% |
| --- |

APR is available at 100% on most agricultural property.

However, only 50% relief is available if a farm is:

*   a tenanted farm; and
*   the lease was taken out before 1 September 1995; and
*   at the date of transfer the owner does not have the right to obtain vacant possession within the next two years.

### Minimum period of ownership

To qualify for APR, the agricultural property must have been held for the following minimum periods:

| Agricultural property farmed by: | Minimum ownership period: |
|---|---|
| the owner | **Two** years |
| a tenant | **Seven** years |

### Exceptions to the minimum period

The same exceptions to the rule for BPR apply to APR (i.e. the replacement property provisions and successive transfers rule).

However, the replacement property rules are slightly different.  APR is available where:

- the individual owned some type of relevant agricultural property for a combined period of ownership of:
  - at least **two** out of the last **five years** if farmed by the owner
  - at least **seven** out of the last **ten years** if farmed by a tenant.

### The interaction of APR and BPR

Where agricultural property forms part of an unincorporated farming business, APR is given before BPR. Double relief is not available on the same value.

However, APR is only available on the agricultural value. Therefore, subject to the relevant conditions for BPR being met, BPR will then be available on any value of the remaining business assets that are not qualifying for APR.

Note that if the farm is tenanted and it is not the owner's farming business, no BPR is available on the remaining business assets as they are investment assets.

### Test your understanding 9

Zac plans to gift his farming business and £20,000 cash to his grandson on the occasion of his marriage. He has made no other lifetime gifts in the preceding seven years.

Zac lives on the farm and has owned and worked the business for the last seventeen years.

A surveyor has recently valued Zac's farm and its land as follows:

|  | £ |
| --- | --- |
| Agricultural value | 600,000 |
| Development value | 400,000 |
|  | ————— |
| Market value of farm land and buildings | 1,000,000 |
| Animals and stock | 150,000 |
| Plant and machinery and motor vehicles | 80,000 |
|  | ————— |
| Market value of farming business | 1,230,000 |
|  | ————— |

**Calculate the chargeable amount of Zac's gift to his grandson.**

## Shares in a farming company

APR is available in respect of shares in a farming company providing that:

- the individual has control of the company
- the minimum period of ownership condition is satisfied.

Note that:

- to determine control, **related property holdings** must be considered (see above)
- APR is only given against the agricultural value that can be attributed to the shares. BPR may be due on some or all of the remainder
- APR will be restricted where the farming company holds excepted assets in the same way as for BPR.

### Example 3 – Agricultural Property Relief

Since 1998, John has owned a 75% shareholding in Arable Ltd, an unquoted trading company which owns farm land.

The farm land has been let to tenants for the previous nine years.

On 31 October 2009 John gifted the shares to his daughter when they were worth £300,000 and the balance sheet of Arable Ltd shows:

|  | £ |
|---|---|
| Farm land | 350,000 |
| Other assets | 150,000 |
|  | 500,000 |

The agricultural value of the farm land was £300,000. The other assets of £150,000 were all used in Arable Ltd's trade.

**Calculate the gross chargeable amount of the gift to John's daughter.**

**Solution**

APR is available as:

- Arable Ltd's farm land has been let out for the previous nine years

- John has a controlling shareholding in the company.

In addition, as the shareholding is in an unquoted company, BPR is available on any amount that does not qualify for APR, subject to the relevant BPR conditions being satisfied.

|  | £ |
|---|---|
| Transfer of value – shares in farming company | 300,000 |
| Less APR on agricultural value (Note) | |
| (£300,000/£500,000) × £300,000 × 100% | (180,000) |
| BPR on Arable Ltd's other assets | |
| (£150,000/£500,000) × £300,000 × 100% | (90,000) |
| AE – 2009/10 | (3,000) |
| – 2008/09 b/f | (3,000) |
| | |
| Gross chargeable amount | 24,000 |

**Note:** APR is only available on the agricultural value of the farm land that can be attributed to the shares transferred.

BPR is available on the value that can be attributed to the business assets in Arable Ltd (i.e. the 'other assets'). BPR is not available on the development value of the farm land attributed to the shares as the farm is tenanted (i.e. not owned and farmed by Arable Ltd).

## Withdrawal of APR on death

In the same way as for BPR, if conditions are not satisfied at the date of death, APR is withdrawn when calculating the IHT payable on lifetime gifts due to the death of the donor.

### Withdrawal of APR on death

For lifetime gifts:

- The conditions for APR are considered at the time of the gift and APR is given at the appropriate rate when calculating the chargeable amount of a CLT or PET.

- If the gift becomes chargeable on death, APR must be considered again at the time of death.

- APR is available again on the death calculation provided:
  - the asset is still relevant agricultural property at the date of death, and

  - the donee still owns the agricultural property (or replacement property) at the date of the donor's death (or at the date of their death, if they predeceased the donor).

- If these two conditions are not satisfied, APR is withdrawn and is not available in the death calculation.

## 9 Summary of reliefs available on lifetime gifts

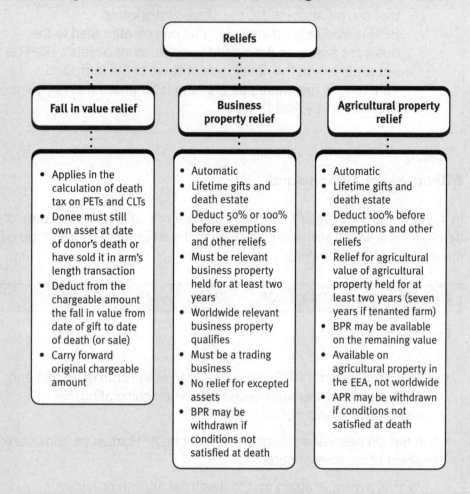

**Reliefs**

**Fall in value relief**
- Applies in the calculation of death tax on PETs and CLTs
- Donee must still own asset at date of donor's death or have sold it in arm's length transaction
- Deduct from the chargeable amount the fall in value from date of gift to date of death (or sale)
- Carry forward original chargeable amount

**Business property relief**
- Automatic
- Lifetime gifts and death estate
- Deduct 50% or 100% before exemptions and other reliefs
- Must be relevant business property held for at least two years
- Worldwide relevant business property qualifies
- Must be a trading business
- No relief for excepted assets
- BPR may be withdrawn if conditions not satisfied at death

**Agricultural property relief**
- Automatic
- Lifetime gifts and death estate
- Deduct 100% before exemptions and other reliefs
- Relief for agricultural value of agricultural property held for at least two years (seven years if tenanted farm)
- BPR may be available on the remaining value
- Available on agricultural property in the EEA, not worldwide
- APR may be withdrawn if conditions not satisfied at death

## 10 Gifts with reservation

A 'gift with reservation of benefit' (GWR) is a lifetime gift where:

- the legal ownership of an asset is transferred, but
- the donor retains some benefit in the asset gifted.

Examples of a GWR include:

- the gift of a house, but the donor continues to live in it
- the gift of shares, but the donor retains the right to receive future dividends
- the gift of assets into a discretionary trust, but the donor is a potential beneficiary of the trust fund.

Special anti-avoidance rules apply to a GWR to ensure that these gifts do not escape from an IHT charge.

**The treatment of GWR**

When an asset is gifted but the donor retains the right to use it without payment of full rent, it falls into the GWR rules.

The gift is effectively ignored, and the asset is still included in the estate of the donor when they die.

Any tax arising is payable by the legal owner of the asset (i.e. the donee).

HMRC have the right to use an alternative treatment if this gives a higher overall IHT liability on the death of the donor.

This recogizises the GWR as though it was a true gift (i.e. a PET or CLT at the time of the gift), and the asset is not then included in the donor's estate.

Usually including the asset in the estate gives the higher IHT charge.This is because capital assets normally appreciate in value and no annual exemptions are available in the death estate.

Exceptions to the GWR are given in the expandable text.

**Exceptions to the GWR rules**

The following gifts will not be treated as a GWR.

- Where full consideration is paid for the benefit derived from the use of the property.

- For example, where a house has been given away but the donor still lives in it, the payment of a commercial rent for the benefit of living in the house will avoid the GWR rules.

- Where the circumstances of the donor have changed in a way that was not foreseen at the time of the gift.

    This situation would be applicable where a house has been given away and the donor moves out of the house. Then, at a later date, the donor becomes ill. If the donor then returns to the house to stay with his or her family because he needs to be cared for, then this will not fall under the GWR rules.

**11 Pre-owned assets**

To counter situations where an individual can give away an asset, retain some benefit from the asset but avoid the GWR rules, further anti-avoidance legislation has been introduced. These rules are known as the 'pre-owned asset' rules.

The provisions apply to:

- gifts of land, chattels and certain types of intangible property, and
- the situation where an individual contributes cash towards the purchase of the asset which they then obtain some benefit of use of in some way.

### The treatment of pre-owned assets

If caught by the pre-owned asset rules, an **annual income tax charge** is levied as follows:

| Asset | Computation of benefit |
|-------|------------------------|
| Land | Annual rental value |
| Chattels | (Market value of the chattel) x official rate of interest at the start of the year |

Alternatively, instead of paying an annual income tax charge, the individual can opt out of the income tax treatment and include the asset in their IHT death estate computation on their death instead.

### Exceptions to the pre-owned asset rules

Transactions that would not be caught by the pre-owned asset rules:

- Transfers caught by the GWR rules
- Gifts to spouses or civil partners
- The disposal of an individual's entire interest in land or chattels in an arm's length transaction
- Where the chargeable amount does not exceed £5,000.

Note that where the chargeable amount exceeds £5,000, the whole amount is taxable.

### Example 4 – Pre-owned assets

Jacob gave his son £70,000 of cash in order to buy a house.

His son purchased the house on 6 April 2009 and Jacob occupied it rent free. The annual rental value of the house is £5,100.

Jacob is a higher rate taxpayer.

**Explain the income tax and inheritance tax implications of Jacob giving the cash to his son.**

**Solution**

As Jacob has gifted an asset (cash) which is used by the son to acquire another asset (land) which Jacob will occupy, the pre-owned asset anti-avoidance legislation applies.

As a result, Jacob must pay income tax on the benefit he receives based on the annual rental value of the property (i.e. the market rent that he might expect to pay for such a property).

In 2009/10 Jacob must pay income tax of £2,040 (£5,100 × 40%) and for each subsequent tax year that he uses the house rent-free.

This anti-avoidance legislation can be avoided if Jacob pays the son full market rent while occupying the property.

For IHT purposes the gift of cash to the son is a PET of £70,000, which means no IHT is payable at the time of the gift but may become chargeable to IHT if Jacob dies within 7 years.

It is possible for Jacob to elect to disapply the income tax charge and have the property treated as subject to a reservation, thus it would become part of Jacob's estate for IHT purposes on his death.

## 12 Summary of special lifetime gifts

```
┌─────────────────────────────┐
│    Special lifetime gifts    │
└─────────────────────────────┘
```

```
┌──────────────────────┐     ┌──────────────────────┐
│ Gifts with reservation│     │   Pre-owned assets    │
│        (GWR)          │     │                       │
└──────────────────────┘     └──────────────────────┘
```

┌──────────────────────────────┐   ┌──────────────────────────────┐
│                              │   │                              │
│ • Legal ownership transferred │   │ • Legal ownership transferred │
│   but benefit retained        │   │   but benefit retained and    │
│ • Treated as part of estate at│   │   GWR rules avoided           │
│   death                       │   │ • Annual income tax charge    │
│ • HMRC may insist on the      │   │   arises on benefit received  │
│   higher total IHT liability  │   │   each tax year               │
│   assuring lifetime gift      │   │ • Can opt out and include     │
│   occurred and asset not in   │   │   asset in IHT death estate   │
│   estate                      │   │   instead                     │
│ • IHT always paid by the      │   │                              │
│   donee                       │   │                              │
│                              │   │                              │
└──────────────────────────────┘   └──────────────────────────────┘

## 13 Chapter summary

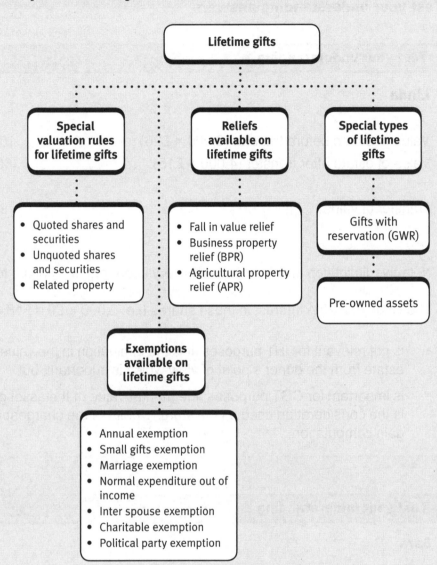

## Test your understanding answers

### Test your understanding 1

#### Linda

| | £ |
|---|---:|
| Value of estate before transfer (6,000 × £26) | 156,000 |
| Value of estate after transfer (4,000 × £15) | (60,000) |
| | |
| Transfer of value | 96,000 |

Note the diminution in value concept is very important and unique to IHT.

The value of a 20% interest in these shares (i.e. 2,000 × £9 = £18,000):

- is not relevant for IHT purposes; it is the diminution in the value of the estate from the donor's point of view which is important, but

- is important for CGT purposes; the market value of the asset gifted is the consideration used as the starting point of the chargeable gain computation.

### Test your understanding 2

#### Sara

Before the gift, Sara and her husband own five chairs between them. After the gift, they own four chairs between them.

Note that the chair owned by the daughter is not related property.

The value of Sara's two chairs before the gift is: = £22,500
[£15,000/(£15,000 + £25,000)] × £60,000

The value of Sara's one chair after the gift is: = £6,667
[£5,000/(£5,000 + £25,000)] × £40,000

The transfer of value is therefore:

|  | £ |
|---|---|
| Value of estate before transfer | 22,500 |
| Value of estate after transfer | (6,667) |
| Transfer of value | 15,833 |

Note that this value is significantly higher than the unrelated value of one chair = £5,000.

## Test your understanding 3

### James

|  | Before the gift No. of shares | After the gift No. of shares |
|---|---|---|
| James | 8,000 | 2,000 |
| Wife | 2,000 | 2,000 |
|  | 10,000 | 4,000 |
| % Holding | 50% | 20% |
| Value per share | £7 | £4 |

The value of James' shares before the gift is:
(8,000 × £7) = £56,000

The value of James' shares after the gift is:
(2,000 × £4) = £8,000

The transfer of value is therefore:

|  | £ |
|---|---|
| Value of Simons Ltd shares before the gift | 56,000 |
| Value of Simons Ltd shares after the gift | (8,000) |
| Transfer of value | 48,000 |

**Test your understanding 4**

### Maggie

1.6.2009 Gift to husband – exempt inter-spouse transfer

6.7.2009 Gift to son on occasion of marriage

|  | £ |
|---|---|
| Transfer of value | 15,000 |
| Less ME | (5,000) |
| AE – 2009/10 | (3,000) |
| – 2008/09 b/f | (3,000) |
| | ——— |
| Chargeable amount | 4,000 |
| | ——— |

The gift is a PET and there is no IHT payable unless Maggie dies within 7 years of the gift.

27.9.2009 Gift to nephew

|  | £ |
|---|---|
| Transfer of value | 20,000 |
| Less AE (already used) | (Nil) |
| | ——— |
| Chargeable amount | 20,000 |
| | ——— |

The gift is a PET therefore no IHT payable unless Maggie dies within 7 years.

24.12.2009 Transfer into discretionary trust

|  | £ |
|---|---|
| Transfer of value | 270,000 |
| Less AE (already used) | (Nil) |
| | ——— |
| Chargeable amount | 270,000 |
| | ——— |

This gift is a CLT and is chargeable during Maggie's lifetime.

However, as she has no other chargeable gifts in the preceding seven years, there will be no IHT to pay as the gift is covered by the NRB of £325,000.

| 1.1.2010 | Gift to the International Red Cross<br>– exempt gift to charity |
|---|---|
| 14.2.2010 | Gift to Labour party<br>– exempt gift to political party |

### Test your understanding 5

**Tim**

**(a) IHT liability arising on the lifetime gift**

**Lifetime IHT**

| **30 April 2007 – CLT** | £ | £ |
|---|---:|---:|
| Transfer of value (100,000 × £3.65) | | 365,000 |
| AE – 2007/08 | | (3,000) |
| – 2006/07 b/f | | (3,000) |
| | | ———— |
| Net chargeable amount (Tim agreed to pay) | | 359,000 |
| NRB at date of gift | 325,000 | |
| GCTs in 7 yrs pre-gift | (Nil) | |
| (30.4.00 to 30.4.07) (no previous gifts) | | |
| | ———— | |
| NRB available | | (325,000) |
| | | ———— |
| Taxable amount | | 34,000 |
| | | ———— |
| Lifetime IHT due (£34,000 × 25%) | | 8,500 |
| (= net gift as Tim paying the tax) | | |
| | | ———— |
| Due date (gift in first half of tax year) | | 30.4.2008 |
| | | |
| GCT c/f (£359,000 + £8,500) | | 367,500 |
| | | ———— |

**IHT payable on death**

| 30 April 2007 – CLT | £ | £ |
|---|---:|---:|
| GCT b/f (above) | | 367,500 |
| **Less Fall in value relief** | | |
| Value at gift (100,000 × £3.65) | 365,000 | |
| Value at Tim's death (100,000 × £3.35) | (335,000) | |
| Alternative calculation (100,000 × (£3.65 – £3.35)) | | (30,000) |
| Revised chargeable amount on death | | 337,500 |
| NRB at death | 325,000 | |
| GCT in 7 yrs pre-gift (30.4.00 to 30.4.07) (no previous gifts) | (Nil) | |
| NRB available | | (325,000) |
| Taxable amount | | 12,500 |
| IHT due on death (£12,500 × 40%) | | 5,000 |
| Less Taper relief (< 3 years before death) | | (Nil) |
| Less IHT paid in lifetime (CLT) | | (8,500) |
| IHT payable on death | | Nil |

There is no repayment of lifetime IHT paid

(b) **Gross chargeable amount to carry forward to the death estate computation**

Note that Tim's cumulative total to carry forward is the original gross chargeable amount per the lifetime IHT calculation.

Gross cumulative total to carry forward = £367,500

KAPLAN PUBLISHING

## Test your understanding 6

### David

(1) There is no entitlement to BPR as ABC plc is a quoted company and David does not have a controlling interest.

(2) BPR is available at the rate of 100% as DEF Ltd is an unquoted trading company.

(3) There is no entitlement to BPR as David is not a partner of the partnership. In this instance, the property is effectively held by David as an investment.

(4) There is no BPR since GHI plc is a quoted company, and David does not have a controlling interest even when taking account of his wife's shares.

(5) 100% BPR is given as Green Ltd is an AIM listed trading company.

## Test your understanding 7

### JKL Ltd

The shares in MNO Ltd have only been held for six months. However, BPR at 100% is available as Marsha has held relevant business property (MNO Ltd shares and JKL Ltd shares) for more than 2 years out of the last five years.

The amount of BPR will be restricted to £110,000 as it cannot exceed the amount of BPR that would have been given on the original property that was replaced.

Therefore, the gross chargeable amount of Marsha's PET to her sister:

|  | £ |
| --- | --- |
| Transfer of value | 160,000 |
| Less BPR | (110,000) |
| AE – 2009/10 | (3,000) |
| – 2008/09 b/f | (3,000) |
| | |
| Gross chargeable amount | 44,000 |

## Test your understanding 8

**Wendy**

31 May 2009 Gift to her niece = PET

|  | £ |
|---|---:|
| Transfer of value | 180,000 |
| Less BPR | |
| 100% × £180,000 × (£450,000 / £500,000) | (162,000) |
| ME | (1,000) |
| AE – 2009/10 | (3,000) |
| – 2008/09 b/f | (3,000) |
| | |
| Gross chargeable amount | 11,000 |

## Test your understanding 9

**Zac**

|  | £ |
|---|---:|
| Transfer of value – Farming business | 1,230,000 |
| – Cash | 20,0000 |
| | |
| | 1,250,000 |
| Less APR on agricultural value | |
| (£600,000 × 100%) | (600,000) |
| BPR on remaining value | |
| (£400,000 + £150,000 + £80,000) × 100% | (630,000) |
| ME (grandparent to grandchild) | (2,500) |
| AE – 2009/10 | (3,000) |
| – 2008/09 b/f | (3,000) |
| | |
| Gross chargeable amount | 11,500 |

**Note:** Items such as the development value of the farm, the farm animals, stock and farming equipment do not qualify for APR.

However, as it is Zac's unincorporated business and he has owned and worked the farm for more than 2 years, BPR is available.

If the farm was owned by Zac but let to tenants who worked the farm, APR would be available on the agricultural value but BPR would not be available on the remainder.

# IHT on the death estate and tax planning

## Chapter learning objectives

Upon completion of this chapter you will be able to:

- prepare a death estate computation for IHT and calculate the IHT liability

- identify the relevant exemptions available to reduce the value of the chargeable estate at death

- recognise the different types of reliefs available on death transfers

- identify the basis of valuation for different types of assets, for death transfers

- calculate the effect of the related party rules on death transfers

- recognise when quick succession relief is available and calculate the effect

- calculate the availability of double taxation relief where there are overseas chargeable assets for IHT

- compute the IHT on a death estate when there is an exempt residue

- state the conditions for there to be a valid variation of a will

- recognise the advantages of varying a will in a given situation and analyse the effect

- explain the advantages and disadvantages of lifetime giving compared to retention of assets at death

- identify and advise on the tax implications of associated operations.

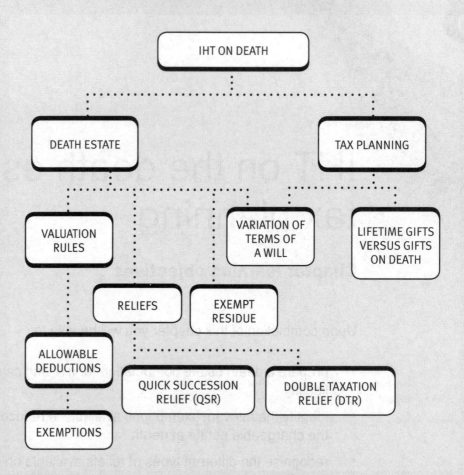

## 1 Introduction

The last two chapters have concentrated on the IHT aspects of lifetime gifts.

This chapter considers:

- the computation of an individual's estate on death and the special valuation rules that apply to certain assets

- the reliefs available on death such as quick succession relief and double taxation relief

- the full computation of IHT on both lifetime transfers and the death estate

- the consequence of leaving exempt legacies and an exempt residue

- tax planning issues.

## 2 The death estate computation

The gross chargeable value of an individual's estate is calculated using the following proforma:

## Proforma death estate computation

| | £ | £ |
|---|---|---|
| Freehold property | X | |
| Less: Repayment mortgage | (x) | |
| | —— | X |
| Foreign property* | X | |
| Less: Expenses | (x) | |
| (restricted to maximum 5% of property value) | | |
| | —— | X |
| Business owned by sole trader/partnership* | | X |
| Farm* | | X |
| Stocks and shares (including ISAs)* | | X |
| Government securities | | X |
| Insurance policy proceeds | | X |
| Death in service policy | | X |
| Leasehold property | | X |
| Motor cars | | X |
| Personal chattels | | X |
| Debts due to the deceased | | X |
| Interest and rent due to the deceased | | X |
| Cash and bank and on deposit | | X |
| | | —— |
| | | X |
| Less: Debts due by the deceased | (x) | |
| Outstanding taxes (e.g. IT, CGT due) | (x) | |
| Funeral expenses | | |
| | —— | (x) |
| | | —— |
| | | X |
| Less: Exempt legacies | | |
| (e.g. to spouse, charity, political party) | | (x) |
| | | —— |
| **Net free estate** | | X |
| Add: Gift with reservation (GWR) | | X |
| Add: Settled Property (interest in a trust fund) | | X |
| | | —— |
| **Gross chargeable estate** | | X |
| | | —— |

* These items may be reduced by BPR/APR if conditions are satisfied (see Chapter 12)

The IHT liability on the estate value is then calculated using the following proforma:

|                                                            | £     |
|------------------------------------------------------------|-------|
| IHT on chargeable estate (per Chapter 11)                  | x     |
| Less: Quick succession relief (QSR)                        | (x)   |
|                                                            | $X_A$ |

Estate rate (ER) = $(X_A$ /chargeable estate$) \times 100$

Less: Double tax relief (DTR)

   Lower of:

     (i) Foreign tax suffered

     (ii) ER × foreign property value in estate      (x)

UK inheritance tax payable      $X_B$

**Allocation of UK IHT payable:**

IHT payable by Beneficiary who receives foreign assets

ER × Value of foreign asset      $X_1$

IHT Payable By Beneficiary who receives the GWR

ER × Value of GWR      $X_2$

IHT Payable By Trustees on the Settled Property

ER × Value of Settled Property      $X_3$

IHT Payable By Executors on the Net Free Estate

ER × Net free estate value (i.e. $X_B - X_1 - X_2 - X_3$)      $X_4$

     $X_B$

KAPLAN PUBLISHING

## 3 Allowable deductions in the death estate computation

### Funeral expenses

The costs of the individual's funeral are allowable providing they are reasonable, even though the cost is incurred after the date of death.

### Costs of administering the estate

The cost of administering the estate is not allowable as it is for professional services carried out after the death.

### Other allowable deductions

Debts are deductible if they:

- were outstanding at the date of death, and

- had been incurred for valuable consideration, or were imposed by law.

This will include all outstanding taxes such as income tax and CGT, although not the IHT due on death itself.

If a debt is secured against specific property it is deducted from the value of that property. This will be the case with a repayment mortgage secured against freehold property.

Note that endowment mortgages are not deducted from the value of the property as the endowment element of the policy should cover the repayment of the mortgage.

### Exempt legacies and reliefs

The only exempt legacies allowable in the death estate are:

- gifts to the spouse or civil partner
- gifts to a charity
- gifts to a qualifying political party.

BPR and APR are available to reduce the value of an individual's death estate. The detail of these exemptions and reliefs have been covered in Chapter 12.

## Test your understanding 1

Tom dies on 30 June 2009 and leaves the following assets:

|  | £ |
| --- | --- |
| House | 200,000 |
| Cottage | 250,000 |
| Unincorporated business | 400,000 |
| Bank account | 75,000 |
| Quoted shares in a trading company | 100,000 |
| Car | 15,000 |

At the date of Tom's death he owes £2,000 on his credit card, and owes £3,000 of income tax and CGT. Tom has owned the business for 20 years.

In Tom's will he leaves

- the business, the house and shares to his wife
- the cottage to his son
- the residue to his daughter.

Tom made a lifetime gift of £115,000 in cash to his son in August 2006.

**Compute the IHT payable on Tom's death.**

## 4 Special valuation rules in the death estate computation

The value of assets brought into an individual's estate computation is normally the **open market value (OMV)** of the asset at the date of death (known as the probate value).

However, there are special rules that apply to the valuation of some assets. This section covers the rules which are frequently examined.

## Quoted shares and securities

As covered in Chapters 8 and 12, the values of quoted shares and securities are usually computed as follows:

Value = Lower of:

(1) 'Quarter Up'
= lower price + ¼ × (higher price – lower price).

(2) Average of the highest and lowest recorded bargains.

The range of prices quoted is usually the 'cum dividend' and 'cum interest' values.

In the examination, always assume shares and securities are quoted 'cum-dividend' and 'cum-interest' unless the question states otherwise.

## Quoted ex-dividend or ex-interest

The capital value of shares and securities quoted ex-dividend or ex-interest is calculated as follows:

| | Shares quoted ex-dividend | Securities quoted ex-interest |
|---|---|---|
| Value using 'lower of' rule | X | X |
| Plus next dividend payment (amount received) | X | |
| Plus next interest payment (amount received) | | X |
| Capital value to include in the estate | X | X |

### Meaning of terminology

### Quoted cum-dividend or cum-interest

When shares in a quoted company are quoted 'cum-dividend' this means that:

- if the shares are sold, they are sold 'with the right to the next dividend payment'

- the shareholder buying the shares will therefore receive the next dividend payment.

Similarly, if securities are quoted 'cum-interest', the person buying the securities will receive the next interest payment.

### Quoted ex-dividend or ex-interest

When shares in a quoted company are quoted 'ex-dividend' this means:

- if the shares are sold in this period, they are sold 'without the right to the next dividend payment'

- the shareholder owning the shares on the date they went 'ex-dividend' will receive the next dividend payment.

Similarly, if securities are quoted 'ex-interest', the owners of the securities on the date they went 'ex-interest' will receive the next interest payment.

Therefore, if an individual dies when shares and securities are quoted 'ex-dividend' or 'ex-interest', that individual's estate will be entitled to the next dividend or interest payment which, in practice, is usually received a few weeks later.

### Test your understanding 2

Jeremy owns £100,000 of 10% debentures in XY plc on the day he died. £100 of the bonds were quoted at £94 – 98 ex-interest. Interest is paid on the bonds every six months on 30 June and 31 December.

(a) **Calculate the value to include in Jeremy's estate in respect of the debentures.**

(b) **Calculate the value to include in Jeremy's estate assuming the securities were Treasury Stock, not company debentures.**

### Unquoted shares and securities

The value of unquoted shares and securities to be used has to be agreed with the HMRC's Share Valuation Division.

In an examination question, the value of unquoted shares and securities to be used is given in the question.

## Unit trusts

Unit trusts are valued at the lowest bid price (not the 1/4 up rule).

## Land and freehold property situated in the UK

When land and property is owned by two or more individuals, they own the property as either 'joint tenants' or 'tenants in common' which means:

|  | **Joint Tenants** | **Tenants in Common** |
|---|---|---|
| On the death of a tenant their share is inherited | • automatically by the other tenant(s) | • in accordance with the terms of their will, or<br>• in accordance with the rules of intestacy. |

The valuation of the UK land and property to be included in the estate computation is the appropriate proportion of the whole for joint tenants. Usually this is one half of the whole as there are normally two joint tenants.

For tenants in common it is 10% lower.

### Example 1 – Special valuation rules in the death estate

A brother and a sister jointly own a property as tenants in common worth £500,000.

**Calculate the value of the brother and sister's share in the property for IHT purposes if they were to consider making a transfer of their share in the property.**

**Solution**

The value of half the property would be on a 'stand-alone' basis. This is the OMV of the half share of the property on the open market which is unlikely to be 50% of the whole value.

However, who would buy half a house?

The Capital Taxes Division of HMRC accepts that a 'tenanted deduction' of 5% to 15% is appropriate for IHT valuation purposes.

**For exam purposes, always assume a deduction of 10%.**

| | £ |
|---|---:|
| Half the value of the property (£500,000 × ½) | 250,000 |
| Less 10% deduction | (25,000) |
| | ——— |
| Value of the half share for IHT purposes | 225,000 |
| | ——— |

### Foreign assets

Overseas assets are valued at OMV on the same basis as assets situated in the UK.

However, note that:

- where the value is provided in foreign currency it is converted into sterling at the exchange rate in force at the date of death which gives the lowest sterling valuation

- when valuing a foreign property to include in a death estate, additional expenses incurred in
  - administration relating to the overseas property or
  - expenses relating to the sale of the overseas property

  may be deducted from the open market value of the property

  - up to a maximum of 5% of the market value of the property

- if IHT is payable and overseas tax has been paid, double tax relief (DTR) may be due (see section 9 in this chapter).

### Life assurance policies

The IHT valuation of a life assurance policy (LAP) is as follows:

| Terms of the policy | Value to include in the estate |
|---|---|
| LAP taken out on one's own life | Actual proceeds received by the estate |
| LAP written specifically for the benefit of a named beneficiary (e.g. the spouse and/or children) under a declaration of trust | Excluded from the estate |

Note that:

- OMV is not necessarily the same as the surrender value.

- For a death in service policy (i.e. an insurance policy taken out by an employer on the life of an employee), in the event that the employee dies, the insurance company will pay out a lump sum to the beneficiaries of the estate. This lump sum forms part of the deceased's death estate.

## Related property

The related property rules covered in Chapter 12 also apply to valuation of an individual's death estate.

Remember that:

- in the examination, the most common related property is **property owned by the donor's spouse**

- property of a similar kind owned by the donor's children or other family members is **not** related property.

## 5 Settled property

The beneficiary of an interest in possession (IIP) trust is known as the 'life tenant' of the trust.

The life tenant is entitled to an interest in the assets of the trust which is usually the right to the income generated by the assets in the trust fund.

For IHT purposes, the life tenant of certain IIP trusts is deemed to own the underlying assets in the trust fund.

For these types of IIP trusts, HMRC require the trust to pay an IHT liability on the death of the life tenant which is calculated as follows:

- The value of the trust fund is included in the individual life tenant's estate computation on death (this is known as 'settled property')

- The IHT on the whole estate is calculated and then the average rate of tax on the estate is calculated

- The trustees pay the IHT relating to the value of the trust fund

- The IHT is payable out of the trust assets.

On the death of the life tenant, the trust fund is usually wound up and the capital assets are distributed to the final beneficiary named in the trust deed, known as the 'remainderman' of the trust.

The remainderman therefore suffers the tax charge levied on the trust following the death of the life tenant.

This treatment applies to the following IIP trusts:

- 'Old' IIP trusts set up before 22 March 2006, and

- 'New' immediate post death interest (IPDI) trusts.

The detailed rules concerning the different types of trusts and the appropriate treatment for IHT purposes are given in Chapter 14.

## 6 Comprehensive example

The following example involves a death estate computation using the special valuation rules.

### Test your understanding 4

Wilma died in a car crash on 4 October 2009.

Under the terms of her will, the estate was left as follows:

- £120,000 to her husband
- £50,000 to charity
- the residue of the estate to her son Joe.

At the date of her death, Wilma owned the following assets.

(i)   Her main residence valued at £243,000.

(ii)  A flat in London valued at £150,000. An endowment mortgage of £70,000 was secured on this property.

(iii) Four shops valued at £50,000 each. Wilma's husband Fred owns two adjacent shops valued at £60,000 each. The combined value of all six shops is £370,000.

(iv)  A villa situated overseas worth $200,000. The exchange rate on 4 October 2009 was $10 to £1.

(v)   A half share of partnership assets which are valued at £400,000 in total. The partnership trades in the UK.

(vi)  20,000 shares in ZAM plc. The shares were quoted at 198p – 206p, with bargains of 196p, 199p and 208p.

(vii) 8,000 units in the CBA unit trust, valued at 130p – 136p.

(viii) Bank balances of £57,850.

Wilma is also the life tenant of an IIP trust set up in 1990. The value of the trust fund on 4 October 2009 was £260,000.

Wilma's outstanding income tax liability was £7,500, and her funeral expenses amounted to £2,000. She had made no lifetime gifts.

(a) **Calculate the IHT that will be payable as a result of Wilma's death.**

(b) **Show who will pay and who will suffer the IHT liability and how the free estate is distributed between the beneficiaries.**

## 7 Reliefs available against the IHT liability on the death estate

There are two tax credit reliefs that **reduce the IHT liability on the death estate** as follows:

|  | £ |
|---|---|
| IHT on chargeable estate | x |
| Less: **Quick succession relief (QSR)** | (x) |
| **Double tax relief (DTR)** | (x) |
|  | |
| UK inheritance tax payable | x |

## 8 Quick Succession Relief

Quick succession relief (QSR) applies where an individual dies and **within the previous five years** they had:

- **inherited an asset** on someone else's death, and IHT was charged on the inheritance, or
- **received a lifetime gift,** and IHT was charged on the gift.

The most common situation is where two members of a family die within a five year period, the first person to die having made a bequest to the second person.

QSR is a **tax credit** against the IHT liability of an estate on the death of the individual receiving the asset.

The amount of QSR where two deaths occur within a five year period is calculated as follows:

QSR = (IHT on first death) × (Appropriate percentage)

The appropriate percentages are as follows:

| Years between the two deaths | | Appropriate percentage |
| More than | Not more than | used in formula above |
| --- | --- | --- |
| 0 | 1 | 100% |
| 1 | 2 | 80% |
| 2 | 3 | 60% |
| 3 | 4 | 40% |
| 4 | 5 | 20% |

The IHT paid on the first death is either given in the question or can be calculated as follows:

$$\frac{\text{Total IHT paid on first death estate}}{\text{Gross chargeable estate value of first death}} \times \text{Value of asset gifted out of the first estate}$$

The following points should be noted.

- **The appropriate percentages are not given in the examination.** However, note that:
  - the closer the two deaths, the greater the percentage
  - each additional year between the gifts reduces the percentage by 20%.

- It is not necessary for the individual who received the asset to still own the property they received on date of their death. Although the same asset is not subject to a double charge to IHT in this case, the relief is still available. This is because the second person's estate will have a higher value following the gift to him whether the original property is retained, exchanged for other property or is converted into cash.

- QSR is given **before** DTR.

### Test your understanding 5

Daisy died on 31 July 2009 leaving an estate of £340,000. She had made no lifetime gifts.

In June 2005, Daisy had been left £28,000 from her brother's estate. Inheritance tax of £75,000 was paid on a total chargeable estate of £450,000 as a consequence of her brother's death.

**Calculate the IHT payable on Daisy's death.**

## 9 Double taxation relief

Double taxation relief (DTR) applies where an asset situated overseas is subject to both UK IHT and tax overseas.

DTR is a **tax credit** against the IHT liability of an estate on the death of the individual which is deducted **after** QSR.

DTR is calculated as follows:

> Lower of:
>
> * the overseas tax suffered (given in the examination), and
> * the UK IHT payable on the overseas asset.

The UK IHT payable on the overseas asset is calculated at the average rate of IHT payable on the gross chargeable estate after QSR as follows:

$$\frac{\text{IHT on the estate after QSR}}{\text{Gross chargeable estate value}} \times \text{Value of asset in estate}$$

The value of the overseas asset brought into the estate is the value after deducting any additional expenses incurred in realising or managing the property (which may be subject to a maximum of 5%).

### Example 2 – QSR and DTR

Peter died on 15 August 2009 leaving an estate valued at £375,000. The estate which included property situated overseas valued at £60,000. Overseas IHT of £18,000 was paid on this property.

The estate also included a 4% interest in quoted shares that Peter inherited on the death of his mother on 10 November 2005. The shares were the total holding of shares held by his mother on her death. At the time of her death the shares were worth £50,000, and on Peter's death they were worth £115,000. IHT of £80,000 was paid on a total estate of £400,000 on his mothers death.

Peter had made no lifetime gifts and he left his entire estate to his son.

**Calculate the IHT payable as a result of Peter's death.**

## Solution

| **15 August 2009** | £ |
|---|---|
| Gross chargeable estate value | 375,000 |
| NRB available | (325,000) |
| | |
| Taxable amount | 50,000 |

| | £ |
|---|---|
| IHT due on death (£50,000 × 40%) | 20,000 |
| Less QSR (W1) | (4,000) |
| | |
| | 16,000 |
| Less DTR (W2) | (2,560) |
| | |
| IHT payable on Peter's estate | 13,440 |

## Workings

### (W1) QSR

QSR = (£80,000/£400,000) × £50,000 x 40% (Note) = £4,000

**Note:** The appropriate percentage is 40% as there are between 3 - 4 years from the legacy and Peter's death.

The current value of the quoted shares is irrelevant to the calculation of quick succession relief QSR.

### (W2) DTR

The rate of IHT on the estate after QSR is 4.267% (£16,000/£375,000 × 100). DTR is therefore the lower of:

| (i) | Overseas tax suffered | £18,000 |
|---|---|---|
| (ii) | UK IHT payable (£60,000 × 4.267%) | £2,560 |

### Test your understanding 6

George died on 15 February 2010, leaving the following free estate.

A farm in Utopia rented out to tenant farmers        £45,000
Other assets after liabilities valued at        £303,250

The farm was left to his brother and the residue was left to his only son.

Additional costs of administering the Utopian farm were £3,500 and Utopian death duties payable amounted to £6,000.

George had made no lifetime transfers.

**Compute the inheritance tax payable, showing clearly the amount payable by George's brother.**

## 10 Payment of IHT

### Normal dates of payment

IHT is payable as follows:

| Transfer | Due Date |
|---|---|
| CLTs between 6 April and 30 September | 30 April in the following year |
| CLTs between 1 October and 5 April | 6 months after the end of the month in which the transfer is made |
| PETs chargeable as a result of death | 6 months after the end of the month of death |
| Additional tax due on CLTs within 7 years before the death | 6 months after the end of the month of death |
| Estate at death | On delivery of the estate accounts to HMRC (unless tax is being paid in instalments, see below). Interest runs from 6 months after the end of the month of death. |

## Responsibility for payment

The tax on a lifetime gift can be paid by the donor or the donee but any additional tax arising on a lifetime gift because the donor dies within 7 years always falls on the donee.

The tax on death is initially paid by the executors. Where there is foreign property, it is then apportioned between the UK and overseas element of the estate.

The tax relating to the overseas property (after DTR) is recovered from the person inheriting the asset.

The remainder of the tax relating to the UK assets is paid from the estate, and so is effectively borne by the person who inherits the residue of the assets after the specific legacies have been paid (known as the residual legatee).

## Payment in instalments

IHT on certain assets can be paid in 10 equal annual instalments, starting on the normal due date for payment.

The tax must arise on any of the following:

* estate at death
* lifetime gifts made within 7 years before the death
* lifetime gifts where the donee has agreed to pay the tax arising.

The assets to which the instalment basis applies are:

* land wherever situated
* shares or securities in a company where the transferor controlled the company immediately before the transfer
* shares or securities in an unquoted company where the tax arises on death, and the amount of tax payable on all instalment assets is at least 20% of the total tax payable on the estate
* shares of an unquoted company with a value in excess of £20,000, which represent 10% or more of the nominal value of the company's shares
* a business or an interest in a business.

The asset must still be owned by the donee, and if it is sold the whole of the outstanding instalments become payable immediately.

## 11 Comprehensive example

The following example involves a comprehensive death estate computation using the special valuation rules and reliefs.

### Test your understanding 7

You have been asked by the chairman of your company for advice on the inheritance tax position on the death of his father. The following information is available:

The chairman's father died on 1 March 2010, and his estate comprised of the following:

(i)   Freehold house and land valued for probate at £630,000. This property was owned jointly by the deceased and his wife (who survived him) as joint tenants.

(ii)  Overseas property with a sterling equivalent of £30,000, left to his daughter. Additional costs of administering the property were £1,800 and death duties payable overseas amounted to £6,500.

(iii) A property situated in Cornwall valued at £340,000.

(iv)  £10,000 8% Corporate bonds valued at 82 – 86p. Interest is payable half yearly on 30 June and 31 December.

(v)   £8,000 6% Treasury stock valued at 72 – 74p ex interest. Interest is payable half yearly on 31 March and 30 September.

(vi)  £10,000 ordinary shares in Able Ltd an unquoted trading company. The shares have been owned for five years. 12% of the company's net assets are investments.

(vii) Bank deposit account £60,635.

(viii)Accrued interest £2,000 (net).

(ix)  Personal chattels £10,000.

(x)   Death in service £200,000. The death in service policy is expressed to be for the benefit of the spouse.

Debts and funeral expenses amounted to £2,665.

By his will apart from leaving the overseas property to his daughter, the chairman's father bequeathed legacies of £5,000 to each of two grandchildren, a legacy of £15,000 and the personal chattels to his widow and the residue to his son, your chairman.

The chairman's father had made one lifetime gift of £139,000 cash into a discretionary trust in November 2008. The chairman's father agreed to pay any IHT, if applicable.

The chairman's father is also the life tenant of an IIP trust set up in 1982. The value of the trust fund on 1 March 2010 was £75,000.

**Prepare a statement showing the amount of inheritance tax payable on the chairman's father's estate, stating who is accountable for the payment and upon whom the burden falls.**

## 12 Legacies left on death

The terms of a person's will are very important in determining the amount of IHT payable on death.

This section summarises rules already covered in relation to exempt legacies and gifts of specific UK assets to a chargeable person, but extends the situation to cover exempt residues where special rules apply.

### Exempt legacy

Gifts to the following persons are exempt from IHT on death:

- Spouse or civil partner.
- Charity.
- Qualifying political party.

Where an exempt person is left a legacy in a will, the amount of the legacy is deducted in the calculation of the gross chargeable estate.

### Specific gift of UK assets left to a chargeable person

Where a chargeable person is left a legacy of a specific UK asset, the IHT on the legacy is borne by the residual legatee (i.e. the person who is left the residue of the estate in the will) not the specific legatee who receives the asset.

For example, if you are left £100,000 in your grandfather's will, you will receive all £100,000. The IHT payable on the gift to you is borne by the person who is left the residue of your grandfather's estate.

This will cause no problems in the calculation of IHT where the residual legatee is a chargeable person. However, where the residual legatee is an exempt person, special rules apply to calculate the IHT on the estate.

### Exempt residue

Special rules known as 'single grossing up' (SGU) are required where the terms of the deceased's will (or the rules of intestacy) leave gifts from the estate as follows:

* specific gift(s) of UK assets are left to a chargeable person(s), and
* the residue of the estate is left to an exempt person.

To find the IHT payable it is necessary to calculate what figure of chargeable assets would be needed so that after the tax was paid, the amount needed to pay the specific legacies is left.

This is then the gross chargeable estate, with the remainder then being allocated to the exempt residual legatee.

### Example 3 – Single grossing up

Edward Ager was a wealthy client of yours.

His estate value is £900,000 and he had made no lifetime gifts.

By his will he left the following gifts.

* Holiday cottage £180,000 to his son.
* Legacies of £110,000 each in cash to his two daughters.
* Legacy of £50,000 cash to charity.
* Residue to his wife.

(a) **Compute the gross chargeable estate value, the IHT payable and the amount of residue which will pass to Edward's wife.**

(b) **Calculate how your answer would differ if Edward had made gross chargeable lifetime gifts of £267,000.**

**Solution**

**(a) Estate computation**

|  | £ |
|---|---|
| Estate value | 900,000 |
| Less Exempt legacies | |
| Charity | (50,000) |
| Spouse (balancing figure) | (400,000) |
| | ———— |
| Gross chargeable estate (W) | 450,000 |
| | ———— |

| | £ |
|---|---|
| IHT liability on the estate value (W) | 50,000 |

| **Distribution of the estate** | £ |
|---|---|
| Residue to wife | 400,000 |
| Gift to charity | 50,000 |
| Cottage to son | 180,000 |
| Legacies to daughters (£110,000 × 2) | 220,000 |
| IHT on legacies to HMRC | 50,000 |
| | 900,000 |

**Working: Single grossing up**

| | £ |
|---|---|
| Specific chargeable legacies | |
| Holiday cottage to the son | 180,000 |
| Legacies to the daughters (£110,000 × 2) | 220,000 |
| Net chargeable estate | 400,000 |

| IHT liability on estate | £ |
|---|---|
| Net chargeable estate value | 400,000 |
| NRB available | (325,000) |
| Taxable amount | 75,000 |
| IHT on death (£75,000 × 40/60) | 50,000 |

| | £ |
|---|---|
| Gross chargeable estate (£400,000 + £50,000) | 450,000 |

**(b) Estate computation**

| | £ |
|---|---|
| Estate value | 900,000 |
| Less Exempt legacies | |
| Charity | (50,000) |
| Spouse (balancing figure) | (222,000) |
| Gross chargeable estate (W) | 628,000 |
| IHT liability on the estate value (W) | 228,000 |

### Distribution of the estate

|  | £ |
|---|---:|
| Residue to wife | 222,000 |
| Gift to charity | 50,000 |
| Cottage to son | 180,000 |
| Legacies to daughters | 220,000 |
| IHT on legacies to HMRC | 228,000 |
|  | ——— |
|  | 900,000 |
|  | ——— |

### Working: Single grossing up

| Specific chargeable legacies | £ |
|---|---:|
| Holiday cottage to the son | 180,000 |
| Legacies to the daughters (£110,000 × 2) | 220,000 |
|  | ——— |
| Net chargeable estate | 400,000 |
|  | ——— |

IHT liability on estate

|  | £ | £ |
|---|---:|---:|
| Net chargeable estate value |  | 400,000 |
| NRB at death | 325,000 |  |
| GCTs in 7 yrs pre-death | (267,000) |  |
| NRB available | ——— | (58,000) |
|  |  | ——— |
| Taxable amount |  | 342,000 |
|  |  | ——— |
| IHT on death (£342,000 × 40/60) |  | 228,000 |
|  |  | ——— |
| Gross chargeable estate (£400,000 + £228,000) |  | 628,000 |
|  |  | ——— |

## Example 4 – Single grossing up

Alex died on 30 September 2009 leaving an estate valued at £664,000.

Under the terms of his will Alex left £331,000 to his son Raymond and the residue of the estate to his widow. Alex had made no lifetime gifts.

(a) **Calculate the IHT payable on Alex's death.**

(b) **Show how Alex's estate will be distributed between the beneficiaries.**

(c) **Show how the situation would change if Alex's widow was left £331,000 and Raymond was left the residue of the estate.**

**Solution**

(a) **Estate computation**

|  | £ |
|---|---|
| Estate value | 664,000 |
| Less Exempt legacies | |
| Spouse (balancing figure) | (329,000) |
| Gross chargeable estate (W) | 335,000 |
| IHT liability on the estate value (W) | 4,000 |

**Working: Single grossing up**

| Specific chargeable legacies | £ |
|---|---|
| Cash to the son = Net chargeable estate | 331,000 |

| IHT liability on estate: | £ |
|---|---|
| Net chargeable estate value | 331,000 |
| NRB available | (325,000) |
| Taxable amount | 6,000 |
| IHT on death (£6,000 × 40/60) | 4,000 |

| Gross chargeable estate (£331,000 + £4,000) | 335,000 |
|---|---|

KAPLAN PUBLISHING

## (b) Distribution of the estate

|  | £ |
|---|---|
| Residue to wife | 329,000 |
| Cash to son | 331,000 |
| IHT on Raymond's legacy to HMRC | 4,000 |
|  | 664,000 |

## (c) Estate computation

|  | £ |
|---|---|
| Estate value | 664,000 |
| Less Exempt legacies |  |
| Spouse | (331,000) |
| Gross chargeable estate | 333,000 |

| IHT liability on estate | £ |
|---|---|
| Gross chargeable estate value | 333,000 |
| NRB available | (325,000) |
| Taxable amount | 8,000 |
| IHT on death (£8,000 × 40%) | 3,200 |

| Distribution of the estate | £ |
|---|---|
| Residue to wife | 331,000 |
| Cash to son (£333,000 - £3,200) | 329,800 |
| IHT on Raymond's legacy to HMRC | 3,200 |
|  | 664,000 |

### 13 Summary of death estate

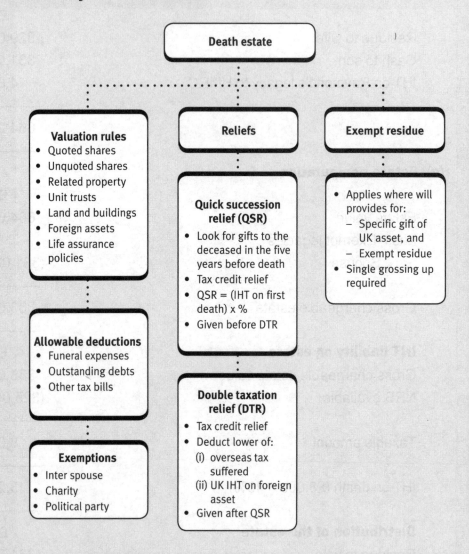

### 14 The variation of a will

There are three ways in which the terms of a will can be varied after the death of an individual.

- A deed of variation.

- A deed of disclaimer.

- Application to the courts by the family and dependants of the deceased if they feel that they have not been adequately provided for under the terms of the deceased's will.

The deed of variation is the most likely form of variation that is examinable.

## Deed of variation

It is possible to change the terms of an individual's will after they have died by entering into a deed of variation (also known as a deed of family arrangement).

In practice, the main reason for entering into a deed of variation is often to redistribute the deceased's estate on a fairer basis. However, a deed of variation can also be used as an effective tax planning tool.

Changes can be made to make the provisions of a will more tax efficient in the following situations.

(i) Where an estate has been left to children who already have sufficient property of their own.

(ii) Part of the estate could be diverted to grandchildren, thus missing out a generation and therefore bypassing a potential charge to IHT on the death of the children.

A parallel election can be made for CGT purposes.

However, the revised terms of a will under a deed of variation will only be effective for tax purposes provided the following conditions are satisfied.

The deed must:

* be in writing and signed by all beneficiaries that are affected by the deed
* not be made for any consideration
* be executed within two years of death
* state that it is intended to be effective for tax (IHT and/or CGT) purposes.

## 15 Lifetime giving versus gifting assets on death

When advising a client of the advantages and disadvantages of lifetime giving versus gifting assets on death in a will, consideration should be given to the relationship between IHT and CGT as follows:

| | CGT | IHT |
|---|---|---|
| Lifetime gift | • no CGT if asset is an exempt asset<br><br>• chargeable gain/ allowable loss arises<br><br>• calculated in normal way using **MV of the asset gifted** as consideration (see below)<br><br>• gift relief may be available<br>  – applies to gifts of business assets, and<br>  – gifts of any asset where there is an immediate charge to IHT (i.e. a CLT)<br><br>• on the subsequent disposal of the asset by the donee, IHT relief may be available (see below) | • no exempt assets for IHT<br><br>• **diminution in value concept** applies to value the gift (see below)<br><br>• if CLT – IHT payable during lifetime<br><br>• if PET – no tax payable during lifetime but IHT payable if death within 7 years<br><br>• valued at time of gift<br><br>• exemptions available on lifetime gifts<br>  – BPR/APR lifetime and death<br><br>• taper relief available if live for more than three years after the gift |
| Gift on death | • no CGT to pay on death | • asset forms part of death estate<br><br>• IHT payable on the market value of the asset at the date of death unless the asset is<br>  – covered by reliefs (e.g. BPR/APR)<br>  – or is left to an exempt beneficiary (e.g. spouse, charity)<br><br>• no other exemptions available on death estate<br><br>• taper relief not available |

## Starting point for calculations

It is important to appreciate that for lifetime gifts, the starting point for the computation of IHT and CGT is different.

- For IHT purposes, lifetime transfers are valued according to the **diminution in value** concept (i.e. the amount by which the donor's estate has diminished as a result of the gift) and the 'related property' rules must be taken into account.
- For CGT purposes, the value of a lifetime transfer (i.e. a gift) is the value of the asset actually gifted. The concept of 'related property' does not apply to CGT.

### Example 5 – Lifetime giving versus gifting assets on death

Eddy owns 100,000 shares (a 10% holding) in WXY Ltd. Eddy's wife owns 50,000 shares in WXY Ltd.

On 31 July 2009 he made a lifetime gift of 50,000 shares in WXY Ltd to his daughter.

The relevant values of WXY Ltd's shares at the time of the gift are as follows:

|       | £  |
|-------|----|
| 5%    | 8  |
| 10%   | 10 |
| 15%   | 13 |

(a) **Calculate the transfer of value for IHT purposes.**

(b) **Calculate the deemed sale proceeds for CGT purposes.**

**Solution**

(a) The transfer of value for IHT purposes will be calculated using the related property valuation rules as follows:

|  | £ |
|---|---|
| Value of shares held before the transfer (based on a 15% holding) 100,000 × £13.00 | 1,300,000 |
| Value of shares held after the transfer (based on a 10% holding) 50,000 × £10.00 | (500,000) |
| Transfer of value | 800,000 |

(b) For CGT purposes, a gift of a 5% shareholding has been made.

The deemed consideration is therefore £400,000 (50,000 × £8).

## Interaction of CGT and IHT

Where an asset is gifted to another individual during the donor's lifetime both IHT and CGT need to be considered.

Where both:

- gift relief is claimed on the gift, and
- IHT is paid in relation to the gift

any IHT paid is allowed as a deduction when calculating the chargeable gain arising on the subsequent disposal of the asset by the donee.

### Example 6 – Lifetime versus gifting assets on death

On 31 December 2007 Yaz made a gift of business property (not in relation to the disposal of the entire business) worth £341,000 to her daughter Jo. Yaz and Jo made a joint gift relief claim to hold over the capital gain of £103,000 arising on the gift.

Assume that the business property did not qualify for BPR and that the IHT annual exemptions have already been used.

Yaz died on 30 April 2009 having made no other lifetime transfers except those to use her annual exemption each year.

Jo sold the business property for £368,000 on 31 August 2009. Jo makes no other disposals in 2009/10.

**Calculate the CGT liability that will arise upon Jo's disposal of the business property on 31 August 2009.**

**Solution**

When calculating her CGT liability, Jo will be able to deduct the IHT payable as a result of the PET becoming chargeable. It is therefore necessary to compute the IHT payable on the PET first.

**IHT payable – during lifetime**

| 31 December 2007 – PET | £ |
|---|---|
| Transfer of value | 341,000 |
| Less: BPR (not applicable per question) | (Nil) |
| Less: AE (not available per question) | (Nil) |
| Gross chargeable amount | 341,000 |
| Lifetime IHT due (PET) | Nil |

**IHT payable – on death**

| | £ |
|---|---|
| Gross chargeable amount (above) | 341,000 |
| NRB available | (325,000) |
| Taxable amount | 16,000 |
| IHT due on death (£16,000 × 40%) | 6,400 |
| Less Taper relief (31.12.2007 to 30.4.2009) (< 3 years before death) | (Nil) |
| Less IHT paid in lifetime (PET) | (Nil) |
| IHT payable on death | 6,400 |

---

### CGT liability – Disposal of asset gifted – 31 August 2009

|  | £ | £ |
|---|---:|---:|
| Sale proceeds |  | 368,000 |
| Base cost of asset to Jo: |  |  |
| MV at date of gift | 341,000 |  |
| Less Gain held over | (103,000) |  |
|  |  | (238,000) |
|  |  | 130,000 |
| Less: IHT paid on PET |  | (6,400) |
| Chargeable gain |  | 123,600 |
| Less: Annual exemption |  | (10,100) |
| Taxable gain |  | 113,500 |
| CGT payable by Jo (£113,500 × 18%) |  | 20,430 |

---

## 16 IHT planning

It is important for an individual to plan their lifetime gifts to be tax efficient and to make a will so that their estate is distributed in a tax efficient way.

There are a number of tax planning measures that can reduce an individual's liability to IHT which can be divided into three areas:

- lifetime tax planning
- death estate planning
- husband and wife planning (and civil partners).

The overall objectives of all IHT tax planning measures are:

- to minimise the amount of tax payable
- to maximise the inheritance of the next generation.

## Lifetime tax planning

IHT planning during an individual's lifetime involves making gifts of wealth as early as possible.

In doing so, an individual should ensure that:

- they maximise the use of their exemptions available against lifetime gifts that are not available against the death estate.

For example, they should maximise the use of the

- – annual exemption of £3,000 each year
- – small gifts exemption of up to £250 per donee per tax year
- – 'normal expenditure out of income' exemption
- – wedding gifts exemption on the marriage of relatives
- they make lifetime gifts to other individuals even if they are not covered by exemptions as:
  - – lifetime gifts to other individuals are PETs
  - – they reduce the value of the individual's estate on death
  - – the gift is completely exempt if the donor dies more than seven years after the gift, and
  - – even if the donor dies within seven years, the IHT payable on the lifetime gift is lower than if the asset had been gifted in the estate because:
    - – the value of the PET is calculated and frozen at the time of the gift
    - – the chargeable amount on death is reduced by fall in value relief if the value has declined since the date of the gift
    - – the annual exemption and other exemptions are available against PETs, but not the death estate
    - – taper relief is available if the donor lives more than three years after the gift
- they carefully choose the assets that are gifted.

  This is because it is better to gift assets which are expected to increase in value due to the value of a gift being fixed at the time the gift is made.

  However, in addition, the implications of CGT must also be considered (see section 15).

An individual should therefore be advised to make lifetime gifts of assets that are:

– appreciating in value, and

– will not generate a significant liability to CGT.

For example, gift assets that are exempt from CGT or assets that are deferred or exempted by available CGT reliefs.

Note however that there is no IHT saving in gifting assets that qualify for BPR or APR at 100%.

## Estate planning

An individual should be advised to draft a tax efficient will ensuring that they:

* fully utilise the NRB, and
* do not incur unnecessary charges to IHT on death.

Rather than leaving property directly to children, it may be more advantageous to miss out a generation and to leave the property to grandchildren instead.

There will be no immediate saving of IHT, but a charge to IHT on the death of the children will be avoided.

Such planning is particularly relevant if the children already have sufficient property in their own right.

The income tax benefits of this arrangement may also be attractive:

* If a parent sets up a source of income for a child, the parent is assessed on the income generated unless the amount is below the de minimis threshold of £100.
* However, if the grandparents set up the source of income, the income is assessed on the child regardless of the amount.

## Husband and wife

### Transfer of unused nil rate band

Any amount of nil rate band that has not been utilised at the time of a persons death can be transferred to their spouse or civil partner:

* provided the second death occurs after 5 October 2007
* it does not matter when the first death took place.

As a result, each spouse or civil partner can now leave the whole of their estate to the surviving spouse or civil partner with no adverse IHT consequences.

- The surviving spouse or civil partner will have the benefit of
  - their own nil rate band, **and**
  - any unused amount of their spouses or civil partners nil rate band.

- The executors of the surviving spouse or civil partner must claim the transferred nil rate band in force on submission of the IHT return
  - within 2 years of the second death.

## Husband and wife tax planning

The advice that could be given to couples (i.e. husband and wife or civil partnerships) is given as follows:

- Where the couple own assets that qualify for BPR and/or APR these assets should not be left to the other spouse or civil partner.

  This is because the legacy would be covered by the inter-spouse exemption and the benefit of BPR/APR would be wasted.

- Therefore BPR and APR assets should be left to non exempt beneficiaries and other assets left to the spouse or civil partner.

  As a result, the benefit of both the relief and inter-spouse exemption will be available to reduce the value of the chargeable estate.

### Example 7 – Husband and wife planning

Joan is 67 years old, and was widowed on the death of her husband six months ago.

The husband had a chargeable estate valued at £800,000, and this was left entirely to Joan, he had made no lifetime transfer.

Joan now has an estate valued at £800,000, which will pass to her two children when she dies. Joan's children are both quite wealthy, and are concerned about the IHT liability that will arise upon Joan's death. Joan had made no lifetime transfers.

Joan has six grandchildren.

**You are to advise Joan and her children of tax planning measures that they could take in order to minimise the impact of IHT.**

### Solution

### Husband's death

On Joan's Husbands death the transfer to Joan is an exempt transfer, no IHT is due on his estate.

### Joan – Death estate

|  | £ |
|---|---|
| Gross chargeable estate | 800,000 |
| Less NRB | (325,000) |
| Less NRB transferred from her husband | (325,000) |
|  |  |
| Taxable amount | 150,000 |
|  |  |
|  |  |
| IHT payable on death (£150,000 × 40%) | 60,000 |

This will be suffered by Joan's children.

- The executors must claim on submission of the IHT return the NRB transferred from Joan's husband within 2 years from her death.

- Since Joan's children are already wealthy, it may be more beneficial for Joan to leave her estate to her grandchildren (via use of a trust). Although this will not save IHT on Joan's death estate, by skipping a generation, IHT on the same wealth will not be due until transfers are made by the grandchildren.

- If Joan dies without considering the above, her children could alter Joan's will by a deed of variation within 2 years from Joan's death.

- Joan should also consider making lifetime gifts to her grandchildren to utilise her annual exemptions and to benefit from the advantages of making PETs

KAPLAN PUBLISHING

## 17 Associated operations

Where there are **two or more transactions which affect the same property** and as a result tax is avoided, special rules may apply.

### Associated operations

Two examples of associated operations are where:

- An asset is transferred piecemeal, so that the total value of the individual transactions is less than the value of the whole asset.

- A person transfers part of an asset which, although of little value, significantly reduces the value of the remainder. The remainder is then transferred at a reduced value thus allowing an asset to be given away at less than its full value.

Where tax is avoided by making a series of transactions and the associated operations rule is applied:

- the associated operations are treated as one transaction, and

- any resulting transfer of value is treated as being made at the time of the last associated operation.

However, note that the rules are not always applied:

- It is much more likely that the associated operations rule will be applied where transactions are with a connected person.

- The longer the length of time between the various transactions, the easier it will be to defend against an allegation of associated transactions.

- It may be possible to argue that there was no intention of making further transactions at the time of the first transaction.

**Situations where the rules will not apply**

The associated operations rules will specifically not apply in respect of:

- leases, where there is more than three years between the grant of a commercial lease and the subsequent transfer of the freehold

- transfers between spouses or civil partners, where property is transferred in order to utilise the AE or the ME provided the donee spouse acts from his or her own choice in making a gift.

For example, where a son or daughter is to get married, both spouses may want to make use of the £5,000 ME. If the husband has no capital, and the wife makes a gift to him of £5,000 in order to make the gift to the son or daughter, then this will not normally be treated as an associated operation.

## 18 Chapter summary

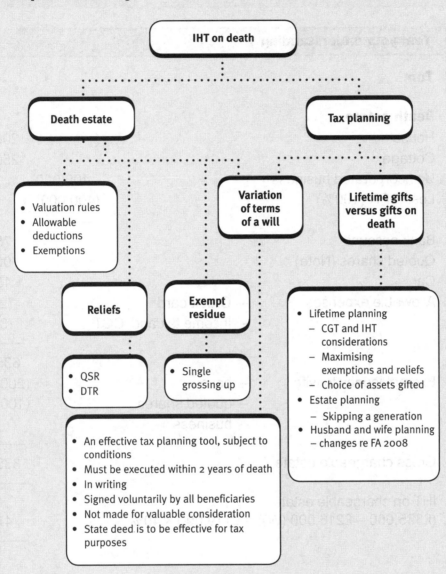

**IHT on death**

**Death estate**

**Tax planning**

- Valuation rules
- Allowable deductions
- Exemptions

**Variation of terms of a will**

**Lifetime gifts versus gifts on death**

**Reliefs**

**Exempt residue**

- QSR
- DTR

- Single grossing up

- Lifetime planning
  - CGT and IHT considerations
  - Maximising exemptions and reliefs
  - Choice of assets gifted
- Estate planning
  - Skipping a generation
- Husband and wife planning
  - changes re FA 2008

- An effective tax planning tool, subject to conditions
- Must be executed within 2 years of death
- In writing
- Signed voluntarily by all beneficiaries
- Not made for valuable consideration
- State deed is to be effective for tax purposes

## Test your understanding answers

### Test your understanding 1

**Tom**

| Death estate | | £ | £ |
|---|---|---:|---:|
| House | | | 200,000 |
| Cottage | | | 250,000 |
| Unincorporated business | | 400,000 | |
| Less BPR (100%) | | (400,000) | |
| | | ———— | Nil |
| Bank account | | | 75,000 |
| Quoted shares (Note) | | | 100,000 |
| Car | | | 15,000 |
| Allowable expenses | – Credit card | | (2,000) |
| | – Income tax and CGT | | (3,000) |
| | | | ———— |
| | | | 635,000 |
| Exempt legacy to wife | – house | | (200,000) |
| | – quoted shares | | (100,000) |
| | – business | | (Nil) |
| | | | ———— |
| Gross chargeable estate | | | 335,000 |
| | | | ———— |
| IHT on chargeable estate | | | |
| (£335,000 – £216,000 (W)) = £119,000 × 40% | | | 47,600 |
| | | | ———— |

**Note:** The quoted shares do not qualify for BPR as it is assumed that Tom does not have a controlling interest in the company.

Always assume that the individual does not have a controlling interest unless the question states otherwise.

| **Working: Lifetime gift to son** | £ |
|---|---:|
| Transfer of value | 115,000 |
| AE – 2006/07 | (3,000) |
| 2005/06 b/f | (3,000) |
| | ———— |
| PET | 109,000 |
| | ———— |

Remaining nil band = (£325,000 – £109,000) = £216,000

## Test your understanding 2

**Jeremy**

(a) **Company debentures**

Capital value = ¼ up method = 94 + (98 – 94) × ¼

= £95 per £100 of debentures

Value of £100,000 debentures:

| | £ |
|---|---|
| £100,000 × 95/100 | 95,000 |
| Add Next **net** interest payment | |
| £100,000 × **6 /12** × 10% × 80% (Note) | 4,000 |
| | ——— |
| Capital value | 99,000 |
| | ——— |

**Note:** 20% income tax is deducted from debenture interest paid to individuals

(b) **Treasury stock**

Value of £100,000 government stock

| | £ |
|---|---|
| £100,000 × 95/100 | 95,000 |
| Add Next **gross** interest payment | |
| £100,000 × 6/12 × 10% (Note) | 5,000 |
| | ——— |
| Capital value | 100,000 |
| | ——— |

**Note:** Government stock interest is received gross

## Test your understanding 3

**Jimmy Harcourt**

Value of 5,000 units = (5,000 × £1.25) = £6,250.

### Test your understanding 4

#### Wilma

|  | £ | £ |
|---|---|---|
| Partnership share (£400,000/2) | 200,000 | |
| Less: BPR | (200,000) | |
|  | ——— | Nil |
| Shares in ZAM plc (20,000 @ 200p) (Note 1) | | 40,000 |
| Units in CBA trust (8,000 @ 130p) | | 10,400 |
| Bank balances | | 57,850 |
| Main residence | | 243,000 |
| Flat (Note 2) | | 150,000 |
| Shops (Note 3) | | 231,250 |
| Villa ($200,000/10) | | 20,000 |
|  | | ——— |
|  | | 752,500 |
| Less: Income tax due | (7,500) | |
| Funeral expenses | (2,000) | |
|  | ——— | (9,500) |
|  | | ——— |
|  | | 743,000 |
| Less: Exempt legacies | | |
| Husband | (120,000) | |
| Charity | (50,000) | |
|  | ——— | (170,000) |
|  | | ——— |
| Net free estate | | 573,000 |
| Settled property | | 260,000 |
|  | | ——— |
| Gross chargeable estate | | 833,000 |
|  | | ——— |

#### IHT liability on the estate value

|  | £ | £ |
|---|---|---|
| Gross chargeable estate | | 833,000 |
| NRB at death | 325,000 | |
| GCTs in 7 yrs pre-death (4.10.02 to 4.10.09) | (Nil) | |
| NRB available | ——— | (325,000) |
|  | | ——— |
| Taxable amount | | 508,000 |
|  | | ——— |
| IHT due on Wilma's death (£508,000 × 40%) | | 203,200 |
|  | | ——— |

### Allocation of the IHT liability on the estate

Average rate of IHT on estate: (£203,200/£833,000) × 100 = 24.394%

| | £ | Paid by: | Suffered by: |
|---|---|---|---|
| Foreign villa (£20,000 × 24.394%) | 4,879 | Executors | Joe (specific legatee) |
| Settled property (£260,000 × 24.394%) | 63,424 | Trustees | Remainderman of trust |
| Free UK estate (£553,000 × 24.394%) | 134,897 | Executors | Joe (residual legatee) |
| | 203,200 | | |

The trustees will pay the trust IHT out of the trust assets.

### Distribution of the net free estate

| | £ |
|---|---|
| Wilma's husband | 120,000 |
| Charity | 50,000 |
| Joe (residual legatee) (Note 4) | 633,224 |
| HMRC (£4,879 + £134,897) | 139,776 |
| | |
| Free estate (£743,000 + £200,000 BPR) | 943,000 |

### Notes:

(1) The shares in ZAM plc are valued at the lower of:

   (i) Quarter up method = 198 + 1/4 (206 − 198) = 200p

   (ii) Average of highest and lowest marked bargains
= ½ × (196 + 208) = 202p

(2) Since the endowment mortgage would have been repaid upon Wilma's death, it is not deducted from the value of the flat.

(3) The shops are valued using the related property rules as follows:

$$\frac{£200,000 \ (£50,000 \times 4)}{£200,000 + £120,000 \ (£60,000 \times 2)} \times £370,000 = £231,250$$

(4) Residual legacy

Joe will receive the residue of the free estate calculated as follows:

|  | £ |
|---|---|
| Value of estate (before BPR and specific legacies) | 943,000 |
| Less: Legacies to husband and charity | (170,000) |
| IHT to HMRC re free UK estate and foreign free estate (as Joe is the specific legatee of the overseas asset) (£4,879 + 134,897 ) | (139,776) |
| Residue of estate | 633,224 |

### Test your understanding 5

**Daisy**

| **31 July 2009** | £ |
|---|---|
| Gross chargeable estate value | 340,000 |
| NRB available | (325,000) |
| Taxable amount | 15,000 |
| IHT on death (£15,000 × 40%) | 6,000 |
| Less QSR (W) | (933) |
| IHT payable on Daisy's estate | 5,067 |

**Working**

QSR = (£75,000/£450,000) × 28,000 × 20% (Note) = £933

**Note:** June 2005 to July 2009 = 4 years

## Test your understanding 6

**George**

### Estate computation

|  | £ |
|---|---|
| Farm in Utopia (Note below) | 45,000 |
| Less Administration expenses (restrict to 5%) | (2,250) |
|  | 42,750 |
| Other assets less liabilities | 303,250 |
| Gross chargeable estate | 346,000 |

### IHT liability on the estate value

|  | £ |
|---|---|
| Gross chargeable estate value | 346,000 |
| NRB available | (325,000) |
| Taxable amount | 21,000 |

|  | £ |
|---|---|
| IHT on death (£21,000 × 40%) | 8,400 |
| Less QSR | (Nil) |
| IHT payable **after** QSR | 8,400 |
| (Estate rate = (£8,400/£346,000) × 100 = 2.428%) |  |
| Less DTR (W) | (1,038) |
| IHT payable on George's estate | 7,362 |

### Allocation of the IHT liability on the estate

| IHT on: | £ | £ | Suffered by: |
|---|---|---|---|
| Foreign property | 1,038 |  |  |
| Less DTR | (1,038) |  |  |
|  |  | Nil | G's brother |
| Other net assets (£303,250 × 2.428%) |  | 7,362 | G's son |
|  |  | 7,362 |  |

## Working: DTR

DTR is the lower of:

| | | |
|---|---|---|
| (a) | Overseas death duties suffered | £6,000 |
| (b) | UK IHT attributable to overseas property<br>(2.428% × £42,750) | £1,038 |

### Note:

- APR is not available because the land is not situated in the EEA, the Channel Islands or the Isle of Man.

- BPR is also not available because the farm is a tenanted farm, which is an investment asset.

## Test your understanding 7

### The chairman's father

**Gross chargeable estate computation**

| | £ | £ |
|---|---:|---:|
| Freehold house | 315,000 | |
| Less: Spouse exemption | (315,000) | |
| | ——— | Nil |
| Overseas property | 30,000 | |
| Less: Administration expenses | | |
| restricted to (5% × £30,000) | (1,500) | |
| | ——— | 28,500 |
| Property in Cornwall | | 340,000 |
| Corporate Bonds | | |
| [10,000 × (82 + ¼ × (86 − 82))] | | 8,300 |
| Treasury stock | | |
| [72 + ¼ × (74 − 72)] × 8,000 | 5,800 | |
| Plus interest (6% × £8,000 × 0.5) | 240 | |
| | ——— | 6,040 |
| Shares in Able Ltd | 10,000 | |
| Less: BPR (100% × £10,000 × 88%) | (8,800) | |
| | ——— | 1,200 |
| Bank account (including accrued interest) | | 62,635 |
| Chattels | | 10,000 |
| Death in service | | 200,000 |
| Less: Funeral expenses | | (2,665) |
| | | ——— |
| | | 654,010 |
| Less: Specific spouse legacies | | |
| Chattels | | (10,000) |
| Cash | | (15,000) |
| Death in service policy | | (200,000) |
| | | ——— |
| Net free estate | | 429,010 |
| Settled property | | 75,000 |
| | | ——— |
| Gross chargeable estate | | 504,010 |

## IHT liability on the estate

|  | £ |
|---|---:|
| Gross chargeable estate value | 504,010 |
| NRB available (W) | (192,000) |
| Taxable amount | 312,010 |

### Working: NRB available

|  | £ |
|---|---:|
| NRB | 325,000 |
| Less: Lifetime CLT in previous 7 years (£139,000 – £3,000 (2008/09) – £3,000 (2007/08) | (133,000) |
| NRB available | 192,000 |

|  | £ |
|---|---:|
| IHT on gross chargeable estate (£312,010 × 40%) | 124,804 |
| Less QSR | (Nil) |
| IHT after QSR | 124,804 |

Estate rate = (£124,804/£504,010) × 100 = 24.762%

Less: DTR
Lower of:

|  |  |  |
|---|---:|---:|
| (1) Foreign tax suffered | 6,500 |  |
| (2) UK IHT on foreign asset (£28,500 × 24.762%) | 7,057 | (6,500) |
| IHT payable on estate |  | 118,304 |

## Allocation of the IHT liability on the estate

| IHT on: | £ | £ | Suffered by |
|---|---:|---:|---|
| Foreign property | 7,057 |  |  |
| Less DTR | (6,500) |  |  |
|  |  | 557 | Daughter |
| Other net assets (£400,510 × 24.762%) |  | 99,175 | Son |
| On Settled Property (£75,000 × 24.762%) |  | 18,572 | Remainderman of the trust |
|  |  | 118,304 |  |

# The taxation of trusts

## Chapter learning objectives

Upon completion of this chapter you will be able to:

- understand the nature of a trust and how it operates

- explain the main types of trust in existence and how they can be recognised

- understand in outline how income tax, capital gains tax and inheritance tax apply to transactions involving trusts

- explain the tax implications of creating a trust now or in the future

- outline the tax implications of property passing to a beneficiary

- explain the inheritance tax consequences of a settlor dying after creating a trust

- explain how trusts can be used in tax and financial planning.

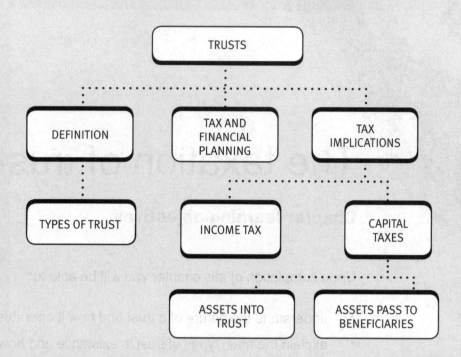

## 1 Introduction

The Finance Act 2006 introduced fundamental changes to the inheritance tax regime relating to trusts. These changes also have an effect on the capital gains tax implications arising when transfers are made into and out of trusts.

Due to the increased complexity of the taxation of trusts, the examiner has summarised the requirements in relation to trusts for the P6 syllabus and has excluded from the syllabus the following areas:

*   The calculation of income tax, capital gains tax and inheritance tax payable **by the trustees** of a trust.

*   The rules concerning trusts for the disabled, trusts for bereaved minors, transitional serial interest trusts and age 18 to 25 trusts.

This chapter therefore just concentrates on the knowledge required by the P6 examiner.

## 2 The nature of a trust

A trust is an arrangement where:

*   property (known as the trust assets or settled property)

*   is transferred by a person (known as the settlor) to the trustees

- to be held for the benefit of one or more specified persons (known as the beneficiaries)

- on specified terms in the trust deed.

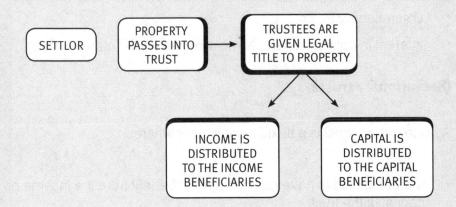

 A trust (sometimes referred to as a settlement) can be created:

- during the settlor's lifetime, or

- on death under the provisions of the settlor's will, or

- following an individual's death under a deed of variation.

The trust deed sets out the trustee's powers and duties.

## The financial planning benefits of a trust arrangement

Trusts are useful arrangements as they allow a settlor to give away the benefit arising from the ownership of property to the beneficiaries of the trust, whilst retaining some control over the property as a trustee.

The trustees are the legal owners of the property.

Separating the beneficial and legal ownership of assets provides financial planning benefits in setting up a trust which include the ability to:

- provide an income from the assets for one group of beneficiaries while preserving and protecting the capital for others

- provide a means for an older generation to protect and make financial provisions for the next generation, particularly where there are young children involved or it is thought that a recipient is financially imprudent

- transfer the benefits of owning property to minors while leaving the control over the assets, together with the responsibilities of managing and maintaining them, with the trustees.

### 3 Types of trust

There are two main types of trust examinable at P6:

- Discretionary trusts, and
- Interest in possession trusts (also known as life interest trusts).

### Discretionary trusts

A discretionary trust is a flexible settlement where

- the beneficiaries have no legal right to benefit from the income or capital of the trust
- any distribution of income or capital out of the trust is at the complete discretion of the trustees.

The trustee can determine how to meet the needs of the beneficiaries as and when they arise.

In a typical discretionary trust the trustees may have power to decide:

- whether or not trust income is to be accumulated or distributed
- how the trust income and the capital of the trust is to be shared between different beneficiaries

### Interest in possession trusts

An interest in possession (IIP trust) exists where:

- a beneficiary has an interest in the assets of the trust.

An interest in possession can be the legal right:

- to receive income generated by the trust assets, and/or
- to use a trust asset or live in a property owned by the trust.

The beneficiary who receives the right to income or use of an asset under an interest in possession is known as the 'life tenant' of the trust. The life tenant is said to have a 'life interest' in the trust.

The beneficiary who receives the capital assets in the trust when the life interest comes to an end at some future date is known as the remainderman.

The remainderman is said to have a 'reversionary interest' in the trust assets as the assets will only revert to them when the trust comes to an end.

IIP trusts are commonly used in a will where one spouse dies and there is a surviving spouse and children. The surviving spouse is usually named as the life tenant and is entitled to the income generated by the assets, but does not have access to the actual capital assets. The children are usually the remaindermen and will receive the capital assets on the death of the surviving spouse.

This form of trust is a popular arrangement to protect the capital assets for the benefit of the children where, for example, the spouse remarries. The capital will eventually be transferred to the children of the first marriage and not to the new spouse and their family.

## Summary

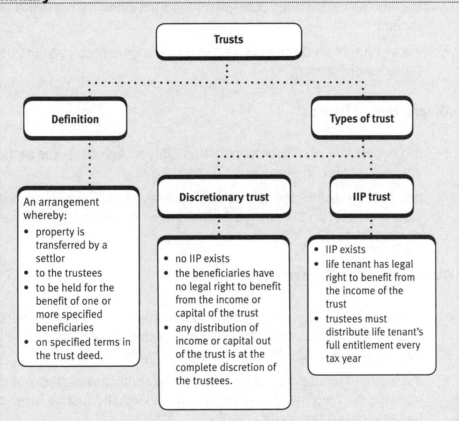

## 4 Income tax and trusts

The trust is a separate legal entity for income tax purposes. The body of trustees is a separate taxable person.

The trustees are subject to income tax on the income arising in respect of trust assets each tax year and distribute income to the beneficiaries.

An understanding of the way in which trust income is taxed is required, however, the calculation of IT payable by the trustees is not examinable.

The taxation of the trust income operates as follows:

- the trustees account for income tax on the receipt of income by the trust each tax year under self assessment
- trustees are taxed at different rates depending on the type of trust
- trustees distribute income to the beneficiaries according to the terms of the trust

## Interest in possession trusts:

- the life tenant of an IIP trust must be distributed his full entitlement to income (i.e. his distributable share) each tax year
- the life tenant is assessed in the tax year of entitlement (i.e. the same tax year as the trustees account for the trust income), not in the year of receipt
- the income of an IIP trust is received by the beneficiary net of 20% tax (10% for dividends)

## Discretionary trusts:

- the beneficiary of a discretionary trust only receives income at the discretion of the trustees
- any income distributed from a discretionary trust is assessed in the tax year of receipt and is always deemed to be received by the beneficiary net of 40% tax

## Taxation of beneficiaries:

- the beneficiaries are taxed on the gross trust income in their personal income tax computations and they can deduct from their income tax liability the tax credit deducted at source by the trustees
- the trustees must give the beneficiaries a certificate each tax year showing the amount of trust income the individual must be taxed on, and the associated tax credit.
- trustees of a discretionary trust can choose to give income generated from the assets to the beneficiaries who are non-taxpayers so that a repayment of income tax paid by the trustees can be claimed.

## 5 The Capital taxes and trusts

The P6 syllabus requires an understanding of the CGT and IHT consequences of:

- a settlor gifting assets **into** a trust, and
- trustees gifting assets **out of** a trust.

Whilst the assets are in the trust, further charges to capital taxes arise as:

- the trustees are subject to CGT on the gains arising in respect of managing the trust assets each tax year at 18%, after deducting an annual exemption of £5,050 (i.e. half the normal annual exemption is available to a trust), and
- they may also be liable to pay IHT in respect of the property held in the trust every ten years (known as the principal charge).

The P6 syllabus requires knowledge of these charges to tax, however, the calculation of CGT and IHT payable by the trustees is not examinable.

### The changes introduced in Finance Act 2006

The Finance Act 2006 introduced fundamental changes to the inheritance tax regime relating to trusts with effect from 22 March 2006 and created new types of trust for IHT purposes.

These changes also have an affect on the capital gains tax implications arising when transfers are made into and out of trusts.

It is therefore necessary to be aware of two sets of rules to understand the IHT and CGT implications of trusts. Consideration of the implications of trusts created both before and after 22 March 2006 is required.

### Trusts created before 22 March 2006 ('Old trusts')

Pre 22 March 2006, there were three types of trusts with different IHT consequences:

- Interest in possession (IIP) trusts
- Discretionary trusts (DT)
- Accumulation and maintenance (A&M) trusts

The definition of IIP trusts and DTs was as defined in section 3.

An A&M trust was a special type of discretionary trust set up for the benefit of young children under the age of 25. These trusts had several conditions to satisfy but the advantage in setting up such a trust was that it was exempt from some charges to IHT.

## Trusts created on or after 22 March 2006 ('New trusts')

With effect from 22 March 2006, there are several types of trusts with different IHT consequences. However, the only trusts examinable at P6 are:

- Immediate post death interest (IPDI) trusts
- Relevant property trusts (RPTs).

An IPDI trust is a special type of IIP trust which can only be created on the death of the settlor.

For the purposes of P6, RPTs are defined as all other new trusts created on or after 22 March 2006.

## Gifts into a trust

A trust can be created:

- during the settlor's lifetime by means of a lifetime gift, and
- on death under the provisions of the settlor's will or under a deed of variation.

The capital tax consequences of a gift into a trust depends on the type of trust as summarised in the following tables.

### Gifts into trusts created before 22 March 2006

The capital tax consequence of a gift into an 'old trust' are as follows:

| Gifts into trust: | IHT | CGT |
|---|---|---|
| **During settlor's lifetime:** | | |
| • **'Old' IIP and A&M trusts** | • PET by settlor | • Not examinable |
| • **'Old' DTs** | • CLT by settlor | • Not examinable |
| **On settlor's death:** | | |
| • **All 'old' trusts** | • Assets form part of the settlor's estate | • Not examinable |
| | • IHT payable on the estate | |
| | • Trust is established after the estate IHT has been paid (i.e. out of post-tax assets) (see note below) | |

**Note:** The IHT payable on an estate is the same whether an individual puts their estate into a trust on death or leaves the estate directly to another individual.

### Gifts into trusts created on or after 22 March 2006

The capital tax consequences of a gift into an 'new trust' are as follows:

| Gifts into trust: | IHT | CGT |
|---|---|---|
| **During settlor's lifetime:** <br><br> • **IPDI trust** | • Not applicable – can only be created on death | |
| • **All other trusts (RPTs)** | • CLT by settlor | • Chargeable disposal of asset at full MV <br><br> • Gift relief available on any asset as there is an immediate charge to IHT <br><br> • Trustees acquire asset at base cost = MV less gift relief |
| **On settlor's death:** <br><br> • **All 'new' trusts** | • Assets form part of the settlor's estate <br><br> • As above for all "old " trusts (see note below) | • No CGT consequences on death <br><br> • Not a chargeable disposal <br><br> • No CGT payable <br><br> • Trustees acquire assets at probate value |

**Note:** The IHT payable on an estate is the same whether an individual puts their estate into an old or new trust on death or leaves the estate directly to another individual.

### Example 1 – The capital taxes and trusts

Toppy died on 19 May 2009 leaving a widower and two children. She had made no lifetime gifts and her estate on death is valued at £422,000.

Under the terms of her will, she requested that a discretionary trust be set up for her children with £325,000 of her estate. The remainder is to go to her husband.

**Calculate the IHT and CGT arising on Toppy's death and show how the estate is to be distributed between the beneficiaries.**

KAPLAN PUBLISHING

## Solution

### Capital gains tax

- There is no CGT to pay on death.

- Any chargeable assets going into the trust have a base cost equal to the probate value.

### Inheritance tax

### Toppy: Estate computation

|  | £ |
|---|---|
| Estate value | 422,000 |
| Less Exempt legacies – Spouse | (97,000) |
|  |  |
| Gross chargeable estate | 325,000 |
|  |  |

This is covered by the NRB available.

| IHT on death | Nil |
|---|---|

### Distribution of the estate

|  | £ |
|---|---|
| Residue to husband | 97,000 |
| Cash to trust | 325,000 |
| IHT to HMRC re-creation of trust | Nil |
|  |  |
|  | 422,000 |

**Note:** Use of discretionary trusts is advantageous if:

- The individual wants to control/divert who the ultimate beneficiary of the trust will be, rather than leave the decision to the surviving spouse

- The assets on the first death are likely to increase in value at a faster rate than the nil rate band. The growth of the assets will be in the trust fund and not be included in the surviving spouse or civil partner's estate

### Gifts out of a discretionary trust

Where a gift of assets is made out of a trust to a beneficiary, the gift is known as a 'capital distribution' and the property passes to the beneficiary 'absolutely' (i.e. the legal title of the property passes to the beneficiary).

The capital tax consequences of making capital distributions out of a trust to the beneficiaries depends on the type of trust as summarised in the following tables.

### Gifts out of trusts created before 22 March 2006

The capital tax consequences of a gift out of an 'old trust' are as follows:

| Gifts out of: | IHT | CGT |
|---|---|---|
| **'Old' IIP trust**<br><br>• **On the death of the life tenant** | • Assets form part of the life tenant's estate = Settled Property<br><br>• IHT payable by the trustees from trust assets | • Not examinable |
| • **On any other occasion** | • PET by life tenant | • Not examinable |
| **'Old' DT** | • Exit charge applies<br><br>• Trustees pay up to a maximum of 6% tax (calculation of liability is not examinable) | • Not examinable |

## Gifts out of trusts created on or after 22 March 2006

The capital tax consequences of a gift out of a 'new trust' are as follows:

| Gifts out of: | IHT | CGT |
|---|---|---|
| **'New' IPDI trust** | | |
| • **On the death of the life tenant** | • Assets form part of the life tenant's estate = Settled Property<br><br>• IHT payable by the trustees from trust assets | • No CGT payable on death<br><br>• Tax free uplift of assets to PV<br><br>• Beneficiary receives assets at their MV on date of the life tenant's death |
| • **On any other occasion** | • if distribution is to another individual = PET by life tenant<br><br>• Exception: if property passes to the life tenant = No IHT<br><br>• Otherwise = CLT by life tenant | • Chargeable disposal of asset at full MV<br><br>• Gift relief available:<br>  – on qualifying assets only (if a PET or exempt from IHT)<br>  – on any asset (if a CLT)<br><br>• Beneficiary acquires asset at base cost = MV less gift relief |
| **All other trusts (RPTs)** | • Exit charge applies<br><br>• Trustees pay up to a maximum of 6% tax (calculation of liability is not examinable) | • Chargeable disposal of asset at full MV<br><br>• Gift relief available on any asset as there is an immediate charge to IHT<br><br>• Beneficiary acquires asset at base cost = MV less gift relief |

## Further charges to the capital taxes

Whilst the assets are in the trust, the trustees are subject to CGT on the gains arising in respect of managing the trust assets each tax year.

Trustees may also be liable to a principal charge which is levied on the following trusts every ten-years following the creation of the trust:

Is there a Principal charge?

**'Old' trusts:**

- **IIP trust**  X
- **DT**  √

**'New' trusts:**

- **IPDI trust**  X
- **RPT**  √

The maximum rate of IHT payable on the principal charge is 6%.

The calculation of the CGT payable and the IHT principal charge payable by the trustees is not examinable.

### Example 2 – Discretionary trust

Windy Miller, a wealthy farmer and landowner has decided to set up a discretionary trust for the benefit of various family members.

- On 6 May 2009 Windy put 50,000 shares in Windmill plc and £400,000 cash into the trust. He originally bought the shares for £20,000 on 1 May 1999. On 6 May 2009 the shares have a market value of £50,000.

  Windy has not made any previous lifetime gifts.

- On 30 November 2012, the trustees distributed the shares to Windy's grandson absolutely. Assume the market value of the shares at that date will be £90,000.

(a) **Explain an advantage for Windy of setting up a discretionary trust during his lifetime.**

(b) **Explain the capital tax consequences resulting from the creation of the discretionary trust on 6 May 2009.**

(c) **Explain the tax consequences arising during the life of the trust.**

(d) **Explain the capital tax consequences of distributing the property out of the trust to Windy's grandson absolutely on 30 November 2012.**

(e) **Explain the capital tax consequences of creating the trust and the distribution to the grandson assuming the discretionary trust had been set up on Windy's death in December 2010, rather than a lifetime gift.**

## Solution

(a) **Advantages of setting up a discretionary trust during lifetime**

Assets placed in the trust can appreciate in value outside of both Windy's and grandson's estates.

If the grandson is a non-taxpayer, a repayment of income tax paid by the trustees may be available.

(b) **Capital tax consequences of the creation of the trust**

**Inheritance tax**

–   Lifetime gift into a RPT = a CLT by Windy Miller
–   Lifetime IHT payable
–   Payable by Windy or trustees by agreement
–   If Windy dies within 7 years: Additional IHT payable on death
–   Death IHT payable by trustees from trust assets

**Capital gains tax**

–   Chargeable disposal of asset at full MV
–   Gift relief available on any asset as there is an immediate charge to IHT
–   Therefore no CGT payable when the assets are put into trust, the gain is held over against the base cost of the shares acquired by the trustees.

| **2009/10** | £ |
|---|---:|
| MV of shares put into trust (May 2009) | 50,000 |
| Cost (May 1999) | (20,000) |
| | |
| Capital gain before reliefs | 30,000 |
| Less: Gift relief | (30,000) |
| | |
| Chargeable gain | Nil |

| **Base Cost of the shares to the Trustees** | £ |
|---|---:|
| MV of shares put into trust (May 2009) | 50,000 |
| Less: Gain held over | (30,000) |
| | |
| Base Cost | 20,000 |

(c) **Tax consequences during the life of the trust**

**Income tax**

The trustees will be subject to income tax on the income received from the trust assets.

The trustees account for income tax each tax year under self assessment.

**Inheritance tax**

IHT at a maximum rate of 6% will be charged every ten years based on the value of the assets in trust on the principal charge date.

The first principal charge will be on 6 May 2019.

**Capital gains tax**

The trustees will manage the trust fund. They will buy and sell capital assets to maintain and grow the fund on behalf of the beneficiaries.

The sale of trust assets will give rise to capital gains which will be subject to CGT.

The trustees account for CGT each tax year under self assessment.

(d) **Capital tax consequences of the distribution to the grandson**

**Inheritance tax**

– An exit charge arises

– Trustees pay a maximum of 6% of the value of the capital distribution

**Capital gains tax**

– Chargeable disposal of asset at full MV

– Gift relief available on any asset as there is an immediate charge to IHT

– Therefore no CGT payable when the assets are distributed out of the trust, the gain is held over against the base cost of the shares acquired by the grandson

| 2012/13 | £ |
|---|---|
| MV of shares (Nov 2012) | 90,000 |
| Less: Base Cost of shares | (20,000) |
| | |
| Capital gain before reliefs | 70,000 |
| Less: Gift relief | (70,000) |
| | |
| Chargeable gain | Nil |

**Base Cost of shares acquired by the grandson**

| | £ |
|---|---|
| MV of shares (Nov 2012) | 90,000 |
| Less: Gain heldover | (70,000) |
| | |
| Base Cost | 20,000 |

(e) **If the discretionary trust is created on Windy's death**

**Capital tax consequences of the creation of the trust**

- Inheritance tax
  - Assets form part of Windy's estate
  - Trust is established after the estate IHT has been paid (i.e. out of post-tax assets)

- Capital gains tax
  - No CGT consequences on death
  - Not a chargeable disposal, no CGT payable
  - Trustees acquire assets at probate value

**Capital tax consequences of the distribution to the grandson**

The same consequences as in part (d).

## 6 Tax planning opportunities

The following tax planning opportunities arise from creating a trust:

- By gifting assets into a trust during the individual's lifetime, the assets will no longer form part of the settlor's estate on death.

- Assets which appreciate in value can be transferred into the trust and will increase in value outside of both the settlor's and the beneficiaries estates.

- The exit charges and principal charges levied on some trusts are a maximum of 6% which may not be significant in the context of the financial planning requirements of the individual settlor.

- Trustees of a discretionary trust can choose to give income generated from the assets to the beneficiaries who are non-taxpayers so that a repayment of income tax paid by the trustees can be claimed.

# 7 Chapter summary

```
                        ┌─────────────────────────┐
                        │  The taxation of trusts  │
                        └─────────────────────────┘
             ┌───────────────────────┴───────────────────────┐
      ┌──────────────┐                              ┌──────────────┐
      │  Income tax  │                              │ Capital taxes │
      └──────────────┘                              └──────────────┘
```

**Income tax**

- Trustees account for IT on income generated by trust assets each tax year under self-assessment
- Beneficiary receives income net of tax:
  - IIP trust income: 20%/10% tax
  - DT income: 40% tax
- Include gross income in IT computation
- Deduct tax credit shown on certificate issued to beneficiary by trustees

**Rules different for trusts created before and after 22 March 2006**

```
┌──────────────┐   ┌──────────────┐   ┌──────────────┐
│  Gifts into  │   │ While assets │   │  Gifts out   │
│    trust     │   │  in trust    │   │  of trust    │
└──────────────┘   └──────────────┘   └──────────────┘
```

**While assets in trust**

- CGT
  = on capital disposals by trustees @ 18% (AE = £5,050 p.a.)
- IHT
  = on some trusts every ten years after the creation of the trust (max 6%)

**Gifts into trust**

- **During lifetime**
  **IHT**
  = PET by settlor
     (Old IIP and A&M trusts)
  = CLT by settlor
     (Old DTs and new RPTs)
  **CGT**
  = Chargeable disposal at MV, gift relief available (RPTs)
  = Not applicable (IPDI trusts)
  = Not examinable
     (Old trusts)
- **On settlor's death**
  **IHT** (all trusts)
  = Assets taxed in estate, Trust set up out of post tax assets
  **CGT** (all trusts)
  = No CGT on death

**Gifts out of trust**

- **Old IIP and IPDI trusts**
  **IHT**
  If due to death of life tenant
  = Settled property in life tenant's estate
  If distribution during life tenant's lifetime and is to an individual = PET by life tenant
  On any other occasion = CLT by life tenant
  **CGT**
  If due to death of life tenant
  = No CGT payable
  If distribution during life tenant's lifetime
  = Chargeable disposal at MV, gift relief maybe available
- **Old DTs and RPTs**
  **IHT**
  = Exit charge applies (max 6%)
  **CGT**
  = No CGT payable if death of life tenant
  = Chargeable disposal at MV, gift relief always available

# Personal financial management

## Chapter learning objectives

Upon completion of this chapter you will be able to:

- describe the principles underlying personal financial management

- compare and contrast the tax treatment of different investment products

- describe and contrast the different forms of finance that may be available to an individual

- calculate the receipts from a transaction, after tax, and compare the results of alternative scenarios and advise on the most efficient course of action.

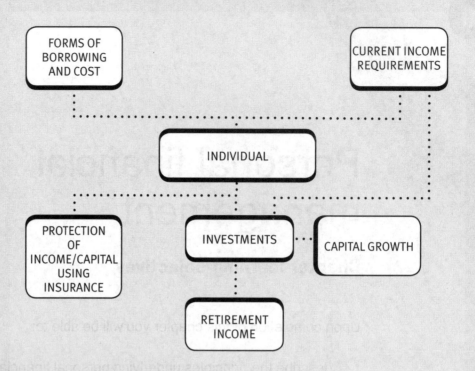

## 1 Personal financial management

The requirements of an individual when considering investments will change during their lifetime, partly as their lifestyle changes but also as their income increases.

When considering investments the main factors that need to be considered are usually:

- what income is available to invest after meeting the current outgoings from their existing income?

- does the taxpayer want to own their own home, and if so how should the purchase be financed?

- where the individual is responsible for children will they need money to fund school fees or university education, and how soon will this be needed?

- are they responsible for supporting their parents now or at some time in the future?

- ensuring there is sufficient income to fund their lifestyle after they have retired from employment or self-employment

- building a portfolio of investments that they may wish the children to inherit after death

- ensuring some investments are readily realisable if there is an unforeseen immediate need for cash e.g a cash ISA

- if it is likely that they will inherit assets from family members at some time in the future, which could be used to fund asset purchases or living expenses during their retirement

- what is the individual's attitude to risk and ethical investment?

These considerations mean that in most cases it will be necessary to balance the requirement for income on an on-going basis, and investing for capital growth to be used to fund retirement.

An important issue is the tax treatment of any income or growth.

As a general rule:

- income will be liable to income tax.
    - however, some income is exempt, or
    - is taxed at source, meaning there is only a further liability for the higher rate taxpayer

- capital growth will be liable to CGT.
    - the annual exemption is a very important factor when deciding what the overall tax charge will be.
    - some investments attract an exemption from CGT.

However, the taxpayer must not allow the tax treatment to cloud their judgement on the nature of the investments they make.

Individuals should also consider:

- the potential risks involved. For example, this could include a market crash affecting equities, property market reversals and future changes in interest rates.

- the timing of the investment. For example, a younger person should not tie up all their money in a pension fund if some of the money will be needed in the near future, as the pension cannot be accessed until the individual is 55.

## 2 Investments

### Investment to generate income

An individual with low income will look to their investments to generate income. This will be the case for many pensioners.

The main examples of investments generating income are:

| Investment | Income |
|---|---|
| Bank and building society accounts | Interest |
| Shares/unit trusts, investment trusts, OEIC's | Dividends |
| Gilts | Interest |
| Corporate Bonds | Interest |
| Government Stock | Interest |
| Pensioners guaranteed income bonds | Interest |
| Investment property | Rent |

In some cases the income generated is exempt from tax (see Chapter 3). These investments are particularly attractive to higher rate taxpayers.

### Investment to generate capital growth

Some investments are more suitable when considering capital growth.

These would include:

- Unit trusts, investment trusts, Open ended investment companies (OEIC's) and shares where the profits are retained to generate growth instead of being distributed.

- Investment property.

- Capital Bonds.

### Choosing the investment

Some types of investment appear under both headings above, for example property. Many people invest in property for capital growth. However, some income is needed to cover the outgoings such as interest on borrowings and the cost of utilities.

For individuals who do not feel confident in their ability to choose the right properties to purchase, or who may wish to invest in a larger development the introduction of the Real estate investment trust (REIT) allows them to buy into property with whatever resources they have available.

Equities (i.e. shares) can be viewed as an income source or a capital investment. Companies will operate different dividend policies and the investor will need to consider these when deciding which shares to acquire.

There are some investment products that attract special tax relief. For example up to £7,200 may be invested each year in an Individual Savings Account (ISA), (£10,200 for those aged 50 and over). Income and gains are then exempt.

Some shares in Enterprise Investment Schemes (EIS) and Venture Capital Trusts (VCT) are exempt from CGT on disposal.

Not everyone will feel able to assess which investments are most suitable. In this case they may invest through a stockbroker or investment trust, relying on the fund manager to decide which investments should be made.

Many funds specialise in certain areas allowing the investor some element of choice. For example, specialising in property companies, overseas companies or technology companies.

Although the stockbroker or fund manager will charge a fee for their services the investor is being given the benefit of their investment expertise.

## Tax efficient investments

There are a number of investments that give tax advantages.

The main ones to consider are:

- Personal pension contributions – Chapter 4.
- Enterprise Investment Scheme – Chapters 3 and 9.
- Venture Capital Trusts – Chapter 3.

Note however that although both EIS and VCT investments produce a reduction in an individual's income tax charge for the year of investment, they are both considered to be a relatively high risk investment.

There are other issues that need to be considered:

- An EIS company will not normally pay a dividend. The profits are usually rolled up to give capital growth, on the assumption that the disposal of the shares will be exempt from CGT.
- EIS companies are unquoted. It may be difficult to withdraw the investment as there is no ready market for the shares.
- These companies tend to be start-up companies, which is a particularly risky area for someone who cannot afford to lose their investment.

- To retain the income tax relief and obtain the CGT exemptions available the shares have to be retained for a minimum of 3 years (EIS) and 5 years (VCT).

## Key Investment products

The situation can be summarised as follows:

| | IT free | CGT free | Risk | Liquidity | Income/ capital growth |
|---|---|---|---|---|---|
| Bank/ B Soc accounts | x | N/A | L | L1 | I |
| National Savings bank | | | | | |
| - Investment account | x | N/A | RF | L1 | I |
| - EASAs | x | N/A | RF | L1 | I |
| National savings certificates | √ | √ | RF | L2 | I |
| Premium bonds | √ | √ | RF | L1 | I |
| Children's bonus bonds | √ | √ | L | L2 | C |
| Qualifying life assurance policies | √ | √ | L | L3 | C |
| EIS scheme (Note 1) | √ | √ | VH | L3 | C |
| VCT scheme | √ | √ | H | L1 | C |
| Pension schemes (Note 2) | √ | √ | M | L3 | C |
| Qualifying Corporate Bonds | x | √ | M | L1 | C/I |
| Gilts | x | √ | L | L1 | I |
| 'Real' property | x | x | M | L3 | C/I |
| REIT | x | x | M | L1 | C/I |
| Investment trusts, unit trusts and OEICs | x | x | M | L1 | C |
| Quoted shares/ securities | x | x | M/H | L1 | C |
| Unquoted shares/ securities | x | x | VH | L3 | C/I |
| ISAs | √ | √ | L/M | L1 | C/I |

Notes:

(1) Tax relief on investment but income taxable

(2) Tax relief on payments

Key to terms:

| I | Income | H | High risk |
| C | Capital growth | VH | Very high risk |
| x | Chargeable | L1 | Immediate access |
| √ | Tax-free | L2 | Access possible but penalty |
| RF | Risk-free | L3 | Non liquid |
| L | Low risk | | |
| M | Medium risk | N/A | Not applicable |

## 3 Raising finance for the individual

There are a number of different ways to raise finance as an individual borrower. A reminder of the key methods is given in expandable text.

### Raising finance

#### Mortgages (long-term source of finance)

Mortgages are a good source of finance when interest rates are low.

If it is thought that the rates may rise it is possible to obtain a fixed rate mortgage, which provides certainty about the cost of the mortgage over the period for which the rate is fixed.

A fixed rate mortgage may at times be more expensive than an ordinary mortgage, however this may be preferable to obtain certainty of cash outflows.

Moving between providers can be expensive as lenders will often charge an early redemption penalty if the mortgage is repaid.

As property prices increase it may be possible to increase the mortgage on the property to use the funds for other purposes, such as starting a new business, buying property to let or as a holiday home.

#### Credit cards

Credit cards are an expensive source of finance, as the interest rates charged are very high. They should really only be considered for short term finance.

Many cards offer interest free periods on balance transfers and these can be used to minimise the cost of interest.

### Bank overdraft (short to medium source of finance)

The interest rate on an overdraft tends to be lower than on a credit card, so this could be a better way to borrow for short or medium term.

### Hire purchase agreements (short to medium source of finance)

This is often used as a method of purchasing household goods. Interest rates tend to be variable, and can be expensive.

## 4 Calculating the net return on an investment

It is difficult to compare the overall returns on different investments if they produce income and capital growth, as one may balance off against the other.

Where the individual needs an amount of income to meet their living expenses it is slightly easier to compare the investment return, as the net of tax return can be calculated for both a basic rate and higher rate taxpayer.

It is more difficult to predict capital growth for the different types of investments.

An elderly taxpayer may prefer a higher rate of income and lower long-term capital growth, as they have no realistic need for the value of their investments to increase during their remaining lifetime.

### Example 1 – Net return

Tim has a bank overdraft of £2,000 and pays interest at 9% but has £5,000 in a deposit account earning interest at 4.7% gross.

**Discuss the financial planning implications and suggest how Tim could increase his disposable income. Assume Tim is a basic rate tax payer.**

### Solution

- Tim is paying bank interest of £180 (9% × £2,000).

- Tim is receiving bank interest of £235 (gross) (4.7% × £5,000) but must pay income tax at 20% on the income as he is a basic rate tax payer. The net interest received is £188 (80% × £235).

- His net disposable income is £8 (£188 – £180).

- Tim should use £2,000 of the capital from his deposit account to repay his bank overdraft, thus saving him £180 of interest.

- The balance of the capital held in the deposit account should be transferred to a mini cash ISA and by shopping around he can receive a high rate of interest which is free of income tax.

- Interest received at 4.7% × £3,000 = £141.

- Tim has increased his disposal income by £133 (£141 – £8).

## Example 2 – Net return

Jeremy has inherited £50,000 from his grandmother.

He has not yet decided what he should do with this money. He is currently in full time employment, and is a higher rate taxpayer.

He is considering investing in either shares or property, as he feels this would produce both income and capital growth.

As part of his considerations he has obtained the following information:

(1) If he bought shares in X plc there would be an annual dividend payment of £1,500 (approx).

(2) Shares in Y plc could be bought. Y plc is a REIT, and it is anticipated that the return would be in the region of £1,743 per annum.

(3) He could buy a small property and let it to students. The rental would be £150 per week with estimated outgoings of £80 per week.

(4) His bank is offering an internet deposit account paying gross interest of 5%.

**Discuss the financial planning implications and consider the ways in which Jeremy's inheritance money could be invested.**

**Solution**

| X plc shares | Net return after tax: | £ |
|---|---|---|
| | Income tax (£1,500 × 100/90 × 32.5%) | 542 |
| | Less Tax credit (£1,500 × 100/90 × 10%) | (167) |
| | Income tax payable | 375 |
| | Net return (£1,500 – £375) | 1,125 |

Capital growth
– possible over a period
– subject to fluctuations of the Stock Market
Easily realisable – yes
– quoted shares can be sold on the Stock Exchange
Risk – Stock Market crash

| | | £ |
|---|---|---|
| Y plc shares | Net return after tax:
Income (£1,743 × 100/80) | 2,179 |
| | Income tax at 40% | 872 |
| | Less Tax credit (20% × £2,179) | (436) |
| | Income tax payable | 436 |
| | Net income (£1,743 – £436) | 1,307 |

Capital growth – possible over a period of time
Easily realisable – yes – quoted shares
Risk – property value crash

| | | £ |
|---|---|---|
| Property | Net return after tax:
Rent received (52 × £150) | 7,800 |
| | Costs (52 × £80) | (4,160) |
| | Net rental income | 3,640 |
| | Tax at 40% | (1,456) |
| | Net return | 2,184 |

Capital growth – yes depending on area

Easily realisable – no – dependent on property market, time to find buyer, process transactions

Risk – rent not paid but expenses still need to be met, property value crash

KAPLAN PUBLISHING

| Bank | Net return after tax: | £ |
|---|---|---|
| | Interest (£50,000 × 5%) | 2,500 |
| | Tax at 40% | (1,000) |
| | | ——— |
| | Net return | 1,500 |
| | | ——— |

Capital growth – none

Easily realisable – yes

Risk – reduction in interest rates

**Note:** Jeremy could increase his return by depositing some of the funds in an ISA, with the shares or cash then held in a tax-free environment.

## 5 Chapter summary

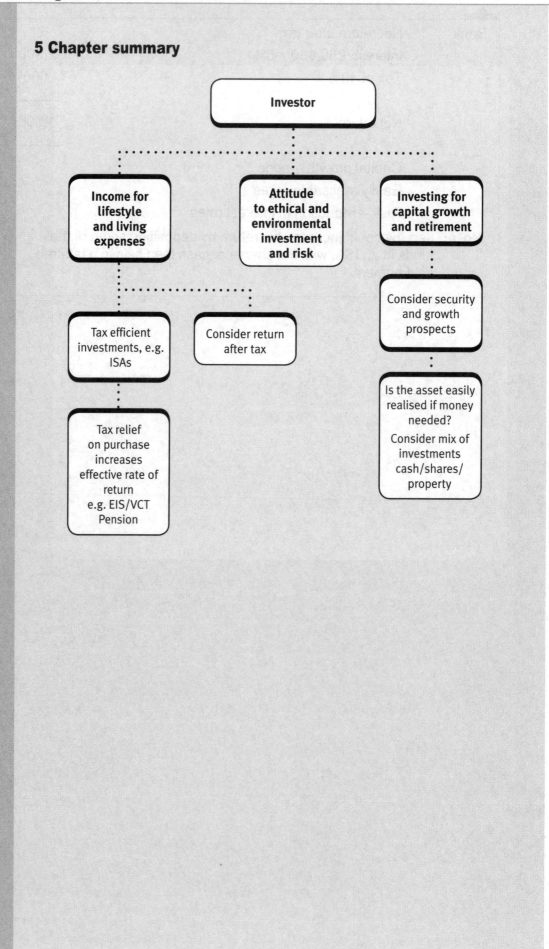

# Ethics and personal tax administration

## Chapter learning objectives

Upon completion of this chapter you will be able to:

- consider the effect of the Association's ethical guidelines when dealing with a client.

- explain the principles of self assessment for an individual including the time limits for notifying/filing returns and claims, due dates of payment and the penalties for non compliance

- list the information and records that taxpayers need to retain for tax purposes and consider the retention period

- explain the circumstances in which HM Revenue and Customs can enquire into a self assessment tax return

- describe the procedures for dealing with appeals and disputes.

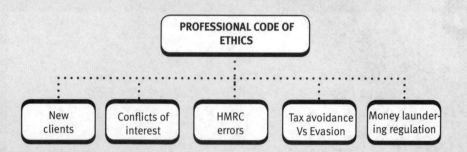

## 1 Introduction

This chapter covers the new area of ethics, which is very likely to feature in the examination as part of a longer question.

An accountant must always consider the ethical guidelines when providing advice to clients, so it is important that you learn the underlying principles and are able to apply them to a given scenario.

## 2 Professional Code of Ethics

### Overview

The ACCA Professional code of ethics was revised in 2006. It sets out the standards of professional conduct expected from the members and students of the Association, and sets a framework of principles that should be applied.

Failure to comply with this code could lead to disciplinary action.

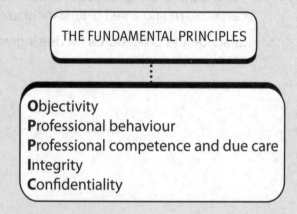

The definitions of the fundamental principles are as follows:

*   **Objectivity**
    Members should not allow a conflict of interest to affect their business decisions.

*   **Professional behaviour**
    Members must comply with relevant laws and avoid actions that may discredit the profession.

- **Professional competence and due care**
  It is important to ensure the member maintains their professional knowledge.

- **Integrity**
  Members should be straightforward and honest in all their professional and business relationships.

- **Confidentiality**
  Information is not disclosed to other parties (including HMRC) without the client's permission.

## New clients

A member is required to exercise their professional expertise when dealing with clients.

Before taking on a new client the member should consider whether:

- acting for the client will pose any risk to the practice in terms of their integrity. This would include assessing the potential client's personal and business circumstances, and attitude to disclosure and compliance with tax law

- the member and their firm have the skills and competence to service the client's requirements

- the potential client is involved in any activity that could be considered as money laundering.

In the case of a limited company, the following information should be gathered:

- Proof of incorporation and primary business address and registered office.

- The structure, directors and shareholders of the company.

- The identities of those persons instructing the firm on behalf of the company and those persons that are authorised to do so.

In the case of an individual, the following information should be gathered:

- Proof of identity and residential address

- Any unincorporated business interests and if so details of the nature and structure and those persons that are authorised to act on behalf of the business (e.g. partners in a partnership)

Once it has been decided that the member can act for the client they should:

- ask permission to contact the old advisors to request the information necessary to decide whether they can act for the client (the old advisor should seek the client's permission before they discuss their situation with the new advisor)

- if the client does not give permission to contact the old advisors the member should give serious consideration as to whether they can act for them.

Assuming the situation is satisfactory and it is decided to act for the client the member should issue a letter of engagement setting out the terms and conditions of the arrangement, and other relevant items.

### Example 1 - New clients

Where a member is asked to replace a client's existing advisors they must request the permission of the prospective client to contact the existing advisor.

**What is the reason for this communication?**

**Solution**

The main purpose of the communication is to ensure that the member:

(i) is aware of any factors that may be relevant to the decision as to whether they accept the work

(ii) is aware of any factors that may have a bearing on ensuring full disclosure of relevant items is made to HMRC

(iii) has the information with regard to filing deadline, elections and claims relating to the client so that no matters are overlooked during the period of the move to the new advisor.

### Conflicts of interest

A member should not put themselves in the position where acting for two clients creates a conflict of interest.

If they become aware of a potential conflict they should act immediately to address it. Where no appropriate action can be taken to avoid the conflict the member should cease to act in the matter where the conflict arose.

Conflicts can occur in the following situations:

- where a member acts for a client and is then asked to act for another party in a transaction

- acting for both parties in a divorce
- acting for the employer and their employees
- where the advisor may benefit from the transaction.

### Test your understanding 1

Steven has been asked to act for both parties to a transaction.

**Describe the three courses of action open to Steven.**

### Test your understanding 2

Simon is about to give some tax advice to his client. If the client acts on this advice Simon will receive commission of £2,000 from a third party.

**What action should Simon take?**

## Dealing with HMRC

It is important to ensure that information provided to HMRC is accurate and complete.

A member must not assist a client to plan or commit any offence.

If a member becomes aware that the client has committed a tax irregularity they must discuss it with the client and ensure that proper disclosure is made.

Examples would include:

- not declaring income that is taxable
- claiming reliefs to which they are not entitled
- not notifying HMRC where they have made a mistake giving rise to an underpayment of tax, or an increased repayment.

Where a client has made an error it will be necessary to decide whether it was a genuine error or a deliberate or fraudulent act.

Once an error (or similar) has been discovered the member should explain to the client the requirement to notify HMRC as soon as possible, and the implications of their not doing so.

The letter of engagement may include a section with regard to disclosure of information to HMRC, if so it would be courteous to inform the client of the intention to disclose.

Should the client refuse to make a full and prompt disclosure to HMRC the member must write and explain the potential consequences. If the client still refuses to make a full disclosure then the member should cease to act for them.

The member must then also write to HMRC informing them that they have ceased to act for the client but without disclosing the reason why.

The member must then consider their position under the Money Laundering Rules (see below).

### Employees

Where the member is an employee they may become aware of irregularities in their employer's dealings with HMRC.

They should raise their concerns with the appropriate person.

If the employer refuses to take any appropriate action the employee should seek advice from the professional body. In addition they need to consider:

*   the need to report to the employer's Money Laundering Officer
*   whether they can continue in their current employment
*   if it is necessary to disclose under the Public Interest Disclosure Act.

Where the employee is responsible for agreeing the employer's tax liabilities with HMRC they are in a similar position to members in practice.

If they discover an error, default or fraud they should bring it to the attention of the employer, and encourage them to disclose the relevant information.

### Tax avoidance or evasion

Tax avoidance is the use of legitimate means to reduce the incidence of tax. A tax advisor may properly advise or assist their clients to reduce their liability to tax. However, the courts are wary of schemes or arrangements the sole purpose of which is to avoid tax.

In recent years, the courts have taken an increasingly firm stance in finding that such schemes do not achieve their purpose.

Tax evasion is unlawful. A taxpayer who dishonestly withholds or falsifies information for tax evasion purposes may be subject to criminal proceedings or suffer civil penalties.

A tax advisor who is a party to tax evasion is subject to the sanctions of the criminal law. Concealment of material facts may constitute tax evasion.

### Test your understanding 3

When you were checking a recent tax computation from HMRC you notice that they have made an error which has resulted in your client receiving a larger repayment than should have been made.

**What actions should you take?**

### Example 2 - Employees

You have recently moved to work in the tax department of a medium sized trading company. You have been reviewing the recently submitted tax return and have identified several material errors.

You have brought this information to the head of the department but he refuses to adjust the figures as this will increase the tax payable for the year, and impact on his bonus.

**What action should you take?**

**Solution**

Taking no action is not permissible, so the following should be considered.

- Is there anyone else in the company with whom it may be appropriate to discuss these concerns?

- Consider taking advice from the ACCA or legal advice on the relevant course of action.

- Consider making a report to the company's money laundering reporting officer, if there is one and, if not, direct to the NCIS.

- Consider looking for alternative employment.

- Consider whether disclosure should be made under the Public Interest Disclosure Act. Does the employer have in place any policies with regard to disclosures under this act? Consider taking legal advice before pursuing this course of action.

The member should keep a record of all action taken to demonstrate that they have acted properly throughout.

## Money Laundering Regulations

Money Laundering is the term used for offences including benefiting from or concealing the proceeds of a crime.

An individual is engaged in money laundering if they:

(i)   conceal, disguise, transfer or remove criminal property from the UK

(ii)  enter into or become concerned in an arrangement that they know or suspect involves the acquisition of criminal property on behalf of another person

(iii) acquire or have possession of criminal property.

Criminal property includes the proceeds of tax evasion.

A member must therefore:

- arrange satisfactory evidence of a client's identity before agreeing to act for them

- ensure their staff are trained and up to date with the relevant regulations

- put in place an appropriate system for reporting suspicious transactions. This includes appointing a Money Laundering Reporting Officer (MLRO) within the firm.

The MLRO will decide whether a transaction should be reported to the National Criminal Intelligence Service (NCIS).

Where a report is made the client should not be informed as this may amount to 'tipping off', which is an offence.

A report to NCIS does not remove the requirement to disclose the information to HMRC.

## 3 Personal tax administration

### The collection of income tax

Income tax may be collected by deduction from the income at source (e.g. interest on building society deposit accounts is paid net of 20% income tax, employment income is received net of income tax under the PAYE system).

However, there are occasions which require the completion of a tax return and these include where:

- deduction at source does not satisfy a taxpayer's higher rate liability

- a taxpayer has income that is not taxed at source.

Self assessment is the system for the collection of tax which is not deducted at source.

## Self assessment

Under the self assessment system for the individual:

- Some taxpayers are sent a self assessment return annually.

- The responsibility for calculating and accounting for income tax and CGT lies with the taxpayer.

- The taxpayer must complete and submit the return to the appropriate district of HMRC.

### Filing the self assessment return

The filing date rules are as follows:

- The taxpayer has the choice of filing a paper return or filing electronically online.

- The date by which a return must be filed depends on the method used.

- All completed and signed paper returns must be filed by:
  - 31 October following the end of the tax year

- All online electronic returns must be filed by:
  - 31 January following the end of the tax year

- The relevant dates for a 2009/10 return are therefore 31 October 2010 and 31 January 2011.

- 31 January following the end of the tax year is known as the 'filing date' regardless of whether the return is filed on paper or electronically.

- This must be distinguished from the date on which the return is filed, known as the 'actual' filing date.

- When a return is not issued until after 31 October following the end of the tax year, filing is required within three months after the date of issue.

A reminder of other key aspects of self assessment which were covered at F6 is given in expandable text and is summarised in the diagram in section 4.

### The format of a tax return

The return should contain all information required to calculate the taxpayer's taxable income (from all sources) and any chargeable gains for the tax year concerned.

Reliefs and allowances will also be claimed in the return.

For self-employed individuals, the return includes a section for standardised accounts information.

For employees who pay their tax liability under PAYE, a self assessment tax return will often not be required because they will have no further tax liability.

Although partners are dealt with individually, a partnership return will have to be completed to aid self assessment on the individual partners. This will give details of the partners, and a partnership statement detailing the partnership's tax adjusted income and how this is allocated between the partners.

Each individual is separately responsible for:

- making a tax return

- declaring all their income to HMRC

- claiming their own allowances and reliefs

- paying any tax due on their own income (and capital gains) or receiving any repayments due.

HMRC will not make any judgement of the accuracy of the figures included in the return, but will merely calculate the tax liability based on the information submitted.

## Amendments to the return

Either party may amend the return:

- HMRC may correct any obvious errors or mistakes within **nine months** of the date that the return is filed with them.

- The taxpayer can amend the return within **12 months** of the filing date. For 2009/10, amendments must therefore be made by 31 January 2012.

If an error is discovered at a later date then the taxpayer can make an error or mistake claim (see later) to recover any tax overpaid.

## Notification of chargeability

Self-assessment places the onus on the taxpayer, therefore:

- Taxpayers who do not receive a return are required to notify HMRC if they have income or chargeable gains on which tax is due.

- The time limit for notifying HMRC of chargeability is six months from the end of the tax year in which the liability arises.

- A standard penalty may be payable if tax is unpaid as a result of failing to notify (see section 9 for the detail on the penalties that can be imposed).

## Penalties for failure to submit a return

HMRC can impose fixed penalties and tax-geared penalties for the failure to submit a return.

See section 9 for the detail on the penalties that can be imposed.

### Determination of tax due if no return is filed

Where a self assessment tax return is not filed by the filing date, HMRC may determine the amount of tax due. The impact of this is:

- This determination is treated as a self assessment by the taxpayer, and will be replaced by the actual self assessment when it is submitted by the taxpayer.

- There is no appeal against a determination, which therefore encourages the taxpayer to displace it with the actual self assessment.

- A determination can be made at any time within **three years** of the filing date.

### Claims

Wherever possible, claims must be included in the self assessment tax return.

A claim for a relief, allowance or repayment must be quantified at the time that the claim is made. For example, if loss relief is claimed, then the amount of the loss must be stated.

### Claims for earlier years

Certain claims will relate to earlier years. The obvious example of this is loss relief claimed for earlier years.

- The taxpayer can make a claim in the return for the later year or can make a separate claim.

- The tax liability for the earlier year is not adjusted. Instead, the tax reduction resulting from the claim will be set off against the tax liability for the later year.

- Alternatively, if a separate claim is made, HMRC will refund the tax due.

- As the claim is only quantified by reference to the earlier year, payments on account based on the relevant amount for the earlier year will not change.

### Error or mistake claims

Where an assessment is excessive due to an error or mistake in a return, the taxpayer can claim relief.

The claim must be made within four years from the end of the tax year. For 2009/10 the claim should be made by 5 April 2014.

### Example 3 – Claims for earlier years

A taxpayer's relevant amount for 2008/09 is £4,400. During 2009/10 the taxpayer made a trading loss of £1,000, and makes a claim to carry this back to 2008/09.

**State the effect on the self-assessment of making the carry-back claim for losses.**

### Solution

The taxpayer's payments on account for 2009/10 are £2,200 (£4,400 × ½), and these will not alter as a result of the carry back of the loss.

The tax refund due will be calculated at the taxpayer's marginal income tax rate(s) for 2008/09.

The tax refund due will then either be set off against the 2009/10 tax liability, or will be repaid.

## 4 Summary

```
            ┌──────────────────────────┐
            │     Self assessment       │
            │    2009/10  tax return    │
            └──────────────────────────┘
                         ⋮
        ┌──────────────────────────────────────┐
        │   Responsibility placed on taxpayer    │
        └──────────────────────────────────────┘
```

**Format of the return**
- Declare income
- Claim allowances and reliefs
- Calculate the tax (optional)

**Notification of chargeability**
- Within six months from end of tax year

- Penalty up to 100% of unpaid tax, depending on taxpayer's behaviour

**Filing dates**

Paper return
- 31 October 2010
- i.e. 31 October following the end of the tax year

Electronic return
- 31 January 2011
- i.e. 31 January following the end of the tax year

If return not issued until after 31 October 2010
- must file within three months after the date of issue

**Amendments to the return**
- HMRC
  - obvious errors and mistakes
  - within 9 months of actual filing date
- Taxpayer
  - by 31 January 2012
  - i.e. within 12 months of filing date

**If no return submitted by filing date**
- HMRC can determine tax due within four, six or twenty years of filing date
- No appeal
- Taxpayer can displace determination with actual self assessment

**Claims**
- Must quantify amount of claims for reliefs, allowances, repayments
- Earlier year claims:
  - tax liability of earlier year not adjusted
  - tax reduction is set against current liability
  - does not affect POAs
- Taxpayer claim
  - for error or mistake
  - must be made by 5 April 2014
  - i.e. within four years of end of tax year

**Penalties**
- Not submitting return by
  - filing date = £100
  - within six months = further £100
  - within 12 months = tax geared
- Daily penalty of £60 can be imposed
- Tax geared penalty can not exceed tax liability

More detail in section 9

## 5 Payment of tax

### Introduction

Any tax due on income which is not deducted at source is payable by self-assessment.

- The payments are due as follows:

|  |  |  |
|---|---|---|
| First payment on account (POA) | – | 31 January during the tax year. |
| Second payment on account (POA) | – | 31 July following the tax year. |
| Balancing payment/repayment | – | 31 January following the tax year. |

- POAs are based on the previous year's tax payable.

- Each POA is 50% of the relevant amount of income tax and Class 4 NIC, if appropriate.

- No POAs are made for CGT liabilities.

---

**Test your understanding 4**

Rebecca's tax payable for 2009/10 was as follows:

|  | £ |
|---|---|
| Income tax | 10,800 |
| Less: Tax deducted at source | (2,500) |
|  | ——— |
|  | 8,300 |
| Class 4 NIC | 800 |
|  | ——— |
| Relevant amount of income tax and Class 4 NICs | 9,100 |
| CGT | 4,600 |
|  | ——— |
|  | 13,700 |
|  | ——— |

Two POAs have been paid on 31 January 2010 and 31 July 2010 of £4,000 each.

**Calculate the amount payable on 31 January 2011.**

---

A reminder of further rules relating to POAs covered at F6 are given in expandable text and are summarised in the diagram in section 6.

## When POAs are not required

POAs are not required where:

- the income tax payable for the previous year was less than £1,000

- more than 80% of the income tax for the previous year was met by deduction of tax at source.

Therefore, most employed people will not have to make POAs, since at least 80% of their tax liability is paid through PAYE.

## Claims to reduce POAs

At any time before the 31 January following the end of the tax year, a taxpayer can claim to reduce the POAs.

- A taxpayer would claim to reduce the POAs if he expected his actual income tax and Class 4 NIC liability (net of tax deducted at source) to be less than the year before.

- The claim must state the grounds for making the claim, and each POAs will be for half of the estimated liability.

- Where a claim is made and the actual tax liability for the current year turns out to be higher than the original POAs, interest will be charged on the tax underpaid.

- Interest is based on the difference between amounts actually paid and amounts that should have been paid.

- The amount that should have been paid is the lower of:
  - The original POAs based on the relevant amount of the previous year

  - 50% of the final tax liability (excluding CGT and net of tax deducted at source) for the current year

- In addition, a penalty will be charged if a taxpayer fraudulently or negligently claims to reduce POAs. The maximum penalty is the difference between the amounts actually paid on account, and the amounts that should have been paid.

### Interest and surcharges

A reminder of the rules for interest and surcharges covered at F6 are given in expandable text and are summarised in the diagram in section 6.

## Interest on tax paid late

Interest will automatically be charged if tax is paid late, whether it is income tax, Class 4 NIC or CGT.

The date from which interest runs depends on the payment made late:

| Payment | Interest runs from |
| --- | --- |
| POAs | Due date of POA (i.e. 31 January or 31 July) |
| Other self assessment payments | Filing date (i.e. 31 January following end of tax year) |
| Penalties | Date the penalty is due |

Interest runs to the day before the date of actual payment.

## Interest on overpaid tax

- Interest is paid by HMRC on any overpayment of tax.
- Interest runs from the later of:
  - due date
  - date of actual payment
- Interest runs to the date of repayment
- Interest is only paid on the amount of tax that should have been paid (i.e. deliberate overpayments will not attract interest).

## Surcharges

- Where a balancing payment is not paid within 28 days after the due date (31 January following the tax year), a surcharge equal to 5% of the tax unpaid is imposed.
- A further 5% surcharge arises if tax is still unpaid after 6 months.
- The surcharge does not apply to POAs.
- If not paid within 30 days of the date imposed, interest is charged on the surcharge.

KAPLAN PUBLISHING

## Example 4 – Interest and surcharges

Rowena's final tax payable (after tax credits but before payments on account) is computed for 2009/10 as follows:

| | |
|---|---|
| IT | £6,000 |
| CGT | £3,000 |

Payments on account of £4,000 in total were made on the relevant dates. The balance of the tax due was paid as follows:

| | |
|---|---|
| IT | 1 March 2011 |
| CGT | 1 April 2011 |

**Calculate the interest and surcharges due, assuming the rate of interest on unpaid tax is 2.5%.**

### Solution

The relevant date for balancing payments is 31 January 2011.
No payments on account are ever required for CGT.

The amounts due were therefore as follows:

| | | |
|---|---|---|
| 31 January 2011 | IT | £2,000 |
| | CGT | £3,000 |

Interest will run as follows:

IT      £2,000 from 31 January 2011 to 28 February 2011:
        i.e. $1/12 \times 2.5\% \times £2,000 = £4.17$

CGT     £3,000 from 31 January 2011 to 31 March 2011:
        i.e. $2/12 \times 2.5\% \times £3,000 = £12.50$

In addition, a surcharge is due on the IT and CGT (as both are more than 28 days late) of 5% of £5,000 = £250.

Total payable = (£4.17 + £12.50 + £250) = £267.

The surcharge may be reduced if HMRC accept there was a reasonable excuse for late payment.

## 6 Summary

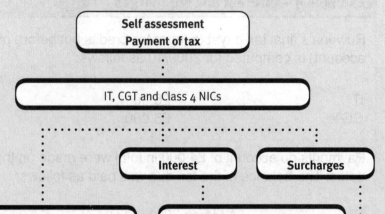

**Self assessment
Payment of tax**

**IT, CGT and Class 4 NICs**

**Interest**

**Surcharges**

---

**Payment dates – 2009/10**

- POA 1
  - 31 January 2010
- POA 2
  - 31 July 2010
- Balancing payment
  - 31 January 2011
- POAs = 50% of relevant amount for previous tax year
- Relevant amount = IT and Class 4 NICs net of tax deducted at source
- No POAs for CGT

**On late paid tax**

- Interest runs from:
  - POAs: Due date of POA
  - Other payments: Filing date
  - Penalties: Due date of penalty
- Interest runs to:
  day before payment made

**On overpaid tax**

- Interest runs from later of:
  - Due date
  - Date actually paid
- Interest runs to:
  - date repayment made

---

**POAs not required if**

- IT payable for previous year ‹ £1000
- › 80% of relevant amount for previous year deducted at source

- Payable in addition to unpaid tax and interest
- No surcharge on POAs
- If balancing payment not paid
  - Within 28 days of due date: 5%
  - Within 6 months: further 5%
- Interest charged on surcharge if not paid within 30 days

---

**Claim to reduce POAs**

- Claim before 31 January following end of tax year
- Must state grounds
- If underestimate payments:
  - Interest charged from due date of POA to date of payment
  - Penalty payable if fraudulent or negligent
  - Maximum penalty = difference between amount paid and amount that should have been paid

# 7 Records

Taxpayers are required to keep and preserve records necessary to make a correct and complete return.

A reminder of the records to keep and the retention periods is given in expandable text.

## Records

**For a business** (including the letting of property), the records that must be kept include records of:

- all receipts and expenses
- all goods purchased and sold
- all supporting documents relating to the transactions of the business, such as accounts, books, contracts, vouchers and receipts.

**Other taxpayers** should keep evidence of income received such as:

- dividend vouchers
- P60s
- copies of P11Ds
- bank statements.

## Retention periods

**For taxpayers with a business** (i.e. the self employed)

- All their records (not just those relating to the business) must be retained until five years after the filing date.
- For 2009/10 records must therefore be retained until 31 January 2016

## For other taxpayers

Records must be retained until the later of:

- 12 months after the filing date (31 January 2012 for 2009/10).
- the date on which an enquiry into the return is completed.
- the date on which it becomes impossible for an enquiry to be started.

### Penalties for not keeping records

A penalty may be charged for failure to keep or retain adequate records.

The maximum penalty is only likely to be imposed in the most serious cases such as where a taxpayer deliberately destroys his records in order to obstruct an enquiry by HMRC.

See section 9 for the detail on the penalties that may be imposed.

## 8 HMRC rights of enquiry

HMRC have the right to enquire into the completeness and accuracy of any self assessment tax return.

### HMRC enquires

An enquiry may be opened for the following reasons:

- a suspicion that income is undeclared or deduction incorrectly claimed
- information in HMRC's possession
- random choice of return.

HMRC do not have to state a reason for the enquiry and are unlikely to do so.

### Enquiry procedures

- HMRC must give written notice before commencing an enquiry.
- The written notice must be issued within 12 months of the date the return was filed. Once this deadline is passed, the taxpayer can normally consider the self assessment for that year as final unless there is fraud or negligence.
- HMRC can demand that the taxpayer produce documents, accounts or other written particulars. This includes being entitled to receive full answers to specific questions.
- The information requested should be limited to that connected with the return.
- The taxpayer has 30 days to comply with the request. An appeal can be made against the request.
- There is the facility for HMRC and the taxpayer to agree to refer any point they are unable to resolve to the Tax Tribunal during the course of the enquiry.

- The enquiry ends when HMRC give a written completion notice stating the outcome of the enquiry. If the taxpayer believes that HMRC have no grounds for continuing an enquiry, he is entitled to ask the Tax Tribunal that a date be set for its completion.

- The completion notice must either include HMRC's amendments to the self-assessment, or state that no amendment is due. The tax payer then has 30 days to appeal against any HMRC amendment. The appeal must be in writing.

## Information and inspection powers

Previously, the separate parts of HMRC, namely Inland Revenue and Customs and Excise, had different powers for inspecting business premises and records. This meant that a business might receive several visits to look at records.

- HMRC will now have unified powers to undertake such compliance checks with one set of powers to inspect business records, assets and premises.

- The new regime covers income tax, capital gains tax, corporation tax, VAT and PAYE.

- HMRC will also have a single approach across all taxes to asking taxpayers for supplementary information, based on formal information notices with a right of appeal. They can also request information from third parties provided either the taxpayer or the new First-tier Tribunal (see section on appeals and the tax tribunal) agrees.

## Discovery assessments

In addition to the enquiries that HMRC can make, a 'discovery assessment' can be raised at a later date to prevent the loss of tax.

- Unless the loss of tax is due to fraud or negligence, a discovery assessment cannot be raised where full disclosure was made in the return.

- HMRC will only accept that full disclosure has been made if any contentious items have been clearly brought to their attention in the 'white space' on the tax return.

- Information in the attached accounts will not constitute full disclosure if its significance is not emphasised.

- Only a taxpayer who makes full disclosure in the self assessment tax return therefore has absolute finality 12 months after the filing date.

The time limit for issuing a discovery assessment is 4 years from the end of the tax year (2009/10 by 5 April 2014), increased to 6 years if there is a careless error (2009/10 by 5 April 2016) or 20 years if there is a deliberate error or failure to notify a chargeability to tax (2009/10 by 5 April 2030).

## 9 Penalties

In addition to interest on the late payment of tax, HMRC can impose penalties.

### Standard penalty

HMRC is standardising penalties across taxes and for different offences. For 2010 exams, the standard penalty applies to two areas:

- inaccuracies in returns – all taxes
- failure to notify liability to tax – income tax, CGT, corporation tax, VAT and PAYE/NIC.

The penalty is calculated as a percentage of 'potential lost revenue' which is generally the tax unpaid as a result of the error or failure to notify.

| Taxpayer behaviour | Maximum penalty (% of revenue lost) |
|---|---|
| Genuine mistake | No Penalty |
| Failure to take reasonable care | 30% |
| Serious or deliberate understatement | 70% |
| Serious or deliberate understatement with concealment | 100% |

Penalties can be reduced where the taxpayer makes full disclosure and cooperates with HMRC to establish the amount of tax unpaid.

| Offence | Penalty |
|---|---|
| **Individuals** | |
| Failure to notify chargeability to tax within 6 months of the end of the tax year | Standard penalty<br>Based on a % of tax unpaid on 31 January following the end of the tax year |
| Late submission of income tax return<br><br>   – within 6 months of due date | £100 fixed penalty |
|    – between 6 -12 months of filing date | Further £100 fixed penalty<br><br>These penalties cannot exceed the amount of tax due per the return |
|    – delay > 12 months | Additional penalty of up to 100% of the tax due per the return |
|    – upon direction by the tribunal | Additional £60 per day<br>from : date of direction<br>to: date return submitted |
| Submission of an incorrect tax return or accounts leading to:<br><br>   – an understatement of tax liability<br>   – a false or inflated statement of a loss<br>   – a false or inflated claim for repayment of tax<br><br>(HMRC may consider charging a penalty where tax has been under-assessed because of a person's failure to send a return, or where a person has discovered an inaccuracy in a document but has not taken reasonable steps to tell HMRC.) | Standard penalty<br>Based on a % of tax unpaid as a result of the error |
| Failing to notify HMRC of an under assessment to tax | Standard penalty<br>Based on a % of the amount of under assessed tax |

| | |
|---|---|
| Deliberately supplying false information to, or deliberately withholding information from, a person with the intention of making that person's document inaccurate | Standard penalty Based on a % of tax unpaid as a result of the error |
| Fraud or negligence on claiming reduced payments on account | POAs actually paid       £<br>                                            X<br>Less POAs if claims  (X)<br>not made<br>                                            X<br>                                            — |
| Failure to keep and retain required records | Up to £3,000 per year of assessment |

### Example 5 – Penalties

A taxpayer was issued with a tax return in April 2010 which relates to the 2009/10 tax year.

Unfortunately, he did not submit his return to HMRC until 10 October 2011. The tax due for 2009/10 amounts to £175.

**Identify the penalties that will be charged.**

**Solution**

Two fixed penalties of £100 will be due as the return is submitted more than six months after the filing date of 31 January 2011.

The penalties will be reduced to the tax due of £175.

If a daily penalty was imposed, then this would run from the date when the Tribunal makes a direction to 10 October 2011.

The second fixed penalty of £100 will not be due if the daily penalties commenced before 31 July 2011 (six months after the filing date).

## 10 Appeals

### Introduction

A taxpayer can appeal against a decision made by HMRC, but they must do so within 30 days of the disputed decision.

Most appeals are then settled amicably by discussion between the taxpayer and HMRC.

However, if the taxpayer is not satisfied with the outcome of the discussions, they can proceed in one of two ways:

- Request that their case is reviewed by another HMRC officer, or
- Have their case referred to an independent Tax Tribunal.

If the taxpayer opts to have their case reviewed but disagrees with the outcome, they can still send their appeal to the Tax Tribunal.

The taxpayer must also apply to postpone all or part of the tax charged. Otherwise they will have to pay the disputed amount.

## Tax Tribunals

The Tax Tribunal is an independent body administered by the Tribunals Service of the Ministry of Justice. Cases are heard by independently appointed tax judges and/or panel members. Each panel is appointed according to the needs of the case.

There are two tiers (layers) of Tax Tribunal system:

- First-tier Tribunal, and
- Upper Tribunal.

### First-tier Tribunal

The First-tier Tribunal will be the first instance tribunal for most issues. They deal with:

- *Default paper cases:* simple appeals (e.g. against a fixed penalty) – will usually be disposed of without a hearing provided both sides agree.
- *Basic cases:* straightforward appeals involving a minimal exchange of paperwork in advance of a short hearing.
- *Standard cases:* appeals involving more detailed consideration of issues and a more formal hearing.
- *Complex cases:* some complex appeals may be heard by the First-tier Tribunal however they will usually be heard by the Upper Tribunal.

If the dispute is not resolved at the First-tier level then the appeal can go to the Upper tribunal.

### Upper Tribunal

The Upper Tribunal will mainly, but not exclusively, review and decide appeals from the First–tier Tribunal on a point of law.

In addition, they will also deal with:

- Complex cases requiring detailed specialist knowledge and a formal hearing – cases involving long and complicated issues, points of principle and large financial amounts which do not go through the First-tier Tribunal stage.
- Judicial review work delegated from the High Court and Court of Session.
- The enforcement of decisions, directions and orders made by Tribunals.

Hearings are held in public and decisions are published.

A decision of the Upper Tribunal may be appealed to the Court of Appeal. However, the grounds of appeal must always relate to a point of law.

The overriding objective of the tribunal rules is to allow cases to be dealt with fairly and justly. The tribunal system aims to avoid delays and unnecessary expense.

### Costs of appeal

Each party (i.e. the taxpayer and HMRC) will normally pay their own costs.

However the Tribunal can award costs in two main situations:

- against a party who has acted unreasonably in bringing or conducting the case, and
- in complex cases (unless the taxpayer has requested that the proceedings be excluded from potential liability for costs or expenses).

Note that the costs of appeal incurred by the taxpayer are not allowable expenses for tax purposes.

### Publication of names of tax offenders

- HMRC will have power to publish the names and details of individuals and companies who are penalised for deliberate defaults leading to a loss of tax of more than £25,000.

- Names will not be published of those who make a full unprompted disclosure or a full prompted disclosure within the required time.

### Monitoring of serious tax offenders

Those who incur a penalty for deliberate evasion in respect of tax of £5,000 or more will be required to submit returns for up to the following 5 years showing more detailed business accounts information and detailing the nature and value of any balancing adjustments within the accounts.

## 11 Chapter summary

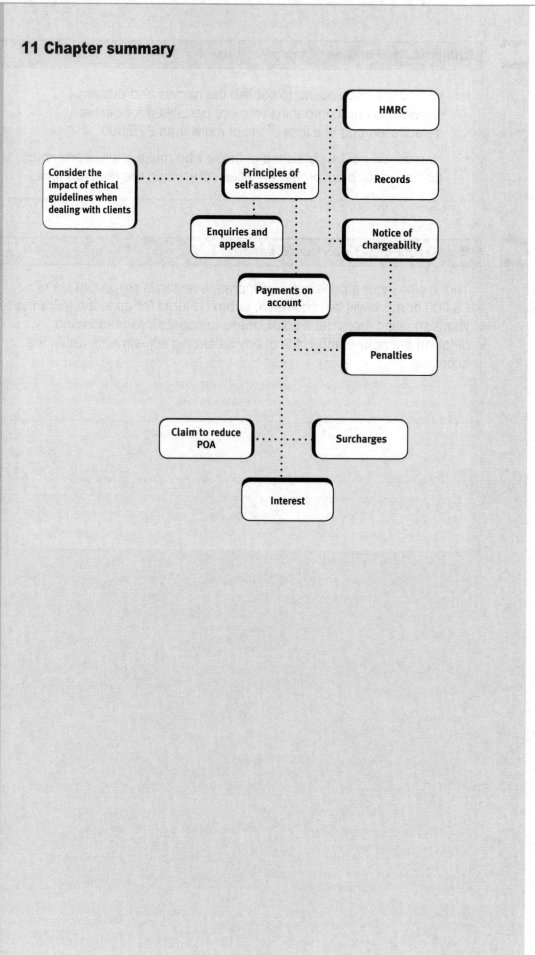

## Test your understanding answers

### Test your understanding 1

**Steven**

(1) Act for neither party

This option may not be in the best interests of everyone but if there is any doubt it is the recommended course of action.

(2) Act for both parties

This may be possible if the facts have been disclosed to both parties involved and they agree. Both clients should be advised to seek independent advice as to whether it is appropriate for the member to act for both parties.

(3) Act for one client

This would normally be the client who first sought advice from the member.

### Test your understanding 2

**Simon**

Simon should inform the client that commission will be receivable, and the amount involved.

He needs to ensure that the commission does not taint his advice, and he preserves the normal standards of care with the advice being in the best interests of the client.

## Test your understanding 3

**HMRC error**

The position should be reviewed carefully to confirm that an error has been made.

The client should be contacted for authority to disclose the error to HMRC, if this authority was not already given within the letter of engagement.

If the authority does not exist in the letter of engagement, the client should be told the consequences of not disclosing the error, including the implication for interest and penalties.

If the client refuses to allow the disclosure it would be necessary to consider whether the amount is material, and if it is, whether you can continue to act for the client.

If it is decided that it is not appropriate to continue acting, the client must be informed in writing. HMRC should also be notified that you have ceased to act, but not the reason why.

It may be necessary to make a report to NCIS under the Money Laundering Legislation.

## Test your understanding 4

**Rebecca**

The balancing payment for 2009/10 due on 31 January 2011 will be as follows:

|  | £ |
|---|---:|
| Total tax liability as above | 13,700 |
| Less: Payments on account | (8,000) |
| Balancing payment due 31 January 2011 | 5,700 |

In addition, the first payment on account for 2010/11 of £4,550 (£9,100 × ½) is due on 31 January 2011.

# New and ongoing unincorporated businesses

## Chapter learning objectives

Upon completion of this chapter you will be able to:

- describe and apply the badges of trade

- prepare the tax adjusted profit / loss given a variety of situations

- compute plant and machinery capital allowances

- recognise the factors that will influence the choice of accounting date for a new business and compute the assessments

- state the conditions that must be met for a change of accounting date to be valid and compute the assessable profits

- understand how to calculate a trading loss for a tax year

- explain how trading losses can be used for an ongoing business and can be relieved in the early years of a trade

- demonstrate the optimum use of trading loss reliefs

- explain the NIC position and calculate the NIC liability

- calculate net receipts from a transaction, compare alternative scenarios and advise on the most tax efficient course of action

- identify and advise on the personal taxes applicable to a given course of action and their impact

- identify suitable tax planning measures in a given scenario to mitigate tax liabilities for an individual

- recognise that alternative courses of action have different consequences and assess the advantages and disadvantages.

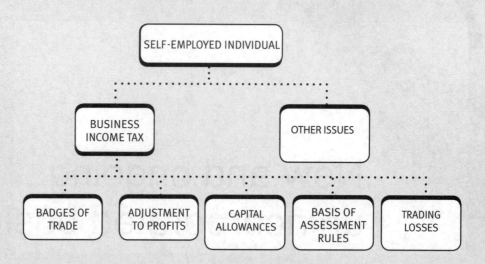

## 1 A revision of basic business income tax

### Introduction

This and the following two chapters deal with the way in which a self-employed individual is taxed on their income derived from an unincorporated business (i.e. a sole trader or partnership).

There is little new knowledge at P6 compared with F6, therefore much of this chapter is a revision of business tax rules covered at F6. However, examination questions will bring many of the business tax topics together in a scenario and will test an in-depth understanding of the different taxes that apply.

Common scenarios are to look at the opening years of a business, the ongoing years where there is a change in the operations or the closing years.

After studying this chapter you should be able to tackle examination questions involving all tax aspects of a new or ongoing business.

The key considerations are as follows:

- Badges of trade – is a trade being carried on?

- Income tax issues for new and ongoing businesses

- Loss reliefs

- NICs

- Expansion: taking on an employee or partner

- VAT

- Self assessment

The new material is only in respect of the emphasis placed on tax planning issues arising from the basic rules.

## The badges of trade

Income arising from a trade, profession or vocation is assessed as trading income in an individual's income tax computation.

In entering into a transaction, or series of transactions, it is not always clear whether an individual is:

- carrying on a trade, and therefore should be assessed to income tax
- making a capital disposal, which may be chargeable to capital gains tax (CGT) or exempt from tax.

### Example 1 – Trading income vs gain

On 1 May 2009 Chow Tong, aged 35, bought a derelict property at an auction for £132,000. She paid cash of £42,000, and borrowed the remaining £90,000 from her bank at an interest rate of 8% pa.

On 15 July 2009 Chow obtained planning permission to convert the property into six holiday apartments, and entered into a contract with a builder to carry out the conversion. The work was completed on 30 September 2009 at a cost of £63,000, and Chow immediately put the six holiday apartments up for sale.

Five of the holiday apartments were sold during November 2009 for £85,000 each. On 30 November 2009 Chow paid her builder and repaid the bank loan. She decided to keep the remaining holiday apartment, valued at £85,000, for her own use. Legal fees of £750 were paid in respect of each of the five holiday apartments sold, and advertising costs amounted to £1,200.

Since the sale of the holiday apartments is an isolated transaction Chow believes that it should be treated as a capital gain rather than as a trade.

Chow has not disposed of any other assets during 2009/10.

**Calculate Chow's net cash position arising from her property activities during 2009/10 if this is treated as:**

(1) **trading income, and**

(2) **a capital transaction.**

You should ignore the implications of NIC and VAT.

**Solution**

**Chow's net tax position treated as if trading income**

If Chow is treated as trading she will be liable to income tax on the trading profit, including the holiday apartment retained by her which is treated as a disposal to her at its market value of £85,000.

Chow's income tax liability will be:

|  | Income tax £ | Net cash £ |
|---|---|---|
| Sale proceeds (5 × £85,000) | 425,000 | 425,000 |
| Market value of property retained (Note 1) | 85,000 | – |
| Cost of property | (132,000) | (132,000) |
| Cost of conversion | (63,000) | (63,000) |
| Loan interest (£90,000 × 8% × 7/12) | (4,200) | (4,200) |
| Legal fees (5 × £750) | (3,750) | (3,750) |
| Advertising | (1,200) | (1,200) |
| Taxable profit | 305,850 | |
| Income tax (40% × £305,850) | 122,340 | (122,340) |
| Net cash after tax | | 98,510 |

**Note 1:** The property retained must be taken into account for tax purposes, but is not real cash income.

**Chow's net tax position if treated as capital**

If Chow is treated as not trading, she will be subject to capital gains tax. The holiday apartment retained by her will not be charged to tax.

Chow's CGT liability will be:

|  | CGT £ | Net cash £ |
|---|---|---|
| Sale proceeds (5 × £85,000) | 425,000 | 425,000 |
| Incidental costs of disposal (£3,750 + £1,200) | (4,950) | (4,950) |
| Net sale proceeds | 420,050 | |
| Cost of property (£132,000 × 5/6) | (110,000) | (132,000) |
| Cost of conversion (£63,000 × 5/6) | (52,500) | (63,000) |
| Capital gain | 257,550 | |
| Annual exemption | (10,100) | |
| Taxable gain | 247,450 | |
| CGT (18% × £247,450) | 44,541 | (44,541) |
| Loan interest (£90,000 × 8% × 7/12) | | (4,200) |
| Net cash after tax | | 176,309 |

**Note 2:** The cash position must take account of property retained.

**Note 3:** Entrepreneurs' relief is not available on the capital disposal as the business it is not a trading business and Chow owned the property for less than 12 months.

**Future position**

Note that if treated as trading, Chow is deemed to have acquired the 6th apartment for £85,000 on the date it is appropriated from stock.

If treated as capital, Chow is also deemed to have acquired the 6th apartment worth £85,000 on 1 May 2009 for a CGT cost of £32,500 ((£132,000 × 1/6) + (£63,000 × 1/6)). This treatment will therefore give rise to a bigger gain in the future.

What constitutes a trade is therefore very important in deciding how profits should be assessed.

The badges of trade produced by the Royal Commission are criteria used to determine whether or not the purchase and resale of property is to be treated as a trading transaction.

The key badges of trade are as follows:

- the subject matter of the transaction (S)
- the length of the period of ownership (O)
- the frequency or number of similar transactions by the same person (F)
- supplementary work, improvements and marketing (I)
- the circumstances responsible for the realisation (R)
- the motive (M).

A reminder of the badges of trade and the full explanation covered at F6 are given in expandable text.

## The badges of trade

It may be helpful to remember the badges of trade by the mnemonic: SOFIRM as denoted by the letters in the brackets in the main text above.

There are a number of other 'badges' which also need to be considered, for example:

- Is the subject matter of the transaction in some way related to the trade otherwise carried on by the taxpayer?
- What was the source of finance for the transaction?
- Was the asset acquired deliberately or unintentionally such as by gift or inheritance?

However, it is vital to appreciate that:

- no single badge of trade will be decisive
- it is necessary to consider all of the facts surrounding the transaction
- in any set of circumstances some badges may indicate trading whilst others may not
- it is the overall impression, taking into account all relevant factors, that is important.

The principles behind each badge of trade and some background information relating to decided cases are given below.

### The subject matter of the transaction (S)

Property which does not yield an income nor gives personal enjoyment to its owner is likely to form the subject matter of a trading transaction.

Other property such as land, works of art and investments are more likely to be acquired for the income and/or personal enjoyment that they provide. The disposal of such items will more often give rise to a gain or loss of a capital nature, rather than a trading profit.

In a decided case, the taxpayer purchased one million rolls of toilet paper for £1,000, which was resold at a profit of £11,000. This was held to be an adventure in the nature of a trade, since it was inconceivable that the rolls of toilet paper were acquired for any purpose other than realising a profit.

## The length of ownership (O)

The sale of property within a short time of its acquisition is an indication of trading.

By itself, however, this is not a strong badge as, for example, stocks and shares will often be bought and sold on an active basis without giving rise to an adventure in the nature of a trade.

## Frequency of similar transactions (F)

Repeated transactions in the same subject matter will be an indication of trading.

This badge is of particular importance when an isolated transaction would not otherwise be treated as an adventure in the nature of a trade.

In a decided case, it was held that although the single purchase and resale of a cotton mill was capital in nature, a series of four such transactions amounted to trading.

Hence, subsequent transactions may trigger a trading profits liability in respect of earlier transactions.

## Improvements to the property (I)

Carrying out work to the property in order to make it more marketable, or taking steps to find purchasers, will indicate a trading motive.

In a decided case, a syndicate was held to be trading when it purchased a quantity of brandy which was then blended, recasked and sold in lots over an 18 month period.

However, a taxpayer is entitled to make an asset more attractive to potential purchasers, without this being an indication of trading.

### Reason responsible for the realisation (R)

A forced sale to raise cash for an emergency will by presumption indicate that the transaction is not an adventure in the nature of a trade.

### Motive (M)

If a transaction is undertaken with the motive of realising a profit, this will be a strong indication of trading. However, the absence of a profit motive does not prevent a person from being treated as trading.

In a decided case, the taxpayer was held to be trading when he bought £200,000 of silver as a hedge against devaluation and later resold it at a profit of £50,000.

## An overview of the trading income assessment for an individual

To calculate the trading income to include in a self-employed individual's income tax computation, the following procedure should be used:

(1) Calculate the tax adjusted trading profits.

(2) Calculate the capital allowances available on:

- plant and machinery; and

- industrial buildings

Deduct capital allowances from the tax adjusted trading profits.

(3) Apply the basis of assessment rules to the tax adjusted trading profit figure after capital allowances have been deducted.

## Proforma tax adjusted trading profits computation

There are four key types of adjustment to be made to the accounting profit to calculate the tax adjusted trading profit as follows:

|  | £ |
|---|---|
| Net profit per accounts | X |
| Add back   Non trading expenses |  |
| (disallowable expenditure) | X |
| Trading income not credited in the accounts | X |
| Deduct   Non trading income | (X) |
| Trading expenses not charged in the accounts | (X) |
| Tax adjusted trading profits before capital allowances | X |
| Less:   Capital Allowances: |  |
| Plant and Machinery | (X) |
| Industrial Buildings Allowances | (X) |
| Tax adjusted trading profits after capital allowances | X |

Note that the detailed rules for adjusting the accounting profits were covered in F6. These are still examinable at P6. However, at P6 it is likely that only a few selected adjustments will be required, not a large adjustment to profits computation or a large capital allowances computation.

## Basis of assessment rules

The basis of assessment rules determine in which tax year the adjusted trading profits will be assessed.

The normal basis of assessment will be the twelve month accounting period ending in the current tax year, known as the 'current year basis' of assessment.

However, special rules apply:

- in the opening years
- in the closing years
- when an unincorporated business changes its accounting date.

## 2 The tax adjusted trading profits computation

A reminder of the key adjustments to profits is given in the diagram below.

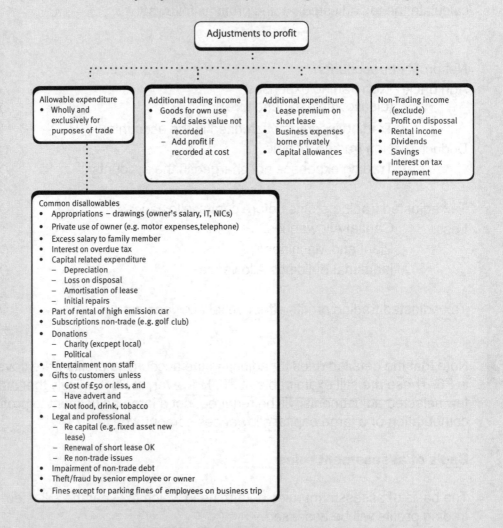

**Adjustments to profit**

**Allowable expenditure**
- Wholly and exclusively for purposes of trade

**Additional trading income**
- Goods for own use
  - Add sales value not recorded
  - Add profit if recorded at cost

**Additional expenditure**
- Lease premium on short lease
- Business expenses borne privately
- Capital allowances

**Non-Trading income (exclude)**
- Profit on disposal
- Rental income
- Dividends
- Savings
- Interest on tax repayment

**Common disallowables**
- Appropriations – drawings (owner's salary, IT, NICs)
- Private use of owner (e.g. motor expenses,telephone)
- Excess salary to family member
- Interest on overdue tax
- Capital related expenditure
  - Depreciation
  - Loss on disposal
  - Amortisation of lease
  - Initial repairs
- Part of rental of high emission car
- Subscriptions non-trade (e.g. golf club)
- Donations
  - Charity (excpept local)
  - Political
- Entertainment non staff
- Gifts to customers  unless
  - Cost of £50 or less, and
  - Have advert and
  - Not food, drink, tobacco
- Legal and professional
  - Re capital (e.g. fixed asset new lease)
  - Renewal of short lease OK
  - Re non-trade issues
- Impairment of non-trade debt
- Theft/fraud by senior employee or owner
- Fines except for parking fines of employees on business trip

## Hiring and leasing an expensive car

There has been a change in the treatment of the cost of leasing a motor car. Previously, the rental or hire charges were restricted where the motor car would have cost more than £12,000 when new.

There is now no adjustment where the $CO_2$ emissions of a leased motor car do not exceed 160 grams per kilometre, regardless of the retail price. Where $CO_2$ emissions are more than 160 grams per kilometre then 15% of the leasing costs are disallowed in calculating taxable profits.

The motor car is the most common asset with private use.  In this case, a further adjustment is required to reflect the private use.

## Allowable element of lease premiums

A business is entitled to deduct a proportion of the amount assessable on the landlord as property business income in calculating the taxable trading profit.

The adjustments for the lease are:

Add: the amortisation charged in the accounts (capital)

Deduct: the property business income assessed on the landlord ÷ period of the lease

## Pre-trading expenditure

Any **revenue** expenditure incurred in the **seven years before a business commences** to trade (which is of the type that would normally be allowed if incurred whilst trading) is treated as an allowable deduction against trading profit on the first day of trading.

**Capital** expenditure incurred within seven years of the start of the trade:

- is treated as incurred on the first day of trading and may be eligible for capital allowances

- however, the actual date of acquisition determines the rate of FYAs and AIA available (if any).

## Comprehensive example

The following example revises the key adjustments to profit covered at F6.

### Test your understanding 1

Olive Green is self-employed running a health food shop. Her profit and loss account for the year ended 31 December 2009 is as follows:

|  | £ | £ |
|---|---|---|
| Gross profit |  | 123,200 |
| Expenses |  |  |
| Depreciation | 2,350 |  |
| Light and heat (note 1) | 1,980 |  |
| Motor expenses (note 2) | 4,700 |  |
| Rent and rates (note 1) | 5,920 |  |
| Sundry expenses (note 3) | 2,230 |  |
| Wages and salaries (note 4) | 78,520 |  |
|  |  | (95,700) |
|  |  | 27,500 |

### Note 1 – Private accommodation

Olive lives in a flat that is situated above the health food shop. 30% of the expenditure included in the profit and loss account for light, heat, rent and rates relates to the flat.

### Note 2 – Motor expenses

During the year ended 31 December 2009 Olive drove a total of 20,000 miles, of which 8,000 were for business purposes.

### Note 3 – Sundry expenses

The figure of £2,230 for sundry expenses includes £220 for a fine in respect of health and safety regulations, £180 for the theft of cash by an employee, £100 for a donation to a political party, and £140 for a trade subscription to the Health and Organic Association.

### Note 4 – Wages and salaries

The figure of £78,520 for wages and salaries includes an annual salary of £14,000 paid to Olive's daughter. She works in the health food shop as a sales assistant. The other sales assistants doing the same job are paid an annual salary of £10,500.

## Note 5 – Goods for own use

Each week Olive takes health food from the shop for her personal use without paying for it. The weekly cost of this food is £30, and it has a selling price of £45.

## Note 6 – Plant and machinery

The only item of plant and machinery is Olive's motor car. The tax written down value of this vehicle at 1 January 2009 was £15,800.

## Note 7 – Patent royalties

Olive pays a patent royalty of £150 (gross) every quarter for the use of equipment that allows her to make her own organic breakfast cereal. This has not been accounted for in arriving at the net profit of £27,500.

## Other income

(1) Olive has a part-time employment for which she was paid a salary of £6,000 during 2009/10. Income tax of £1,320 has been deducted from this figure under PAYE.

(2) During 2009/10 Olive received building society interest of £1,440 and dividends of £1,080. These were the actual cash amounts received.

(3) On 30 November 2009 Olive sold some investments, and this resulted in a capital gain of £11,800.

## Other information

(1) During 2009/10 Olive paid interest of £220 (gross) on a loan taken out on 1 January 2008 to purchase equipment for use in her part-time employment.

(2) Olive contributed £2,600 (gross) into a personal pension scheme during 2009/10.

(3) Olive's payments on account of income tax in respect of 2009/10 totalled £4,900.

(a) **Calculate Olive's tax adjusted trading profit for the year ended 31 December 2009.**

(b)

    (i) **Calculate the income tax and capital gains tax payable by Olive for 2009/10;**

    (ii) **Calculate Olive's balancing payment for 2009/10 and her payments on account for 2010/11, stating the relevant due dates.**
    **Ignore national insurance contributions.**

(c) **Advise Olive of the consequences of not making the balancing payment for 2009/10 until 30 April 2011.**

## 3 Capital allowances for plant and machinery

This section covers capital allowances for plant and machinery only. It is possible that industrial buildings allowances may also be available to an unincorporated business, but as these are more likely to feature in questions involving companies, they are revised in Chapter 23.

The detailed rules for calculating capital allowances were covered in F6. These rules are still examinable at P6 and are summarised here, however there have been two main changes to the capital allowances regime for plant and machinery in FA2009.

The changes apply to both unincorporated businesses and companies and are effective from 6 April 2009 for unincorporated businesses and from 1 April 2009 for companies.

- A temporary first year allowance (FYA) of 40% will apply for expenditure in the main pool in excess of the annual investment allowance (AIA) limit of £50,000.

- Capital allowances for cars purchased after the date of change are to be calculated by reference to their $CO_2$ emissions. Note however that the treatment of cars purchased before the date of change will continue as before.

Further details are set out below.

Note that other than these two changes, there is little new technical knowledge on capital allowances at P6 compared with F6. The only new areas introduced at P6 are tax planning, and the awareness that the AIA is split between related businesses.

## Basis of the calculation

Capital allowances are calculated on an accounting period basis.

If the accounting period is not 12 months long, the AIA and WDA must be time apportioned. Note that FYAs are never time apportioned.

## Summary of the capital allowances available for cars

The following table sets out the treatment of cars following the changes introduced in FA2009.

| Cars purchased pre 6 April 2009 | Cars purchased on/after 6 April 2009 |
|---|---|
| • Cost < £12,000<br>  – Went into general pool<br>  – WDA 20% for 12 month period | • Emissions 111 – 160 g/km<br>  – Put in general pool<br>  – WDA 20% for 12 month period |
| • Cost ≥ £12,000<br>  – Keep separate<br>  – WDA 20% for 12 month period<br>  – Max £3,000 for 12 month period<br>  – BA or BC will arise on disposal | • Emissions > 160 g/km<br>  – Put in special rate pool<br>  – WDA 10% for 12 month period |
| • Private use cars<br>  – Keep separate<br>  – WDA 20% for 12 months period<br>  – Max £3,000 for 12 month period<br>  – BA or BC will arise on disposal | • Private use cars<br>  – Keep separate<br>  – WDA 20%/10% for 12 month period depending on emissions<br>  – BA or BC will arise on disposal |

Note that:

- Cars are never eligible for AIAs

- Cars are not eligible for FYAs, unless a low emission car

- Cars with emissions of 110g/km or less are low emission cars, and regardless of the date of purchase, continue to qualify for a 100% FYA.

### The procedure for calculating capital allowances

For plant and machinery capital allowances, adopt the following step-by-step approach:

(1) Read the information in the question and decide how many columns / pools you will require.

(2) Draft the layout and insert the TWDV b/f (does not apply in a new trade).

(3) Insert additions not eligible for the AIA or FYAs into the appropriate column taking particular care to allocate cars into the correct column according to cost or $CO_2$ emissions as relevant.

(4) Insert additions eligible for the AIA in the first column, then allocate the AIA to the additions.

Allocate the AIA to 'special rate pool' additions in priority to additions of plant and machinery in the general or special asset pools.

Within the general pool, allocate the AIA to expenditure that does not qualify for a 40% FYA in priority.

(5) Any 'special rate pool' additions in excess of the AIA must be added to the 'special rate pool' column to increase the balance available for 10% WDA.

Any general pool expenditure, in excess of the AIA, which has been incurred between 6.4.09 to 5.4.10 should be carried forward to the FYA section as it qualifies for 40% FYA.

Otherwise the excess should be added to the general pool to increase the balance qualifying for 20% WDA.

(6) Deal with any disposal by deducting the lower of cost or sale proceeds.

(7) Work out any balancing charge / balancing allowance for assets in individual pools.

Remember to adjust for any private use.

(8) Consider if the small pools WDA applies to the general pool and / or the 'special rate pool'.

(9) Calculate the WDA on each of the pools at the appropriate rate (20% or 10%). Remember to:

- time apportion if the accounting period is not 12 months

- adjust for any private use if an unincorporated business (not relevant for companies)

(10) Insert additions eligible for FYAs - the balance of any general pool expenditure (excluding cars) in excess of the AIA will get an FYA of 40% (the balance should then be transferred to the general pool) and any cars with emissions of 110 g/km or less will get 100% FYA.

(11) Calculate the TWDV to carry forward to the next accounting period and add the allowances column.

(12) Deduct the total allowances from the tax adjusted trading profits.

## Proforma capital allowances computation

| | Notes | £ | General pool £ | Special rate pool £ | Short life asset £ | Private use asset £ (Note 3) | Expensive car £ (Note 1) | Allowances £ |
|---|---|---|---|---|---|---|---|---|
| TWDV b/f | | | X | X | X | | X | |
| **Additions:** | | | | | | | | |
| Not qualifying for AIA or FYA: | | | | | | | | |
| Cars (111–160 gm/km) | (2) | | X | | | | | |
| Cars (over 160 gm/km) | | | | X | | | | |
| Car with private use | | | | | | X | | |
| Qualifying for AIA but not FYA: | | | | | | | | |
| Special rate pool expenditure | | X | | | | | | |
| Less AIA (Max £50,000 in total) | (4) | (X) | | | | | | |
| Transfer balance to special rate pool | | | | X | | | | |
| Plant and machinery (purchased pre 6.4.09 and post 5.4.10) | | X | | | | | | |
| Less AIA (Max £50,000 in total) | | (X) | | | | | | |
| Transfer balance to general pool | | | X | | | | | |
| Qualifying for AIA and FYA: | | | | | | | | |
| Plant and machinery (purchased between 6.4.09 and 5.4.10) | | X | | | | | | |
| Less AIA (Max £50,000 in total) | | (X) | | | | | | |
| Balance of AIA qualifying expenditure (see below) | (5) | B | | | | | | |
| Disposals (lower of original cost or sale proceeds) | (5) | | (X) | (X) | (X) | (X) | | |
| | | | X | X | X | X | | |
| BA / (BC) | (6) | | | | X / (X) | | | X / (X) |
| Small pools WDA | (1) | | (X) | (X) | | | | X |
| WDA at 20% | | | X | | | | | X |
| WDA at 20% (max £3,000) | | | | | | | (X) | X |
| WDA at 10% | | | | (X) | | | | X |
| WDA at 10%/20% (depending on emissions) | | | | | | (X) × BU% | | X |
| Additions qualifying for FYAs: | (5) | | | | | | | |
| Balance of AIA qualifying expenditure (see B above) eligible for FYA at 40% | | X | | | | | | |
| Low emission cars (up to 110 gm/km) | | | Nil | | | | | |
| Less FYA at 100% | | (X) | X | | | | | X |
| TWDV c/f | | | X | X | X | X | X | |
| Total allowances | | | | | | | | X |

## Notes to the proforma capital allowances computation

(1) Cars purchased before 1 April 2009 (companies) or 6 April 2009 (sole traders and partnerships) continue to be dealt with under the old rules (see above). The P6 examiner has confirmed that questions may have an 'old' expensive car with a TWDV b/f, however he will not have the purchase of a car pre 6 April 2009.

(2) Cars purchased on/after 1 April 2009 (companies) and 6 April 2009 (unincorporated businesses) are now pooled according to their $CO_2$ emissions into either the 'general' or 'special rate' pool.

   Low emission cars continue to receive 100% FYA.

(3) Cars with private use are de-pooled regardless of the date of purchase, and only the business proportion of allowances can be claimed. However, the date of purchase (pre or post April 2009) is important in determining the rate of WDA available.

(4) Allocate the AIA to the 'special rate' pool expenditure in priority to plant and machinery assets as a WDA of only 10% is available on the 'special rate' pool as opposed to 20% available on 'general' pool items.

(5) Pre April 2009, expenditure qualifying for AIA in the general pool but exceeding the level of AIA available, was eligible for a WDA of 20%. However, with effect from April 2009, expenditure qualifying for AIA in the general pool but exceeding the level of AIA available, is eligible for a FYA at 40% provided it is purchased in the year ending 31 March 2010 (companies) or in the year ending 5 April 2010 (unincorporated businesses).

(6) Small pools WDA: where the balance on the general pool and/or 'special rate pool' before calculation of the WDA is ≤ £1,000, all of the balance can be claimed as a WDA.

(7) Remember that private use asset pools are not relevant to companies.

(8) The taxpayer does not have to claim all or any of the AIA or WDA.

### The Annual Investment Allowance (AIA)

The Annual Investment Allowance (AIA) is a 100% allowance for the first £50,000 of expenditure incurred by a business on plant and machinery.

The key rules for the allowance are as follows:

- available to **all** businesses regardless of size;

- available on acquisitions of general plant and machinery and acquisitions of 'special rate pool' items (see later);

- **not** available on cars;

- limited to a maximum of £50,000 expenditure incurred in each accounting period of 12 months in length;

- for long and short accounting periods the £50,000 allowance is pro-rated;

- not available in the accounting period in which trade ceases.

Where a business spends more than £50,000 in a 12 month accounting period on assets qualifying for the AIA:

- the expenditure above the £50,000 limit will immediately qualify for further allowances (see below).

Note also that:

- the taxpayer does not have to claim all / any of the AIA if he does not want to

- any unused AIA can not be carried forward or carried back, the benefit of the allowance is just lost.

Expenditure on plant and machinery in the main pool not qualifying for AIA will qualify for writing down allowances (WDA).

## Expenditure in excess of the AIA limit

Expenditure on plant and machinery in the main pool qualifying for AIA but falling above the £50,000 AIA limit will qualify for further allowances as follows:

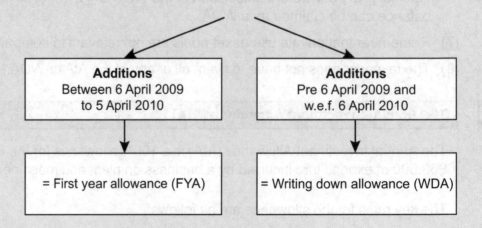

Note that the business can choose the expenditure against which the AIA is matched.

It will therefore be most beneficial for the AIA to be allocated against expenditure in the following order:

(1) Expenditure eligible for the WDA: 10% then 20%

(2) Expenditure eligible for the temporary 40% FYA

### AIA for related business

- The AIA must be split between related businesses.

  Businesses owned by the same individual will be regarded as related where they are engaged in the same activities or share the same premises.

  In such circumstances the owner of the businesses can choose how to allocate a single AIA between them.

- Unrelated businesses owned by the same individual will each be entitled to the full AIA.

### Points to note

- If VAT registered, include:
  - all additions of plant and machinery at the VAT exclusive price
  - except cars which are included at the VAT inclusive price.
- If not VAT registered, include all additions at the VAT inclusive amounts.
- Pre-trading capital purchases:
  - include if incurred in the seven years before trade commenced
  - treated as acquired on the first day of trade at its market value on that day.
  - but AIA only available for expenditure after 5 April 2008 and FYA only available for expenditure after 5 April 2009.

### Special rate pool

The 'special rate pool' is a pool of expenditure eligible that operates in the same way as the general pool except that:

- the WDA is 10% for a 12 month period (rather than 20%)
- the temporary FYA of 40% is not available.

Note that:

- the AIA is available against this expenditure (except on cars with emissions > 160 g/km), and

- the business can choose the expenditure against which the AIA is matched.

It will therefore be most beneficial for the AIA to be allocated against expenditure in the following order:

(1) the 'special rate pool' (as assets in the 'special rate pool' are not eligible for the temporary FYA and are eligible for 10% WDA, whereas general plant and machinery is eligible for the FYA of 40%).

(2) the general pool

(3) short life assets

(4) private use assets.

## Special rate pool - qualifying expenditure

The 'special rate pool' groups together expenditure incurred on the following type of assets:

- long-life assets
- 'integral features' of a building or structure
- thermal insulation of a building
- cars purchased on/after 6 April 2009 with emissions > 160 g/km.

Qualifying expenditure includes

- initial cost, and
- replacement expenditure.

Qualifying replacement expenditure is expenditure which is more than 50% of the replacement cost of the integral feature at the time the expenditure is incurred.

It also includes situations where less than 50% is spent initially but further spending in the next twelve months takes the total over 50%.

This rule prevents businesses gradually replacing integral features and claiming the cost as a repair.

### Long-life assets

- Long-life assets are defined as those with:
  - an expected working life of **25 years or more**
  - **total cost of £100,000** or more in a 12 month accounting period (the limit is scaled down for accounting period of less than 12 months)

- If the definition is satisfied, the items **must** be treated as long-life assets.

- Expected life:
  - from date first brought into use to the date it ceases to be capable of being used by anyone (i.e. not just the expected life in the hands of the current owner).

- Examples of long-life assets:
  - aircraft, agricultural equipment, air-conditioning units.

- Motor cars and plant and machinery situated in a building used as a retail shop, showroom, hotel or office can never be classified as a long-life asset.

### Integral features of a building or structure and thermal insulation

'Integral features of a building or structure' include expenditure incurred on the following:

- electrical (including lighting) systems;
- cold water systems;
- space or water heating systems;
- powered systems of ventilation, air cooling or air purification;
- lifts and escalators.

Thermal insulation in all business buildings (except residential buildings in a property business) is also included in the special rate pool.

### The small pool WDA

Where the balance immediately before the calculation of the WDA:

- on the general and/or 'special rate' pool
- is ≤ £1,000

the balance can be claimed as a small pool WDA and immediately written off in that year.

The £1,000 limit is for a 12 month accounting period, it is therefore pro rated for long and short accounting periods.

The claim is optional. However, the taxpayer will want to claim the maximum allowances available and reduce the balance on the pool to £Nil.

## Hire purchase assets

For **hire purchase** contracts:

- the individual is treated **as if** they had purchased the asset outright

- when the contract was taken out (even though they do not legally own the asset until they make the final payment)

- the hire purchase interest is treated as an allowable trading expense of the period of account in which it accrues

- capital allowances are **based on the cash price** (excluding interest), regardless of the actual instalments paid in the period of account.

## Comprehensive example

### Example 2 – Capital allowances computation

Ashley runs a manufacturing business and prepares accounts to 30 April each year.

During the year ending 30 April 2010 Ashley incurred the following expenditure:

1 May 2009     Spent £120,000 on a new air-conditioning system for the factory which is expected to last 30 years.

1 June 2009    Purchased new machinery for £40,000.

3 June 2009    Purchased a car with $CO_2$ emissions of 109 g/km for £17,000.

15 July 2009    Purchased a new car for with $CO_2$ emissions of 146 g/km for £18,000.

In addition on 1 July 2009 Ashley sold an old machine for £10,000 (original cost £15,000) and the expensive car for £7,000, which had originally cost £15,000.

As at 1 April 2009 the tax written down values were as follows:

General pool                          £64,000
Expensive car                        £9,000

## Calculate Ashley's capital allowances for the year ended 30 April 2010.

### Solution

### Capital allowances computation

|  | | General pool | Special rate pool | Expensive car | Allow-ances |
|---|---|---|---|---|---|
|  | £ | £ | £ | £ | £ |
| **y/e 30 April 2010** | | | | | |
| TWDV b/f | | 64,000 | Nil | 9,000 | |
| Additions: | | | | | |
| Not qualifying for AIA or FYA: | | | | | |
| Car (CO$_2$ emissions 146 g/km) | | 18,000 | | | |
| Qualifying for AIA but not FYA: | | | | | |
| Integral features | 120,000 | | | | |
| Less: AIA (Max) | (50,000) | | | | 50,000 |
| | | | 70,000 | | |
| Qualifying for AIA and FYA: | | | | | |
| Plant and machinery | 40,000 | | | | |
| Less: AIA (Max used) | (Nil) | | | | |
| | 40,000 | | | | |
| Disposal (lower of Cost and SP) | | (10,000) | | (7,000) | |
| | | 72,000 | 70,000 | 2,000 | |
| Balancing allowance | | | | (2,000) | 2,000 |
| Less: WDA (20%) | | (14,400) | | | 14,400 |
| WDA (10%) | | | (7,000) | | 7,000 |
| Less: FYA (40%) | (16,000) | | | | 16,000 |
| | | 24,000 | | | |
| Car (CO$_2$ < 110 g/km) | 17,000 | | | | |
| Less: FYA (100%) | (17,000) | | | | 17,000 |
| | | Nil | | | |
| TWDV c/f | | 81,600 | 63,000 | Nil | |
| Total allowances | | | | | 106,400 |

**Note:** The AIA is allocated to the additions in the 'special rate pool' (WDA 10%) in priority to the additions in the general pool (WDA 20%).

## Tax Planning measures to reduce tax liabilities

### Introduction

An individual has scope within the capital allowance rules to ensure that:

* the amount of and use of allowances, reliefs and losses are maximised
* the tax liabilities of an individual are minimised.

Key opportunities which may arise:

* the ability to waive the right to some, or all, of the capital allowances available , to enable more capital allowances to be claimed in future
* the ability to accelerate capital allowances with a short life asset election.

### Waiver of capital allowances

An individual does not have to claim the full capital allowances to which they are entitled if it would be advantageous not to do so.

A claim can be made in the self-assessment tax return for the whole or just part of the capital allowances available.

If a partial claim is made in one year:

* WDAs in subsequent years will be calculated on a higher TWDV figure than if the allowances had previously been claimed in full
* As a consequence, relief for the expenditure incurred will be delayed.
* However note any unused AIA cannot be carried forward or carried back, the benefit of the AIA is lost.

It may be advantageous to waive the right to capital allowances:

* to make full use of the individual's personal allowance
* to reduce a trading loss and claim higher allowances in the future, rather than having to waste losses against income already covered by personal allowances.

### Example 3 – Waiver of capital allowances

John has been trading for many years. His assessable trading income for the year ended 31 December 2009 is £7,000 before taking account any claim for capital allowances.

The TWDV of plant and machinery at 1 January 2009 is £10,000. He has made no additions or disposals in the year.

John is single and has no other income or outgoings.

**Advise John on how much of his capital allowances he should claim for the year ended 31 December 2009.**

**Solution**

John could claim a WDA of £2,000 (£10,000 × 20%), leaving a TWDV to carry forward of £8,000 (£10,000 – £2,000).

However, if he claimed the maximum allowance, his taxable income would be as follows:

|  | £ |
|---|---|
| Trading Income (£7,000 – £2,000) | 5,000 |
| Less: Personal allowance | (6,475) |
|  | Nil |

He will have no taxable income, but will waste £1,475 (£6,475 – £5,000) of his personal allowance.

He should therefore restrict the claim for capital allowances to £525 to prevent the wastage of his personal allowance for 2009/10.

His taxable income for 2009/10 will then be:

|  | £ |
|---|---|
| Trading Income (£7,000 – £525) | 6,475 |
| Less: Personal allowance | (6,475) |
|  | Nil |

Although his taxable income is still £Nil, the TWDV carried forward is increased from £8,000 to £9,475 (£10,000 – £525), which will enable him to claim higher relief for capital allowances in subsequent periods.

The amount of capital allowances claimed is a particularly important tax planning tool in a trading loss situation. This is covered in more detail later in this chapter.

## Accelerating capital allowances

The 'de-pooling' election to treat an asset as a short life asset enables a trader to accelerate capital allowances on certain types of short-life plant or machinery, for example, computers.

However, if eligible for the AIA, there will be no expenditure left to 'de-pool' and the short life asset election will not be made. This means that there is no need to even consider the election unless the business has expenditure > £50,000 in a 12 month period.

Note that:

- If there is expenditure in excess of the maximum £50,000 on expenditure eligible for the AIA, it may be advantageous for the AIA to be allocated against the general pool expenditure rather than a short life asset and for the de-pooling election to be made.

- The de-pooling election is:
    - beneficial if a BA arises on the disposal as it accelerates the capital allowances claim
    - not beneficial if it accelerates the crystallisation of a balancing charge.

- The de-pooling election must be made within 12 months of 31 January following the end of the tax year in which the trading period of acquisition ends.

- If no disposal is made within four years from the end of the accounting period in which the asset is acquired:
    - the balance on the separate short-life asset column must be transferred back to the general pool
    - WDAs are claimed in the future in the normal way in the general pool

In order to determine whether making the election is beneficial, the trader must decide within two years whether they anticipate selling the asset for more or less than its TWDV.

As the election is irrevocable and binding, if they find that the disposal will crystallise a balancing charge, they should wait to dispose of the asset after five years as it will then be included in the general pool and will not crystallise a charge.

**Example 4 - Short life asset**

Gina has traded for many years preparing accounts to 31 March each year. The TWDV on the general pool was £15,000 on 1 April 2009.

In May 2009, she acquired a new machine costing £10,000. She anticipated that the machine would last two years and she eventually sold it on 30 June 2011, for £1,750.

In August 2009, she acquired general plant and machinery for £52,000.

**Calculate the allowances available for each year, illustrating whether or not an election to treat the new machine as a short life asset would be beneficial.**

**Solution**

**Capital allowances computation**
**– without making a short life asset election**

| | £ | General pool £ | Allowances £ |
|---|---|---|---|
| **y/e 31 March 2010** | | | |
| TWDV b/f | | 15,000 | |
| Additions: | | | |
| Qualifying for AIA and FYA: | | | |
| Plant and machinery (£52,000 + £10,000) | 62,000 | | |
| Less: AIA | (50,000) | | 50,000 |
| | ——— | | |
| | 12,000 | | |
| Less: WDA (20%) | | (3,000) | 3,000 |
| | | ——— | |
| | | 12,000 | |
| Less: FYA (40%) | (4,800) | | 4,800 |
| | ——— | 7,200 | |
| | | ——— | |
| TWDV c/f | | 19,200 | |
| | | | ——— |
| Total allowances | | | 57,800 |
| | | | ——— |
| **y/e 31 March 2011** | | | |
| Less: WDA (20%) | | (3,840) | 3,840 |
| | | ——— | |
| TWDV c/f | | 15,360 | |
| | | | ——— |
| Total allowances | | | 3,840 |
| | | | ——— |

**y/e 31 March 2012**

| | | |
|---|---|---|
| Disposal (lower of Cost and SP) | (1,750) | |
| | ———— | |
| | 13,610 | |
| Less: WDA (20%) | (2,722) | 2,722 |
| | ———— | |
| TWDV c/f | 10,888 | |
| | ———— | |
| Total allowances | | 2,722 |
| | | ———— |

## Capital allowances computation – with a short life asset election

| | General pool | Short life asset | Allowances |
|---|---|---|---|
| | £ | £ | £ |
| **y/e 31 March 2010** | | | |
| TWDV b/f | 15,000 | | |
| Additions: | | | |
| Qualifying for AIA and FYA: | | | |
| Plant and machinery | 52,000 | 10,000 | |
| Less: AIA | (50,000) | (Nil) | 50,000 |
| | ———— | ———— | |
| | 2,000 | 10,000 | |
| Less: WDA (20%) | (3,000) | | 3,000 |
| | | ———— | |
| | 12,000 | | |
| Less: FYA (40%) | (800) | (4,000) | 4,800 |
| | ———— | 1,200 | |
| | | ———— | |
| TWDV c/f | 13,200 | 6,000 | |
| | | | ———— |
| Total allowances | | | 57,800 |
| | | | ———— |
| **y/e 31 March 2011** | | | |
| Less: WDA (20%) | (2,640) | (1,200) | 3,840 |
| | ———— | ———— | |
| TWDV c/f | 10,560 | 4,800 | |
| | | | ———— |
| Total allowances | | | 3,840 |
| | | | ———— |
| **y/e 31 March 2012** | | | |
| Disposal (lower of cost and SP) | | (1,750) | |
| | ———— | ———— | |
| | 10,560 | 3,050 | |
| Balancing allowance | | (3,050) | 3,050 |
| | | ———— | |
| Less: WDA (20%) | (2,112) | | 2,112 |

KAPLAN PUBLISHING

|  |  |
|---|---|
| TWDV c/f | 8,448 |
| Total allowances | 5,162 |

The total allowances claimed without making the election are £64,362 (£57,800 + £3,840 + £2,722). In the event Gina makes the election, the allowances available for the three years are £66,802 (£57,800 + £3,840 + £5,162)

Note that the election just accelerates the allowances available and only changes the timing of the allowances. The total allowances available will eventually be the same, however, without the election, it will take considerably longer to get there relief.

Therefore, if not covered by the AIA, it is recommended that the short life treatment is taken but only if it is expected that a balancing allowance can be accelerated. It is not advantageous to accelerate a balancing charge.

### Test your understanding 2

On 1 January 2010, Gordon commenced in self-employment running a music-recording studio. He prepared his first set of accounts for the 3 months to 31 March 2010.

The following information relates to the 3 months of trading to 31 March 2010:

(1) The tax adjusted trading profit for the period is £22,590. This figure is before taking account of capital allowances.

(2) Gordon purchased the following assets:

|  |  | £ |
|---|---|---|
| 1 January 2010 | Recording equipment | 21,625 |
| 15 January 2010 | Motor car with $CO_2$ emissions of 162 g/km (used by Gordon – 60% business use) | 15,800 |
| 20 February 2010 | Motor car with $CO_2$ emissions of 156 gkm (used privately by employee – 20% private use) | 10,400 |
| 4 March 2010 | Recording equipment (expected to be scrapped in 2 years) | 3,250 |

**Calculate Gordon's taxable trading income for the period ended 31 March 2010.**

## Summary of capital allowances for plant and machinery

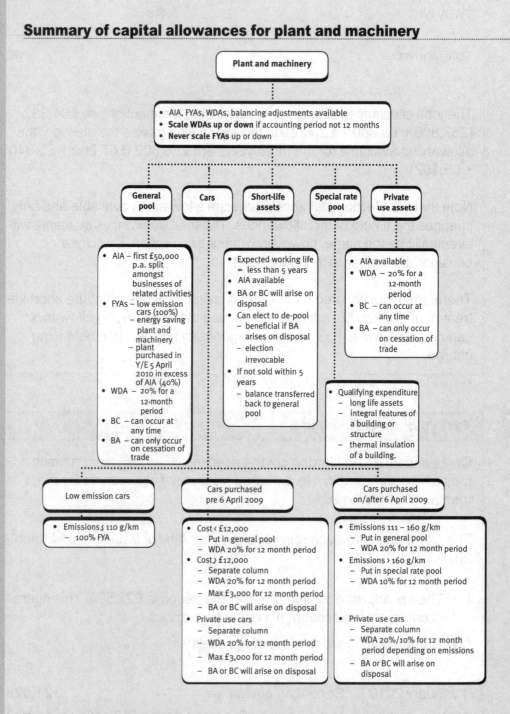

## Examination questions

Note that at P6:

- large capital allowance computations with many additions and disposals as seen at F6 are unlikely, less complicated computations will probably be required

- all of the knowledge in this chapter needs to be retained, however the computations are likely to focus on only a few aspects

- in some questions, it may be quicker and advisable to calculate allowances in single computations / workings rather than constructing a full proforma.

### 4 Basis of assessment rules

The basis of assessment rules determine in which tax year the adjusted trading profits will be assessed.

#### Ongoing basis rules

On an ongoing basis, the profits assessed are those of the twelve month accounting period ending in that tax year.

For example, the profits of the year ended 28 February 2010 are assessed in 2009/10 as the accounting period ends in that tax year (6 April 2009 to 5 April 2010).

#### Opening year rules

A reminder of the opening year rules and overlap profits covered at F6 are given in the table below.

| Year of assessment | Basis of assessment |
|---|---|
| **First tax year** (tax year in which trade starts) | Date of commencement to following 5 April |
| **Second tax year** The accounting period ending in the tax year is: | |
| (i)  12 months | That period of account |
| (ii)  less than 12 months | The first 12 months of trade |
| (iii)  more than 12 months | 12 months to the accounting date ending in the second tax year |
| There is no accounting period ending in the second tax year | Actual profits in the second tax year: From 6 April to 5 April |
| **Third tax year** | 12 months to the accounting date ending in the third tax year |
| **Fourth tax year onwards** | Normal current year basis |

Note that where apportionment of trading profits is required, calculations should be performed to the nearest month.

### Overlap profits

In the opening years, unless the trader has a 31 March or 5 April accounting end date, some of the profits are assessed in more than one tax year. These are known as 'overlap profits'.

Overlap profits:

- can arise in any of the first three tax years of assessment
- are carried forward, and are normally deducted from:
  - the assessment for the period in which the business ceases; or
  - possibly on an earlier change of accounting date.

### Test your understanding 3

John started to trade on 1 July 2009. He prepared accounts with tax adjusted trading profits after capital allowances as follows.

| | |
|---|---|
| Year ended 30 June 2010 | £24,000 |
| Year ended 30 June 2011 | £30,000 |

**Calculate the trading income assessments to include in John's income tax computations for the first three tax years of assessment and calculate the overlap profits to carry forward.**

### Test your understanding 4

Eric started to trade on 1 July 2009. He prepared accounts with tax adjusted trading profits as follows.

| | |
|---|---|
| 1 July 2009 to 30 April 2010 | £20,000 |
| Year ended 30 April 2011 | £38,400 |

**Calculate the trading income assessments to include in Eric's income tax computations for the first three tax years of assessment and calculate the overlap profits to carry forward.**

**Test your understanding 5**

Edwina commenced trading on 1 July 2008. She prepared accounts to 31 March 2010 and annually thereafter.

Her adjusted trading profits for the first two periods were as follows:

| | |
|---|---|
| 21 months ended 31 March 2010 | £42,000 |
| Year ended 31 March 2011 | £27,000 |

**Calculate the trading income assessments to include in Edwina's income tax computations for the first three tax years of assessment and calculate the overlap profits to carry forward.**

## Choice of accounting date

This is an important consideration at paper P6 as choice of an appropriate accounting date at the commencement of a business can affect:

- the level of profits to be taxed in a particular tax year
- the overlap profits created
- the timing and amount of tax payments.

**Choice of accounting date**

Over the life of the business, regardless of the accounting date chosen, the individual will be charged on all of the profits earned.

However, tax planning can have an advantageous impact on:

- cash flow
- can result in profits being assessed at a lower marginal rate of tax (depending on the individual's other income in each of the years).

The following important factors should be considered when choosing the optimum accounting date.

- An accounting date of just after, rather than just before, 5 April (such as 30 April) will ensure the maximum interval between earning profits and having to pay the related tax liability.
- However, an accounting date just after 5 April will result in increased overlap profits upon the commencement of trading (there are no overlap profits with a 31 March accounting date).

- Choosing alternative dates in the opening period can influence the level of profits to be taxed in the earlier years.

Note that the choice of an optimum accounting date depends on the implications of these factors in the given scenario. There is unlikely to be a clear cut recommendation. All of the facts have to be considered.

The common debate in examinations is the choice between an accounting date ending early in the tax year (e.g. 30 April) or late in the tax year (e.g. 31 March).

A summary of the preferred choice for each consideration is as follows:

| | 31 March | 30 April |
|---|---|---|
| Avoiding overlap profits | √ | |
| Time to prepare accounts and calculate tax | | √ |
| Time lag between earning income and paying tax | | √ |
| Minimise final year's tax liability | √ | |
| Simplicity | √ | |

### Example 5 – Choice of accounting date

A trader commences to trade on 1 January 2007 and is considering preparing his first accounts to 31 March 2008 or 30 April 2008.

His estimated tax adjusted trading profits after capital allowances are:

£2,000 per month for the first 12 months
£3,000 per month for the second 12 months
£4,000 thereafter per month.

(a) **Calculate the assessable profits under each alternative for the first five tax years.**

(b) **Calculate the overlap profits.**

(c) **State when the income tax is due for payment for the accounts ending in 2009.**

## Solution

### Accounting periods: 31 March date

| Periods ended 31 March: | 2008 | 2009 | 2010 | 2011 |
|---|---|---|---|---|
| Months: | (15) | (12) | (12) | (12) |
| | £ | £ | £ | £ |
| (£2,000 × 12) + (£3,000 × 3) | 33,000 | | | |
| (£3,000 × 9) + (£4,000 × 3) | | 39,000 | | |
| (£4,000 × 12) | | | 48,000 | 48,000 |

### Accounting periods: 30 April date

| Periods ended 30 April: | 2008 | 2009 | 2010 |
|---|---|---|---|
| Months: | (16) | (12) | (12) |
| | £ | £ | £ |
| (£2,000 × 12) + (£3,000 × 4) | 36,000 | | |
| (£3,000 × 8) + (£4,000 × 4) | | 40,000 | |
| (£4,000 × 12) | | | 48,000 |

| Basis periods | 31 March | 30 April |
|---|---|---|
| 2006/07 | 1.1.07 – 5.4.07 | 1.1.07 – 5.4.07 |
| | 3/15 × £33,000 | 3/16 × £36,000 |
| | £6,600 | £6,750 |
| 2007/08 | y/e 31.03.08 | No a/c period |
| | 12/15 × £33,000 | 12/16 × £36,000 |
| | £26,400 | £27,000 |
| 2008/09 | y/e 31.3.09 | 12m to 30.4.08 |
| | £39,000 | 12/16 × £36,000 |
| | | £27,000 |
| 2009/10 | y/e 31.3.10 | y/e 30.4.09 |
| | £48,000 | £40,000 |
| 2010/11 | y/e 31.3.11 | y/e 30.4.10 |
| | £48,000 | £48,000 |

### Total assessable trading profits

| | £ | £ |
|---|---|---|
| In 1st 5 tax years | 168,000 | 148,750 |
| | | |
| Overlap profits | | Nil |
| 11/16 × £36,000 | | £24,750 |

| Tax due for accounts ending in 2009 | y/e 31.3.09 | y/e 30.4.09 |
|---|---|---|
| Assessed in | 2008/09 | 2009/10 |
| Tax due in Instalment (1) | 31.1.09 | 31.1.10 |
| (2) | 31.7.09 | 31.7.10 |
| Final balance | 31.1.10 | 31.1.11 |

## Tax planning in opening years

It is usually beneficial to ensure that profits for the first period of trading, which are assessed more than once under the commencement rules, are kept to a minimum.

Profits can be minimised by increasing costs in the opening year, for example by:

- ensuring account is taken of any allowable pre-trading expenditure

- renting or leasing equipment for the first period of trading rather than purchasing it, if the rental / lease deduction exceeds the capital allowances available in the first year

- consider timing of purchases to bring forward revenue deductions or capital allowances.

However, it is important to note that simply delaying the issue of sales invoices, or accruing non bona fide expenses would not constitute normal tax avoidance. This would cross the boundary of tax evasion and is illegal.

## 5 Change of accounting date

A self-employed trader may change their accounting date if they wish. However, for tax purposes:

- conditions have to be met for a change to be a valid change of accounting date

- special rules apply to calculate the assessable trading profits in the tax year of the change.

### Conditions for a valid change of accounting date

A reminder of the conditions to be met and the calculation of assessable profits covered at F6 are given in expandable text and are summarised in the diagram below.

## Summary of change of accounting date rules

**Change of accounting date**

**Conditions:**
- Accounts to new date **must not exceed 18 months**
- No other COAD in last five years unless genuine commercial reason
- Notify HMRC by **31 January following tax year** of change

Where the new accounting date is **earlier in the tax year** than the old accounting date

Where the new accounting date is **later in the tax year** than the old accounting date

- The basis period must be for 12 months
- Assess:
  **12 months to the new accounting date**
- **Overlap profits** are **created**

- The basis period must be for 12 months
- Assess:
  **Accounts not yet assessed up to the new accounting date**
- **Deduct** the appropriate number of months' worth of **overlap profits** to ensure that the equivalent of only 12 months' profits are assessed

### Conditions to be met

All of the following conditions must be satisfied.

(1) The change of accounting date must be notified to HMRC on or before 31 January following the tax year in which the change is to be made.

(2) The first accounts to the new accounting date must not exceed 18 months in length.

If the period between the old accounting date and the proposed new accounting date is longer than 18 months; two sets of accounts will have to be prepared (12 months plus the balance).

(3) There must not have been another change of accounting date during the previous five tax years **unless** HMRC accept that the present change is made for genuine commercial reasons.

Not surprisingly, obtaining a tax advantage is not accepted as a genuine commercial reason.

If **all** of the above conditions are not met:

- the old accounting date will continue to apply for tax purposes
- if accounts are prepared to the new accounting date; the figures will have to be apportioned accordingly.

### The principle behind the calculations

The length of the accounting period required to change the accounting date of a business will be either less than or more than 12 months.

For example, if a trader has previously prepared accounts to 30 June and changes his accounting date to 30 September, the next set of accounts will be either three months in length or fifteen months in length.

For tax purposes, other than for the first and the final tax years, the basis of assessment rules only seek to assess twelve months of profits in any tax year. Therefore, on a change of accounting date, special rules apply to ensure that regardless of the length of accounting period, in any tax year only twelve months' profits will be assessed.

There are two key sets of rules to consider depending on whether the new accounting date is earlier or later in the tax year than the original accounting date.

In applying the rules, further overlap profits may arise or existing overlap profits may be relieved.

### New accounting date earlier in the tax year

The length of the accounting period to change the accounting date to a date **earlier in the tax year** can be less than or more than 12 months.

Regardless of the length of the accounting period, where the new accounting date is **earlier in the tax year** than the old accounting date:

- the basis period for the "tax year of change" will be the **12-month period** ending with the new accounting date
- as a result, some profits will be assessed more than once and overlap profits will arise.

These overlap profits are carried forward and offset in exactly the same way as overlap profits arising upon the commencement of trading.

The "tax year of change" is defined as the earlier of:

(i) the first tax year in which the accounts are made to the new accounting date, or

(ii) the first tax year in which the accounts are not made to the old accounting date.

In many cases, the first tax year in which both of the above events occur is the same. However, they could be different and if this is the case, the earlier tax year is the important year of change.

For example, if an individual prepares accounts to 28 February 2009 and then changes the accounting date to 30 April 2010.

The tax year of change is 2009/10, determined as the earlier of:

(i) the first tax year in which the accounts are made to the new accounting date (2010/11)

(ii) the first tax year in which the accounts are not made to the old accounting date (2009/10).

The following two examples show how the rules are applied if the new accounting date is earlier in the tax year:

- firstly by producing accounts for a period of less than 12 months

- secondly by producing accounts of more than 12 months.

### Example 6 – New date earlier in the tax year

(a) Andrea, a sole trader, has always prepared her accounts to 31 March. She decides to change her accounting date to 30 June by preparing accounts for the three-month period to 30 June 2009.

Andrea's tax adjusted profits after capital allowances are as follows:

|  | £ |
| --- | --- |
| Year ended 31 March 2009 | 60,000 |
| Three months to 30 June 2009 | 20,000 |
| Year ended 30 June 2010 | 85,000 |

**Calculate Andrea's trading income assessments for 2007/08 to 2009/10.**

(b) Assume that instead of producing a three month set of accounts, Andrea had decided to change her accounting date to 30 June by preparing accounts for the fifteen-month period to 30 June 2010 with tax adjusted profits of £105,000.

**Calculate Andrea's trading income assessments for 2008/09 to 2010/11 and prove that the result would be virtually the same.**

**Solution**

(a) The accounting date has moved from March to June. The accounting date is moving to earlier in the tax year.

The tax year of change is 2009/10, determined as the earlier of:

(i) the first tax year in which the accounts are made to the new accounting date (2010/11)

(ii) the first tax year in which the accounts are not made to the old accounting date (2009/10).

| Tax year | Basis period | Trading income £ |
|---|---|---|
| 2008/09 | Year to 31.3.09 | 60,000 |
| | | |
| 2009/10 | 12-month period to new accounting date of 30.6.09 | |
| | Year to 31.3.09: (£60,000 × 9/12) | 45,000 |
| | Period to 30.6.09 | 20,000 |
| | | 65,000 |
| 2010/11 | Year to 30.6.10 | 85,000 |

**Note:** The change in accounting date has created further overlap profits of £45,000, as the 9 months to March 2009 are assessed in both 2008/09 and 2009/10.

(b) The tax year of change is 2009/10, determined as the earlier of:

(i) the first tax year in which the accounts are made to the new accounting date (2010/2011)

(ii) the first tax year in which the accounts are not made to the old accounting date (2009/10).

| Tax year | Basis period | Trading income £ |
|---|---|---|
| 2008/09 | Year to 31.3.09 | 60,000 |
| 2009/10 | 12-month period to new accounting date of 30.6.09 (Note 1) | |
| | Year to 31.03.09: (£60,000 × 9/12) | 45,000 |
| | Period to 30.06.09: (£105,000 × 3/15) | 21,000 |
| | | 66,000 |
| 2010/11 | Year to 30.6.10 (Note 2) (£105,000 × 12/15) | 84,000 |

**Notes**

(1) The tax year in which the change takes place is 2009/10 as Andrea does not adopt her normal 31 March year end in that year. As all the criteria are met, she is treated as having accounts to the new accounting date in this year. This means that she is assessed on a deemed 12 month set of accounts to the new accounting date (i.e. year to 30 June 2009).

(2) In 2010/11, Andrea will be assessed **as if** she had prepared accounts for the year ended 30 June 2010.

(3) Overlap profits in respect of 9 months, as before = £45,000.

## New accounting date later in the tax year

The length of the accounting period to change the accounting date to a date **later in the tax year** can be less than or more than 12 months.

Regardless of the length of the accounting period, where the new accounting date is **later in the tax year** than the old accounting date:

- the basis period for the "tax year of change" will be the period **not yet assessed** ending with the new accounting date (whatever the length of that period)

- as this period will be more than 12 months, to ensure that the equivalent of only 12 months profits are assessed, an appropriate amount of overlap profits are deducted from the assessment.

The following two examples show how the rules are applied if the new accounting date is later in the tax year:

- Firstly by producing accounts for a period of more than 12 months.

- Secondly by producing accounts of less than 12 months.

### Example 7 – New date later in the tax year

Peter, a sole trader, commenced trading on 1 July 2006, and has always prepared his accounts to 30 June.

He has now decided to change his accounting date to 30 September by preparing accounts for the 15-month period to 30 September 2009.

Peter's tax adjusted trading profits after capital allowances are:

|  | £ |
|---|---|
| Year ended 30 June 2007 | 18,000 |
| Year ended 30 June 2008 | 24,000 |
| Period ended 30 September 2009 | 30,000 |
| Year ended 30 September 2010 | 36,000 |

**Calculate Peter's trading income assessments for all of the years affected by the results.**

**Solution**

**Peter**

The tax year of change is 2009/10, determined as the earlier of:

(i) the first tax year in which the accounts are made to the new accounting date (2009/10)

(ii) the first tax year in which the accounts are not made to the old accounting date (2009/10).

| Tax year | Basis period | Trading income £ |
|---|---|---|
| 2006/07 | 1.7.06 to 5.4.07 (£18,000 × 9/12) (Note 1) | 13,500 |
| 2007/08 | Year to 30.6.07 | 18,000 |

| 2008/09 | Year to 30.6.08 | 24,000 |
|---------|-----------------|--------|
| 2009/10 | Period not yet assessed, ending on the new accounting date | |
| | 15 month period to 30.9.09 (Note 2) | 30,000 |
| | Less: Overlap profits (£13,500 × 3/9) | (4,500) |
| | | 25,500 |
| 2010/11 | Year to 30.9.10 | 36,000 |

**Notes:**

(1) The overlap profits in the opening years are £13,500, representing 9 months profits (01.07.06 to 05.04.07) that have been taxed twice.

(2) In 2009/10 the period of account not yet assessed and ending with the new accounting date is 15 months. As no assessment can exceed 12 months, Peter is allowed to offset 3 months worth of his overlap profits.

(3) The remaining 6 months of overlap profits are carried forward as normal and are available for relief, either on a further change in accounting date or on the cessation of trade.

## 6 Trading losses for new and ongoing business

There is little new technical knowledge in respect of trading loss reliefs at P6 compared with F6, however FA 2009 introduced an extended carry back relief against trading profits.

The key difference at P6 is that examination questions at this level will usually involve giving tax advice and recommending a particular course of action to ensure the optimum use of trading losses in a particular scenario.

Common scenarios are to look at losses in the opening years of business, the ongoing years, where there is a change in operations or the closing years (see Chapter 18).

It is necessary to have a firm grasp of the basic trading loss rules in order to:

• identify the suitable tax planning measures available

• be able to recognise the consequences, advantages and disadvantages of taking different courses of action.

### The calculation of a trading loss

A trading loss occurs when the normal tax adjusted trading profit computation gives a negative result.

Where a trading loss occurs:

- the individual's trading income assessment will be £Nil
- a number of loss relief options are available to obtain relief for the loss.

#### Calculation of trading loss

A trading loss can occur in two situations, as follows:

|  | £ | £ |
|---|---|---|
| Tax adjusted trading profit / (loss) before capital allowances | X | (X) |
| Less: Plant and Machinery Allowances | (X) | (X) |
| Industrial Buildings Allowances | (X) | (X) |
| Trading loss | (X) | (X) |

Note that:

- capital allowances are taken into account in calculating the amount of the trading loss available for relief
- capital allowances:
  - can increase a tax adjusted trading loss; and
  - can turn a tax adjusted trading profit into a trading loss.

## 7 Loss relief options available

An individual trader has the following choice of options:

| | Opening years | Ongoing years | Closing years |
|---|---|---|---|
| Relief against total income | √ | √ | √ |
| Relief against chargeable gains | √ | √ | √ |
| Carry forward of trading losses | √ | √ | x |
| Opening years loss relief | √ | x | x |
| Terminal loss relief | x | x | √ |
| Incorporation relief | x | x | √ |

### Loss relief options in ongoing years

If an individual makes a trading loss in the ongoing years, they initially have to decide whether to claim relief against total income or carry forward all of the loss.

Where a claim against total income is made, any remaining loss is automatically carried forward unless the individual then makes a claim to:

- set the loss against chargeable gains, or
- extend the loss carry back against trading profits of the previous three years..

Note that a claim against gains and extended carry back claim can only be made after a claim against total income has been made. Any remaining loss is automatically carried forward.

The choices can be summarised as follows:

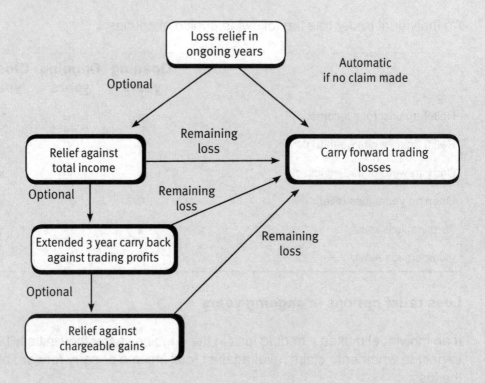

## A revision of the rules for relief against total income and carry forward

The key rules relating to the above reliefs are unchanged from F6 and are summarised as follows:

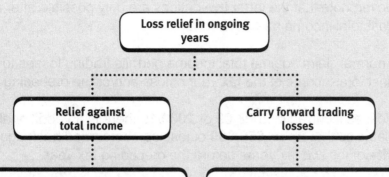

## Extended carry back against trading profits

If any loss remains after a claim against total income, a taxpayer can make:

- an extended claim against **trading profits** (see below), and/or
- a claim against **chargeable gains** (section 5).

However, note that the latter two options are only possible after a claim against total income has been made.

The normal claim against total income permits trading losses to be offset against total income of the tax year of loss and/or the preceding tax year.

For losses incurred in 2008/09 or 2009/10 there is an additional relief available so that **up to £50,000** of loss can be carried back against **trading profits** of the two tax years before the preceding tax year.

The extended relief will operate as follows:

- Trade losses of 2008/09 or 2009/10 can be subject to an extended carry back claim, although for examination purposes you will not have to deal with losses arising in 2008/09.

- The extended relief is optional and does not have to be claimed.

- A claim against total income must be made for the loss first, before an extended carry back claim can be made.

- The taxpayer has the usual choice of whether to claim one year or both years against total income.

- The claim need not be made if the taxpayer has no income in the two years of a possible claim; he does not have to claim in both years before an extended claim can be made.

- If a loss remains after the normal claim has been made against total income, then:
    - the loss can be carried back
    - against **trade profits**
    - of the **three years** preceding the loss.

- The carry back to the preceding year is unlimited.

- A **maximum** of **£50,000** can be carried back for two further years.

- The carry back is on a **LIFO basis**.

- Hence a loss of 2009/10 can be carried back against trade profits firstly of 2008/09 (if the claim against total income did not include that year) then 2007/08 and finally 2006/07.

- This is an extra relief and does not affect the ability of the taxpayer to use the loss in any other way that they choose.

- These rules also apply to losses on furnished holiday lettings which are treated as trade losses.

## Test your understanding 6

Gertrude has been in business for many years and until recently her business had been profitable. The results for the last four years, as adjusted for tax purposes, are as follows:

| | |
|---|---|
| Year ended 30 September 2006 | £72,000 |
| Year ended 30 September 2007 | £39,000 |
| Year ended 30 September 2008 | £28,000 |
| Year ended 30 September 2009 | £92,000 loss |

Gertrude has £5,500 of property business income each year but no other income.

**Show how she could obtain relief for his loss as efficiently as possible**

## A revision of the rules for relief against chargeable gains

The key rules relating to relief against chargeable gains are unchanged from F6 and can be summarised as follows:

> **Relief against chargeable gains**

- A claim against chargeable gains can **only be made if a claim against total income has been made** in that tax year first
- Claim is **optional**
  - if not claimed, the remaining loss is automatically carried forward.
- Amount of claim against chargeable gains = **lower** of:

|  | £ |
|---|---|
| (i) Total gains in year | X |
| All capital losses in the year | (X) |
| All capital losses brought forward | (X) |
|  | X |
| (ii) Remaining loss after claim against total income | X |

- If claimed, treat the trading loss **as if** it is a **current year capital loss** in the capital gains tax computation
- **Claim** can be **made in the same tax years as a claim** against total income
- If claimed
  - must **set off maximum amount possible**
  - **cannot restrict set-off** to preserve the annual exemption
  - therefore the benefit of the annual exemption may be wasted if a claim is made
- Relief must be **claimed in writing**
- For 2009/10 loss, the claim must be made **by 31 January 2012**

Note that there is no need to make an extended carry back claim before considering relief against gains.

### Example 8 - Relief against chargeable gains

Diana prepares her accounts to 31 December each year.

Her recent results have been as follows:

|  | £ |
|---|---|
| y/e 31.12.2009 Tax adjusted trading profit | 4,500 |
| y/e 31.12.2010 Trading loss | (18,500) |

Diana has received bank interest of £2,760 and dividends of £297 in 2009/10.

She realised the following chargeable gains in the year 2009/10:

|  | £ |
|---|---|
| Asset 1 | 16,000 |
| Asset 2 | 14,360 |

She has capital losses brought forward of £1,675.

**Calculate Diana's taxable income and taxable gains for 2009/10, assuming that she decides to claim relief for her losses against her total income and against her gains in 2009/10 only.**

**Solution**

Diana's loss occurs in y/e 31 December 2010 = in 2010/11

Note that:

- She is entitled to claim relief against total income in 2010/11 and/or 2009/10.
- She has decided to claim relief in 2009/10 only.
- Therefore she is only allowed to claim relief against gains in 2009/10.

### Income tax computation - 2009/10

| | £ |
|---|---:|
| Trading income | 4,500 |
| Bank interest (£2,760 x 100/80) | 3,450 |
| Dividends (£297 x 100/90) | 330 |
| | ——— |
| Total income | 8,280 |
| Less: Loss relief | (8,280) |
| | ——— |
| Net income | Nil |
| PA | (wasted) |
| | ——— |
| Taxable income | Nil |
| | ——— |

| **Amount of claim against chargeable gains** = lower of: | £ |
|---|---:|
| (i)   Total gains in year | 30,360 |
|     All capital losses in the year | (Nil) |
|     All capital losses brought forward | (1,675) |
| | ——— |
| | 28,685 |
| | ——— |
| (ii)  Remaining loss after claim against total income (£18,500 - £8,280) | 10,220 |
| | ——— |

Therefore, claim £10,220 relief and treat it as if it is a current year capital loss in the capital gains computation as follows:

### Capital gains tax computation - 2009/10

| | £ |
|---|---:|
| Asset 1 | 16,000 |
| Asset 2 | 14,360 |
| | ——— |
| Total chargeable gains | 30,360 |
| Less: Trading loss relief | (10,220) |
| Less: Capital loss b/f | (1,675) |
| | ——— |
| Net chargeable gains | 18,465 |
| AE | (10,100) |
| | ——— |
| Taxable gains | 8,365 |
| | ——— |

**Note:** The trading loss is treated as a current year capital loss and therefore must be set off before capital losses brought forward.

### Loss relief options in opening years

The options available in the opening years of trade are exactly the same as those available to an ongoing business, but with one extra option available: three year carry back against total income.

The choices can be summarised as follows:

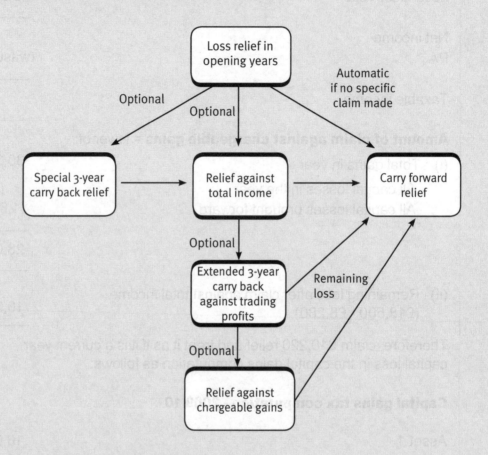

### Extended carry back relief in opening years

The extended relief claim is not possible in the first two years of business, and is unlikely to be made in the third year. This is because the relief is against trading profits of the three years preceding the year of the loss, when profits are likely to be minimal.

The extended carry back is therefore unlikely to feature in opening year questions.

#### Choice of loss relief in opening years

If an individual makes a trading loss in the opening years, they initially have to decide whether to claim normal relief against total income, special opening year loss relief or carry forward all of the loss.

Where a normal claim against total income is made, any remaining loss is automatically carried forward unless the individual decides to make an extended carry back claim against trading profits, a claim against chargeable gains or an opening year claim against total income.

Note that an individual can claim both normal relief against total income and opening year relief if there are sufficient losses. However, they must utilise the maximum amount of loss under one claim first, and can only make the other claim with the remaining loss.

Where a special opening year claim is made, any remaining loss is automatically carried forward unless the individual decides to make a normal claim against total income (and a possible extended carry back and/or extension against gains can then be considered).

Note that a claim against chargeable gains and extended carry back claim can only be made after a normal claim against total income has been made.

---

**Special opening year relief against total income**

- Optional claim
- Applies to loss arising in any of **first 4 years** of trading
- If claimed, set loss against
  - **total income**
  - **in 3 tax years** before tax year of loss
  - on a FIFO basis (i.e. earliest year first)
- There is no need for the trade to have been carried on in the earlier years
- **One claim** covers all 3 years
- For example:
  Loss in y/e 31.12.09 (2009/10) will be set off in:
  1. 2006/07
  2. 2007/08
  3. 2008/09
- If claimed
  - Must set off **maximum amount possible**
  - Cannot restrict set-off to preserve the personal allowance
  - Therefore, the benefit of the personal allowance may be wasted if a claim is made
- Relief must be claimed in writing
- For 2009/10 loss, the claim must be made by 31 January 2012

### Calculation of loss in opening years

- Losses are matched to tax years in exactly the same way as profits by applying the opening year assessment rules
- However, a loss may only be relieved once. If a loss has been taken into account in one year, it is treated as nil in the next assessment.

**Example 9 – Opening year loss**

Geraldine starts trading on 1 August 2008. Her results, as adjusted for tax purposes, are:

| | | |
|---|---|---|
| 10 months to 31 May 2009 | Loss | (£20,000) |
| Year ended 31 May 2010 | Profit | £48,000 |

**Calculate Geraldine's assessable profits for 2008/09 and 2009/10. State the amount of loss relief available in each year.**

| Solution | Assessable profits | Loss Available |
|---|---|---|
| | £ | £ |
| **2008/09** (Actual basis) | | |
| 01.08.08 – 05.04.09 | | |
| 8/10 × (20,000) = (£16,000) | Nil | 16,000 |
| | | |
| **2009/10** (First 12 months) | | |
| 01.08.08 – 31.07.09 | | |
| Loss (10 m/e 31.05.09) | (20,000) | |
| Less: Taken into account in 2008/09 | 16,000 | |
| | (4,000) | |
| 2 months of y/e 31.05.10 | | |
| Profits (2/12 × 48,000) | 8,000 | |
| | 4,000 | |
| Loss relief claim (Note) | | Nil |

**Note:** The £4,000 loss relief is automatically given in 2009/10 by reducing the assessment from £8,000 to £4,000.

## The procedure for dealing with questions involving losses

The following procedure should be adopted when answering questions:

(1) Determine the tax adjusted profits and losses after capital allowances for each accounting period.

(2) Determine when losses arise and therefore when loss relief is available (i.e. in which tax years).

(3) Set up a proforma income tax computation for each tax year side by side and leave spaces for the loss set off to be inserted later.

(4) Set up a loss memo working for each loss to show how it is utilised.

(5) If more than one loss – consider in chronological date order.

(6) Consider each option – be prepared to explain the options, the consequences of making a claim, the advantages and disadvantages.

(7) Set off losses according to the requirements of the question, or in the most beneficial way if it is a tax planning question.

## Proforma income tax losses computation

For a new business starting in 2009/10 where loss arising in 2009/10

|  | 2006/07 | 2007/08 | 2008/09 | 2009/10 | 2010/11 |
|---|---|---|---|---|---|
|  | £ | £ | £ | £ | £ |
| Trading income (Note) |  |  |  | Nil | X |
| Loss relief b/fwd |  |  |  |  | (x) |
|  |  |  |  |  |  |
|  |  |  |  | Nil | X |
| Employment income | X | X | X | X | X |
| Other income | X | X | X | X | X |
|  |  |  |  |  |  |
| Total income | X | X | X | X | X |
| Normal relief |  |  | (x) | (x) |  |
| Opening years relief | (x) | (x) | (x) |  |  |
|  |  |  |  |  |  |
| Net income | X | X | X | X | X |
| PA (if applicable) | (x) | (x) | (x) | (x) | (x) |
|  |  |  |  |  |  |
| Taxable income | X | X | X | X | X |

|  | 2009/10 |
|---|---|
| **Loss working** | £ |
| Trading Loss | x |
| Utilisation of loss | |
| Opening years relief against total income (strict FIFO order) | (x) |
| Normal relief against total income (any order) | (x) |
| | ——— |
| C/fwd against future trading profits | x |
| | ——— |

**Note:** The extended carry back against trading profits would not be possible here, as no trading profits arose before 2009/10. Where extended carry back relief is claimed, the loss would be set against trading income.

## Tax planning with trading losses

### The primary aims of tax planning for trading losses

When planning relief for trading losses, careful consideration needs to be given to the personal circumstances of the individual.

Tax advice should aim to satisfy the following goals of a taxpayer:

- Obtain tax relief at the highest marginal rate of tax.

- Obtain relief as soon as possible.

- Ensure that the taxpayer's personal allowances are not wasted, if possible.

It may not be possible to satisfy all of these aims, for example:

- in order to get a higher rate of relief, the taxpayer may have to waste their personal allowance

- carrying losses forward may give a higher rate of relief, but the cash flow implications of claiming relief now rather than waiting for relief, may be more important to the taxpayer.

In examination questions you will be given a scenario and the tax advice must address the specific facts of the situation presented.

### Factors to consider

In understanding the position of the taxpayer, it is important to understand the key features of the reliefs available.

## Test your understanding 7

Jeremy aged 35 and single started in business on 1 July 2008 and decided to prepare accounts to 30 June.

The results for his first two trading periods are as follows:

|  | £ |
|---|---|
| Year ended 30.6.2009 : Trading loss | (20,000) |
| Year ended 30.6.2010 : Trading profit | 9,000 |

Prior to setting up in business he was employed and his employment income has been as follows:

|  | £ |
|---|---|
| 2005/06 | 13,000 |
| 2006/07 | 13,000 |
| 2007/08 | 14,000 |
| 2008/09 | 4,000 |

He had rental income of £1,000 for the years 2005/06 and 2009/10 only.

(a) **Show the loss claims if loss relief is claimed in the most beneficial way.**

(b) **Comment briefly on the result obtained under the alternative scenarios.**

## 8 NICs payable in respect of self employed individuals

A reminder of the rules for Class 2 and Class 4 contributions covered at F6 is given in expandable text and are summarised in the diagram below.

### Summary of total NICs payable

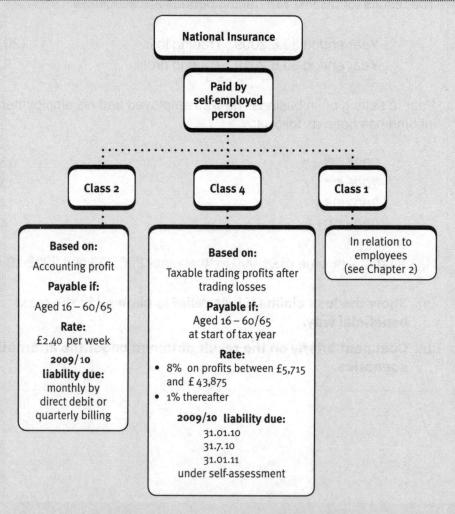

**Class 2 contributions**

Provided the individual does not have a certificate of exemption, Class 2 contributions are payable by individuals:

- aged 16 or over **until** attaining pensionable age (65 for a man, 60 for a woman).

The key facts to remember about Class 2 NICs are as follows.

- Class 2 contributions are a flat rate payment of £2.40 per week.
- The maximum total Class 2 NICs payable for 2009/10 is therefore £125 (£2.40 × 52 weeks).

- Class 2 contributions are paid to HMRC on a monthly basis by direct debit, or by quarterly billing in arrears.

- Class 2 contributions are not an allowable deduction for the purposes of calculating the individual's income tax liability.

- Class 2 contributions are not a deductible expense when calculating the business' taxable trading profits.

- A certificate of exemption can be obtained if 'earnings' are equal to or below the low earnings threshold of £5,075 for 2009/10.

- "Earnings' for Class 2 purposes are the financial accounting net profit actually falling into the tax year, not the taxable trading profits.

- The individual does not have to obtain the exemption and can pay Class 2 NICs voluntarily if they wish.

## Class 4 contributions

In addition to Class 2 NICs, a self-employed individual may also be liable to Class 4 NICs.

Class 4 contributions are payable by self employed individuals who:

- **at the start of the tax year**, are aged 16 or over.

They continue to pay until:

- **the end of the tax year** in which they attain pensionable age (65 for a man, 60 for a woman).

The key facts to remember about Class 4 NICs are:

- Class 4 NICs are a percentage-based contribution levied on the 'profits' of the individual in excess of £5,715 for 2009/10.

- Contributions payable are calculated as follows:
  - 8% on profits between £5,715 and £43,875 per annum
  - 1% on profits in excess of £43,875.

- Class 4 contributions are not an allowable deduction for the purposes of calculating the individual's income tax liability.

- Class 4 contributions are not a deductible expense when calculating the business' taxable trading profits.

- 'Profits' for the purposes of Class 4 NICs consist of:
  - the taxable trading profits of the individual which are assessed to income tax
  - **after** deducting trading losses (if any).

  Note that 'profits' for Class 4 NICs are before deducting the individual's personal allowance which is available for income tax purposes.

- If the individual has more than one business, the aggregate of all profits from all self employed occupations are used to calculate the Class 4 NIC liability.

- Class 4 contributions are paid to HMRC at the same time as the individual's income tax due under self assessment, as follows:

| Payment | Due date | Amount |
|---|---|---|
| Payments on account | • 31 January in the tax year (i.e. 31.1.2010 for 2009/10) <br><br> • 31 July following the end of the tax year (i.e. 31.7.2010 for 2009/10) | Two equal instalments of: <br><br> • 50% of the amount paid by self assessment in the preceding year |
| Balancing payment | • 31 January following the end of the tax year (i.e. 31.1.2011 for 2009/10) | Under or overpayment for the year |

### Test your understanding 8

James has been trading as a self-employed painter and decorator since 1998. His taxable trading profits for 2009/10 are £55,000 and he has trading losses brought forward of £10,000.

His wife, Poppy, is a part-time mobile hairdresser. Her taxable trading profits for 2009/10 are £6,350.

**Calculate the Class 2 and Class 4 NICs payable by James and Poppy for 2009/10.**

**NICs: Self employed individuals**

A self-employed individual pays both Class 2 and Class 4 NICs.

If the self-employed individual employs staff, they will be required to account for:

- Class 2 and Class 4 NICs in respect of their trading profits; and
- Class 1 primary, Class 1 secondary and Class 1A NICs in respect of earnings and benefits provided to employees.

## 9 Employee versus partner

A popular scenario in the examination is the consideration of expanding the business and taking on an individual, often a spouse, as either an employee or a partner.

This section sets out a summary of the tax implications.

### Employment of individuals in the business

- Employment costs (salaries, cost of providing benefits, employer's NICs) are tax deductible expenses for the employer.
- Employer's NICs can be avoided or reduced by taking on fewer full time staff and more part time staff because of the threshold at which NIC becomes payable.
- However, there is an increased administrative burden of employing staff.
- Alternatively, work could be subcontracted to self-employed individuals, avoiding the need to pay employer's NICs.

### Employee

| | Implications for sole trader | Implications for employee |
|---|---|---|
| **Salary** | • Allowable deduction from trading profits<br><br>• Employer's Class 1 secondary NICs payable at 12.8% on earnings over £5,715 per annum (allowable deduction from trading profits)<br><br>• PAYE compliance burden | • Taxed on employment income – receipts basis<br><br>• Employee's Class 1 primary NICs payable at 11% (£5,715 – £43,875 per annum and 1% thereafter) – deducted under PAYE |

| Provision of car | • Capital allowances 100% FYA or WDA of 20% or 10% depending on emissions. | • Benefit under employment income rules (if earning > £8,500 pa) based on $CO_2$ emissions |
|---|---|---|
| | • Allowable deduction from trading profits | • Reduction in benefit for contribution toward private use |
| | • No private use restriction for employee usage | |
| | • Running costs allowable in full as deduction from trading profits | |
| | • Employers Class 1A NICs at 12.8% of assessable benefit – allowable deduction from trading profits | |

### Setting up a partnership or taking on a partner

- Where two or more individuals are in partnership (rather than in the sole trader and employee relationship) then there is a NIC saving and a spreading of the tax burden.

- A partner
    - shares profit allocation
    - there is no employer's NIC to pay

    Each partner is subject to the trading profit basis period rules and is responsible for his or her own income tax, Class 2 and Class 4 NICs.

    The detailed rules covering how partnerships are taxed are set out in Chapter 19

**Partner**

| | Implications for sole trader (exisiting partner) | Implication for new partner |
|---|---|---|
| **Salary (profit share)** | <ul><li>Not allowable deduction from trading profits</li><li>Trading assessment on share of profits</li><li>No additional NICs</li></ul> | <ul><li>Trading assessment on share of profits – opening year rules basis</li><li>Class 2 NICs payable – £2.40 per week</li><li>Class 4 NICs payable – 8% on share of profits (£5,715 – £43,875 and 1% thereafter)</li><li>Tax and Class 4 NICs payable under self-assessment</li></ul> |
| **Provision of car** | <ul><li>Capital allowances for partners' cars 100% FYA or WDA of 20% or 10% depending on emissions, based on cost.</li><li>Allowable deduction from trading profits of the partnership</li><li>Private use restriction for partners' usage – only claim business use proportion</li><li>Running costs allowable as deduction from trading profits – business use proportion only</li><li>No NICs on cars (as no employment)</li></ul> | |

**Test your understanding 9**

Henry has been in business as a sole trader for a number of years, and makes annual profits of £100,000.  He wants to involve his wife Mary in the business, either as an employee or as a partner, and is considering the following options:

(i)   Employing Mary at a gross salary of £30,000 per annum

(ii)  Running the business in equal partnership with Mary

Both Henry and Mary had rental income each year of £6,475.

(a) **Calculate the total annual tax payable by Henry as a sole trader**

(b) **Calculate the total annual tax saving for the couple under each of the suggested alternatives**

## 10 VAT

The key issues that may be relevant to a new or ongoing unincorporated business are:

- Registration
- Pre registration input VAT
- Special accounting schemes

These areas are all covered in detail in Chapter 20

## 11 Self assessment

Another important area in examination scenarios is likely to be advising the client on their duties under self assessment, particularly:

- Notification of chargeability
- Payment of tax
- Submission of tax returns
- Record keeping

These areas are all covered in detail in Chapter 16.

## 12 Chapter summary

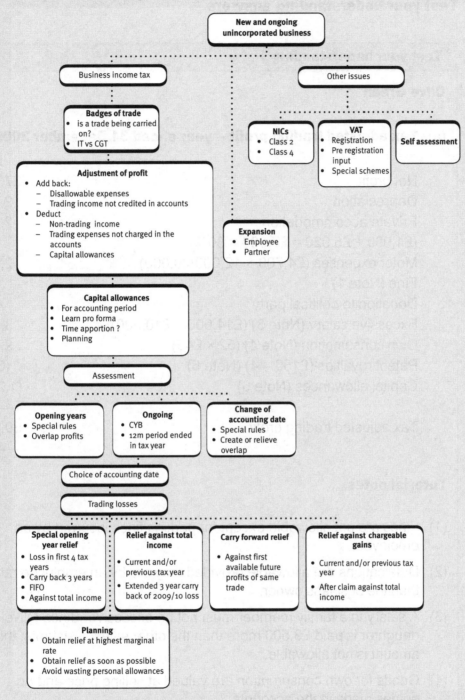

## Test your understanding answers

### Test your understanding 1

**Olive Green**

(a) **Tax adjusted trading profit – year ended 31 December 2009**

| | £ |
|---|---:|
| Net profit | 27,500 |
| Depreciation | 2,350 |
| Private accommodation | 2,370 |
| (£1,980 + £5,920 = £7,900 × 30%) | |
| Motor expenses (£4,700 × 12,000/20,000) | 2,820 |
| Fine (Note 1) | 220 |
| Donation to political party | 100 |
| Excessive salary (Note 3) (£14,000 – £10,500) | 3,500 |
| Own consumption (Note 4) (52 × £45) | 2,340 |
| Patent royalties (£150 × 4) (Note 5) | (600) |
| Capital allowances (Note 6) | (1,200) |
| | |
| Tax adjusted trading profit | 39,400 |

**Tutorial notes:**

(1) Fines are not allowable except for parking fines incurred by an employee.

(2) Defalcations are allowable provided they are by an employee rather than the business owner.

(3) A salary to a family member must not be excessive. Since Olive's daughter is paid £3,500 more than the other sales assistants, this amount is not allowable.

(4) Goods for own consumption are valued at selling price and no entries made in the accounts.

(5) The patent royalties have been paid wholly and exclusively for the purposes of the trade and are therefore deductible from trading profits.

(6) Capital allowances for Olive's motor car are restricted to £3,000, with the business proportion being £1,200 (£3,000 × 8,000/20,000). The treatment of motor cars already owned at 6 April 2009 is unaffected by the changes introduced in Finance Act 2009.

## (b) **Income tax computation – 2009/10**

| | Total £ | Other £ | Savings £ | Dividends £ |
|---|---|---|---|---|
| Trading income | 39,400 | 39,400 | | |
| Employment income | 6,000 | 6,000 | | |
| Building society interest | | | | |
| (£1,440 × 100/80) | 1,800 | | 1,800 | |
| Dividends (£1,080 × 100/90) | 1,200 | | | 1,200 |
| Total income | 48,400 | 45,400 | 1,800 | 1,200 |
| Reliefs: | | | | |
| Loan interest (Note 1) | (220) | (220) | | |
| Net income | 48,180 | 45,180 | 1,800 | 1,200 |
| Personal allowance | (6,475) | (6,475) | | |
| Taxable income | 41,705 | 38,705 | 1,800 | 1,200 |

| £ | | £ |
|---|---|---|
| 38,705 | at 20% (other income) | 7,741 |
| 1,295 | at 20% (savings) | 259 |
| 40,000 | Extended band (Note 2) | |
| 505 | at 40% (savings) | 202 |
| 1,200 | at 32.5% (dividends) | 390 |
| 41,705 | | |

| | |
|---|---|
| Income tax liability | 8,592 |
| Less: Tax suffered at source | |
| Dividends (£1,200 at 10%) | (120) |
| PAYE | (1,320) |
| Building society interest (£1,800 at 20%) | (360) |
| Income tax payable | 6,792 |

### Notes:

(1) The loan interest qualifies as a relief deductible from total income since the loan was used by Olive to finance expenditure for a qualifying purpose. It is paid gross.

(2) The personal pension contribution results in Olive's basic rate tax band threshold being extended to £40,000 (£37,400 + £2,600).

### Olive's CGT liability for 2009/10

= £306 (£11,800 − £10,100 = £1,700 at 18%).

### Balancing payment for 2009/10 due on 31 January 2011

= £2,198 (£6,792 + £306 − £4,900).

### Payments on account for 2010/11

Payments on account are not required for CGT, so the payments on account for 2010/11 will be £3,396 (6,792 × 50%). These will be due on 31 January and 31 July 2011.

### Consequences of paying balancing payment late

(1) Interest is charged where a balancing payment is paid late. This will run from 31 January 2011 to 30 April 2011.

(2) The interest charge will be £14 (£2,198 × 2.5% × 3/12).

(3) In addition, a 5% surcharge of £110 (£2,198 at 5%) will be imposed as the balancing payment is not made within 28 days of the due date.

## Test your understanding 2

### Gordon

### Period ended 31 March 2010

| | £ |
|---|---|
| Adjusted profit | 22,590 |
| Less: Capital allowances (W) | (18,207) |
| Trading profit | 4,383 |

### Working: Capital allowances computation

| | General pool £ | Short life asset £ | Private use car £ | Business use £ | Business use % | Allow-ances £ |
|---|---|---|---|---|---|---|
| Additions: | | | | | | |
| Not qualifying for AIA or FYA: | | | | | | |
| Car (CO$_2$ 156 g/km) (Note 1) | | 10,400 | | | | |
| Private use car | | | 15,800 | | | |
| Qualifying for AIA and FYA: | | | | | | |
| Equipment | 21,625 | 3,250 | | | | |
| Less: AIA (Max) (Note 2) | (12,500) | (Nil) | | | | 12,500 |
| | 9,125 | 3,250 | | | | |
| | | 10,400 | 15,800 | | | |
| Less: WDA (20% × 3/12) | | (520) | | | | 520 |
| WDA (10% × 3/12) (CO$_2$ > 160 g/km) | | | (395) | × 60% | | 237 |
| Less: FYA (40%) | (3,650) | (1,300) | | | | 4,950 |
| | | 5,475 | | | | |
| TWDV c/f | | 15,355 | 1,950 | 15,405 | | |
| Total allowances | | | | | | 18,207 |

### Notes:

(1)   Private use by an employee is not relevant. A separate private use asset column is only required where there is private use by the owner of the business.

(2)   The AIA is pro-rated for the three month period. The maximum allowance is therefore £12,500 (£50,000 x 3/12). The AIA is allocated to the general plant and machinery in priority to the short life asset.

### Test your understanding 3

**John**

| Tax year | Basis period | Trading income £ |
|---|---|---|
| 2009/10 | 1 July 2009 to 5 April 2010 (9/12 × £24,000) | 18,000 |
| 2010/11 | Year ending 30 June 2010 | 24,000 |
| 2011/12 | Year ending 30 June 2011 | 30,000 |

**Overlap profits**

| | |
|---|---|
| 1 July 2009 to 5 April 2010 (9/12 × £24,000) | £18,000 |

### Test your understanding 4

**Eric**

| Tax year | Basis period | Trading income assessment £ |
|---|---|---|
| 2009/10 | 1 July 2009 to 5 April 2010 (9/10 × £20,000) | 18,000 |
| 2010/11 | 1 July 2009 to 30 June 2010 (£20,000 + 2/12 × £38,400) | 26,400 |
| 2011/12 | Year ending 30 April 2011 | 38,400 |

**Overlap profits**

| | £ |
|---|---|
| 1 July 2009 to 5 April 2010 (9/10 × £20,000) | 18,000 |
| 1 May 2010 to 30 June 2010 (2/12 × £38,400) | 6,400 |
| | 24,400 |

**Test your understanding 5**

**Edwina**

| Tax year | Basis period | Trading income assessment |
|---|---|---|
| | | £ |
| 2008/09 | 1 July 2008 to 5 April 2009 (42,000 × 9/21) | 18,000 |
| 2009/10 | Year ended 31 March 2010 (42,000 × 12/21) (Note) | 24,000 |
| 2010/11 | Year ending 31 March 2011 | 27,000 |

**Note:** There is an accounting date in the second year of assessment so the assessment is the 12 months ending on that accounting date.

Overlap profits: There are no overlap profits.

## Test your understanding 6

### Gertrude

**Computation of taxable income**

|  | 2006/07 £ | 2007/08 £ | 2008/09 £ | 2009/10 £ |
|---|---|---|---|---|
| Trading income | 72,000 | 39,000 | 28,000 | Nil |
| Extended carry back relief | (11,000) | (39,000) |  |  |
|  | 61,000 | Nil |  |  |
| Property income | 5,550 | 5,500 | 5,500 | 5,500 |
| Total income | 66,500 | 5,500 | 33,500 | 5,500 |
| Less: Loss relief | - | - | (33,500) | Nil |
| Net income | 66,500 | 5,500 | Nil | 5,500 |
| Less PA | (6,475) | (5,500) | - | (5,500) |
| Taxable income | 60,025 | Nil | Nil | Nil |

### Loss memorandum

|  | £ |
|---|---|
| Loss for year ending 30 September 2009 | 92,000 |
| Less: Relief against total income: |  |
| 2009/10 (no claims as income covered by PA) | Nil |
| 2008/09 | (33,500) |
|  | 58,500 |
| Less: Extended carry back claims: |  |
| 2007/08 | (39,000) |
| 2006/07 (£50,000 max – £39,000) | (11,000) |
| Loss remaining to carry forward | 8,500 |

**Note:** The claim against total income could be made in 2009/10 instead of 2008/09. This would waste the 2009/10 PA, but would mean only £28,000 of loss would be utilised against trading income in 2008/09. In this example there is no net effect, however the choice of year for the claim could be significant if there are varying levels of other income.

## Test your understanding 7

**Jeremy**

**Step 1** **Find the loss available, and the trading income assessments of the new business**

|  |  | Trading Profits | Loss |
|---|---|---|---|
|  |  | £ | £ |
| 2008/09 | 01.07.08 – 05.04.09 | NIL | |
|  | 9/12 × £20,000 | | 15,000 |
| 2009/10 | y/e 30.06.09 | NIL | |
|  | Loss is (£20,000 – £15,000) | | 5,000 |
| 2010/11 | y/e 30.06.10 | 9,000 | |

**Step 2** **Set up income tax computations before loss reliefs**

| | 2005/06 | 2006/07 | 2007/08 | 2008/09 | 2009/10 | 2010/11 |
|---|---|---|---|---|---|---|
| Income: | £ | £ | £ | £ | £ | £ |
| Employment | 13,000 | 13,000 | 14,000 | 4,000 | | |
| Trading | | | | Nil | Nil | 9,000 |
| Rental | 1,000 | | | | 1,000 | |
| | | | | | | |
| Total | 14,000 | 13,000 | 14,000 | 4,000 | 1,000 | 9,000 |

**Step 3** **Using special opening year relief only**

(a) Loss in 2008/09 of £15,000 can be set against total income of 2005/06 – 2007/08 with earliest year first.

(b) Loss in 2009/10 of £5,000 can be used against total income of 2006/07 – 2008/09.

(c) No restrictions to preserve PA.

| | 2005/06 | 2006/07 | 2007/08 | 2008/09 |
|---|---|---|---|---|
| | £ | £ | £ | £ |
| Total income | 14,000 | 13,000 | 14,000 | 4,000 |
| 2008/09 loss | (14,000) | (1,000) | | |
| 2009/10 loss | | (5,000) | | |
| | | | | |
| Net income | Nil | 7,000 | 14,000 | 4,000 |
| | | | | |
| PA | Wasted | Available in full | | |

**Step 4**  **Alternatively claim normal relief against total income and carry forward relief**

(a) Relief can be claimed agaist total income in the year of the loss and/or the previous year. For 2008/09 loss relief is available in 2008/09 and/or 2007/08. There is no point making 2008/09 claim as total income is covered by PA. Therefore use £14,000 in 2007/08 and then c/fwd £1,000 against trading income of 2010/11.

(b) The 2009/10 loss can be used in that year and/or 2008/09. In both years PA is available to cover total income. Therefore carry forward £5,000 against trading profit of 2010/11. This will still however result in some wastage of PA.

**Step 5**  **The effect is as follows**

|  | 2007/08 £ | 2008/09 £ | 2009/10 £ | 2010/2011 £ |
|---|---|---|---|---|
| Trading profit | 14,000 | 4,000 | nil | 9,000 |
| Less: Loss relief b/f |  |  |  | (1,000) |
|  |  |  |  | (5,000) |
| Other income |  |  | 1,000 |  |
|  | 14,000 | 4,000 | 1,000 | 3,000 |
| Less: Loss relief | (14,000) |  |  |  |
| Net income | nil | 4,000 | 1,000 | 3,000 |
| PA | Wasted | Part Wasted | Part Wasted | Part Wasted |

Using special opening year relief relieves the losses immediately as they were carried back. There is a wastage of PA in 2005/06 only but repayments of tax at 20% will result.

Using normal relief against total income/carry forward wastes PA in 2007/08 and partially in other years. It does not relieve the loss immediately and tax saved is at 20% tax rates. Therefore on balance route (1) is preferred as loss is relieved quickly at a higher rate with minimum PA wastage.

## Test your understanding 8

**James**

| | £ |
|---|---|
| **Class 2 NICs** | |
| (£2.40 × 52 weeks) | 125 |

James' profits for Class 4 purposes are as follows:

| | £ |
|---|---|
| Taxable trading profits for 2009/10 | 55,000 |
| Less Trading losses brought forward | (10,000) |
| Profits for Class 4 purposes | 45,000 |

| | |
|---|---|
| **Class 4 NICs** | |
| (£43,875 – £5,715) × 8% | 3,053 |
| (£45,000 – £43,875) × 1% | 11 |
| | 3,064 |

**Poppy**

| | £ |
|---|---|
| **Class 2 NICs** | |
| (£2.40 × 52 weeks) | 125 |

| | |
|---|---|
| **Class 4 NICs** | |
| (£6,350 – £5,715) × 8% | 51 |

## Test your understanding 9

**Henry and Mary**

| Operating as a sole trader | | | Total tax |
|---|---|---|---|
| | £ | £ | £ |
| Income tax on profit of £100,000 (PA used by rental income) | | | |
| Basic rate band | 37,400 @ 20% | 7,480 | |
| Higher rate bank | 62,600 @ 40% | 25,040 | |
| | 100,000 | | |
| Income tax liability | | | 32,520 |
| NICs | | | |
| Class 2 (52 weeks @ £2.40 per week) | | | 125 |
| Class 4 (£43,875 – £5,715) × 8% | | 3,053 | |
| (£100,000 – £43,875) × 1% | | 561 | |
| | | | 3,614 |
| Total tax and NIC liability | | | 36,259 |

**Employing Mary at a gross salary of £30,000 p.a.**

| | £ | £ |
|---|---|---|
| Employer's NICs re Mary payable by Henry | | |
| Class 1 secondary contributions (£30,000 - £5,715) x 12.8% | | 3,108 |
| Tax payable by Henry on profits from the business | | |
| Profits | 100,000 | |
| Adjustment to profits | | |
| Mary's salary | (30,000) | |
| Employer's secondary NICs | (3,108) | |
| Tax adjusted profits | 66,892 | |
| Income tax | | |
| Basic rate band | 37,400 @ 20% | 7,480 |
| Higher rate bank | 29,492 @ 40% | 11,797 |
| | 66,892 | |
| Income tax liability | | 19,277 |

NICs

    Class 2  As above                                  125

    Class 4  (£43,875 – £5,715) × 8%         3,053
             (£66,892 – £43,875) × 1%         230
                                      ————  3,283

                                              25,793

## Tax payable by Mary re her salary

As rental income covers her personal allowance, Mary will be assessed to tax on £30,000 taxable income (all non-savings) as follows:

|  | £ | £ |
|---|---|---|
| Income tax |  |  |
| Basic rate band | 30,000 @ 20% | 6,000 |
|  | 30,000 |  |
| Income tax liability |  | 6,000 |
| NICs |  |  |
| Class 1 Primary | (£30,000 – £5,715) × 11% | 2,671 |
| Total tax and NIC liability |  | 34,464 |

**Tax saved by employing Mary (£36,259 – £34,464) = £1,795**

## Running the business in equal partnership with Mary

Both Henry and Mary will be assessed to tax on £50,000 (£100,000 x 50%) taxable income (all non-savings) as follows:

|  | £ | £ | Total tax £ |
|---|---|---|---|
| Income tax on profit of £50,000 | | | |
| Basic rate band | 37,400 @ 20% | 7,480 | |
| Higher rate band | 12,600 @ 40% | 5,040 | |
| | 50,000 | 12,520 | |
| Income tax liability (£12,520 × 2) | | | 25,040 |
| NICs | | | |
| Class 2 (52 weeks @ 2.40 per week) × 2 | | | 250 |
| Class 4 (£43,875 – £5,715) × 8% | | 3,053 | |
| (£50,000 – £43,875) × 1% | | 61 | |
| | | 3,114 | |
| Class 4 NIC liability (£3,114 × 2) | | | 6,228 |
| Total tax and NIC liability | | | 31,518 |

**Tax saved by taking Mary on as equal partner (£36,259 - £31,518) = £4,741**

**Note:** If the examiner asks you to calculate 'total tax', you need to consider all the taxes that will apply, i.e. income tax and NICs in this question.

# 18

# Cessation of an unincorporated business

## Chapter learning objectives

Upon completion of this chapter you will be able to:

- recognise the factors that will influence the choice of cessation date and compute the assessments

- explain the range of loss reliefs available on the cessation of a business

- identify suitable tax planning measures in a given scenario to mitigate tax liabilities for an individual

- recognise that alternative courses of action have different tax consequences and assess the advantages and disadvantages

- demonstrate the optimum use of trading loss reliefs for an individual

- consider the tax implications of incorporating an existing business, and to advise on planning issue that may arise.

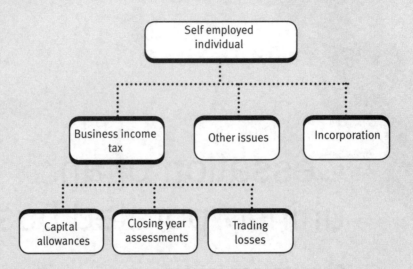

## 1 Introduction

This chapter covers the popular examination scenario of the cessation of an unincorporated business. There is scope for a wide variety of questions due to the various ways in which an unincorporated business can cease:

- A sole trader sells his business to another sole trader
- A sole trader gifts his business
- A sole trader retires or dies
- A partner leaves the partnership
- A sole trader sells his business to a company (incorporation)

As in the previous chapter, we need to consider all of the possible tax implications of these scenarios.

The main considerations are as follows:

- Income tax issues on cessation
- Loss reliefs
- VAT issues on cessation
- Capital gains tax issues on cessation
- Incorporation of a business

## 2 A revision of basic business income tax

If the business ceases to trade, the key differences in the calculation of taxable trading profits will be:

- Calculating the capital allowances for the final accounting period
- Applying the closing year rules for assessment of profits

## 3 Capital allowances in the closing years

The final accounting period before cessation is usually not 12 months in length, however there is no need for any time apportionment as:

- there are no WDAs, FYAs, or AIAs in the final period
- all additions are brought in, then the disposals on cessation are dealt with
- the disposals will give rise to BCs and BAs
- the capital allowances computation is then closed off
- if an owner takes over an asset, the disposal proceeds will be the market value
- if the business is being transferred as a going concern to a connected person, an election is available to transfer the assets at their TWDV and thereby avoid BCs and BAs.

### Successions to trade between connected persons

If the predecessor and successor to a trade are connected, the approach for capital allowances purposes is broadly to ignore the change of ownership:

- the actual sale price (if any) is ignored
- the plant and machinery is deemed to have been sold for the predecessor's written down value
- consequently no balancing charge or allowance arises on the predecessor
- the successor uses the same written down values to begin his computation.

This is a privileged treatment and so there are conditions attached.

These are:

- an election must be made jointly by the predecessor and successor within two years of the time the succession took place
- both parties must be within the charge to UK tax on the profits of the trade
- the assets must be in use in the trade immediately before and after the succession.

If no election is made assets are deemed to have been sold at market value as normal.

## Test your understanding 1

Julia, aged 28, has been trading as a sole trader since 2002 and has always prepared her accounts to 31 December. Her business is becoming more and more profitable, so she has decided to incorporate at the end of March 2010. She will transfer all her business assets to a new company to be formed, which is to be called Jules Ltd. Julia will be the sole shareholder of Jules Ltd.

The values of her plant and machinery are as follows:

|  | TWDV b/f at 1 January 2010 £ | MV at 31 March 2010 £ |
|---|---|---|
| General pool items | 24,000 | 37,000 |

After incorporation, Julia will become a director of Jules Ltd. The company will prepare its accounts to 31 March.

The tax adjusted trading profits of the business are as follows:

|  | £ |
|---|---|
| Year ended 31 December 2009 (after capital allowances) | 72,300 |
| Forecast for 3 months ended 31 March 2010 (before capital allowances) | 20,250 |
| Forecast for year ended 31 March 2011(before capital allowances | 85,000 |

Julia has overlap profits from commencement of £3,500.

**Explain the options available with regard to capital allowances. You should consider the effect on both Julia and Jules Ltd, including illustrative calculations, and advise on which alternative is best.**

## 4 Basis of assessment rules

### Closing year rules

Special rules are applied to the 'trading profits' in the last tax years of assessment.

The last tax year is the tax year in which the trade ceases.

The penultimate tax year is assessed on the current year basis as normal, however the rules for the final closing tax year ensure that:

- any profits not previously assessed are included in the final year

- any overlap profits from the commencement of trade are relieved in the final year.

### Test your understanding 2

Michael ceased trading on 31 March 2010. His adjusted trading profits for the final three periods are as follows:

|  | £ |
|---|---|
| Year ended 30 April 2008 | 40,000 |
| Year ended 30 April 2009 | 42,000 |
| Period ended 31 March 2010 | 38,000 |

Assume his overlap profits are £27,000.

**Calculate Michael's taxable trading profit assessments for all of the years affected by the above results.**

### Choice of cessation date

This is an important consideration at paper P6.

If an individual dies, or a business is failing, the luxury of choosing a cessation date is not necessarily an available option.

However, where an individual is planning to:

- sell or gift the business to another person, or
- incorporate the business into a company

the choice of an appropriate cessation date could be important and can affect:

- the level of profits to be taxed in a particular tax year, and
- the timing and amount of tax payments.

Tax planning can have an advantageous impact on:

- cash flow, and
- can result in profits being assessed at a lower marginal rate of tax.

The appropriate advice will depend on whether profits are increasing or declining, and the level of the individual's other income.

### Example 3 – Choice of cessation date

Susan starts trading on 1 June 2006 and prepares her first accounts to 31 May 2007.

Her tax adjusted trading profits after capital allowances are as follows:

| | |
|---|---:|
| Year ended 31 May 2007 | £24,000 |
| Year ended 31 May 2008 | £31,000 |
| Year ended 31 May 2009 | £44,000 |

She is planning to retire in 2010 and has asked whether she should prepare her final accounts to 31 March 2010 or 30 April 2010.

From 1 June 2009 she estimates that her monthly tax adjusted profits will be £3,500.

**Calculate Susan's taxable trading profit assessments for all of the years affected by the above results under the following alternative cessation dates:**

(a) **She ceases trading on 31 March 2010**

(b) **She ceases trading on 30 April 2010.**

**Solution**

Susan's trading income assessable in the first three years of her business are:

| Tax year | Basis period | Trading income assessment £ |
|---|---|---:|
| 2006/07 | 1 June 2006 – 5 April 2007 (10/12 × £24,000) | 20,000 |
| 2007/08 | Year ending 31 May 2007 | 24,000 |
| 2008/09 | Year ending 31 May 2008 | 31,000 |

Overlap profits

| | £ |
|---|---:|
| 1 June 2006 – 5 April 2007 (10/12 × £24,000) | 20,000 |

**Ceases trading 31 March 2010 (2009/10)**

|         |                              |         |
|---------|------------------------------|---------|
|         |                              | £       |
| 2009/10 | 1 June 2008 – 31 March 2010  |         |
|         | Year ended 31 May 2009       | 44,000  |
|         | Period to 31 March 2010      |         |
|         | (£3,500 × 10)                | 35,000  |
|         | Less Overlap profits         | (20,000)|
|         |                              | 59,000  |

**Ceases trading 30 April 2010 (2010/11)**

|         |                              |         |
|---------|------------------------------|---------|
|         |                              | £       |
| 2009/10 | Year ending 31 May 2009      | 44,000  |
|         |                              |         |
| 2010/11 | 1 June 2009 – 30 April 2010  |         |
|         | (£3,500 × 11)                | 38,500  |
|         | Less Overlap profits         | (20,000)|
|         |                              | 18,500  |

By ceasing to trade one month later, a further £3,500 profits are assessed.

However, there is a lower assessment in 2009/10 and a small assessment in 2010/11, rather than all of the profits being assessed in 2009/10.

Depending on her level of other income in these years, she could save income tax by continuing to trade.

## 5 Trading losses

### Loss relief options in closing years

The options available in the closing years of trade are exactly the same as those available to an ongoing business, except that:

- the option to carry forward losses is not available as there will be no further trading profits once the trade ceases

- an extra option for terminal loss relief is available

- an additional option for incorporation relief is available if the business is ceasing because it is being incorporated.

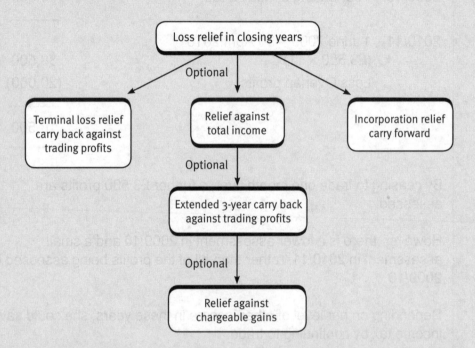

If an individual makes a trading loss in the closing years, they therefore have to decide whether to claim relief against total income and then whether to extend the claim against their chargeable gains.

If there are remaining losses, the individual can claim terminal loss relief.

## A revision of the rules for relief against total income and terminal loss relief

The key rules relating to the above reliefs in the closing years can be summarised as follows:

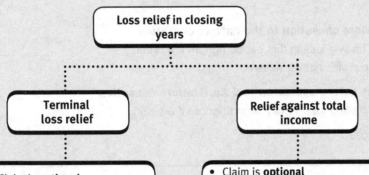

**Loss relief in closing years**

**Terminal loss relief**

- Claim is **optional**
  - however will normally be claimed
  - otherwise the benefit of the loss will be lost
- Relief is to set the **'terminal loss'** against **'trading income'**
  - of the **last tax year** (if any), and then
  - **carry back three tax years**
  - on a **LIFO basis**
- No £50,000 restriction as for extended carry back
- Terminal loss = **loss of the last 12 months** (see below)
- Relief must be **claimed in writing**
- For 2009/10 loss, the claim must be made **by 5 April 2014**

**Relief against total income**

- Claim is **optional**
- Loss in the last tax year can be **set against total income** in
  - the last tax year **and/or**
  - the preceding tax year
- Extended carry back for loss in 2009/10
- As for ongoing business
- Relief must be **claimed in writing**
- For 2009/10 loss, the claim must be made **by 31 January 2012**

**Extension of claim against chargeable gains**

- Claim is **optional**
- Loss in the last tax year can be **set against chargeable gains** in
  - the last tax year, **and/or**
  - the preceding tax year
- As for ongoing business
- Relief must be **claimed in writing**
- For 2009/10 loss, the claim must be made **by 31 January 2012**

### The calculation of the terminal loss

The terminal loss is the loss of the **last 12 months of trading**.

It has three elements which are calculated as follows:

| | £ |
|---|---|
| **6 April before cessation to the date of cessation** | |
| (1) Actual trading loss in this period (ignore if a profit) | X |
| (2) Overlap profits not yet relieved | X |
| **12 months before cessation to 5 April before cessation** | X |
| (3) Actual trading loss in this period (ignore if a profit) | —— |
| Terminal loss | X |
| | —— |

Note that in the closing years, it is not compulsory to make a claim against total income before claiming terminal loss relief.

However, where losses included in the above terminal loss calculation have already been relieved under another claim (i.e. against total income or chargeable gains), the amount of the terminal loss must be reduced.

### Extended carry back relief in closing years

It is possible to claim the extended carry back relief in the closing years of business.

However it is unlikely to be beneficial as the relief is the same as terminal loss relief (i.e. set off against trading profits of the three years preceding the year of the loss) but with terminal loss relief there is no £50,000 maximum restriction and relief is available for the losses of the last 12 months trading, not just the loss of the last tax year.

### Test your understanding 3

Jim Luck ceased trading on 30 June 2009. His results were:

| | | £ |
|---|---|---|
| Year ended 31 December | 2006 | 30,000 |
| | 2007 | 24,000 |
| | 2008 | 20,000 |
| Period to 30 June | 2009 loss | (19,000) |

Jim had overlap profits on commencement of the business of £11,500.

**Calculate the terminal loss and show how it is relieved.**

## A revision of the rules for relief on incorporation

When an unincorporated business ceases, the individual will seek to obtain relief from any losses as soon as possible.

They will therefore consider relief against total income and against chargeable gains first, then claim terminal loss relief next. Normally, if there are any unrelieved losses remaining after these claims, the loss is lost.

However, where the business is ceasing due to incorporation, these unrelieved losses can be relieved against future income derived from the company.

The key rules relating to incorporation relief are unchanged from F6 and can be summarised as follows:

> **Incorporation relief against future income from the company**

- Incorporation relief is available where an unincorporated business
  - is **transferred to a company**
  - **'wholly or mainly'** in exchange **for shares**, and
  - the company is controlled by the former owner of the business
- 'Wholly or mainly' it usually taken to mean that **at least 80%** of the consideration received from the business from the company is in the form of shares
- The relief is to **carry the losses forward**
  - indefinitely
  - provided the owner retains the shares throughout the whole tax year in which the loss relief is given, and
  - provided the company continues to carry on the trade of the former unincorporated business
- Losses are **set against**
  - the **first available income** the individual derives **from the company** (e.g. salary, interest, dividends)
  - Set off against types of income from the company in any order
  - Most beneficial order will be from employment income first, then savings income, then dividends
- Note that the losses cannot be set against the future profits of the company

### Test your understanding 4

On 1 January 2009 Mr Percival transferred his business that he started on 1 May 1995 to a newly formed limited company, Atkinson Ltd, in exchange for shares. He had incurred trading losses in the opening years and £83,000 remained unrelieved at 1 January 2009.

Mr Percival owns all the share capital of Atkinson Ltd and plans to draw a salary of £20,000 per annum from the company and pay himself a dividend of £9,000 in June each year.

His other income comprises dividends of £2,700 per annum from other UK companies.

**Calculate Mr Percival's net income after reliefs for all relevant years, showing how he will obtain incorporation relief against future income from the company for the losses from his business.**

## 6 Capital gains tax

Whether a sole trader sells his business, gifts his business or incorporates, this will represent a disposal for capital gains tax purposes.

Separate gains or losses will be calculated for each chargeable asset of the business, using market value as the proceeds where assets are either given or exchanged for shares in a company.

Typical examples of chargeable assets are:

- Goodwill
- Land and buildings
- Investments

But not:

- Motor cars
- Plant and machinery falling under the £6,000 chattels exemption
- Plant and machinery sold at a loss (no capital loss if claimed capital allowances)

For a reminder of the basic calculation of gains/losses see Chapters 7 and 8.

### Reliefs available

There are a number of reliefs to consider, depending on the scenario:

- Rollover relief
- Gift relief
- Incorporation relief
- Entrepreneurs' relief
- EIS reinvestment relief

All of these reliefs were covered in detail in Chapter 9.

Gains may also be reduced by:

- Capital losses
- The annual exemption

## 7 VAT

The key issues that may be relevant to a business which is ceasing are:

- Deregistration
- Transfer of a business as a going concern

These areas are all covered in detail in Chapter 20

## 8 Inheritance tax

If the sale of the business is at an arms length price, then as there is no diminution in value of the owner's estate there are no IHT implications.

If there is a loss in value to the estate (i.e. the gift of the business or sale at undervalue), then there will be potential IHT implications:

- Gift to an individual – potentially exempt transfer (PET)
- Gift to a trust – chargeable lifetime transfer (CLT)
- Gift to spouse – exempt.

### Reliefs

The key IHT relief to consider is business property relief (see Chapters 11 – 13 for a reminder of the IHT rules).

## 9 Incorporation

### Introduction

A sole trader or partnership may decide that they would be in a better position if they traded through a company, and therefore incorporate the business.

The shares in the company would be owned by the individual trader (or the partners).

Once the company has been set up the assets and trade will be transferred from personal ownership to the company.

In most cases the proprietors will then receive shares in the company, equal to the value of the assets transferred.

### Tax implications of transferring a business to a limited company

Transferring the assets to a limited company has the following tax consequences:

### Income Tax

- The business will cease at the date of the incorporation.
- The closing year rules will apply, and any overlap profit will be deducted.
- For capital allowances, incorporation is treated as an open market value disposal. However, as the trader and the company are connected, they may claim that the assets are transferred to the company at their tax written-down value.

  Which method is chosen will depend on whether a market value disposal would produce balancing charges or allowances.

  In either situation the company will then claim capital allowances, although no AIA or FYAs (if applicable) would be available.

- If the business had unrelieved losses at the time of the incorporation they can be relieved against future income derived from the company.

### National insurance contributions

As a sole trader the individual will have paid Class 2 & 4 NIC.

- As a director/employee of the company the individual will have to pay Class 1 primary NICs.
- The company also pays Class 1 secondary NICs and Class 1A NICs if benefits are provided.

### Capital Gains Tax

- The assets of the business are treated as being sold to the company for their market value.

- The gains can be deferred with incorporation relief or gift relief.

### VAT

- Providing the company is registered for VAT the transfer of assets will be a transfer of a going concern, and so outside the scope of VAT.

- For ease of administration the company may take over the trader's VAT registration.

### Stamp Duty Land Tax

- Where there is a property involved, SDLT will be payable by the company, assuming the property is worth in excess of the SDLT threshold.

- This charge can be avoided by not transferring the property to the company but CGT incorporation relief would not then be available, as it requires all assets to be transferred.

- In this case, the relevant assets could be gifted to the company, and a claim made to hold-over the gain under the gift relief provisions.

### Corporation Tax

- It is probable that the company will be a close company, and the implications of this are discussed in Chapter 26.

### Inheritance tax

- There should be no IHT implication, as there is no gratuitous intent involved in an incorporation.

- Furthermore, the individual still owns the assets they did before but through a company, so there should be no fall in value in their estate.

## Summary

| Tax | Considerations |
| --- | --- |
| Income tax | Cessation of business<br>Capital allowances and disposal value<br>Trading losses |
| NIC | Change from Classes 2 & 4 to Class 1 |
| CGT | Disposal at open market value<br>Methods of deferring gain until later disposal |
| VAT | Transfer of going concern |
| SDLT | Company liable if property transferred |
| CT | Company will probably be a close company |
| IHT | Not applicable |

### Test your understanding 5

Isaac has owned a business for 4 years, and is considering transferring the business to a limited company in exchange for shares.

The gains would be as follows:

| | |
| --- | --- |
| Goodwill | £50,000 |
| Freehold | £80,000 |

It is anticipated that the property will increase in value by 50% in the next 2 years at which time it is likely to be sold and larger premises will then be rented.

**Consider the alternative courses of action available to achieve the incorporation of the business and explain any immediate and future taxation impact including any advantages and disadvantages.**

## 10 Comprehensive example

### Test your understanding 6

Mavis has been trading for a number of years, but at the age of 55 decides that the time has come to retire.

She ceases trading on 31 March 2010, and has the following adjusted profits (after deducting capital allowances) for her final accounting periods:

| | |
|---|---|
| Year ended 30 June 2009 | £45,250 |
| 9 months ended 31 March 2010 | £35,187 |

The TWDVs at 1 July 2009 for capital allowances are:

| | £ |
|---|---|
| General pool | 15,637 |
| Car (private use 40%) | 12,700 |

No assets were purchased during the final accounting period, and on 31 March 2010 all assets in the pool were sold for £13,255, none for more than the original cost. Mavis decided to keep the car, which was worth £13,000.

Mavis's overlap profits from commencement were £7,800.

The following information is also available regarding the sale of the business on 31 March 2010:

| | |
|---|---|
| Value of office | £170,000 |
| Cost of office (January 1989) | £35,000 |
| Value of goodwill | £200,000 |

After cessation, Mavis will receive a pension of £9,000 per annum.

(a)

   (i)   **Calculate Mavis's taxable profits for 2009/10**

   (ii)  **Advise Mavis of the income tax implications of ceasing on 6 April 2010 (assume no profits are made between 31 March 2010 and 6 April 2010).**

(b)

   (i)   **Calculate the capital gains tax payable on the sale of the business**

   (ii)  **Explain the capital tax implications if Mavis were to give the business to her son instead.**

(c)  Mavis has just received an offer from Jumbo plc to purchase her business for £400,000 broken down as follows:

|  | £ |
|---|---|
| Office | 170,000 |
| Plant and machinery | 13,255 |
| Car | 13,000 |
| Net current assets | 3,745 |
| Goodwill | 200,000 |
|  | ——— |
| Adjusted profit for accounting period | 400,000 |
|  | ——— |

Mavis would receive £150,000 in cash and £250,000 worth of shares in Jumbo plc.

Assume plant and machinery is sold at less than cost.

**Calculate the CGT payable, assuming that all available reliefs are applied, and advise Mavis why it may be beneficial to elect to disapply incorporation relief**

Assume the 2009/10 rates and allowances apply throughout

## Chapter summary

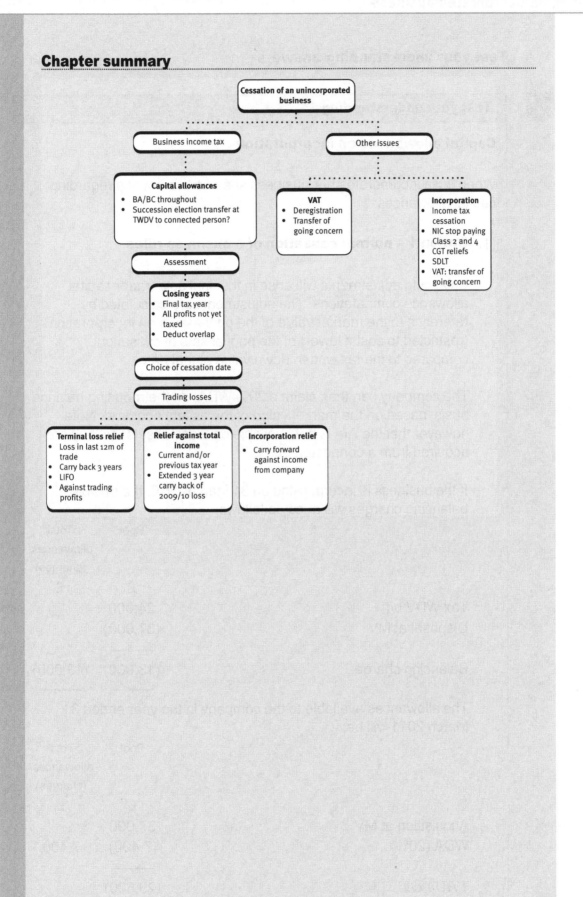

**Test your understanding answers**

### Test your understanding 1

**Capital allowances on incorporation**

When Julia incorporates her business she has two options regarding capital allowances:

(1) **Option 1 – normal cessation of a business rules**

Balancing adjustments will arise in the final sole trader capital allowance computations. The adjustments are calculated by reference to the market value of the pool assets on incorporation (restricted to cost if lower) of the pool assets at cessation, compared to the tax written down value at that date.

The company can then claim a 20% WDA, on the reducing balance basis, based on the market value of the assets acquired. Note however that the AIA is not available on these assets, as they are acquired from a connected party.

If the business is incorporated on 31 March 2010, the taxable balancing charges will arise as follows:

|  | Pool | Total allowances/ (charges) |
|---|---|---|
|  | £ | £ |
| Tax WDV b/f | 24,000 | |
| Disposal at MV | (37,000) | |
| | ——— | |
| Balancing charge | (13,000) | (13,000) |
| | ——— | ——— |

The allowances available to the company in the year ended 31 March 2011 will be:

|  | Pool | Total allowances/ (charges) |
|---|---|---|
|  | £ | £ |
| Acquisition at MV | 37,000 | |
| WDA (20%) | (7,400) | 7,400 |
| | ——— | |
| TWDV c/f | (29,600) | |
| | ——— | ——— |
| Total allowances | | 7,400 |
| | | ——— |

(2) **Option 2 – succession election**

An election (known as the succession election) can be made for the assets in the general pool and the car to be transferred to the company, Jules Ltd, at tax written down value rather than the market value at the date of incorporation.

This is because the trade has passed between connected persons.

As a result, no balancing adjustments arise on the unincorporated business.

The company can then claim a 20% WDA, on the reducing balance basis, based on the TWDV of the assets acquired.

The allowances available to the company in the year ended 31 March 2011 will be:

|  | Pool | Total allowances/ (charges) |
|---|---|---|
|  | £ | £ |
| Transfer at TWDV | 24,000 |  |
| WDA (20%) | (4,800) | 4,800 |
|  | ——— |  |
| TWDV c/f | 19,200 |  |
|  | ——— | ——— |
| Total allowances |  | 4,800 |
|  |  | ——— |

**Note:** Where a succession election is made, the assets are deemed to be transferred to the company at their TWDV at the end of the penultimate accounting period.

There are no capital allowances available to Julia in the final accounting period.

## Recommendation

The succession election will be beneficial to Julia as:

- Without the election, the balancing charges of £13,000 would have the effect of increasing Julia's taxable trading profits. This would be avoided if the succession election is taken.

- Given her current level of profits, avoiding the increase in profits and loss of capital allowances would save income tax at 40% and Class 4 NICs at 1%.

- The total saving by Julia would be £5,330 (£13,000 x 41%).

- However, the company would be able to claim £2,600 (£7,400 – £4,800) less capital allowances in the year ended 31 March 2011.

- Given the level projected profits of the business, this would result in an increase in corporation tax payable of £546 (£2,600 x 21%).

- The net tax saving is the succession election is made would be £4,784 (£5,330 – £546).

For this reason it would appear that a succession election would be beneficial to Julia.

The succession election will need to be made by 31 March 2012 (i.e. within two years of the date of incorporation).

## Test your understanding 2

**Michael**

| Tax year | Basis period | Trading income assessment £ |
|---|---|---|
| 2008/09 | Year ended 30 April 2008 | 40,000 |
| 2009/10 | 23 months from 1 May 2008 to 31 March 2010: | |
| | Year ended 30 April 2009 | 42,000 |
| | Period ended 31 March 2010 | 38,000 |
| | | 80,000 |
| | Less Overlap profits | (27,000) |
| | | 53,000 |

## Test your understanding 3

**Jim Luck**

(a) **Terminal loss**

Loss of last 12 months (01.07.08 – 30.06.09)

|  | £ | £ |
|---|---|---|
| **6 April 2009 – 30 June 2009 (3 month period)** | | |
| Actual trading loss in this period (£19,000) × 3/6 | | (9,500) |
| Overlap profits | | (11,500) |
| **1 July 2008 to 5 April 2009** | | |
| Actual trading loss in this period | | |
| (£19,000) × 3/6 | (9,500) loss | |
| £20,000 × 6/12 | 10,000 profit | |
| Overall profit – ignore | 500 | Nil |
| Terminal loss | | (21,000) |

(b) **Terminal loss relief (TLR)**

|  | 2006/07 £ | 2007/08 £ | 2008/09 £ | 2009/10 £ |
|---|---|---|---|---|
| Trading income | 30,000 | 24,000 | 20,000 | Nil |
| Less: TLR | – | (1,000) | (20,000) | Nil |
| Final assessments | 30,000 | 23,000 | Nil | Nil |

### Test your understanding 4

**Mr Percival**

| | 2008/09 £ | 2009/10 £ | 2010/11 £ | 2011/12 £ |
|---|---|---|---|---|
| Employment income | 5,000 | 20,000 | 20,000 | 20,000 |
| Less: Loss relief | (5,000) | (20,000) | (20,000) | (18,000) |
| Atkinson dividend × (100/90) | – | 10,000 | 10,000 | 10,000 |
| Less: Loss relief | | (10,000) | (10,000) | |
| Other dividends × (100/90) | 3,000 | 3,000 | 3,000 | 3,000 |
| Net income | 3,000 | 3,000 | 3,000 | 15,000 |

| **Loss working** | £ |
|---|---|
| Unrelieved losses b/f | 83,000 |
| Less: Incorporation relief | |
| 2008/09 | (5,000) |
| 2009/10 | (30,000) |
| 2010/11 | (30,000) |
| 2011/12 (balance of loss) | (18,000) |
| | Nil |

### Test your understanding 5

**Isaac**

- As Isaac is transferring the whole business the gains will be automatically deferred against any share consideration he receives under incorporation relief.

- On a future disposal of the shares the CGT base cost (the market value of the shares at incorporation) will be reduced by the gains now deferred.

- Entrepreneurs' relief will be available on a future disposal of the shares, if Isaac owns > 5%, is an employee of the limited company, and owns the shares for at least 12 months.

- There is a risk that if Isaac sells the shares within 12 months, he will lose the entitlement to Entrepreneurs' relief.

- Isaac could consider disapplying incorporation relief with the effect that the gains of £130,000 (£50,000 + £80,000) are subject to Entrepreneurs' relief on 4/9ths of the gains.

  The taxable gain would therefore be £62,122 (£72,222 (W) less annual exemption £10,100).

  To disapply incorporation relief, an election must be made. The consequence is that some capital gains tax will still be payable at 18%.

- Isaac could consider incorporating the business and receive consideration in the form of a mix of shares and loan account/ cash. As a result, part of the gain is automatically chargeable on incorporation. With planning, the amount of cash consideration to take can be calculated to ensure the maximum use of any capital losses and the annual exemption.

- A more long term disadvantage of using incorporation relief is the fact that the property is transferred to the company. If the property continues to appreciate in value significantly, then on a sale by the company there will be an element of double taxation: a corporation tax charge on the company, and in extracting the profits a further income tax charge on the individual.

- If Isaac were to keep the property in personal ownership and not rent it to the company then he would be eligible for Entrepreneurs' relief on a disposal of the property as long it was disposed of at the same time as the personal company shares. However incorporation relief would not then be available to defer the gains on the goodwill.

- An alternative would be to gift the goodwill (and other non-capital assets as relevant) to the company and claim gift relief to defer that gain so enabling the retention outside the company.

- Alternatively, the goodwill could remain within the charge to CGT at 10% / 18% with the company claiming relief for the cost of the goodwill at its marginal rate.

  **Working: Chargeable gain**

  |  | £ |
  | --- | --- |
  | Gains on incorporation | 130,000 |
  | Less: Entrepreneurs' relief (4/9) | (57,778) |
  |  | |
  | Chargeable gain | 72,222 |

## Test your understanding 6

**Mavis**

(a)

### (i) Taxable profits for 2009/10

The first step is to calculate capital allowances for the final accounting period:

**Capital allowances computation – 9 m/e 31 March 2010**

|  | General pool | Private use car (B.U. 60%) | | Allowances |
|---|---|---|---|---|
|  | £ | £ | | £ |
| TWDV b/f | 15,637 | 12,700 | | |
| Disposal | (13,255) | (3,000) | | |
|  | 2,382 | (300) | | |
| Balancing allowance | (2,382) | | | 2,382 |
| Balancing charge | | (300) | 60% | (180) |
| TWDV c/f | Nil | Nil | | |
| Total allowances | | | | 2,202 |

The capital allowances are then deducted from the profit for the 9 months ending 31 March 2010.

|  | £ |
|---|---|
| Adjusted profit before capital allowances | 35,187 |
| Less: Capital allowances (w) | (2,202) |
| Adjusted profit for accounting period | 32,985 |

Then the adjusted profits can be matched to tax years using the closing year rules.

**Assessments**

| **2009/10 (tax year of cessation)** | £ |
|---|---|
| Year ended 30 June 2009 | 45,250 |
| Period ended 31 March 2010 (above) | 32,985 |
| Less: Overlap profits | (7,800) |
| Total taxable trading profit for 2009/10 | 70,435 |

## (ii) Cessation on 6 April 2010

If Mavis ceased trading on 6 April 2010, her tax year of cessation would be 2010/11 giving the following assessments:

### Assessments

| | £ |
|---|---|
| **2009/10 (penultimate tax year)** | |
| Year ended 30 June 2009 | 45,250 |
| | |
| **2010/11 (tax year of cessation)** | |
| Period ended 6 April 2010 (above) | 32,985 |
| Less: overlap | (7,800) |
| Total taxable profit for 2010/11 | 25,185 |

This would be beneficial for the following reasons:

- The £25,185 which is now taxable in 2010/11 will now fall into the basic rate band and will be taxed at 20% instead of 40%, assuming that Mavis has no other income apart from her pension.

- There will also be an extra year to pay the tax due on the profit assessable in 2010/11, as the balancing payment will not be due until 31 January 2012.

(b)

## (i) Capital gains tax payable on sale of the business

Gains will arise only on the office and the goodwill as follows:

| | £ | £ |
|---|---|---|
| **Office** | | |
| Proceeds | 170,000 | |
| Less: Cost | (35,000) | |
| | | 135,000 |
| **Goodwill** | | |
| Proceeds | 200,000 | |
| Less: Cost | (Nil) | |
| | | 200,000 |
| Total gains before reliefs | | 335,000 |
| Less: Entrepreneurs' relief (4/9 × £335,000) | | (148,889) |
| Chargeable gains | | 186,111 |

| | |
|---|---:|
| Less: Annual exemption | (10,100) |
| Taxable gains | 176,011 |
| CGT payable (18% × £176,011) | 31,682 |

(ii) **Capital tax implications of gift of business**

Note that if the examiner asks you to talk about the "capital taxes" he means not just CGT, but also IHT and stamp duty.

**Capital gains tax**

- The assets would be deemed to be sold at market value

- Gains would arise as above

- However, Mavis and her son could jointly claim gift relief to defer the gains before Entrepreneurs' relief

- The gains would then be deducted from the cost of the assets for Mavis's son, giving him bigger gains on the eventual sale

**Inheritance tax**

- The gift of the business would be a potentially exempt transfer (PET)

- There would be no tax payable during lifetime

- The gift would only become chargeable if Mavis were to die within 7 years

- As Mavis would be giving a whole business which she has owned for more than 2 years, 100% business property relief (BPR) would be available, leaving no IHT to pay

- However, if Mavis's son sold the business before Mavis's death, the BPR would be withdrawn

**Stamp duty land tax**

- There would be no SDLT payable on the gift of the office as there would be no consideration.

(c) **CGT on transfer of business to Jumbo plc**

Again, the assets would be deemed to be sold for their market values and gains would arise on the chargeable assets as before.

As the business would be transferred to a company as a going concern, in exchange partly for shares, incorporation relief would automatically apply.

A proportion of the gain before Entrepreneurs' relief would be deferred until the shares were sold.

|  | £ |
|---|---|
| Total gains before reliefs (as above) | 335,000 |

Less: Incorporation relief:

$$\text{Gains} \times \frac{\text{Value of share consideration}}{\text{Total consideration}}$$

| £335,000 × £250,000/£400,000 | (209,375) |
|---|---|
|  | 125,625 |
| Less: Entrepreneurs'relief (4/9 × £125,625) | (55,833) |
| Chargeable gains | 69,792 |
| Less: Annual exemption | (10,100) |
| Taxable gains | 59,692 |
| CGT payable (18% × £59,692) | 10,745 |

It may be beneficial for Mavis to elect to disapply the incorporation relief in order to take advantage of Entrepreneurs' relief on the full gain of £335,000.

The reason for this is that as Mavis is receiving shares in a plc, it is unlikely that she will own the 5% required to qualify for Entrepreneurs' relief on the eventual sale of the shares, giving a higher tax charge on disposal.

# Partnerships: income tax and capital gains tax

## Chapter learning objectives

Upon completion of this chapter you will be able to:

- explain how a partnership is assessed to tax

- show the allocation of trading profits / losses between partners for the accounting period in a variety of business scenarios

- calculate the assessable profit for ongoing / new and ceasing partners

- describe the alternative loss relief claims that are available to partners

- explain the loss relief restriction that applies to the partners of a limited liability partnership

- recognise the basis of allocation of partnership investment income between partners for tax purposes

- recognise how qualifying payments of a partnership are allocated between partners and how they are relieved

- identify the occasions when a capital gain will arise on partnership transactions and show how each partner is assessed to capital gains tax on partnership gains.

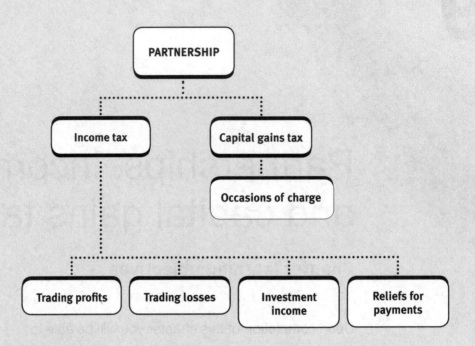

## 1 Introduction

This chapter starts with a revision of the treatment of partnerships. Much of the technical content in this section has been covered at F6.

A brief reminder of F6 content is given in expandable text and revision examples are provided to check your retention of F6 knowledge.

The new P6 topics introduced are:

- the treatment of partnership investment income and reliefs
- the taxation of partnership capital gains.

## 2 Trading income assessments for partners

A partnership is a body of persons carrying on business together with a view to profit.

Despite the fact that a partnership is a single trading entity, the partnership itself is not liable to tax.

For tax purposes, each partner:

- is treated as trading in their own right, as if they were a sole trader running their own business, and
- is taxed individually on their share of the partnership profits, investment income and capital gains, and

- is responsible for paying their own income tax, NICs and capital gains tax arising from their share of the partnership.

The partnership is therefore merely a collection of sole traders operating together.

## Adjusted profits and allocation between partners

A reminder of the calculation of adjusted profits for a partnership and the allocation between partners covered at F6 is given in expandable text and is summarised in the diagram in section 6.

### Partnership adjusted profits

The tax adjusted trading profits of a partnership are calculated in exactly the same way as for a sole trader:

- The accounting net profit is adjusted for disallowable expenditure, non-trading income etc in the normal way.

- Capital allowances are calculated in the normal way and deducted from the tax adjusted profits.

- If applicable, industrial buildings allowances are calculated as normal and deducted from the tax adjusted profits.

Note that:

- Partner's salaries and interest on capital are often charged through the profit and loss account. These are not allowable deductions and need to be added back, as they are an appropriation of profit and not an expense of the business.

- Capital allowances can be claimed on assets owned personally by the partners if they are used in the partnership. However, the individual partners cannot claim the capital allowances on their own behalf. The capital allowances are an allowable expense against the partnership profits as a whole.

### The allocation between partners

Profits are allocated:

- according to the **profit sharing arrangements** in force;
- during the **accounting period** in which the profits are earned.

Once the partners have been allocated their share, each partner is assessed on their share of the trading profits according to the basis of assessment rules in the normal way, as if they were a sole trader.

Profit sharing arrangements (PSA) usually provide for a combination of three types of allocation:

*   Salaries (a fixed allocation of profit).

*   Interest on capital introduced into the business (a fixed percentage return on capital).

*   Profit sharing ratio (PSR) (an agreed ratio to share the balance of profits).

The terms "salaries" and "interest" are just an allocation of profit, they are not assessed to income tax as employment income and savings income.

Whatever terms are used to describe the allocation method, the total amount allocated to each partner is assessed to income tax as trading income.

### Test your understanding 1

Alan and Brian formed a partnership in June 2006. They agreed to share profits equally after charging interest of 10% p.a. on their fixed capital accounts of £8,000 and £5,000 respectively, and paying a salary to Alan of £5,000.

The tax adjusted trading profits for the y/e 31 December 2009 were £15,000.

**Show the allocation of profits for the y/e 31 December 2009.**

### Change to profit sharing agreement

The profit sharing agreement between partners may change for a number of reasons:

*   The existing partners may decide to allocate profits in a different way. This may be as a result of a change in duties, seniority or simply by agreement of the parties concerned.

*   The membership of a partnership may change as the result of the admission, death or retirement of a partner.

Where there is a change in the PSA during the accounting period:

- The accounting period must be time apportioned into two or more parts (depending on the number of changes).
- Each part is then allocated separately between the partners according to the partnership agreement in place at that time.

## Test your understanding 2

Xavier and Yvonne started in partnership on 1 January 2008 sharing profits equally, after allowing for a salary for Yvonne of £10,000 p.a. The partnership accounts are prepared to 31 December each year.

On 1 July 2009 Zack is admitted as a new partner, the profits continuing to be shared equally but with no salary allowance for Yvonne.

On 30 September 2010, Xavier retired from the partnership. Yvonne and Zack agreed to shares profits in the ratio of 3:2.

The tax adjusted trading profits for the first three accounting periods are:

| | |
|---|---|
| Year ended 31 December 2008 | £50,000 |
| Year ended 31 December 2009 | £90,000 |
| Year ended 31 December 2010 | £150,000 |

**Show the allocation of profits between the partners for the three accounting periods.**

## The calculation of assessable trading income for each partner

Each partner is taxed on their share of the partnership profits as if they were a sole trader who runs a business that:

- starts when they join the partnership
- ceases when they leave the partnership and
- has the same accounting periods as the partnership.

A brief reminder of the calculations required is given in expandable text and is summarised in the diagram in section 6.

## Assessable trading income

To calculate the trading income assessments arising from the partnership allocations the following rules should be applied:

| Event | Treatment |
|---|---|
| Commencement of the partnership. | • the opening year rules apply to all partners who set up the business<br>• each partner has their own overlap profits arising. |
| New partner joins an existing partnership (Note 1). | • the existing partners continue to be assessed on a CYB basis<br>• opening year rules apply to the new partner<br>• new partner has their own overlap profits arising. |
| Partner leaves the partnership (Note 2). | • continuing partners continue to be assessed on a CYB basis<br>• closing year rules apply to the partner leaving<br>• leaving partner deducts their own overlap profits. |

**Notes:**

(1) The same approach and rules apply if a sole trader takes on a partner and the business becomes a partnership.

(2) The same approach and rules apply if one partner leaves a two partner partnership so that the remaining individual now operates the business as a sole trader.

### Test your understanding 3

Use the facts in Test Your Understanding 2 for Xavier, Yvonne and Zack.

**Calculate the trading income assessments arising for each partner for all of the years affected by the results.**

### Test your understanding 4

Alex, Arsene and Jose have been in partnership for a number of years. Their recent results and projected results into the future are as follows:

| Year ended 30 September: | £ |
|---|---|
| 2008 | 103,500 |
| 2009 | 128,000 |
| 2010 | 140,000 |
| 2011 | 180,000 |
| 2012 | 210,000 |

The relationship is often fractious and there have been a number of disputes over the years. In an attempt to improve the dynamics, on 1 January 2009, Rafa was admitted to the partnership.

However, the disputes continued. Alex accepts that he is the cause of most of the arguments and has therefore agreed that he will leave the partnership at the end of March 2012. Alex has £15,000 of overlap profits from when he joined the partnership.

The profit sharing ratio prior to the admission of Rafa had been equal after allocating the following salaries and interest on capital.

| Partner | Salary £ | Capital Balance £ | Rate of Interest on Capital |
|---|---|---|---|
| Alex | 15,000 | 100,000 | 5% |
| Arsene | 12,000 | 80,000 | 5% |
| Jose | 10,000 | 40,000 | 5% |

Rafa's admission changed the profit sharing arrangements as follows:

| Partner | Salary £ | Capital Balance £ | Rate of Interest on Capital | Profit Share |
|---|---|---|---|---|
| Alex | 20,000 | 100,000 | 5% | 35% |
| Arsene | 18,000 | 80,000 | 5% | 30% |
| Jose | 15,000 | 40,000 | 5% | 25% |
| Rafa | 10,000 | Nil | n/a | 10% |

When Alex leaves the partnership, the salary and interest arrangements will remain in place, but the rest of the profit will then be split equally between the three remaining partners.

**Calculate the assessable trading income for each of the partners from 2008/09 to 2012/13.**

# 3 Partnership trading losses

## The calculation and allocation of partnership trading losses

Each partner is:

- allocated his share of the tax adjusted trading losses (including capital allowances)
- according to the **partnership agreement** in the **accounting period**
- in exactly the same way as profits.

## Loss relief options available

Each partner is treated as a sole trader and can therefore utilise his share of the partnership loss:

- under the normal trading loss rules
- in the most tax efficient manner
- according to their own personal circumstances.

The options available can be summarised as follows:

| Partner joining | Ongoing partners | Partner leaving |
|---|---|---|
| Relief against total income | Relief against total income | Relief against total income |
| Extended carry back relief for loss arising in 2009/10 | Extended carry back relief for loss arising in 2009/10 | Extended carry back relief for loss arising in 2009/10 |
| Relief against gains | Relief against gains | Relief against gains |
| Carry forward | Carry forward | |
| **In addition:** | | **In addition:** |
| Opening year relief | | Terminal loss relief |
| | | Incorporation relief |

See Chapters 17 and 18 for a reminder of the loss relief rules.

## Example 1 – Partnership losses

Peter, Paul and Mary are in partnership preparing accounts to 5 April.

During 2009/10 Paul left the partnership and Maggie joined in his place.

For the year ended 5 April 2010 the partnership made a tax adjusted trading loss (after taking account of capital allowances) of £20,000.

**State the loss relief claims available to each of the partners.**

**Solution**

Paul will be entitled to terminal loss relief since he has actually ceased trading.

Maggie will be entitled to claim opening years relief since she has actually commenced trading.

Peter and Mary will not be entitled to either of the above reliefs.

All the partners will be entitled to relief against total income (together with extended carry back relief against trading income) and, if applicable, an extension of relief against chargeable gains in the current and/or previous tax years, provided a claim against total income is made first.

All the partners except Paul will be entitled to carry forward relief.

## Limited liability partnerships

A limited liability partnership (LLP) is a special type of partnership where the amount that each partner may be required to contribute towards the partnership losses, debts and liabilities is limited to their investment in the partnership.

LLPs are:

- taxed in the same way as other partnerships, and
- if applicable, the normal loss reliefs are available.

However, there is a restriction on the amount of loss that may be set against income **not derived from the partnership**.

The set off of losses is limited to the **amount of capital that the partner has contributed** to the partnership.

### Example 2 – Limited liability partnerships

John and Angela are partners in a limited liability partnership (LLP) to which they contributed capital of £50,000 and £15,000 respectively.

The LLP prepares its accounts to 31 March each year and John and Angela share profits and losses in the ratio 2:1.

For the year to 31 March 2010 the LLP made a trading loss of £60,000.

**State how much of the loss John and Angela can offset against other income in 2009/10.**

#### Solution

#### John

- John will be entitled to £40,000 (£60,000 × 2/3) of the loss arising in the year ended 31 March 2010.

- As this figure is less than the capital that he has contributed, the full amount of the loss (£40,000) is available for offset against John's non-partnership income for 2009/10.

#### Angela

- Angela will be entitled to £20,000 (£60,000 × 1/3) of the loss arising in the year ended 31 March 2010.

- However, the amount of the loss that may be set against income not deriving from the partnership in 2009/10 is limited to £15,000, being the amount of capital that she has contributed to the LLP.

- The balance of the loss £5,000 (£20,000 – £15,000) can be offset against partnership income under the extended carry back provisions or carried forward.

KAPLAN PUBLISHING

## 4 Partnership investment income

If a partnership has non-trading income, it is allocated between the partners as follows:

| Income received | Examples | Allocation according to: |
|---|---|---|
| **Gross** | Rental income, gilt-edged security interest, NSB interest | PSR in the **accounting period** |
| **Net** | Bank and building society interest | PSR in the **tax year of receipt** |

Each partner must:

- include their share of the partnership's non-trading income in their own personal income tax computation, in addition to the trading income assessment; and

- tax it in the normal way at the appropriate rates.

### Example 3 – Partnership investment income

Harry and Ellis have been operating in partnership for many years with an accounting year end of 31 December.

They have agreed to share profits in the ratio 35%:65% until 30 September 2009. Thereafter they will share profits equally.

The partnership has tax adjusted trading profits for the year ended 31 December 2009 of £100,000. The partnership also received bank interest of £2,500 on 30 June 2009.

**Calculate the amounts of trading income and savings income to be included in each partner's income tax computation in 2009/10.**

## Solution

### Allocation between partners

| 2009/10 | Harry | Ellis | Total |
|---|---|---|---|
| | £ | £ | £ |
| Trading income (W) | 38,750 | 61,250 | 100,000 |
| Bank interest | 1,094 | 2,031 | 3,125 |
| (£2,500 × 100/80) = £3,125 allocated (35%:65%) | | | |

### Note:

As Ellis is a higher rate taxpayer based on trading income, he will be assessed to income tax at 40% on his share of the bank interest which is taxed as normal savings income. Harry is a basic rate taxpayer so will have no further tax to pay on his savings income.

### Working: Allocation of trading profits

| Y/e 31/12/09 | Harry | Ellis | Total |
|---|---|---|---|
| | £ | £ | £ |
| 01/01/09 – 30/09/09 | | | |
| Shared (35%:65%) | 26,250 | 48,750 | 75,000 |
| 01/10/09 – 31/12/09 | | | |
| Shared (50%:50%) | 12,500 | 12,500 | 25,000 |
| | | | |
| Total | 38,750 | 61,250 | 100,000 |

## 5 Qualifying payments made by the partnership

If a partnership pays qualifying payments eligible for relief, such as an annuity to a retired partner, the payment is allocated to partners according to the PSR in the **tax year of payment**.

Each partner will:

- deduct their share of the partnership's payment in their own personal income tax computation;

- as a relief from total income before considering loss relief.

## 6 Summary of partnership income tax

```
           ┌─────────────────┐
           │  Partnership    │
           │  income tax     │
           └─────────────────┘
```

**Each partner:**
- taxed in his own right on his share of the partnership income
- responsible for paying his own income tax and NICs

```
┌──────────────┐   ┌──────────────┐   ┌──────────────┐
│ Trading      │   │ Trading      │   │ Investment   │
│ income       │   │ losses       │   │ income       │
└──────────────┘   └──────────────┘   └──────────────┘
```

**Trading income**

- Adjust profits as normal
- Allocate between partners
  - according to PSA
  - in accounting period
- Apply basis of assessment rules
- CYB (ongoing partners)
- Opening year rules (new partners)
- Closing year rules (partners leaving)
- Assessed as trading income in each partner's income tax comp

Change in PSA and/or membership of partners
- Time apportion the profit allocation
- Apply **PSA** to each part separately

**Investment income**

Received gross:
- Allocate per **PSR** in **accounting period**

Received net:
- Allocate per **PSR** in **tax year of receipt**

**Qualifying payments by partnership**

- Allocate per **PSR** in tax year of payment

**Trading losses**

- Calculate tax adjusted trading loss in the same way as for profits
- Loss relief options
  = same as for sole trader
- LLP
  - Loss relief restricted
  - Maximum set off against non-partnership income
    = amount of capital contributed

## 7 Partnership capital gains tax

### The basis of assessment to CGT on partnership gains

Each partner:

- is deemed to own a fractional share of the partnership assets, and

- is assessed separately to CGT according to their own personal circumstances, if they dispose of some or all of their fractional share in a partnership asset.

The fractional share is determined by the agreed capital profit sharing ratio in the partnership agreement.

This ratio is usually taken as:

- the PSR used to allocate the balance of profits for income tax purposes as stated in the partnership agreement

- unless the agreement says otherwise.

Each partner will:

- include their share of the partnership gains in their CGT computation, along with gains from the disposals of other assets;

- if the entire partnership share is being disposed of, Entrepreneurs' relief will be available if the partnership business has been owned for at least 12 months;

- deduct the annual exemption of £10,100 against the total chargeable gains of the individual in the normal way;

- calculate the CGT at 18%.

### Capital gains tax reliefs

As partnership assets are business assets, CGT reliefs are also available in the normal way, for example:

- rollover relief

- gift relief.

Note that with rollover relief and gift relief, each partner can decide independently whether or not they wish to make a claim.

If a partner decides to make a rollover relief claim:

- their share of a gain is rolled over (i.e. deferred)
- against their share of the cost of the replacement asset.

## The occasions of charge to CGT on partnership disposals

The occasions of charge to CGT for partnerships are as follows:

- The disposal of a partnership asset to a third party.
- The distribution of a partnership asset to a partner.
- The change in a partnership agreement (i.e. either a change in the PSR and/or a change in membership of the partnership).

## Disposal of a partnership asset to a third party

Strictly, each partner should have their own separate capital gains computation for each partnership disposal.

A separate gain computation should be calculated allocating the sale proceeds and cost of the asset between the partners.

However, it is usually acceptable to calculate the gain arising on the asset and then allocate this one figure between the partners.

### Test your understanding 5

In January 2002, Paul and Phil commenced in partnership. They introduced capital into the business of £30,000 and £20,000 respectively and agreed to share profits in the ratio 60%:40%.

The partnership purchased freehold premises for £125,000 in January 2002. In September 2009 the partnership sold the premises for £495,000 and continued to trade in rented premises.

**Calculate the capital gains arising on Paul and Phil in 2009/10 in respect of the partnership disposal.**

### The distribution of a partnership asset to a partner

If a partner takes over an asset, the partnership is deemed to sell the asset to the partner at market value:

- a capital gain arises on the partners giving up their fractional share in the asset, calculated using the market value of the asset
- a gain also arises on the partner taking over the asset as he takes ownership of it privately:
    - but it is not charged at the time
    - the gain is deferred against the base cost of the asset acquired
    - until they subsequently dispose of the asset.
- the partner taking over the asset acquires the asset at a base cost equal to its market value less the deferred gain.

### A change in the partnership agreement

Where there is a change in the PSR, the partners are changing their relative ownership of the capital assets.

In effect, there is a disposal of part of an asset between the partners. One or more partners must be giving up a fractional share of an asset if another partner has an increased share.

For CGT purposes, this could be taken to be a disposal of an interest in an asset to a connected person. However, special rules apply in this case.

A change in the partners' PSR and the change in membership of a partnership:

- **does not give rise to a charge to CGT** at the time of the change in agreement;
- **unless** the change occurs **after there has been a revaluation** of the partnership asset in the accounts.

If there has been a revaluation in the accounts prior to a change in the partnership agreement:

- a normal capital gains computation is calculated
- using consideration equal to the value of the asset in the balance sheet
- at the date of the change in the agreement.

## Example 4 – Change in agreement

Cathy and Des have been in partnership since 1997. They allocate profits equally. In June 2007 they admitted Eve as a partner. Profits were still allocated equally.

At the date that Eve was admitted to the partnership, goodwill was valued at £120,000, but was not revalued in the partnership balance sheet. The goodwill has a nil CGT base cost.

The partners decided to cease trading in May 2009 and sold the goodwill for £150,000.

**Calculate the capital gains that will be assessed on the partners as a result of the changes in membership in the partnership.**

### Solution

On Eve's admission to the partnership there was no charge to CGT since goodwill was not revalued in the partnership balance sheet.

The cessation in May 2009 is a straightforward disposal of a partnership asset resulting in a capital gain of £150,000.

As the whole of the business is being disposed of and each partner has owned assets for more than 12 months, Entrepreneurs' relief will be available = £66,667 (4/9 × £150,000), leaving a chargeable gain of £83,333 (£150,000 – £66,667).

This will be shared equally between the three partners (£27,778 each), and will be assessed in 2009/10.

## Test your understanding 6

Adam and Barry have been in partnership for many years.

In December 2006 they decided to include the value of the partnership goodwill in their balance sheet at a value of £100,000.

The partners have always allocated profits and losses equally, but decided to change the allocation in December 2009 to Adam 70% and Barry 30%.

**Calculate the capital gains that will be assessed on the partners as a result of the change in the PSR.**

## Summary of partnership capital gains

```
                        ┌─────────────────────┐
                        │    PARTNERSHIP      │
                        └─────────────────────┘
```

**Each partner:**
- **Deemed to own a fractional share** of every partnership asset
- Fractional share = according to PSR used in partnership agreement
- **taxed in his own right** on his share of the partnership gains along with his gains on his own assets
- annual exemption and CGT reliefs available in the normal way
- responsible for paying his own CGT

```
┌──────────────────────┐  ┌──────────────────────┐  ┌──────────────────────┐
│ Disposal to third    │  │ Distribution to      │  │ Change in partnership│
│ party                │  │ partner              │  │ agreement after a    │
│                      │  │                      │  │ revaluation          │
└──────────────────────┘  └──────────────────────┘  └──────────────────────┘
```

- Calculate gain as normal
- Allocate the gain between partners

- Chargeable gains arises on partners giving up a share
- Partner taking over the asset
  - Gain deferred against base cost of asset

- No charge to CGT unless occurs after a revaluation in the accounts
- If there has been a revaluation
  - Normal gain computation
  - Using balance sheet value of asset as consideration

# 8 Chapter summary

**PARTNERSHIP**

Each partner
- taxed in his own right on his share of the partnership income and gains
- responsible for paying his own income tax, NICs and CGT

**INCOME TAX**

**CAPITAL GAINS TAX**

Trading profits and losses

Other income and qualifying payments

Occasions of charge
- Disposal to third party
- Distribution to partner
- Change in partnership agreement after a revaluation in the accounts

- Adjusted profits and capital allowances calculated as normal
- Profits/losses allocated between partners
  - according to **PSA**
  - in **accounting period**
- Apply basis of assessment rules in normal way
- Assessed as trading income in each partner's income tax comp
- If applicable, loss relief options:
  - same as for sole trader
  - except LLPs
    = loss relief restricted to capital contributed

Investment income
Received gross:
- Allocate per **PSR** in **accounting period**
Received net:
- Allocate per **PSR** in **tax year of receipt**
Qualifying payments
- Allocate per **PSR** in **tax year of payment**

## Test your understanding answers

### Test your understanding 1

**Alan and Brian**

| Y/e 31/12/2009 | Alan £ | Brian £ | Total £ |
|---|---|---|---|
| Interest on capital | 800 | 500 | 1,300 |
| Salary | 5,000 | – | 5,000 |
| Balance shared (1:1) | 4,350 | 4,350 | 8,700 |
| Allocation of profits | 10,150 | 4,850 | 15,000 |

### Test your understanding 2

**Xavier and Yvonne**

| Y/e 31/12/08 | Xavier £ | Yvonne £ | Zack £ | Total £ |
|---|---|---|---|---|
| Salary | – | 10,000 | – | 10,000 |
| Balance shared (1:1) | 20,000 | 20,000 | – | 40,000 |
| Allocation of profits | 20,000 | 30,000 | Nil | 50,000 |
| **Y/e 31/12/09** | | | | |
| 01/01/09 – 30/06/09 | | | | |
| Salary | – | 5,000 | – | 5,000 |
| Balance shared (1:1) | 20,000 | 20,000 | – | 40,000 |
| | 20,000 | 25,000 | – | 45,000 |
| 01/07/09 – 31/12/09 | | | | |
| Balance shared (1:1:1) | 15,000 | 15,000 | 15,000 | 45,000 |
| Total | 35,000 | 40,000 | 15,000 | 90,000 |

| Y/e 31/12/10 | Xavier £ | Yvonne £ | Zack £ | Total £ |
|---|---|---|---|---|
| 01/01/10 – 30/09/010 Balance shared (1:1:1) | 37,500 | 37,500 | 37,500 | 112,500 |
| 01/10/10 – 31/12/10 Balance shared (3:2) | Nil | 22,500 | 15,000 | 37,500 |
| Total | 37,500 | 60,000 | 52,500 | 150,000 |

## Test your understanding 3

### Xavier

Xavier started to trade in partnership in 2007/08 and left the partnership in 2010/11. He will be assessed to the opening and closing year rules as follows:

| Tax year | Basis period | £ | Trading income £ |
|---|---|---|---|
| 2007/08 | 1 January 2008 to 5 April 2008 (3/12 × £20,000) | | 5,000 |
| 2008/09 | y/e 31 December 2008 (first 12 months) | | 20,000 |
| 2009/10 | y/e 31 December 2009 | | 35,000 |
| 2010/11 | Profits not yet assessed | 37,500 | |
| | Less overlap profits | (5,000) | |
| | | | 32,500 |

### Yvonne

Yvonne started to trade in partnership in 2007/08 and is still a partner. Her assessments will be as follows:

| Tax year | Basis period | Trading income £ |
|---|---|---|
| 2007/08 | 1 January 2008 to 5 April 2008 (actual) (3/12 × £30,000) | 7,500 |
| 2008/09 | y/e 31 December 2008 (first 12 months) | 30,000 |
| 2009/10 | y/e 31 December 2009 | 40,000 |
| 2010/11 | y/e 31 December 2010 | 60,000 |

Overlap profits

| | |
|---|---|
| 1 January 2008 to 5 April 2008 (3/12 × £30,000) | 7,500 |

### Zack

Zack joined the partnership in 2009/10 and is still a partner. The opening year rules apply to his shares of the profits assuming his first set of accounts run from 1 July 2009 to 31 December 2009.

His assessments will be as follows:

| Tax year | Basis period | Trading income £ |
|---|---|---|
| 2009/10 | 1 July 2009 to 5 April 2010 £15,000 + (3/12 × £52,500) | 28,125 |
| 2010/11 | y/e 31 December 2010 (12 months ending in 2nd year) | 52,500 |

Overlap profits

| | |
|---|---|
| 1 January 2010 to 5 April 2010 (3/12 × £52,500) | 13,125 |

## Test your understanding 4

**Alex, Arsene and Jose**

Allocate of profits between the partners:

|  | Total £ | Alex £ | Arsene £ | Jose £ | Rafa £ |
|---|---|---|---|---|---|
| **Y/e 30.09.08** |  |  |  |  |  |
| Salary | 37,000 | 15,000 | 12,000 | 10,000 |  |
| Interest at 5% | 11,000 | 5,000 | 4,000 | 2,000 |  |
| PSR (1:1:1) | 55,500 | 18,500 | 18,500 | 18,500 |  |
| **Total** | **103,500** | **38,500** | **34,500** | **30,500** |  |
| **Y/e 30.09.09** |  |  |  |  |  |
| **01.10.08 – 31.12.08** |  |  |  |  |  |
| £128,000 x 3/12 = £32,000 |  |  |  |  |  |
| Salary (3/12) | 9,250 | 3,750 | 3,000 | 2,500 |  |
| Interest at 5% (x 3/12) | 2,750 | 1,250 | 1,000 | 500 |  |
| PSR (1:1:1) | 20,000 | 6,667 | 6,667 | 6,666 |  |
|  | 32,000 | 11,667 | 10,667 | 9,666 |  |
| **01.01.09 – 30.09.09** |  |  |  |  |  |
| £128,000 x 9/12 = £96,000 |  |  |  |  |  |
| Salary (9/12) | 47,250 | 15,000 | 13,500 | 11,250 | 7,500 |
| Interest at 5% (x 9/12) | 8,250 | 3,750 | 3,000 | 1,500 | Nil |
| PSR (35%:30%:25%:10%) | 40,500 | 14,175 | 12,150 | 10,125 | 4,050 |
|  | 96,000 | 32,925 | 28,650 | 22,875 | 11,550 |
| **Total** | **128,000** | **44,592** | **39,317** | **32,541** | **11,550** |
| **Y/e 30.09.10** |  |  |  |  |  |
| Salary | 63,000 | 20,000 | 18,000 | 15,000 | 10,000 |
| Interest at 5% | 11,000 | 5,000 | 4,000 | 2,000 | Nil |
| PSR (35%:30%:25%:10%) | 66,000 | 23,100 | 19,800 | 16,500 | 6,600 |
| **Total** | **140,000** | **48,100** | **41,800** | **33,500** | **16,600** |

|  | Total £ | Alex £ | Arsene £ | Jose £ | Rafa £ |
|---|---|---|---|---|---|
| **Y/e 30.09.11** | | | | | |
| Salary | 63,000 | 20,000 | 18,000 | 15,000 | 10,000 |
| Interest at 5% | 11,000 | 5,000 | 4,000 | 2,000 | Nil |
| PSR (35%:30%:25%:10%) | 106,000 | 37,100 | 31,800 | 26,500 | 10,600 |
| **Total** | **180,000** | **62,100** | **53,800** | **43,500** | **20,600** |

|  | Total £ | Alex £ | Arsene £ | Jose £ | Rafa £ |
|---|---|---|---|---|---|
| **Y/e 30.09.12** | | | | | |
| **01.10.11 – 31.03.12** | | | | | |
| 210,000 x 6/12 = 105,000 | | | | | |
| Salary (6/12) | 31,500 | 10,000 | 9,000 | 7,500 | 5,000 |
| Interest at 5% (x 6/12) | 5,500 | 2,500 | 2,000 | 1,000 | Nil |
| PSR (35%:30%:25%:10%) | 68,000 | 23,800 | 20,400 | 17,000 | 6,800 |
|  | 105,000 | 36,300 | 31,400 | 25,500 | 11,800 |
| **01.04.12 – 30.09.12** | | | | | |
| 210,000 x 6/12 = 105,000 | | | | | |
| Salary (6/12) | 21,500 | | 9,000 | 7,500 | 5,000 |
| Interest at 5% (x 6/12) | 3,000 | | 2,000 | 1,000 | Nil |
| PSR (1:1:1) | 80,500 | | 26,834 | 26,833 | 26,833 |
|  | 105,000 | | 37,834 | 35,333 | 31,833 |
| **Total** | **210,000** | **36,300** | **69,234** | **60,833** | **43,633** |

## Trading income assessments

Arsene and Jose will be assessed on a current year basis for each tax year. Their trading income assessments will be as follows:

| Tax year | Basis period | Arsene £ | Jose £ |
|---|---|---|---|
| 2008/09 | y/e 30 September 2008 | 34,500 | 30,500 |
| 2009/10 | y/e 30 September 2009 | 39,317 | 32,541 |
| 2010/11 | y/e 30 September 2010 | 41,800 | 33,500 |
| 2011/12 | y/e 30 September 2011 | 53,800 | 43,500 |
| 2012/13 | y/e 30 September 2012 | 69,234 | 60,833 |

Rafa will be treated as commencing on 1 January 2009, and will be assessed on his share of the partnership profits as follows:

| Tax year | Basis period | Trading income £ |
|---|---|---|
| 2008/09 | 1 January to 5 April 2009 (£11,550 x 3/9) | 3,850 |
| 2009/10 | First 12 months trading £11,550 + (£16,600 x 3/12) | 15,700 |
| 2010/11 | y/e 30 September 2010 | 16,600 |
| 2011/12 | y/e 30 September 2011 | 20,600 |
| 2012/13 | y/e 30 September 2012 | 43,633 |

Rafa will carry forward overlap profits of £8,000 (£3,850 + £4,150).

Alex will be treated as ceasing to trade on 31 March 2012, he will be assessed on his share of partnership profits as follows:

| Tax year | Basis period | £ | Trading income £ |
|---|---|---|---|
| 2008/09 | y/e 30 September 2008 | | 38,500 |
| 2009/10 | y/e 30 September 2009 | | 44,592 |
| 2010/11 | y/e 30 September 2010 | | 48,100 |
| 2011/12 | y/e 30 September 2011 | 62,100 | |
| | p/e 31 March 2012 | 36,300 | |
| | | ——— | |
| | | 98,400 | |
| | Less: Overlap profits | (15,000) | |
| | | ——— | 83,400 |

**Test your understanding 5**

**Paul and Phil**

|  | Paul £ | Phil £ | Total £ |
|---|---|---|---|
| Sale proceeds (60%:40%) | 297,000 | 198,000 | 495,000 |
| Less: Cost (60%:40%) | (75,000) | (50,000) | (125,000) |
| Chargeable gain | 222,000 | 148,000 | 370,000 |

The partnership asset is not part of the disposal of the entire business, so Entrepreneurs' relief is not available.

**Note:** To save time in the examination, it is acceptable to compute the total gain of £370,000 and allocate it 60%:40% to the partners.

However, it is an important principle to appreciate that each partner technically owns a fractional share and that each partner should do their own capital gains computation.

### Test your understanding 6

**Adam and Barry**

The inclusion of goodwill in the balance sheet in December 2006 does not give rise to a chargeable gain.

The subsequent change in profit sharing in December 2009 will result in a chargeable gain based on the value of goodwill reflected in the balance sheet of £100,000.

**Barry**

Barry's share of goodwill is reduced from 50% to 30% and so he will be treated as making a disposal of 20%, as follows:

| | £ |
|---|---:|
| Share of goodwill before change in profit sharing | |
| £100,000 × 50% | 50,000 |
| Share of goodwill after change in profit sharing | |
| £100,000 × 30% | (30,000) |
| | ——— |
| Deemed proceeds | 20,000 |
| | ——— |

Since the goodwill has no cost, he will be treated as having a capital gain of £20,000 for 2009/10.

**Adam**

Adam's share of the goodwill is increased from 50% to 70% and he will have an increased base cost for goodwill equivalent to Barry's deemed proceeds of £20,000.

# VAT: outline

## Chapter learning objectives

Upon completion of this chapter you will be able to:

- state the scope and nature of VAT

- explain the significance of the different types of supply for VAT

- list the principal zero rated and exempt supplies

- identify the two situations which require compulsory VAT registration

- discuss the advantages and disadvantages of voluntary registration

- identify when pre registration VAT can be recovered

- explain when a person must compulsorily/may voluntarily deregister for VAT

- explain how VAT is accounted for under the special schemes available

- outline the alternative VAT treatments on the sale of a business

- identify the value of a supply and calculate the relevant VAT

- identify recoverable and non recoverable input VAT on key purchases and expenses

- compute the relief that is available for impairment losses on trade debts

- advise on the meaning and impact of the disaggregation of business activities for VAT purposes

- advise on the VAT implications of the supply of land and buildings in the UK

- identify when partial exemption applies and calculate the impact

- state the purpose of the capital goods scheme and demonstrate how it operates.

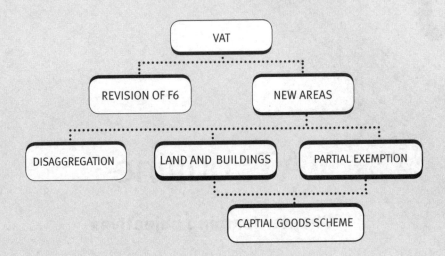

## 1 A revision of basic VAT

### Introduction

This chapter and the next cover Value Added Tax (VAT).

The first part of this chapter revises the basic rules of VAT covered at F6. The new topics introduced at P6 shown in the diagram above.

### The scope and nature of VAT

VAT is an indirect tax. It is levied on **taxable supplies** made by a **registered person** in the **course of business.**

| Key terms |
| --- |

- A **taxable person** is one who is or should be registered for VAT. A person can be an individual or a legal person such as a company.

- A **taxable supply** is all supplies which are not exempt or outside of the scope of VAT.

- For VAT to apply, the taxable supply must be made in the course or furtherance of a business carried on by a taxable person.

A taxable person must account for VAT on a regular basis as follows:

- Input VAT is paid by businesses on purchases and imports of goods and services.

- Input VAT is reclaimable from HMRC.

- Output VAT is charged on the supply of taxable goods and services. This includes gifts of goods (with some exceptions dealt with later) but not gifts of services. It also includes imports (Chapter 21).

- Output VAT is payable to HMRC.

> - Every month or quarter the input and output VAT is netted off and paid to or recovered from HMRC.

## Types and supply

VAT is charged on taxable supplies, but not on exempt supplies or those outside the scope of VAT.

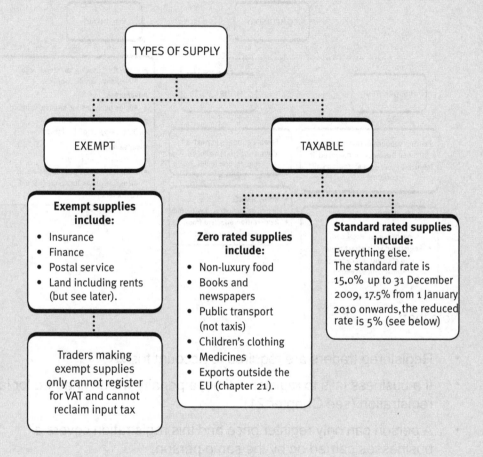

Note that:

- Some taxable supplies, mainly domestic or charitable use, are charged at the reduced rate. These are not important for the examinations.

- Some supplies are outside the scope of VAT. These include wages, dividends, other taxes (e.g. road fund licence), transfer of a business as a going concern and sales between companies in a VAT group.

## VAT registration

If a person's taxable supplies (excluding the sale of capital assets) exceeds the registration limit, registration is compulsory.

Voluntary registration is possible. This is particularly useful for businesses as it allows the recovery of input VAT.

However care should be taken when selling to the public as VAT will then be added to the selling price.

A reminder of registration rules:

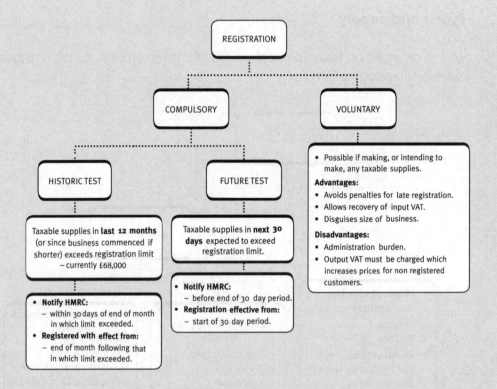

Note that:

- Registered traders are required to account for VAT.

- If a business fails to register in time, a penalty will be charged for late registration (see Chapter 21).

- A person can only register once and this registration covers all businesses carried on by the same person.

- A partnership is a separate person, therefore a partnership registration will cover all the businesses which are carried on by the same partners, but not any businesses they operate individually as sole traders.

## Pre-registration input VAT

Pre-registration input VAT can be recovered on the following:

- Goods (e.g. stock and fixed assets):
    - if acquired for business purposes
    - in the last four years, and
    - goods are still in hand at the date of registration.

- Services:
    - if supplied for business purposes
    - in the six months prior to registration.

## Deregistration

Deregistration is compulsory when a business ceases or is sold, although it is possible (by joint election) to transfer a registration to a new owner who assumes all rights and obligations in respect of the registration. Voluntary deregistration is also possible.

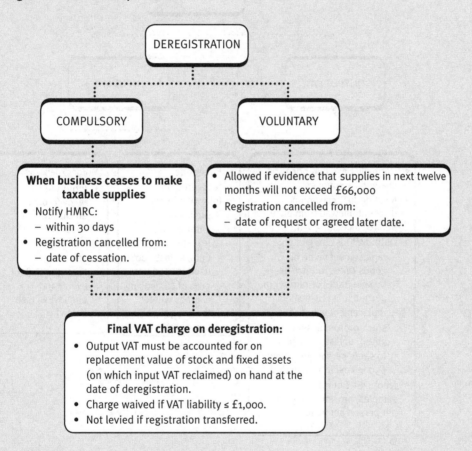

## VAT on the sale of a business

When a business is sold it will be necessary to charge VAT on the sale proceeds. This is avoided if the transfer of going concern rules apply, in which case the sale is outside the scope of VAT and no VAT needs to be charged (although see interaction with land and buildings below).

Conditions for transfer of going concern are as follows:

- The business is sold as a going concern.
- There is no significant break in trading.
- The same type of trade is carried on by the new owner.

- The new owner is, or immediately becomes, VAT registered.

## Input and output VAT

This section deals with some of the special rules for determining the value of an output and reminds you of the purchases and expenses incurred by a business on which input VAT is not recoverable.

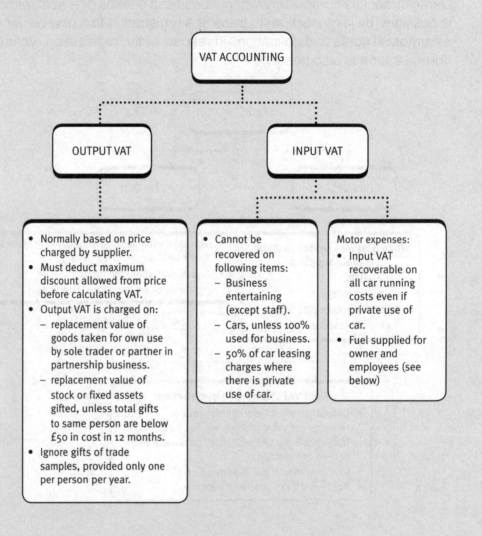

VAT ACCOUNTING

OUTPUT VAT

INPUT VAT

**OUTPUT VAT**
- Normally based on price charged by supplier.
- Must deduct maximum discount allowed from price before calculating VAT.
- Output VAT is charged on:
  - replacement value of goods taken for own use by sole trader or partner in partnership business.
  - replacement value of stock or fixed assets gifted, unless total gifts to same person are below £50 in cost in 12 months.
- Ignore gifts of trade samples, provided only one per person per year.

**INPUT VAT (cannot be recovered)**
- Cannot be recovered on following items:
  - Business entertaining (except staff).
  - Cars, unless 100% used for business.
  - 50% of car leasing charges where there is private use of car.

**Motor expenses:**
- Input VAT recoverable on all car running costs even if private use of car.
- Fuel supplied for owner and employees (see below)

## Motor expenses – private fuel supplied by business

The basis for charging output tax on the provision of private fuel is based on the $CO_2$ emissions of the car.

Scale charges exist for 21 bandings of $CO_2$ emissions. If required in the examination, the appropriate scale charge will be given in the question.

The treatment of the scale charge is as follows:

- The VAT scale charge must be added to outputs in the VAT return, and output VAT borne by the business

- The output VAT can be avoided
  - if no input VAT is recovered on the fuel, or
  - no private fuel supplied.

## Bad debt relief

Normally, VAT output tax is accounted for when an invoice is issued. If the sale becomes a bad debt, the seller has paid VAT to HMRC and never recovers this from the customer.

This position is addressed by the seller being able to claim VAT bad debts relief provided the following conditions are satisfied:

- **At least 6 months** must have elapsed since payment from the debtor was due.
- The debt must have been written off in the seller's books.
- Relief is obtained by adding the VAT element of the bad debt to the input tax claimed.
- Claims for bad debt relief are subject to a **four-year** time limit.

If there has been a series of supplies, any payments made by the customer must be allocated on a FIFO basis unless the customer allocated a payment to a particular supply and paid in full.

### Test your understanding 1

(1) Wilf Evans is a systems analyst who has recently started his own business. He has supplied you with the following information:

 (a) His sales revenue for his first year ending 31 December 2009 is estimated to be £92,000 accruing evenly over the year. All Wilf's customers are VAT registered businesses and all Wilf's turnover is of taxable supplies.

 (b) He purchased computer equipment for £3,525 including VAT on 14 January 2009.

 (c) His business telephone bills are estimated to be £400 per quarter including VAT.

 (d) He uses a room at his home as his office. His house has five main rooms and the electricity bill for the whole house for the year is estimated as £1,500 including VAT of £70.

(e) He has a 1,800 cc petrol engine car which he uses 75% for business. Wilf bought the car in October 2008 for £15,000 including VAT. It was valued at £13,500 when he started his business on 1 January 2009. The car emits 190g/km of $CO_2$ and annual running costs excluding petrol are £1,100 per year which includes £115 of VAT. He charges all his petrol costs through the business and these amount to £100 per month.

(f) Prior to starting in business, Wilf paid his accountant £400 plus VAT on 1 December 2008 for drawing up cash flow projections. His annual accountancy preparation costs are estimated to be £600 plus VAT.

**Wilf has not yet registered for VAT. He wishes you to advise him when he will have to register compulsorily for VAT and whether it would be beneficial to register before that date.**

(2) In his second year Wilf has problems collecting a debt from XYZ Ltd. He has invoiced that company £3,500 including VAT on 15 Mar 2010. In September 2010 he receives £1,000 from XYZ Ltd in partial settlement of the debt but in October 2010 he writes off the rest of the debt as bad.

**Advise Wilf of the VAT position on this debt.**

(3) In his third year of trading, Wilf decides to offer a discount for prompt payment to try to improve his cash flow. The discount offered is 5% for payments within 14 days and 2.5% for payments within 30 days.

**Explain to Wilf what action he should take for VAT purposes when invoicing his customers.**

(4) In his fourth year of business Wilf receives an offer for his business of £450,000.

**Wilf wants you to advise him whether VAT needs to be charged on this amount and whether there are any other actions he should take. The projected sale date for the business is 31 May 2013.**

Assume all VAT rules remain as they are in 2009/10. The VAT scale charge for a car with 190g/km of $CO_2$ emissions is £53.47 per quarter.

## 2 Special Accounting Schemes

There are three special VAT accounting schemes that are examinable and were covered at F6, namely:

- Cash Accounting scheme
- Annual Accounting scheme
- Flat rate scheme.

A brief reminder of these schemes is given in expandable text and is summarised in the diagram below.

### Cash accounting

Under this scheme VAT is accounted for on the basis of amounts received and paid in the VAT period rather than the normal basis.

To be eligible for cash accounting the following conditions must be satisfied:

- Businesses must have an annual taxable sales revenue (excluding sales of capital assets) of less than £1,350,000 per annum.
- The business must leave the scheme if its taxable sales revenue exceeds £1,600,000.
- The business must be up to date with its VAT returns and payments and must have no convictions for VAT offences or penalties for dishonest conduct.

The main advantages of cash accounting are:

- where customers are slow payers or there are bad debts no VAT is payable until the money is received
- the information for the VAT return can be taken from the cash book, and no detailed cut-off procedures are required.

### Annual Accounting

This scheme alleviates the burden of administration of VAT and helps the cash flow of the business.

To be eligible to use the annual accounting scheme the same conditions as above must be satisfied.

The consequences of joining the scheme are as follows:

- One VAT return is prepared for the year, and payments are made on an estimated basis.

- Payments can be either:
  - 9 instalments of 1/10th of the estimated amount, with a final payment equal to the balance of the amount due or
  - 3 instalments of 25% of the estimated amount due, with a final payment of the balance.

- The first payment is due at the end of month 4, and the return is due with the final payment 2 months after the end of the year.

- Payments must be made electronically or by standing order.

- Annual accounting may be calculated on a cash basis.

### Flat rate scheme

Businesses with a sales revenue (excluding VAT) of £150,000 or less, may account for VAT using the flat rate scheme.

The consequences of the scheme are as follows:

- VAT is accounted for using a flat % of total sales revenue. The total sales revenue used is the VAT inclusive amount including exempt and zero rated supplies.

- Different %'s apply for each business sector and if appropriate will be given in the examination.

- No input VAT is recovered on purchases, although a claim can be made to recover VAT on purchases of fixed assets that cost more than £2,000.

- The standard %'s are reduced for the first 12 months the trader uses the scheme.

- Businesses are eligible to stay in the scheme until annual income (cash received if using cash accounting or invoiced sales revenue if using invoice basis) exceeds £225,000.

## Summary

**SMALL BUSINESS VAT SCHEMES**

**Cash accounting**
- Same conditions as the annual accounting scheme
- Account on cash paid/cash received basis, not accruals
- Advantages
  - Automatic bad debt relief
  - Easier administration

**Conditions:**
- Annual taxable sales revenue (excluding capital) < £1,350,000
- Up to date with returns and payments
- Leave scheme if taxable sales revenue > £1,600,000

**Annual accounting**
- Same conditions as the cash accounting scheme
- One VAT return for year
- Pay regularly by standing order or electronically:
  - 9 monthly instalments of 10%, or
  - 3 quarterly instalments of 25%
  - plus balancing payment
- First instalment = end of month 4
- Final payment = 2 months after year end
- Advantages
  - Regular cash outflows
  - Easier administration

**Flat rate scheme**
- VAT payment = (fixed % x VAT inclusive total turnover)
- Conditions:
  - Taxable sales revenue (excluding VAT) ≤ £150,000
- Advantages
  - No need for detailed records of sales and purchases
  - Easier administration
- Leave scheme if taxable sales revenue > £225,000

## Comprehensive example

### Test your understanding 2

Vector Ltd is registered for VAT, and is in the process of completing its VAT return for the quarter ended 31 March 2010. The following information is available.

(1) Sales invoices totalling £128,000 were issued in respect of standard rated sales. Vector Ltd offers its customers a 2.5% discount for prompt payment.

(2) On 15 March 2010 Vector Ltd received an advance deposit of £4,500 in respect of a contract that is due to be completed during April 2010. The total value of the contract is £10,000. Both figures are inclusive of VAT.

(3) Standard rated expenses amounted to £74,800. This includes £4,200 for entertaining customers.

(4) On 31 March 2010 Vector Ltd wrote off £12,000 due from a customer as a bad debt. The debt was in respect of three invoices, each of £4,000, that were due for payment on 15 August, 15 September and 15 October 2009 respectively.

(5) On 1 January 2010 the company purchased a motor car costing £9,800 for the use of its sales manager. The sales manager is provided with free petrol for private mileage. The car has $CO_2$ emissions of 205 g/km and the relevant quarterly scale charge is £400. Both figures are inclusive of VAT.

Unless stated otherwise all of the above figures are exclusive of VAT.

**Required:**

(a) Calculate the amount of VAT payable by Vector Ltd for the quarter ended 31 March 2010.

(b) State the conditions that Vector Ltd must satisfy before it will be permitted to use the cash accounting scheme, and advise the company of the implications of using the scheme.

Assume the VAT rate of 17.5% applies throughout.

## 3 Disaggregation

There is a provision to prevent a business from being artificially split into small units thereby avoiding VAT registration because one or more units fall below the turnover limits.

- Where HMRC are satisfied that persons are carrying on separate activities which could properly be regarded as part of a single business, then they will issue a direction.

- There is no requirement for HMRC to establish that the main reason for the separation of the activities was to avoid registration for VAT.

- The direction will state that the persons named therein are carrying on the activities listed together, i.e. a partnership is deemed to exist. However, a direction cannot have retrospective effect.

- For example, if a husband and wife run a pub together, but the wife operates the pub catering separately, both activities will be considered as one business if a direction is made. The sales revenue from both activities will be taken into account for the registration limits.

# 4 Land and buildings

## Types of supply

Supplies of land and buildings in the UK can be either be zero-rated, standard-rated or exempt.

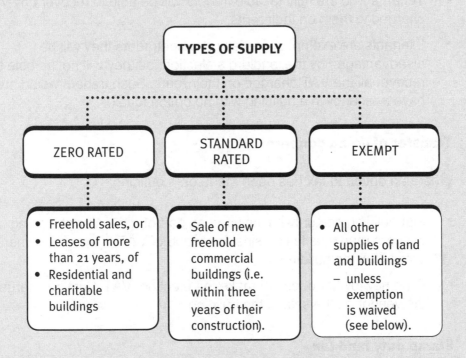

**TYPES OF SUPPLY**

**ZERO RATED**
- Freehold sales, or
- Leases of more than 21 years, of
- Residential and charitable buildings

**STANDARD RATED**
- Sale of new freehold commercial buildings (i.e. within three years of their construction).

**EXEMPT**
- All other supplies of land and buildings
  - unless exemption is waived (see below).

## Opting to tax

A VAT registered vendor or lessor of a building can opt to waive the exemption of the building. This is usually referred to as 'opting to tax.'

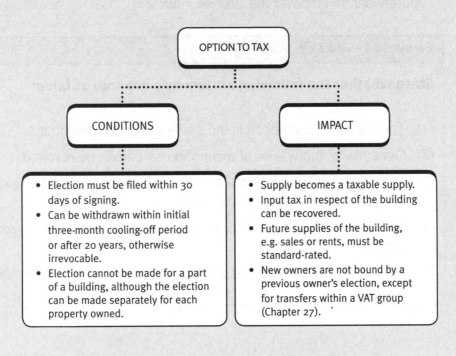

**OPTION TO TAX**

**CONDITIONS**
- Election must be filed within 30 days of signing.
- Can be withdrawn within initial three-month cooling-off period or after 20 years, otherwise irrevocable.
- Election cannot be made for a part of a building, although the election can be made separately for each property owned.

**IMPACT**
- Supply becomes a taxable supply.
- Input tax in respect of the building can be recovered.
- Future supplies of the building, e.g. sales or rents, must be standard-rated.
- New owners are not bound by a previous owner's election, except for transfers within a VAT group (Chapter 27).

Note that opting to tax is particularly useful for landlords letting out commercial property which would normally be an exempt supply.

- By opting to tax the building, the landlord can recover any input tax on the purchase and running costs of the building.

- Tenants who are fully taxable traders will be able to recover any VAT charged to them on their rents.

- If tenants are exempt or partially exempt traders they will be disadvantaged by the landlord's election, as they will not be able to recover all the VAT charged on their rents. Such traders would prefer to have a tenancy in a building with no option to tax.

### Transfer of going concern

Where an option to tax has been made on a building:

- that building can only be included as part of a transfer of a going concern (and thus fall outside the scope of VAT) if the new owner also opts to tax the building.

- If the new owner does not make the election, VAT must be charged by the vendor on the sale of the building.

### Stamp duty land tax

SDLT is charged on

- the purchaser of the building
- on the consideration for the building including VAT (even if the purchaser can recover the VAT as input tax).

| Example 1 – VAT on property |
| --- |

**State whether the following statements are true or false:**

(1) The waiver of exemption is the same thing as opting to tax.

(2) Once made, the waiver of exemption can never be revoked.

(3) If you buy a building which the previous owner has opted to tax, you are obliged to continue the option.

(4) The sale of second hand commercial buildings is always an exempt supply.

(5) The supply of new freehold buildings is always a standard rated supply.

### Solution

(1)  Yes.

(2)  No – the waiver can be withdrawn within an initial three month cooling off period or after 20 years, otherwise it is irrevocable.

(3)  No – the only time this is true is if the sale takes place within a VAT group.

(4)  No – because the owner may have opted to tax the building.

(5)  No – if the building is for residential or charitable use the sale will be zero rated.

### Test your understanding 3

(1)  X plc purchases a new factory building for use in its manufacturing trade from a builder, paying £700,000.

(2)  Y plc is granted a 25 year lease on an office block which is intended for use in Y's trade.

(3)  Z plc sells a 15 year old freehold building.

Assume that X, Y and Z plc are all registered traders, all transactions take place within the UK and the standard rate of VAT is 17.5%.

**State the VAT implications of the above transactions.**

## 5 Partial exemption

### Introduction

Traders who make both taxable and exempt supplies are given credit for only part of the input tax they incur. This section deals with the calculation of the recoverable input tax credit.

### Methods of determining recoverable input tax

The standard method for determining the amount of recoverable input VAT is as follows:

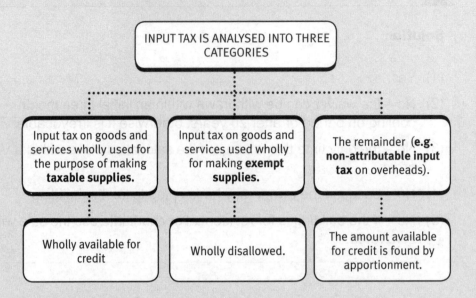

- The non-attributable input tax available for credit is found by using the fraction:

$$\frac{\text{Total taxable supplies}}{\text{Total supplies}}$$

- The taxable and total supplies exclude VAT and supplies of capital goods are excluded when calculating this proportion.

- The ratio is computed as a percentage and, if not a whole number, it is rounded up to the next whole number.

- If input tax wholly or partly attributed to exempt supplies is below the following de minimis limits, all input tax is available for credit.

The exempt input tax must not exceed:

- **£625 per month** on average for any VAT account period, and
- **50% of the input tax** incurred on all purchases.

Any other reasonable method of apportionment can be agreed with HMRC.

The percentage used during the year is generally the annual percentage from the previous year.

Alternatively, the business can choose to calculate the percentage each quarter based on supplies for that quarter. Whichever method is used, it must be used consistently throughout the year.

In either case, an annual adjustment will be made at the end of the accounting period.

## Annual adjustment

The amount available for credit is calculated for each VAT return period separately, i.e. usually for each quarterly return.

- At the end of the accounting period, an annual adjustment calculation must be performed to ensure that the correct amount of credit has been claimed for the year as a whole.

- Any under or over-declaration is then accounted for to HMRC or reclaimed from them on the first VAT return of the next year.

- Alternatively, the business can opt to bring forward the annual adjustment calculation to the last VAT return of the year (for example, if there was a repayment due).

### Example 2 – Partial exemption

Arnold carries on activities which give rise to both taxable supplies and exempt supplies for which input tax is wholly disallowed.

Arnold prepares accounts to 31 December each year.

Relevant figures for the quarter ended 30 June 2009 are:

| Activity | Attributable input tax £ |
|---|---|
| Standard rated supplies (£96,000) | 10,500 |
| Zero rated supplies (£32,000) | 3,500 |
| Exempt supplies (£37,200) | 4,000 |
| | 18,000 |
| Overheads | 5,000 |
| Total input tax | 23,000 |

**Calculate the recoverable input tax for the quarter ended 30 June 2009, assuming Arnold chooses to calculate the percentage based on supplies for the quarter.**

**Solution**

| Quarter to 30 June 2009 | Total £ | Recover £ | Disallow £ |
|---|---|---|---|
| Relating to taxable supplies (£10,500 + £3,500) | 14,000 | 14,000 | |
| Relating to exempt supplies | 4,000 | | 4,000 |
| Relating to overheads | 5,000 | 3,900 | 1,100 |
| | 23,000 | 17,900 | 5,100 |

**De minimis test**

The average exempt monthly input tax is £1,700 (£5,100 ÷ 3).

As this exceeds £625, it is not de minimis and cannot be recovered.

Recoverable input VAT is therefore £17,900.

**Annual adjustment**

At the end of the year, when calculating the recoverable input VAT for the quarter ended 31 December 2009, the same calculation needs to be performed on an annual basis. Any under or over claims for the previous quarters are made in this last return period.

**Working:** Percentage apportionment of input VAT on overheads:

$$\frac{£96,000 + £32,000}{£96,000 + £32,000 + £37,200} \times 100 = 78\% \text{ (Note)}$$

**Note:** The percentage is rounded up to the nearest whole percentage.

### Test your understanding 4

Toby's input tax and supplies made in the quarter to 31 December 2009 are analysed as follows:

|  | £ |
|---|---|
| Input tax wholly re-taxable supplies | 23,250 |
| Input tax wholly re-exempt supplies | 14,000 |
| Non-attributable input tax | 28,000 |
| Value (excluding VAT) of taxable supplies | 250,000 |
| Value of exempt supplies | 100,000 |

**Calculate the deductible input tax assuming that Toby uses the standard method of attribution and chooses to calculate the percentage based on supplies for the quarter.**

## 6 The capital goods scheme

### Introduction

The capital goods scheme applies to partially exempt businesses that spend large sums on land and buildings or computers and computer equipment.

- Where the scheme applies, the initial deduction of input tax is made in the ordinary way and then reviewed over a set adjustment period.

- This is to stop businesses manipulating their proportion of taxable and exempt supplies in the period of purchase in order to reclaim more input tax.

### Assets covered by the scheme

The assets dealt with by the scheme are as follows:

| Item | Value | Adjustment period |
|---|---|---|
| Land and buildings | £250,000 or more | 10 years (5 years where subject to a lease of less than 10 years at acquisition) |
| Computers and computer equipment | £50,000 or more | 5 years |

A trader making say 70% taxable supplies and 30% exempt supplies can initially reclaim 70% of the input VAT charged in respect of a building.

Adjustments are made over the next 10 (or 5) years if the proportion of exempt supplies changes.

The annual adjustment is:

$$\frac{\text{Total input tax}}{\text{10 or 5 years}} \times (\text{\% now} - \text{\% in the original year})$$

### Example 3 – Capital goods scheme

Confusion plc is a company that buys a new freehold building for £5,875,000 including VAT at 17.5%. 40% of the building is used in making exempt supplies and 60% taxable. After 7 years this changes to 50%: 50%.

**Explain how Confusion plc can recover input VAT on the purchase of the building.**

**Solution**

The purchase of the building is subject to the capital goods scheme as it is a building costing £250,000 or more. The adjustment period is 10 years as it is a freehold purchase.

The initial recovery of input tax is:

60% × £5,875,000 × 7/47 = £525,000

For years 1 – 7 of the adjustment period there is no need to make any adjustment.

For each of years 8, 9,10 the company will have part of its initial input tax recovery clawed back as follows:

£875,000 × 1/10× (50% – 60%) = £8,750 owed to HMRC

### Example 4 – Capital goods scheme

Delta plc is a partially exempt trader and makes 30% exempt and 70% taxable supplies.

On 1 March 2010 Delta plc buys a freehold building for £2 million including VAT which is used in the same proportion. After two years Delta plc's percentages and use of the building change to 40% exempt and 60% taxable. After a further 3 years Delta plc ceases the exempt trade and makes only taxable supplies from thereon.

**Calculate the input VAT relief that can be obtained by Delta plc.**

**Solution**

The purchase of the building is subject to the capital goods scheme as it is a building costing £250,000 or more. The adjustment period is 10 years as it is a freehold purchase.

The initial recovery of VAT is:

70% × 7/47 × £2,000,000 = £208,511.

There are no adjustments required for years 1 and 2 but for years 3 – 5 the company must repay part of its input tax relief as follows:

£2,000,000 × 7/47 × 1/10 × (60% – 70%)

= £2,979 due to HMRC for each of years 3,4,5.

For years 6 – 10 the company will be able to reclaim further input tax relief as follows:

£2,000,000 × 7/47 × 1/10 × (100% – 70%)

= £8,936 due to Delta plc each year.

## 7 Chapter summary

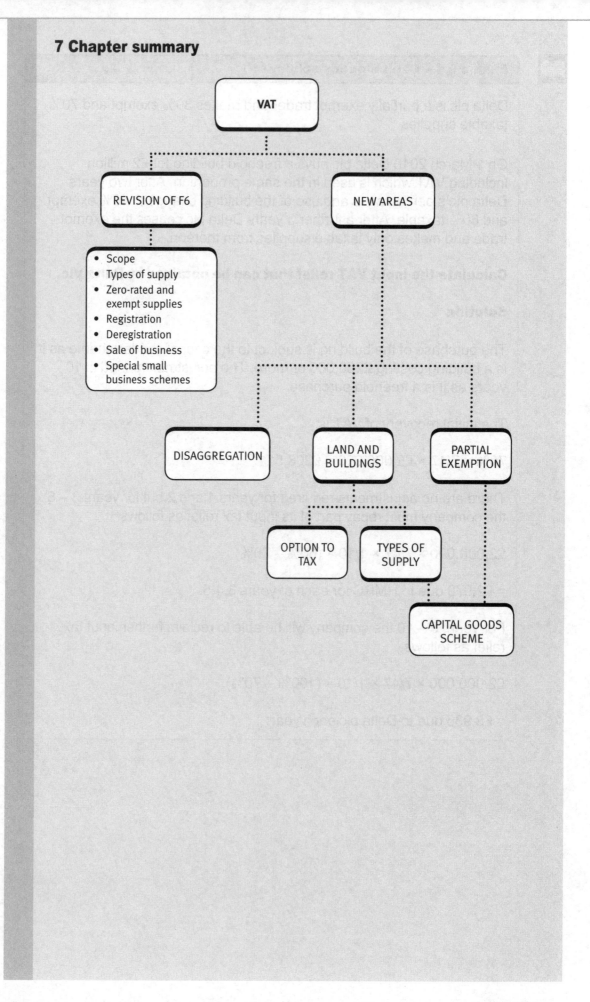

VAT

REVISION OF F6

NEW AREAS

- Scope
- Types of supply
- Zero-rated and exempt supplies
- Registration
- Deregistration
- Sale of business
- Special small business schemes

DISAGGREGATION

LAND AND BUILDINGS

PARTIAL EXEMPTION

OPTION TO TAX

TYPES OF SUPPLY

CAPITAL GOODS SCHEME

# Test your understanding answers

## Test your understanding 1

### Wilf Evans

### (1) Registration

- Wilf will become liable to compulsory registration for VAT when his taxable supplies for any 12 month period exceed £68,000. His turnover is £7,667 per month starting on 1 January 2009 so he will exceed £68,000 after 9 months i.e. at the end of September 2009.

- He will need to notify HMRC by 30 October 2009 and will be registered with effect from 1 November 2009 or an earlier agreed date.

- As Wilf is selling to VAT registered traders, there should be no disadvantage to registering for VAT voluntarily before 1 November 2009. His customers will be able to reclaim any VAT charged by Wilf.

- The main advantage of registering early is that Wilf will be able to reclaim input VAT as follows:

  (i) Computer equipment – even if purchased before registration, the VAT can be recovered provided Wilf still owns the computer at the date of registration. Reclaim £460 (£3,525 x 15/115).

  (ii) Business telephone – reclaim £52 per quarter (£400 x 15/115).

  (iii) Use of home as office – Wilf can reclaim VAT on the business proportion of his electricity bills £14 (£70 x 1/5) for the year.

  (iv) Wilf cannot recover VAT on his car purchase. He can recover VAT on the running expenses £115 and VAT on his petrol of £13 per month (£100 x 15/115). If he recovers input tax on the petrol, he will have to account for a VAT fuel charge. For a car with $CO_2$ emissions of 190g/km, the amount VAT scale charge is £53.47 per quarter, which must be added to the output tax for each quarter. This fuel charge can be avoided if Wilf does not claim any VAT input tax in respect of fuel.

  (v) If Wilf registers by 1 June 2009 he will be able to reclaim the input VAT on his accountant's fee for preparing his cash flow projections. This is because he can recover input VAT on services supplied in the six months prior to registration.

(2) **Bad debts**

In the quarter which includes October 2010 Wilf can make a claim for the VAT on his outstanding debt. This will be £372 (£2,500 x 7/47). This is permitted because Wilf has written off the debt in his books and it is more than 6 months since the date payment was due.

(3) **Discounts**

Wilf must charge VAT on the discounted amount as if the full discount of 5% had been taken. Hence for an invoice for £1,000 excluding VAT, the VAT charged should be:

17½% x 95% x £1,000 = £166

(4) **Sale of business**

There are two issues to consider here:

(i) No VAT needs to be charged if Wilf sells his business as a going concern provided:

– the new owner is or becomes VAT registered

– the assets sold are used in the same trade in the future, and

– there is no significant break in the trading.

(ii) Wilf must

– deregister unless his registration is transferred to the new owner. This is unlikely if they are unconnected third parties.

– notify HMRC that he has ceased to make taxable supplies. This notification must be within 30 days of cessation.

– account for VAT on the replacement values of his stock (if any) and tangible fixed assets on hand at the date of deregistration. However it seems likely that there will be no charge as amounts below £1,000 are not collected.

### Test your understanding 2

**Vector Ltd**

(a) **VAT Return – Quarter ended 31 March 2010**

|  | £ |
|---|---:|
| Output VAT: | |
| Sales (£128,000 × 97.5% × 17.5%) | 21,840 |
| Advance payment (£4,500 × 17.5/117.5) | 670 |
| Motor car scale charge (£400 × 17.5/117.5) | 60 |
|  | ——— |
|  | 22,570 |
| Input VAT: | |
| Expenses (£74,800 – £4,200 = £70,600 × 17.5%) | (12,355) |
| Bad debt relief (£4,000 + £4,000 = £8,000 × 17.5%) | (1,400) |
|  | ——— |
| VAT payable | 8,815 |
|  | ——— |

**Notes:**

(1) The calculation of output VAT on sales must take into account the discount for prompt payment, even if customers do not take advantage of it.

(2) Input VAT on business entertainment is not recoverable.

(3) Relief for a bad debt is not given until six months from the time that payment is due. Therefore relief can only be claimed in respect of the invoices due for payment on 15 August and 15 September 2009.

(4) Input VAT cannot be recovered in respect of the motor car as it is not used exclusively for business purposes.

**Tutorial note:** Although the examiner uses a VAT fraction of 17.5/117.5 it could be less cumbersome and equally valid to use a VAT fraction of 7/47 from 1 January 2010. Prior to this use a fraction of 15/115 or 3/23 as the standard rate of VAT is 15% until 31 December 2009.

(b) **Cash accounting scheme**

(1) Vector Ltd can use the cash accounting scheme if its expected taxable sales revenue for the next 12 months does not exceed £1,350,000.

(2) In addition, the company must be up to date with its VAT returns and VAT payments.

(3) The scheme will result in the tax point becoming the date that payment is received from customers.

(4) This will provide for automatic bad debt relief should a customer not pay.

(5) However, the recovery of input VAT on expenses will be delayed until payment is made.

### Test your understanding 3

**VAT on property**

(1) **X plc**
The builder will charge VAT on the sale of a new commercial building. As it says that X plc paid £700,000 it can be assumed that this is the VAT inclusive price. The VAT of £104,255 (7/47 × £700,000) can be reclaimed by X plc as they plan to use the building to make taxable supplies. The net cost of the building £595,745 will be examined for a possible IBA claim.

(2) **Y plc**
Unless the landlord has opted to tax the transaction, this will be an exempt supply. Y plc will not incur any input tax.

(3) **Z plc**
Normally the sale of a building more than 3 years old will be an exempt supply and no VAT will be charged. However, if Z plc has opted to tax the building then they will have to charge VAT on the disposal.

## Test your understanding 4

**Toby**

| | Total £ | Recover £ | Disallow £ |
|---|---|---|---|
| Relating to taxable supplies | 23,250 | 23,250 | |
| Relating to exempt supplies | 14,000 | | 14,000 |
| Relating to overheads (W) | 28,000 | 20,160 | 7,840 |
| | 65,250 | 43,410 | 21,840 |

### De Minimis test

The exempt input tax is £21,840 and as this amounts to more than £625 per month on average none of it is recoverable.

The recoverable input VAT is therefore £43,410.

### Working: Allocate non-attributable VAT

Taxable % apportionment

$$= \frac{£250,000}{£250,000 + £100,000} \times 100 = 72\% \text{ (round up to whole \%)}$$

# VAT: administration and overseas aspects

## Chapter learning objectives

Upon completion of this chapter you will be able to:

- identify how a default surcharge penalty arises and calculate it

- explain the procedure and effect when errors on earlier VAT returns are identified

- describe the penalty for submission of an incorrect VAT return and state the amount of the penalty

- describe the penalty regime for failure to notify liability for registration or change in nature of supplies by persons exempted from registration

- describe when a default interest charge will arise and calculate it

- advise on the VAT implications of imports and exports

- advise on the VAT implications of acquisitions and supplies within the EU.

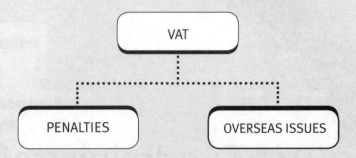

## 1 Introduction

This chapter revises the rules for penalties and interest covered at F6, however note that there have been some significant changes recently in the penalty regime.

The chapter also covers the main new topic at P6, namely the overseas aspects of VAT.

## 2 Electronic filing of VAT returns

HMRC plans to phase out paper VAT Returns from April 2010.

After that date, if the business has annual sales revenue of £100,000 or more, or is newly VAT registered, the VAT return will have to be submitted online and the VAT paid electronically.

## 3 The default surcharge

The rules for default surcharges were covered at F6 and are unchanged. A brief reminder of the rules is given in expandable text and is summarised in the diagram below.

### Default surcharge

A default occurs if a return is not submitted on time or a payment is made late. The sequence for the default surcharge is as follows:

- On the first default, HMRC serve a surcharge liability notice on the taxpayer.

- The notice specifies a surcharge period, starting on the date of the notice and ending in twelve months time.

- If a trader defaults in the surcharge period, there are two consequences.

    - the surcharge period is extended to the 12 month anniversary of the VAT period to which the new default relates

    - a surcharge penalty can be levied if the default results in the late payment of VAT.

- The amount of surcharge depends on the number of defaults in the surcharge period:

| Default in the surcharge period | Surcharge as a % of tax unpaid at the due date |
|---|---|
| First | **2%** |
| Second | **5%** |
| Third | **10%** |
| Fourth | **15%** |

- Surcharge assessments at rates below 10% will not be issued for amounts of less than **£400.**

- Where the rate of surcharge is 10% or more, an assessment will be issued for either £30 or the actual amount of the calculated surcharge, whichever is the greater.

- The surcharge liability period only ends when a trader submits four consecutive quarterly returns on time, and pays any tax due on time.

### Example 1 – Default surcharge

Mark's return for 30 June 2009 is late, and the tax of £14,500 is not paid until 16 August 2009. His return for the following period is submitted late and the tax of £16,200 is not paid until 9 November 2009.

**Explain the consequences for Mark.**

**Solution**

(1) **Return period ended 30 June 2009**

First default: surcharge liability notice issued. The surcharge period runs from the date of the notice to 30 June 2010.

(2) **Return period ended 30 September 2009**

First default within the surcharge period. Penalty of £324 (£16,200 × 2%) is due but as the amount is less than £400 an assessment will not be issued.

The surcharge period is extended to 30 September 2010.

## 4 Errors on a VAT return

VAT is a self-assessed tax. The trader calculates their own liability or repayment.

- HMRC make occasional control visits to check that returns are correct.

- HMRC have the power to enter business premises, inspect documents, including profit and loss accounts and balance sheets, take samples, and inspect computer records (see Chapter 16 for HMRC information and inspection powers).

### Errors on earlier VAT returns

If a trader realises that there is an error this may lead to a standard penalty as there has been a submission of an incorrect VAT return. If, however, the error is below the de minimus level and voluntarily disclosed no default interest will be charged.

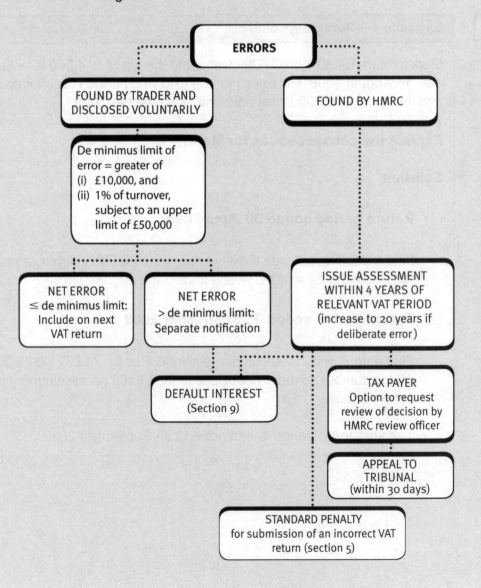

## 5 Penalties

### Standard penalty

HMRC is standardising penalties across taxes and for different offences. For 2010 exams, the standard penalty applies to two areas:

- inaccuracies in returns – all taxes
- failure to notify liability to tax – income tax, CGT, corporation tax, VAT and PAYE/NIC.

The penalty is calculated as a percentage of 'potential lost revenue' which is generally the tax unpaid as a result of the error or failure to notify.

| Offence | Penalty |
|---|---|
| Submission of an incorrect VAT return leading to: <br><br> – an understatement of VAT liability <br><br> – a false or inflated claim for repayment of tax | Standard penalty <br> Based on a % of VAT underpaid |
| Failure to notify liability for registration or change in nature of supplies by person exempted from registration | Standard penalty <br> Based on a % of VAT lost during the period from when the notification should have been made until actually made |
| Default surcharge | See section 3 |

## 6 Default interest

Interest is charged, if HMRC raise an assessment, or an error is voluntarily disclosed by the trader, as the net error exceeds the de minimus limit.

Interest is charged:

from:   – the date that the outstanding VAT should have been paid
to:        – the actual date of payment.

Any interest charged by HMRC is limited to a maximum of three years prior to the date of the assessment or voluntary disclosure.

### Example 2 – Penalties and interest

Hopeless Ltd has recently had a control visit from HMRC. During the visit it has been discovered that on their previous VAT return for the quarter to 31 March 2010, Hopeless Ltd forgot to include output VAT on £500,000 (VAT exclusive) of taxable supplies.

The actual output and input tax included in the return were as follows.

|  | £ |
| --- | --- |
| Output tax | 100,000 |
| Input tax | 30,000 |
| Due to HMRC | 70,000 |

Hopeless paid the underpaid VAT on 6 June 2010.

**State whether a penalty for submission of an incorrect return will be levied on Hopeless Ltd and, if so, discuss the maximum penalty that will be imposed. State the position with respect to default interest. Assume a rate of default interest of 2.5%.**

### Solution

The error Hopeless Ltd has made is to under declare output VAT of:

$$(17\frac{1}{2}\% \times £500,000) = £87,500.$$

This means the VAT return for the quarter to 31 March 2010 is incorrect due to an understatement of the VAT liability.

The standard penalty therefore applies and is determined according to:

- The amount of tax understated.
- The reason for the understatement.
- The extent of disclosure by the taxpayer.

The level of the penalty is a percentage of the revenue lost as a result of the inaccuracy or under assessment and depends on the behaviour of the taxpayer as follows:

| Taxpayer behaviour | Maximum penalty (% of revenue lost) |
|---|---|
| Genuine mistake. | No penalty |
| Failure to take reasonable care. | 30% |
| Serious or deliberate understatement. | 70% |
| Serious or deliberate understatement with concealment. | 100% |

The penalties may be reduced depending on the type of penalty and whether the taxpayer makes an unprompted disclosure.

As Hopeless Ltd have not voluntarily disclosed the error (as it was discovered by HMRC), no reduction is likely to be made for unprompted disclosure.

Where the return is incorrect through deliberate intention of a third party, the penalty can be charged on the third party.

Default interest will also be charged from the date the VAT should have been paid (30 April) until the actual date of payment on 6 June (37 days).

The charge will be: (37/365 × 2.5% × £87,500) = £222

## Summary

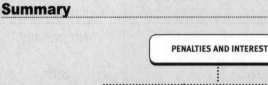

**PENALTIES AND INTEREST**

**DEFAULT SURCHARGE**
- Return or payment late
- First default:
  surcharge liability notice served
  = 12 months from notice date
- Default in surcharge period:
  1st = **2%**
  2nd = **5%**
  3rd = **10%**
  4th = **15%**
- Surcharge period extended by
  12 months
- If rate < 10%, amount < £400:
  – No penalty payable
- If rate ≥ 10%
  – Penalty = greater of £30 or
  actual amount calculated

**STANDARD PENALTY**
- Penalty subject to the behaviour
  of the taxpayer and is a percentage
  of the revenue lost

**Errors**
- If net error less than or equal to the greater of
  – £10,000 and
  – 1% of turnover (subject to an upper limit of £50,000)
  include in next VAT return
- If net error more than the greater of
  – £10,000 and
  – 1% of turnover (subject to an upper limit of £50,000)
  advise VAT office
- Can lead to penalty for submission of incorrect VAT returns

**Default interest**
- Interest charged if net error more than the default surcharge limit
  – HMRC raise assessment or error voluntarily disclosed
- Runs from: date should have paid
- Runs to: date paid
- Maximum 3 years interest charged

## 7 Overseas aspects of VAT

### Introduction

VAT is a tax levied within the European Union (EU) only. It is therefore necessary to distinguish imports and exports from outside the EU from transactions within the EU.

### Imports from outside the EU

VAT is charged on goods imported from outside the EU as if it were a customs duty. It is normally collected direct from the importer at the place of importation, such as a port or airport.

- If the imported goods are immediately placed in a bonded warehouse or free zone, then VAT is postponed until the goods are removed from the warehouse or zone.

- Approved traders can pay all their VAT on imports through the Duty deferment system. This allows all VAT on imports to be paid on the 15th of the month following the month of importation. This assists the traders' cash flow and is more convenient than having to be paid at the point of import.

## Exports outside the EU

These are zero-rated supplies.

This is a favourable treatment for the exporter as it allows them to recover input tax. It also means the customer is not charged VAT.

## Transactions within the EU

The following table summarises the two situations which can occur when trading between EU countries.

|  | **Transactions** | **Accounting for VAT** |
|---|---|---|
| Supplier and customer registered (the destination system). | Zero-rated in country of origin.<br><br>Chargeable at the appropriate rate in force in country of destination. | (a) Supplier does not account for output VAT.<br><br>(b) Customer must account for output VAT on their VAT return at the rate in force in customer's country.<br><br>(c) The tax point is the earlier of:<br><br>– the fifteenth of the month following the month of acquisition, and<br><br>– the date of issue of the invoice<br><br>(d) VAT suffered by customer may be reclaimed by them as input VAT on the same VAT return, thus cancelling the output VAT (unless the customer is partially exempt - see Chapter 20). |

| Supplier registered but not customer (the origin system). | Chargeable at the appropriate rate in force in the country of origin. | (a) Supplier accounts for output VAT.<br><br>(b) Where supplies to the destination country exceed an EU threshold,<br><br>(the 'distance selling' threshold) the supplier will have to register for VAT in that country.<br><br>(c) No input VAT recoverable by the customer. |
|---|---|---|

### Test your understanding 1

Overseas Ltd has been importing computers from Ruritania since 1 January 2010. Ruritania is not currently a member of the European Union but is expected to join in the near future. Overseas Ltd makes only taxable supplies. For the quarter ended 31 March 2010 imports of £100,000 have been made. This amount excludes any VAT or duties.

**Explain how Overseas Ltd will have to account for VAT on the computers imported from Ruritania.**

**State how will this change if Ruritania becomes a member of the European Union and show the entries required on Overseas Ltd's VAT return in this case.**

### Test your understanding 2

Foreign Ltd, a UK resident company registered for VAT, has the following international transactions.

(a) Sale of children's toys to a customer in Germany, who is VAT registered.

(b) Sale of ladies' handbags to Venezuela.

(c) Sale of men's ties to an Italian customer, who is not VAT registered.

(d) Purchase of silk fabric from Hong Kong.

**Outline the VAT treatment in each case for Foreign Ltd. Note that Germany and Italy are EU countries.**

## Place of supply of services

The rules determining the place of supply of services have changed.

The new basic (or general) place of supply for business to business supplies will be where the customer is established.

The basic rule for supplies to non-business customers will remain unchanged, i.e. it will be where the supplier is established.

The result for UK business customers is that they will be liable to account for UK VAT on most services provided by their overseas supplier under the reverse charge provisions, rather than the supplier charging VAT.

## Time of supply for cross border supplies of services

Under the old rules, the time of supply (or tax point) for cross border supplies was normally when the supply was paid for.

The new rules are governed primarily by when a service is performed and a distinction is made between single and continuous supplies.

- For single supplies, the tax point will occur when the service is completed or when it is paid for if this is earlier.
- In the case of continuous supplies, the tax point will be the end of each billing or payment period.

## 8 Chapter summary

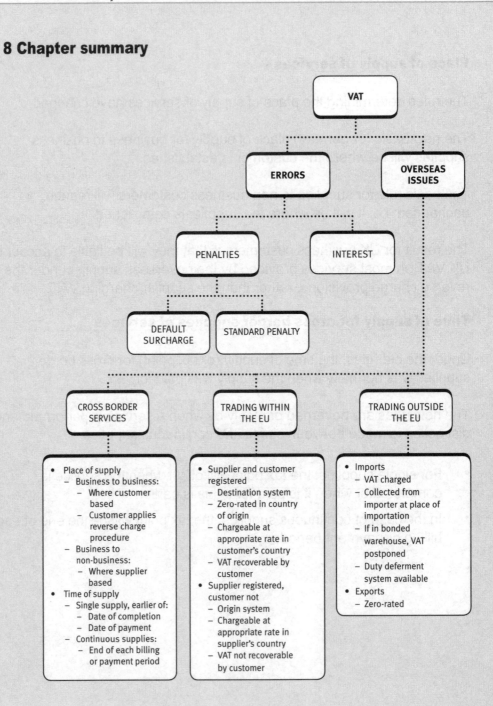

# Test your understanding answers

**Overseas Ltd**

(1) **Ruritania is not in the EU**

Overseas Ltd will have to account for VAT on the value of the computers (including any carriage and import charges) at the point of importation. This will amount to £17,500. Overseas Ltd can then claim input tax relief of £17,500 on their next VAT return.

Overseas Ltd may be able to defer the payment of VAT on import under the duty deferment scheme and pay monthly on the 15th of the month following the month of importation.

(2) **Ruritania is in the EU**

The goods will be zero-rated supplies in Ruritania and Overseas Ltd will be responsible for paying over the output VAT on the computers at the rate in force in the UK. This is essentially the same as if Ruritania were not in the EU, except that the VAT does not have to be paid over immediately at the date of importation.

The output VAT will be due on the earliest of:

– The date the invoice is issued; or

– The 15th of the month following that in which the goods are removed.

As before, Overseas Ltd will be able to reclaim the VAT as input VAT on their next VAT return which will therefore include the following:

Output tax

    On acquisition from Ruritania         £17,500

Input tax

    On acquisition from Ruritania         £17,500

**Test your understanding 2**

**Foreign Ltd**

(a) Foreign Ltd will charge VAT at zero rate because it is an EU transaction, and the customer is VAT registered.

(b) The transaction is zero rated as an export outside EU.

(c) The transaction must be charged in the UK at the standard rate as the customer is not VAT registered.

(d) VAT will be paid at point of entry into UK. Foreign Ltd will then recover VAT through the quarterly system.

# Corporation tax: computations and administration

## Chapter learning objectives

Upon completion of this chapter you will be able to:

- identify the accounting period rules and their significance for corporation tax

- prepare the corporation tax computation and liability for a UK resident company

- explain the principles of company self assessment including the time limits for notifying/filing returns and claims and the penalties for non compliance

- list the information and records that taxpayers need to retain for tax purposes together with the retention period

- state when corporation tax is due for non large companies and any penalties for non compliance

- define a large company and explain how they are required to pay corporation tax on a quarterly basis and the penalties for non compliance

- understand and explain the impact of taxation on the cash flows of a business

- list the key conditions and purpose of the corporate venturing scheme

- show the reliefs available to an investing company and how they are given and withdrawn.

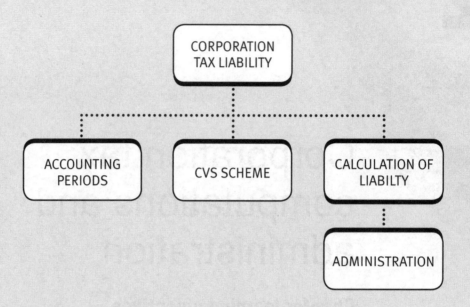

## 1 Introduction

This and the following two chapters deal with the way in which companies are subject to corporation tax.

This chapter sets out the basis upon which companies are assessed to corporation tax and explains how a company's corporation tax liability is calculated. Much of this chapter is a revision of rules covered in F6.

The main new topic introduced at P6 and covered in this chapter is the corporate venturing scheme (CVS).

### Basis of assessment

UK resident companies are assessed to corporation tax on their profits chargeable to corporation tax (PCTCT) arising in an accounting period.

PCTCT = income and chargeable gains less Gift Aid donations.

**Chargeable accounting period**

- Chargeable accounting period (CAP) = the period for which a charge to corporation tax is made
    - usually = 12 months and is the same as the company's period of account
    - can be less than 12 months
    - cannot exceed 12 months

Note that a company's 'period of account' is the period for which the company prepares its financial statements. It is usually 12 months but can be shorter or longer than 12 months.

- If company's period of account exceeds 12 months, need to split into two corporation tax CAPs:
  - first 12 months of period of account
  - followed by balance of period of account = short CAP

- A CAP **starts** when
  - a company starts to trade; or
  - the profits of a company first become liable to corporation tax; or
  - the previous CAP ends

- A new company must notify HMRC of its establishment **within 3 months** of the start of its first CAP. There is a separate obligation to notify HMRC of chargeability to tax within 12 months from the end of its accounting period.

- A CAP **ends** on the earliest of:
  - **12 months after it started**
  - the end of the period of account
  - when the company ceases to trade, to be UK resident or ceases to be liable to corporation tax
  - commences /ceases administration or winding up proceedings.

## Example 1 – Chargeable accounting periods

AB Ltd was incorporated on 15 July 2009 and commenced to trade on 1 September 2009. The company chose 30 June as their accounting year end and prepared their first financial statements to 30 June 2010 and then for the twelve months to 30 June 2011.

**State the dates of AB Ltd's first two chargeable accounting periods.**

**Solution**

First CAP:   1 September 2009 – 30 June 2010
             (date of commencing trade until end of period of account).

Second       1 July 2010 – 30 June 2011
CAP:         (immediately after the end of the previous CAP until the
             end of the period of account).

## Example 2 – Chargeable accounting periods

XY plc has been trading for many years making up their financial statements to 31 December each year. On 1 February 2010 the board of directors decided to change the year end to 30 April.

**State the chargeable accounting periods for XY plc if it**

(a) **prepared one set of financial statements covering the sixteen months to 30 April 2011, or**

(b) **two sets of financial statements covering the four months to 30 April 2010 and the twelve months to 30 April 2011.**

**Solution**

(a) One set of financial statements prepared covering sixteen months:

   – must be divided into a 12 month period to 31 December 2010 and a 4 month period to 30 April 2011.

(b) Two sets of financial statements prepared:

   – the CAPs will be the same as the financial statements:

      – 4 months to 30 April 2010

      – 12 months to 30 April 2011

## Corporation tax computation

**Name of company**

**Corporation tax computation – for year ended:**

|  | £ |
|---|---|
| Trading profits | X |
| Interest income | X |
| Property income | X |
| Miscellaneous income | X |
| Net chargeable gains | X |
| **Total Profits** | X |
| Less Gift Aid donations (gross amount paid) | (X) |
| **Profits chargeable to corporation tax (PCTCT)** | X |
| Corporation tax (CT) calculated at relevant rates | X |
| Less Marginal relief (if applicable) | (X) |
| **Corporation tax liability** | X |
| Less CVS relief (section 3) | (X) |
| Double taxation relief (DTR) (Chapter 28) | (X) |
| **Corporation tax payable** | X |

**Due date** 9 months and one day after end of CAP (unless 'large company' which pays in instalments – section 5)

**File date** 12 months after end of period of account

**Note:**

Trading profits, interest income and property income includes income from foreign sources.

All income is included in the computation **gross**.

The detailed rules for computing PCTCT are in Chapter 23.

## 2 The corporation tax liability

### Determining the relevant rate of corporation tax

Corporation tax (CT) is payable on a company's PCTCT at the relevant rate.

- The rate of corporation tax is determined by comparing a company's 'profits' to statutory limits.

- 'Profits' are calculated as follows:

|  | £ |
|---|---|
| PCTCT | X |
| Franked investment income (FII) | |
| (Dividends received × 100/90) | X |
| | ___ |
| 'Profits' | X |
| | ___ |

**Note: FII excludes** dividends from associated companies.

### Calculating the corporation tax liability

- The rate of corporation tax is fixed for each Financial Year (FY) which runs from 1 April to the following 31 March.

- The rates of corporation tax needed for the P6 examination are:

| | FY2007 | FY2008 | FY2009 |
|---|---|---|---|
| Small companies rate (SCR) | 20% | 21% | 21% |
| Full rate (FR) | 30% | 28% | 28% |
| Lower limit (LL) | £300,000 | £300,000 | £300,000 |
| Upper limit (UL) | £1,500,000 | £1,500,000 | £1,500,000 |
| Marginal relief (MR) fraction | 1/40 | 7/400 | 7/400 |

- The full statutory limits are compared to 'profits' unless:

  - Short AP: time apportion

  - Associated companies: divide by the number of associated companies in the group

- Marginal relief is available if 'profits' fall between the upper and lower limits and is calculated as follows:

> Marginal relief fraction × (Upper limit – Profits) × PCTCT/Profits

## Example 3 – Corporation tax liability

Sycamore Ltd has the following results for the y/e 31 March 2010.

| | |
|---|---|
| PCTCT | £330,000 |
| Dividends from UK companies (amount received) | £18,000 |

**Calculate the CT liability and state when it will be payable.**

**Solution**

| | £ |
|---|---|
| PCTCT | 330,000 |
| Plus FII (£18,000 × 100/90) | 20,000 |
| | ———— |
| 'Profits' | 350,000 |
| | ———— |
| | |
| Corporation tax on PCTCT (£330,000 × 28%) | 92,400 |
| Less: Marginal relief | |
| 7/400 × (£1,500,000 – £350,000) × £330,000/£350,000 | (18,975) |
| | ———— |
| Corporation tax payable | 73,425 |
| | ———— |
| Due date | 1 January 2011 |

## Example 4 – Corporation tax liability

Beech Ltd has the following results for the 9 m/e 31 March 2010.

| | |
|---|---|
| PCTCT | £330,000 |
| Dividends from UK companies (amount received) | £18,000 |

**Calculate the CT liability and state when it will be payable.**

---

**Solution**

|  | £ |
|---|---|
| PCTCT | 330,000 |
| Plus FII (£18,000 × 100/90) | 20,000 |
| | |
| 'Profits' | 350,000 |

MR limits must be scaled down as the AP is only 9 months.

|  | £ |
|---|---|
| Lower limit (£300,000 × 9/12) | 225,000 |
| Upper limit (£1,500,000 × 9/12) | 1,125,000 |

MR applies as 'profits' are in between the limits.

|  | £ |
|---|---|
| Corporation tax on PCTCT (£330,000 × 28%) | 92,400 |
| Less:      Marginal relief | |
|         7/400 × (£1,125,000 – £350,000) × £330,000/£350,000 | (12,787) |
| | |
| Corporation tax payable | 79,613 |

---

## Straddling Financial Years

When a company's chargeable accounting period falls into two Financial Years, then the corporation tax liability must be calculated in two parts if:

- the corporation tax rate changes, or
- the statutory limits change.

Where a company's accounting period straddles 31 March 2009, there is no need to split the computation as the same rates apply in the FY2008 and FY2009.

However, where a company's accounting period straddles 31 March 2008, part of the accounting period will fall into FY2007 and part into FY2008.

The corporation tax liability must be calculated for each FY applying the appropriate rates of tax for each year.

**Example 5 – Straddling financial years**

Oboe Ltd had PCTCT of £100,000 and FII of £20,000 for the year ended 31 December 2008.

**Calculate Oboe Ltd's CT liability for the y/e 31 December 2008.**

**Solution**

|  | £ |
|---|---|
| PCTCT | 100,000 |
| Plus FII | 20,000 |
| | |
| 'Profits' | 120,000 |

As 'profits' are below the lower limit of £300,000 the SCR applies.

The company's accounting period straddles 31 March 2008.

Three months (1 January 2008 to 31 March 2008) fall into FY2007 and nine months (1 April 2008 to 31 December 2008) fall into FY2008.

The CT liability is calculated as follows:

|  | £ |
|---|---|
| FY2007 : £100,000 x 3/12 x 20% | 5,000 |
| FY2008 : £100,000 x 9/12 x 21% | 15,750 |
| | |
| Corporation tax liability | 20,750 |

**Test your understanding 1**

Flute Ltd had PCTCT of £400,000 and received dividends from non associated companies of £45,000 in the year ended 30 September 2008.

**Calculate Flute Ltd's CT liability for the y/e 30 September 2008.**

## 3 Corporate venturing scheme

### Introduction

The corporate venturing scheme (CVS) is similar to the EIS for individuals. It was introduced to encourage companies to subscribe for shares in small, unquoted trading companies which often find it difficult to obtain finance.

Corporation tax reliefs are given to the investing company if conditions are satisfied. The conditions are very similar to the EIS conditions.

### Conditions for the relief

There are two sets of conditions to consider:

| Investing company | Investee company |
|---|---|
| • Must be a trading company.<br>• Can be quoted or unquoted | • Must be an unquoted trading company |
| • Can be of any size | • The 'gross assets' of the issuing company must not exceed<br>　– **£7 million** immediately before the issue of the shares and<br>　– **£8 million** immediately afterwards<br>• If the issuing company is the parent company of a trading group, these limits apply to the group as a whole |
| • Must not have a material interest in the issuing company, that is own no more than 30% of their shares | • Must have at least 20% of its shares held by independent individuals<br>• Directors and employees of the investing company, and their relatives, are not independent |
| • Can be part of a trading group or the holding company of a trading group | • Must not be controlled by another company |

## Reliefs available to the investing company

There are three key reliefs available:

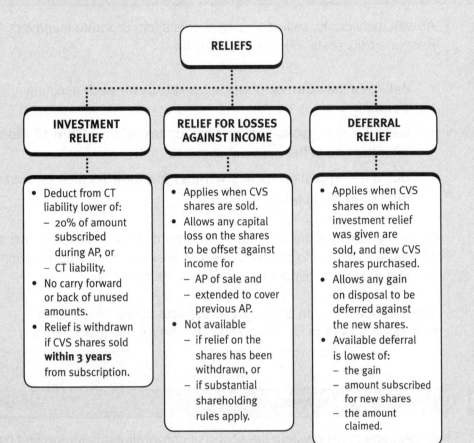

RELIEFS

**INVESTMENT RELIEF**

- Deduct from CT liability lower of:
  - 20% of amount subscribed during AP, or
  - CT liability.
- No carry forward or back of unused amounts.
- Relief is withdrawn if CVS shares sold **within 3 years** from subscription.

**RELIEF FOR LOSSES AGAINST INCOME**

- Applies when CVS shares are sold.
- Allows any capital loss on the shares to be offset against income for
  - AP of sale and
  - extended to cover previous AP.
- Not available
  - if relief on the shares has been withdrawn, or
  - if substantial shareholding rules apply.

**DEFERRAL RELIEF**

- Applies when CVS shares on which investment relief was given are sold, and new CVS shares purchased.
- Allows any gain on disposal to be deferred against the new shares.
- Available deferral is lowest of:
  - the gain
  - amount subscribed for new shares
  - the amount claimed.

### Test your understanding 2

PQ plc, which has an accounting year end of 31 December, subscribes £300,000 for a 15% shareholding in Minor Ltd on 1 September 2009. This is a qualifying investment under the CVS scheme. PQ plc sells the shares for £375,000 on 15 October 2012 making a chargeable gain of £65,000. On 1 December 2012 PQ plc invests a sum of £80,000 in a CVS qualifying investment and claims investment relief.

(a) **Calculate the tax relief for PQ plc for its investment in 2009.**

(b) **State how PQ plc can defer its gain arising in 2012.**

## 4 Self assessment for companies

### Introduction

As with individuals, self-assessment exists for corporate taxpayers. Responsibility rests with the company to:

- calculate their own corporation tax liability for each accounting period
- submit a self-assessment corporation tax return **within 12 months** after the end of the accounting period
- pay any corporation tax due **within nine months** after the end of the accounting period.

Given the timing of the due date for payment of tax, in practice, many companies will aim to complete the self-assessment tax return prior to the nine-month deadline for paying the corporation tax.

The following session considers all aspects concerning the self-assessment system for companies and the related procedures.

### Notification of chargeability

A company coming within the scope of corporation tax for the first time must notify HMRC when its first accounting period begins, **within three months** of the start of its first accounting period.

Companies that do not receive a tax return are required to notify HMRC if they have income or chargeable gains on which tax is due.

The time limit for notifying HMRC of chargeability is **12 months** from the end of the accounting period in which the liability arises.

A standard penalty may be imposed for failure to notify HMRC of chargeability.(See section 6).

## The self assessment tax return

The self-assessment tax return must be submitted either:

- **within 12 months** after the end of the accounting period; or
- **three months** after the issue of the return (if this is later than the normal submission date).

The return should contain all information required to calculate the company's profits chargeable to corporation tax.

A company has to submit a copy of its financial accounts together with the self-assessment tax return.

The return must include a self-assessment of the amount of corporation tax payable for that accounting period.

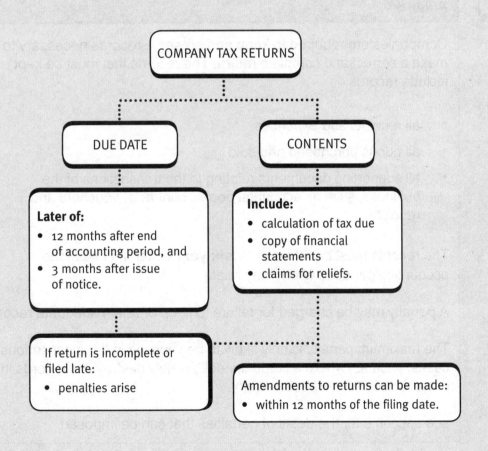

## Determination assessments

To prevent companies deliberately delaying the submission of the return, HMRC have the following actions available:

- HMRC may determine the amount of corporation tax due by issuing a determination assessment.

- The determination assessment is treated as a self-assessment by the company, and will be replaced by the actual self-assessment when it is submitted by the company.

- There is no appeal against a determination assessment. Instead, the company must displace it with the actual self-assessment return.

- A determination assessment can be raised at any time **within four years** of the filing date.

## Records

Companies are required to keep and preserve records necessary to make a correct and complete return. The records that must be kept include records of:

- all receipts and expenses

- all goods purchased and sold

- all supporting documents relating to the transactions of the business, such as accounts, books, contracts, vouchers and receipts.

The records must be retained for **six years** after the end of the accounting period to which they relate.

A penalty may be charged for failure to keep or retain adequate records.

The maximum penalty is only likely to be imposed in the most serious cases, such as, where a company deliberately destroys its records in order to obstruct a HMRC enquiry.

see section 6 for the detail of penalties that can be imposed.

## Personal liability of senior accounting officers of large companies and groups

- A designated Senior Accounting officer will have to:
  - ensure that the company's accounting systems will be adequate for the purposes of accurate tax reporting
  - certify annually that the accounting systems are adequate, or
  - specify the inadequacies and confirm that the auditors have been informed.

- These rules only apply to 'large' companies and groups, i.e. not small or medium sized per CA 2006.

- Penalties (personal and corporate) can be levied for careless or deliberate failure of these obligations.

### Amendments and errors

#### Amendments to the return

- HMRC may correct any obvious errors or mistakes **within nine months** of the date that the return is filed with them. For example, they will correct arithmetical errors or errors of principle. This process of repair does not mean that HMRC has necessarily accepted the return as accurate.

- A company can amend the return **within 12 months** of the filing date. For an accounting period ending on 31 March 2010, the filing date is 31 March 2011, and so the company has until 31 March 2012, to make any amendments.

- If an error is discovered at a later date, then the company can make an error or mistake claim to recover any corporation tax overpaid.

#### Error or mistake claims

- Where an assessment is excessive due to an error or mistake in a return, the company can claim relief.

- The claim must be made **within four years** of the accounting period to which it relates.

- A claim can be made in respect of errors made, and mistakes arising from not understanding the law.

### Enquiries into returns

HMRC have the right to enquire into the completeness and accuracy of any self-assessment tax return and issue discovery assessments. The procedures and rules are similar to those for individuals.

The enquiry may be initiated as a result of:

- suspicion that income is undeclared or a deduction incorrectly claimed
- information in HMRC's possession
- the choice of return as part of a random selection process.

Additionally:

- HMRC do not have to state a reason for the enquiry and are unlikely to do so.
- HMRC must give written notice before commencing an enquiry.
- The written notice must be issued **within 12 months** of the actual delivery of the tax return to HMRC.
- Once this deadline is passed, the company can normally consider the self-assessment for that accounting period as final.

### Enquiry procedures

HMRC can demand that the company produce:

- documents
- accounts
- other written particulars
- full answers to specific questions.

The information requested should be limited to that connected with the return.

- The company has 30 days to comply with the request. An appeal can be made against the request.
- The enquiry ends when HMRC give written notice that it has been completed.
- The notice will state the outcome of the enquiry.
- Refer to Chapter 16 for details about appeal procedures.

- A company has 30 days from the completion of the enquiry to amend its self-assessment.

- If the company declines to do so or makes an amendment that is not to the satisfaction of HMRC, HMRC have a further 30 days to impose their amendment. The company then has a further 30 days to appeal against HMRC's amendment. The appeal must be in writing.

### Discovery assessments

HMRC has the capacity to raise additional assessments, referred to as discovery assessments. The key points are:

- The use of a discovery assessment is restricted where a self-assessment return has already been made. However, although enquiries must normally begin **within 12 months** of the actual submission date, a discovery assessment can be raised at a later date to prevent the loss of corporation tax.

- Unless the loss of corporation tax is due to fraud or negligence, a discovery assessment cannot be raised where full disclosure was made in the return, even if this is found to be incorrect.

- HMRC will only accept that full disclosure has been made if any contentious items have been clearly brought to their attention – perhaps in a covering letter.

- Only a company that makes full disclosure in the self-assessment tax return, therefore, has absolute finality 12 months after the actual submission date.

- The time limit for making a discovery assessment is **four years** from the end of the accounting period. This is extended to **six years** if there is a careless error, and **twenty years** from the end of the accounting period, in the case of deliberate error.

- A discovery assessment may be appealed against.

## 5 Payment of tax

### Due date

- Companies not paying tax at the full rate pay all their tax nine months and one day after their accounting period.

- Companies paying tax at the full rate of 28% pay their tax by quarterly instalments (see exceptions below).

### Quarterly instalments

Instalments are based on the expected corporation tax liability for the current accounting period.

For a twelve month accounting period, instalments are due on the **14th day** of months **7, 10, 13 and 16** following the start of the accounting period.

Special rules apply if the accounting period is less than 12 months.

### Exception to instalments

Companies paying tax at the full rate which do not have to pay by instalments are as follows:

- companies that are paying at the full rate but whose liability for the year is below **£10,000**

- companies that have become full rate companies during the year provided

    (i)   they were not paying at the full rate last year; and

    (ii)  their profits for the year do not exceed **£10 million**. This limit is shared between associated companies.

### Interest

Interest runs from the due date on any tax paid late and is deducted from interest income in the PCTCT computation.

Any repayment of tax made by HMRC will attract interest from the original payment date. This interest is included in interest income.

### Impact of taxation on the cash flows of a business

Companies need to take account of their tax payments when considering their cash flow forecasts for the year.

This will be a particular problem when the company changes to quarterly instalments for the first time.

### Example 6 – Payments of tax

Q plc is a single company with no associated companies. On 1 February 2009 Q plc estimates that its PCTCT will be £2 million for the year ended 31 October 2009. Its PCTCT for the year ended 31 October 2008 was £1,700,000 and for the year ended 31 October 2007 £1,200,000. Q plc does not receive any dividends.

(a) **Calculate Q plc's corporation tax liabilities for the years ended 31 October 2008 and 31 October 2009 and explain how they will be paid. Assume you are writing in February 2009.**

(b) **In July 2009 the company revises its forecast profit figure to £2,200,000. State the difference, if any, this will make to their corporation tax payments.**

**Solution**

(a) **Corporation tax liabilities**

With PCTCT of £2 million in the y/e 31 October 2009, the company will be liable to tax at the full rate of 28% as follows:

FY2008 and FY2009: £2,000,000 × 28%          £560,000

(b) **Payment dates**

The company was also a full rate company in the y/e 31 October 2008, but would not have had to make quarterly instalments in that year.

This is because a company does not have to make instalment payments in the first year that they start paying at the full rate provided the profits of that year do not exceed £10 million.

The liability for the y/e 31 October 2008 of £490,167 (£1,700,000 × 30% × 5/12) + (£1,700,000 × 28% × 7/12) will be due on 1 August 2009.

For the y/e 31 October 2009, as the company is paying at full rate for the second year running, they will have to pay the £560,000 liability in quarterly instalments as follows:

| **Due date** | £ |
|---|---|
| 14 May 2009 | 140,000 |
| 14 August 2009 | 140,000 |
| 14 November 2009 | 140,000 |
| 14 February 2010 | 140,000 |
| | 560,000 |

Interest will be charged from the due date until the date of payment for any instalments paid late. This interest is a deduction from interest income.

(b) **If Q plc revises its forecast**

If the profit forecast is revised upwards the company will have to revise its forecast tax payments.

The corporation tax liability will increase to £616,000 (£2,200,000 × 28%).

Quarterly payments should therefore be £154,000 (£616,000 × 1/4).

Therefore an extra £14,000 (£154,000 – £140,000) will be due for each instalment.

As the instalment for May has already been paid, the additional £14,000 will attract interest from 14 May 2009 until it is paid.

## 6 Penalties

In addition to interest on the late payment of tax, HMRC can impose penalties.

### Standard penalty

HMRC is standardising penalties across taxes and for different offences. For 2010 exams, the standard penalty applies to two areas:

- inaccuracies in returns – all taxes
- failure to notify liability to tax – income tax, CGT, corporation tax, VAT and PAYE/NIC.

The penalty is calculated as a percentage of 'potential lost revenue' which is generally the tax unpaid as a result of the error or failure to notify.

| Taxpayer behaviour | Maximum penalty (% of revenue lost) |
|---|---|
| Genuine mistake | No Penalty |
| Failture to take reasonable care | 30% |
| Serious or deliberate understatement | 70% |
| Serious or deliberate understatement with concealment | 100% |

Penalties can be reduced where the taxpayer makes full disclosure and cooperates with HMRC to establish the amount of tax unpaid.

| Offence | Penalty |
|---|---|
| **Companies** | |
| Failure to notify chargeability to tax within 12 months of the end of the accounting period | Standard penalty<br>Based on a % of tax unpaid 12 months after the end of the accounting period |
| Late submission of corporation tax return | |
|     – up to 3 months after the filing date | £100 fixed penalty (£500 for persistent failure) |
|     – more than 3 months after the filing date | £200 fixed penalty (£1,000 for persistent failure) |
|     – ≥18 but < 24 months after end of the return period | Additional tax geared penalties 10% of tax unpaid at 18 months after the end of the return period |
|     – > 24 months after end of the return period | 20% of tax unpaid at 18 months after end of return period |
| Submission of an incorrect tax return or accounts leading to:<br><br>    – an understatement of tax liability<br>    – a false or inflated statement of a loss<br>    – a false or inflated claim for repayment of tax | Standard penalty<br>Based on a % of tax unpaid as a result of the error |
| Failing to notify HMRC of an under assessment to tax | Standard penalty<br>Based on a % of the amount of under assessed tax |
| Deliberately supplying false information to, or deliberately withholding information from, a person with the intention of making that person's document inaccurate | Standard penalty<br>Based on a % of tax unpaid as a result of the error |
| Failure to keep and retain required records | Up to £3,000 per year of assessment |

# 7 Chapter summary

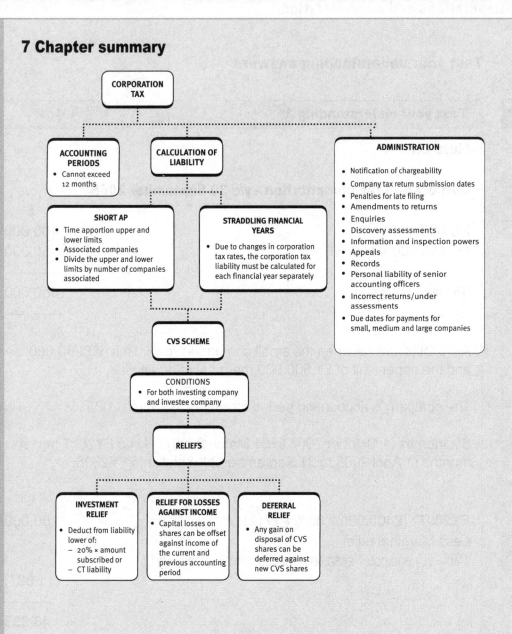

**CORPORATION TAX**

**ACCOUNTING PERIODS**
- Cannot exceed 12 months

**CALCULATION OF LIABILITY**

**ADMINISTRATION**
- Notification of chargeability
- Company tax return submission dates
- Penalties for late filing
- Amendments to returns
- Enquiries
- Discovery assessments
- Information and inspection powers
- Appeals
- Records
- Personal liability of senior accounting officers
- Incorrect returns/under assessments
- Due dates for payments for small, medium and large companies

**SHORT AP**
- Time apportion upper and lower limits
- Associated companies
- Divide the upper and lower limits by number of companies associated

**STRADDLING FINANCIAL YEARS**
- Due to changes in corporation tax rates, the corporation tax liability must be calculated for each financial year separately

**CVS SCHEME**

**CONDITIONS**
- For both investing company and investee company

**RELIEFS**

**INVESTMENT RELIEF**
- Deduct from liability lower of:
  - 20% × amount subscribed or
  - CT liability

**RELIEF FOR LOSSES AGAINST INCOME**
- Capital losses on shares can be offset against income of the current and previous accounting period

**DEFERRAL RELIEF**
- Any gain on disposal of CVS shares can be deferred against new CVS shares

## Test your understanding answers

### Test your understanding 1

**Flute Ltd**

**Corporation tax computation - y/e 30 September 2008**

|  | £ |
|---|---|
| PCTCT | 400,000 |
| FII (£45,000 × 100/90) | 50,000 |
| 'Profits' | 450,000 |

As 'profits' are between the small companies lower limit of £300,000 and the upper limit of £1,500,000 marginal relief applies.

The company's accounting period straddles 31 March 2008.

Six months (1 October 2007 to 31 March 2008) fall into FY2007 and six months (1 April 2008 to 31 September 2008) fall into FY2008.

|  |  | £ |
|---|---|---|
| FY2007 : (£400,000 × 30% × 6/12) |  | 60,000 |
| Less Marginal relief |  |  |
| 1/40 × (£1,500,000 – £450,000) × £400,000/£450,000 × 6/12 |  | (11,667) |
|  |  | 48,333 |
| FY2008 : (£400,000 × 28% × 6/12) | 56,000 |  |
| Less Marginal relief |  |  |
| 7/400 × (£1,500,000 – £450,000) × £400,000/£450,000 × 6/12 | (8,167) |  |
|  |  | 47,833 |
| Corporation tax liability |  | 96,166 |

### Test your understanding 2

**PQ plc**

(a) **Investment relief**

PQ plc can deduct £60,000 (£300,000 × 20%) from its CT liability for the year ended 31 December 2009, provided the company has a liability of at least this amount.

If its liability were only £50,000 then the relief would be limited to £50,000 and the unused relief of £10,000 would be lost.

(b) **Deferral relief**

PQ's gain of £65,000 arising in 2012 can be deferred due to the new CVS investment made.

As the gain is less than the amount reinvested, full deferral of the £65,000 can be claimed unless PQ wishes to claim less.

# Calculation of corporation tax: income and gains

## Chapter learning objectives

Upon completion of this chapter you will be able to:

- prepare a comprehensive computation of PCTCT for a company

- recognise qualifying and non qualifying expenditure for industrial buildings purposes

- compute the industrial buildings allowances for a new building with both industrial and non industrial use

- distinguish the key differences in computing gains for a company

- explain the conditions required for the sale of shares by a company to be treated as an exempt transaction for capital gains

- identify qualifying research and development expenditure and determine the amount of relief by reference to the size of the individual company/group

- recognise the tax treatment of intangible assets and determine the appropriate treatment for a given company

- understand the purpose of transfer pricing rules and identify the companies/transactions where they will impact

- understand the issue of thin capitalisation and advise on the impact where a company is affected

- prepare a corporation tax computation for a company with investment business.

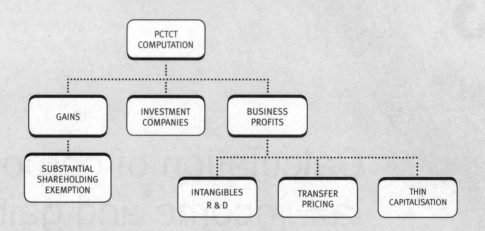

# 1 Introduction

This chapter revises the rules for computing a company's PCTCT and introduces the new topic areas at P6 shown in the diagram above.

A brief reminder of F6 content is given in expandable text and revision examples are provided to check your retention of the required F6 knowledge.

# 2 Computation of PCTCT

## Pro-forma computation

**Name of company**

**Corporation tax computation – for chargeable accounting period ended:**

|  | £ |
|---|---|
| *Trading profits (adjusted profits less capital allowances) | X |
| *Interest income (non-trading loan relationships) (gross) | X |
| *Property income | X |
| Miscellaneous income | X |
| Net chargeable gains (chargeable gains less allowable losses) | X |
| **Total Profits** | X |
| Less Gift Aid donations (gross amount paid) | (X) |
| **Profits chargeable to corporation tax (PCTCT)** | X |

\* Including overseas income (gross of overseas tax suffered)

## Trading profits

As for a sole trader, the net profit per the accounts must be adjusted for tax purposes.

The main adjustments are summarised in Chapter 17.

The key differences that apply to adjusting a company's profits are:

- There are no private use adjustments (including the capital allowances computation).

- Any interest received or paid for trading reasons is included in trading profit.

- If the interest is received or paid for a non trading purpose then it is included in interest income (see below).

- Dividends payable are not an allowable trading expense.

- Enhanced deductions are available for research and development expenditure if conditions are satisfied (section 4).

- A tax deduction is available to a company which issues shares to its employees, provided the employee is taxed on the shares or would be if the share acquisition was not from an approved share scheme.

  The available tax deduction is the market value of the qualifying shares issued to the employee, less any amounts paid for them.

## Capital allowances

Capital allowances apply to companies in the same way as unincorporated businesses with the following additional points to note:

## Annual investment allowance

- The AIA must be split between related companies.

  Companies owned by the same individual will be regarded as related where they are engaged in the same activities or share the same premises.

  - This could be the case if an individual runs two companies from home, the AIA will be spilt between the two companies.

  - In such circumstances the owner of the companies can choose how to allocate a single AIA between them.

- Unrelated companies owned by the same individual will each be entitled to the full AIA.

- Only one AIA is available to a group of companies.

  Note that:

  - A 'group' for this purpose is defined by the Companies Act and essentially applies where a parent company holds a simple majority shareholding (> 50%) in another company or companies at the end of the accounting period.

  - Therefore if there are associated companies, the allocation of the AIA between the group members will need to be considered.

  When allocating the AIA:

  - the group members can allocate the maximum £50,000 AIA in any way across the group

  - the AIA does not have to be divided equally between them

  - all of the allowance can be given to one company, or any amount can be given to any number of companies within the group.

### Special rate pool

- The 10% special rate of writing down allowances in respect of plant and machinery that is integral to a building applies to both **initial and replacement** expenditure.

- Replacement expenditure occurs where more than 50% of an asset is replaced in a 12-month period.

  This prevents a tax deduction being claimed for the repair of such assets where such repairs are substantial and the asset can be used in the trade.

- Previously, a deduction against trading income for repairs expenditure on an asset was allowed if it could be used in the trade before the "repairs" were carried out. This deduction is no longer available for plant and machinery integral to a building; instead tax relief is spread via the special rate writing down allowance.

### Energy saving plant and machinery

- Expenditure on energy saving or environmentally beneficial plant and machinery qualifies for a 100% first year allowance.

- Where a company has made a loss, it may surrender that part of the loss that relates to such allowances in exchange for a payment from HMRC equal to 19% of the loss surrendered. (This is similar to research and development expenditure loss credits.)

Such a claim can only be made where the company is unable to use the losses in the current accounting period against its own profits or via group relief. The claim is made in the company's corporation tax return.

The maximum payment that a company can claim is the higher of £250,000 and its total PAYE and NIC liabilities for the relevant accounting period.

Where any of the qualifying plant and machinery is sold within four years of the end of the relevant accounting period, there will be a claw-back of an appropriate part of the payment made and a reinstatement of the loss.

## Industrial buildings allowances

### Introduction

Industrial buildings allowances (IBAs) are being phased out from 2008/09 onwards and no allowances will be available from 2011/12.

### Basis of the calculation

Relief for IBAs is given as a trading expense and is deducted in the adjustment to profits computation, together with capital allowances on plant and machinery.

A reminder of the basis of calculation, the definition of an industrial building and the qualifying cost for IBAs is given in expandable text and is summarised in the diagram at the end of this section.

### Basis of calculation

IBAs, like capital allowances on plant and machinery, are calculated on an **accounting period basis**.

The date the expenditure is incurred determines in which accounting period the transaction belongs.

The allowances are calculated according to the **length of the accounting period**, not the length of ownership of the industrial building.

Where the accounting period is not 12 months, the WDA must be scaled down or up as with capital allowances for plant and machinery.

### Definition of an industrial building

Industrial buildings are those used for the purposes of a qualifying trade.

**Qualifying trades**

The more important of these qualifying trades are:

- a trade carried on in a mill, factory or similar premises
- a trade that consists in the manufacture of goods or materials or the subjection of goods or materials to any process
- a trade which consists in the storage of:
  - goods or materials used for manufacturing purposes, or which are to be subjected to any process
  - finished goods or materials that have been manufactured or subjected to any process.

In addition, the following structures are also industrial buildings:

- any building or structure provided by the company carrying on one of the above trades for the welfare of its employees, for example, a canteen or workplace nursery
- a drawing office used for the preparation of plans for manufacturing or processing operations.

**Qualifying hotels**

A hotel is treated as a qualifying industrial building, provided it satisfies **all** the following conditions:

- the building must be a hotel:
- it must be open for
  - at least 4 months (120 days)
  - in the season (1 April to 31 October each year).
- when open in the season:
  - the hotel must have at least 10 bedrooms that are available for short-term letting to the public
  - the rooms must not be let for > 30 days per letting period
  - the services provided for guests must normally include breakfast, evening meal, room cleaning and bed making.

## Qualifying cost of construction

IBAs are available on the qualifying cost that includes and excludes the following costs:

| Includes | Excludes |
|---|---|
| • Cost of preparing the land to lay foundations and construct the building.<br><br>• Cutting, tunnelling and levelling the land.<br><br>• Professional fees relating to the construction of the building (e.g. architects fees).<br><br>• All expenditure incurred in the construction of the building.<br><br>• Capital expenditure on alterations to an existing industrial building. | • Cost of the land.<br><br>• Legal and other associated fees relating to the land<br><br>• Cost of constructing:<br>  – dwelling houses<br>  – retail or wholesale premises<br>  – showrooms<br>  – general offices<br>  **unless**<br>  – an integral part of the industrial building<br>  **and**<br>  – cost of this non-qualifying part does not exceed:<br><br>(25% x 'total cost of building'). |
| **Note:**<br><br>If the building is acquired from a builder:<br><br>Qualifying cost = purchase price<br><br>If the building is acquired from any other vendor:<br><br>Qualifying cost = Lower of<br><br>(i) purchase price<br>(ii) construction expenditure incurred | **Note:**<br><br>'Total cost of building' for this purpose:<br><br>• excludes land, but<br>• includes all of the building costs. |

## Test your understanding 1

Harriet Ltd acquired a new factory at a cost of £400,000 on 1 January 2009. It was brought into industrial use on the same day.

The total cost of the new factory was as follows:

|  | £ |
|---|---|
| Land | 80,000 |
| Levelling the land | 9,200 |
| Architects' fees | 24,300 |
| Heating system | 12,800 |
| Fire alarm system | 7,200 |
| Strengthened concrete floor to support machinery | 16,500 |
| General offices | 62,500 |
| Factory | 187,500 |
|  | ——— |
|  | 400,000 |
|  | ——— |

(a) **Calculate the expenditure qualifying for IBAs.**

(b) **Calculate the qualifying expenditure if the offices had cost £82,500 and the factory cost £167,500 so that the total cost is still £400,000.**

## Calculating IBAs for a new building

### Where the building is always used for industrial purposes

The allowances available to the first user of an industrial building are:

| Writing down allowance (WDA) | Disposal of building |
|---|---|
| • 2% for a 12 month period<br><br>• Calculated on a straight line basis<br><br>• based on qualifying cost<br><br>• the building must be in industrial use on the last day of the accounting period (temporary disuse is ignored)<br><br>• only available during "tax life of the building"<br><br>• tax life of building<br>   – starts when the building is first brought into industrial use<br>   – ends 25 years later | • there are no capital allowance implications for the vendor in the year of sale<br>   – no WDA for the vendor<br>   – no balancing adjustment arises on the disposal |

### Where the building has periods of non-industrial use

The allowances available are as follows:

| Writing down allowance (WDA) | Disposal of building |
|---|---|
| • If building is not in industrial use on the last day:<br>   – no WDA can be claimed,<br>   – the TWDV must be written down by a notional WDA<br><br>• Notional WDA<br>= same as normal WDA | • there are no capital allowance implications for the vendor in the year of sale<br>   – no WDA for the vendor<br>   – no balancing adjustment arises on the disposal |

### Example 1 – Industrial buildings allowances

Henry Ltd acquired a building for a qualifying cost of £340,000 on 1 June 2007 and immediately brought it into industrial use.

The company used it throughout its ownership for industrial purposes, with the exception of the period between 1 September 2008 and 31 January 2010 when the building was used as a retail premises.

On 30 June 2010 the company sold the building.

Henry Ltd prepares accounts to 31 March each year.

**Calculate the IBAs available to Henry Ltd for each of the years concerned assuming he sold the building for £500,000 (including £100,000 for the land).**

You should assume that FA2009 rates apply throughout.

**Solution**

|  | £ |
|---|---|
| **Year ended 31 March 2008** | |
| WDA (2% × £340,000) | 6,800 |
| –   in industrial use on 31 March 2008 | |
| **Year ended 31 March 2009** | |
| Notional WDA – non industrial use on 31 March 2009 | Nil |
| **Year ended 31 March 2010** | |
| WDA (2% × £340,000) | 6,800 |
| – in industrial use on 31 March 2010 | |
| | ——— |
| Total allowances | 13,600 |
| | ——— |

**Year ended 31 March 2011 – year of disposal**

No WDA and no  balancing adjustment on the disposal.

However, the sale is for more than cost, therefore a capital gain will arise on the capital profit.

## Test your understanding 2

Chris Ltd commenced to trade on 1 January 1993 and prepares accounts to 31 March each year.

The company acquired a new industrial building on 1 September 2008 and brought it into industrial use on 1 June 2009.

The total cost of £112,500 was made up as follows:

| | £ |
|---|---|
| Land | 12,500 |
| Site clearance | 2,500 |
| Foundation | 7,500 |
| General office | 5,000 |
| Drawing (design) office | 2,500 |
| Canteen | 3,750 |
| Accounts office | 4,500 |
| Other allowable costs | 74,250 |
| | ——— |
| Total Expenditure | 112,500 |
| | ——— |

On 1 July 2010 Chris Ltd sold the building to Freddy Plc, for £130,000.

**Compute the IBAs available to Chris Ltd for all relevant years.**

You should assume that FA2009 rates apply throughout.

## Summary of IBAs

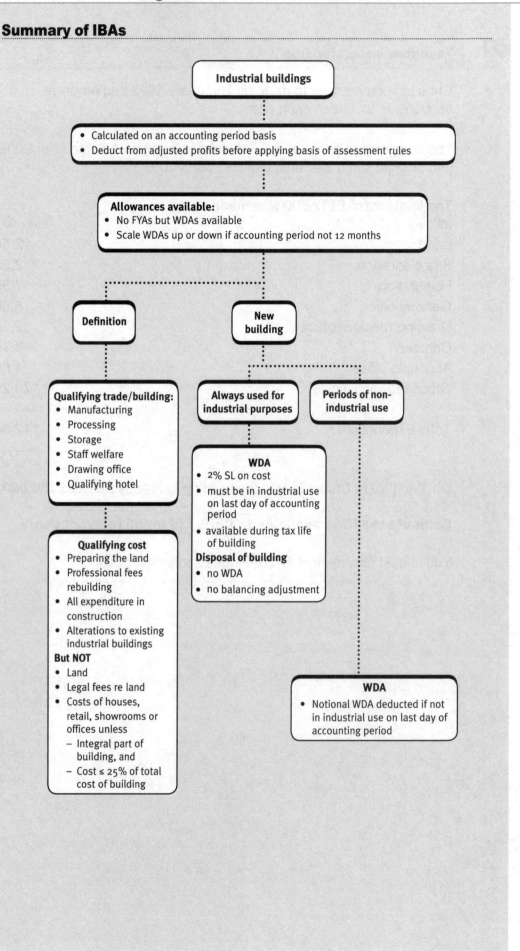

**Industrial buildings**

- Calculated on an accounting period basis
- Deduct from adjusted profits before applying basis of assessment rules

**Allowances available:**
- No FYAs but WDAs available
- Scale WDAs up or down if accounting period not 12 months

**Definition**

**New building**

**Qualifying trade/building:**
- Manufacturing
- Processing
- Storage
- Staff welfare
- Drawing office
- Qualifying hotel

**Always used for industrial purposes**

**Periods of non-industrial use**

**WDA**
- 2% SL on cost
- must be in industrial use on last day of accounting period
- available during tax life of building

**Disposal of building**
- no WDA
- no balancing adjustment

**Qualifying cost**
- Preparing the land
- Professional fees rebuilding
- All expenditure in construction
- Alterations to existing industrial buildings

**But NOT**
- Land
- Legal fees re land
- Costs of houses, retail, showrooms or offices unless
  - Integral part of building, and
  - Cost ≤ 25% of total cost of building

**WDA**
- Notional WDA deducted if not in industrial use on last day of accounting period

## Interest income

Loan relationship rules apply to all costs and revenues associated with lending or borrowing money.

- Interest receivable

  Generally, all interest receivable by a company is treated as non-trade interest, unless it is the company's trade to lend money (e.g. a bank).

  Interest receivable should therefore be deducted in the adjustment to profits computation and shown separately in PCTCT as interest income.

- Interest payable

  Money borrowed for the trade is a trading expense and so no adjustment is required. Examples would be

  (i)  working capital requirements

  (ii)  purchase of fixed assets.

  Where the loan is for a non-trading purpose (e.g. purchase of investments), it is a non-trade item. It is therefore added back in the adjustment of profits and deducted from interest income.

  If there is no (or insufficient) interest income the excess is a deficit, eligible for loss relief (Chapter 24).

- Interest on overpaid/underpaid corporation tax

  Interest received from HMRC is taxable as interest income. Interest paid to HMRC is an allowable deduction from interest income.

  Note for sole traders interest from HMRC is exempt income and interest paid to HMRC is not allowable for income tax.

## Overseas income

- Any income from overseas (such as interest or rents) must be included in PCTCT as under the appropriate heading.  Dividends from overseas are excluded as all dividends received by a company are exempt from corporation tax.

- Profits from overseas branches are included in trading profits.

- Overseas tax deducted must be added back to include the gross income in PCTCT.

- Double tax relief may be available (Chapter 28).

## Property income

Property income is calculated in the same way as for individuals except:

- assessed on income in the accounting period, not tax year
- interest on a loan to buy let property is treated as a deduction from interest income, not property income
- losses can be relieved against other profits, not just property income (Chapter 24).

## Miscellaneous income

Miscellaneous income is uncommon. The most likely items are as follows:

- Patent royalties received /paid for a non-trading purpose (e.g. held as investments). If for a trade purpose then the amounts are included in trade profits. In both cases the amounts are included on the accruals basis.
- Profits on the sale of goodwill and other intangible assets are included here if the asset is not held for trading purposes (section 5).

## Chargeable gains

Chargeable gains are calculated in the same way as for individuals, with the following key differences:

### Indexation allowance

- An indexation allowance (IA) is available to companies.

  The IA gives a company some allowance for the effects of inflation in calculating a chargeable gain.

  The aim is to ensure that capital gains are subject to tax only to the extent that they represent an increase in real terms of an asset's value on disposal and to eliminate the effects of inflation.

- The rules for the IA are as follows:
    - the IA is based on the cost of the asset and the movement in the retail price index
    - it is available:
        - from the month of purchase
        - to the month of disposal
    - the IA is calculated separately for each item of expenditure (e.g. calculate a different IA for the original acquisition cost and any enhancement expenditure because they have different purchase dates).
    - the IA cannot create or increase a capital loss.

- The IA is calculated as follows:

  IA = indexation factor x allowable cost

- The indexation factor is calculated as follows:

$$\frac{\text{RPI @ date of disposal} - \text{RPI @ date of acquisition}}{\text{RPI @ date of acquisition}}$$

The indexation factor must be rounded to three decimal places.

  - If the RPI falls between acquisition and disposal, the IA is £Nil.

- The relevant RPIs will be given in the exam question, but a full list of RPIs is given in the introduction to this manual.

### Test your understanding 3

Stella Ltd sold an office building on 12 September 2009 for £3,500,000. The company had acquired the building on 3 June 1990 for £700,000 and an extension was built on 13 October 1996, costing £200,000. Stella Limited has a 31 December year end.

**Calculate the chargeable gain to include in Stella Ld's corporation tax computation for year ended 31 December 2009.**

### Capital losses

- All capital losses must be netted off against capital gains.
  - any net gain is chargeable as part of PCTCT
  - net capital losses are carried forward against the first available future net gains

- The following steps should be carried out to compute the chargeable gains to be included in a company's PCTCT computation:
  (1) Calculate the capital gains / allowable loss arising on the disposal of each chargeable asset separately
  (2) Calculate the total net capital gains arising in the accounting period = (capital gains less allowable losses)
  (3) Deduct capital losses brought forward = total net chargeable gains
  (4) Include in PCTCT computation

## Annual exemption

- Note that there is no annual exemption available to companies, the total net chargeable gains is simply included in the company's PCTCT computation.

## Shares and securities

- The matching rules for the disposal of shares is different for companies. Disposals should be matched as follows:

    (1) Same day acquisitions

    (2) Acquisitions in the previous nine days

    (3) Acquisitions from the share pool

- The share pool for companies is different as follows:

    – the pool contains shares in the same company, of the same class, purchased up to 9 days before the date of disposal.

    – the pool keeps a record of the:

        – number of shares acquired and sold

        – cost of the shares, and

        – indexed cost of the shares (i.e. cost plus indexation allowance)

    – The calculation of cost and indexed cost in the share pool is not examinable.

    – When shares are disposed of out of the share pool, the appropriate proportion of the cost and indexed cost which relates to the shares disposed of is calculated on an average cost basis.

### Test your understanding 4

ST Limited sold 5,000 shares in JM Ltd for £50,000 on 12 January 2010. They had been acquired as follows:

| | | |
|---|---|---|
| Share pool | 3,900 shares costing | £6,638 |
| 4 January 2010 | 2,000 shares costing | £4,500 |

The indexed cost of the share pool at 12 January 2010 is £9,345.

**Calculate the chargeable gain to include in the corporation tax computation.**

- Special rules apply to the disposal of shares out of a substantial shareholding are exempt (section 3).

- Rollover relief and holdover relief (i.e. reinvestment into depreciating assets) are the only capital gains reliefs available for companies.

  These reliefs are not available for gains on disposal of shares.

## Gift Aid Donations

Relief for Gift Aid donations is given as an allowable deduction from the total profits of the company.

- Companies pay Gift Aid donations gross.

- Deduct the gross amount paid in the accounting period.

## Summary

**PCTCT**

**Trading income**
Differences for companies:
- The 10% special rate WDA on P&M that is integral to a building applies to the initial and replacement expenditure
- Expenditure on energy saving or environmentally beneficial P&M qualifies for 100% FYA. The company can then surrender any loss created by the FYA in exchange for a payment up to 19% of the loss surrendered
- No private use
- Interest paid and received for non-trading purposes = interest income
- Enhanced R&D deductions allowed
- Cost of share issues to employees allowable

**Gift Aid donations**
- Paid gross
- Deduct gross amount paid

**Property income**
Differences for companies:
- Accounting period basis of assessment
- Interest on buying property = deduct from interest income
- Loss relief available against other profits

**Foreign income**
- Include gross amount
- DTR available
- Dividends excluded

**Chargeable gains**
- IA to reduce gains
- Offset all capital losses
- Share matching rules
  - same day
  - previous 9 days
  - share pool with cumulative indexation allowance
- Exemption for disposal of some shares
- Rollover relief and reinvestment into depreciating assets = only reliefs available to companies

**Interest income**
- All interest receivable
- Deduct interest payable for non-trading purposes
- If deficit = loss relief available

## Comprehensive examples

### Test your understanding 5

PQR Ltd, a manufacturing company in the UK has one associated company. Its profit and loss account for the accounting year ended 30 September 2009 shows a net profit before taxation of £329,700, after accounting for the following items:

| Expenditure | £ | |
|---|---:|---|
| Debenture interest | 12,000 | Note 1 |
| Loan interest | 6,000 | Note 2 |
| Patent royalties | 10,000 | |
| Depreciation | 11,000 | |
| Gift Aid payments made 1 August 2009 | 5,000 | |

| Income | | |
|---|---:|---|
| Loan interest receivable | 8,000 | Note 3 |
| Rents accrued | 7,000 | Note 4 |
| Insurance recovery | 6,800 | Note 5 |
| Profit on disposal of old headquarters building | 100,000 | Note 6 |
| Patent royalties received during year | 30,000 | |
| Dividend received | 8,000 | |

### Notes:

(1) This represents interest on debentures issued by PQR Ltd in 2000 to provide funds to build a factory extension. The figure of £12,000 includes accrued interest of £3,000.

(2) This represents interest paid on a ten-year loan raised by PQR Ltd to purchase property which is currently let to another company.

(3) The loan interest receivable is in respect of a loan made by PQR Ltd to a supplier.

(4) The rents receivable relate to the property let by PQR Ltd.

(5) This represents an amount recovered from the company's insurers during the year in respect of goods destroyed in a fire last year. The cost of these goods was written off and allowed as an expense last year.

(6) On 14 July 2009 the company sold its old headquarters building for £490,450. The building had been purchased in June 1986 for £150,000. At the time of its disposal, the building was held in the financial statements at a value of £375,000 due to a revaluation in 2002.

(7) Capital allowances of £34,700 are available.

(a) **Compute the adjusted trading profit stating clearly your treatment of any interest paid or received.**

(b) **Compute the corporation tax liability of PQR Ltd for the year ended 30 September 2009.**

**Test your understanding 6**

Arable Ltd commenced trading on 1 April 2009 as a manufacturer of farm equipment, preparing its first accounts for the nine-month period ended 31 December 2009. The following information is available:

**Trading profit**

The tax adjusted trading profit is £284,543. This figure is before taking account of capital allowances and any deduction arising from the premiums paid in respect of leasehold property.

**Industrial building**

Arable Ltd had a new factory constructed at a cost of £400,000 that the company brought into use on 1 May 2009. The cost was made up as follows:

|  | £ |
|---|---|
| Land | 120,000 |
| Site preparation | 14,000 |
| Professional fees | 6,000 |
| Drawing office serving the factory | 40,000 |
| Showroom | 74,000 |
| Factory | 146,000 |
|  | ——— |
|  | 400,000 |
|  | ——— |

### Plant and machinery

Arable Ltd purchased the following assets in respect of the nine-month period ended 31 December 2009.

|  |  | £ |
|---|---|---|
| 15 February 2009 | Machinery | 32,000 |
| 18 February 2009 | Building alterations necessary for the installation of the machinery | 3,700 |
| 20 April 2009 | Lorry | 22,000 |
| 12 June 2009 | Motor car (1) (emissions 135g/km) | 11,200 |
| 14 June 2009 | Motor car (2) (emissions 171g/km) | 14,600 |
| 17 June 2009 | Motor car (3) (emissions 108g/km) | 13,000 |
| 29 October 2009 | Computer | 4,400 |

The company will not make any short life asset elections.

### Leasehold property

On 1 April 2009 Arable Ltd acquired two leasehold office buildings. In each case a premium of £75,000 was paid for the grant of a 15-year lease.

The first office building was used for business purposes by Arable Ltd throughout the period ended 31 December 2009.

The second office building was empty until 30 September 2009, and was then sub-let to a tenant. On that date Arable Ltd received a premium of £50,000 for the grant of a five-year lease, and annual rent of £14,800 which was payable in advance.

### Loan interest received

Loan interest of £6,000 was received on 30 September 2009, and £3,000 was accrued at 31 December 2009. The loan was made for non-trading purposes.

### Dividends received

During the period ended 31 December 2009 Arable Ltd received dividends of £18,000 from Ranch plc, an unconnected company. This figure was the actual cash amount received.

### Profit on disposal of shares

On 5 December 2009 Arable Ltd sold 10,000 £1 ordinary shares in Ranch plc for £37,574. Arable Ltd had a share pool containing 20,000 shares in Ranch plc, with a total cost of £23,250. The indexed cost of the share pool at 5 December 2009 was £23,490. Arable Ltd's shareholding never represented more than a 1% interest in Ranch plc.

### Other information

Arable Ltd has two associated companies.

(a) **Calculate Arable Ltd's corporation tax liability for the nine-month period ended 31 December 2009.**

(b) **State the date by which Arable Ltd's self-assessment corporation tax return for the period ended 31 December 2009 should be submitted, and explain how the company can correct the return if it is subsequently found to contain an error or mistake.**

## Long period of account

A company requires permission from the Registrar of Companies if it wishes to extend its period of account beyond twelve months.

- A chargeable accounting period (CAP) can never exceed 12 months.
- Therefore, if a company prepares accounts for a period which exceeds 12 months, the period must be split into two CAPs:
  - one for the first 12 months, the other for the balance of the time.

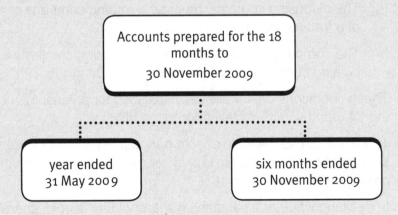

- Profits are split between the chargeable accounting periods as follows:

| Income | Method of allocation |
|---|---|
| Adjusted trading profit | Time-apportion |
| Capital allowances | Separate computations (where the AP is less than 12 months, the WDA and AIA is reduced accordingly) |
| Interest and property income | Compute accrued amount for each period separately (Note) |
| Chargeable gains | According to date of disposal |
| Gift aid donations | According to date paid |
| FII for 'profits' purposes | According to date received |

**Note:** If information to apply the strict basis is not available; time apportion

- Two separate corporation tax computations are then prepared.

## 3 Substantial shareholding exemption

Any gain on the disposal by a company of shares out of a substantial shareholding in another company is exempt, and any loss is not allowable.

- A substantial shareholding is defined as a holding
  - of ≥ 10%
  - owned for at least 12 months in the two years before the disposal.

- The conditions are as follows:

  (i) The disposing company must be a trading company or a member of a trading group.

  (ii) The company disposed of must be a trading company or the holding company of a trading group or sub group.

- These conditions must have been satisfied for at least 12 months out of the 24 months immediately prior to the disposal.

- The effect of this rule is to enable part disposals out of a substantial shareholding to continue to qualify for relief even after the vendor company owns less than 10%.

- In deciding whether a substantial shareholding is held, shareholdings held by other group members may be taken into account.

- Where there has been a qualifying share-for-share exchange, the holding period of the original shares is effectively amalgamated with the holding period of the replacement shares in determining whether the '12 month' rule has been satisfied.

### Test your understanding 7

Omega Ltd owns 15% of the shares issued by Epsilon Ltd, a shareholding qualifying for the substantial shareholding exemption (SSE). The shares were acquired on 1 January 2004.

On 30 June 2009 it disposed of a 10% holding in Epsilon Ltd.

The remaining 5% holding was disposed of on 31 December 2009.

**State which of these disposals qualify for the exemption.**

## 4 Research and development expenditure

### Introduction

In order to encourage more spending on research and development (R&D), additional tax reliefs are given for qualifying revenue expenditure incurred by companies.

There are separate schemes for small or medium sized enterprises (SMEs) and large companies.

For R&D purposes, the question in the exam will state whether or not the company is a SME.

### Scheme for SMEs

The scheme works as follows:

- Expenditure must be on qualifying R&D, as defined by generally accepted accounting principles (GAAP) and DTI Guidelines.

- Enhanced relief is available if the company spends £10,000 or more in any year on qualifying R&D (note that limit reduced if accounts < 12m).

- SMEs can deduct an additional 75% of qualifying expenditure for tax purposes.

- If the deduction creates a loss it may be surrendered in return for a cash payment from HMRC = 14% of the surrendered amount (but the repayment is restricted to an amount equal to the total PAYE/NIC paid in the year if lower).

- If surrendered in return for cash, the loss cannot also be carried forward for future relief.

- Intellectual property rights arising from R&D must belong to the company.

Qualifying R&D expenditure must be revenue expenditure on a project that seeks to achieve an advance in science or technology that is relevant to the trade.

It can include expenditure on the following:

- staffing costs, including NIC (Class 1 and Class 1A) and pension contributions but excluding assessable benefits

- agency staff for R&D

- materials, water, fuel and power for R&D

- software directly used in R&D

- payments to subcontractors (Note that only 65% of this expenditure will be eligible for the enhanced tax credit).

It cannot include:

- contributions to other bodies for independent research

- expenditure covered by a grant or subsidy.

### Scheme for large companies

The scheme for large companies is similar to the scheme for SMEs.

The differences are as follows:

- large companies can claim an additional 30% of the amount spent as a deduction from trading profits (not 75%)

- there is no option of surrendering losses for cash repayments for large companies

- large companies cannot claim relief for payments made to SME's

- large companies can claim relief for contributions made to a qualifying body such as a charity or a university for independent research provided the research is relevant to the company's trade.

## Example 2 – R&D expenditure

(1) Curzon plc is a large company for the purposes of R&D expenditure. In the year ended 31 March 2010 they have spent £60,000 on qualifying R&D expenditure.

(2) Gul Ltd is a small sized company for the purposes of R&D expenditure. In the year ended 31 December 2009 they spent £8,500 on qualifying R&D expenditure.

**Advise the companies of any tax relief available in respect of their expenditure.**

**Solution**

(1) Curzon plc will be able to claim 130% relief on the £60,000 qualifying expenditure giving a deduction of £78,000 in total.

(2) Gul Ltd will not be able to claim any extra relief on their R&D expenditure as it is less than £10,000. Therefore they will be able to claim just the amount spent of £8,500 against their business profits.

## Test your understanding 8

Dax plc is a profitable company manufacturing audio visual equipment. Dax plc is a small enterprise for the purposes of R&D.

The company has recently decided to investigate the market for a radically new type of classroom projection equipment and has spent the following amounts in the year ended 31 December 2009 on the project:

|  | £ |
|---|---|
| Market research | 8,000 |
| Staff directly involved in researching the project | 20,000 |
| Administrative support for the R&D department | 5,000 |
| Heat and light in the R&D department | 9,000 |
| New software | 4,000 |
| An agency for temporary R&D staff | 10,000 |

**Advise the company of any tax relief available in respect of its expenditure.**

## 5 Intangible assets

### Introduction

Since 1 April 2002, the tax treatment of intangible assets broadly follows the accounting treatment. This is providing the accounting treatment is in accordance with GAAP (either UK or international).

Intangible assets include the following items:

- purchased goodwill (not goodwill on consolidation)
- patents, copyrights and trademarks
- brands
- intellectual property and know-how.

### Tax treatment of costs

Expenditure relating to intangibles which has been charged in the company's profit and loss account is allowable for tax purposes.

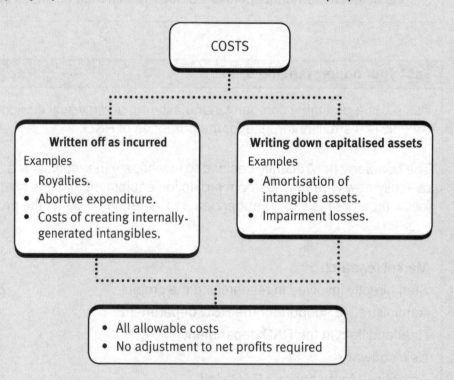

### Election – alternative tax treatment

Instead of allowing the amounts charged in the accounts, an election can be made:

- to write off the cost of a capitalised intangible asset / intellectual property against profit for tax purposes at a rate of 4% per annum

- any accounting debts for amortisation or impairment losses would then be disallowed.

This is useful where:

(1) the asset has a long expected life and is being amortised at a rate of less than 4%

(2) the asset is not amortised in the accounts.

The allowable amount is pro-rated for accounting periods of less than twelve months.

The election is:

- irrevocable, and

- must be made within two years of the end of the accounting period in which the asset was acquired or created.

---

### Test your understanding 9

On 1 December 2009 Rom plc purchased the trade and assets of another company in the same business sector. They paid £2 million that included £35,000 for a patent with a ten-year life remaining. Goodwill is valued at £200,000.

The patent is capitalised and will be written off on a straight-line basis over 10 years on a month-by-month basis.

The goodwill is capitalised but not amortised. The acquisition is expected to significantly increase Rom's profitability.

The company prepares its accounts to 31 March annually.

**What relief is available to Rom plc for its spending on intangible assets?**

---

## Disposals

On the disposal of an intangible asset, the proceeds of sale are compared with the written down value to give profit/loss.

- Any profit or loss made on disposal of an intangible asset
  - will give rise to an identical tax profit or loss
  - unless the tax value at the time of disposal differs from the accounts value
  - this can occur when the 4% election has been made.

### Test your understanding 10

Assume that Rom plc in the previous illustration decides to sell the business that it bought on 1 December 2009. The consideration includes £38,000 for the patent and £250,000 for the goodwill. The sale is made on 1 April 2012.

**State the effect for tax purposes of the disposal of the intangible assets.**

- If a new IFA is acquired within 12 months before or up to 36 months after disposal:
  - part of the taxable credit may be deferred.
- The maximum deferral is:
  - the disposal proceeds (or amount reinvested if lower) in excess of the cost of the original IFA.

## 6 Transfer pricing

### Aim of the legislation

Transfer pricing adjustments may be necessary for transactions between companies where:

- one company controls the other, or
- both are controlled by the same person.

The transfer pricing rules apply to both transactions with non UK resident companies and UK transactions.

HMRC want to ensure that companies cannot reduce total UK corporation tax by substituting a transfer price that is below or above an arm's length price.

- The transfer pricing legislation covers not only sales but also lettings/hiring of property and loan interest.
- Where transfer pricing policies are under review the basic aim is to ensure transactions are recorded at an arm's length price.

- Arm's length means the price which might have been expected if the parties had been independent persons dealing with each other in a normal commercial manner unaffected by any special relationship between them.

- An adjustment may be necessary to increase the profits of the advantaged company (i.e. the one benefiting from the favourable price).

## Companies covered by the legislation

Not all companies are affected by the legislation. The following diagram summarises the position:

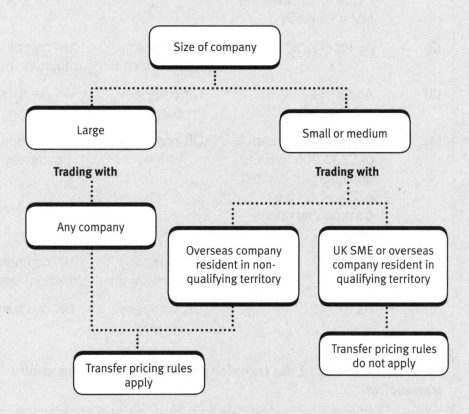

The definition of 'large and 'small or medium' is the same as for research and development expenditure. The question in the exam will state if the company is 'large' or 'small' or 'medium'.

A medium sized company will be brought within the rules if there is 'manipulation'. For example, there is a deliberate attempt to divert profits to a company paying at lower tax rate.

A non-qualifying territory means one that is:

- not in the UK

- has no DTR agreement with the UK, or

- if it does have an agreement then that agreement has no non-discrimination clause.

It is also possible for the Treasury to designate countries as non-qualifying.

### Test your understanding 11

| Transaction | | A Ltd | Subsidiary (B Ltd) |
|---|---|---|---|
| (1) | A Ltd sells 5,000 units to B Ltd at £1.50 each when the MV = £3 each | UK company (large) | Overseas company |
| (2) | As for (1) | UK company (medium/small) | UK company (medium/small) |
| (3) | As for (1) | UK company (large) | UK company |
| (4) | A Ltd makes a loan of £200,000 to B Ltd and charges interest at 2% when the commercial rate is 8%. | UK company (large) | Overseas company |
| (5) | As for (4) | UK company (medium/small) | UK company (medium/small) |
| (6) | As for (4) | UK company (large) | UK company |

**Explain the effect of the transfer pricing legislation on each transaction.**

## Thin capitalisation

### Introduction

When a UK company pays a dividend, there is no tax relief for the payment. When it pays loan interest, the interest is tax allowable. This means that companies would prefer to be financed through loans (debt) rather than through shares (equity).

The thin capitalisation rules aim:

- to stop UK companies from getting excessive tax relief on interest.

This occurs:

- usually because they have received a loan from a related party that exceeds the loan a third party borrower would be prepared to lend.

The rules ensure that:

- interest on the part of the loan that an independent third party would be prepared to lend the company is allowable.
- the excess is disallowed.
- the borrowing capacity of the individual company and its subsidiaries is considered (but not the rest of the group).

## Factors determining thin capitalisation

HMRC will usually look at two areas to determine whether they believe a company is thinly capitalised:

(1) Gearing

- This is the relationship of debt to equity.
- In the UK this is usually around 50:50.
- A higher proportion of debt could cause thin capitalisation problems.

(2) Interest cover

- This is the ratio of earnings before tax and interest to loan interest.
- It measures how risky the loan is for the lender.
- Many commercial lenders will look for a ratio of around 3.

### Test your understanding 12

Archer plc is a wholly owned subsidiary of Berry Inc, a company resident in Babylonia. Archer borrows £100,000 from Berry Inc paying a market rate of interest of 8%. Archer had to borrow from Berry Inc as their UK bankers were not prepared to lend them more than £60,000.

**Advise Archer plc of how much loan interest they are likely to have relieved for tax purposes.**

## 7 Companies with investment business

### Introduction

A company with investment business is a company 'whose business consists wholly or partly in the making of investments'. This includes any company that makes and holds investments, regardless of whether or not it also carries on a trade.

The costs incurred by such a company in managing its investments are allowable when computing its corporation tax liability in accordance with the rules set out below.

### Profits of a company with investment business

The PCTCT of a company with investment business:

- are calculated in the same way as for a trading company
- the same rules for the various sources of income and capital gains apply (for example, that costs relevant to a property business will be deducted from the property income).

### Management expenses

Management expenses are incurred in managing the company's investments and can be deducted from the company's 'total profits'.

Expenses which the courts have allowed as management expenses include:

- directors' fees and commissions, provided they are not excessive
- salaries of management
- audit fees
- office rent and rates
- bank interest.

Excess management expenses can be

- carried forward and treated as management expenses of the next accounting period
- group relieved if part of a 75% group (Chapter 27).

### Rate of corporation tax

Companies with investment business are taxed in the same way as other companies, and can take advantage of the small companies' rate and marginal relief.

However, if the company is a 'close investment company' (CIC) (Chapter 26) all profits, whatever their level, will be taxed at the full rate of corporation tax.

**Test your understanding 13**

Cheetah Ltd has the following results for the year ended 31 March 2010:

| | £ |
|---|---|
| Rental income | 70,000 |
| Deposit account interest receivable | 20,000 |
| Chargeable gains | 3,000 |
| Management expenses: | |
|     Property management | 35,000 |
|     Other | 60,000 |
| Capital allowances: | |
|     On property | 2,300 |
|     Other | 1,600 |
| Loan stock interest payable (gross) | 2,000 |
| Directors' remuneration | 3,000 |

**Calculate Cheetah Ltd's CT liability for y/e 31 March 2010.**

## 8 Chapter summary

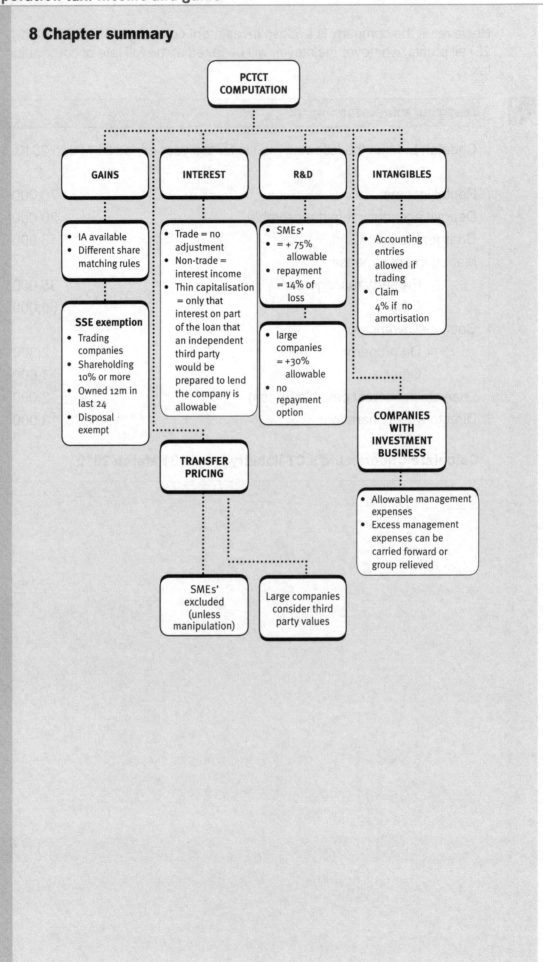

## Test your understanding answers

### Test your understanding 1

**Harriet Ltd**

**(a) Qualifying expenditure**

|  | £ |
|---|---:|
| Total cost | 400,000 |
| Less: | |
| Land | (80,000) |
| Heating system (plant and machinery) | (12,800) |
| Fire alarm system (plant and machinery) | (7,200) |
| Potential qualifying cost | 300,000 |

Check whether the cost of the office qualifies:
(£300,000 × 25%) = £75,000
General office cost £62,500 < £75,000 = allowed

| Total qualifying cost | 300,000 |
|---|---:|

**(b) Qualifying expenditure – if office cost £82,500**

| As in part (a), the total potential qualifying cost | 300,000 |
|---|---:|

Check whether the cost of the office qualifies:
(£300,000 × 25%) = £75,000
General office cost £82,500 > £75,000 = not allowed

| Total qualifying cost (£300,000 – £82,500) | 217,500 |
|---|---:|

**Test your understanding 2**

**Chris Ltd**

£

**Y/e 31 March 2009**

Building is not in industrial use at the end of this POA.                    Nil

**Y/e 31 March 2010**

WDA @ (2% × £100,000 (W))                                                     2,000

Building is in industrial use at the end of this POA.

**Y/e 31 March 2011**

Year of disposal – no WDA, no balancing adjustment

**Note:**  The excess proceeds over original qualifying cost is a capital profit. This may give rise to a chargeable gain for Chris Ltd.

**Workings: Qualifying cost**

|  | £ |
|---|---|
| Total cost | 112,500 |
| Less : Land | (12,500) |
| Potentially qualifying cost | 100,000 × 25% = £25,000 |
| General office | 5,000 |
| Accounts office | 4,500 |
| Total | 9,500 < £25,000 therefore allowed |

**Test your understanding 3**

**Stella Ltd**

|  | £ |
|---|---|
| Sale proceeds | 3,500,000 |
| Less: Cost | (700,000) |
| Enhancement expenditure | (200,000) |
| | |
| Unindexed gain | 2,600,000 |
| Less: Indexation allowance | |
| On Cost: | |
| 212.5 – 126.7/126.7 = 0.677 × £700,000 | (473,900) |
| On Enhancement expenditure: | |
| 212.5 – 153.8/153.8 = 0.382 × £200,000 | (76,400) |
| | |
| Chargeable gain | 2,049,700 |

**Test your understanding 4**

**ST Ltd**

| | | | Shares |
|---|---|---|---|
| (1) | Same day | | Nil |
| (2) | Previous 9 days | 4 Jan 2009 | 2,000 |
| (3) | Share pool | | 3,000 |
| | | | |
| | | | 5,000 |

| **Gain on shares acquired in last 9 days:** | £ |
|---|---|
| Proceeds (2,000/5,000 × £50,000) | 20,000 |
| Less: Cost | (4,500) |
| | |
| Chargeable gain | 15,500 |

| **Gain on shares in share pool** | £ |
|---|---|
| Proceeds (3,000/5,000 × £50,000) | 30,000 |
| Less: Indexed cost | (7,188) |
| | |
| Chargeable gain | 22,812 |

### Total chargeable gains on sale of 5,000 shares in JM Ltd:

|  | £ |
|---|---:|
| Previous nine days | 15,500 |
| Share pool | 22,812 |
|  | |
| Total chargeable gains | 38,312 |

| Working: share pool | Number | Cost £ | Indexed cost £ |
|---|---:|---:|---:|
| Pool per question | 3,900 | 6,638 | 9,345 |
| Sales Jan 2009 | (3,000) | (5,106) | (7,188) |
|  | | | |
| Balance in share pool | 900 | 1,532 | 2,157 |

### Test your understanding 5

**PQR Ltd**

(a) **Adjusted trading profits – y/e 30 September 2009**

|  | £ |
|---|---:|
| Profit before tax | 329,700 |
| Add: Loan interest payable | 6,000 |
| Depreciation | 11,000 |
| Gift Aid payments | 5,000 |
|  | |
|  | 351,700 |
| Less: Rents receivable | (7,000) |
| Profit on disposal of building | (100,000) |
| Dividend | (8,000) |
| Loan interest receivable | (8,000) |
| Capital allowances | (34,700) |
|  | |
| Adjusted trading profits | 194,000 |

KAPLAN PUBLISHING

(b) **Corporation tax computation – y/e 30 September 2009**

| | £ |
|---|---:|
| Trading profits (above) | 194,000 |
| Interest income (£8,000 – £6,000) | 2,000 |
| Rental profits | 7,000 |
| Chargeable gain (W1) | 165,100 |
| | 368,100 |
| Less Gift Aid | (5,000) |
| PCTCT | 363,100 |

| | £ |
|---|---:|
| FY2008 and FY2009 (£363,100 × 28%) | 101,668 |
| Less: Marginal relief | |
| 7/400 × (£750,000 – £371,989) × £363,100/£371,989 | (6,457) |
| Corporation tax liability | 95,211 |

**Workings:**

(1) **Chargeable gain on headquarters building**

| | £ |
|---|---:|
| Proceeds (July 2009) | 490,450 |
| Less: Cost (June 1986) | (150,000) |
| Unindexed gain | 340,450 |
| Less: IA from June 1986 to July 2009 | |
| (212.1 – 97.79)/97.79 = 1.169 × £150,000 | (175,350) |
| Chargeable gain | 165,100 |

(2) **Rate of corporation tax**

| | £ |
|---|---:|
| PCTCT | 363,100 |
| Plus FII (£8,000 × 100/90) | 8,889 |
| 'Profits' | 371,989 |
| Upper limit (£1,500,000 × 1/2) | 750,000 |
| Lower limit (£300,000 × 1/2) | 150,000 |

Marginal relief applies. Although the year straddles 31 March 2009, there is no need to split the CT computation as there was no change in rates from FY2008 to FY2009.

## Test your understanding 6

**Arable Ltd**

(a) **Corporation tax computation – p/e 31 December 2009**

| | £ |
|---|---:|
| Trading profit | 284,543 |
| Capital — IBA (W1) | (3,090) |
| allowances | |
| — P & M (W2) | (63,115) |
| Deduction for lease premium (W3) | (2,700) |
| Trading income | 215,638 |
| Property business income (W4) | 31,700 |
| Interest — Loan interest (£6,000 + £3,000) | 9,000 |
| income | |
| Chargeable gain (W5) | 25,829 |
| PCTCT | 282,167 |

| | £ |
|---|---:|
| Corporation tax (£282,167 at 28%) | 79,007 |
| Less: Marginal relief | |
| 7/400 × (£375,000) – £302,167) × £282,167/£302,167 | (1,190) |
| Corporation tax liability | 77,817 |

**Workings**

**(W1) Industrial buildings allowance**

| | £ |
|---|---:|
| Site preparation | 14,000 |
| Professional fees | 6,000 |
| Drawing office | 40,000 |
| Factory | 146,000 |
| Eligible expenditure | 206,000 |
| WDA = (£206,000 at 2% = £4,120 × 9/12) | 3,090 |

**Notes:**

The cost of the land does not qualify.

(1)  The showroom does not qualify as it cost £74,000 which is more than £70,000 (i.e. 25% of the total qualifying cost (£400,000 – £120,000 = £280,000 × 25% = £70,000)).

Note in practice some of the other costs may be treated as relating to the showroom and would therefore not qualify. This approach would be awarded equivalent marks.

| (W2) **Plant and machinery** | General pool £ | Special rate pool £ | Total allowances £ |
|---|---|---|---|
| **P/e 31 December 2009** | | | |
| Additions: | | | |
| Not qualifying for AIA or FYA: | | | |
| Cars (111 – 160 g/km) | 11,200 | | |
| Cars (over 160 g/km) | | 14,600 | |
| Qualifying for AIA and FYA: | | | |
| Plant and machinery (Note 1) | 62,100 | | |
| Less: AIA ( Note 2) | (37,500) | | 37,500 |
| | ———— | | |
| | 24,600 | | |
| | ———— | ———— | |
| | 11,200 | 14,600 | |
| Less: WDA (20% × £11,200 × 9/12) | (1,680) | | 1,680 |
| Less: WDA (10% × £14,600 × 9/12) | | (1,095) | 1,095 |
| Less: FYA (40%) | (9,840) | | |
| | ———— | | |
| | 14,760 | | |
| Low emission car | 13,000 | | |
| Less: FYA (100%) | (13,000) | | 13,000 |
| | ———— | | |
| | | Nil | |
| | ———— | ———— | |
| TWDV c/f | 24,280 | 13,505 | |
| | ———— | ———— | ———— |
| Total allowances | | | 63,115 |
| | | | ———— |

### Notes:

(1) Plant qualifying for AIA is £62,100 (£32,000 + £3,700 + £22,000 + £4,400).

(2) The maximum AIA is 9/12 of £50,000 = £37,500 as the accounting period is only 9 months long.

### (W3) Deduction for lease premium

The first office building has been used for business purposes, and so a proportion of the lease premium assessed on the landlord can be deducted.

The amount assessed on the landlord calculated as follows:

£75,000 × [(51 – 15)/50] = £54,000

This is deductible over the life of the lease, so the deduction for the nine-month period ended 31 December 2009 is:

(£54,000/15 = £3,600 × 9/12) = £2,700

**(W4) Property business income**

| | £ |
|---|---:|
| Assessed as property income | |
| £50,000 × [(51 – 5)/50] | 46,000 |
| Less: Relief for premium paid for head lease | |
| £54,000 × 5 /15 | (18,000) |
| | 28,000 |
| Rent receivable (£14,800 × 3/12) | 3,700 |
| | |
| Property business income | 31,700 |

**(W5) Chargeable gain**

| | £ |
|---|---:|
| Disposal proceeds | 37,574 |
| Less: Cost (see below) | (11,625) |
| | |
| Unindexed gain | 25,949 |
| Less: Indexation (£11,745 – £11,625) (see below) | (120) |
| | |
| Chargeable gain | 25,829 |

| **Share Pool** | Number | Cost | Indexed cost |
|---|---:|---:|---:|
| | | £ | £ |
| Pool b/f | 20,000 | 23,250 | 23,490 |
| Disposal (December 2009) | | | |
| Cost × 10,000/20,000 | (10,000) | (11,625) | (11,745) |
| | | | |
| Balance c/f | 10,000 | 11,625 | 11,745 |

**(W6) Rate of corporation tax**

| | £ |
|---|---:|
| PCTCT | 282,167 |
| Plus FII (£18,000 × 100/90) | 20,000 |
| | |
| Profits | 302,167 |

### Limits for determining rate of tax

(1) Since the accounting period is nine months long, the upper limit is reduced to £1,125,000 (£1,500,000 × 9/12) and the lower limit to £225,000 (300,000 × 9/12).

(2) They are then further reduced to £375,000 (£1,125,000/3) and £75,000 (£225,000/3) as Arable Ltd has two associated companies.

The company is therefore a marginal relief company. The accounting period falls entirely within FY2009.

**(b) Self assessment corporation tax return**

Arable Ltd's self-assessment corporation tax return for the period ended 31 December 2009 must be submitted by 31 December 2010.

It will be possible for Arable Ltd to amend its return at any time before 31 December 2011, being 12 months after the filing date.

If an error or mistake in a return is subsequently discovered, then Arable Ltd can make a claim for relief before 31 December 2013, being four years from the end of the accounting period.

### Test your understanding 7

**Omega Ltd**

Both of these disposals will qualify for the SSE.

- The first disposal of the 10% holding has been held for a 12 month period in the two years prior to disposal.

- The second disposal also qualifies, despite it being made out of only a 5% holding, because Omega Ltd held at least a 10% holding throughout a 12 month period beginning in the two years prior to this second disposal.

## Test your understanding 8

### Dax plc

Dax plc is an SME; they can claim R&D tax credits on most of their expenditure, but not all.

The amount they can claim against their taxable profits is as follows:

|  | £ |
|---|---|
| Allowable expenses but not qualifying for the special relief: | |
| Market research | 8,000 |
| Administrative staff | 5,000 |
|  | 13,000 |
| Qualifying for R&D relief: | |
| Staff | 20,000 |
| Heat and light | 9,000 |
| Software | 4,000 |
| Agency staff | 10,000 |
|  | 43,000 |
| Allowable amount (£43,000 x 175%) + £13,000 | 88,250 |

**Note:** £88,250 is the total allowable amount, but the actual expenses of £56,000 (£43,000 + £13,000) will already have been charged in the account. Therefore an additional £32,250 (£88,250 – £56,000) is deducted in the adjustment to profits computation.

## Test your understanding 9

### Rom plc

(1) Patent

– This is being amortised at 10% per annum.

– This will also be the tax allowable amount.

– Therefore £3,500 (£35,000 x 10%) will be the amortisation and tax allowable amount.

(2)  Goodwill

–   This is not being amortised.

–   It will be beneficial for the company to elect to write this off for tax purposes at 4% per annum.

–   An allowance of £8,000 (£200,000 × 4%) will be available

**Note:** Full annual allowances are available as the accounting period is 12 months in length.

### Test your understanding 10

**Rom plc continued**

| **Patent** | £ |
|---|---:|
| Original cost | 35,000 |
| Less:  Amounts written off | |
| Year ended 31.3.10 | (1,167) |
| Year ended 31.3.11 | (3,500) |
| Year ended 31.3.12 | (3,500) |
| | ———— |
| Tax written down value at 1 April 2012 | 26,833 |
| Proceeds | 38,000 |
| | ———— |
| Profit (included in taxable trading profits) | 11,167 |
| | ———— |

**Goodwill**

Any accounting profit is deducted for tax purposes in the adjustment of profits computation and is replaced with the following taxable profit.

| | £ |
|---|---:|
| Original cost | 200,000 |
| Less:  Amounts written off | |
| Year ended 31.3.10 | (8,000) |
| Year ended 31.3.11 | (8,000) |
| Year ended 31.3.12 | (8,000) |
| | ———— |
| Tax written down value at 1 April 2012 | 176,000 |
| Proceeds | 250,000 |
| | ———— |
| Profit (included in taxable trading profits) | 74,000 |
| | ———— |

### Test your understanding 11

**A Ltd and B Ltd**

(1) The transfer pricing legislation applies.

   A Ltd must increase its PCTCT by £7,500 (£1.50 × 5,000).

(2) The transfer pricing legislation does not apply, unless a medium company and HMRC consider profits are being manipulated.

(3) The transfer pricing legislation applies.

   A Ltd must increase its profits by £7,500 and B Ltd may make an equal and opposite adjustment to its profits as it is UK resident.

(4) The transfer pricing legislation applies.

   A Ltd must increase its PCTCT by £12,000 (6% × £200,000).

(5) The transfer pricing legislation does not apply.

(6) The transfer pricing legislation applies.

   A Ltd must increase its PCTCT by £12,000 and B Ltd may make an equal and opposite adjustment to its profits as it is UK resident.

### Test your understanding 12

**Archer plc**

A third party was only prepared to lend Archer plc £60,000.

As they have borrowed £100,000 from their parent company, it is likely that interest on the excess £40,000 will be disallowed for tax purposes.

Of the £8,000 interest they pay to Berry Inc, only £4,800 is likely to be allowed for tax.

**Test your understanding 13**

**Cheetah Ltd**

**Corporation tax computation – year ended 31 March 2010**

|  | £ |
|---|---|
| Property income (W1) | 32,700 |
| Interest income (£20,000 – £2,000) | 18,000 |
| Chargeable gains | 3,000 |
| Total profits | 53,700 |
| Less Management expenses (restricted) (W2) | (53,700) |
| PCTCT | Nil |
| Corporation tax liability | Nil |

**Workings**
**(W1) Property income**

|  | £ |
|---|---|
| Rents | 70,000 |
| Less: Capital allowances | (2,300) |
| Property management expenses | (35,000) |
| Property income | 32,700 |

**(W2) Management expenses**

|  | £ |
|---|---|
| General management expenses | 60,000 |
| Directors' remuneration | 3,000 |
| Capital allowances | 1,600 |
|  | 64,600 |
| Less: Total profits | (53,700) |
| Excess management expenses | 10,900 |

Excess management expenses are carried forward and treated as management expenses of y/e 31 March 2011.

# Corporation tax losses

## Chapter learning objectives

Upon completion of this chapter you will be able to:

- explain and show the alternative methods for relieving a range of losses in a single company

- identify the factors that influence the choice of a loss relief claim and advise on the effect of alternative courses of action

- recognise the circumstances when the use of losses may be restricted on a change of ownership of a company and state the effect.

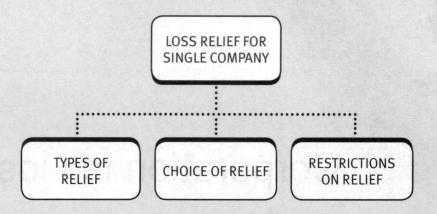

## 1 Introduction

This chapter covers the rules for loss reliefs available to a single company.

Much of this chapter is a revision of rules covered at F6. A brief reminder of F6 content is given in expandable text and revision examples are provided to check your retention of the required F6 knowledge.

The new areas at P6 are

- the treatment of non-trading loan relationship deficits, and
- the restrictions for the use of some losses.

There is however a much greater emphasis at P6 in choosing the most tax efficient use of loss reliefs available and tax planning for companies with losses.

## 2 Loss reliefs for a single company

### A revision of loss relief available

The following diagram summarises the trading loss relief options to a single company covered at F6:

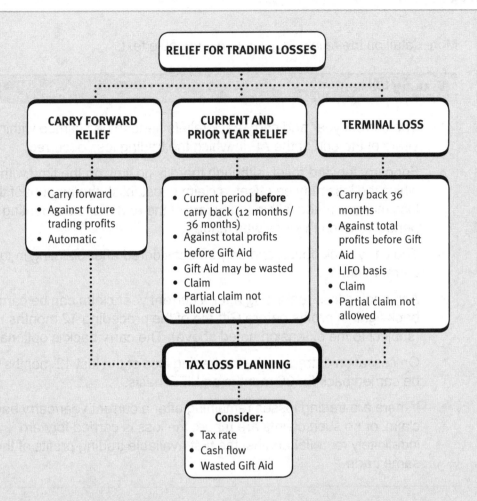

The loss reliefs available for companies remain essentially unchanged, except for the following rule which was introduced in FA2009:

**Extended loss relief**

- A trading loss can normally be carried back and set against profits of the preceding 12 months.

- However, for loss making accounting periods ending between 24 November 2008 and 23 November 2010 this relief is extended to 36 months.

- The extended relief is exactly the same as that given for terminal losses, except that the extended loss relief is restricted to a maximum of £50,000.

- The £50,000 limit is apportioned if a loss making period is shorter than 12 months. For example, for a 6-month loss making period the extended relief would be restricted to a maximum of £25,000 (6/12 x £50,000)

- The £50,000 restriction only applies to losses carried back past the normal 12 month carry back period.

- As with relief for terminal losses, where extended relief is claimed the losses are carried back for 36 months on a LIFO basis.

More detail on the reliefs is given in expandable text.

> ### Trading losses
>
> - The current year and carry back reliefs need to be claimed within 2 years of the end of the AP in which the trading loss occurred.
>
> - For carry forward relief, although there is no limit on the time within which the loss may be offset, a claim to establish the amount of the loss must be made within four years of the end of the accounting period in which the loss was made.
>
> - The carry back option can only be considered after claiming in the current period.
>
> - Any trading loss remaining after a current year claim can be carried back against profits before Gift Aid of the preceding 12 months (subject to the extension noted above). The carry back is optional.
>
> - On cessation of trade only, the trading loss of the last 12 months can be carried back for 36 months on LIFO basis.
>
> - If there are trading losses remaining after a current year/carry back claim, or no such claims are made, the loss is carried forward indefinitely for relief against the first available trading profits of the same trade.

## Trading losses – pro-forma computation

When dealing with losses it is necessary to have a neat and logical layout for computations.

### Pro forma: Corporation tax losses

| (Loss arises in 2009) | 2006 £ | 2007 £ | 2008 £ | 2009 £ | 2010 £ |
|---|---|---|---|---|---|
| Trading profit | X | X | X | Nil | X |
| Less: Loss relief b/f | | | | | (X) |
| | | | | | X |
| Other income | X | X | X | X | X |
| Chargeable gains | X | X | X | X | X |
| Total profits | X | X | X | X | X |
| Less: Loss relief | | | | | |
| – Current year offset | | | | (X) | |
| – 12 month c/back | | | (X) | | |
| – Extended c/back (Max £50,000) | (X) | (X) | | | |
| | X | Nil | Nil | Nil | X |
| Gift Aid | (X) | Wasted | Wasted | Wasted | (X) |
| PCTCT | X | Nil | Nil | Nil | X |

**Note:** The carry back claims are on a LIFO basis
(i.e. 12 m/e 31 December 2008, then 2007, then 2006).

### Loss-making period of less than 12 months

The length of the loss-making period is usually not important:

* Full relief is given against the current period total profits.
* The remaining loss can be carried back in full in the normal way.

However, remember that the £50,000 maximum limit for the extended relief must be apportioned according to the length of the loss-making accounting period.

### Short accounting periods prior to year of loss

- If any of the accounting periods falling in the carry back period is less than 12 months:

- The profits of the accounting period that falls partly into the carry back period must be time apportioned.

- The loss can only be offset against those profits which fall within the carry back period.

- Remember, the loss is offset on a LIFO basis (i.e. against the later accounting period first).

### Illustration 1 – Short accounting period prior to the loss

If the preceding AP before the loss making year ended 31 December 2010 is only 8 months to 31 December 2009, then the loss can be carried back:

- Against 8 months to 31 December 2009, and then if sufficient loss;

- Against 4/12 of the profits before Gift Aid of the 12 months to 30 April 2009.

**Note:** It does not matter if the accounting period of loss is less than 12 months.

### Non trading losses

In addition to trading losses three other types of loss can occur.

The following diagram summarises the non-trading loss relief options to a single company:

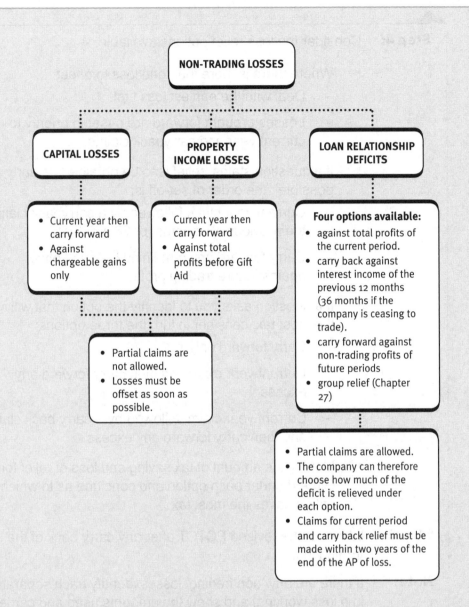

## Approach for loss computations

A question involving company losses often covers several years; therefore a methodical approach is important.

**Step 1:** Write out the skeleton PCTCT proforma, lay out the years side by side.

**Step 2:** Fill in the pro forma with the PCTCT information provided, ignoring loss relief. In the year of the loss, the trading income is £Nil.

**Step 3:** Keep a separate working for the 'trading loss'. If there are losses in more than one AP, then keep a separate loss working for each and update the workings as the loss is relieved.

**Step 4:** Consider the loss relief options available.

- Where there is more than one loss to offset:
    - Deal with the earliest loss first.
    - Losses brought forward are offset in priority to current year and carryback claims.

- If a question states 'relief is to be obtained as early as possible', the order of set-off is:
    - Current year claim followed by a carryback claim to the previous 12 months (or 36 months).
    - Carry forward any remaining loss and offset against future trading profits.

- If a question asks you to identify the option that will save the most tax, consider in turn the three options:
    - Carry forward only.
    - Current year claim and then carry forward any excess.
    - Current year claim, followed by a carry back claim and then carry forward any excess.

- Identify the amount of tax saving and loss of relief for Gift Aid under each option and conclude as to which option saves the most tax.

**Step 5:** Work out the revised PCTCT after any carry back of the trading loss.

**Note:** If there are any 'non trading' losses identify each separately, in a loss working, and show the amounts used and carried forward. Deal with property losses and loan relationship deficits before using the trading loss.

### Example 1 – Loss computation

Daffodil Ltd has the following results for the four accounting periods ended 31 March 2010.

| Year ended: | 31.03.07 | 31.03.08 | 31.03.09 | 31.03.10 |
|---|---|---|---|---|
| | £ | £ | £ | £ |
| Trading profit/(loss) | 14,000 | 10,000 | 23,500 | (25,000) |
| Interest income | 2,200 | 1,800 | 2,000 | 2,400 |
| Property business income | 800 | 1,100 | (800) | 800 |
| Chargeable gains | Nil | (700) | Nil | 2,600 |
| Gift Aid payments | 200 | 200 | 200 | 200 |

There was a trading loss brought forward at 1 April 2006 of £7,000. Daffodil continues to trade after 31.03.10.

**Calculate the PCTCT, assuming that loss relief is claimed as early as possible.**

**Solution**

- There are two trading losses to consider:
    - £7,000 brought forward at 1 April 2006
    - £25,000 in the year ended 31 March 2010

    The phrase "as early as possible" in the requirements means that a current year claim must be made, then a carry-back claim, for the loss of £25,000. Relief must be given for earlier trading losses before relief is obtained for later losses.

- The capital loss must be carried forward and used against future gains only.

- The property income loss must be deducted from profits before Gift Aid of the accounting period of loss.

- The losses should be dealt with in the order that they arose, and as each loss is relieved the loss memorandum should be completed.

**Corporation tax computations**

| Year to: | 31.03.07 | 31.03.08 | 31.03.09 | 31.03.10 |
|---|---|---|---|---|
| | £ | £ | £ | £ |
| Trading profit | 14,000 | 10,000 | 23,500 | Nil |
| Less: Loss b/f | (7,000) | | | |
| | ——— | | | |
| | 7,000 | | | |
| Interest income | 2,200 | 1,800 | 2,000 | 2,400 |
| Property income | 800 | 1,100 | Nil | 800 |
| Chargeable gains | Nil | Nil | Nil | 1,900 |
| | ——— | ——— | ——— | ——— |
| Total profits | 10,000 | 12,900 | 25,500 | 5,100 |
| Property income loss | | | (800) | |
| Less: Loss relief | | | | |
| - current AP | | | | (5,100) |
| - carried back | | | (19,900) | |
| | ——— | ——— | ——— | ——— |
| | 10,000 | 12,900 | 4,800 | Nil |
| Less Gift Aid payments | (200) | (200) | (200) | Wasted |
| | ——— | ——— | ——— | ——— |
| PCTCT | 9,800 | 12,700 | 4,600 | Nil |
| | ——— | ——— | ——— | ——— |

| Loss memorandum – trading losses | £ |
|---|---|
| Loss carried forward at 01.04.06 | 7,000 |
| Less: Used in y/e 31.03.07 | (7,000) |
| | Nil |
| Loss for y/e 31.03.10 | 25,000 |
| Less: Used in current period – y/e 31.03.10 | (5,100) |
| Used in 12 month carry back – y/e 31.03.09 | (19,900) |
| | Nil |

| Loss memorandum – non-trading losses | £ |
|---|---|
| Capital loss for y/e 31.03.08 | 700 |
| Less: Deducted from capital gains for y/e 31.03.10 | (700) |
| | Nil |
| Property business income loss for y/e 31.03.09 | 800 |
| Less: Used against total profits of y/e 31.03.09 | (800) |
| | Nil |

### Test your understanding 1

Loser Ltd's results for the four accounting periods to 31 March 2009 are as follows:

| | y/e 30.06.06 | y/e 30.06.07 | p/e 31.03.08 | y/e 31.03.09 | y/e 31.03.10 |
|---|---|---|---|---|---|
| | £ | £ | £ | £ | £ |
| Trading profit/(loss) | 95,400 | 56,600 | (25,700) | 27,300 | (105,900) |
| Property income | 7,100 | - | 4,500 | 8,100 | 5,600 |
| Chargeable gain/ (capital loss) | (3,000) | - | - | 9,500 | - |
| Gift Aid payments | (1,600) | (1,400) | (800) | (1,200) | (1,100) |

There was a trading loss brought forward at 1 July 2005 of £2,000.

Loser Ltd does not have any associated companies.

> (a) **Assuming that Loser Ltd claims relief for its losses as early as possible, compute the company's PCTCT for the five accounting periods to 31 March 2010.**
>
> Your answer should clearly identify the amount of any losses that are unrelieved.
>
> (b) **Explain how your answer to (a) above would have differed if Loser Ltd had ceased trading on 31 March 2010.**

## 3 Choice of loss reliefs

### Factors to consider

The following factors will influence the loss relief chosen:

- Tax saving
- Cash flow
- Wastage of Gift Aid relief

### Tax saving

The company will want to save (or get a refund at) the highest rate of tax.

The effective corporation tax rates for profits in the margin for FY2007 to FY2009 are as follows:

| Level of profits | Effective rate | | | Ranking |
|---|---|---|---|---|
| | FY2007 | FY2008 | FY2009 | |
| Up to £300,000 | 20% | 21% | 21% | 3rd |
| £300,001 to £1,499,999 | 32.5% | 29.75% | 29.75% | 1st |
| £1,500,000 + | 30% | 28% | 28% | 2nd |

### Cash flow

A company's cash flow position may affect its choice of loss relief.

A company may be prepared to accept loss relief at a lower marginal rate, if it results in an earlier receipt of cash.

Note that when a loss is carried back, it will lead to a repayment of tax for the earlier period.

### Example 2 – Choice of loss relief

Lion Ltd prepares its accounts to 31 March 2008 but has since changed to a 30 September accounting date, and prepared a set of accounts to 30 September 2008.

The company has suffered declining results in recent years, and is therefore planning to restructure its business operations during September 2009 by closing three branches of its business, and disposing of the related assets which will lead to gains of £100,000.

You should assume that today's date is 1 August 2009.

Lion Ltd forecasts a substantial tax adjusted trading loss for the current year to 30 September 2009 of £300,000. A small trading profit is forecast for the following year to 30 September 2010, with steadily increasing profits thereafter.

The company's tax adjusted trading profits for recent years have been:

| | |
|---|---|
| Year ended 31 March 2008 | £550,000 |
| Period ended 30 September 2008 | £70,000 |

(i) **Advise Lion Ltd as to which loss relief claims would be the most beneficial.**

(ii) **Advise Lion Ltd as to whether it would be beneficial for tax purposes to delay its restructuring until after 30 September 2009.**

**Solution**

(i) **Most beneficial loss relief claims**

Lion Ltd is forecasting only small trading profits for the near future and is likely only to be paying tax at 21%.

The rate of tax applicable in year ended 30 September 2009 and the period ended 30 September 2008 will be 21%.

However, for the year ended 31 March 2008, marginal relief will apply and the profits are taxed at the marginal rate of 32.5%.

If the company makes a claim against current year profits and then carries it back twelve months, the loss and rate of tax saving will be as follows:

| y/e 31.03.08 | p/e 30.09.08 | y/e 30.09.09 | y/e 30.09.10 |
|---|---|---|---|
| £130,000 (Note) | £70,000 | £100,000 | Nil |
| 32.5% | 21% | 21% | |

**Note:** The full loss can be used against 6/12 of the profit for the year ended 31 March 2008 which is a maximum of £275,000 (6/12 × £550,000).

However, there is only £130,000 of the loss remaining to carry back into this period, so all of the loss can be offset. If Lion Ltd had excess losses, extended relief would be available to carry an additional £50,000 (max) back for 36 months (i.e. a further 24 months).

## Delay of restructuring

If Lion Ltd delays its restructuring until after 30 September 2009, the gains of £100,000 will fall into the year ended 30 September 2010. Given the expected low level of other profit, the gains are likely to be taxed at 21%.

This will allow a further £100,000 of the loss to be carried back into year ended 31 March 2008.

All of the £230,000 loss can be offset in that year as it is below £275,000 (Note above).

A claim for £230,000 relief will save tax at 32.5% as even with the loss relief, the company's PCTCT for that year will be £320,000 (£550,000 – £230,000) which exceeds the lower limit of £300,000.

The higher rate of tax saving on the loss will be more than the extra tax payable on the gains in the year ended 30 September 2010. Accordingly, the company should delay its restructuring if possible.

## Test your understanding 2

Crocus Ltd has the following results.

| Year ended: | 31.3.09 | 31.3.10 | 31.3.11 (estimated) |
| --- | --- | --- | --- |
| | £ | £ | £ |
| Trading profit/(loss) | 340,000 | (150,000) | 300,000 |
| Property income | 14,000 | 25,000 | 28,000 |
| Chargeable gains / (capital loss) | Nil | 40,000 | (15,000) |
| Gift Aid payments | 3,000 | 3,000 | 3,000 |

The directors wish to relieve their losses as efficiently as possible.

**Advise the directors which loss claim or combination of claims will achieve their objective and quantify the tax saving and any repayments due.**

Assume that you are advising the directors in December 2010.

## 4 Restrictions on loss relief

### Introduction

In order to prevent avoidance of tax, there are restrictions on the carry forward or carry back of trading losses when there is a change in the ownership of a company.

### Change in ownership

A change in ownership means that more than one half of the ordinary share capital of the company is acquired by a person, or persons, ignoring any person acquiring 5% or less.

For example, an individual shareholder owns 10% of the shares and purchases a further 60% making his total holding 70%. As more than half (in this case 60%) of the shares have changed hands then this is a change in ownership.

### Restrictions

The restrictions apply in two situations:

- where there is **both** a **change in ownership** and a **major change** in the **nature or conduct of the trade** within a period of **three years** (see below); or

- when **at any time** after the scale of **activities** of the trade has become **small or negligible**, and before any considerable revival of the trade, there is a change in the ownership of the company.

The **three-year period,** where there is a major change in the nature or conduct of trade, can be either **before or after** the change of ownership.

The restrictions prevent:

- losses from before the change in ownership from being carried forward against profits arising after the change in ownership,

- losses incurred after the date of change of ownership from being carried back before the change of ownership.

## Major change in the nature or conduct of the trade

It is important to understand that the trade itself has not changed, just the nature or conduct of trade. Major changes include:

- a major change in the type of property dealt in or services provided; and

- a major change in customers, outlets or markets.

### Test your understanding 3

All the share capital of H Ltd has recently been acquired by Richard. H Ltd manufactures mobile phone accessories which it sells to large retailers. H Ltd has made heavy losses for the last two years. Richard wants to make the following changes to the company over the next three years.

- Relocate most of the manufacturing activity overseas.

- Expand the company's product range.

- Start to sell direct to the public over the internet.

- Appoint two new sales directors.

**State the effect these changes are likely to have on the company's corporation tax loss position.**

## 5 Chapter summary

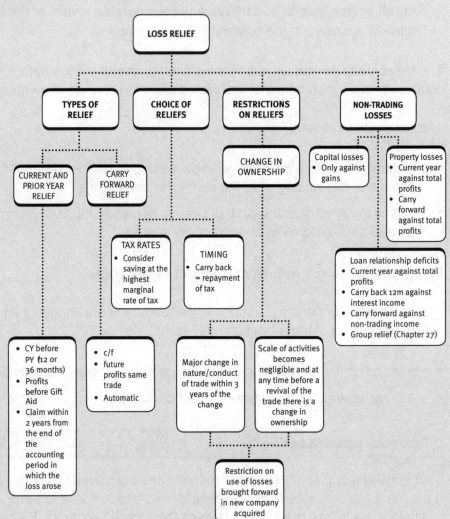

# Test your understanding answers

## Test your understanding 1

### Loser Ltd

(a) **Loser Ltd – Profits chargeable to corporation tax**

| | y/e 30.06.06 £ | y/e 30.06.07 £ | p/e 31.03.08 £ | y/e 31.03.09 £ | y/e 31.03.10 £ |
|---|---|---|---|---|---|
| Trading profit | 95,400 | 56,600 | Nil | 27,300 | Nil |
| Less: Loss b/f | (2,000) | - | - | - | - |
| Property income | 7,100 | - | 4,500 | 8,100 | 5,600 |
| Net chargeable gain | - | - | - | 6,500 | - |
| Total profits | 100,500 | 56,600 | 4,500 | 41,900 | 5,600 |
| Less: Loss relief | | | | | |
| – Current year | | | (4,500) | | (5,600) |
| – Carry back 12 mths | | (21,200) | | (41,900) | |
| – Extended carry back (Max £50,000) | (14,600) | (35,400) | - | | |
| | 85,900 | Nil | Nil | Nil | Nil |
| Less: Gift Aid | (1,600) | Wasted | Wasted | Wasted | Wasted |
| PCTCT | 84,300 | Nil | Nil | Nil | Nil |

### Notes

- The balance of the trading loss for the period ended 31 March 2008 of £21,200 (£25,700 – £4,500) is carried back to the year ended 30 June 2007.

- The amount of unrelieved trading loss for the year ended 31 March 2010 is £8,400 (£105,900 – £5,600 – £41,900 – £35,400 – £14,600). This is available to carry forward against future trading profits of the same trade

- There is no restriction to the amount of loss relief for the year ended 31 March 2009 as this is within the normal 12 month carry back period.

- For the year ended 30 June 2006 loss relief is limited to £14,600 (£50,000 – £35,400) being the balance of the £50,000 limit. This is less than the maximum possible relief of £25,125 (£100,500 x 3/12) or the loss remaining of £23,000.

(b) **If Loser Ltd ceased to trade on 31 March 2010**

- The trading loss of the final 12 months could be relieved against total profits for the previous 36 months.
- Relief for the trading loss of the last 12 months of £105,900 would have been given in exactly the same way except that the relief for the year ended 30 June 2006 would have been £23,000 instead of £14,600, since the £50,000 limit would not then apply.

### Test your understanding 2

**Crocus Ltd**

- The capital loss must be carried forward for offset against future chargeable gains. It may not be set against income and it cannot be carried back.

- Relieving losses as efficiently as possible means the trading loss must be relieved to save the maximum amount of tax. This means that, where possible, the loss should be relieved against profits taxed at the marginal rate.

- In the y/e 31 March 2010 the company is paying tax at the SCR of 21%. However, in the y/e 31 March 2009 and 2011 marginal relief applies (W1).

- In order to relieve the marginal profits of the y/e 31 March 2009, the company must first claim against the profits of 2010.

  This uses £65,000 of the loss leaving £85,000 to be carried back.

  The tax saving with current year and carryback claims is:

| | Loss used £ | Tax rate (W1) | Tax saving £ |
|---|---|---|---|
| y/e 31 March 2010 | 65,000 | 21% | |
| (£65,000 – £3,000) × 21% | | | 13,020 |
| y/e 31 March 2009 | 51,000 | 29.75% | 15,172 |
| | 34,000 | 21% | 7,140 |
| | | | ———— |
| Total saving | | | 35,332 |
| | | | ———— |

- If all the loss is carried forward, the saving is:

|  | Loss used £ | Tax rate (W1) | Tax saving £ |
|---|---|---|---|
| y/e 31 March 2011 | 25,000 | 29.75% | 7,438 |
|  | 125,000 | 21% | 26,250 |
| Total saving |  |  | 33,688 |

- If a current year claim is made, but not the carryback claim, so that the remaining loss is carried forward the tax saving would be:

|  | Loss used £ | Tax rate (W1) | Tax saving £ |
|---|---|---|---|
| y/e 31 March 2010 | 65,000 | 21% |  |
| (as above) |  |  | 13,020 |
| y/e 31 March 2011 | 25,000 | 29.75% | 7,438 |
|  | 60,000 | 21% | 12,600 |
| Total saving |  |  | 33,058 |

**Conclusion**

The directors should claim relief in the loss making year and carry back the loss to y/e 31 March 2009 as it gives the highest tax saving.

This also gives earliest relief and will lead to a repayment of tax for the year ended 31 March 2009 of £22,312 (£15,172 + £7,140) or (£78,172 (W1) – £55,860(W2)).

## Workings

### (W1) Corporation tax payable before loss relief

| Year ended | 31.03.09 | 31.03.10 | 31.03.11 |
|---|---|---|---|
| | £ | £ | £ |
| Trading profit | 340,000 | Nil | 300,000 |
| Property income | 14,000 | 25,000 | 28,000 |
| Chargeable gains | Nil | 40,000 | Nil |
| | 354,000 | 65,000 | 328,000 |
| Gift Aid | (3,000) | (3,000) | (3,000) |
| PCTCT | 351,000 | 62,000 | 325,000 |
| Status | Marginal | Small | Marginal |
| | £ | £ | £ |
| CT at 28%/21%/28% | 98,280 | 13,020 | 91,000 |
| Less Marginal relief | | | |
| 7/400 × (£1,500,000 – £351,000) | (20,108) | | |
| 7/400 × (£1,500,000 – £325,000) | | | (20,563) |
| CT payable before relief | 78,172 | 13,020 | 70,437 |

## (W2) Corporation tax payable after recommended claims

| Year ended | 31.03.09 | 31.03.10 | 31.03.11 |
|---|---|---|---|
| | £ | £ | £ |
| Trading profit | 340,000 | Nil | 300,000 |
| Property income | 14,000 | 25,000 | 28,000 |
| Chargeable gains | Nil | 40,000 | Nil |
| | ——— | ——— | ——— |
| Total profits | 354,000 | 65,000 | 328,000 |
| Less: Loss relief | (85,000) | (65,000) | |
| | ——— | ——— | ——— |
| | 269,000 | Nil | 328,000 |
| Gift Aid | (3,000) | Wasted | (3,000) |
| | ——— | ——— | ——— |
| PCTCT | 266,000 | Nil | 325,000 |
| | ——— | ——— | ——— |
| Status | Small | Small | Marginal |
| | £ | £ | £ |
| CT at 21%/28% | 55,860 | Nil | 91,000 |
| Less Marginal relief | | | |
| (as above) | | | (20,563) |
| | ——— | ——— | ——— |
| CT payable after relief | 55,860 | Nil | 70,437 |
| | ——— | ——— | ——— |

Note there is no repayment of tax for the year ended 31 March 2010 as the tax is not due for payment until 1 January 2011.

---

### Test your understanding 3

#### H Ltd

The changes that Richard proposes are likely to be taken by HMRC as a major change in the nature or conduct of H Ltd's trade.

As the changes occur within three years of Richard buying the company (a change in ownership) they will have the result of disallowing H Ltd's loss relief.

Losses will no longer be available to carry forward against profits arising after the change in ownership.

# 25

# Business financial management

## Chapter learning objectives

Upon completion of this chapter you will be able to:

- discuss the methods of financing a business by means of investment by individuals and other corporate bodies, and explain the impact for tax of these various methods, including the effect on the investor and the business that is raising the finance

- compare the different methods of financing the fixed assets of a business from a tax and commercial viewpoint

- describe the various methods available to defer or reduce tax liabilities for an individual or a business.

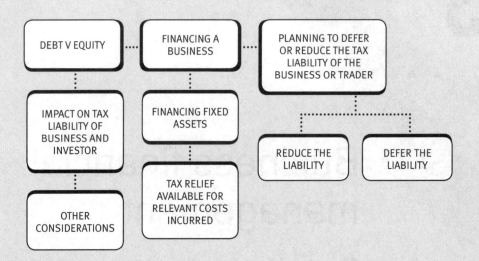

## 1 Introduction

This chapter deals with the way in which a company can raise finance, and financing for a sole trader or partnership. Fixed asset financing is also considered.

The tax implications and other commercial considerations that should be borne in mind when deciding how to finance the business are discussed.

## 2 Business finance

### Financing a company – long term finance

A company can raise long-term finance to fund its activities from two main sources:

- Shareholders (Equity).

- Third party loan finance, sometimes by way of an issue of loan stock or debentures (Debt).

The effect of each of these is different from the company's perspective.

However, the requirements of the investors also need to be taken into account, and these will vary depending on whether they are individuals or other companies.

The main considerations for the company will then be:

- funding the interest or dividends that will be required

- what security will be required by the lenders – they may require a charge on the assets which would be exercised if the company failed to meet its obligations with regard to income and/or capital repayments.

## Comparison between the use of equity or debt

A summary of the main differences between using these two methods of finance is as follows:

| | Equity | Debt |
|---|---|---|
| Amount | The maximum issued share capital is<br><br>• specified in the Articles when the company is formed<br><br>• usually well in excess of what it is anticipated the company will need. | There is no limit to the amount of finance that can be raised in debt, other than the amount the investors are prepared to invest. |
| Return | Dividends<br><br>• The company must have distributable profits to pay a dividend.<br><br>• The dividend payment is not allowable for corporation tax. | Interest<br><br>• Interest can be paid irrespective of the company's profitability.<br><br>• It is deductible on an accruals basis.<br><br>• Interest is paid net of 20% tax if it is paid to an individual.<br><br>• Companies receive interest gross. |
| Corporate Investors | • No CT on dividends received. | • Interest income (on an accruals basis) = part of PCTCT. |
| Individual Investors | • A basic rate taxpayer<br>– no liability on UK dividends received.<br><br>• A higher rate taxpayer<br>– additional tax to pay. | • A basic rate tax payer<br>– no further liability as interest paid net of 20% tax<br><br>• A higher rate payer<br>– further liability to pay. |

| | Equity | Debt |
|---|---|---|
| Other points | • Companies that are not listed on the Stock Exchange may find it difficult to raise finance with a new issue of shares.<br><br>• However, for an owner managed business the existing shareholders may not be prepared to accept outside shareholders that could dilute their control of the company.<br><br>• In this case new share issues will probably be to existing shareholders and their family members. | • A lender may require a charge on assets as security for the debt.<br><br>• If the company defaults on either the interest or the capital that charge can be called in, and the assets of the company sold to finance the outstanding amounts. |

### Example 1 – Debt vs Equity

M Ltd is a trading company set up a number of years ago with 1,000 £1 ordinary shares issued at par. In order to expand the production facilities it needs to raise a further £50,000.

There are **two** possibilities:

(1) The company will issue a further 50,000 5% preference shares, which have a nominal value of £1 and a market value of £1 each.

(2) £50,000 loan stock will be issued at par. It will carry interest of 5% payable annually.

(a) **Calculate the retained profit for the year ended 31 December 2009 on the assumption that:**

- **the shares or loan stock will be issued on 1 January 2009**

- **a full year's preference dividend will be paid in the year**

- **no dividend is paid on the ordinary shares in the year**

- **the profit before interest, tax and dividends is £150,000.**

(b) **Calculate the net return for the investor on the assumption that:**

- **the investor is a company that pays tax at 28%**

- **the investor is an individual who is a higher rate taxpayer.**

**Solution**

(a) **Retained profit – y/e 31 December 2009**

| | Equity £ | Debt £ |
|---|---|---|
| Profit | 150,000 | 150,000 |
| Less: Interest (5% × £50,000) | | (2,500) |
| | 150,000 | 147,500 |
| Less: CT at 21% | (31,500) | (30,975) |
| | 118,500 | 116,525 |
| Less: Dividend (5% × £50,000) | (2,500) | |
| Retained profit | 116,000 | 116,525 |

(b) **Return for the investor**

**Individual**

| | | |
|---|---|---|
| Dividend received (£2,500 × 100/90) | 2,778 | |
| Interest received (£2,000 × 100/80) | | 2,500 |
| IT at 32.5% on dividend | 903 | |
| IT at 40% on interest | | 1,000 |
| IT credit 10%/20% | (278) | (500) |
| IT payable | 625 | 500 |
| Net income: | | |
| Dividend (£2,500 – £625) | 1,875 | |
| Interest (£2,000 – £500) | | 1,500 |

**Company**

| | | |
|---|---|---|
| Dividend received | 2,500 | |
| Interest received | | 2,500 |
| CT at 28% | Nil | (700) |
| After tax income | 2,500 | 1,800 |

## Incentives to invest in shares

Where the issuing company meets certain conditions their shares may be issued under special schemes that allow the investor tax relief on the investment, and/or when the shares are sold.

The most important of these are:

|  |  | Chapter | Applies to |
| --- | --- | --- | --- |
| Enterprise Investment Scheme | EIS | 3 and 9 | Individuals |
| Venture Capital Trusts | VCT | 3 | Individuals |
| Corporate Venturing Scheme | CVS | 22 | Companies |
| Substantial Shareholding Exemption | SSE | 23 | Companies |

If the investment is wholly by way of equity, no return can be received by the investing company until the company becomes profitable. Interest can always be paid.

As a result a company may well invest using a mix of debt and equity, especially where they are investing in a new company, which may not yet have distributable profits, as no dividend can be paid until the company becomes profitable.

## Financing a sole trader or partnership

There are two main sources of finance for unincorporated businesses (i.e. where the business is owned by the individual sole trader or partners in a partnership):

- the individuals themselves
- loans from banks and other financial institutions.

**Financing by the individuals:**

- An individual may have funds that they can invest in the business.
- If they are sole traders there is no interest charged as they are entitled to all of the profits of the business.
- In a partnership the profit sharing arrangements would reflect the amount invested by each partner in the business.

**Financing from a loan:**

- A bank may be prepared to lend money to an individual to invest in their business. Interest relief is available on this borrowing where it is to acquire fixed assets, in the year of purchase and the following three years.

- Relief is also available where an individual borrows money to invest in a partnership, of which they are a partner.

- Many sole traders rely on short term financing such as bank overdrafts. The interest is deducted from the business profits as an expense.

- Most lenders will require some form of personal guarantee before they will lend money or allow an overdraft facility to a sole trader or partnership. If the business fails the individual will then be responsible for repaying the debt from their personal resources.

## Short term finance

Sources of short-term finance are:

- bank overdraft – interest allowed as a deduction from trading profits

- short term loans – as for debt except interest is paid gross to individuals and companies

- trade credit – not utilising cash balances to pay for purchases increases a credit balance or reduces the overdraft

- invoice discounting

- debt factoring

- HP and leasing.

Invoice discounting is where a company sells its debtors to a factor who pays them an amount after deducting a service charge. The company will have to reimburse the money if the debt becomes irrecoverable.

Debt factoring is where the company sells its debt outright, and the debt factors take the risk of bad debts. The cost charged to the company is usually higher than where they use invoice discounting.

## Summary

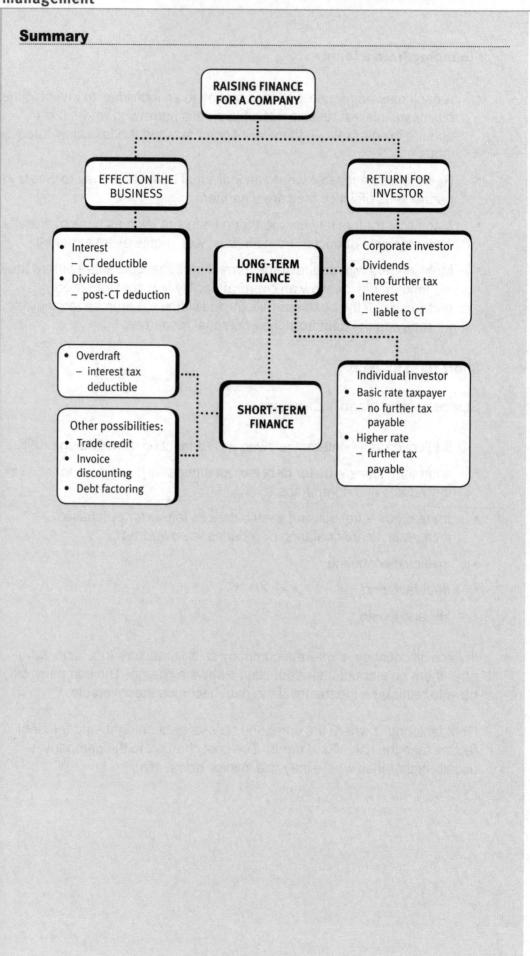

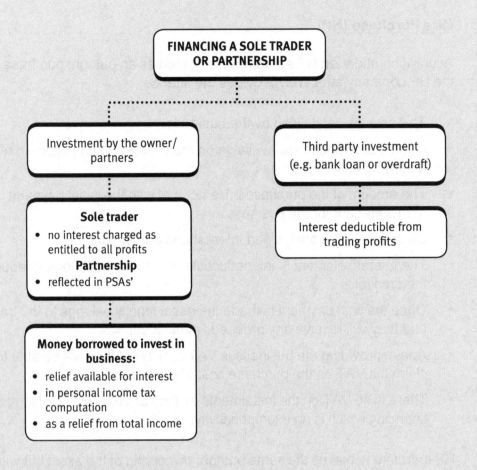

## 3 Financing fixed assets

### Introduction

Most businesses will require the use of fixed assets to function efficiently.

There are three main ways of financing the purchase:

- Outright purchase.
- Hire purchase.
- Leasing.

### Outright purchase

If the asset is bought by the business from its existing resources:

- Many of these assets will qualify for capital allowances, with businesses entitled to the AIA in the year of purchase (Chapters 17 and 18).

- The initial cost has to be met up front but the trader will receive the proceeds of sale when the asset is sold.

- VAT will be recoverable providing the business is registered and it is not irrecoverable VAT (e.g. cars).

### Hire Purchase (HP)

Acquisition under an HP agreement is treated as an outright purchase but the HP company effectively provides the finance.

- The asset is capitalised by the business.

- Capital allowances are available on the cost (excluding interest) of the qualifying assets.

- The amount of the purchase price not met with the initial payment is then a creditor for the business.

- Each instalment paid is part interest and part capital.

- The interest element is tax deductible, and the capital portion reduces the creditor.

- Once the final payment is made the asset legally belongs to the trader, and they will receive any proceeds of disposal.

- Again, providing the business is VAT registered they will be able to claim the VAT on the purchase cost of the asset.

- There is no VAT on the instalments as they are effectively relating to financing which is an exempt activity.

HP therefore achieves the same outright ownership of the asset but without the up-front cost. The overall cost will be greater as the interest has to be paid but it is spread over the period of the HP contract.

### Leasing

Where an asset is leased:

- The business pays a rent, which is deductible for tax purposes.

- The relief is given when the payments are debited to the profit and loss account, and these are spread using the normal accounting principles.

- The asset returns to the leasing company at the end of the lease. Accordingly, there are
  - no proceeds of sale
  - no problems trying to find a buyer when the asset is no longer required.

- VAT is recovered by a VAT registered business.

- Where the asset is a car there is a restriction on the tax relief available on the rental payments if $CO_2$ emissions exceed 160g/km. In addition, usually only 50% of the VAT can be reclaimed on any car lease payments.

## Summary

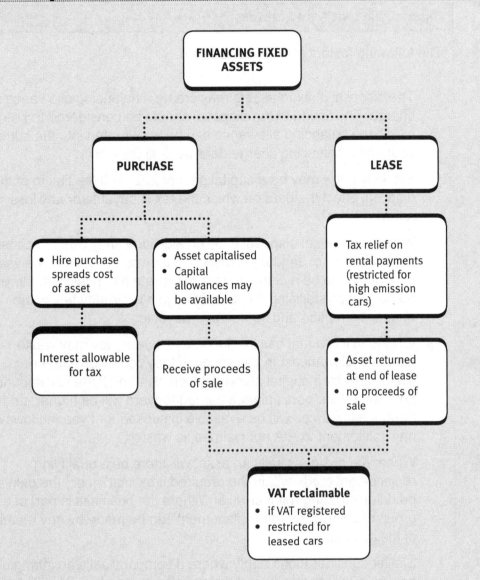

## 4 Deferring or reducing the tax liability of a business

There are a number of ways of reducing or deferring a tax liability incurred by a business.

For a quoted company it is necessary to also consider the effect of these measures on the company's net profit as this will affect their ability to pay dividends, and possibly their share price.

Factors to consider have been covered in detail in earlier chapters. A reminder of the key factors to consider is given in expandable text and the considerations are summarised in the diagram in the chapter summary.

## Expandable text – Key factors

The following factors may be considered:

- The disposal of fixed assets may create a balancing allowance or charge. The timing of the disposal should be considered to see whether a balancing allowance can be accelerated into the current year and a balancing charge delayed until the next.

- Similarly there may be a capital gain or loss. Will the timing of the disposal affect the date on which the tax is payable or any loss relieved?

- Where the capital disposal is by an individual they need to consider the availability of annual exemption. If they have a gain in the year, and there is to be a disposal that will create a capital loss, there is no point in crystallising the loss if the gain is already below the annual exemption and so no tax is payable.

- Where an individual has low income in a year they may waste personal allowances. In this situation they could consider not claiming all their capital allowances entitlement. If the full amount is not claimed the pool balance carried forward will be higher, and so greater allowances will be available in subsequent years. However, any entitlement to AIA not claimed, is wasted.

- Where the business sells an asset will there be a qualifying replacement made within the required time limit? If so, the gain can be deferred using rollover relief. Where the business is part of a group of companies the replacement can be made by any member of the gains group.

- Similar considerations apply where a company sells an intangible asset (usually goodwill) and replaces it with a further intangible asset. For an individual goodwill is included in the assets on which rollover relief is available.

- EIS Investment Relief reduces the current year's income tax liability. However, it is difficult to withdraw from an EIS investment as they are unquoted shares. In addition, EIS companies tend not to pay dividends and retain their profits to increase the gain on disposal, as the gain should be exempt if the conditions are met.

- An investment in EIS shares may allow a gain on another disposal to be deferred. It will become chargeable when the EIS shares are sold.

- VCTs are a better investment in this context as they will pay dividends, and because they are quoted companies it should be possible to realise the investment when needed. However, they are considered to be a risky investment and should not be used by someone who cannot afford to lose their investment as they are relying on it to fund their lifestyle or retirement.

## 5 Chapter summary

```
┌─────────────┐     ┌─────────────┐     ┌─────────────────┐
│   COMPANY   │·····│ FINANCING THE│·····│  SOLE TRADER/   │
│             │     │   BUSINESS  │     │   PARTNERSHIP   │
└─────────────┘     └─────────────┘     └─────────────────┘
       :                   :                    :
┌─────────────┐     ┌─────────────┐     ┌─────────────────┐
│ Equity v debt│     │ FIXED ASSETS│     │Personal v third party│
│             │     │             │     │   investment    │
└─────────────┘     └─────────────┘     └─────────────────┘
       :                   :
┌─────────────┐     ┌─────────────┐
│Impact on company│  │ Lease or buy?│
│ and investor │     │             │
└─────────────┘     └─────────────┘
```

**PLANNING ISSUES**

**DEFERRING LIABILITIES**

- Altering the timing of a disposal can affect when balancing allowances and gains/losses are recognised
- Gains on certain asset sales can be deferred if a qualifying reinvestment occurs in the specified time limit

Quoted companies must also consider impact on reported profits and ability to pay dividends

**REDUCING LIABILITIES**

- Crystallising a capital loss for an individual in a year when the other net gains are below the AE is not tax efficient as they save no tax

- Individual may not claim full capital allowances if income below personal allowance
- Higher allowances will be available in later years
- Could lead to wasting AIA

- Qualifying investment can allow deferral of gains on asset disposals

**EIS**
- Qualifying investment reduces IT liability for investors
- Disposal may be CGT exempt

**VCT**
- Qualifying investment reduces IT liability for investors
- Dividends received not taxable
- Disposal may be CGT exempt

**CVS**
- Reduces CT payable by investing company

# Family companies and related planning scenarios

## Chapter learning objectives

Upon completion of this chapter you will be able to:

- describe the various business vehicles available to individuals who want to start their own business

- identify companies that may fall within the close company regime, and set-out the implications for the company and its shareholders

- discuss the different ways of extracting profits from a company, identifying the various tax issues that may arise

- identify personal service companies (PSC) and advise on the tax consequences of the company being treated as a PSC

- discuss the various methods available to shareholders who wish to withdraw their investment from a company.

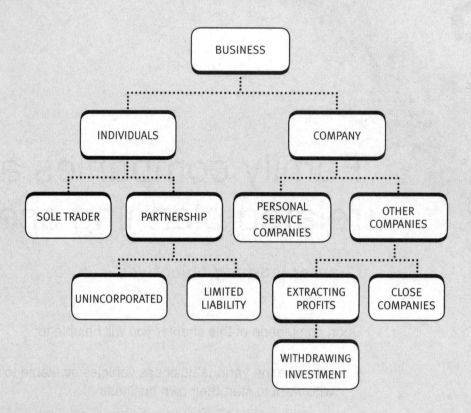

## 1 Introduction

This chapter considers multi-tax scenarios from a business aspect and introduces tax planning measures to minimise tax liabilities.

Much of the content of this chapter is covered in more detail in other chapters. However, this chapter aims to show how various ideas and taxes interact and form the basis of multi-tax scenario examination questions.

Areas covered in this chapter which primarily draw from previous knowledge include:

- Choosing the appropriate business vehicle when starting to trade.
- Extracting profits from a company.

The new areas at P6 introduced in this chapter include:

- Close companies.
- Personal service companies.
- Exit strategies such as the purchase of own shares by a company and putting the company into liquidation.

## 2 Business vehicle

### Introduction

When an individual decides to start their own business, one of the most important factors they have to consider is how they should own it.

Direct ownership will be as sole trader, or if there is more than one person involved, a partnership.

The alternative is to set up a limited company, and own the assets through the company. The individuals involved will then be shareholders and (probably) directors of the company.

Each method has its own tax implications.

The main areas that need to be considered are:

- What amounts does the individual pay tax on?
- Is there a liability to NIC?
- When is any tax payable?
- Any other commercial considerations.

### Summary of differences

The differences between operating as an unincorporated business or as a company can broadly be summarised as follows:

| | **Sole trader** | **Company** |
|---|---|---|
| Taxation of profits | Trading profit assessed on a current year basis under income tax rules.<br><br>Adjustments for private use.<br><br><br><br><br>Capital allowances with private use adjustments.<br><br>Personal allowance.<br><br>Tax at:<br>20%/40%.<br><br>Class 4 NICs<br>= 8% of profits (£5,715 to £43,875) and 1% thereafter.<br><br>Class 2 NICs<br>= £2.40 per week | Corporation tax on PCTCT – after the individual has paid themselves a salary.<br><br>No adjustments for private use when calculating trading profit – instead the individual is taxed on benefits received.<br><br>Capital allowances in full (no private use adjustments).<br><br>No personal allowance.<br><br>Tax at:<br>21% (small companies rate)<br>28% (full rate). |
| Relief for losses | Relief available against total income.<br><br>Opening years relief – loss in any of first four tax years, set against total income of 3 preceding tax years (FIFO).<br><br>Relief against total income of current/previous tax year/extended carry back against trading profit.<br><br>C/fwd against trading profit of same trade. | Loss relieved against company's profits only.<br><br>Current year – set against total profits of current CAP.<br><br>Prior year – set against total profits of previous 12 months/36 months.<br><br>C/fwd – against future trading profits of same trade. |

|  | **Sole trader** | **Company** |
|---|---|---|
| Withdrawal of funds | No tax implications<br><br>– all profits assessed on the individual as trading profit. | Salary/Bonus<br><br>• Employment income for individual.<br><br>• Allowable deduction for the company.<br><br>• Class 1 primary NIC for employee.<br><br>• Class 1 secondary NIC for company (allowable deduction).<br><br>Dividend<br><br>• UK dividend income for individual, grossed up at 100/90.<br><br>• Tax at 10%/32½% with 10% tax credit (i.e. no extra tax unless higher rate taxpayer).<br><br>• Dividends not an allowable deduction from trading profit for a company.<br><br>• Company must have distributable profit. |
| VAT | Individual registers. | Company registers. |
| Disposal of business | Gains on individual chargeable assets:<br><br>• Gains are business assets:<br> – for Gifts relief<br> – for Entrepreneurs' relief if disposal of the entire business.<br><br>IHT – 100% BPR on gift/legacy. | Gain on shares:<br><br>• Shares in an unquoted trading company will usually be business assets.<br><br>• Gifts relief if shares gifted.<br><br>• Entrepreneurs' relief on disposal.<br><br>IHT – 100% BPR on gift/legacy. |

## Considerations when choosing the relevant structure

Intention to withdraw profits:

- A sole trader is required to pay tax on the profits made, not the amount drawn out of the business.

- Where it is not intended to withdraw all the profits, and the company is paying tax at 21%, it will probably be more advantageous to operate as a company, allowing the retained profits to be taxed at the lower rate.

### Initial losses

- If the business will start with losses it may be preferable to structure it initially as a sole trader, allowing the losses to be used against the owner's personal income.

- Once the business becomes profitable, it may be incorporated if a company is the preferred structure.

### Liability

- Where liability is an issue, a company will probably be preferred as a company structure will limit the individual's potential liability.

- However, it should be remembered that some businesses are not allowed to incorporate. In this case a Limited Liability Partnership (LLP) may be used.

### Limited liability partnership

- An LLP is taxed in the same way as an unincorporated partnership, with each partner paying tax on their share of the profits.

- Each partner's liability is limited to their investment in the LLP. However, each partner has no limit to their liability for the work that they are responsible for.

## Summary

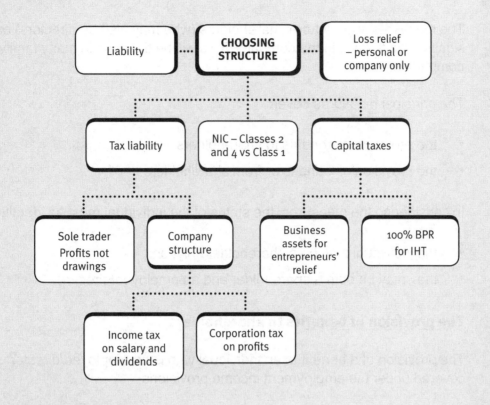

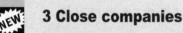

## 3 Close companies

### Definition of a close company

Many 'Owner Managed Businesses' will be close companies.

A close company is a company controlled by either:

- any number of directors; or
- five or fewer participators.

A participator is primarily a shareholder.

To decide whether a group of individuals has control of the company it is necessary to include the shares of their associates.

Associates are taken to be the spouse, children and issue, parents and remoter ancestors, brothers and sisters.

A company which is a subsidiary takes its status from the holding company. So, if the holding company is a close company, the subsidiary is a close company.

## Implications of close company status

The measures apply where shareholders (who may also be directors) have significant influence in the company. This will be the case in many family companies.

The principal measures cover:

* the provision of benefits to shareholders
* the provision of loans to or from shareholders.

In considering the measures, the status of the individual must be identified.

* the individual may be a shareholder only, or
* they may be both a shareholder and an employee/director.

## The provision of benefits to shareholders

The provision of a benefit to an individual who is an employee/director is covered under the employment income provisions.

* For the company, the cost of providing the benefit is an allowable expense and reduces trading profits.
* For the individual, the benefit is calculated using employment income rules.

The tax implications for the company and the individual shareholder of the provision of a benefit to a shareholder (or his associate) who is not an employee/director are as follows:

| Individual (shareholder) | Company |
|---|---|
| No employment income charge possible as no office or employment. | The company is deemed to have paid a dividend. |
| The value of the benefit is treated as a **net** dividend. | The **amount** (i.e. value) of the dividend is determined using the benefit rules. |
| This will be grossed up × 100/90 and taxed in the year the benefit is provided.<br><br>Dividend income is taxed at the rate of 10% if the individual is a basic rate taxpayer, or 32.5% if higher rate.<br><br>The tax credit on dividends is not repayable. | No trading profit deduction for the cost of providing the benefit as it is treated as a dividend. |

**Test your understanding 1**

Malcolm and Helen are shareholders of Houghton Ltd, a close trading company. Malcolm is also a director.

Houghton Ltd provided each of them during the current accounting period with a petrol engine company car, list price £20,000 and a $CO_2$ emission rate of 191 gms/km. They each travel 5,000 miles; 3,000 miles of Malcolm's mileage is on company business. The company does not pay for private petrol.

Houghton Ltd is a profitable company paying tax at 21% in its year ended 31 March 2010.

**Explain the taxation implication on the company and the individuals.**

## The provision of a loan to a shareholder

The provision of a loan to a shareholder, irrespective of employment status, has the following implications:

**For the company**

- There is a tax charge of 25% of the amount of the loan.

- This charge is paid at the same time as the mainstream corporation tax (i.e. 9 months and one day after the end of the accounting period).

- No tax is payable if the loan has been repaid before that due date.

- Where the tax charge has been paid, it becomes repayable when:

  (1) the loan is repaid:

      – where part of the loan is repaid a proportion of the tax is repayable

  (2) the loan is written off:

      – the company can reclaim the tax paid when the loan was made.

      – there is no deduction for the write-off against the company's profits for CT purposes.

      – at this point the individual becomes liable for tax (see below).

- No tax is payable by the company where the loan fulfils three requirements:

  (1) The amount of the loan is less than or equal to £15,000, and

  (2) The individual is a full-time working employee, and

(3) The individual (including associates' interests) owns less than 5% of the shares.

**For the shareholder**

- There are no immediate tax implications for the individual when the company makes them a loan.

- If the loan is written off, they then become taxable on the amount written off as though it was a dividend received at the date of the write-off.

**Interest**

Where the company does not charge interest of at least the official rate, (currently 4.75%, there will be an assesable benefit. The rules for the provision of benefits apply (see above).

- For an employee, this benefit will be taxed as earnings.

- Where the individual is not an employee, the benefit will be treated as a dividend distribution.

### Test your understanding 2

Sally and Claire are both shareholders and full time employees in White Ltd, a close company. The company prepares its accounts to 31 March annually.

Sally owns 15% of the company, whilst Claire owns 3%. They are not connected with each other. The company lends each of them £10,000, on 6 April 2009. Claire repays £4,000 on 31 December 2009. Interest of 2% is charged on the loans.

The official rate of interest is 4.75%.

**Explain the taxation implications for both White Ltd and its employees Sally and Claire.**

## The provision of loans from shareholders to the close company

A shareholder may take out a personal loan in order to make a loan to or buy shares in a close company.

Income tax relief on interest paid on such borrowing is available as a relief deducted from total income.

The conditions are that the individual:

- has a material interest (more than 5%) in the company, or
- is a full-time working officer or employee involved in the management of the company.

## Close investment holding company (CIC)

All close companies are close investment companies (CIC) unless their main activity is trading, or letting property to unconnected persons.

The tax consequences of a CIC are as follows:

- CIC's are required to pay corporation tax at the full rate (i.e. 28%), irrespective of the level of their profits.
- The shares will not be treated as business assets for both IHT and CGT.
- Tax relief will not be available to an individual if they borrow money to invest in a CIC.

## Summary

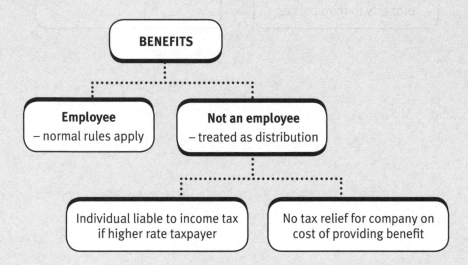

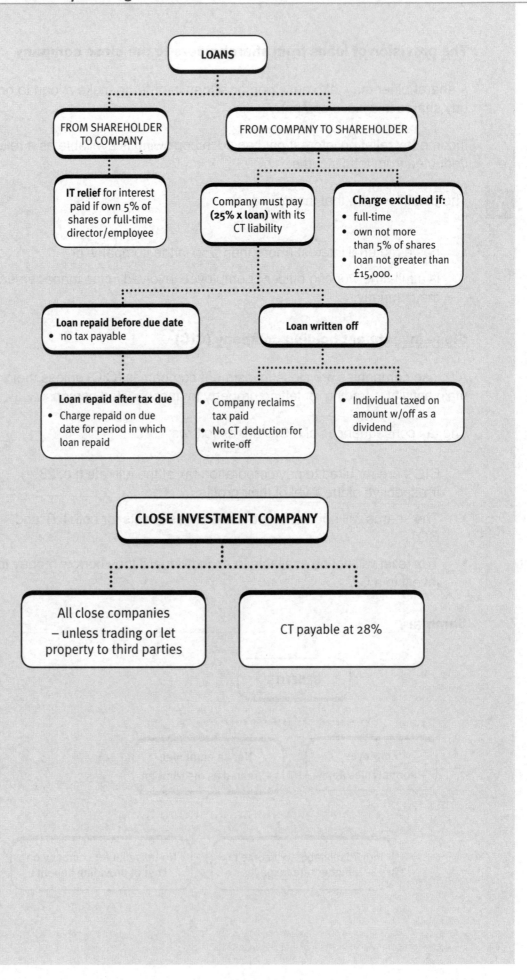

## 4 Extracting profits from a company

### Introduction

Many UK companies are small to medium sized family trading companies, and consideration is often given to tax efficient means of extracting profits in an income or capital form.

This section considers the methods of extracting profits from a company and the implications for both the company and the individual shareholder and/or director.

### Salary v dividend

| | Salary | Dividend |
|---|---|---|
| Rates of IT | 20%/40% | 10%/32.5% |
| NICs paid by individual | Individual must pay Class 1 primary NIC on the salary at 11% or 1%. | No NIC is payable on dividends. |
| NICs paid by Company | Employer must pay Class 1 secondary NIC on the salary at 12.8%. | No NIC is payable on dividends. |
| CT implications for company | The salary paid to the employee and the NIC paid by the company are treated as staff costs. This reduces the trading profit of the company and the CT payable. | None. |
| Pension contributions | Salary is earned income and can be used to make contributions to a pension plan. | Dividends are not earned income and cannot be used to make contributions to a pension plan. |
| Formalities | If a bonus is accrued at the end of the accounting period it must:<br><br>• be paid within 9 months of the end of the accounting period; and<br><br>• must comply with FRS 12. | The company must have distributable profits to be able to pay a dividend. |

## Test your understanding 3

Norman is the only shareholder of Fletcher Ltd. He has been paid a salary of £60,000.

It has been decided that there are £50,000 of profits before corporation tax that can be used to either pay a bonus to Norman, or a dividend. The £50,000 is to include any employer's NIC liability.

The company pays corporation tax at 21% on its profits.

**Calculate the amount Norman will receive after all taxes have been paid.**

## Other possibilities

There are a number of other possible ways of extracting profits, depending on the individual situation which include:

- charging rent
- charging interest, and
- funding a pension scheme.

Further details of these extraction methods are given in expandable text.

## Rent

- Where property is to be bought for the use of the company it may be preferable to consider owning it personally and charging the company rent for its use.

- The rent would be an allowable deduction for corporation tax, providing it was at no more than a commercial rent.

- When the individual retires they may sell the property with the shares or might consider retaining it so that the rent received would supplement their pension income.

- A further advantage of direct ownership is that if the company owns the asset there will be two charges to tax before the individual receives the proceeds of the sale:

    (1) The company pays corporation tax on any gain arising.

    (2) The individual would then be taxable when the profits were extracted from the business.

- A slight drawback of holding the property outside the business is that if IHT became an issue, BPR would only be available at 50%. However, as it is likely that the business would be sold before the individual dies this would not create a problem. If there was a concern about a charge, insurance could be taken to cover any liability that may arise on death.

- Further, on the disposal of the property it would not qualify for Entrepreneurs' relief even if sold at the same time as the disposal of the company shares.

## Interest

- Where the individual has lent money to the company interest may be paid. The rate applied cannot be in excess of a commercial rate.

- There may be a timing advantage as the company will deduct the interest on an accruals basis but the individual is not taxed until it is received.

- Consider a company with a year ended 31 March 2010. Interest can be accrued within the accounts for that period but providing it is not paid until 6 April 2010 it will only be taxed on the individual in 2010/11.

- Where the individual and the company are connected the interest must be paid within 12 months of the end of the accounting period to be allowable as a deduction for the period in which it is accrued. If it is not, it only becomes an allowable deduction for corporation tax when it is paid.

## Pension contributions

- The company may make contributions to the pension scheme on behalf of the individual. Providing they fell within the approved limits there would be no income tax or NIC liability.

- The main drawback of this method of extraction is that the funds cannot be accessed until the individual is at least 55.

## Summary

| Type of Payment | Liable to IT? | NIC | Pensionable | CT deductible? |
|---|---|---|---|---|
| Salary | Yes | Class 1 | Yes | Yes – providing paid within 9m of end of the AP and complies with FRS 12 |
| Dividend | Yes if higher rate taxpayer | No | No | No |
| Rent | Yes | No | No | Yes – providing at commercial rate |
| Interest | Yes | No | No | Yes – providing not at > commercial rate and paid <12 months of end of CAP |
| Pension contributions | No | No | No | Yes when paid |

## 5 Personal service companies (PSC)

### The purpose of the PSC legislation

The purpose of the legislation on personal service companies (PSC) is to counter practices of tax avoidance which were becoming widespread.

Reference is sometimes made to these rules as the IR35 legislation, which is the original Revenue Press release issued that set out the objectives of the legislation.

The schemes the legislation aims to combat are as follows:

- Many businesses have been reluctant to pay an individual for their services directly as a self-employed individual because if HMRC reclassify them as employees there can be substantial costs and penalties incurred by both the self-employed business and the business employing their services (the client).

- As a result:
  - individuals who were self-employed have been encouraged to set up companies and the client would then contract with, and pay the company for the individual's services. Where the client is paying a company it would be more difficult to argue that the individual was a direct employee of that client.

- companies have encouraged existing employees to resign, set up a company, and the client would then use their services through that company, resulting in a major saving of NIC for that client.

The company owned by the individual worker is referred to as a Personal Service Company (PSC).

## Advantages to the individuals

Individuals realised that operating through a company could have advantages as follows:

(1) The PSC invoices for the individual's services (plus VAT, if appropriate) and

- the client pays the invoices gross without having to apply the PAYE regulations

- there are no employer's NIC contributions payable.

(2) The PSC pays CT at probably only 21% on profits net of any expenses wholly and exclusively incurred for the trade.

(3) The individual is an employee of the PSC, or better still, a director without a contract of employment thereby side-stepping the National Minimum Wage regulations.

(4) The individual could draw sufficient remuneration (or director's fees)

- to exceed the lower earnings limit for NIC purposes thereby creating entitlement to benefits

- but below the primary threshold so that no Class 1 liabilities arise.

The individual can then draw out the rest of the profits of the business as dividends.

(5) There is scope for dividing the shareholding of the PSC with the spouse so that two basic rate bands are utilised before higher rate income tax is payable.

(6) Income could be rolled up indefinitely net of a 21% CT charge so that good and bad years can be evened out and the individual need never pay higher rate tax unless they so choose.

As a result HMRC introduced rules to combat what they perceived was a loss of tax/NIC arising where individuals used a company to bill their services to a client.

## What makes a company a PSC?

HMRC look at the relationship between the client and the worker.

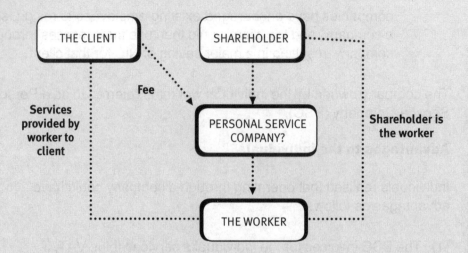

HMRC will ask the question: if the company was not there, would the worker be an employee of the client or self-employed? The normal rules for deciding employment or self-employment are used.

If the situation is considered to be one of employment the company owned by the worker is then a PSC, and the special legislation applies.

### The scope of PSC rules

The rules only apply to 'relevant engagements'. These are contracts between the company and the client which would have been a contract of employment in the absence of the PSC.

Although the client of the PSC is a significant beneficiary of the abuse, they are not the focus of the provisions.

The PSC has to

- treat the income from relevant engagements arising in a tax year **as if it were paid out as salary** to the employee, and

- account for the notional income tax and NIC on 19 April following the end of the tax year.

This **notional** salary is deemed paid at the end of the tax year.

The notional salary is the income from the relevant engagements, reduced by the following:

- any actual salary and benefits received in the year

- expenses incurred by the company which would have been deductible under the employment income rules if the individual had incurred them personally

- contributions made by the company to an occupational pension scheme

- employer's NIC paid during the year on actual salary and on the notional salary

- 5% of gross payments from relevant engagements as a flat rate deduction to cover such things as overheads and training, whether or not the money is spent.

To avoid a double charge to tax:

- The notional salary and NIC is allowable for calculating corporation tax profits.

- Where dividends are subsequently paid out of this income they are ignored as part of the individual's taxable income.

**Pro-forma for notional salary calculation**

|  |  | £ |
|---|---|---|
| Amount received in tax year |  | $X_A$ |
| Less: | Statutory deduction (5% × $X_A$) | (X) |
|  | NICs paid by employer | (X) |
|  | Pension contributions by employer | (X) |
|  | Salary paid by employer | (X) |
|  |  | ——— |
| Deemed salary including employer's NICs |  | $X_B$ |
| Less: Employer's NICs [$X_B$ × (12.8/112.8)] |  | (X) |
|  |  | ——— |
| Notional salary |  | X |
|  |  | ——— |

### Test your understanding 4

Brian is a consultant trading through a personal service company, Conrad Ltd. He owns all of the shares of the company.

During 2009/10 Brian is occupied almost full-time under a contract with Wilson Ltd. The value of the contract is £70,000.

During 2009/10 Brian draws a salary of £25,000 which is taxed via PAYE and employer's NICs of £2,468 were paid.

(a) **Calculate the employment income, income tax and employer's NICs to be assessed.**

(b) **Calculate the corporation tax payable by Conrad Ltd in year ending 31 March 2010, assuming IR35 applies.**

## Summary

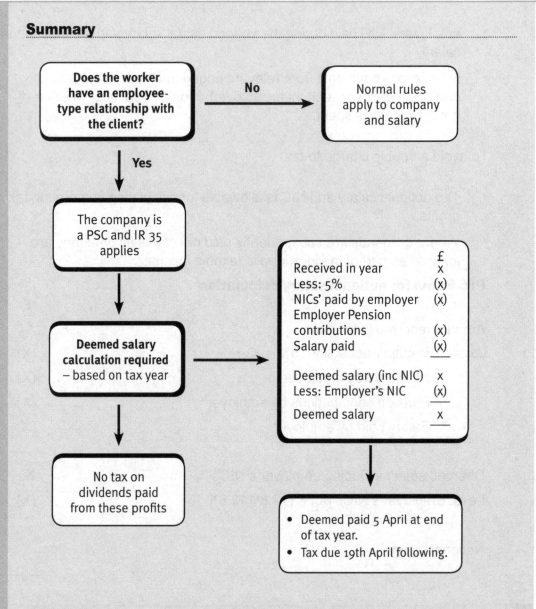

Does the worker have an employee-type relationship with the client?

— No → Normal rules apply to company and salary

— Yes ↓

The company is a PSC and IR 35 applies

↓

Deemed salary calculation required – based on tax year →

| | £ |
|---|---|
| Received in year | x |
| Less: 5% | (x) |
| NICs' paid by employer | (x) |
| Employer Pension contributions | (x) |
| Salary paid | (x) |
| Deemed salary (inc NIC) | x |
| Less: Employer's NIC | (x) |
| Deemed salary | x |

↓

No tax on dividends paid from these profits

↓

- Deemed paid 5 April at end of tax year.
- Tax due 19th April following.

## 6 Withdrawing investment from the company

### Overview

When a shareholder wishes to withdraw their investment from a company there are a number of exit strategies available.

- They could sell their shares.

- The company could purchase the shares back from the shareholder.

- The company could be put into liquidation.

### Sale of shares

The simplest method of withdrawing investment in a company is to sell the shares.

- This may not be as easy as it sounds as there is no ready market for shares in unquoted companies. They can usually only be sold to the other shareholders, or with their permission to a third party.

- If the shares are sold the main tax to consider will be CGT, and the availability of Entrepreneurs' relief.

  Most shares in unquoted trading companies will be business assets if the individual has been a full time employee or director of the company. Therefore, if they have been owned for at least 12 months, Entrepreneurs' relief would apply.

- Before the shares are sold it may be possible to pay a dividend (assuming the company has distributable profits). This would reduce the value of the shares on sale.

  To decide if this is worthwhile it will be necessary to consider the tax rates that apply to the amounts received by the shareholder.

  - A basic rate taxpayer would prefer a dividend, as they have no further liability on the income received.

  - A higher rate taxpayer will pay income tax on the dividend, equal to an effective rate of 25% as follows:

| | |
|---|---:|
| Gross dividend (£18,000 × 100/90) | £20,000 |
| | |
| | £ |
| Income tax at 32.5% | 6,500 |
| Income tax credit at 10% | (2,000) |
| | |
| Tax payable | 4,500 |

  Rate of IT payable = 25% (£4,500/£18,000)

- Where Entrepreneurs' relief is relevant (ignoring the annual exemption) CGT will be payable at an effective rate of 10% on the first £1 million of gains (5/9 × 18%) for a taxpayer. After the first £1 million of gains the effective rate is 18%.

  Therefore, a higher rate taxpayer would not benefit from a dividend being paid before the shares are sold.

## Purchase of own shares

Where it is not possible to sell the shares to another person, it may be possible for them to be bought by the company.

Depending on how the transaction is structured the amount received for the shares will be treated:

- as an income distribution (dividend), or
- a capital payment.

The income distribution will trigger a tax liability for an individual who is a higher rate taxpayer. Again, assuming Entrepreneurs' relief is available it may be better structured as a capital disposal, where the effective tax rate becomes 10%/18%.

## Conditions for treatment as a CGT disposal

(1) The company must be an unquoted trading company (companies quoted on the AIM are treated as unquoted).

(2) The shareholder must be resident and ordinarily resident in the UK.

(3) The shares must normally have been owned by the shareholder for at least five years.

(4) The shareholder must either dispose of their entire interest in the company or their interest must be substantially reduced. This means they own less than 75% of their holding from before the purchase once the shares have been bought back.

(5) The shareholder must not immediately after the purchase be connected with the company (i.e. be able to control it or be in possession of > 30% of the voting power).

(6) The purchase must be for the benefit of the trade.

If **any** of the above provisions do not apply the payment will be treated as a distribution.

Note that the taxpayer cannot choose which treatment is to apply. If the specified conditions are fulfilled it **must** be treated as a capital disposal, and if not it **will be** an income distribution.

## Tax treatment

If treated as a capital disposal, a normal CGT computation applies.

If treated as an income distribution, the amount of its distribution is the excess of the payment over the amount originally subscribed for the shares.

Where the person whose shares are being purchased is a company HMRC will always treat the event as a capital disposal.

Note that any legal costs and other expenditure incurred by the company in purchasing its own shares will **not** be allowable against the company's profits for corporation tax.

## Test your understanding 5

You act as tax advisor for Bliss Ltd (which operates a successful marriage bureau) and its managing director, Mr Crippen.

The company has made tax-adjusted trading profits in excess of £250,000 pa over the previous five years. It has now built up a substantial reserve of cash, since its policy has been not to pay out any dividends. The company has not made any chargeable gains in recent years and has always prepared accounts to 30 April.

Mr Crippen informs you that he and Mr Bluebeard, his fellow shareholder, are in serious disagreement about the future strategy of the company and that this is having a very harmful effect on the running of the business.

It has therefore been decided that Mr Bluebeard should no longer be involved in the management of the company and that the company will purchase all of his shares from him.

**Further relevant information**

(1)  Mr Bluebeard has worked in the company as a full-time director since it was incorporated on 1 June 1998, when he acquired 10% of the ordinary shares for £3,000.

(2)  Mr Bluebeard has a private income of £50,000 per annum.

(3)  The company has agreed to buy back Mr Bluebeard's shares at market value of £600,000 on 1 April 2010.

(4)  All of Bliss Ltd's assets are in use for the purposes of the trade.

**Set out the tax implications for Mr Bluebeard if:**

(a)  **HMRC treat the purchase as a qualifying distribution;**

(b)  **HMRC do not consider it as a qualifying distribution.**

## Liquidation

Many people associate liquidation with a company that has gone bankrupt. This is not always the case. A liquidation can be an effective way of extracting the final value from the company where:

*   the net assets of the company are worth more than the shares on a going concern basis, or

*   no one wishes to buy the shares in the company as it stands.

The process of liquidation is normally as follows:

(1)  The liquidator is appointed, and the trade ceases.

(2)  The assets of the company are sold, the debtors collected, and the liabilities paid.

(3)  There will be corporation tax due on any profits and gains made on the disposal of the assets, and this must be paid.

(4)  The liquidator pays out the balance of the funds to the shareholders, and the shares are cancelled.

(5)  The shareholders pay any tax due on the amounts received.

If payments are made to the shareholders

- **before** the liquidator is appointed they are taxed as dividends

- **after** the liquidator is appointed they are treated as capital receipts for the disposal of the shares.

Whichever of these two the taxpayer prefers will, again, depend on their relevant income tax rates, and CGT position.

Where the company is a personal trading company, and the shares will qualify for Entrepreneurs' relief, a higher rate taxpayer will prefer a capital distribution with the effective tax rate of 10%/18%.

### Test your understanding 6

Simon set up an unquoted trading company on 1 July 2003, and acquired 100% of the shares for £1,000.

The business has been successful but he has decided that now is the time to retire.

A liquidator will be appointed on 1 January 2011, to oversee the disposal of the assets and the winding-up of the company.

It is anticipated that after the assets have been sold the balance sheet will be as follows:

| | £ |
|---|---|
| Bank and cash | 840,000 |
| Creditors (inc corporation tax due on profit) | (120,000) |
| | 720,000 |
| Share Capital | 1,000 |
| Retained profits | 719,000 |
| | 720,000 |

Simon is a higher-rate taxpayer, and has realised substantial gains already in the current year.

**Calculate the impact of extracting the profits as follows:**

(i) **£180,000 before the liquidation commences, with the remaining £540,000 paid on 1 April 2011.**

(ii) **The whole £720,000 is paid out on 1 April 2011.**

## Winding-up

The costs of appointing and paying a liquidator can be high.

Where the business is profitable it is possible to wind-up the company without the formal appointment of a liquidator.

HMRC will allow payments made to shareholders to be treated as capital, even though no liquidator has been appointed, providing:

* the company is being wound-up, and
* all liabilities are agreed and subsequently paid (including the individual's personal liability on any distribution by the company).

## Summary

A major element in the planning of a liquidation is deciding whether the investment should be withdrawn in a form treated as income, or capital.

For an individual who is a higher rate taxpayer the capital route would normally be preferred if they are eligible for Entrepreneurs' relief, as this gives an effective tax rate of 10% on the first £1 million of capital gains.

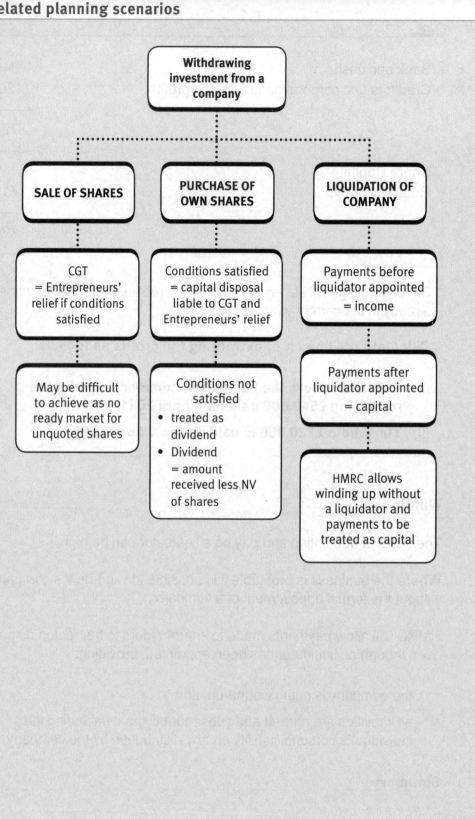

## 7 Chapter summary

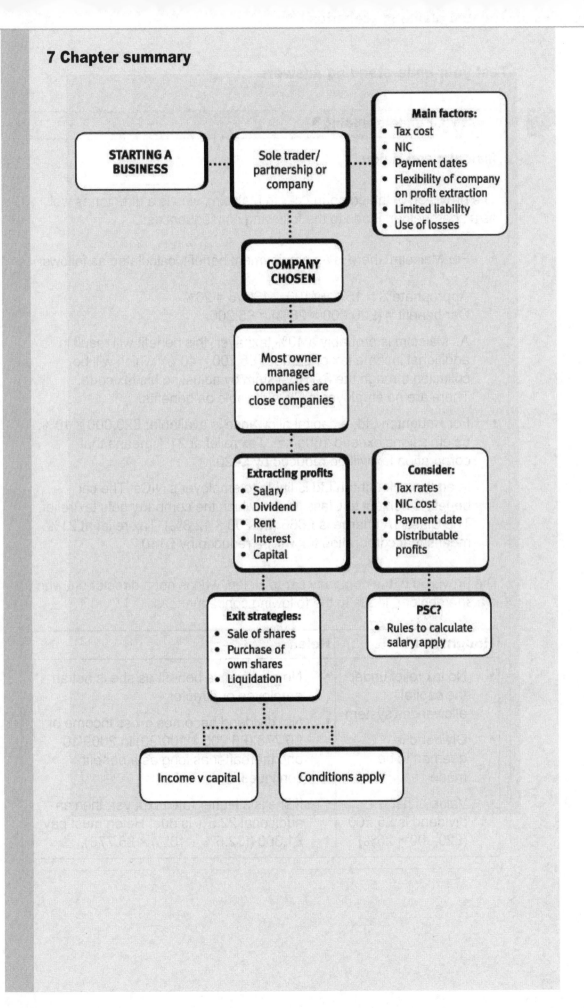

## Test your understanding answers

### Malcolm and Helen

The provision of the company car to Malcolm, who is a director as well as a shareholder, leads to the following consequences:

- For Malcolm, there is an employment benefit, calculated as follows:

  Appropriate% = 15% + (190 – 135)/5 = 26%
  Car benefit = (£20,000 × 26%) = £5,200.

- As Malcolm is probably a 40% taxpayer, this benefit will result in additional income tax of £2,080 (£5,200 × 40%), which will be collected through the PAYE system by adjusting his tax code. There are no employee's NICs payable on benefits.

- For Houghton Ltd, a capital allowance is available: £20,000 × 10%, as emissions exceed 160g/km. Tax relief at 21% means that corporation tax will be reduced by £420.

- In addition Houghton Ltd is liable to employer's NICs. The car benefit is subject to Class 1A, on which the company gets tax relief. The Class 1A charge is £666 (£5,200 × 12.8%). Tax relief at 21% means that corporation tax will be reduced by £140.

The provision of the company car to Helen, who is not a director but who is a shareholder, leads to the following consequences.

| Houghton Ltd | Helen |
|---|---|
| • No tax relief under the capital allowances system | • No assessable benefit as she is not an employee or director |
| • Dividend is deemed to be made | • Net dividend becomes gross income of £5,778 (£5,200 × 100/90) in 2009/10 and thereafter as long as a benefit continues. |
| • Value of net dividend is £5,200 (£20,000 × 26%) | • If she is a higher rate taxpayer, then an additional 22.5% is due. Helen must pay £1,300 ((32.5% – 10%) × £5,778). |

## Test your understanding 2

### Sally and Claire

|  | Sally | Claire |
|---|---|---|
| Is the amount loaned less than or equal to £15,000? | Yes | Yes |
| Is the individual is a full-time working employee? | Yes | Yes |
| Does the individual own less than 5% of the shares? | No | Yes |

### Sally

She has received the benefit of a low interest loan, for which under the employment income rules there is a benefit charge each tax year of average loan £275 (£10,000 × (4.75% – 2%)).

The loan to Sally is caught by the provisions as she has > 5% of the shares. Therefore White Ltd will be required to pay £2,500 (£10,000 × 25%) tax charge to be paid on 1 January 2011. If any part of the loan is repaid before 1 January 2011 then this tax charge is reduced accordingly.

The £2,500 will be recoverable when the loan is repaid, or written off.

### Claire

The loan is not caught by the close company provisions (see above), but it will still be caught by the employment income benefit provisions.

Using the average method the benefit is calculated as:

Average loan = (£10,000 + £6,000) × 1/2 = £8,000

|  | £ |
|---|---|
| Interest on average loan (4.75% × £8,000) | 380 |
| Less: Interest actually paid (£10,000 × 2% × 9/12) + (£6,000 × 2% × 3/12) | (180) |
| Loan benefit | 200 |

Claire may elect for the precise method to be used if the benefit is lower.

HMRC also have the right to impose the precise method but would only do so if the repayment pattern was uncommercial or designed to reduce the benefit. This does not appear to be the case here.

**Test your understanding 3**

**Fletcher Ltd**

|                                          | Salary £ | Dividend £ |
|------------------------------------------|----------|------------|
|                                     £    |          |            |
| Profit available                         | 50,000   | 50,000     |
| Salary                              44,326 |        |            |
| Employer's NIC                           |          |            |
| (12.8/112.8 × £50,000)              5,674  |        |            |
|                                          | (50,000) |            |
|                                          | Nil      | 50,000     |
| Corporation tax at 21%                   | Nil      | (10,500)   |
| Profit for dividend                      | Nil      | 39,500     |

**Norman**

|                                          | Salary £ | Dividend £ |
|------------------------------------------|----------|------------|
| Salary                                   | 44,326   |            |
| Dividend (£39,500 × 100/90)              |          | 43,889     |
| Income tax                               |          |            |
| (£44,326 × 40%)                          | 17,730   |            |
| (£43,889 × 32.5%)                        |          | 14,264     |
| Class 1 NIC (1% × £44,326)               | 443      | Nil        |
|                                          | 18,173   | 14,264     |
| Tax credit (10% × £43,889)               |          | ( 4,389)   |
|                                          | 18,173   | 9,875      |
| Net after tax income                     |          |            |
| Salary (£44,326 – £18,173)               | 26,153   |            |
| Dividend (£39,500 – £9,875)              |          | 29,625     |

**Test your understanding 4**

**Brian**

(a) **Employment income, income tax and employer's NICs**

|  | £ |
|---|---|
| Total contract value earned | 70,000 |
| Less: Statutory deduction (5%) | (3,500) |
|  | ——— |
|  | 66,500 |
| Less: Salary | (25,000) |
| Employer's NICs | (2,468) |
|  | ——— |
| Deemed salary including employer's NICs | 39,032 |
| Employer's NICs (£39,032× 12.8/112.8) | (4,429) |
|  | ——— |
| Deemed employment income | 34,603 |
|  | ——— |

Income tax:

| £ | £ |
|---|---|
| 18,875 × 20% (W) | 3,775 |
| 15,728 × 40% | 6,291 |
| ——— |  |
| 34,603 |  |
| ——— | ——— |
| Income tax on deemed employment income | 10,066 |
|  | ——— |

**Working: Basic rate band remaining**

|  | £ |
|---|---|
| BR band | 37,400 |
| Taxable income (£25,000 – £6,475) | (18,525) |
|  | ——— |
| BR band remaining | 18,875 |
|  | ——— |

(b) **Conrad Ltd**
**Corporation Tax Liability – Year ending 5 April 2010**

|  | £ |
|---|---:|
| Trading profit | 70,000 |
| Less: Staff costs (£25,000 + £2,468) | (27,468) |
| IR35 costs (£34,603 + £4,429) | (39,032) |
| PCTCT | 3,500 |
| Corporation tax at 21% | 735 |

## Test your understanding 5

**Bliss Ltd**

(a) **HMRC treat the payment as a qualifying distribution**

Mr Bluebeard will be treated as receiving a dividend on 1 April 2010 and will be subject to income tax in 2009/10 as follows:

|  | £ |
|---|---|
| Cash received | 600,000 |
| Less: Original subscription price | (3,000) |
| | |
| Net distribution | 597,000 |
| | |
| Gross dividend received (£597,000 × 100/90) | 663,333 |
| | |
| Income tax (£663,333 × (32.5% − 10%)) | 149,250 |

Alternative calculation = (£597,000 × 25%) = £149,250

| Due date | 31 Jan 2011 |
|---|---|

(b) **HMRC do not treat it as a qualifying distribution**

Mr Bluebeard will be liable to capital gains tax as follows:

|  | £ |
|---|---|
| Sale proceeds | 600,000 |
| Less: Cost | (3,000) |
| | |
| Capital gain | 597,000 |
| Less: Entrepreneurs' relief: (4/9 × £597,000) | (265,333) |
| | |
| Chargeable capital gain | 331,667 |
| Less Annual exemption | (10,100) |
| | |
| Taxable gain | 321,567 |
| | |
| Capital gains tax (£321,567 × 18%) | 57,882 |
| | |
| Due date | 31 Jan 2011 |

## Test your understanding 6

### Solution

(i) **Option 1**
**Pre-liquidation dividend – Income Tax**

| | £ | £ |
|---|---:|---:|
| Dividend received (£180,000 × 100/90) | 200,000 | |
| | | |
| Income tax: (32.5% × £200,000) | 65,000 | |
| Less: Tax credit | (20,000) | |
| | | |
| Income tax payable | 45,000 | 45,000 |

**Post-liquidation distribution – CGT**

| | £ | £ |
|---|---:|---:|
| Proceeds | 540,000 | |
| Less: Cost | (1,000) | |
| | | |
| | 539,000 | |
| Less: Entrepreneurs' relief (4/9 × £539,000) | (239,555) | |
| | | |
| Chargeable gain | 299,445 | |
| Less AE (already used) | (Nil) | |
| | | |
| Taxable gain | 299,445 | |
| | | |
| CGT payable (18% × £299,445) | | 53,900 |
| | | |
| Total tax payable | | 98,900 |

(ii) **Option 2 – CGT**

| | £ |
|---|---:|
| Proceeds | 720,000 |
| Less: Cost | (1,000) |
| | |
| | 719,000 |
| Less: Entrepreneurs' relief (4/9 × £719,000) | (319,555) |
| | |
| Chargeable gain | 399,445 |
| | |
| CGT payable (18% × £399,445) | 71,900 |

# Groups and consortium

## Chapter learning objectives

Upon completion of this chapter you will be able to:

- define an associated company and recognise the effect for corporation tax

- distinguish the different 75% group relationships which exist for corporation tax and gains purposes and identify the relevant groups from the information provided

- recognise the reliefs available when provided with a group scenario and advise on the effect of alternative courses of action

- determine the effects on loss relief availability where arrangements exist for a company to leave a group and recognise when relief is available for trading losses incurred by an overseas subsidiary

- define a consortium and recognise how consortium loss relief operates

- advise on the tax consequences of a transfer of tangible and intangible assets within a group and advise on the tax consequences of a transfer of trade and assets where there is common control; recognise when a degrouping charge will arise in connection with asset transfers

- determine pre-entry losses and understand their tax treatment

- identify the availability of any stamp duties exemption / relief in connection with group transactions;explain the taxation implications for a company of a scheme of reconstruction

- define the relationship required for group VAT registration, explain the effects and outline any advantages or disadvantages of group VAT registration and explain the purpose of divisional registration for VAT.

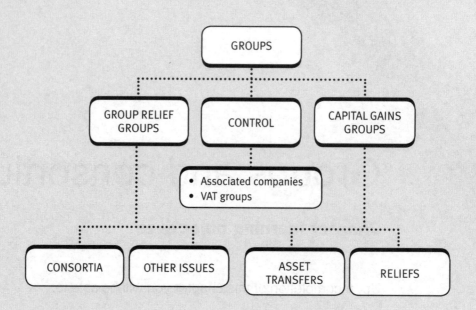

## 1 Introduction

This chapter deals with the tax position of groups of companies, where one company owns shares in another.

Remember that for corporation tax purposes:

- each company within the group is treated as a separate entity

- each company is required to submit its own tax return based on its individual results

- but being a member of a group provides opportunities for tax planning to save tax and improve the cash flow of the group as a whole.

Much of this chapter is a revision of the rules covered in F6, however there is a much greater emphasis at P6 in the tax planning aspects of groups:

- choosing the most tax efficient group structure for the business

- effective use of loss reliefs

- effective crystallisation or deferral of chargeable gains, and

- giving tax advice on proposed strategies.

The new areas at P6 are:

- Consortia relief

- The degrouping charge

- Pre-entry capital losses

- Transfers of a trade and assets

- VAT groups.

## 2 Associated companies

### Definition of an associated company

A company is associated with another in either of the following situations:

- One company controls the other(s), or
- Both are controlled by the same 'person' (company or individual).

**Examples of each situation:**

- One company controls the other(s)

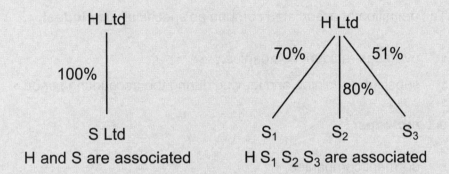

- Both are controlled by the same 'person' (company or individual).

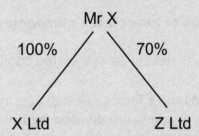

X Ltd and Z Ltd are associates. Mr X is the controlling link, although as an individual he is not included in the number of associated companies.

### Control

Control means that the person has > 50% of

- the issued share capital of another company, **or**
- the voting power, **or**
- the right to receive distributable profits, **or**
- the right to receive the net assets in the event of a winding up.

Note that control can be exercised directly or indirectly:

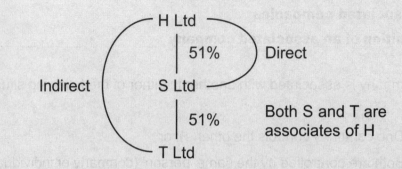

It is not necessary to have an effective interest of > 50% for associates therefore it does not matter that H Ltd's effective interest in T Ltd is only 26.01% (0.51 × 0.51).

The definition of associated companies specifically **includes:**

- overseas resident companies.
- subsidiaries joining and leaving during the accounting period.

but **excludes:**

- dormant companies.
- non-trading holding companies.

### The consequences of associated companies

The consequences of having an associated company are:

- The **upper and lower limits,** used to determine the appropriate rate of corporation tax to apply, are **divided by the total number of associated companies**, thereby potentially increasing the effective rate of tax each company pays.

- **Dividends received** from associated companies (UK and overseas) are **excluded from FII** in the calculation of 'profits'.

- A group of companies is entitled to a single AIA for capital allowances, but can choose how to allocate the AIA between group companies.

**Test your understanding 1**

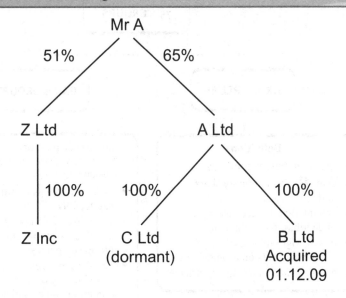

All companies except Z Inc are UK resident and prepare financial statements to 31 March 2010.

A Ltd has PCTCT of £270,000 for the year ended 31 March 2010. A Ltd also receives dividends of £40,000 from B Ltd in January 2010.

(a) **State the number of associates that A Ltd has for corporation tax purposes for the year ended 31 March 2010.**

(b) **Calculate the corporation tax liability of A Ltd for the year ended 31 March 2010.**

## 3 75% groups

### Identification of 75% groups

The identification of the appropriate 75% groups for corporation tax purposes is essential before any tax planning advice can be given.

A reminder of the key rules covered at F6 is given in the following diagram:

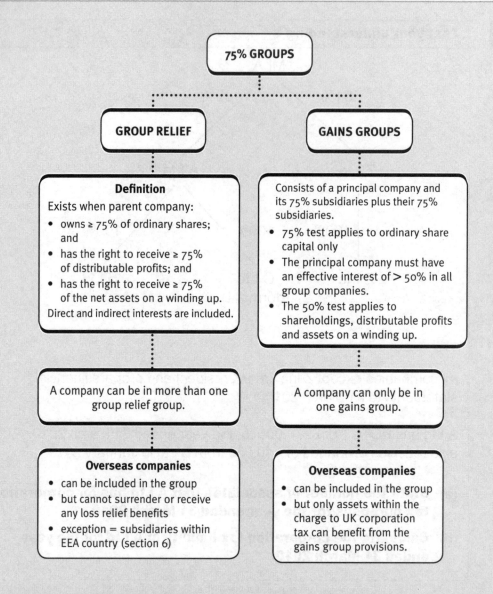

**75% GROUPS**

**GROUP RELIEF**

**Definition**

Exists when parent company:

- owns ≥ 75% of ordinary shares; and
- has the right to receive ≥ 75% of distributable profits; and
- has the right to receive ≥ 75% of the net assets on a winding up.

Direct and indirect interests are included.

A company can be in more than one group relief group.

**Overseas companies**

- can be included in the group
- but cannot surrender or receive any loss relief benefits
- exception = subsidiaries within EEA country (section 6)

**GAINS GROUPS**

Consists of a principal company and its 75% subsidiaries plus their 75% subsidiaries.

- 75% test applies to ordinary share capital only
- The principal company must have an effective interest of > 50% in all group companies.
- The 50% test applies to shareholdings, distributable profits and assets on a winding up.

A company can only be in one gains group.

**Overseas companies**

- can be included in the group
- but only assets within the charge to UK corporation tax can benefit from the gains group provisions.

**Example 1 – 75% groups**

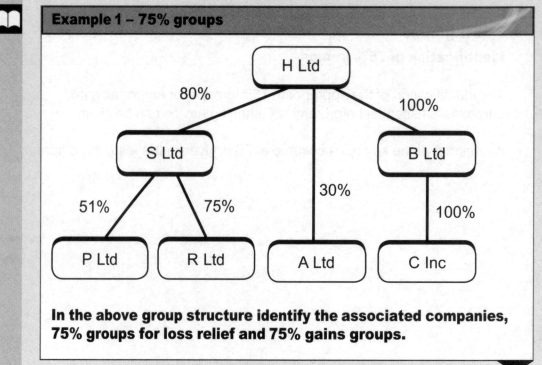

In the above group structure identify the associated companies, 75% groups for loss relief and 75% gains groups.

## Solution

(i) **The associated companies are:**

H, S, P, R, B and C Inc.

(ii) **Groups for group loss relief**

- Group 1: H plc, S Ltd, B Ltd and C Inc (although C Inc may not receive any loss relief).
- Group 2: S Ltd and R Ltd

H plc has only a 60% (80 × 75) indirect interest in R Ltd and hence R Ltd cannot be in a group with H plc.

(iii) **Capital gains group**

R Ltd can be included in the main group which now consists of H plc, S Ltd, R Ltd, B Ltd and C Inc (although the reliefs only apply to assets within the charge to UK corporation tax).

---

### Test your understanding 2

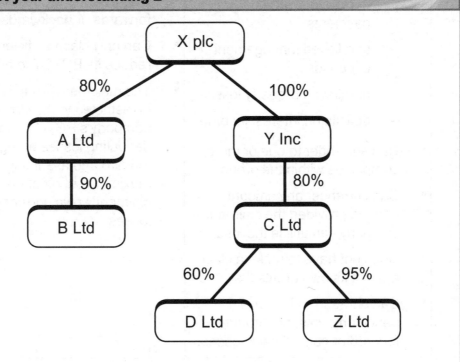

In the above group structure identify the associated companies, 75% groups for loss relief and 75% gains groups.

### 4 Group relief

- Members of a group relief group may surrender losses to other profitable group members for corresponding accounting periods.

- Losses surrendered must be set against the claimant company's profits of a 'corresponding' accounting period.

  A corresponding accounting period = any accounting period falling wholly or partly within the surrendering company's accounting period.

  Where the companies do not have coterminous (same) year ends, the available profits and losses must be time apportioned to find the relevant amounts falling within the corresponding accounting period.

- Rules apply to both the surrendering and the claimant companies as follows:

| Surrendering company | Claimant company |
|---|---|
| • Can surrender current period:<br>  – trading losses<br>  – unrelieved Gift Aid payments<br>  – unrelieved management expenses<br>  – unrelieved property losses<br>  – deficits on interest income.<br><br>• Can surrender to one or more companies within the group.<br><br>• Can surrender any amount desired provided the claimant company can utilise the loss.<br><br>• Does not have to make a claim against its own profits first.<br><br>• Can only surrender current period amounts, not brought forward or carried back losses. | • Offsets the surrendered loss against its PCTCT.<br><br>• Cannot carry group relief forwards or backwards.<br><br>• Can only claim sufficient to reduce its PCTCT to nil.<br><br>• The maximum group relief claim is restricted to the claimant company's PCTCT after deducting losses brought forward and assuming maximum set off of the claimant's own current period losses. |

---

**Test your understanding 3**

A Ltd and B Ltd are members of the same 75% group.

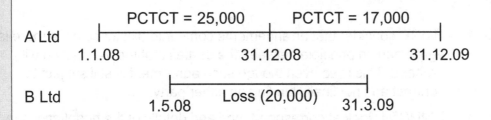

(a) **Calculate the maximum amount of loss that B Ltd can surrender to A Ltd for use in year ended 31.12.08 and compute the revised PCTCT of A Ltd assuming B Ltd surrenders the maximum amount of loss.**

(b) **Calculate the maximum amount of loss that B Ltd can surrender to A Ltd for use in year ended 31.12.09 and compute the revised PCTCT of A Ltd assuming B Ltd surrenders the maximum amount of loss.**

---

- Tax planning primarily seeks to ensure losses are used within the group to save the most tax. Accordingly, losses are first set against profits taxed at the marginal rate.

- It is usual, particularly where there is a minority shareholder, for the claimant company to pay for group relief. Such payments subject to a maximum of £1 per £1 of loss claimed, are ignored for tax purposes.

## 5 Effect on group relief of changes in group structures

### Companies joining a group

There are several areas to consider:

- Group relief is only available for losses and profits generated after a company joins a group.

- It is not possible to have group relief for pre-acquisition losses or to relieve pre-acquisition profits.

- A corresponding accounting period begins when a company joins a group.

- When a loss making company joins a group there is a 'change in ownership' of that company, and consequently there may be a restriction on the use of its brought forward losses against its own profits if there is also a major change in the nature or conduct of trade (Chapter 24).

## Companies leaving a group

Group relief ceases to be available once arrangements are in place to sell the shares of a company. This will usually occur some time before the actual legal sale of the shares.

- HMRC consider that arrangements come into existence once there is agreement in principle between the parties that the transaction will proceed. This is so even though such agreement is still subject to contract and not finally binding on either party.

- HMRC will look at correspondence and details of the negotiations to determine the date of any arrangements coming into force.

- For computational exam questions you should be given the date on which a company is deemed to leave a group.

### Test your understanding 4

Romeo Ltd owns 80% of the ordinary share capital of Juliet Ltd. These shares were acquired during 1994. Both companies are UK resident for tax purposes and neither has any other associated companies. Their most recent results have been:

|  | Romeo Ltd 12m/e 31/12/09 £ | Juliet Ltd 9m/e 31/03/10 £ |
|---|---|---|
| Tax adjusted trading profit | 890,000 |  |
| Tax adjusted trading losses |  | (102,000) |
| Capital gains |  | 15,000 |
| Capital loss | (20,000) |  |
| Bank interest received | 6,000 | 4,000 |
| Property business profit | 2,000 | 8,000 |
| Dividends from other UK companies |  | 32,000 |
| Dividend from Juliet Ltd | 27,000 |  |
| Gift Aid donation | 4,000 | 5,000 |

**Compute the corporation tax payable by each company for the above accounting periods, on the assumption that maximum possible group relief is claimed by Romeo Ltd, before taking into account any notional transfer of assets.**

## 6 Losses of overseas subsidiaries

Group relief is normally only allowed between UK resident group companies.

- However, overseas losses can be group relieved to the UK, but only if:

  (i)   the overseas subsidiary is either resident in, or has a permanent establishment in, the European Economic Area (EEA); and

  (ii)  losses can not be relieved in any other way.

- Note that losses may only be surrendered by European Subsidiaries to a UK parent and not from the parent to the subsidiary.

- This new rule was introduced following the judgement in the much publicised Marks and Spencer case in 2005.

The examiner has stated that if an overseas subsidiary sustains a trading loss, the question will state whether the company is, or is not, resident in an EEA country.

## 7 Consortia

### Introduction

Further loss relief is available if companies are structured as a consortium.

The tax reliefs available between qualifying companies where a consortium is involved are more limited than for a 75% loss group.

### Definition of a consortium

There are several elements to the definition:

- A consortium exists where two or more companies (UK or overseas) between them own at least 75% of another company. Each company must own at least 5% but less than 75%.

- Ownership includes ordinary shares and assets and profits as for a 75% group.

- The investing company is known as a consortium member.

- The target company is known as a consortium company.

**Test your understanding 5**

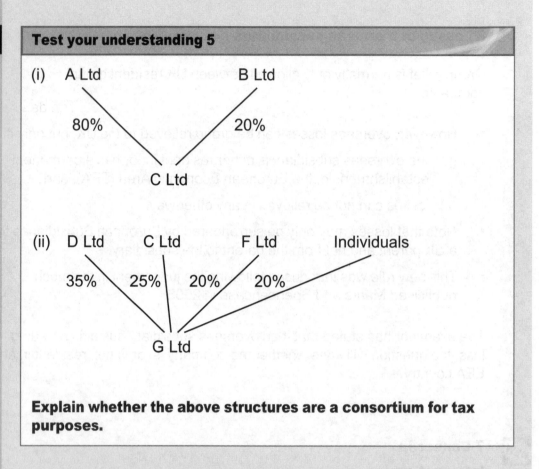

**Explain whether the above structures are a consortium for tax purposes.**

## Effect of being in a consortium

Consortium relief (a form of loss relief) is available between a UK consortium company and its UK members, for current period qualifying losses.

Corresponding accounting period rules apply as they do for group relief.

- Losses can be **surrendered upwards** from the consortium company to the consortium members:
    - But only up to the percentage interest that the consortium member has in the consortium company.
    - The loss must first be relieved against current period profits in the consortium company.

- Losses can also be **surrendered downwards** from consortium members to the consortium company to relieve
    - up to their percentage of the consortium company's PCTCT.
    - the loss does not have to be relieved in the consortium members computation first.

- The maximum consortium loss relief available for surrender is: the lower of:

  (i) the results of the consortium member;

  (ii) the consortium members' percentage entitlement to the results of the consortium company.

- Losses cannot be exchanged between consortium members.

- Consortium members can be resident anywhere in the world but only a UK resident consortium member can claim or surrender losses.

### Test your understanding 6

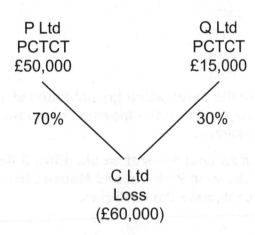

**Calculate the maximum consortium relief available for P Ltd and Q Ltd. Assume all companies have coterminous year end dates.**

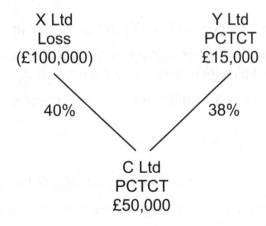

**Explain how X Ltd can relieve its loss within the consortium. Assume all companies shown have coterminous year end dates.**

**Test your understanding 7**

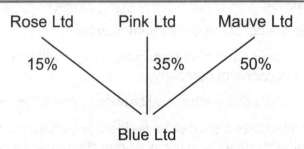

In the year ended 31 March 2010 their results were:

|  |  | £ |
|---|---|---|
| Rose Ltd | loss | (90,000) |
| Pink Ltd | loss | (126,000) |
| Mauve Ltd | profit | 55,000 |
| Blue Ltd | profit | 300,000 |

(i) **Calculate the corporation tax liabilities of all companies, on the assumption that the maximum amount of consortium relief is claimed.**

(ii) **Explain how your answer would differ if Rose Ltd owned 80% of Blue Ltd, with Pink Ltd and Mauve Ltd owning 10% each. Do not recalculate the liabilities.**

## 8 Capital gains groups

### Introduction

When an asset is sold to another gains group member:

- this is a no gain/no loss transfer (regardless of any actual price paid)
- the receiving company acquires the asset at a base cost equal to its original cost plus indexation up to the point of transfer
- this treatment is automatic, no election is needed.

No gain arises until either:

- the receiving company sells the asset outside the group, or
- the group company receiving the asset leaves the group (degrouping charge).

## Disposals of assets outside the group

A normal capital gain or loss is calculated.

### Test your understanding 8

Green Ltd acquired an asset on 1 April 1983 for £100,000. The asset is transferred to Jade Ltd, a wholly owned subsidiary on 1 October 1993 for £120,000, when the asset was worth £180,000.

On 1 December 2009 Jade Ltd sells the asset outside the group for £350,000.

**Calculate any chargeable gains arising on the disposal of the asset.**

## Degrouping charge

A degrouping charge arises when a group company:

- leaves a group
- still owning an asset that it had received via a no gain/no loss transfer from a fellow group company
- within the last **six years**.

| Degrouping charge | Other issues |
|---|---|
| • The company leaving the group is deemed to have sold and re-purchased any assets acquired from other group members at their **MV on the day of the intergroup transfer** (not the MV when it leaves the group).<br><br>• The gain is treated as accruing in the **AP in which the company leaves the group**.<br><br>• Degrouping gains can be:<br>  – reallocated to another UK resident member of the original group, provided both companies agree. The election must be made within two years of the end of the AP in which the company leaves the group.<br>  – rolled over, providing an amount equal to the market value of the asset being degrouped is reinvested into new assets to be used in the trade of the selling company. | • Note that if the company leaves the group within **three years** of the original transfer, then the original exemption for SDLT is withdrawn, with duty becoming payable.<br><br>• The holding company that is selling the shares is likely to benefit from the substantial shareholding exemption in respect of any gain or loss on the disposal of the shares.<br><br>• A similar charge arises when a company leaves the group still owning an intangible asset acquired in the previous six years from another group company.<br><br>• This can be reallocated to another company in the original group by joint election within two years from the end of the accounting period in which the company leaves the group. |

### Example 2 – Degrouping charge

Shelley plc bought a freehold office block on 15 May 1990 for £350,000. On 10 June 2004 Shelley sold the office block to its wholly owned subsidiary company Wordsworth Ltd, for £400,000 when the true market value of the office block was £620,000.

On 1 March 2010 Wordsworth Ltd sold the office block for £800,000.

Both companies prepare financial statements to 31 March each year.

(i) **Calculate the gain realised by Wordsworth Ltd in March 2010.**

(ii) **Rather than have Wordsworth sell its office block, Shelley plc sells its entire shareholding in Wordsworth Ltd for £5 million. Advise the group of the gains (if any) that will arise as a result of this sale and any reliefs available.**

**Solution**

| **Inter group transfer: nil gain/nil loss:** | £ |
|---|---|
| Cost | 350,000 |
| Plus: IA (May 1990 to June 2004) | |
| $((186.8 - 126.2)/126.2) = 0.480 \times £350,000$ | 168,000 |
| | ——— |
| Base cost to Wordsworth Ltd | 518,000 |
| | ——— |

**Sale of asset outside the group**

| | £ |
|---|---|
| Proceeds | 800,000 |
| Less: Base Cost | (518,000) |
| | ——— |
| Unindexed gain | 282,000 |
| Less: IA (June 2004 to March 2010) | |
| $((213.7 - 186.8)/186.8) = 0.144 \times £518,000$ | (74,592) |
| | ——— |
| Chargeable gain | 207,408 |
| | ——— |

**Sale of Wordsworth Ltd**

- Degrouping charge arises
- Wordsworth Ltd is treated as if it had sold the building on 10 June 2004 at its MV, and then immediately reacquired it.

| | £ |
|---|---|
| Proceeds | 620,000 |
| Less Base cost to Wordsworth Ltd (as above) | (518,000) |
| | ——— |
| Chargeable gain | 102,000 |
| | ——— |

This gain is assessed on Wordsworth Ltd in year ended 31 March 2010 (i.e. the accounting period when it leaves the group).

- Shelley plc and Wordsworth can make a joint election for the gain to be reallocated to Shelley plc.

- Alternatively, provided at least £620,000 is spent on new qualifying assets, the gain can be rolled over.

- Shelley plc sells its shares in Wordsworth Ltd for £5 million. Any gain is likely to be exempt under the substantial shareholding rules as they have owned 100% of the shares for more than 12 months.

- SDLT would not have been charged when the office block was sold between the group companies.

- It is not charged retrospectively when Wordsworth leaves the group as this is more than three years after the original disposal.

### Test your understanding 9

Yellow Ltd sold its wholly owned subsidiary, Orange Ltd, on 15 April 2009. Yellow Ltd had purchased a building on 1 August 1990 for £180,000. On 1 December 2003, the building was transferred to Orange Ltd for £230,000. Its market value on the date of the transfer was £375,000. Orange Ltd still owned the building on 15 April 2009.

Both companies prepare accounts to 31 March each year.

**Explain the effect of the sale of Orange Ltd.**

## Matching election

Companies within a gains group can elect to reallocate gains/losses between group companies.

This election allows groups to achieve the following:

- Capital gains and losses can be matched together within one company.

- Gains can be realised in the group company which has capital losses brought forward (but beware of the restrictions on pre-entry losses).

- Gains can be realised in the group company which is paying the lowest rate of corporation tax.

The election must be made within two years of the end of the accounting period of disposal. This allows groups time to plan how best to treat capital gains and losses.

**Test your understanding 10**

During the year ended 31 March 2010 Violet Ltd is to dispose of an asset that will result in a capital loss of £75,000. Mauve Ltd, a 100% subsidiary of Violet Ltd, is to dispose of an asset that will result in a capital gain of £100,000.

The results of Mauve Ltd and Violet Ltd for the y/e 31 March 2010 are:

|  | Mauve Ltd | Violet Ltd |
| --- | --- | --- |
| Trading profits | £30,000 | £250,000 |

**Show the PCTCT for the year ended 31 March 2010 for each group company assuming the group wants to minimise the corporation tax of the group as a whole.**

## Rollover relief

For the purposes of rollover relief, the gains group is treated as a single trade.

This means that gains on disposal of a qualifying asset in one group company can be rolled against the purchase of qualifying assets, within the permitted time period, by another group company.

## 9 Comprehensive example

**Test your understanding 11**

The Apple Ltd group structure as at 31 March 2010 is as follows:

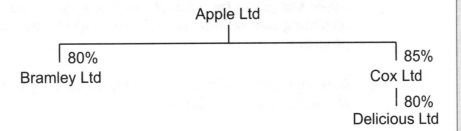

Apple Ltd has owned 80% of the ordinary share capital of Bramley Ltd and 85% of the ordinary share capital of Cox Ltd since these two companies were incorporated on 1 April 2008. Cox Ltd acquired 80% of the ordinary share capital of Delicious Ltd on 1 April 2009, the date of its incorporation.

The tax adjusted trading profits/(losses) of each company for the years ended 31 March 2009, 2010 and 2011 are as follows:

| Year ended 31 March | 2009 | 2010 | 2011 (forecast) |
|---|---|---|---|
| | £ | £ | £ |
| Apple Ltd | 620,000 | 250,000 | 585,000 |
| Bramley Ltd | (64,000) | 52,000 | 70,000 |
| Cox Ltd | 83,000 | (58,000) | 40,000 |
| Delicious Ltd | n/a | 90,000 | (15,000) |

The following information is also available:

(1) Apple Ltd sold a freehold office building on 10 March 2010 for £380,000, and this resulted in a capital gain of £120,000.

(2) Apple Ltd sold a freehold warehouse on 5 October 2010 for £365,000, and this resulted in a capital gain of £80,000.

(3) Cox Ltd purchased a freehold factory on 20 September 2010 for £360,000.

(4) Delicious Ltd sold an investment property on 10 January 2011 for £180,000 and this resulted in a capital loss of £90,000.

**(a) (i) Explain the group relationship that must exist for trading losses to be surrendered between group companies.**

**Distinguish this from the relationship that must exist for chargeable assets to be transferred between two companies in a group without incurring a chargeable gain or an allowable loss.**

**(ii) Explain the factors that should be taken into account by the Apple Ltd group when deciding which group companies the trading losses should be surrendered to.**

**(b) (i) Calculate the PCTCT for each of the companies in the Apple Ltd group for each of the three years concerned assuming that reliefs are claimed as efficiently as possible.**

**(ii) Give an explanation of why you have chosen the reliefs as applied above in (b)(i).**

Assume that the FY2009 corporation tax rates apply for all years.

## 10 Transfers of assets within a group

### No gain/no loss transfers

As seen before, generally a transfer between companies would be a chargeable event giving rise to an allowable loss or a chargeable gain.

However, companies in a 75% capital gains group:

- Make intra-group transfers of chargeable assets at nil gain/nil loss.
- This is regardless of any price actually paid.
- The transferee company takes over the asset at cost plus indexation to the date of transfer.
- This treatment is automatic, no election is needed.

### Transfers of intangible assets

Where intangible fixed assets, such as goodwill, are acquired on or after 1 April 2002 they fall outside the capital gains regime.

However, various reliefs which apply to capital gains groups are mirrored in the rules for intangible fixed assets held within groups. Groups in this case are defined in the same way as capital gains groups.

Transfers of intangible fixed assets between companies within groups are made on a 'tax neutral' basis. This means that the acquiring company takes over the asset at its written down value.

### Stamp duty

Three key points need to be remembered in relation to stamp duty and groups:

- There is no charge to stamp duty or stamp duty land tax where assets are transferred between two gains group companies.
- This relief is not available where, at the time the assets are transferred, arrangements exist for the purchasing company to leave the group.
- Any relief given in respect of stamp duty land tax is withdrawn, with duty becoming payable, if the transferee company leaves the group within **three years** of the transfer whilst still owning the land transferred.

### Transfer of trade within a group

Special reliefs apply under the rules of s343 ICTA 1988 when a company sells its trade and assets to another company that is under 75% common control.

Transfers between gains group members will meet this condition, as will transfers between companies with the same shareholders as follows:

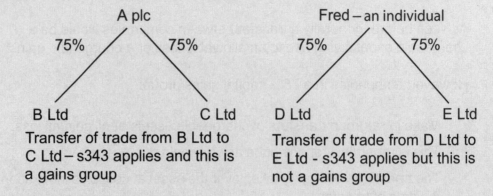

Transfer of trade from B Ltd to C Ltd – s343 applies and this is a gains group

Transfer of trade from D Ltd to E Ltd - s343 applies but this is not a gains group

The same person or persons must have owned at least 75% of the trade:

- at some time within one year before the transfer of the trade, and

- on or at any time within two years after that transfer.

Normally when the trade and assets of a company are transferred to another company:

- any losses remain with the original company

- assets are transferred at market value, therefore
    - balancing adjustments arise for capital allowances
    - capital gains arise.

However, if s343 applies, the following reliefs apply:

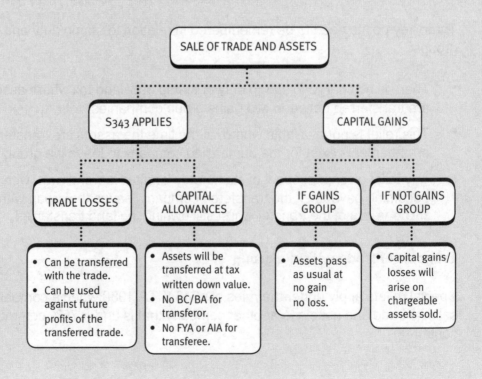

It may be that a company wishes to separate a particular business by transferring it to a newly created subsidiary company. This is often referred to as a **'hive down'**.

In such a situation the above tax reliefs will also be available if all relevant conditions are satisfied.

## 11 Pre-entry capital losses

### Introduction

The rules on pre-entry capital losses are designed to prevent a group from purchasing a company in order to use its capital losses incurred in the period before it joins a gains group via the nil gain/nil loss transfer mechanism.

Where a company joins a gains group it must identify its capital losses (realised and unrealised) at the point of entry.

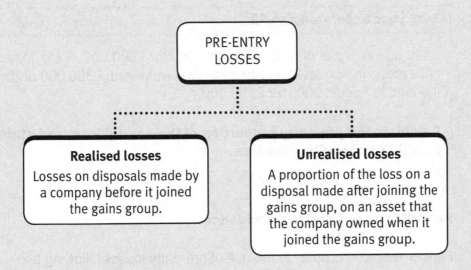

### Calculation of the pre-entry portion of a loss

There are two ways of calculating the unrealised losses at the point of entry into the group:

(i) Calculate the actual capital loss and then time apportion it into the period before and after joining the group.

(ii) Elect for the pre-entry loss to be calculated as the **lower** of

– the loss that would have been made if the asset had been sold for its MV on the date the company joined the group, and

– the actual loss.

This election:

- will only be made if it produces a smaller pre-entry loss
- must be made within two years of the end of the AP of disposal.

## Using the loss

Pre-entry losses can only be used by the company that joins the group. They can use them to relieve gains on assets:

- sold before joining the group (but in the same AP as the loss)
- owned when joining the group and sold later
- bought after joining the group from third parties (i.e. not other group members) and used in their own trade.

### Test your understanding 12

S Ltd bought a plot of land in August 2000 for £500,000. S Ltd joined H Ltd's group in August 2005 when the land was worth £350,000 and sold the land in August 2009 for £300,000.

**Calculate the pre-entry proportion of the capital loss, and state how S Ltd can utilise the loss.**

## Pre-entry losses and tax avoidance

Further restrictions apply to the use of pre-entry losses following tax avoidance schemes invented in the past.

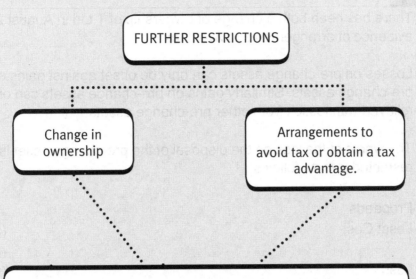

- The entire capital loss on a pre-change asset can only be deducted from a gain arising on another pre-change asset and vice versa.
- A pre-change asset = an asset owned by a company before a change of ownership

## Example 3 – Pre-change asset

T Ltd bought a plot of land in August 2000 for £500,000. T Ltd joined the X Group in August 2009, when the land was worth £350,000. The land was then sold in March 2010 for £320,000.

The circumstances of the change of ownership indicate that there was an intention to deduct this loss to obtain a tax advantage.

T Ltd also sold two further assets during the same accounting period generating gains of £30,000 and £50,000. The gain of £30,000 arose on an asset acquired in August 2005 and the gain of £50,000 on a speculative investment acquired from a third party in September 2009 and sold in March 2010.

**State the tax implications of the above transactions.**

### Solution

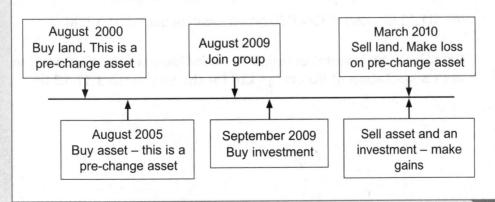

There has been both a change of ownership of T Ltd in August 2009 and evidence of arrangements to avoid tax.

Losses on pre-change assets can only be offset against gains on other pre-change assets. Similarly gains on pre-change assets can only be relieved with losses from other pre-change assets.

The whole of the loss on the disposal of the pre-change asset is a restricted loss as follows:

|  | £ |
|---|---|
| Proceeds | 320,000 |
| Less: Cost | (500,000) |
| Loss | (180,000) |

This loss can be utilised against the pre-change asset gain but not against the asset acquired post entry.

Therefore, £30,000 of the loss will be relieved, leaving £150,000 to carry forward against gains on any other pre-change assets.

Note that there is no time apportionment of the pre-change asset loss.

### Test your understanding 13

Coleridge Ltd became a wholly owned subsidiary of the Poets group of companies on 1 June 2009.

Coleridge had the following gains and losses during its accounting period of 12 months ended 31 December 2009.

(1) 01.02.09: gain of £35,000 on asset acquired in 1998

(2) 01.04.09: loss of £56,000 on an asset acquired 01.02.2003

(3) 01.07.09: gain of £70,000 on an asset acquired from Keats Ltd (also a wholly owned subsidiary of the Poets group)

(4) 01.12.09: loss of £24,000 on an asset acquired 01.12.06.

**Calculate the amount of gains to be included in the corporation tax computation of Coleridge Ltd for the year ended 31.12.09.**

## 12 Reconstructions and reorganisations

The term reconstruction is used to describe a number of situations. In general terms these are transactions in which:

- one company takes over another company, or

- one company takes over the business of another company.

However, because shares or debentures are issued to the original shareholders they retain an interest in the company or its business.

The detailed rules for share for share exchanges are given in expandable text.

### Share for share exchange

When an individual shareholder receives new shares in exchange for existing shares, then share for share exchange rules apply (Chapter 8).

The rules for companies are the same as for individuals except where the substantial shareholding exemption (SSE) rules apply.

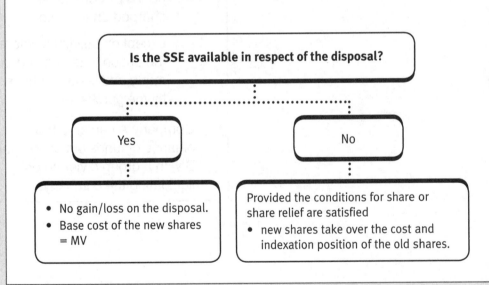

### Sale of shares or assets

A group may also choose to reorganise its business by selling its shares in a subsidiary, or simply by selling the trade and assets of the subsidiary, to a third party.

The main implications of company A selling its shares in company B as opposed to company B selling its trade and assets are as follows:

| Company A sells its shares in company B | B sells its trade and assets |
|---|---|
| • Company A makes gain/loss on disposal of company B shares **unless** SSE is available.<br><br>• Stamp duty at 0.5% is payable on share sales by the purchaser.<br><br>• If company B was associated with A, it will continue to be associated until the end of the CAP.<br><br>• If the companies are in a gains group, there may be degrouping charges when company B leaves the group. | • Company B makes gains/losses on its chargeable assets (e.g. freehold land and buildings).<br><br>• Gains may be rolled over elsewhere if Company B is in a gains group.<br><br>• Taxable credits or allowable debits will arise on the sale of intangible assets.<br><br>• If Company B sells its only trade, then it will cease to trade:<br>  – A CAP will end.<br>  – Terminal loss relief may be available.<br><br>• For VAT, the transfer of going concern rules will probably apply. Therefore<br>  – no VAT needs to be charged on the sale<br>  – except on buildings where the option to tax has been made and is not continued by the purchaser.<br><br>• Company A can strip the balance of funds out of company B with a group dividend or by liquidating the company. |

## 13 VAT

### VAT groups

Companies that are under common control can elect for a group VAT registration, provided that all the companies are UK resident or are trading in the UK via a permanent establishment.

The effect of a group VAT registration is as follows:

- Goods and services supplied by one group company to another are outside the scope of VAT.

- Where there is a registration in force the VAT group appoints a representative member who is responsible for accounting for all input and output VAT.

- The representative member submits a single VAT return covering all group members, but all companies are jointly and severally liable for the VAT payable

- The normal time limits apply for submission of VAT returns.

- An application for group VAT registration has immediate effect, although HMRC has 90 days during which they can refuse the application.

### Advantages and disadvantages of group VAT registration

| Advantages | Disdvantages |
|---|---|
| • VAT on intra-group supplies eliminated. | • All members remain jointly and severally liable. |
| • Only one VAT return required. | • A single return may cause administrative difficulties collecting and collating information. |
| • Flexible: do not have to include all group companies. | • The inclusion of a net repayment company (i.e. a company making wholly or mainly zero rated supplies) would result in loss of monthly repayments. |
| • Companies which make exempt supplies can be included (but see disadvantages). | • Inclusion of an exempt company would cause the group to become partially exempt. This may restrict input tax recovery. |

## Test your understanding 14

Stewart plc owns 100% of the share capital of Enterprise Ltd. Both companies are UK resident trading companies.

All of Stewart's supplies for VAT purposes are taxable. Only 25% of the supplies of Enterprise are taxable and 75% exempt.

Their VAT details for the year ended 31 March 2010 are as follows:

|  |  | £ |
|---|---|---|
| Stewart plc | Total supplies excluding VAT | 600,000 |
|  | Input tax: |  |
|  | Relating to taxable supplies | 60,000 |
|  | Relating to share of group overheads | 5,000 |
| Enterprise Ltd |  |  |
|  | Total supplies excluding VAT | 950,000 |
|  | Input tax: |  |
|  | Relating to taxable supplies | 40,000 |
|  | Relating to exempt supplies | 115,000 |
|  | Relating to share of group overheads | 18,000 |

**Explain whether a group VAT registration would be worthwhile.**

## Divisional registration

In some cases a large enterprise operates not as a group of companies but as a single company with a number of divisions.

If the divisions are largely autonomous units dealing in different products and having separate accounting systems, it may be difficult to produce one VAT return for the whole company.

In these circumstances the company can apply to be registered in the name of its separate divisions.

## 14 Chapter summary

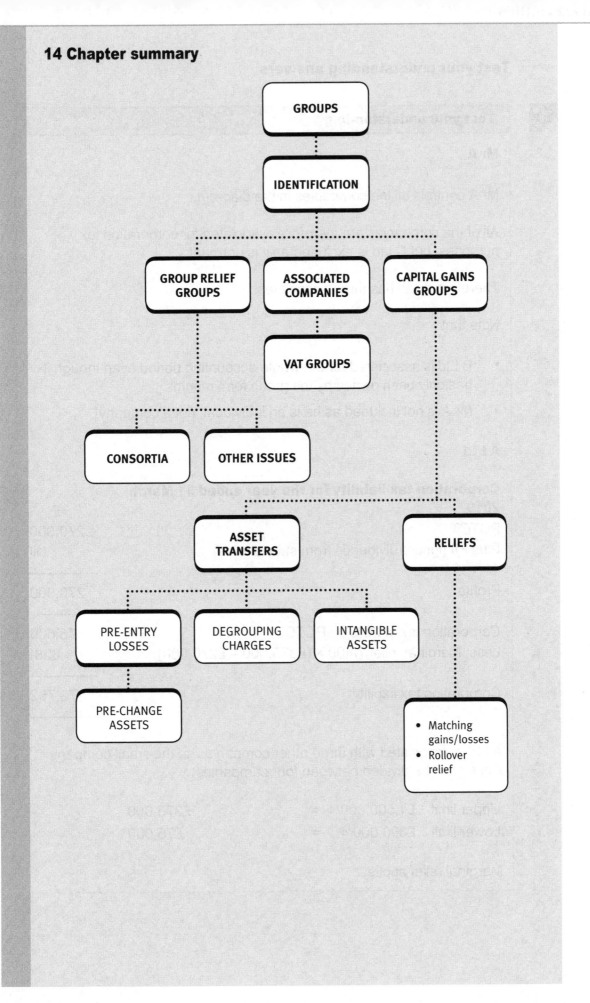

## Test your understanding answers

### Test your understanding 1

**Mr A**

Mr A controls all the companies in the diagram.

All of the companies are therefore associated for corporation tax purposes, but C Ltd is excluded as it is dormant.

Therefore A Ltd has three associates.

Note that:

*   B Ltd is associated for the whole accounting period even though it has only been owned by the group for 4 months.

*   Mr A is not included as he is an individual, not a company!

**A Ltd**

**Corporation tax liability for the year ended 31 March 2010**

|  | £ |
|---|---|
| PCTCT | 270,000 |
| Plus FII (ignore dividends from subsidiaries) | Nil |
| Profits | 270,000 |
| Corporation tax at 28% on PCTCT | 75,600 |
| Less: Marginal relief 7/400 × (£375,000 – £270,000) | (1,838) |
| Corporation tax liability | 73,762 |

A Ltd is associated with three other companies so the small company limits must be divided between four companies:

| | | | |
|---|---|---|---|
| Upper limit | £1,500,000/4 | = | £375,000 |
| Lower limit | £300,000/4 | = | £75,000 |

Marginal relief applies.

**Test your understanding 2**

## X plc

(i) **Associated companies**

All the companies are associated, as they are all under the control of X plc.

Note it does not matter that X plc's indirect interest in D Ltd is only 48% (100 × 80 × 60), it is sufficient that a chain of control has been established.

(ii) **Group loss relief group**

There are two group relief groups.

Group 1: X plc and its 75% directly and indirectly owned subsidiaries Y Inc, C Ltd, A Ltd and Z Ltd.
Note that B Ltd cannot be included in this group as X plc's indirect interest is only 72% (80 × 90).

Group 2: A Ltd and B Ltd.

(iii) **Capital gains group**

The gains group consists of:
X plc, A Ltd, B Ltd, Y Inc, C Ltd and Z Ltd.

B Ltd can be included in the main group with X plc as A Ltd has a holding ≥ 75% in B Ltd and X plc has an indirect interest in B Ltd of > 50%.

Note that although Y Inc (the overseas company) must be included in the definition of the groups, it cannot enjoy any group advantages.

**A Ltd and B Ltd**

(a) **Maximum group relief – y/e 31.12.08**

Lower of:

(1) A Ltd's profit in corresponding period
$$8/12 \times £25,000 = £16,667$$

(2) B Ltd's loss in corresponding period
$$8/11 \times £20,000 = £14,545$$

**Y/e 31.12.08 – A Ltd's revised PCTCT calculation**

|  | £ |
|---|---:|
| PCTCT | 25,000 |
| Less Group relief | (14,545) |
| Revised PCTCT | 10,455 |

(b) **Maximum group relief – y/e 31.12.09**

Lower of:

(1) A Ltd's profit in corresponding period
$$3/12 \times £17,000 = £4,250$$

(2) B Ltd's loss in corresponding period
$$3/11 \times £20,000 = £5,455$$

**Y/e 31.12.09 – A Ltd's revised PCTCT calculation**

|  | £ |
|---|---:|
| PCTCT | 17,000 |
| Less Group relief | (4,250) |
| Revised PCTCT | 12,750 |

**Romeo Ltd**

| Corporation tax computations | Romeo Ltd 12 months to 31/12/2009 £ | Juliet Ltd 9 months to 31/3/2010 £ |
|---|---|---|
| Trading profit | 890,000 | Nil |
| Interest income | 6,000 | 4,000 |
| Property business profit | 2,000 | 8,000 |
| Chargeable gains | | 15,000 |
| | | |
| Total profits | 898,000 | 27,000 |
| Less: Loss relief | | (27,000) |
| Gift Aid donation | (4,000) | (Wasted) |
| | | |
| | 894,000 | Nil |
| Less: Group relief (W2) | (68,000) | |
| | | |
| PCTCT | 826,000 | Nil |
| | | |
| Corporation tax (28% × £826,000) | 231,280 | Nil |

**Notes:**

(i) The capital loss £20,000 in Romeo Ltd must be c/fwd for set off against future chargeable gains.

(ii) There is no FII for Romeo Ltd as dividends from associated companies are excluded

**Workings:**

**(W1) Upper and lower limits for corporation tax for Romeo Ltd**

There are two companies under common control.

Romeo Ltd – 12 months AP to 31.12.2009 is in FY 2008 and FY 2009 but the main limits are identical.

The applicable upper and lower limits are therefore:

£1,500,000 × 1/2 = £750,000
£300,000 × 1/2 = £150,000

## (W2) Loss available for group relief

The common/corresponding accounting period, is 6 months to 31 December 2009 (1.7.2009 to 31.12.2009).

Juliet Ltd         1.7.2009                               31.3.2010

**6 months CAP**

Romeo Ltd ——————————————————

         1.1.2009                      31.12.2009

Therefore, maximum group relief = lower of:

| | | | |
|---|---|---|---|
| (a) | Loss of Juliet Ltd | £102,000 × 6/9 | £68,000 |
| (b) | Romeo Ltd's 'profits' | (6/12 × £894,000) | £447,000 |

## Test your understanding 5

### A Ltd and B Ltd

(i)   This is not a consortium.

     A Ltd has ≥ 75% of C Ltd so this is a 75% group.

(ii)   This is a consortium. D Ltd, C Ltd and F Ltd own ≥ 75% of G Ltd and each own ≥ 5%.

     G Ltd is the consortium company and D Ltd, C Ltd and F Ltd are consortium members.

## Test your understanding 6

| P Ltd and Q Ltd | P Ltd | Q Ltd |
|---|---|---|
| | £ | £ |
| Maximum CR = lower of | | |
| (1) Available profits of members | 50,000 | 15,000 |
| (2) Available loss of consortia company | | |
| 70% × £60,000 | 42,000 | |
| 30% × £60,000 | | 18,000 |
| | | |
| Maximum amount | 42,000 | 15,000 |

### X Ltd and Y Ltd

X Ltd can use part of its loss to relieve up to 40% of C Ltd's PCTCT = £20,000. X Ltd cannot surrender any of its loss to Y Ltd.

## Test your understanding 7

### Blue Ltd, Rose Ltd, Pink Ltd and Mauve Ltd

(i) **Corporation tax computations**

| Blue Ltd | £ |
|---|---|
| Trading profit | 300,000 |
| Consortium relief (W): | |
| – From Rose Ltd | (45,000) |
| – From Pink Ltd | (105,000) |
| | |
| PCTCT | 150,000 |
| | |
| CT Liability (£150,000 × 21%) | 31,500 |

| Rose Ltd | |
|---|---|
| CT liability | Nil |
| | |
| Loss carried forward (W) | 45,000 |

| Pink Ltd | |
|---|---|
| CT liability | Nil |
| | |
| Loss carried forward (W) | 21,000 |

**Mauve Ltd**

| | |
|---|---:|
| PCTCT | 55,000 |
| CT liability (£55,000 × 21%) | 11,550 |

**Note:** Mauve Ltd has exactly 50% of the share capital of Blue Ltd (not more than 50%), and so they are not associated companies.

**Working: Maximum consortium relief**

| | Rose Ltd £ | Pink Ltd £ |
|---|---:|---:|
| Lower of | | |
| (i) Consortium member loss | 90,000 | 126,000 |
| (ii) % of consortium company profits | | |
| 15% × £300,000 | 45,000 | |
| 35% × £300,000 | | 105,000 |
| | | |
| Loss left to c/f | 45,000 | 21,000 |

(ii) **If Rose Ltd owned 80% of Blue Ltd**

The two companies would be associated and form a group relief group.

The whole of Rose Ltd's loss would be available as group relief to reduce the PCTCT of Blue Ltd to £210,000 (£300,000 – £90,000). With one associated company this would make Blue Ltd a marginal company.

Pink's loss would no longer be available to Blue Ltd and would have to be used by Pink Ltd only.

Mauve Ltd would be unaffected.

---

**Test your understanding 8**

**Green Ltd**

| | £ |
|---|---:|
| **Intergroup transfer:** | |
| Cost | 100,000 |
| Plus Indexation Allowance: (April 1983 to October (1993) | |
| ((141.8 – 84.28)/84.28) = 0.682 × £100,000 | 68,200 |
| | |
| Base cost | 168,200 |

**Sale outside the group:**

|  | £ |
|---|---|
| Proceeds | 350,000 |
| Less: Base cost | (168,200) |
| Unindexed gain | 181,800 |
| Less: IA (October 1993 to December 2009) | |
| $((213.1 - 141.8)/141.8) = 0.503 \times £168,200$ | (84,605) |
| Chargeable gain | 97,195 |

### Test your understanding 9

**Orange Ltd**

When Orange Ltd leaves the group, the company still owns an asset which it had acquired from Yellow Ltd in the six years preceding Orange Ltd's departure.

Orange Ltd is treated as if it had sold the building on 1 December 2003 at its market value on that date, and then immediately reacquired it.

|  | £ |
|---|---|
| Proceeds | 375,000 |
| Less: Base Cost: (Note): | |
| Cost to Yellow Ltd | (180,000) |
| IA (Aug 1990 – Dec 2003) | |
| $((183.5 - 128.1)/128.1) = 0.432 \times £180,000$ | (77,760) |
| Chargeable gain | 117,240 |

The chargeable gain is assessed on Orange Ltd in the y/e 31 March 2010 (i.e. in the accounting period in which Orange Ltd left the group).

**Note:** Orange Ltd's cost is the original cost to Yellow Ltd plus the indexation allowance from the date of purchase by Yellow Ltd to the date of transfer to Orange Ltd.

**Mauve Ltd and Violet Ltd**

**Year ended 31 March 2010 – PCTCT computation**

The statutory limits with two associated companies:

Upper Limit = £750,000
Lower Limit = £150,000

Violet Ltd is therefore paying CT at the marginal rate of 29.75% with profits of £250,000. Mauve Ltd is a small company paying CT at 21% with profits of £30,000.

To minimise tax for the group as a whole:

- Violet Ltd and Mauve Ltd should dispose of their chargeable assets realising their capital gain and capital loss.

- The group should then make an election by 31.3.2012 to reallocate the capital loss in Violet to Mauve Ltd.

- As a result the capital gain and capital loss are treated as being realised by Mauve Ltd.

- The group will therefore suffer CT at 21% on the £25,000 gain.

- If the net gain had been assessable on Violet Ltd the group would suffer corporation tax at 29.75%.

|  | Mauve Ltd £ | Violet Ltd £ |
|---|---|---|
| Trading profits | 30,000 | 250,000 |
| Capital gain (£100,000 – £75,000) | 25,000 | |
| PCTCT | 55,000 | 250,000 |

**Test your understanding 11**

**Apple Ltd**

(a) (i) **Group relationships**

*Group relief*

For group relief purposes, two companies are members of a 75% group where one of them is a 75% subsidiary of the other, or both of them are 75% subsidiaries of the holding company.

To qualify as a 75% subsidiary, the holding company must hold 75% or more of the subsidiary's ordinary share capital, and have the right to receive 75% or more of its distributable profits and net assets (were it to be wound up). The 75% holding must be an effective interest that is held directly or indirectly.

*Capital gain*

For the purposes of transferring chargeable assets between two companies without incurring a chargeable gain or an allowable loss, the definition of a 75% subsidiary is 'less rigorous' than for group relief. The 75% holding must only be met at each level in the group structure, subject to the principal company having an effective interest of over 50%.

(ii) **Surrender of trading losses**

The most important factor that should be taken into account when deciding which group companies the trading losses should be surrendered to is the rate of corporation tax applicable to those companies.

Surrender should be made initially to companies subject to corporation tax at the marginal rate of 29.75%. The amount surrendered should be sufficient to bring the claimant company's profits down to the lower limit.

Surrender should then be to those companies subject to the full rate of corporation tax of 28%, and lastly to companies subject to corporation tax at the small company rate of 21%.

The ability of companies with minority interests to compensate for group relief surrenders will be another factor.

(b)  (i)  **Profits chargeable to coporation tax**

| | Apple Ltd £ | Bramley Ltd £ | Cox Ltd £ | Delicious Ltd £ |
|---|---|---|---|---|
| **Y/e 31 March 2009** | | | | |
| Trading profit | 620,000 | Nil | 83,000 | |
| Group relief (B to A) | (64,000) | | | |
| PCTCT | 556,000 | Nil | 83,000 | |
| **Y/e 31 March 2010** | | | | |
| Trading profit | 250,000 | 52,000 | Nil | 90,000 |
| Capital gain (part (ii)) | | | 20,000 | |
| Group relief (C to A) | (58,000) | | | |
| Loss relief s393A | | | | (15,000) |
| PCTCT | 192,000 | 52,000 | 20,000 | 75,000 |
| **Y/e 31 March 2011** | | | | |
| Trading profit | 585,000 | 70,000 | 40,000 | Nil |
| Capital gain (part (ii)) | | | | Nil |
| PCTCT | 585,000 | 70,000 | 40,000 | Nil |

(ii)  **Explanation of claims used**

– For the year to 31 March 2009 there are three associates.

   *Small company rate*
   LL      £30,000 × 1/3 = £100,000
   UL      £1,500,000 × 1/3 = £500,000

– For the years to 31 March 2010 and 2011 there are four associates.

   *Small company rate*
   LL      £30,000 × 1/4 = £75,000
   UL      £1,500,000 × 1/4 = £375,000

– Delicious Ltd is part of the Apple Ltd capital gains group.

– Delicious Ltd is only grouped with Cox Ltd for group relief purposes (85% × 80% = 68%).

**Reliefs claimed to maximise corporation tax saving:**

(1) A claim for rollover relief is possible because the reinvestment by Cox Ltd on 20 September 2010 took place within three years of Apple Ltd selling both of its freehold buildings.

Only one of the following claims is possible:

– *Claim against 10 March 2010 disposal:*
 – Only £20,000 (£380,000 – £360,000) not reinvested.
 – Gain rolled over £100,000 (£120,000 – £20,000).
 – Marginal tax saving 29.75%.

– *Claim against 5 October 2010 disposal:*
 – Only £5,000 (£365,000 – £360,000) not reinvested.
 – Gain rolled over £75,000 (£80,000 – £5,000).
 – Marginal tax saving 28%.
 – Can use Delicious Ltd's capital loss to fully shelter this gain in any case (see below).

Claim against 10 March 2010 disposal preferable. Remaining gain of £20,000 is reallocated to Cox Ltd so only taxed at 21%.

(2) Apple Ltd's gain of £80,000 in the year ended 31 March 2011 is reallocated to Delicious Ltd:

– Delicious Ltd's capital loss of £90,000 set against the gain.
– Net chargeable gain is £Nil.
– Capital loss carried forward in Delicious Ltd is £10,000 (£90,000 – £80,000).

(3) Bramley Ltd's loss of £64,000 for the year ended 31 March 2009 is surrendered to Apple Ltd saving tax at 28%. The alternatives would be:

– group relief to Cox Ltd saving tax at 21% in the year ended 31 March 2009;
– carry forward in Bramley Ltd saving tax at 21% with two years of delay until fully relieved.

(4) Cox Ltd's loss of £58,000 for the year ended 31 March 2010 is surrendered to Apple Ltd, rather than being carried back or surrendered to Bramley Ltd. Relief is at the marginal rate of 29.75% in Apple Ltd in the year ended 31 March 2010 rather than at the small company rate of 21% in Bramley Ltd or in Cox Ltd in the year ended 31 March 2009.

(5) Delicious Ltd's loss of £15,000 for the year to 31 March 2011 is relieved at the marginal rate of 29.75% by making a carry back claim. A group relief claim to Cox Ltd in the year to 31 March 2011 would only save tax at 21%. Group relief is not possible to any other company.

## Test your understanding 12

**S Ltd**

| | £ |
|---|---|
| Proceeds | 300,000 |
| Less: Cost | (500,000) |
| | |
| Total loss | (200,000) |

Time apportioned pre-entry loss:

$$£200,000 \times \frac{\text{Aug 2000} - \text{Aug 2005}}{\text{Aug 2000} - \text{Aug 2009}} = £200,000 \times 5/9 \qquad 111,111$$

**Loss with the election:**

| | | £ |
|---|---|---|
| (a) | Loss if sold on date of joining group | |
| | Notional proceeds | 350,000 |
| | Less: Cost | (500,000) |
| | | |
| | Notional loss | (150,000) |
| | | |
| (b) | Loss on the actual sale | 200,000 |
| | | |
| | Lower loss | 150,000 |

## Conclusion

S Ltd wants the pre-entry portion of the loss to be as small as possible because the use of that part of the loss is restricted. It will therefore not make the election and the pre-entry loss will be £111,111.

S Ltd's pre-entry loss can only be used against gains directly connected with S Ltd's own business.

The balance of S Ltd's loss £88,889 (£200,000 – £111,111) can be used as a normal capital loss without restriction.

## Test your understanding 13

### Coleridge Ltd

Provided there are no arrangements to avoid tax or obtain a tax advantage, the computation is as follows:

*   The loss of £56,000 is a pre-entry loss.
*   Part of the £24,000 loss is also pre-entry.
*   These losses can be used against the gain of £35,000 realised before Coleridge Ltd joined the group reducing that gain to £Nil.
*   The post entry portion of the £24,000 loss can be used against the gain of £70,000 on the asset acquired from another group company.

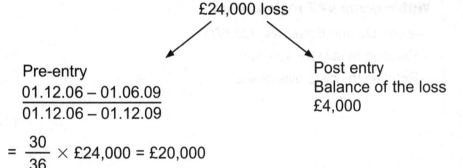

£24,000 loss

Pre-entry

$$\frac{01.12.06 - 01.06.09}{01.12.06 - 01.12.09}$$

$$= \frac{30}{36} \times £24,000 = £20,000$$

Post entry
Balance of the loss
£4,000

*   Chargeable gains for the year ended 31.12.09 are £66,000 (£70,000 – £4,000).

Note that if there had been evidence of arrangements to avoid tax, then the £4,000 loss would be on a pre-change asset and could not be used against the £70,000 gain.

**Stewart plc**

**Without a group registration:**

Both companies account for VAT separately and the input tax recovery would be as follows:

|  | £ |
|---|---:|
| Stewart plc (can recover all input VAT) | 65,000 |
| Enterprise Ltd (W1) | 44,500 |
| Recoverable input VAT | 109,500 |

**With a group VAT registration:**

Stewart plc and Enterprise Ltd (W2)

|  | £ |
|---|---:|
| – Relating to taxable supplies | 100,000 |
| – Relating to group overheads | 12,650 |
|  | 112,650 |

**Conclusion**

It is worthwhile for Stewart plc and Enterprise Ltd to form a VAT group as it allows a higher recovery of input VAT of £3,150 (£112,650 – £109,500).

**Working**

| (W1) **Enterprise Ltd** | Total | Recover | Disallow |
|---|---:|---:|---:|
|  | £ | £ | £ |
| Relating to taxable supplies | 40,000 | 40,000 |  |
| Relating to exempt supplies | 115,000 |  | 115,000 |
| Relating to overheads (25%/75%) | 18,000 | 4,500 | 13,500 |
|  | 173,000 | 44,500 | 128,500 |

**De minimus test:** The exempt input tax is £128,500 and as this amounts to more than £625 per month on average it is all irrecoverable.

**(W2) Group position**

| | Total £ | Recover £ | Disallow £ |
|---|---|---|---|
| Relating to taxable supplies (£60,000 + £40,000) | 100,000 | 100,000 | |
| Relating to exempt supplies | 115,000 | | 115,000 |
| Relating to overheads (£5,000 + £18,000) (see below for split) (55% / 45%) | 23,000 | 12,650 | 10,350 |
| | 238,000 | 112,650 | 125,350 |

**Split of non-attributable VAT**

Taxable supplies = £600,000 + (25% × £950,000) = £837,500

Total supplies = £600,000 + £950,000 = £1,550,000

Taxable % apportionment

£837,500 ÷ £1,550,000 × 100 = 55% (rounded up to whole %)

**De minimus test:** The exempt input tax is £125,350 and as this amounts to more than £625 per month on average it is all irrecoverable.

# 28

# Overseas aspects of corporation tax

## Chapter learning objectives

Upon completion of this chapter you will be able to:

- explain how the residence of a company is determined and state the impact

- recognise the impact of the OECD model double tax treaty on corporation tax

- explain the meaning of and implications of a permanent establishment

- advise on the tax position of a non UK resident company trading in the UK

- determine the corporation tax liability when a UK company has overseas chargeable profits and calculate the double taxation relief available

- identify and advise on the tax implications of controlled foreign companies.

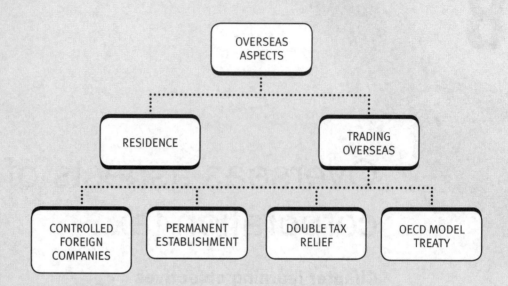

# 1 Introduction

This chapter considers the overseas aspects of corporation tax. Much of the content of this chapter is covered at F6, however, at P6 a more detailed knowledge of this area is required.

This chapter aims to show the impact of:

- UK resident companies trading overseas via a branch or an overseas company set up for the purpose, and

- overseas companies trading in the UK.

The main new area introduced at P6 is the legislation on controlled foreign companies.

## 2 Company residence

### Determining UK residence

Under UK law, a company is resident in the UK if

- it is incorporated in the UK, or

- has its place of central management and control in the UK.

The centre of management and control is where the key operational and financial decisions are made. HMRC will look at factors such as:

- the location of the board meetings

- where the effective day-to-day management decisions are made.

- the residence status of the directors.

No one factor is conclusive in determining the centre of management and control.

Note that other countries may have different definitions to determine residency status. Therefore, it is possible for a company to have dual residence status.

For example, a company incorporated in another country may be treated as resident there, but if it were centrally managed and controlled in the UK it would also be treated as resident here in the UK.

## Implications of UK residence

A UK resident company is chargeable to corporation tax on its worldwide profits. This includes;

- all UK profits
- overseas branch profits
- dividends received from overseas subsidiaries and investments
- other overseas income (e.g. rental income) and capital gains.

## 3 OECD model tax treaty

### Introduction

The OECD (Organisation for Economic Cooperation and Development) is an organisation of developed countries whose main purpose is to maintain financial stability and the expansion of world trade.

In order to help avoid double taxation between countries, the OECD has published a model Double Taxation Convention with an accompanying commentary.

### Significance of the OECD model double tax treaty

The UK has a large number of double tax treaties with other countries. Whenever a new treaty is drawn up or an old treaty is renegotiated, the OECD model is used as a guide.

Detailed knowledge of treaties is not required in your examination but you are required to understand the impact of the OECD model double tax treaty on corporation tax.

The main function of any treaty is to avoid double taxation and to decide which country shall have the right to tax income.

### Contents of the model treaty

Some of the main areas covered in the treaty are as follows:

| | |
|---|---|
| Article 1: | states that companies which are covered by the treaty are those resident in one or both of the countries involved. |
| Article 4: | explains that residence is determined by the laws of a state (i.e. not by the model treaty itself). Includes a 'tie breaker' clause to be applied when a company appears to be resident in two countries. |
| | In this case, residence is where the place of 'effective management' is situated. This is usually where the head office, main company records and senior staff are located. |
| Article 5: | deals with the meaning of 'permanent establishment' – see below for more detail. |
| Articles 6 to 22: | deal with the treatment of different types of income. |
| Article 23: | explains the two methods of giving relief for double taxation |

- exempting the income in one state and taxing it only in the other, or

- the credit method which gives credit in one state for the tax levied by the other. The credit method (also known as unilateral relief) is covered in section 5.

## 4 Trading overseas

### The taxation of overseas trading income

The normal provision in tax treaties (based on the OECD model treaty) is that a foreign country will usually only tax income arising in its country from the commercial operation of a UK resident company if:

(a)  a trade is carried on **within its boundaries**; and

(b)  the profits are derived from a **permanent establishment** set up for that purpose.

The term 'within a country's boundaries' is important, because trading **with**, as opposed to **within**, another country will avoid any liability to overseas profits taxes.

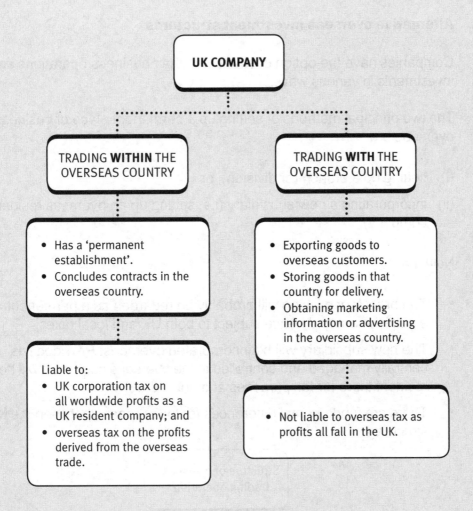

## Permanent establishment

The term 'permanent establishment' within an overseas country includes

- a place of management
- a branch
- an office
- a factory, a workshop or any mine or other place of extraction of natural resources.

A UK resident company that has a permanent establishment trading within an overseas country will normally:

- be charged to tax on its overseas profits arising,
- by both HMRC under the UK residence rule, and
- the overseas tax authority under their own tax code.

Double tax relief (DTR) will be available (section 5).

## Alternative overseas investment structures

Companies have the option of structuring their business operations and investments in various ways.

The two principal methods of setting up a permanent place of business overseas are:

(i)  setting up a branch (or division); or

(ii) incorporating a new subsidiary (i.e. setting up an overseas resident company).

Note that:

- The branch or division will probably be regarded as a permanent establishment and hence subject to both UK and local taxes.

- The new subsidiary will be incorporated overseas. Provided it is centrally managed and controlled in the overseas country, it will be resident there for tax purposes and not in the UK.

- There are fundamental differences for tax purposes between the two structures.

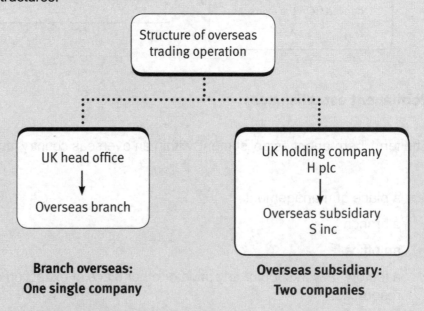

## Overseas dividends

Overseas dividends are treated in the same way as UK dividends:

- They are exempt from corporation tax

- They are included in FII, unless dividends received from associated companies, in which case they are ignored completely for corporation tax purposes.

The tax implications of both structures:

| | Overseas branch | Overseas subsidiary |
|---|---|---|
| **Scope and basis of charge** | • Extension of UK operations.<br><br>• All profits arising assessed on UK company.<br><br>• If the branch is controlled from the UK:<br>　– then its trading profit is added to UK trading profit.<br><br>• If trade is the same as in UK:<br>　– included in trading income, and available for relief of b/f trading losses. | • Foreign company profits not assessable in UK.<br><br>• Profits remitted to UK may be chargeable when received (e.g. foreign interest but not foreign dividends) |
| **Trading loss relief** | • Can relieve trading losses against UK profits:<br>　– unless the loss can be relieved in the country in which it arose. | • UK trading loss<br>　– cannot be surrendered to overseas subsidiary.<br><br>• Overseas loss from 75% subsidiary in EEA<br>　– can be surrendered to UK parent if no alternative relief in overseas country. |
| **Capital allowances and IBAs** | • Available on overseas located assets purchased and used by overseas branch. | • Not available under UK tax rules. |

|  | **Overseas branch** | **Overseas subsidiary** |
|---|---|---|
| **Chargeable gains** | • Capital gains computed using UK rules<br><br>• Rollover relief is available on reinvestment<br><br>• Capital losses can be utilised. | • Not assessed in UK. |
| **Impact on tax rates** | • None (as not a separate entity). | • As an associated company, the upper and lower limits for marginal relief are reduced. |

## Tax planning

Where a new overseas operation is expected to make losses initially, it may be advantageous to set it up as a branch.

Once the overseas operation expects to be profitable, its trade can be transferred to an overseas resident subsidiary company so that its profits are not taxable in the UK (if paid as dividends).

* Starting as a branch would enable the UK company to offset the losses against its other profits.

* The transfer of the trade represents a disposal of the assets of the branch at MV which may lead to:
    – balancing adjustments in respect of assets qualifying for capital allowances, and
    – chargeable gains.

* Where all of the assets of the branch (excluding cash) are transferred to the overseas company in exchange for shares:
    – an election is available
    – to defer any gains arising until the overseas company is sold.

* The deferred gains will also be charged if the overseas company disposes of the assets transferred to it within six years of acquisition.

* Consideration should be given as to whether or not it is necessary to obtain the consent of the Treasury for the transfer of the trade to the overseas company. This is because it is generally illegal for a UK resident company to permit a non-UK resident company over which it has control to create or issue shares.

### Example 1 – Branch vs subsidiary

**Explain the advantages for taxation purposes of operating overseas through a branch rather than through an overseas subsidiary.**

**Solution**

**Advantages of operating through an overseas branch**

(1)  Relief is usually available in the UK for trading losses if incurred by an overseas branch, but no UK relief is available for trading losses incurred by an overseas subsidiary unless the overseas subsidiary is resident in the EEA.

(2)  UK capital allowances are available in respect of plant and machinery purchased by an overseas branch.

(3)  Unlike an overseas subsidiary, an overseas branch cannot be an associated company. The UK corporation tax limits will therefore not be reduced.

### Worldwide debt cap

For accounting periods commencing on/after 1 January 2010, there is a potential restriction on the amount of finance expense that UK group members can deduct, the 'worldwide debt cap'.

Broadly speaking, it will be limited to the consolidated gross finance expense. You are not expected to know any further details for this exam.

### Foreign companies trading in the UK

A non-UK resident company can be liable to UK corporation tax on trading profits if it trades **within** the UK, but not for trading **with** the UK.

*   Trading within the UK means either trading through a permanent establishment or concluding contracts in the UK.

*   Trading with the UK means activities such as exporting goods to UK customers, storing goods in the UK for customers and advertising and marketing activities in the UK.

Corporation tax is generally charged at the full rate unless there is a double taxation treaty specifying a lower rate.

### Example 2 – Trading in the UK

Morn Inc is a large company resident in Shortland. Morn Inc manufactures mobile telephones in Shortland, and has been selling these in the UK since 1 September 2009.

Initially, Morn Inc sold the telephones through a UK based agent and stored the telephones in a rented warehouse. On 1 February 2010 Morn Inc rented an office and showroom in London which were staffed initially by two sales managers and an administrator from Shortland.

Morn Inc intends to incorporate a UK subsidiary company on 31 December 2010 to operate the UK business.

There is no double tax treaty between the UK and Shortland.

**Advise Morn Inc of its liability to UK corporation tax during the period from 1 September 2009 to 31 December 2010.**

**Solution**

Morn Inc will be liable to UK CT if it is trading through a permanent establishment in the UK (i.e. trading within the UK). The company will not be liable to UK CT if it is merely trading with the UK.

From 1 September 2009 to 31 January 2010, Morn Inc employed a UK agent, and maintained a stock of telephones in the UK. Provided that contracts for the sale of the telephones are concluded in Shortland, Morn Inc will probably not be liable to UK CT on profits made during this period.

On 1 February 2010, Morn Inc would appear to have opened a permanent establishment in the UK by renting an office and showroom, and it is likely that the sales managers will be empowered to conclude contracts in the UK.

Morn Inc will therefore be liable to UK CT on the profits made in the UK during the period from 1 February 2010 to the date that the trade is transferred to the new company (presumably 31 December 2010).

CT will be at the full rate regardless of the level of profits made in the UK, or by Morn Inc, since there is no double taxation treaty between the UK and Shortland.

## 5 Double taxation relief

### Introduction

UK resident companies can get relief for overseas taxes suffered in the following ways:

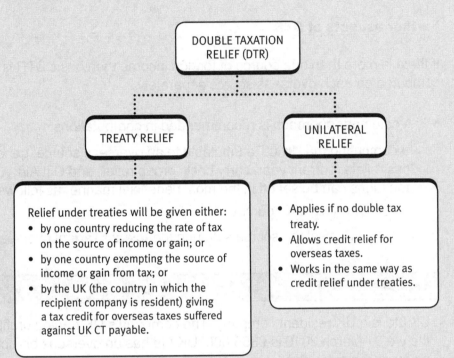

### Calculation of tax credit

All overseas income must be included in the PCTCT computation gross (i.e. including any overseas taxation suffered).

Relief is available for overseas withholding tax (WHT) as follows:

- WHT = any overseas tax deducted at source from foreign income.

- If the **amount** of WHT is given
  - simply add it back to the net income to give the gross amount.

- If the **rate** of WHT is given
  - gross up as normal.

There is no longer any relief for underlying tax, as overseas dividends are now not taxable in the UK.

DTR is the **lower of:**

(i)  overseas tax suffered; and

(ii)  UK CT attributable to the overseas income (using effective rate).

### Further aspects of DTR

If there is more than one source of foreign income then basic DTR is computed on each overseas source separately.

- A columnar approach is recommended in computations.
- In computing the UK CT attributable to an overseas source, general loss reliefs (current year, carry back, group relief) and Gift Aid donations can be set off in the most beneficial manner as follows:
    - first against UK sources
    - then against the source suffering the **lowest rate** of overseas tax.

### Example 3 – DTR

UK Ltd is a UK resident company. The company's UK trading profit for the y/e 31 March 2010 is £355,000. UK Ltd has an overseas branch and an overseas subsidiary.

**Overseas branch**

The branch is controlled from overseas. It has a trading profit of £65,000 for the y/e 31 March 2010. The overseas corporation tax on these profits is £26,000.

**Overseas subsidiary**

UK Ltd owns 80% of the share capital of Overseas Inc, a company that is resident overseas. UK Ltd received a dividend of £80,750 during the y/e 31 March 2010. This dividend was net of withholding tax of £4,250.

UK Ltd did not receive any other dividends.

**Calculate UK Ltd's CT liability for the y/e 31 March 2010.**

## Solution

| | Total £ | UK £ | Branch £ |
|---|---|---|---|
| Trading profits | 420,000 | 355,000 | 65,000 |
| PCTCT | 420,000 | 355,000 | 65,000 |
| CT @ 28% | 117,600 | | |
| Less MR (W1) | (5,775) | | |
| | 111,825 | 94,519 | 17,306 |
| DTR(W3) | (17,306) | | (17,306) |
| CT liability | 94,519 | 94,519 | Nil |

### (W1) Corporation tax rate

Overseas Inc is an associated company, so the upper limit for corporation tax purposes is £750,000 (£1,500,000/2).

The dividend received from Overseas Inc is group income, and is therefore not included as FII.

PCTCT = Profits, as UK Ltd has no FII.

Marginal relief applies.

MR = 7/400 × (£750,000 – £420,000) = £5,775

Effective rate of tax = (£111,825/£420,000) × 100 = 26.625%

### (W2) DTR

| | £ |
|---|---|
| Lower of: | |
| (i) Overseas tax (W1) | 26,000 |
| (ii) UK CT (26.625% × £65,000) | 17,306 |

---

### Test your understanding 1

Z plc has the following income for the year ended 31 March 2010

| | |
|---|---|
| Trading profit | £200,000 |
| Foreign dividends received 1 March 2010 (net of 29% WHT) | £5,680 |
| Foreign rents received (net of 17% WHT) | £4,980 |

Z plc paid a Gift Aid donation of £100,000.

The foreign dividends are received from an overseas company in which Z plc has a 5% interest.

**Compute the corporation tax payable by Z plc.**

### Test your understanding 2

R plc has received rent of £119,000 in the year ended 31 March 2010 from a foreign company in which it has a 20% interest.

A WHT rate of 15% has been applied to the rent received by R plc.

**Compute the CT payable by R plc, on the assumption that R plc has trading profits of £900,000 in the year ended 31 March 2010 in addition to the overseas income but no other income, or gains.**

### Unrelieved overseas tax

Initially DTR is dealt with on a source by source basis. This can lead to overseas tax being only partly relieved.

Utilise the excess overseas taxes according to the following:

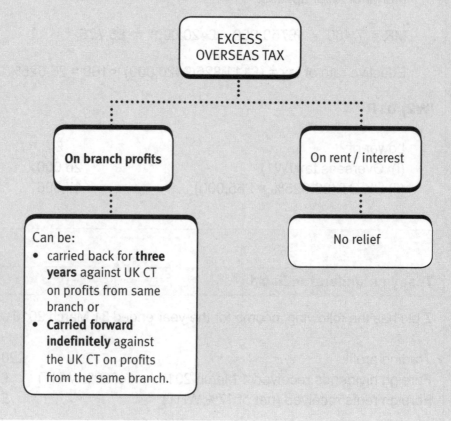

## 6 Controlled foreign companies

### Introduction

If a UK company is considering setting up an overseas subsidiary, it will be attracted to countries with low rates of tax (known as tax havens).

There is anti avoidance legislation in place to prevent UK companies diverting profits out of the UK to countries charging low rates of tax. These companies are called Controlled Foreign Companies (CFCs).

### Definition of a CFC

A CFC is a company:

- resident outside the UK

- controlled by persons resident in the UK

- subject to a lower level of taxation (less than 75% of the UK rate).

### Effect of a CFC

The aim of the anti-avoidance provisions is to charge the same rate of tax on profits of CFCs as in the UK.

- This is achieved by legislating that any UK company having at least a **25% interest** in the CFC may suffer a UK tax charge in respect of its share of the extra tax that would have been payable in the UK.

- UK companies are required to self assess their liability and complete a supplementary form to accompany the CT600 return giving:
  - details of the CFC
  - country of residence
  - % holding, and
  - taxes paid.

- This apportionment can be avoided if the foreign company meets any **one** of the following **three** conditions:

  (1) **Motive test**

  The foreign company does not exist wholly or mainly to reduce UK tax by diverting profits out of the UK.

  (2) **Profit**

  The foreign company's profits are £50,000 or less in a 12-month period.

### (3) **Exempt activities test**

- The foreign company must be involved in exempt activities. A normal trading company will be exempt.

- Examples of non exempt activities are:
  (i) an investment company, or
  (ii) a company involved mainly in goods for delivery to or from the UK company.

- This exemption does not apply to holding companies, except for local holding companies.

---

## Example 4 – Controlled foreign companies

X plc is a large UK company with annual profits of £10 million. They are considering investing overseas and have identified two possible alternative investments in Farland where the corporate tax rate is only 10%.

X plc plan to buy a 70% stake in Dorn Inc, an investment company resident in Farland. Dorn Inc makes regular annual profits of £2 million. Alternatively, they could invest in Burton Inc which is a trading company but only produces profits of £1 million.

There is no double tax treaty between the UK and Farland.

**Advise the tax considerations that X plc should take into account before making their investment.**

**Solution**

**Dividends**

- Any dividends paid by the foreign companies to X plc will be exempt for X plc.

- As X plc plans to acquire more than 50%, the dividends will not be included as FII.

### Controlled foreign companies

- Both of the potential investments will be classed as CFCs. They are:

  (i) resident outside the UK

  (ii) controlled by persons resident in the UK

  (iii) subject to a lower level of taxation (10% is < 75% of the UK rate).

- This means that X plc could have an additional tax charge at 28% on their 70% share of profits.

- However, Burton Inc is a trading company and should be exempt from the apportionment charge.

### Loss relief

It is not possible for losses to be surrendered from an overseas company to a UK company unless:

(i) the UK company has at least 75% interest in the overseas company's shares

(ii) no other method of relieving the loss exists

(iii) the company is resident in the EEA.

In this case there cannot be any relief for losses made in Farland as the company proposes to buy only a 70% stake. The other points are unknown.

### Test your understanding 3

**Explain which of the following companies are likely to give rise to an apportionment under the CFC rules:**

(1) Alcock Inc – resident in Ruritania where the CT rate is 8%. Alcock Inc is an investment company producing profits of £40,000 p.a.

(2) Barbauld SA – resident in Narnia where the CT rate is 25%. Barbauld SA is an investment company producing profits of £2 million p.a.

(3) Blake Inc – resident in Albion where the CT rate is 5%. Blake Inc manufactures nursery accessories and makes profits of £750,000 p.a.

## 7 Chapter summary

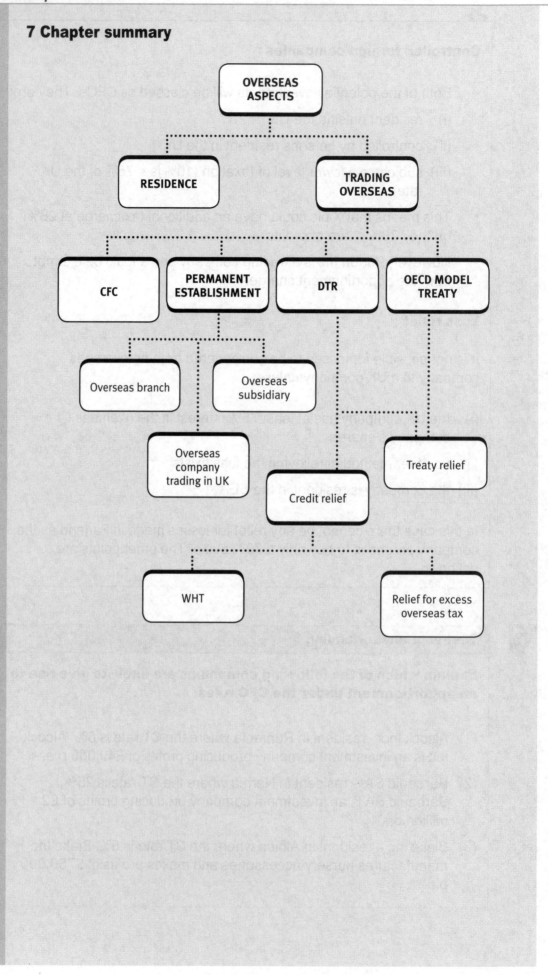

## Test your understanding answers

**Z plc**

**Corporation tax computation – year ended 31 March 2010**

|  | UK Income £ | Foreign Rent £ | Total £ |
|---|---|---|---|
| Income (W1) | 200,000 | 6,000 | 206,000 |
| Less: Gift Aid | (100,000) | – | (100,000) |
| PCTCT | 100,000 | 6,000 | 106,000 |
| CT @ 21% (W2) | 21,000 | 1,260 | 22,260 |
| Less: DTR(W3) | – | (1,020) | (1,020) |
| CT liability | 21,000 | 240 | 21,240 |

**Workings**

**(W1) Gross overseas rental income**

|  | £ |
|---|---|
| Amounts received | 4,980 |
| Add WHT (£4,980 × 17/83) | 1,020 |
| Gross overseas income | 6,000 |

**(W2) Rate of corporation tax**

|  | |
|---|---|
| PCTCT | 106,000 |
| Plus FII (£5,680 × 100/90) | 6,311 |
| Profits | 112,311 |

As Z plc owns < 50% of the voting power of the overseas company, the overseas dividend will be included as FII.

The overseas company is not an associated company, therefore the full limits apply and the appropriate tax rate based on profits is 21%.

**(W3) DTR on overseas rental income**

|  | £ |
|---|---|
| Lower of: | |
| (i)  Overseas tax suffered | 1,020 |
| (ii) UK CT on overseas income | 1,260 |
| Unrelieved overseas tax suffered | Nil |

## Test your understanding 2

**R plc**

**Corporation tax computation – year ended 31 March 2010**

|  | UK £ | Foreign Income £ | Total £ |
|---|---|---|---|
| Trading profit | 900,000 | | 900,000 |
| Overseas rent (W1) | | 140,000 | 140,000 |
| PCTCT | 900,000 | 140,000 | 1,040,000 |
| CT @ 28% | | | 291,200 |
| Less: MR (W2) | | | (8,050) |
| | 245,034 | 38,116 | 283,150 |
| Less: DTR (W2) | | (21,000) | (21,000) |
| CT liability | 245,034 | 17,116 | 262,150 |

**Workings**

**(W1) Gross overseas rent**

|  | £ |
|---|---|
| Rent received | 119,000 |
| Add WHT (15/85 × £119,000) | 21,000 |
| Overseas rent | 140,000 |

## (W2) Marginal relief

R plc has no associated companies, therefore the full limits apply.

PCTCT = Profits, as it has no FII

Marginal relief therefore applies:
7/400 × (£1,500,000 – £1,040,000) = £8,050

Effective rate of tax = (£283,150/£1,040,000) × 100 = 27.226%

## (W3) DTR

|  | £ |
|---|---|
| Lower of (i) Overseas tax suffered | 21,000 |
| (ii) UK CT(£27.226% × £1,400,000) | 38,116 |

### Test your understanding 3

**Alcock Inc**

All the companies should be exempt as follows:

(1) Alcock Inc has profits below £50,000.

(2) Barbauld SA is resident in a country where the tax rate is > 75% of the UK full rate.

(3) Blake Inc is a trading company.

# Planning for companies

## Chapter learning objectives

Upon completion of this chapter you will be able to:

- identify and advise on the taxes applicable to a given course of action and their impact on a business scenario

- identify and advise on the types of investment and other expenditure that will result in a reduction of tax liabilities for a business

- recognise that alternative courses of action have different tax consequences and assess the advantages and disadvantages

- identify suitable tax planning measures in a given scenario to mitigate tax liabilities for a company

- identify relevant procedures, time limits and claims for transactions with a tax impact.

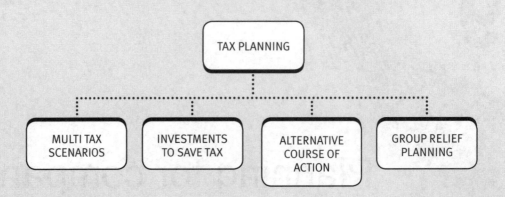

## 1 Tax planning

### Introduction

The purpose of this chapter is to consider tax planning in the context of multi tax corporate scenarios.

It concentrates on corporate aspects of planning, the most likely taxes to consider being corporation tax, VAT and stamp duty/stamp duty land tax. However, the income tax and NIC implications of employing staff can also feature in an examination question.

None of the content in this chapter is new. However, the chapter aims to show how to advise clients and deal with a selection of corporate taxation scenarios that may form the basis for an examination question.

### Purchase of a building

Companies often need to buy buildings. These can be bought freehold or leasehold and have a number of tax implications to consider.

|  | **Freehold** | **Leasehold** |
|---|---|---|
| IBAs | • Available if industrial building within its tax life.<br>• WDA = 2% for new buildings from 1 April 2009 to 31 March 2010. | • IBA normally given to the landlord. |
| VAT | • Charged if<br>  – building less than 3 years old, or<br>  – if previous owner opted to tax building.<br>• Recoverable by registered purchaser using the building to make taxable supplies. | • Charged if previous owner opted to tax<br>• Otherwise an exempt supply.<br>• Recoverable by registered trader using the building to make taxable supplies. |

|  | **Freehold** | **Leasehold** |
|---|---|---|
| Tax relief on cost | • Capital asset.<br>• Price paid is the cost for future capital disposals.<br>• IBAs may be available. | • Tax relief on:<br>  – rents paid, and<br>  – a portion of premium if lease is less than 50 years. |
| Rollover relief | • Qualifying asset if used for the trade. | • If lease has less than 60 years to run when purchased:<br>  – it is a depreciating asset<br>  – gains cannot be rolled over into it,<br>  – gains are deferred for up to 10 years. |
| SDLT | • Payable on cost. | • Payable on lease premium (note stamp duty on leases is not examinable). |

### Test your understanding 1

Ariel Ltd is a medium-sized unquoted company which makes refrigerators. The company was set up five years ago and has been expanding rapidly ever since. It now requires a new factory building.

Two alternative options have been identified as follows:

(i) A suitable factory is available for rent. The owners of the factory are prepared to grant a 30 year lease for a premium of £600,000. The annual rent payable will be £47,000. The owners will exercise their option to tax the grant of the lease, and it will therefore be standard rated. Both figures are inclusive of VAT where applicable. Assume SDLT of £24,000 is payable on the premium.

(ii) A new factory can be purchased from a building company. This will cost £600,000 excluding SDLT. The cost has been broken down as follows:

|  | £ |
|---|---|
| Land | 100,000 |
| Levelling the land | 15,000 |
| Access roads | 25,000 |
| Car park surfacing | 15,000 |
| Architects and legal fees | 30,300 |
| Central heating and air conditioning systems | 20,000 |
| Fire alarm and sprinkler system | 8,400 |
| General offices | 75,000 |
| Factory | 221,938 |
| VAT | 89,362 |
|  | 600,000 |
| SDLT (4%) | 24,000 |
|  | 624,000 |

In order to finance the purchase of either the lease or the freehold building it is necessary for the company to raise funds.

The company will borrow £274,000 from the bank on a 10 year loan at a fixed rate of 8% and will sell its old factory for £350,000 which includes £50,000 for land. The old factory was bought new 5 years ago for £200,000 plus £40,000 for land. Use an RPI factor of 0.220 for this disposal.

Ariel Ltd is registered for VAT.

**Advise Ariel Ltd of the tax implications arising from the two alternatives, and from the financing of whichever alternative is chosen.**

## Expenditure that reduces tax

Certain types of investment and other expenditure can result in a reduction of tax liabilities for a company. The detailed tax rules in respect of these types of expenditure are dealt with in earlier chapters. The main points only are mentioned below.

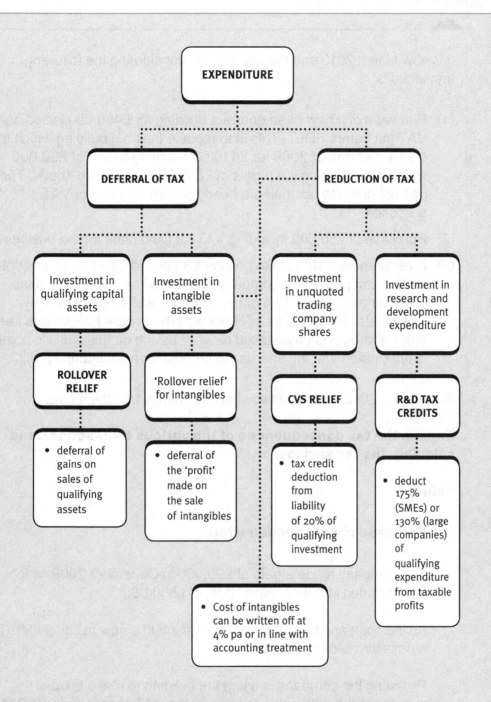

Note that capital allowances on plant and industrial buildings can also reduce tax liabilities but are not considered further here.

### Example 1 – Investments by a company

Rose plc is a profitable trading company that prepares its accounts to 31 December each year. It is not part of a group. In the year ended 31 December 2009 the company had taxable profits of £800,000 and is budgeting £1,200,000 for the year ended 31 December 2010 before considering any of the transactions mentioned below.

It is now March 2010 and the company is considering the following transactions:

(1) Purchase of a new head quarters building for £450,000 including VAT but before SDLT. This is to replace their old building which they sold in December 2009 for £410,000 making a gain of £90,000 which is included in the profits of £800,000 mentioned above. They had not opted to tax their old headquarters building for VAT purposes.

(2) Purchase of £50,000 including VAT, of fixed plant for the business.

(3) Investment in a 10% stake costing £30,000 in Lisa Ltd, an unquoted trading company. This company has issued new shares to raise funds for expansion. 40% of the company's shares are held by individuals. The directors of Rose plc are not sure how long to keep these shares and have asked for your advice on this specific point. It is anticipated that the shares will be sold for a substantial profit.

Assume FY 2009 rates and allowances continue into the future.

**Explain the tax consequences of the various transactions and calculate the tax savings.**

**Solution**

(1) **Purchase of new headquarters**

The company made a gain of £90,000 in December 2009 which was included in their taxable profit of £800,000.

As the company has made an investment in a new building there is a possible rollover relief claim.

Providing the company is using the building to make taxable supplies it should be able to recover the VAT charged of £67,021 (7/47 of £450,000).

SDLT will be payable at 3% on £450,000 = £13,500.

Hence the overall cost of the building is £396,479 (£450,000 – £67,021 + £13,500).

| Rollover claim | £ |
|---|---|
| Proceeds of sale of old building | 410,000 |
| Less Cost of new building | (396,479) |
| | |
| Proceeds not reinvested | 13,521 |

| | £ |
|---|---:|
| Gain on old building | 90,000 |
| Gain rolled over | (76,479) |
| | |
| Gain remaining (= proceeds not spent) | 13,521 |
| | |
| Base cost of new building: | |
| Original cost | 396,479 |
| Less Gain rolled over | (76,479) |
| | |
| | 320,000 |

This claim will reduce the PCTCT for the year ended 31 December 2009 by £76,479 which will save the company tax at 29.75%.

Therefore, Rose plc will have £22,753 (£76,479 × 29.75%) less to pay at the normal payment date for the y/e 31 December 2009 of 1 October 2010.

The claim must be made within 4 years from 31 December 2009.

## (2) Purchase of fixed plant

The purchase of fixed plant has two tax consequences:

– The cost net of recoverable VAT is £42,553 (40/47 × £50,000).

– The company may claim the AIA (subject to other acquisitions) on £50,000, otherwise a WDA at 20% can be claimed. This will save the company tax at 29.75% for the year ended 31.12.10.

The tax saving is therefore:
(£42,553 × 29.75%) = £12,660, if the AIA is available.

In addition, the company has made a purchase of fixed plant which is eligible for rollover deferral relief. In excess of £13,521 has been spent on the fixed plant, which allows the balance of the gain of £13,521 on the old headquarters building to be deferred until the earliest of three events:

– The plant ceases to be used in the trade.

– The plant is sold.

– 10 years after the plant is purchased.

This will save the company tax of £4,022 (29.75% × £13,521) in y/e 31.12.09.

(3) **Investment in Lisa Ltd**

Provided the investment qualifies under the CVS it will result in a reduction of tax liability of £6,000 for the year ended 31 December 2010 (i.e. 20% of the amount invested, 20% of £30,000).

The shares should be retained for three years to keep this relief.

On sale the substantial shareholding exemption should exempt the gain.

## Alternative courses of action

This section looks at the different levels of investment that can be made in other companies and the tax effects.

| Stake purchased in UK company | < 50% | > 50% but < 75% | ≥ 75% |
|---|---|---|---|
| CVS relief | Possible if subscribe ≤ 30% | No | No |
| Associated | No | Yes | Yes |
| Can join VAT group | No | Yes | Yes |
| Group relief group | No | No | Yes |
| Consortium relief | Possible * | Possible * | No |
| Gains group | No | No | Yes |
| Other issues<br><br>1) Losses b/f<br><br>2) Stamp duty | ½% on share purchases | Possible bar to losses being brought forward if major change in nature/conduct of trade or revival of negligible activities.<br><br>As for < 50% | As for > 50%<br><br>As for < 50% |

**\* Note:** It depends on ownership of remaining shares. For a consortium at least 75% of the shares in the consortium company must be owned by companies, each of whom has at least a 5% stake.

| | Joining a 75% group | Leaving a 75% group |
|---|---|---|
| Associated company | • Associated for whole of CAP in which purchase takes place. | • Associated for whole of CAP in which sale takes place. |
| Group relief | • Only possible from date of joining group.<br>• No relief for pre acquisition losses. | • Ceases from date 'arrangements' come into force for company to leave group. |
| Capital losses | • Pre acquisition capital losses cannot be used to relieve gains in other group companies.<br>• This rule extends to the pre-entry proportion of a capital loss realised after joining group. | • No relief against group gains for capital losses realised after leaving group. |
| Degrouping charge | • Not applicable. | • Arises if company leaves gains group still owning asset which it received from another gains group member on a no gain/no loss transfer within the last 6 years.<br>• Degrouping gain can be transferred to another gains group member or rolled over.<br>• Similar rule for intangibles. |
| VAT | • No VAT on share sales or purchases.<br>• Can join a VAT group but this is not automatic. | • No VAT on share sales or purchases.<br>• Will leave VAT group unless parent company still owns > 50%. |

| | Joining a 75% group | Leaving a 75% group |
|---|---|---|
| Stamp duty levied | • Paid by purchaser at ½% on share purchases. | • No stamp duty for vendor. |
| Stamp duty 'group' | • Transfers of property between gains group members exempt from stamp duty and SDLT. | • May be a claw back of stamp duty or SDLT exemption if leave group owning an asset transferred in by another group member with SD/SDLT exemption within last 3 years. |

### Example 2 – Corporate tax planning

You act as a tax advisor to Northanger Ltd, a UK company specialising in the manufacture and sale of kitchen appliances. Northanger Ltd has a 31 March year end and is registered for VAT because all of its supplies are taxable supplies for VAT purposes.

The company has been very successful since its formation seven years ago and now has taxable profits of £1 million. The board of directors are considering several opportunities for expansion. They have asked you to report to them on the taxation consequences of both of the possible projects they have under review.

The details of the projects are as follows:

(1) **Buy a stake in Fridgco Ltd**

This is a small company which has developed a new food storage product. At present, Fridgco Ltd is wholly owned by Mrs Austin who is willing to sell Northanger Ltd a 60% stake in Fridgco for £350,000 although she is prepared to consider offers for a higher stake in Fridgco. Mrs Austin will continue to own the shares that she does not sell to Northanger.

Fridgco Ltd has made losses in the past although it is expected to be profitable in future. At 1 April 2010, the company had trade losses brought forward of £70,000 and a capital loss of £55,000 on the sale of its headquarters building on 1 June 2010.

Since that sale, the company has used rented office space in addition to its manufacturing plant. For the accounting period to 31 March 2011, the company expects to make a trading loss of £48,000.

Mrs Austin thinks that the purchase price of £350,000 should be increased to take account of the value of these losses.

Assume any share purchase will take place on 1 February 2011.

(2) **Set up a new branch to expand sales**

This branch could be located in the UK but as the directors are keen to expand exports, they feel it would be better to locate it overseas in Bajoria, a country outside the EU which has no double tax treaty with the UK.

The branch operation is expected to be loss making initially and then produce profits of £200,000 per annum. Components would be shipped from the UK and sold through the branch. The Bajorian tax system operates in a similar way to the UK and levies tax on branch profits at 24%.

One of the directors has raised the possibility of operating in Bajoria through a company rather than a branch.

**Write a report to the board of directors which covers the tax consequences of these two projects. Include any suggestions that you consider would improve the company's tax position.**

**Assume that FY 2009 rates and allowances continue into the future.**

**Solution**

**Report**

| | |
|---|---|
| **To:** | The board of directors |
| **From:** | An Advisor |
| **Subject:** | Tax consequences of two new investments |

**Buy stake in Fridgco Ltd**

The current proposal is to buy a 60% stake in Fridgco Ltd. This will have the following consequences:

(1) The company will be associated with Northanger for the whole of its accounting period of purchase. This will increase the tax payable by Northanger as it will be subject to tax at the full rate of 28%. The increased tax on taxable profits of £1 million will be £8,750 (W1). In addition, as a full rate company, Northanger will have to start paying tax by instalments but not until year ended 31 March 2012.

Northanger and Fridgco Ltd can join a VAT group. This will be useful if there is to be much trading between the two companies, as supplies within the group are ignored for VAT.

Any dividends paid by Fridgco Ltd to Northanger Ltd will be classed as group income and ignored.

No group relief or capital gain advantages are available with a 60% stake. A consortium does not exist because this requires at least 75% of the shares to be owned by companies. Mrs Austin could incorporate a company to hold her shares and then a consortium would exist allowing Northanger Ltd to claim 60% of Fridgco's loss from 1 February onwards.

The purchase represents a change of ownership for Fridgco Ltd (more than half the shares have changed hands). If this is followed within 3 years by major changes to the nature and conduct of the trade, then the trading losses of £70,000 brought forward plus £40,000 losses accruing from 1 April 2010 to 1 February 2011 (10/12 of £48,000) will lapse and will not be available to carry forward against future profits.

Provided Northanger Ltd holds the shares in Fridgco Ltd for at least 12 months, any capital gain on the sale of the shares will be exempt under the substantial shareholding rules.

(2)    Increase purchase to at least 75%.

If Northanger buys at least 75% of Fridgco Ltd, then all of the above consequences will occur but it will also be possible to create a group relief and capital gains group. This would enable group relief to be claimed by Northanger for Fridgco Ltd's losses from 1 February 2011.

£8,000 could be surrendered to use against Northanger's taxable profits for the year ended 31 March 2011.

It is not possible for Northanger Ltd to make use of Fridgco's trading losses brought forward as group relief, nor can they make use of the capital losses brought forward. These are designated as pre entry losses and can only be used by Fridgco Ltd against gains on assets it owned when it joined the group or purchased subsequently from third parties.

Although in gains groups it is possible to roll gains made by one company on land and buildings used for the trade over against qualifying assets purchased in another gains group company, this is not possible for Fridgco's gain as it was incurred before it joined the gains group.

**Advice** - the company should negotiate with Mrs Austin to buy at least 75% of Fridgco Ltd.

## Set up overseas branch

The profits of an overseas branch are taxed in the UK as part of trading profits. The initial losses will be relievable against UK profits of Northanger Ltd. The extra £200,000 profits that are expected would be subject to tax at 28% in the UK although credit would be given for the 24% tax payable in Bajoria.

Bajoria is outside the EU therefore no VAT is charged in that country. Any goods shipped from the UK to sell in Bajoria will be zero rated supplies in the UK.

If a company is set up instead of a branch then there will be no relief for the initial losses. They will remain in Bajoria.

When profitable, any profits paid up to the parent company will be in the form of a dividend and will be exempt in Northanger's computation of taxable profits. As Northanger will own 100% of the shares, the dividend will not be included as FII

Although the tax rate is Bajoria is lower, this should not cause any problems under the CFC rules as the new subsidiary will be a trading company and the tax rate in Bajoria is more than 75% of the UK rate.

A subsidiary in Bajoria will be an associated company which will further reduce the small company marginal limits.

As the UK has no double tax treaty with Bajoria, any trading between UK companies of any size, and related companies in Bajoria will be subject to the transfer pricing rules. Northanger Ltd will have to ensure that any goods sold to the new subsidiary are sold at an arm's length price.

**Advice** – start the overseas operation as a branch to obtain relief for its expected losses. Once profitable it could be transferred to a company structure.

---

### Working: Increased tax payable by Northanger Ltd

|  | £ |
|---|---|
| PCTCT = Profits = MR company | 1,000,000 |
| Corporation tax @ 28% | 280,000 |
| Less Marginal Relief | |
| (£1,500,000 – £1,000,000) × 7/400 | (8,750) |
| Corporation tax liability | 271,250 |

With one associated company, the upper limit for small company marginal relief will be divided in half and become £750,000.

With profits of £1 million, Northanger Ltd would pay tax at 28% and lose its marginal relief.

---

## Approach to a complex group losses question

Where there are qualifying losses for group relief, they need to be allocated for the benefit of the **group** as a whole (i.e. to save as much tax as possible).

The approach (as a general rule) should be:

(i) Prepare a diagram of the group structure.

(ii) Determine the number of associates, 75% group(s) and consortia.

(iii) State the upper and lower limits for CT purposes.

(iv) Set up a tabular proforma for PCTCT and "profits" (if relevant).

(v) Complete the computations down to PCTCT, separating out any losses to loss memoranda.

(vi) Determine the best use of any qualifying losses to save tax rates and revise PCTCT.

(vii) Where there are a number of losses in a question, deal with the losses with the most restricted set off first.

(viii) Compute CT liability on revised PCTCT.

(ix) Show CT payable and any losses or surpluses to be carried forward.

Factors to consider:

- Saving tax at the highest rate is the primary factor in using company losses.

  Consideration should always be given to all alternatives such as carrying back a trading loss (after current period relief) in the loss making company as an alternative to group relief, if this saves more tax.

- Cash flow.
- Wastage of Gift Aid donations.
- Another factor that should be taken into account is whether a group company has **double taxation relief** available as the surrender of losses to such a company may waste the DTR credit available.

## Test your understanding 2

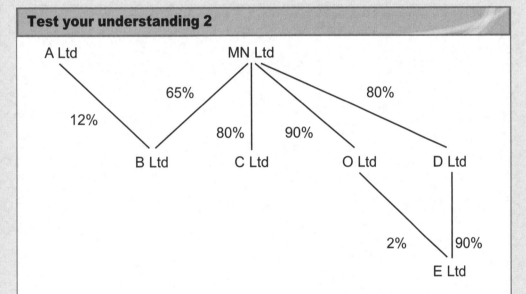

As shown in the group structure above, MN Ltd, a UK resident company, has the following holdings of ordinary shares in other companies, which, apart from O Ltd, are all UK resident.

> 65% in B Ltd
> 80% in C Ltd
> 90% in O Ltd (a foreign resident company)
> 80% in D Ltd

D Ltd holds 90% of the ordinary shares of E Ltd, A Ltd holds 12% of the shares in B Ltd and O Ltd holds 2% of the shares in E Ltd.

No company had any other source of income or gains.

The trading results for each company for the year ended 31 March 2010 were as follows:

|        |        | £       |
|--------|--------|---------|
| A Ltd  | Loss   | 60,000  |
| B Ltd  | Profit | 58,000  |
| MN Ltd | Profit | 53,000  |
| C Ltd  | Loss   | 10,000  |
| D Ltd  | Profit | 293,000 |
| E Ltd  | Loss   | 5,000   |
| O Ltd  | Loss   | 10,000  |

**Assuming the above losses are used in the most efficient manner, compute the corporation tax payable by each of the above companies for the 12 months ended 31 March 2010.**

## 2 Chapter summary

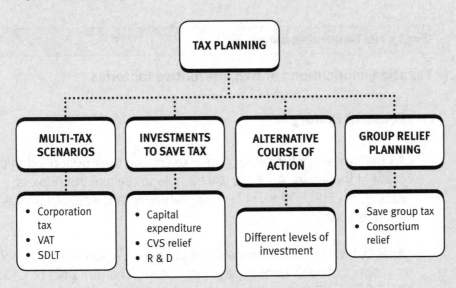

## Test your understanding answers

### Test your understanding 1

**Taxation implications of two alternative factories**

#### (1) Lease of factory

As the owners of the factory have exercised their option to tax the grant of the lease, Ariel Ltd will be able to reclaim input tax of £89,362 (£600,000 × 7/47). This assumes that Ariel Ltd is making taxable supplies.

Ariel Ltd will be able to reclaim input tax of £7,000 (£47,000 × 7/47) in respect of each annual payment of rent. The rent paid of £40,000 (£47,000 − £7,000) will be deductible for corporation tax purposes.

The proportion of the premium assessed on the owners as property business income will be deductible for CT purposes spread over the period of the lease, as follows:

| | |
|---|---:|
| Assessment on the owners<br>= £600,000 × 40/47 × [(51 − 30)/50] | £214,468 |
| Relief available to the payer of the premium:<br>(£214,468 × 1/30) | £7,149 pa |

The deduction of £7,149 will be restricted for the CAP in which it is paid according to the length of the period from the date of payment to the end of that CAP.

**(2)** **Construction of new factory**

|  | £ |
|---|---|
| Total cost | 624,000 |
| Less: Land | (100,000) |
| Central Heating | (20,000) |
| Fire Alarm | (8,400) |
| VAT | (89,362) |
| Eligible cost | 406,238 |

IBAs of £8,125 (£406,238 × 2%) will be given if purchased in the y/e 31 March 2010, provided the factory is brought into use in that period.

The central heating and fire alarm are eligible for plant and machinery capital allowances. Subject to other acquisitions, the Annual Investment Allowance of £50,000 per annum may be used against the acquisitions. Otherwise, WDA at 10% for the central heating (an integral feature) and 20% for the fire alarm will be available.

The AIA will be £28,400 (assuming other acquisitions are less than £50,000).

**(3)** **Bank loan**

Loan interest is deducted from trading profits on the accruals basis as the loan is raised for a trading purpose.

The annual deduction will therefore be £21,920 (£274,000 at 8%).

**(4) Sale of old factory**

|  | £ |
|---|---:|
| Sale proceeds (including land) | 350,000 |
| Less: Cost | (240,000) |
| Unindexed gain | 110,000 |
| Less: Indexation (£240,000 × 0.220) | (52,800) |
| Chargeable gain | 57,200 |

**Replacement of business asset:**

- **If the new factory is bought:**
  - The gain on sale of the old factory can be rolled over against the base cost of the new factory.
  - There is no restriction on the amount of the gain that can be rolled over, as the full proceeds of £350,000 will be reinvested.
  - This is provided that the new factory is purchased within the reinvestment period of 12 months before and up to three years after the disposal of the old factory.

- **If the factory is leased:**
  - The gain can only be held over for a maximum of 10 years from the date of purchase.
  - This is because the replacement asset will be a depreciating asset with a life of less than 60 years.
  - The gain will crystallise in 10 years time unless the asset is sold or ceases to be used in the business within the next 10 years.

**Industrial Building Allowance:**

- As the disposal is after 21 March 2007, there are no consequences on Ariel Ltd for IBAs on the disposal of the old factory.

### Test your understanding 2

**Corporation tax computations – Year ended 31 March 2010**

|  | A Ltd £ | B Ltd £ | MN Ltd £ | C Ltd £ | D Ltd £ | E Ltd £ |
|---|---|---|---|---|---|---|
| Trading profits | Nil | 58,000 | 53,000 | Nil | 293,000 | Nil |
| Group relief |  |  |  |  |  |  |
| (1) |  |  |  |  | (5,000) |  |
| (2) |  |  | (3,000) |  |  |  |
| (3) |  |  |  |  | (7,000) |  |
| (4) (W3) |  | (6,960) |  |  |  |  |
| PCTCT | Nil | 51,040 | 50,000 | Nil | 281,000 | Nil |
| Corporation tax |  |  |  |  |  |  |
| £51,040 × 28% |  | 14,291 |  |  |  |  |
| £50,000 × 21% |  |  | 10,500 |  |  |  |
| £281,000 × 28% |  |  |  |  | 78,680 |  |
| Less: MR (W4) |  | (3,482) |  |  |  |  |
| Corporation tax | Nil | 10,809 | 10,500 | Nil | 78,680 | Nil |

Generally claims should be made within 2 years of the end of the accounting period of claim (i.e. by 31 March 2012).

**Workings**

**(1) Analysis of group structure**

| | | |
|---|---|---|
| Associated cos. | = | 6 |
| Upper limit | = | £250,000 |
| Lower limit | = | £50,000 |
| No. of 75% groups | = | 2 |
| Group 1 | = | MN Ltd, C Ltd, D Ltd, O Ltd (but O Ltd resident outside the EEA, therefore no loss relief) |
| Group 2 | = | D Ltd, E Ltd |
| Consortium | = | 1 |
| Members | = | A Ltd, MN Ltd |
| Consortium company | = | B Ltd |

| (2) **Loss working** | A Ltd | C Ltd | E Ltd |
|---|---|---|---|
| | £ | £ | £ |
| Loss | 60,000 | 10,000 | 5,000 |
| Group relief | | | |
| – to D Ltd | | | (5,000) |
| – to MN Ltd | | (3,000) | |
| – to D Ltd | | (7,000) | |
| Consortium relief (W3) | (6,960) | | |
| Loss to c/f | 53,040 | Nil | Nil |

(3) **Consortium relief to B Ltd**

Lower of: £

(1) A Ltd's loss       60,000

(2) % of B's profit (12% × £58,000)    6,960

(4) **Marginal relief**

7/400 × (£250,000 − £51,040) = £3,482

# Questions and Answers

## 1 Income tax: Computation

### Norman

#### Question 1

Norman, aged 45, has the following income, outgoings and allowances for the year ended 5 April 2010.

| | £ |
|---|---|
| Salary and commission from his employer 'Flyhigh Ltd' | 39,630 |
| Benefits, assessable as employment income | 2,100 |
| Building society interest received | 2,000 |
| UK dividends received | 207 |
| Qualifying loan interest paid to buy shares in 'Flyhigh Ltd' | 1,500 |

On 15 November 2009 Norman and his wife Kate jointly bought a property that has been let out as unfurnished accommodation. The assessable property income for 2009/10 is £4,100. No declaration has been made in respect of this source of income.

#### Required:

Calculate the income tax payable by Norman for 2009/10.

**(5 marks)**

## 2 Employment income and related NIC

### Mr Darcy

#### Question 1

Mr F Darcy, managing director of the Pemberley Trading Co Ltd, is paid an annual salary of £37,000 and also bonuses based on the company's performance.

Mr Darcy pays 7% of his basic salary to a registered occupational pension scheme.

Pemberley's accounting year ends on 31 December each year and the bonuses are normally determined and paid on 31 May thereafter.

In recent years bonuses have been:

| | £ |
|---|---|
| Year to 31 December 2007 | 4,000 |
| Year to 31 December 2008 | 8,000 |
| Year to 31 December 2009 | 4,000 |

He uses a company car (3,500cc) purchased in 2006 at its list price of £20,000, for 25,000 miles during 2009/10, of which 25% is for non-business use. Running expenses, including petrol paid by the company, were £4,600 in the year and the car has a carbon dioxide emission rating of 232 g/km.

Under the terms of the company's all employee share scheme Mr Darcy was allotted 1,000 ordinary £1 shares of the company, the market value of which is £3 per share, on 21 January 2010. He purchased 478 partnership shares during the year, £125 being deducted from his salary each month to pay for the shares. The company allotted him a further 717 matching shares at a total cost of £2,250.

**Required:**
Compute Mr Darcy's income tax liability for 2009/10.

Briefly give reasons for your treatment of items included or excluded in arriving at Mr Darcy's taxable income.

**(8 marks)**

## Hubert

### Question 2

Hubert, a bachelor, was born on 19 May 1969. In 2009/10 he received the following income:

|  | £ |  |
|---|---|---|
| Salary | 23,000 | PAYE £4,500 |
| Pension from former employer | 5,000 | PAYE £1,100 |
| Profits from a partnership interest | 9,480 | |
| Treasury stock interest received | 250 | |
| Bank deposit account interest received | 1,680 | |
| Building society interest received | 92 | |
| UK dividends received | 578 | |
| Foreign property income (gross) | | |
| (no overseas tax suffered) | 1,200 | |

The following information is also available:

(1) In March 2001, Hubert was granted unapproved share options to buy 25,000 shares at £7. The shares were worth £7.50 at that time. In January 2010, Hubert exercised his options, bought 25,000 shares and sold them on the same day for £200,000.

(2) Hubert paid subscriptions of £360 to the Institute of Builders. He worked for a property development company.

(3) He also received the following benefits of employment:

- A company car was provided for the whole year. The car has a list price of £20,000 and $CO_2$ emissions of 190 g/km.

- Petrol for private use of the company car was paid for by the employer.

- The employer reimbursed expenses of £1,960. Hubert had incurred the expenses on accommodation while on business trips abroad.

- Hubert uses his employer's tools occasionally during the course of his work. During 2009/10 he used one of his employer's cement mixers throughout the whole year whilst building his property overseas. The cement mixer cost the company £1,200 two years ago.

**Required:**

Calculate the income tax payable by Hubert for 2009/10.

**(15 marks)**

### Chalk and Cheese

### Question 3

Alice Chalk and Zara Cheese, aged 37, are twin sisters. Although having the same levels of earned and investment income, they are surprised that their total income tax and NIC liabilities for 2009/10 are not the same.

The following information is available for 2009/10:

**Alice Chalk**

(1) Alice is employed by Tesbury plc as a manager in one of the company's nationwide chain of retail grocery shops. She is paid a gross annual salary of £40,000.

(2) Throughout 2009/10 Alice was provided with an 1800cc petrol powered motor car which has a list price of £14,600. Alice made a capital contribution of £2,000 towards the cost of the motor car when it was first provided. The official $CO_2$ emission rate for the motor car is 197 grams per kilometre. Tesbury plc paid for all of the motor car's running costs of £5,400 during 2009/10, including petrol used for private journeys.

(3) Tesbury plc has provided Alice with living accommodation since 2008. The property was purchased in 2004 for £105,000, and was valued at £120,000 when first provided to Alice. It has an annual value of £3,895, and Tesbury plc pays for the annual running costs of £3,200.

(4) Alice contributes 6% of her gross salary of £40,000 into Tesbury plc's approved occupational pension scheme.

(5) In 2009/10 Alice received building society interest of £1,800 (net).

**Zara Cheese**

(1) Zara is self-employed running a retail grocery shop. Her profit and loss account for the year ended 5 April 2010 is as follows:

|  | £ | £ |
|---|---|---|
| Gross profit |  | 120,105 |
| Depreciation | 12,425 |  |
| Motor expenses (note 2) | 5,400 |  |
| Property expenses (note 3) | 9,600 |  |
| Other expenses (all allowable) | 52,680 |  |
|  |  | (80,105) |
| Net profit |  | 40,000 |

(2) During the year ended 5 April 2010 Zara drove a total of 12,000 miles, of which 4,000 were for private journeys. Zara's motor car originally cost £12,600, and at 6 April 2009 had a tax written down value of £9,600. She does not own any other assets that qualify for capital allowances.

(3) Zara purchased her grocery shop in 2001 for £105,000. She lives in a flat that is situated above the shop, and one-third of the total property expenses of £9,600 relate to this flat.

(4) Zara contributed £2,400 (gross) into a personal pension scheme during 2009/10.

(5) During 2009/10 Zara received dividends of £1,800 (net).

**Required:**

(i)  Calculate Alice's income tax liability and Class 1 NIC for 2009/10.

**(11 marks)**

(ii) Calculate Zara's liability to income tax, Class 2 NIC and Class 4 NIC for 2009/10.

**(10 marks)**
**(Total: 21 marks)**

### 3 Property and investment income

**Muriel Grand**

### Question 1

On 31 December 2009 Muriel Grand, aged 52, made a gift of a house in London to her brother Bertie, aged 53.

Bertie is to rent out the house in London, either unfurnished or as furnished holiday accommodation. In either case, the roof of the house must be repaired at a cost of £24,000 before it will be possible to let the house. The roof was badly damaged by a gale on 5 December 2009.

If the house is let unfurnished, then Bertie will have to decorate it at a cost of £3,600. The forecast rental income is £28,000 per annum.

If the house is let as furnished holiday accommodation, then the house will be converted into two separate units at a cost of £41,000. The total cost of furnishing the two units will be £9,000.

This expenditure will be financed by a £50,000 bank loan at an interest rate of 8% per annum. The total forecast rental income is £45,000 per annum, although 22.5% of this will be deducted by the letting agency. Other running costs, such as cleaning, will amount to £3,500 per annum in total.

Bertie is a higher rate taxpayer and plans to sell the house when he retires at age 60, and anticipates making a substantial capital gain.

**Advise Bertie of the tax implications of letting out the house in London either (i) unfurnished, or (ii) as furnished holiday accommodation.**

**Your answer should include details of the tax advantages of letting the house as furnished holiday accommodation.**

## Anthony & Cleopatra

### Question 2

Anthony, aged 48, has the following income and outgoings for the year ended 5 April 2010.

|  | £ |
|---|---|
| Salary from 'Roma publications' | 50,000 |
| (PAYE £20,000) | |
| Rental income from an apartment in Bath | 12,000 |
| Building society interest received | 42,120 |
| UK dividends received (Note 6) | 67,890 |
| Qualifying loan interest paid to buy equipment for Roma publications | (550) |

The following information is also available for the year ended 5 April 2010:

(1) Anthony is the sales manager of Roma publications and is entitled to an annual bonus based on the company's results for each year ending 31 December. The bonuses are determined at the April board meetings following the end of the year and are paid on 30 April each year.

Bonuses were as follows:

| y/e 31 December 2008 | £2,000 |
|---|---|
| y/e 31 December 2009 | £2,100 |

(2) One of Anthony's clients, Julius, gave him a cash tip of £1,000 after Anthony arranged for his assignment to be dealt with as a priority.

(3) Anthony had the use of a company computer. The state of the art laptop and accessories cost the company £3,000 on 31 May 2009. Anthony uses the laptop at home and lets his children use the computer as much as possible to help with their studies.

(4) Anthony had the use of a company car, which was imported to the UK from Rome at a cost of £25,000. The list price of this care is £30,000 and $CO_2$ emissions are 143 g/km. The car has a diesel powered engine and all fuel was paid for by the company on a company credit card. Anthony makes no payment for any private use of the vehicle.

(5) Roma publications own a villa in Italy which cost the company £65,000. The villa has an annual value of £2,250. The family are allowed to use the villa at any time during the year. Anthony pays the company £120 per month for this privilege.

(6) On 6 April 2009 Anthony has invested £20,000 in an unquoted trading company, in the UK, that qualifies for relief under the Enterprise Investment Scheme. Of the £67,890 dividends received by Anthony, £2,700 relates to the EIS shares.

Cleopatra, aged 45, has the following income and outgoings for the year ended 5 April 2010.

| | £ |
|---|---:|
| Salary from her part-time employment with 'The Spa' | 12,500 |
| Allowable subscriptions to the 'Institute of Beauty' | (400) |
| Interest from an ISA account | 500 |

Cleopatra has inherited some cash from her father and decided to invest £20,000 in a Venture Capital Trust company. She received dividends of £1,000 from the VCT company during 2009/10.

### Required:

(a) Calculate Anthony and Cleopatra's income tax payable (or repayable) for 2009/10.

(b) Advise Anthony and Cleopatra of any tax planning they may wish to use to reduce future tax liabilities assuming their income remains the same in the future.

**(20 marks)**

## 4 Pensions

### Enid, Tom and Norman

### Question 1

(a) Enid is the sole shareholder and director of Enid Limited, a trading company which prepares accounts to 31 March each year.

Enid has had a successful year to date the company's tax adjusted trading profits for the year ended 31 March 2010 have been forecast at £85,000 after paying a gross salary to Enid of £26,000. Apart from this salary, Enid currently has no other income.

Assume that today's date is 2 April 2010 and Enid has not yet made any pension contributions in 2009/10.

She is contemplating making a lump sum payment into her personal pension scheme and is also arranging for the company, Enid Limited, to make a lump sum premium into the same scheme for her benefit.

**Required:**

Write brief notes advising Enid of the taxation implications of the proposed lump sum pension scheme contributions in 2009/10.

**(5 marks)**

(b) Tom, who was born on 30 June 1976, is a self-employed computer consultant and has just inherited £150,000.

He has decided to invest some of his inheritance into his personal pension plan and to use the balance to pay off his mortgage. Tom has never made any contributions to a pension plan before.

Assume today's date is 14 January 2010 and Tom's trading profits for 2009/10 are £50,000.

**Required:**

Calculate the maximum gross amount that Tom can contribute into his personal pension plan on which tax relief can be obtained in 2009/10.

Explain how Tom will obtain tax relief for any contributions paid.

**(4 marks)**

(c) Norman has inherited £125,000 and decided to invest some of the proceeds to provide for an additional entitlement to a pension.

From 6 April 2009 Norman has been employed at an annual salary of £20,000. He was also provided with a petrol engine car with $CO_2$ emissions of 174 g/km and a list price of £30,000. He drives a total of 12,000 miles. Norman's employer pays for all of the fuel for the car and Norman contributes £50 per month towards the car (£10 of which is towards the fuel).

Norman pays 6% of his salary into his employer's registered company pension scheme. The company contributes a further 5%.

**Required:**

Advise Norman as to the additional contribution he should make into the registered company pension scheme in 2009/10.

**(5 marks)**
**(Total: 14 marks)**

## Clive Scott

### Question 2

Assume today's date is 1 January 2010.

Clive Scott, who was born on 28 March 1961, has approached you for some advice concerning pensions. He is single and has no children and informs you that he owns all of the shares in Scott Engineering Limited, a company which has been trading since April 1996.

The company pays corporation tax at 21% and prepares its accounts to 31 March each year.

Whilst the profits in the earlier years of the business have been reinvested back into the firm, Scott Engineering Limited is now more established and over the last few years Clive has been withdrawing more funds from the business.

He is now keen to put money aside for his retirement in ten to twelve years time and wants to know more about the options open to him.

Clive's expected income from the company for 2009/10 is a salary of £15,000 and dividends of £46,350. Clive has no income other than from Scott Engineering Limited.

**Required:**

(a) Assuming Clive wishes to set up a personal pension scheme in 2009/10 advise him of:

   (i) The maximum pension contributions that Clive can make in 2009/10 and by when these should be paid to obtain relief.

   **(3 marks)**

   (ii) The way in which tax relief will be given if he pays the pension contributions personally. Your answer to this part should include a calculation of the effect of making such contributions on his 2009/10 income tax liability.

   **(3 marks)**

   (iii) The tax implications of Scott Engineering Limited making contributions into his personal pension scheme and the factors to be considered in deciding whether he or the company should pay these contributions. Detailed calculations are not required for this question part.

   **(6 marks)**

(b) Briefly advise Clive of any alternative HMRC registered pension arrangements that could be made.

You are not required to comment on the benefits that may ultimately be received under such arrangements.

**(3 marks)**
**(Total: 15 marks)**

## 5 Income tax planning

### Ethel Jones

### Question 1

Assume today's date is 30 June 2010.

Ethel Jones is aged 69 years. She is married to George, who is independently wealthy in his own right. They have one child, Simone.

Ethel owns the following assets:

(1) 10,000 ordinary £1 shares in Bluebird plc, a quoted UK resident trading company with an issued share capital of 1 million ordinary shares. The company prepares its accounts to 31 March each year.

Ethel was a director of this company for many years until she had to retire for health reasons on 31 May 2009. During 2009/10 she earned £10,900 in director's fees from Bluebird plc.

The company has paid the following dividends in recent years:

| Year ended | Dividend | Payment date |
|---|---|---|
| 31 March 2009 | 25 pence per share | 30 April 2009 |
| 31 March 2010 | 30 pence per share | 30 April 2010 |

(2) A 25% beneficial interest in £100,000 10% loan stock in Chaffinch plc, a quoted UK resident trading company. This loan stock is held jointly with George who has always owned the remaining 75% beneficial interest in it.

The couple has not made a declaration of beneficial interest to HMRC in respect of this asset. This loan stock is a qualifying corporate bond.

(3) Cash deposits amount to £145,000, which generated net interest receipts in 2009/10 of £4,200.

**Required:**

(a)  Calculate Ethel's 2009/10 income tax liability.

**(5 marks)**

(b)  Advise Ethel and George whether it would be beneficial to make a declaration of beneficial interest to HMRC in respect of the loan stock held in Chaffinch plc.

Detailed calculations are not required for this part of the question.

**(3 marks)**

**(Total: 8 marks)**

## 6 CGT: Computations and stamp duty land tax

### Julie

### Question 1

Julie made the following disposals in 2009/10:

(1)  On 19 June 2009 she sold a concert grand piano for £12,500. She bought the piano in September 1997 for £8,750. She uses the piano to play at home purely for pleasure.

(2)  On 23 September 2009 she sold her car, a Renault Espace for £8,700. She bought the car for £18,000 in March 2004.

(3)  On 25 December 2009 she sold an investment property for £485,000. She bought the property for £156,000 in August 2003. Legal costs, estate agent fees and stamp duty land tax totalled £2,700 at the time of purchase and £4,075 on the sale of the property.

(4)  On 4 January 2010 she sold an asset for £37,000. She purchased the asset for £4,000 in October 2007. The asset had been used for the purposes of her self-employed business for the whole period of ownership. The disposal was not part of a disposal on the whole of the business.

Julie has capital losses brought forward at 6 April 2009 of £3,250.

**Required:**

Calculate Julie's capital gains tax liability for 2009/10.

**(10 marks)**

## 7 CGT: Variations to computations

### Spangle

#### Question 1

During December 2009 Spangle had the following capital transactions:

(a) He sold for £24,000 a desk which he had acquired in April 1983 for £7,000.

(b) He sold for £220,000 a house bought in April 1983 for £58,000. The house had at no time been his main residence. Spangle had built an extension to the house in October 1985 which had cost £4,000.

(c) He sold for £17,200 an antique table that he bought for £10,000 in July 1985.

(d) He also gave away a greyhound which he had bought assuming that it had a good pedigree for £8,000 in 2000. It had come last in every race it had been entered in and had no value when he gave it away.

(e) Spangle had some unquoted shares which he sold for £6,000. These had been left to him in his uncle's will in July 1985 when the probate value was £7,500.

(f) Spangle bought a 24 acre plot of land for £130,000 in March 2002 for investment purposes.

   In June 2008, Spangle sold four acres of the land for £30,000. The remaining 20 acres were worth £150,000.

   In December 2009 Spangle sold the remaining 20 acres for £205,000.

#### Required:

Calculate the capital gains tax payable by Spangle for 2009/10 and state the due date of payment.

**(15 marks)**

**Darren**

## Question 2

Darren made the following disposals during the y/e 5 April 2010:

(1) On 9 May 2009 he sold a three acre paddock for £15,000. It has never been used for business purposes.

He originally bought this land as a four acre paddock in January 1988 for £5,000. One acre was sold in March 1994 for £4,000 when the value of the remaining three acres was £12,500.

(2) Darren had bought a classic Mini Cooper in August 1988 for £500 and sold this to a friend on 21 April 2009 for £3,000.

(3) He purchased a painting for £9,000 on 14 May 1993 which was destroyed in a flood on 25 December 2009. He received insurance proceeds of £50,000 and decided not to buy more paintings.

(4) After the shock of losing the painting, Darren gifted his only other antique, a ring worth £1,000 to his mother on Boxing Day, 26 December 2009. He had acquired this from a flea market in the summer (July) of 2005 for £5.

(5) Darren purchased a lease with 39 years to run on 12 February 2002 for £200,000. Darren used the property wholly for the purposes of his trade until 19 October 2009 when he sold the lease for £275,000.

This was not part of the disposal of the whole of the business.

### Required:
Calculate Darren's capital gains tax payable for 2009/10.

**(15 marks)**

## 8 Shares and securities for individuals and stamp duty

**Emma**

### Question 1

Emma made the following disposals during the year ended 5 April 2010:

(1) On 9 February 2010 she sold 1,050 shares in Apple plc for net proceeds of £95,000.

The history of this shareholding is as follows:

| | |
|---|---|
| March 2006 | purchased 400 shares for £10,000 |
| January 2007 | took up 1 for 4 rights issue at £30 per share |
| December 2008 | purchased a further 200 shares for £8,000 |
| January 2009 | Bonus issue of 1 for every 2 shares |

Emma does not work for the company and her shares are a very small percentage of the shares in issue.

(2) On 19 March 2009 she gifted to her sister three out of her shareholding of ten shares in Willow Ltd, her unquoted personal trading company. The value of the three shares gifted was £50,000.

Emma acquired the shares at a cost of £100 per share when she set up the company in February 1988. Emma had never worked for the company.

(3) On 15 September 2009, she sold National Savings Certificates worth £600. Emma acquired the certificates from her grandfather's estate following his death in August 2007. The shares were valued at £500 at that time.

(4) Emma had acquired 100 ordinary shares in Bridge plc for £9,200 in June 1999. She had never worked for Bridge plc. In January 2010, Bridge plc was subject to a takeover.

In return for each share Emma received the following:

£350 cash, and a loan note in Poker plc worth £50.

**Required:**
Calculate Emma's capital gains tax payable for 2009/10.

**(15 marks)**

## 9 CGT: Reliefs for individuals

### Mr Harry

#### Question 1

(a) Mr Harry, who is aged 49, owns 60 per cent of the ordinary share capital of X Ltd, an unquoted trading company.

He acquired his holding on 1 January 1996 at a cost of £70,000 and since that date he has been a full-time working director of the company.

The following information has been extracted from the balance sheet of X Ltd at 30 November 2009.

|  | £ |
|---|---|
| Buildings | 480,000 |
| Investments in other companies (not in the same industry) | 80,000 |
| Plant and machinery | 16,000 |
| Net current assets | 32,333 |

The plant and machinery consists entirely of movable plant with no single item costing, or having a current value of, more than £6,000.

Assume today's date is 1 December 2009.

On 1 January 2010 Mr Harry intends to retire from the company, and plans to gift his entire share holding to his daughter. The market value of the shareholding is estimated to be worth £365,000.

In November 2009 Mr Harry sold his house for net proceeds of £503,000. The house cost £38,000 in September 1988. He intends to use the proceeds received from the sale of his house to build a new flat in Spain.

Mr Harry lived in the house throughout his ownership except for a period of one year, six years ago. He moved out and let the property while he lived and worked as the manager of the local pub. He returned to his house one year later.

#### Required:

Compute the expected taxable gains for 2009/10 assuming Mr Harry gifts the shares to his daughter and assuming all available reliefs are claimed, which are beneficial.

**(6 marks)**

(b) The building owned by X Ltd was originally purchased by Mr Harry and he sold it to the company on 1 April 2009. Mr Harry has already paid the capital gains tax liability for 2008/09 arising on the disposal.

Mr Harry is now considering buying some commercial property with a view to setting up a new business. He would like to know if there are any CGT advantages in purchasing new property and setting up a new business.

**Required:**

Prepare notes for a meeting with Mr Harry covering the CGT advantages of his proposal and any conditions he needs to bear in mind.

**(10 marks)**

**(Total: 16 marks)**

## Bangle

### Question 2

Barbara Bangle, aged 45, has carried on her retail jewellery business as a sole trader since April 1983. On 1 July 2009 she transferred the business as a going concern to Bangle Ltd, an unquoted company she formed for that purpose. Bangle Ltd allotted 200,000 £1 ordinary shares, valued at par, in settlement of the consideration for the transfer.

The net assets transferred to the company were as follows:

|  | Cost/MV | Acquisition date | Market value 1 July 2009 |
|---|---|---|---|
|  | £ |  | £ |
| Freehold trade premises | 65,000 | (1.4.1983) | 165,000 |
| Shop fittings | 6,000 | (1.4.1983) | 5,000 |
| Shop front and canopy | 13,165 | (1.7.1984) | 8,000 |
| Stocks |  |  | 109,000 |
| Bank/cash |  |  | 3,000 |
|  |  |  | 290,000 |
| Less current liabilities |  |  | (90,000) |
| Net assets transferred |  |  | 200,000 |

**Required:**

(a)    (i)   Compute the chargeable gain arising after incorporation relief as a result of the transfer, and the base cost of the shares received by Barbara.

**(5 marks)**

        (ii)   Compute the taxable gains arising in 2009/10 if, in March 2010, Barbara sold 80,000 of her new shares for net proceeds of £90,000.

**(3 marks)**

(b)    Show what difference it would have made to the computations

- Had the consideration for the transfer been settled by
  - the allocation of 150,000 £1 ordinary shares at par, and
  - the balance being left on loan account, and

- Barbara had, in March 2010, sold 80,000 shares to her sister for £81,000 when their true value was, as before, £90,000.

**(6 marks)**

(c)    Briefly explain any alternative tax efficient method of transferring the chargeable assets of Barbara's business to Bangle Ltd.

You are not to consider the possibility of Bangle Ltd registering as an Enterprise Investment Scheme company.

**(4 marks)**
**(Total: 18 marks)**

## 10 Overseas aspects of income tax and capital gains tax

### Simon White

### Question 1

Simon was born in Australia but has lived in the UK for many years since his parents emigrated to the UK when he was a child. Simon regards the UK to be his permanent home and does not intend to return to Australia.

For the past five years Simon has been employed in the UK but is now about to take up a secondment to his employer's Paris office.

The proposed secondment dates are from 1 February 2009 to 31 July 2010.

Simon will need to return to the UK so that he can report back to the UK company. He plans to make two visits, each one week long. He will receive remuneration from the UK company of £1,600 for these visits.

For the duration of his secondment in Paris, Simon will be paid £3,500 per month (gross) by the French company for his duties for them. He suffers 20% French tax at source.

Simon's only other income is rental income of £12,600 p.a. (net of expenses) from an unfurnished property in the UK.

**Required:**

(a) Calculate Simon's UK income tax payable for 2009/10.

**(5 marks)**

(b) Explain Simon's tax position for 2009/10 if the secondment to Paris began on 1 October 2008 and ended on 31 March 2010 with the same pattern of UK visits.

**(10 marks)**
**(Total: 15 marks)**

### Mr and Mrs Posh

### Question 2

Mr and Mrs Posh are domiciled in Switzerland but have been resident in the UK for the last 12 years. Their income for 2009/10 is as follows:

|  | Mr Posh | Mrs Posh |
|---|---|---|
|  | £ | £ |
| Overseas rental income | 39,200 | 423,000 |
| Remitted to the UK | 15,640 | 108,900 |

**Required:**
Advise Mr and Mrs Posh as to whether they should elect for the remittance basis to apply in 2009/10 and justify your reasons.

**(10 marks)**

## Darwin

### Question 3

Darwin, a UK domiciled, resident and ordinarily resident individual, received the following income in 2009/10.

|  | £ |
|---|---|
| Salary from Darwin's personal company (PAYE deducted £6,105) | 37,000 |
| Bank interest received from UK bank | 2,840 |
| Erewhon bank interest (45% Erewhon tax paid) (gross amount) | 1,265 |
| Narnia rental income (15% Narnian tax paid) (gross amount) | 690 |

Other relevant information for 2009/10 is as follows:

(1) Darwin's company provided him with a company car and diesel fuel for private use. The car has a list price of £32,000 and $CO_2$ emissions of 213 g/km.

(2) Darwin received goods from his company when a new shipment came in. If sold to a customer they would be valued at £500 but the cost of the goods was £300.

(3) Darwin paid £9,840 into a personal pension scheme on 13 May 2009.

**Required:**

Calculate Darwin's income tax payable for 2009/10.

**(13 marks)**

## Peter Singer

### Question 4

Peter Singer moved to the UK to work at his company's head quarters in Manchester in January 2009. He was born and lived until then in Portugal.

The terms of his contract are that he will be paid £44,000 per annum by the UK company, but will continue to have his Portuguese salary (UK equivalent) of £28,000 paid by his original employer into his Portuguese bank account. This will allow him to keep his house which his family will use whilst he is in the UK.

Peter's employment package includes the following:

(1) Company car – costing £28,000 with $CO_2$ emissions of 203g/km. All petrol will be provided by the company.

(2) Private medical insurance - costing £1,800 for him and his family.

(3) The company has bought a flat for his use, costing £187,000. The rateable value of the property is £4,500. The company will meet all the expenses of running the flat which are estimated to be in the region of £5,700 per annum. The company have furnished the flat at a cost of £49,000. Peter will pay rent of £1,300 per month to the company for the use of the flat.

(4) The company has arranged for Peter's children to attend a local nursery school starting on 5 September 2009. The cost will be £1,250 per month.

(5) Peter is provided with a mobile phone, and it is estimated that he spends about £135 per month on calls.

(6) Employees of the company are allowed to use a corporate membership at the local health club costing £220 per month.

(7) As his wife is staying in Portugal, the company will pay for her to fly to England every month at a cost of £650 for each trip. During 2009/10 she will make 10 trips.

Peter also has a number of investments in the UK and overseas which have yielded income as follows:

|  | £ | Remitted to the UK £ |
|---|---|---|
| UK dividends | 3,600 | |
| Portuguese dividends | 3,150 | 2,250 |
| Portuguese rental income | 2,900 | 1,300 |
| UK bank interest | 880 | |

The figures for the Portuguese income are shown before the deduction of withholding tax at 10%.

**Required:**

(i) Discuss the factors HMRC will use to decide whether Peter is resident, ordinarily resident and domiciled in the UK, and the impact of this on his income tax computation.

**(9 marks)**

(ii) Calculate Peter's income tax payable for 2009/10, on the basis of the information given above.

The official rate of interest for 2009/10 is 4.75%.

**(16 marks)**
**(Total: 25 marks)**

### Roberta

#### Question 5

Roberta has always been resident in the UK until February 2007 when she left the UK to work abroad. She plans to return to the UK in June 2011.

In May 2009 she sold an asset for £195,000 that she bought in June 2006 for £76,000.

In July 2010 she plans to sell another asset for £26,500. She bought the asset in February 2006 for £54,000.

**Explain how Roberta will be assessed on her chargeable gains.**

**(10 marks)**

## 11 An introduction to inheritance tax

There are no questions for this chapter.

## 12 Further aspects of IHT affecting lifetime gifts

### Mary Day

#### Question 1

Mary Day is a wealthy widow who has asked for your advice in respect of a number of gifts that she is planning to make in the near future.

Her only previous gift was one of £335,000 into a discretionary trust two years ago.

The proposed gifts are as follows:

(a) A gift of a holiday cottage worth £100,000 to her nephew Paul.

   As a condition of the gift, Mary would have the free use of the cottage for six months each year.

(b) A gift of an antique clock worth £10,000 to her granddaughter Jane in respect of her forthcoming wedding.

(c) A gift of 20,000 £1 ordinary shares in DEF Ltd into a discretionary trust for the benefit of her nieces and nephews.

Mary currently holds 30,000 shares in the company. She acquired the shares one year ago.

DEF Ltd is an unquoted trading company with a share capital of 200,000 £1 ordinary shares.

A 5% holding is worth £10 per share, whilst 10% and 15% holdings are worth £13 and £16 per share respectively.

(d)  A gift of agricultural land and buildings with an agricultural value of £160,000 to her son David.

The land was bought ten years ago, and has always been let out to tenants.

The most recent tenancy agreement commenced in 2004, and comes to an end in six months' time. Mary has obtained planning permission to build ten houses on the land.

The value of the land with planning permission is £280,000.

David owns the neighbouring land, and the value of this will increase from £200,000 to £250,000 as a result of the gift.

Mary will pay the inheritance tax arising from the gift into the discretionary trust. Any inheritance tax arising on the other gifts will be paid for by the respective donee.

**Required:**
Advise Mary of the inheritance tax implications arising from the above gifts, ignoring annual exemptions.

**(12 marks)**

## Gerry Generous

## Question 2

Gerry Generous is a wealthy individual aged 57, married to Jane, aged 54. The couple have two children, Jack, aged 34 and Jill, aged 37, who both have children of their own.

Gerry currently owns 60% of the issued share capital of GG Limited, a UK resident trading company, which he set up in 1984. The remaining shares are held, 20% by his daughter Jill and 20% by unconnected third parties.

Gerry has made the following gifts during his lifetime. Gerry agreed that he would pay any inheritance tax arising on these gifts.

| | |
|---|---|
| 4 June 2002 | £331,000 cash gift to a discretionary trust. |
| 4 March 2004 | £10,000 cash as a wedding gift to his son Jack. |
| 4 March 2004 | 20% of the shares in GG Limited to his daughter Jill. |

At this time the GG Limited shares were valued as follows:

| | £ |
|---|---|
| 20% | 100,000 |
| 60% | 450,000 |
| 80% | 600,000 |
| 100% | 800,000 |

4 June 2008    A further £100,000 cash gift to the discretionary trust created on 4 June 2002.

**Required:**

Explain the IHT implications arising from the lifetime gifts made between 4 June 2002 and 4 June 2008.

Your answer should include a calculation of any IHT payable and an explanation of any exemptions or reliefs available.

You are not required to explain the implications for the trustees of the discretionary trust.

You should assume that the rates and allowances for 2009/10 apply throughout this part of the question.

**(12 marks)**

## 13 IHT on the death estate and tax planning

**Martin**

### Question 1

Martin died on 31 July 2009. At the time of his death, Martin owned the following assets:

(1)  15,000 £1 ordinary shares in ABC Ltd, an unquoted trading company with an issued share capital of 100,000 shares.

Martin's wife also owns 15,000 shares in ABC Ltd.

Both these shareholdings were acquired five years ago.

The relevant values of ABC Ltd's shares, as agreed by HMRC, are:

| Shareholding | Value per share |
|---|---|
| 15% | £10 |
| 30% | £13 |

ABC Ltd has assets worth £3,000,000 of which £500,000 are investments in quoted shares.

(2)  100,000 £1 ordinary shares in DEF plc, a quoted trading company with an issued share capital of 20,000,000 shares.

DEF plc's shares were quoted on the Stock Exchange at 208 – 216p on 31 July 2009, with recorded bargains of 196p, 222p and 228p for that day.

(3)  A holiday cottage valued at £120,000.

Martin had inherited this 18 months ago on the death of his uncle.

The value of the cottage on the date of his uncle's death was £67,500. IHT of £22,500 was paid on his uncle's estate which had a gross chargeable value of £90,000.

(4)  Bank and cash balances of £150,000.

(5)  Other assets valued for IHT purposes at £208,000.

Under the terms of his will, Martin left £100,000 in cash to his wife, and the residue of his estate to his daughter.

Martin's wife is not domiciled in the UK.

Martin is also the life tenant of an IIP trust set up in 2001. The value of the trust fund on 31 July 2009 was £88,000.

Martin made no lifetime gifts.

**Required:**

Calculate the IHT liability arising as a result of Martin's death.

State how much of the liability is payable by the trustees of the IIP trust.

**(10 marks)**

## Jane Macbeth

### Question 2

(a) Jane Macbeth, aged 61, died on 20 November 2009. At the date of her death Jane owned the following assets:

(1) A main residence valued at £235,000. This has an outstanding repayment mortgage of £40,000.

(2) Building society deposits of £87,000.

(3) 10,000 £1 ordinary shares in Banquo plc. On 20 November 2009 the shares were quoted at 945p–957p, with bargains on that day of 937p, 961p and 939p.

Jane inherited the shares as a specific gift on the death of her sister on 10 August 2007 when they were valued at £68,000. The sister's executors paid IHT of £54,000 on an estate valued at £360,000.

(4) A life assurance policy on her own life. Immediately prior to the date of Jane's death, the policy had an open market value of £86,000. Proceeds of £104,000 were received following her death.

(5) Agricultural land valued at £168,000, but with an agricultural value of £110,000. The land was purchased during 1993, and it has always been let to tenant farmers. The most recent tenancy commenced on 1 January 2005.

Jane made the following gifts during her lifetime (any IHT arising was paid by Jane):

(1) On 28 November 2001 she made a cash gift of £105,000 into a discretionary trust.

(2) On 15 April 2005 she made a gift of 50,000 shares in Shakespeare Ltd, an unquoted trading company, to her son as a wedding gift. The shares were valued at £155,000, and were originally acquired by Jane in 1992. Her son still owned the shares on 20 November 2009. Shakespeare Ltd has 20% of the value of its total assets invested in quoted shares.

(3) On 10 March 2006 she made a cash gift of £268,000 into a discretionary trust.

Jane's husband Duncan is wealthy in his own right. Under the terms of her will Jane has therefore left a specific gift of £100,000 to her brother, with the residue of the estate being left to her children.

KAPLAN PUBLISHING

**Required:**

(a)

   (i)   Calculate the IHT that will be payable as a result of Jane's death. Assume that the tax rates and allowances for 2009/10 apply throughout.

**(15 marks)**

   (ii)  State who is primarily liable for the tax, the due dates of the IHT liabilities, the amount of IHT that can be paid under the instalment option, and the amount of inheritance that will be received by Jane's children.

**(4 marks)**

(b)  Jane's husband Duncan is aged 58. He is in good health, and expects to live for at least ten more years.

The Macbeth family appreciate that Jane's estate may not have been distributed in a tax efficient manner. They have therefore agreed that the terms of her will are to be varied so that the entire estate is left to Duncan.

Duncan will then make gifts totalling £500,000 to the children and Jane's brother during 2010 and 2011.

**Required:**

   (i)   State the conditions that must be met in order that the variation of the terms of Jane's will is valid for IHT purposes.

**(2 marks)**

   (ii)  Advise the Macbeth family of the IHT implications of the proposed plan.

You are not expected to calculate the revised IHT liability or to consider anti-avoidance legislation.

**(4 marks)**
**(Total: 25 marks)**

## Paul

### Question 3

Paul, due to ill health, is expected to die in the near future. You should assume that today's date is 31 December 2009.

The current value of his estate, and a forecast value for 12 months time, is as follows:

| | Present value £ | Forecast value £ |
|---|---|---|
| 20,000 shares (1% holding) in BCD plc a quoted company | 50,000 | 45,000 |
| 8,000 shares (2% holding) in GHI plc a quoted company | 70,000 | 85,000 |
| 30,000 shares (10% holding) in NOP Ltd an unquoted company | 65,000 | 60,000 |
| Main residence | 330,000 | 350,000 |
| Holiday cottage | 130,000 | 110,000 |
| | 645,000 | 650,000 |

All of these assets have been owned for at least two years.

Under the terms of his will, Paul has left all of his assets to his son. His son has two children.

Paul's wife is also ill, and is not expected to live for more than three months. She does not have any assets of her own, but Paul is confident that his son will look after her upon his death.

Paul has made the following transfers of value during his lifetime:

(i) On 1 November 2001, he made a gift of £203,000 into a discretionary trust. The trust paid any IHT arising on the gift.

(ii) On 1 October 2006, he gave his son £150,000 as a wedding gift.

(iii) On 1 November 2006, he gave his son a business valued at £250,000. Paul had run the business for 10 years, and his son has continued to run it since.

**Required:**

(a) Calculate the IHT liabilities that would arise if Paul were to die on 31 December 2009. Your answer should show the relevant due dates of payment.

**(8 marks)**

(b) Explain why it might be beneficial to change the terms of Paul's will.

If the changes were not made by Paul, explain whether it would be possible for his son to subsequently make the changes after the date of Paul's death.

**(4 marks)**

(c) Paul's son is considering selling the business that was given to him by Paul for its current value of £175,000.

Explain the IHT implications if the sale was before Paul's death.

**(2 marks)**

(d) Explain:

(i) The main advantages in lifetime giving for IHT purposes.

(ii) The main factors that need to be considered in deciding which assets to gift.

**(6 marks)**
**(Total: 20 marks)**

## Henry

### Question 4

Henry, aged 70, died on 5 October 2009. He was survived by his wife, Sally, also aged 70, and two children, Cecil and Ida.

Sally is herself in a frail condition and not expected to live for much longer. Both Cecil and Ida have children of their own and are relatively wealthy in their own right.

Henry owned the following assets:

(1) 100,000 £1 ordinary shares in Peel plc a quoted company with an issued share capital of 10,000,000 £1 ordinary shares.

On 5 October 2009 the price for these shares was quoted at 200 – 208p per share with marked bargains on that day of 201p, 204p and 207p.

A dividend of 9p per share had been paid on 30 September 2009.

(2) £20,000 10% Government Stock quoted at 95p – 97p ex interest. Interest is payable half yearly on 30 April and 31 October.

(3) The following capital deposits both of which have been held for several years:

– £25,000 deposited with a building society.

– £18,000 invested in an ISA account.

The following interest was received during 2009/10.

| | |
|---|---|
| Building Society | £320 on 30 June 2009 with a further £304 on 31 December 2009. |
| ISA | £350 on 30 June 2009 with a further £358 on 31 December 2009. |

All interest figures relate to the actual amount received.

(4) A house valued on 5 October 2009 at £450,000. This property was his and Sally's family home but was owned outright by Henry.

Under the terms of his will Henry has left £20,000 each to Cecil and Ida with the remainder of his estate left to his wife. Sally's will currently leaves her estate equally to their two children.

The only gifts made by Henry during his lifetime were cash gifts of £181,000 on 1 January 2002 and £164,000 on 1 January 2005 respectively. Both gifts were made to a discretionary trust. Henry had agreed to pay any inheritance tax arising on these lifetime gifts.

The only other taxable income Henry received during the period 6 April 2009 to 5 October 2009 was a State Retirement Pension of £5,460 and gross annuity income of £7,200. Basic rate income tax at the rate of 20% was deducted from the annuity income. The annuity did not have any capital value on Henry's death.

**Required:**

(a) Explain how Henry's income will be taxed in 2009/10, the tax year of his death, and calculate the income tax payable for this tax year.

**(7 marks)**

(b) Calculate the inheritance tax liabilities arising:

(i) from the lifetime gifts of cash to the discretionary trust; and

(ii) arising as a consequence of Henry's death on 5 October 2009.

**(10 marks)**

(a) Explain any action that could be taken following Henry's death to reduce or defer any inheritance tax liability that may become payable upon the future death of his wife, Sally.

Your answer should state any qualifying conditions that need to be satisfied and, where the information permits, include a calculation of any potential tax savings.

**(8 marks)**

You should assume that the rates and allowances for 2009/10 apply throughout parts (b) and (c).

**(Total: 25 marks)**

## Thelma

### Question 5

Assume today's date is 30 June 2010.

Thelma is aged 78 years. She is married to Gordon, who is independently wealthy in his own right. They have one child, Louise.

Thelma has unfortunately recently become terminally ill and is expected to live for only another four years.

She owns the following assets:

(1)  10,000 ordinary £1 shares in Blackbird plc, a quoted UK resident trading company with an issued share capital of 1 million ordinary shares. The company prepares its accounts to 31 March each year.

   The shares are currently quoted at 1460p – 1468p. Thelma acquired 5,000 of her shares in June 1997 for £25,000. The remainder of the shares were acquired by way of a rights issue in June 2004 for a further £50,000.

   Thelma was a director of this company for many years until she had to retire for health reasons on 31 May 2009.

(2)  A 25% beneficial interest in £100,000 10% loan stock in Robin plc, a quoted UK resident trading company.

   This loan stock is currently quoted at 102p – 106p and is held jointly with Gordon who has always owned the remaining 75% beneficial interest in it. This loan stock was acquired in June 2004 for £90,000.

(3)  Main residence valued at £500,000.

(4)  Three antique plates which are part of a set of six. Thelma bought her three plates in June 2004 for £2,500. On the same day Gordon bought two of the plates for £1,500 whilst Louise bought the remaining plate for £750.

   The value of the plates are currently as follows:

|  | £ |
|---|---|
| 1 plate | 1,000 |
| 2 plates | 2,200 |
| 3 plates | 3,800 |
| 4 plates | 6,000 |
| 5 plates | 10,000 |
| 6 plates | 20,000 |

(5)  Cash deposits amount to £145,000.

(6)  Sundry personal chattels collectively worth £20,000 with no individual asset worth more than £5,000.

Under the terms of Thelma's will, all of her assets are to be left to Louise with the exception of the house and her sundry personal chattels which are bequeathed to Gordon.

Due to her failing health, Thelma and her family are currently considering whether she should either:

(i)  gift all of her assets, with the exception of the house and her sundry personal chattels, to Louise upon her death in four years time, or

(ii)  make these gifts to Louise now.

In four years time her assets are expected to be valued at the following amounts for inheritance tax purposes:

|  | £ |
|---|---|
| Blackbird plc shareholding | 200,000 |
| 100% of the Robin plc loan stock | 100,000 |
| Residence | 600,000 |
| Antique plates | 10,000 |
| Cash deposits | 160,000 |
| Sundry personal chattels | 20,000 |
|  | 1,090,000 |

The only previous gift made by Thelma was a cash gift, net of annual exemptions, of £360,000 made to Louise in September 2008.

**Required:**
Advise Thelma whether she should

(i)  make the transfers of the selected assets to Louise upon her death in four years time, or

(ii) make the transfers now.

Your answer should consider the likely IHT and CGT implications and should include a calculation of any capital taxes likely to arise under each option.

Stamp duty and stamp duty land tax should be ignored.

You should assume that the rates and allowances for 2009/10 apply throughout.

**(18 marks)**

## 14 The taxation of trusts

### The Wood Discretionary Trust

#### Question 1

You are a member of the tax team in the firm 'Tax & Co'. In a few days time you have a meeting set up with potential new clients.

The clients are about to become the trustees of 'The Wood Discretionary Trust' which is to be set up under the terms of Tom Wood's will following his recent death.

#### Required:
Make brief notes for the meeting with the potential trustees detailing.

(a) The income tax implications of distributing income to the beneficiaries

(b) The CGT and IHT implications of distributing capital to the beneficiaries.

**(15 marks)**

## 15 Personal financial management

There are no questions for this chapter.

## 16 Ethics and personal tax administration

### Fred Foyle

### Question 1

Fred was employed until 31 March 2009. He purchased an existing business on 1 June 2009. Accounts have been prepared for the ten-month period to 5 April 2010. The results show a marked decline compared to the results of the previous owner for the y/e 31 May 2009.

|  | Previous owner y/e 31 May 2009 £ | Fred p/e 5 April 2010 £ |
|---|---|---|
| Sales – Cash | 600,000 | 400,000 |
| – Credit | 120,000 | 100,000 |
| Gross profit | 300,000 | 150,000 |
| Net profit | 216,000 | 80,000 |

Fred included the figures in his self assessment tax return for 2009/10 which was submitted on 31 January 2011.

HMRC proceeded to carry out an enquiry into Fred's 2009/10 return, and have stated that they consider the sales shown in the accounts to be understated by £100,000.

HMRC gave written notice that the enquiry was complete on 31 July 2011 and amended Fred's self assessment accordingly. Fred did not raise an appeal, and paid the additional tax due on 31 August 2011.

Fred is single, and has no other income or outgoings.

### Required:

(a) State the likely reasons why HMRC have investigated Fred's 2009/10 tax return.

State possible criteria that he could put forward in order to justify the fall in profits from those of the previous owner.

**(5 marks)**

(b) Calculate the interest on overdue tax (assuming a rate of 2.5%).

**(2 marks)**

(c) State the maximum amount of penalty that HMRC can charge Fred, and state the factors that will be taken into account in deciding if this maximum amount should be mitigated.

**(2 marks)**
**(Total: 9 marks)**

## 17 New and ongoing unincorporated businesses

### Lucinda Luck

### Question 1

Lucinda Luck set up her sweet shop 'Lucie's Lollies' on 1 June 2008, in time for the school holidays.

The first set of accounts has been prepared to 31 December 2008. The tax adjusted results for the first period were as follows:

|  | £ |
| --- | --- |
| Adjusted profits before capital allowances | 18,960 |
| Capital allowances | 5,000 |

Her accounts for the year ended 31 December 2009 have not yet been adjusted for tax purposes and the results are as follows:

| | £ | | £ |
| --- | --- | --- | --- |
| Rent and business rates | 9,600 | Gross profit b/d | 70,260 |
| Light and heat | 1,200 | Profit on the sale of | |
| Permanent employee's | | equipment | 400 |
| salary | 8,090 | Bank deposit interest | 160 |
| Repairs to premises | | Dividends | |
| (Note 1) | 5,020 | (amount received) | 262 |
| Motor expenses | 531 | | |
| Depreciation | | | |
| – motor van | 700 | | |
| – shop equipment | 1,300 | | |
| Amortisation of lease | 220 | | |
| Professional charges | | | |
| (Note 2) | 1,125 | | |
| Interest paid on business | | | |
| bank account (Note 3) | 782 | | |
| Sundry expenses (Note 4) | 1,524 | | |
| Salary | | | |
| – Lucinda Luck | 12,000 | | |
| – Emma (part-time) | 2,000 | | |
| Net profit | 26,990 | | |
| | 71,082 | | 71,082 |

The following information is given:

(1) Repairs to premises

|  | £ |
|---|---|
| Decorating and repairs | 370 |
| Demolition of wall to extend the shop area | 4,650 |
|  | 5,020 |

(2) Professional charges

|  | £ |
|---|---|
| Accountancy | 600 |
| Legal costs of obtaining new lease (Note 5) | 460 |
| Debt collection | 65 |
|  | 1,125 |

(3) Interest paid on the business bank account

|  | £ |
|---|---|
| Interest paid on the current account overdraft to purchase stock | 1,392 |
| Interest received from the reserve account | (610) |
| Net interest paid | 782 |

(4) Sundry expenses

|  | £ |
|---|---|
| Lucinda's parking fine | 60 |
| Subscription to 'Sweetie' a monthly periodical | 30 |
| Entertaining customers | 1,336 |
| Miscellaneous allowable expenses | 98 |
|  | 1,524 |

(5) For the first seven month period, Lucinda took out a temporary lease on the shop. However, on 1 January 2009 she was granted a 10 year lease. She paid a premium of £50,000 which was charged to the leasehold property account.

(6) During the year Lucinda used some of her stock for Christmas presents for her family. The cost of this stock was £240. The business makes a uniform gross profit of 50% on selling price. No entry had been made in the books in respect of the goods taken, other than the resulting reduction in closing stock.

(7) Capital allowances for the year ended 31 December 2009 have already been calculated and amount to £4,500.

**Required:**

(a) Calculate Lucinda's trading income assessments for the first two tax years of business and calculate the amount of overlap profits.

**(10 marks)**

(b) Calculate Lucinda's income tax liability for 2009/10.

**(5 marks)**

**(Total: 15 marks)**

## William

## Question 2

William recently set up his own small business, repairing aircraft, on 1 March 2009.

He has decided to prepare his accounts to 30 April each year.

The adjusted profit (before capital allowances) for the first period of account to 30 April 2010 was £71,440.

In this period William made the following transactions:

| | |
|---|---|
| 1 March 2009 | He brought into the business a Peugeot car with emissions of 149 g/km worth £13,100 which he used 15% privately. He also purchased equipment worth £8,400. |
| 15 July 2009 | He purchased some plant and machinery for £28,400. |
| 1 August 2009 | He sold the Peugeot for £6,000 and purchased a Land Rover for £30,000. His private use continued to be 15%. The Land Rover has emissions of 165 g/km. |
| 30 September 2009 | He bought some additional equipment for £150. |
| 1 April 2010 | Purchased some painting equipment for £2,600, used to sign-write the aircraft. |

**Required:**

Calculate William's trading income assessments for the first three tax years and any overlap profits arising in the opening years.

**(8 marks)**

Assume the FA2009 rules for capital allowances apply throughout.

### Ali

## Question 3

Ali has been in business as a sole trader for many years as a publisher.

He had an illness at the end of 2009 which resulted in his profits falling unexpectedly. The results for the last few years, and the projected profits for the next accounts, are as follows:

| Year ended: | | £ |
|---|---|---|
| 31 December 2008 | Profit | 55,000 |
| 31 December 2009 | Loss | (18,000) |
| 31 December 2010 (forecast estimate) | Profit | 26,000 |

Ali also had other income and outgoings as follows:

| | 2008/09 | 2009/10 | 2010/11 |
|---|---|---|---|
| | £ | £ | £ |
| Bank interest (gross amount) | 8,690 | 5,050 | Nil |
| Income from property | 9,200 | 6,820 | 6,840 |

During 2009/10, to realise some cash funds, he sold one of the properties that he let and made a capital gain of £19,400. The property was purchased in 1990.

Ali had unused capital losses of £8,750 at the beginning of 2009/10.

**Required:**

Advise Ali of the best method of utilising the loss for the year ended 31 December 2009 and calculate the taxable income and taxable gains for all relevant tax years assuming your advice is taken.

Assume rates and allowances for 2009/10 apply throughout.

**(10 marks)**

## 18 Cessation of an unincorporated business

### Jane Seemore

### Question 1

You should assume today's date is 1 March 2010.

Jane Seemore, aged 42, has been running a small restaurant business as a sole trader since 1 September 1999. She has decided to sell her business, and needs some advice concerning the tax implications.

**Offer for sale of business:**

- Jane has accepted an offer from Hollywood Ltd, an unconnected company quoted on the Alternative Investment Market, to purchase her business.

- Hollywood Ltd would like to complete the purchase on 31 March 2010.

- The purchase consideration will consist of either cash or ordinary shares in Hollywood Ltd, or a mixture of cash and shares.

- Jane will become an employee of Hollywood Ltd from 1 April 2010 on an annual salary of £30,000.

- If the consideration is taken wholly in the form of shares in Hollywood Ltd, then Jane's holding will represent 7.5% of the company's total share capital.

**Trading results:**

- Jane's trading profits and losses are as follows:

|  | £ |
|---|---|
| Year ended 31 August 2006 | 15,000 |
| Year ended 31 August 2007 | 6,000 |
| Year ended 31 August 2008 | 15,000 |
| Year ended 31 August 2009 | 10,000 |
| Period ended 31 March 2010 (before adjustments for capital allowances and sale of stock) | (21,500) |

- Jane has overlap profits brought forward of £2,815.

**Forecast market values of Jane's business assets:**

- The market values of the assets to be sold, at 31 March 2010 are:

|  | £ |
|---|---|
| Premises (bought for £335,000 in 2007) | 365,000 |
| Goodwill | 50,000 |
| Stock (cost plus 5%) | 8,300 |
| Shelving and restaurant fittings (all below cost) | 10,000 |
| Van (used 85% for business purposes) | 4,700 |
| Total value | 438,000 |

**Capital allowances:**

- The tax written down value on capital allowances general pool at 31 August 2009 was £15,050.

- Jane purchased equipment for £820 in November 2009.

- The written down value of the van at 31 August 2009 was £4,130.

**Other income:**

- Jane currently has no other income. Her investment income will exceed £40,000 pa for 2010/11 onwards, regardless of whether the consideration is taken as cash or shares.

**Required:**

(a) (i) Explain the capital allowances implications for Jane on the transfer of the business, with supporting calculations.

**(3 marks)**

(ii) Calculate Jane's trading income assessments for all relevant tax years, and calculate the amount of the trading loss.

**(3 marks)**

(iii) Outline briefly the loss relief options available and explain their relative merits in Jane's situation.

**(6 marks)**

(b) Explain why there would be no capital gains tax liability on the transfer of Jane's business in exchange for shares.

Calculate the maximum cash proceeds that Jane could receive without giving rise to a capital gains tax liability, and suggest how much cash Jane should actually receive.

**(6 marks)**

You should assume that the tax rates and allowances for 2009/10 apply throughout.

**(Total: 18 marks)**

## 19 Partnerships – income tax and capital gains tax

**Alf and Bob**

### Question 1

Alf, aged 56 and Bob, aged 57 have been in partnership together since 1 December 1998.

The partners sold their business on 30 November 2009 for its market value of £520,000.

The partnership assets at 30 November 2009, and the capital gains arising on the disposal, were as follows:

|  | Market value | Capital gain |
|---|---|---|
|  | £ | £ |
| Freehold property | 322,000 | 97,000 |
| Goodwill | 100,000 | 100,000 |
| Plant and machinery | 58,000 | – |
| Net current assets | 40,000 | – |
|  | 520,000 | 197,000 |

The assessable trading income for the final four tax years, before allocation between the partners, was as follows:

|  |  |  | £ |
|---|---|---|---|
| 2006/07 | Y.e. 30.11.06 | Profit | 15,000 |
| 2007/08 | Y.e. 30.11.07 | Profit | 14,000 |
| 2008/09 | Y.e. 30.11.08 | Profit | 11,200 |
| 2009/10 | Y.e. 30.11.09 | Loss | (33,500) |

Profits and losses have always been shared 40% to Alf and 60% to Bob.

Alf is single and had employment income from a part time job as follows:

|  | £ |
|---|---|
| 2006/07 | 5,000 |
| 2007/08 | 7,000 |
| 2008/09 | 9,000 |

He has capital losses brought forward at 6 April 2009 of £25,000.

Bob is single and also has no other income or outgoings apart from bank interest of £3,850 (gross) received on 1 December 2009 from investing the proceeds of sale of his holiday cottage. The cottage had been sold in June 2009, and the capital gain was £5,500.

Assume the 2009/10 rates and allowances apply to all years. Ignore overlap relief.

**Required:**

(a) Calculate the chargeable gains in respect of the partnership that will be assessed on Alf and Bob for 2009/10.

**(3 marks)**

(b) (i) Advise the partners of the possible ways of relieving the partnership loss for 2009/10 and which loss relief claims would be the most beneficial.

**(5 marks)**

(ii) After taking into account the advice in (i), calculate the partners' taxable income for 2006/07 to 2009/10 and their taxable gains for 2009/10.

**(5 marks)**
**(Total: 13 marks)**

## 20 VAT: outline

### Ken and Cindy

#### Question 1

(a) Ken has a market stall selling clocks and watches.

He started trading on 1 March 2009, and his turnover has accrued evenly over time as follows:

|  | £ |
|---|---|
| One month ended 31 March 2009 | 35,000 |
| Quarter ended 30 June 2009 | 51,000 |
| Quarter ended 30 September 2009 | 53,000 |
| Quarter ended 31 December 2009 | 59,000 |

**Required:**
Advise Ken if he should register for VAT and, if so, when HMRC should be notified.

**(3 marks)**

(b) Cindy's input tax and supplies made in the quarter to 31 December 2009 are analysed as follows:

|  | £ |
|---|---|
| Input tax wholly re-taxable supplies | 25,575 |
| Input tax wholly re-exempt supplies | 15,400 |
| Non-attributable input tax | 30,800 |
| Value (excluding VAT) of taxable supplies | 275,000 |
| Value of exempt supplies | 120,000 |

**Required:**

Calculate the deductible input tax assuming that Cindy uses supplies for the current quarter for attributing input tax.

**(3 marks)**

**(Total: 6 marks)**

## 21 VAT: administration and overseas aspects

### Alan and Roger

### Question 1

Alan and Roger commenced in partnership as chartered architects on 1 February 2009 and the values of their supplies were as follows:

| Month | Fees for services invoiced | Sales of unsuitable office equipment |
|---|---|---|
| 2009 | £ | £ |
| February | 3,950 | |
| March | 6,200 | |
| April | 3,900 | |
| May | 3,700 | |
| June | 3,500 | |
| July | 2,200 | |
| August | 6,100 | |
| September | 6,800 | 1,500 |
| October | 8,200 | |
| November | 10,200 | |
| December | 13,400 | |
| 2010 | | |
| January | – | |
| February | 35,700 | |
| March | 29,400 | |

Alan and Roger informed HMRC of their liability to register by telephone on 12 October 2010 and submitted the VAT Registration Form on 28 November 2010.

**Required:**
Discuss when Alan and Roger are liable to be registered for VAT.

**(6 marks)**

### Sandy Brick

### Question 2

Sandy Brick has been a self-employed builder since 2003. He registered for VAT on 1 January 2010, and is in the process of completing his VAT return for the quarter ended 31 March 2010.

The following information is relevant to the completion of this VAT return:

(1) Sales invoices totalling £44,000 (excluding VAT) were issued to VAT registered customers in respect of standard rated sales. Sandy offers his VAT registered customers a 5% discount for prompt payment.

(2) Sales invoices totalling £16,920 were issued to customers that were not registered for VAT. Of this figure, £5,170 was in respect of zero-rated sales with the balances being in respect of standard rated sales. Standard rated sales are inclusive of VAT.

(3) On 10 January 2010 Sandy received a payment on account of £5,000 in respect of a contract that was completed on 28 April 2010. The total value of the contract is £10,000. Both of these figures are inclusive of VAT at the standard rate.

(4) Standard rated materials amounted to £11,200, of which £800 were used in constructing Sandy's private residence.

(5) Since 1 December 2008 Sandy has paid £120 per month for the lease of office equipment. This expense is standard rated.

(6) During the quarter ended 31 March 2010 £400 was spent on mobile telephone calls, of which 30% relates to private calls. This expense is standard rated.

(7) On 20 February 2010 £920 was spent on repairs to a motor car. The motor car is used by Sandy in his business, although 20% of the mileage is for private journeys. This expense is standard rated.

(8) On 15 March 2010 equipment was purchased for £6,000. The purchase was partly financed by a bank loan of £5,000. This purchase is standard rated.

Unless stated otherwise all of the above figures are exclusive of VAT.

**Required:**

(a) State the VAT rules that determine the tax point in respect of a supply of services.

**(3 marks)**

(b) State the circumstances in which Sandy is required to issue a VAT invoice, and the period during which such an invoice should be issued.

**(2 marks)**

(c) Calculate the amount of VAT payable by Sandy for the quarter ended 31 March 2010.

**(10 marks)**
**(Total: 15 marks)**

## 22 Corporation tax: computations and administration

There are no questions for this chapter.

## 23 Calculation of corporation tax income and gains

### Springvale Ltd

#### Question 1

Springvale Ltd has been carrying on a manufacturing business since 1970 and the following is a summary of the profit and loss account for the year to 31 March 2010.

| | £ | | £ |
|---|---|---|---|
| Directors' remuneration | 37,840 | Trading profit | 362,372 |
| Loan stock interest payable (gross) | 480 | Loan stock interest receivable (gross) | 1,200 |
| Depreciation | 44,400 | Bank deposit interest | |
| Entertaining expenses (all customers) | 420 | receivable | 359 |
| | | Dividend from UK trade | |
| Gift Aid paid to charity | 4,150 | investment (excluding | |
| Salaries and wages | 16,460 | tax credit) | 400 |
| Rent and business rates | 1,650 | | |
| Audit fee | 350 | | |
| Trade expenses | 15,418 | | |
| Net profit before taxation | 243,163 | | |
| | 364,331 | | 364,331 |

The loan stock interest is payable in respect of a trade related loan. Interest of £80 was accrued at 31 March 2010. There was no opening accrual. Debenture interest is receivable annually on 31 March.

The trade expenses include the following items:

| Christmas gifts | £ |
|---|---|
| Wines and spirits for UK customers | 320 |
| 5,000 ball-point pens with company's name | 250 |
| Legal costs | |
| Re long-term trade related loan finance secured by a floating charge | 500 |
| Re staff service agreements | 90 |

The Tax WDV on 1 April 2009 of plant and machinery was £24,220.

On 10 July 2009 the company purchased a new lathe for £1,200 and plant for £2,000. On 1 December 2009 plant that had cost £11,000 was sold for £1,500.

On 1 February 2010 plant costing £5,200 and a motor car costing £13,000 with emissions of 139 g/km were purchased (the private use of this car by the sales director was estimated at one-third).

During the year the company made a chargeable gain of £51,160.

**Required:**
Calculate the PCTCT for the year ended 31 March 2010.

**(10 marks)**

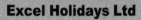

## Excel Holidays Ltd

### Question 2

Excel Holidays Ltd operates a holiday camp. In order to reflect more effectively the seasonal nature of the trade, it changed its accounting date from 31 March to 30 September.

Accordingly, accounts were drawn up for the year ended 31 March 2008 and for the 18 months ended 30 September 2009, as follows:

|  | y/e 31 March 2008 £ | 18 m/e 30 September 2009 £ |
|---|---|---|
| Trading profit | 150,000 | 183,000 |
| Less: Repairs and renewals | (15,000) | (12,000) |
| Travelling | (2,000) | (3,000) |
| Sundry expenses | (4,000) | (5,000) |
| Depreciation | (8,000) | (10,000) |
|  | 121,000 | 153,000 |
| Deposit account interest | 1,000 | 3,000 |
|  | 122,000 | 156,000 |

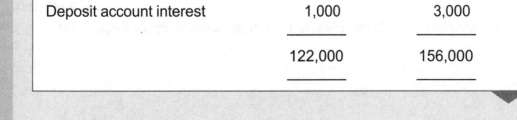

The following transactions had taken place.

(a) Sundry expenses:

included in the y/e 31 March 2008

|  |  | £ |
|---|---|---|
| (i) | theft by staff | 1,000 |
| (ii) | travelling expenses of two directors to the French Riviera to attend a conference on holiday camp management | 3,000 |

included in the 18 m/e 30 September 2009

| (i) | entertainment of overseas supplier | 500 |
|---|---|---|
| (ii) | fines for serving contaminated food | 1,500 |

(b) Interest on the bank deposit account was credited as follows.

|  | £ |
|---|---|
| 30 September 2007 | 400 |
| 31 March 2008 | 600 |
| 30 September 2008 | 500 |
| 31 March 2009 | 600 |
| 30 September 2009 | 1,900 |

(c) Included in the 18 m/e 30 September 2009, under repairs and renewals, is an accrual of £4,000 for painting and decorating. This work was completed during September 2009 but not invoiced until October 2009.

(d) The general pool Tax WDV of plant and machinery at 1 April 2007 was £nil, and additions were as follows:

|  |  | £ |
|---|---|---|
| 30 April 2007 | second hand coach | 25,000 |
| 31 May 2008 | swimming pool extension | 41,000 |
| 30 September 2009 | two gas-fired barbecues | 3,125 |

**Required:**

Calculate the CT liabilities for all accounting periods covered by the periods of account ended 31 March 2008 and 30 September 2009.

**(12 marks)**

Assume the FA2009 rules for capital allowances apply throughout.

## 24 Corporation tax losses

### Iris Ltd

#### Question 1

Iris Ltd has the following results for the periods to 31 August 2010:

|  | y/e 31.12.08 £ | 8 m/e 31.8.09 £ | y/e 31.8.10 £ |
|---|---|---|---|
| Trading profit/(loss) | 170,000 | 78,000 | (176,100) |
| Property income | 10,000 | 11,000 | 12,000 |
| Interest income | 2,500 | 3,600 | 4,100 |
| Gift Aid donation | 3,000 | 3,000 | 3,000 |

**Required:**

Calculate the PCTCT for all three periods, assuming that as much of the loss as possible is relieved against total profits.

State the amount of unrelieved loss at 1 September 2010.

**(8 marks)**

### Cosmet Ltd

#### Question 2

(a) Cosmet Ltd is a company that manufactures cosmetics. The recent results of Cosmet Ltd are as follows:

|  | y/e 31.5.07 £ | y/e 31.5.08 £ | p/e 31.12.08 £ | y/e 31.12.09 £ |
|---|---|---|---|---|
| Trading profit | 750,250 | 500,500 | 101,999 | |
| Trading loss | | | | (232,790) |
| Property income | 10,000 | 10,000 | 10,000 | 11,000 |
| Bank interest receivable | 8,460 | 7,526 | 5,076 | 5,275 |
| Capital (loss)/gain | 1,622 | (4,000) | 2,990 | 60,400 |

**Required:**

(i) Calculate the PCTCT for all four periods, assuming that relief is obtained for the loss against total profits.

**(6 marks)**

(ii) Calculate the tax repayments arising from the claim.

**(3 marks)**

(b) The company director is thinking about the company's options and has arranged a meeting with you and your tax partner.

He is considering one of the following two options:

(1) merging with another company which will buy the shares in Cosmet Ltd, that is keen to acquire the goodwill and clients of Cosmet Ltd and utilise the losses, or

(2) changing the products that Cosmet Ltd currently make, and moving into the more lucrative market of making beauty products for Spa Hotels.

**Required:**

Make brief notes for your meeting with the director on the effect on trading losses of the two options being considered.

**(6 marks)**

**(Total: 15 marks)**

## 25 Business Financial Management

There are no questions for this chapter.

## 26 Family companies and related planning scenarios

### Bream

### Question 1

Bream is a participator in, but not an employee of, Test Valley Ltd, a close trading company that prepares accounts to 31 December each year.

In June 2007 the company loaned Bream £72,000 for the purchase of a yacht. In January 2009 Bream repaid £20,000 and in March 2010 the company waived the outstanding amount of the loan.

**Required:**

Show the effect of these transactions on Test Valley Ltd and on Bream.

**(5 marks)**

## Joe

### Question 2

Joe subscribes for 100,000 £1 shares in his family company, Grange Ltd, at par in November 1986. This represents a 25% holding in the company. Joe is not an employee or Grange Ltd.

In August 2009 Joe sells the shares back to the company at £7.30 per share, as he is aged 58 and ready to retire, and the family do not want the shares to go to outsiders.

Joe has earned income of £50,000 in 2009/10 and made no other capital disposals during the year. Grange Ltd is an unquoted trading company.

**Required:**

Advise Joe of how the sale of shares will affect his tax liability for 2009/10 if:

(a) the transaction is treated as a distribution; and

(b) the transaction is not treated as a distribution.

(c) Explain the effect of satisfying the exemption from treatment as a distribution.

**(6 marks)**

## John

### Question 3

Assume that today's date is 1 March 2009.

John is a 52 year old single man who does not have any children.

John will resign from the job, in which he has been employed since 1996, earning a salary of £6,000 per month, on 31 March 2009.

John intends to start trading on 1 April 2009 producing VAT exempt goods. His business plan shows expected profits of £100,000 per annum net of wages to his employees. He is undecided whether he should incorporate or not as he does not understand the differences in the taxation of a sole trader and a company.

The business needs funds in the order of £100,000 to start up, but John does not want to use his own capital.

He expects that funds will be easier to raise if he incorporates, but is confused about the taxation implications of equity versus loan finance.

John estimates that he needs £20,000 per year to cover his living expenses, in addition to the £6,475 property business income that he receives annually. John has not made any pension provision to date.

**Required:**

(a) Identify the main differences between the taxation of John as a sole trader and the taxation of John's company and John as an employee and shareholder

Calculate the income tax (IT), corporation tax (CT) and national insurance contributions (NIC) payable by John and (where applicable) John's company for the tax year 2009/10 or for the year ended 31 March 2010, under each of the following options:

(i) John trades as a sole trader;

(ii) John incorporates and takes a net dividend of £20,000 as his only income from the company; and

(iii) John incorporates and takes a gross annual salary of £28,074 as his only income from the company.

Ignore the odd five days at the start of the accounting period (i.e. assume that it matches the tax year 2009/10).

**(8 marks)**

(b) Describe the taxation implications of both equity and loan finance from the point of view of:

(i) a company, and

(ii) an individual investor.

**(6 marks)**

(c) Assuming that John decides to incorporate on 1 April 2009, taking an annual salary of £25,000 and annual dividends of £9,000 (cash received), briefly describe the options available to John for investing in a pension. Indicate which of the options identified is preferable in his case and calculate the maximum contributions he could make before 31 December 2009.

**(8 marks)**
**(Total: 22 marks)**

## 27 Groups and consortium

### Longbow

#### Question 1

Longbow Ltd wishes to acquire Minnow Ltd and has made an offer to the shareholders of that company which it would like to finalise on 1 October 2009. The share capital of Minnow Ltd is owned equally by A Ltd, B Ltd and C Ltd.

The forecast results of Longbow Ltd and Minnow Ltd for the year ended 31 March 2010 are as follows:

|  | Longbow Ltd | Minnow Ltd |
|---|---|---|
|  | £ | £ |
| Adjusted trading profit/(loss) | 220,000 | (140,000) |
| Trading losses brought forward | – | (9,000) |
| Capital gain | – | 50,000 |
| Interest received on Loan Stocks (gross) | 5,250 | – |

Longbow Ltd purchased £150,000 of 7% Loan Stock issued by an unrelated company on 1 August 2009. On 30 April 2010 the company is to purchase a new freehold factory for £120,000.

Minnow Ltd's capital gain is in respect of the proposed sale of a freehold office building for £150,000 on 10 February 2010. One-quarter of the building has never been used for the purposes of the company's trade.

**Required:**

Calculate the corporation tax liability for both Longbow Ltd and Minnow Ltd for the year ended 31 March 2010 if:

(a) Longbow Ltd acquires one-third of Minnow Ltd's share capital from A Ltd on 1 October 2009.

**(4 marks)**

(b) Longbow Ltd acquires two-thirds of Minnow Ltd's share capital from A Ltd and B Ltd on 1 October 2009.

**(3 marks)**

(c) Longbow Ltd acquires all of Minnow Ltd's share capital from A Ltd, B Ltd and C Ltd on 1 October 2009.

**(4 marks)**
**(Total: 11 marks)**

## Willow Group

### Question 2

Willow Ltd, a UK resident company, has holdings of ordinary shares in other companies, which, apart from Beech Inc, are all UK resident.

> 90% in Beech Inc (an overseas resident company not in EEA)
> 90% in Fig Ltd
> 85% in Oak Ltd
> 55% in Pine Ltd

Fig Ltd holds 75% of the ordinary shares of Cherry Ltd, Ash Ltd holds 45% of the shares in Pine Ltd and Beech Inc holds 5% of the shares in Cherry Ltd.

Trading results for each company for the year ended 31 March 2010:

|  |  | £ |
|---|---|---|
| Ash Ltd | Loss | (160,000) |
| Pine Ltd | Profit | 158,000 |
| Willow Ltd | Profit | 153,000 |
| Oak Ltd | Loss | (107,000) |
| Fig Ltd | Profit | 294,000 |
| Cherry Ltd | Loss | (15,000) |
| Beech Inc | Loss | (110,000) |

No company had any other source of income or gains.

### Required:

Assuming losses are used in the most efficient manner, calculate the UK corporation tax payable by each of the UK companies for the year ended 31 March 2010.

**(10 marks)**

## 28 Overseas aspects of corporation tax

## X Ltd

### Question 1

X Ltd is a UK resident company which has, to date, traded only in the UK. The directors have decided to establish a factory overseas and seek advice on the taxation implications of this proposal.

In particular, they wish to know whether the overseas trade should be conducted through a foreign-based subsidiary or simply as a branch of the UK company.

**Required:**

Draft an appropriate memorandum to the board of the company highlighting the taxation implications of each of the two alternatives.

**(6 marks)**

### Bertie Overseas

### Question 2

You have recently met with Bertie, a UK resident individual, who requires some preliminary advice concerning setting up an overseas operation.

You ascertain during the course of the meeting that Bertie owns 30% of the share capital and is the managing director of Bertie Limited a successful UK resident trading company which manufactures lawnmowers in the UK. The remaining shares are held by other third party individuals.

Bertie Limited operates on a wholesale basis and currently only sells products in the UK. Bertie, however, believes the time is right for overseas expansion and is considering setting up a distribution operation in the country of Picea (a non EEA country) ('Bertie Overseas') which will be wholly owned by Bertie Limited. It is planned that Bertie Overseas will also operate on a wholesale basis and will only buy lawnmowers from Bertie Limited.

The following additional information is available:

(1)  Bertie Limited currently pays corporation tax at the full rate.

(2)  The rate of Picean corporation tax is 10%, irrespective of whether the trading entity is a branch or a company incorporated in Picea. Picean tax law only allows the offset of trading losses generated against other profits earned in the same period. Under Picean tax law no withholding tax is deductible on overseas profits remittances. There is no double tax treaty between the UK and Picea.

(3)  The mark up currently achieved by Bertie Limited, after all selling and distribution costs, on sales to its UK customers is 100%. The mark up on sales to Bertie Overseas will be 80%. Bertie Overseas will be responsible for all of its own selling and distribution costs including meeting carriage costs from the UK. Bertie believes that, in the absence of Bertie Overseas, Bertie Limited would achieve a comparable mark up on sales to Picea of 85%.

(4) Setting up the Picean operation will involve the acquisition of some freehold premises as well as necessary vehicles and equipment.

(5) Local Picean management will be appointed to run the day to day operations of Bertie Overseas. Bertie is considering retaining a high level of ultimate control over Bertie Overseas.

(6) Bertie Limited is planning to charge Bertie Overseas interest on any loan finance provided at the rate of 4% per year. If Bertie Overseas were to arrange its own loan finance via an independent bank it would have been charged 6% per year.

(7) The business plans produced indicate that Bertie Overseas is likely to make a loss for its first trading period and will then produce progressively stronger profits. Once profits are being generated it is planned to remit 25% of these to Bertie Limited.

Bertie has asked that you write to him setting out the principal business tax issues that need to be considered in advance of a future meeting where these issues will be discussed in more detail.

**Required:**

Write a letter to Bertie identifying the principal business tax issues that can be identified from the above information regarding the setting up of Bertie Overseas.

You are not required to discuss any employee or sales tax issues.

The points covered should include (but not be restricted to) an analysis of whether Bertie Overseas should be set up as a branch or a limited company, the anti-avoidance legislation that HMRC could use to tax the overseas profits in the UK and whether relief will be available in the UK for any Picean taxes paid.

Marks will be awarded for presentation, structure and format.
Ignore VAT.

**(25 marks)**

## 29 Planning for companies

### North and South

### Question 1

Bertrand owns 100% of the issued share capital of two UK resident trading companies, North Limited and South Limited. Both companies operate in the retail sector and commenced trading on 1 April 2009.

The actual and forecast results for both companies are as follows:

|  | Trading Profit/(Loss) |
| --- | ---: |
|  | £ |
| North Limited |  |
| Actual for the year ended 31 March 2010 | 10,000 |
| Forecast for the year ended 31 March 2011 | (114,000) |
| South Limited |  |
| Actual for the year ended 31 March 2010 | 160,000 |
| Forecast for the year ended 31 March 2011 | 200,000 |

It is the accounting policy of both North Limited and South Limited to amortise goodwill at the rate of 2% per year, except in the year of disposal when no amortisation is charged. The trading profit figures above, for both companies, are stated before any adjustments for goodwill.

Due to the losses forecast for North Limited some restructuring of the two companies is required. This is planned to take place at the end of the Financial Year ending 31 March 2011.

The forecast figures given above for both companies are stated before the effects of this proposed restructuring, which will comprise:

(1) North Limited selling one of its retail outlets to a third party for £160,000 with the consideration allocated as follows:

|  | £ |
| --- | ---: |
| Freehold property | 120,000 |
| Stock (cost £6,000) | 10,000 |
| Goodwill | 30,000 |
|  | ——— |
|  | 160,000 |
|  | ——— |

At the date of sale the freehold property will have an indexed cost of £80,000. The goodwill was originally acquired on 1 April 2009 for £10,000. This is the only purchased goodwill that North Limited has acquired.

(2) As South Limited has sufficient cash resources it will acquire a replacement retail outlet costing £120,000 with the consideration allocated as follows:

|  | £ |
|---|---|
| Freehold property | 100,000 |
| Stock | 20,000 |
|  | 120,000 |

The goodwill will cost £20,000 and will be the only purchased goodwill that South Limited has acquired. However, in May 2010, South Limited incurred £2,000 on an abortive attempt to acquire the goodwill of another retail outlet.

**Required:**

(a) Calculate the actual and forecast corporation tax liabilities of North Limited and South Limited for the years ended 31 March 2010 and 31 March 2011 assuming that the objective is to minimise the total tax liability for these years.

Your answer should clearly identify any unrelieved losses carried forward at 31 March 2011.

**(7 marks)**

(b) Explain the weaknesses of the above group structure and advise as to how this position could be improved by making one company a wholly owned subsidiary of the other company.

Your answer should include a summary of the procedures involved in altering the group structure to a more tax efficient basis together with an explanation of any relieving provisions which can be used in this group restructuring.

**(9 marks)**

(c) Recalculate the corporation tax liabilities of North Limited and South Limited for the years ended 31 March 2010 and 31 March 2011 assuming that the group restructuring identified at part (b) had been implemented with effect from 1 April 2010 and the objective is again to minimise the total tax liability for these years.

**(9 marks)**

You should assume that the rates and allowances for the Financial Year 2009 apply throughout.

**(Total: 25 marks)**

## Test your understanding answers

**Norman**

### Answer 1 – Chapter 1

**Income tax computation – 2009/10**

|  | £ |
|---|---:|
| Employment income (£39,630 + £2,100) | 41,730 |
| Building society interest (£2,000 x 100/80) | 2,500 |
| Property income (Note 1) | 2,050 |
| UK dividends received (£207 x 100/90) | 230 |
| | ——— |
| Total income | 46,510 |
| Less Relief – Qualifying loan interest | (1,500) |
| | ——— |
| Net income | 45,010 |
| Less PA | (6,475) |
| | ——— |
| Taxable income | 38,535 |
| | ——— |

### Analysis of income

**Dividends  Savings  Other income**

£230        £2,500   (£38,535 – £230 – £2,500) = £35,805

|  |  |  | £ |
|---|---|---|---:|
| 35,805 | x 20% | Other income | 7,161 |
| 1,595 | x 20% | Savings | 319 |
| ——— | | | |
| 37,400 | | | |
| 905 | x 40% | Savings | 362 |
| 230 | x 32½% | Dividends | 75 |
| ——— | | | |
| 38,535 | | | |
| ——— | | | ——— |
| Income tax liability | | | 7,917 |
| Less Tax credits | | | |
| Dividends (10% x £230) | | | (23) |
| Interest (20% x £2,500) | | | (500) |
| | | | ——— |
| Income tax payable | | | 7,394 |
| | | | ——— |

## Mr Darcy

### Answer 1 – Chapter 2

**Income tax computation – 2009/10**

| | £ |
|---|---|
| Salary | 37,000 |
| Bonus (Note 1) | 8,000 |
| Car benefit (Note 2) | 6,800 |
| Fuel benefit (Note 2) | 5,746 |
| | 57,546 |
| Less Pension contributions (7% x £37,000) | (2,590) |
| Partnership shares (12 x £125) (Note 3) | (1,500) |
| Employment income | 53,456 |
| Less PA | (6,475) |
| Taxable income (all 'other income') | 46,981 |

| £ | | £ |
|---|---|---|
| 37,400 | x 20% | 7,480 |
| 9,581 | x 40% | 3,832 |
| 46,981 | | |
| Income tax liability | | 11,312 |

**Notes:**

(1) Under the receipts basis for directors the bonus is treated as received, and therefore taxed, when it is determined. Thus the bonus determined in May 2009 is taxable in 2009/10.

(2) Car and fuel benefit

$CO_2$ emission 232g/km, available all year

Appropriate percentage:

$(232 - 135) \div 5 = 19\% + 15\%$ (petrol car) = 34%

| Car benefit = 34% x £20,000 | £6,800 |
|---|---|
| Fuel benefit = 34% x £16,900 | £5,746 |

(3)  The free shares and the matching shares are allotted tax free under the all employee share scheme. The cost of partnership shares is an allowable deduction against employment income (and would have been deducted before applying PAYE).

## Hubert

### Answer 2 – Chapter 2

**Income tax computation – 2009/10**

|  | £ | £ |
|---|---|---|
| Employment income (W1) |  | 57,474 |
| Pension |  | 5,000 |
| Trading income |  | 9,480 |
|  |  | 71,954 |
| Bank interest (£1,680 x 100/80) | 2,100 |  |
| Building society interest (£92 x 100/80) | 115 |  |
| Treasury stock interest (gross) | 250 |  |
|  |  | 2,465 |
| Foreign income (gross) |  | 1,200 |
| UK dividends received (£578 x 100/90) |  | 642 |
| Total income |  | 76,261 |
| Less PA |  | (6,475) |
| Taxable income |  | 69,786 |

Analysis of income:

| **Dividends** | **Savings** | **Other income** |
|---|---|---|
| £642 | £2,465 | (£69,786 – £642 – £2,465) = £66,679 |

Income tax:

| £ | | | £ |
|---|---|---|---|
| 37,400 x 20% | (other income) | | 7,480 |
| 29,279 x 40% | (other income) | | 11,712 |
| 66,679 | | | |
| 2,465 x 40% | (savings) | | 986 |
| 642 x 32½% | (dividends) | | 209 |
| 69,786 | | | |

| | £ |
|---|---|
| Income tax liability | 20,387 |
| Less Tax credits | |
| Dividends (10% × £642) | (64) |
| Interest (20% × (£2,100 + £115)) | (443) |
| PAYE (£4,500 × £1,100) | (5,600) |
| Income tax payable | 14,280 |

**Workings**

**(W1) Employment income**

| | £ |
|---|---|
| Salary | 23,000 |
| Car benefit (W2) | 5,200 |
| Fuel benefit (W2) | 4,394 |
| Business expenses (Note) | 1,960 |
| Use of assets (W3) | 240 |
| | 34,794 |
| Less Professional subscriptions | (360) |
| Business expenses (Note) | (1,960) |
| | 32,474 |
| Unapproved share options (W4) | 25,000 |
| Employment income | 57,474 |

**Note:** The business expenses reimbursed by the employer offsets the business expenses allowable: the position is tax neutral.

**(W2)** **Car and fuel benefit**

$CO_2$ emission 195 g/km, available all year

Appropriate percentage:

$(190 - 135) \div 5 = 11\% + 15\%$ (petrol car) = 26%

| | |
|---|---:|
| Car benefit = 26% x £20,000 | £5,200 |
| Fuel benefit = 26% x £16,900 | £4,394 |

**(W3)** **Use of assets**

| | |
|---|---:|
| Use of cement mixer (20% x £1,200) | £240 |

**(W4)** **Unapproved share options**

| | £ |
|---|---:|
| Charge on exercise (MV at that time) | 200,000 |
| Less Price paid (25,000 x £7) | (175,000) |
| | |
| Income tax charge | 25,000 |

No capital gain arises on the disposal of the shares as the sale proceeds received are equal to the base cost of the shares acquired.

## Chalk and Cheese

### Answer 3 – Chapter 2

**Alice Chalk**
**Income tax computation – 2009/10**

|  | Total £ | Other income £ | Savings £ |
|---|---|---|---|
| Salary | 40,000 | | |
| Pension contribution (£40,000 × 6%) | (2,400) | | |
| | 37,600 | | |
| Car benefit (W1) | 3,402 | | |
| Fuel benefit (£16,900 × 27%) | 4,563 | | |
| Living accommodation (W2) | 8,520 | | |
| Employment income | 54,085 | 54,085 | |
| Building society interest | | | |
| (£1,800 × 100/80) | 2,250 | | 2,250 |
| Total income | 56,335 | 54,085 | 2,250 |
| Personal allowance | (6,475) | (6,475) | |
| Taxable income | 49,860 | 47,610 | 2,250 |

| £ | | £ |
|---|---|---|
| 37,400 x 20% (other income) | | 7,480 |
| 10,210 x 40% (other income) | | 4,084 |
| 2,250 x 40% (savings) | | 900 |
| 49,860 | | |
| Income tax liability | | 12,464 |

### Class 1 NICs

Alice's Employee Class 1 NIC will be:
(£40,000 – £5,715) x 11%    £3,771

Class 1 NIC is payable on gross earnings, before any deductions for allowable expenses and pension contributions.

### Total income tax and NIC liability

Alice's total income tax and NIC liability for 2009/10 is £16,235 (£12,464 + £3,771).

**Workings**

**(W1) Car benefit**

(1) The list price of the motor car is reduced to £12,600 (£14,600 – £2,000) as Alice's capital contribution is less than £5,000.

(2) The $CO_2$ emission figure is rounded down to 195. The relevant percentage is therefore 27% (15% + 12% (195 – 135 = 60/5)).

(3) The motor car was available throughout 2009/10 so the benefit is £3,402 (£12,600 × 27%).

**(W2) Living accommodation**

|  | £ |
|---|---|
| Rateable value | 3,895 |
| Additional benefit | 1,425 |
| (£105,000 – £75,000 = £30,000 at 4.75%) | |
| Running costs | 3,200 |
| | 8,520 |

- There is an additional benefit as the property cost is in excess of £75,000.

- Since the property was not purchased more than six years before first being provided, the benefit is based on the cost of the property.

**Zara Cheese**

**Income tax computation – 2009/10**

| | Total £ | Other income £ | Dividends £ |
|---|---|---|---|
| Net profit | 40,000 | | |
| Depreciation | 12,425 | | |
| Motor expenses (£5,400 × 4,000/12,000) | 1,800 | | |
| Private accommodation (£9,600 × 1/3) | 3,200 | | |
| | 57,425 | | |
| Capital allowances (W) | (1,280) | | |
| Trading profit | 56,145 | 56,145 | |
| Dividends (£1,800 × 100/90) | 2,000 | | 2,000 |
| Total income | 58,145 | 56,145 | 2,000 |
| Personal allowance | (6,475) | (6,475) | |
| Taxable income | 51,670 | 49,670 | 2,000 |

Income tax

| £ | | £ |
|---|---|---|
| 39,800 x 20% (other income) (Note) | | 7,960 |
| 9,870 x 40% (other income) | | 3,948 |
| 49,670 | | |
| 2,000 x 32.5% (dividends) | | 650 |
| 5,1670 | | |

| | |
|---|---|
| Income tax liability | 12,558 |
| **Class 2 NICs** (52 × £2.40) | 125 |
| **Class 4 NICs** | |
| (£43,875 – £5,715) x 8% | 3,053 |
| (£56,145 – £43,875) x 1% | 123 |
| | 3,176 |

**Total income tax and NIC liability**

Zara's total income tax and NIC liability for 2009/10 is £15,859 (£12,558 + £125 + £3,176).

**Note:** The personal pension contribution results in Zara's basic rate tax band threshold being extended to £39,800 (£37,400 + £2,400).

**Working: Capital allowances**

Car: (£9,600 x 20% x 8,000/12,000) = £1,280

## Muriel Grand

### Answer 1 - Chapter 3

**Tax implications of letting property**

In either case, Bertie will be assessed on the profits of a business of letting property. The assessment will be on an actual basis from 6 April to 5 April, and will be calculated in accordance with most of the rules used in calculating assessable trading profits.

**Repairs to roof**

The roof was damaged before Muriel transferred the house to Bertie. Since the roof must be repaired before the house can be let, the house would not appear to be usable at the time of the transfer. The cost of repair of £24,000 is therefore likely to be classed as capital expenditure as it is pre-acquisition expenditure. This will increase Bertie's base cost for CGT purposes.

**Let as unfurnished accommodation**

The cost of decoration would normally be a revenue expense. However, some of the expenditure may be classed as capital if the house was in a bad state of repair on 31 December 2009. The decoration will presumably be carried out before letting commences, and so will be pre-trading expenditure. This will be allowed as an expense on the first day of business.

Any capital gain arising on the disposal of the house when Bertie retires at 60, will be fully chargeable.

### Let as furnished holiday accommodation

The cost of converting the house into two separate units will be mainly capital expenditure, and this will increase Bertie's base cost for CGT purposes. The figure of £41,000 may include some revenue expenditure, such as decorating costs, and this will be treated as above. The £9,000 cost of furnishing the two units will be capital expenditure.

Bertie will be able to claim the following deductions from his annual gross rents of £45,000:

(1)  the loan interest of £4,000 (£50,000 at 8%)

(2)  capital allowances in the form of the Annual Investment Allowance up to £50,000 p.a. The allowance in this case will be £9,000.

(3)  the letting agency fees of £10,125 (£45,000 at 22.5%)

(4)  the other running costs of £3,500.

Expenses will be restricted if Bertie occupies the house for his own use.

Given Bertie's level of rental income the letting is likely to qualify for the special rules applicable to furnished holiday lettings.

This will mean that:

*   capital allowances will be available on plant and machinery, such as furniture and kitchen equipment.

*   the property business profit will qualify as relevant earnings for personal pension purposes

*   loss relief will be available against total income

*   Entrepreneurs' relief will be available provided that all qualifying conditions are met

*   rollover relief available on disposal.

The letting of holiday accommodation is standard rated for VAT purposes. The forecast rental income of £45,000 is below the VAT registration limit of £68,000, but the impact of VAT will have to be considered if Bertie is already registered for VAT, or if there is an increase in rental income.

### Conclusion

Letting the house as a furnished holiday letting will produce annual income of approximately £18,375 (£45,000 – £4,000 – £10,125 – £9,000 – £3,500), compared to £28,000 (given in the question) if the house is let unfurnished.

It will also be necessary to incur additional expenditure of £46,400 (£41,000 + £9,000 – £3,600).

This must be compared against the potential CGT saving upon the disposal of the house arising from Entrepreneurs' relief available for furnished holiday letting which is not available for unfurnished property.

## Anthony & Cleopatra

### Answer 2 – Chapter 3

(a) **Income tax payable computations**

**Anthony**

**Income tax computation – 2009/10**

|  | £ |
|---|---:|
| Employment income (W1) | 63,221 |
| Building society interest (£42,120 x 100/80) | 52,650 |
| Rental income (gross) | 12,000 |
| UK dividends received (£67,890 x 100/90) (Note) | 75,433 |
| | |
| Total income | 203,304 |
| Less Reliefs – Qualifying loan interest | (550) |
| | |
| Net Income | 202,754 |
| Less PA | (6,475) |
| | |
| Taxable income | 196,279 |

Analysis of income:

**Dividends  Savings  Other income**

£75,433    £52,650    (£196,279– £75,433 – £52,650) = £68,196

**Note:** Dividends from an EIS investment are taxable as normal dividends.

| | £ | £ |
|---|---|---|
| 37,400 x 20% (other income) | | 7,480 |
| 30,796 x 40% (other income) | | 12,318 |
| 68,196 | | |
| 52,650 x 40% (savings) | | 21,060 |
| 75,433 x 32½% (dividends) | | 24,516 |
| 196,279 | | |
| | | 65,374 |
| Less EIS investment relief (20% × £20,000) | | (4,000) |
| Income tax liability | | 61,374 |
| Less Tax credits | | |
| Dividends (10% × £75,433) | | (7,543) |
| Interest (20% × £52,650) | | (10,530) |
| PAYE | | (20,000) |
| Income tax payable | | 23,301 |

**Cleopatra**

**Income tax computation – 2009/10**

| | £ |
|---|---|
| Employment income (£12,500 – £400) | 12,100 |
| ISA interest (exempt) | Nil |
| VCT dividends (exempt) | Nil |
| Total income | 12,100 |
| Less PA | (6,475) |
| Taxable income (all other income) | 5,625 |

|  | £ |
|---|---|
| £5,625 x 20% | 1,125 |
| Less VCT investment relief | |
| (30% x £20,000 = £6,000)  (part wasted) | (1,125) |
| | ——— |
| Income tax liability | Nil |
| Less Tax credits | (Nil) |
| | ——— |
| Income tax payable | Nil |
| | ——— |

**Note:** VCT investment relief is restricted to the income tax liability, the remaining relief is wasted. It cannot be paid in cash, nor carried forward or back to other years.

(b) **Tax planning**

**Transferring capital assets to Cleopatra**

Anthony is a higher rate taxpayer, however Cleopatra is a basic rate taxpayer. The couple should be advised to transfer capital assets from Anthony to Cleopatra, to ensure that her personal allowance and basic rate bands are used each year.

Transferring the property giving rise to the rental income and cash from the bank and building society accounts will save the couple 20% income tax (40% – 20%).

Transferring shares giving rise to the dividend income will save the couple income tax at 22½% (32½% – 10%).

**Note:** The transfer of capital assets will not give rise to CGT as inter spouse transfers are at nil gain/nil loss, and no IHT arises as inter spouse transfers are exempt from IHT.

**Choice of investments**

Cleopatra has invested in the VCT shares and wasted part of the 30% income tax relief available, and Anthony has only received 20% tax credit in relation to his EIS investment, the investments should be switched with Anthony investing in VCT shares and Cleopatra EIS shares.

If the couple plan to make further investments in the future, they should consider carefully which of them is to invest and ensure that the maximum tax relief can be obtained.

**Workings**

(W1)  **Employment income**                                £

      Salary                                              50,000

      Bonus (W2)                                           2,000

      Gift from client (W3)                                1,000

      Computer benefit (W4)                                  500

      Company car benefit (W5)                             5,700

      Fuel benefit (W5)                                    3,211

      Accommodation benefit (W6)                             810

                                 —————

      Employment income                                   63,221

                                 —————

(W2)  **Bonus**

The bonus for the year ended 31 December 2008 was determined at the Board meeting in April and paid on 30 April 2009. It is therefore assessed in 2009/10.

(W3)  **Gift from a client**

Any form of payment including tips and gratuities whilst in the course of carrying out one's employment duties will be taxable as earnings, if they can be converted into cash.

(W4)  **Computer benefit**

(£3,000 x 20% x 10/12)                               £500

                                 —————

**Note:** The laptop was only available for private use for 10 months in 2009/10.

(W5)  **Car and fuel benefit**

$CO_2$ emission 143 g/km, available all year

Appropriate percentage:

(143 – 135) ÷ 5 = 1% + 18% (diesel car) = 19%

Car benefit (19% x £30,000)                          £5,700

                                 —————

Fuel benefit (19% x £16,900)                         £3,211

                                 —————

| (W6) **Accommodation benefit** | £ |
|---|---:|
| Annual value | 2,250 |
| Less Contributions made by Anthony (£120 x 12) | (1,440) |
| | |
| Assessable benefit | 810 |

## Enid, Tom and Norman

### Answer 1 – Chapter 4

(a) **Enid – Brief notes on the tax implications of lump sum pension contributions**

The tax treatment of making lump sum contributions into an occupational pension scheme will depend upon whether or not the scheme is a registered scheme with HMRC.

If the scheme is a registered scheme, significant tax advantages can accrue:

– The employer's payment made on Edith's behalf will be an exempt benefit.

– Enid Limited will obtain a tax deduction at its marginal corporation tax rate on the contribution paid.

– Enid will be able to make and obtain income tax relief on additional employee contributions of up to 100% of her earned income. Such contributions will not, however, attract relief from Class 1 NIC.

– If Enid contributes 100% of her earnings and the company contribute £20,000, the total contributions will not exceed the annual allowance of £245,000. Therefore full relief is available for both contributions and no further tax consequences arise.

– The funds will be invested in a tax free environment.

– Upon retirement Enid will be able to take a tax free lump sum payment of up to 25% of the lower of the fund value at that time and the lifetime allowance (£1,750,000 for 2009/10).

Such advantages will not accrue if the scheme is not a registered scheme with HMRC.

(b) **Tom – Maximum gross contribution into a private pension**

The maximum gross amount Tom can contribute into a private pension in 2009/10 and obtain tax relief is:

Greater of:
- £3,600
- 100% x relevant earnings of the tax year = £50,000

To obtain tax relief for £50,000 in 2009/10, Tom would need to have paid £40,000 (80% x £50,000) into the pension scheme before 6 April 2010.

Basic rate tax relief (20%) is given at source and HMRC will give the pension scheme £10,000 (£50,000 x 20%).

Higher rate relief is given by extending Tom's basic rate band in his income tax computation by £50,000 from £37,400 to £87,400.

(c) **Norman – Additional contributions payable by employee**

Norman is in pensionable employment. He therefore has a number of choices if he wants to make an additional contribution to a registered pension plan.

He can either contribute into an AVC run by his employer, or into a FSAVC run by an insurance company.

The maximum additional amount that Norman can contribute into a registered pension plan is:

|  | £ |
|---|---|
| 100% x Employment income (see below) | 29,838 |
| Less: Amount already contributing (6% × £20,000) | (1,200) |
| Maximum additional contributions | 28,638 |

**Working: Employment income**

Car and fuel benefit:

$CO_2$ emission 174 g/km, available all year

Appropriate % = (170 – 135) ÷ 5 + 15% (petrol car) = 22%

| Benefits: | Car £ | Fuel £ |
|---|---|---|
| (£30,000 x 22%) | 6,600 | |
| (£16,900 x 22%) | | 3,718 |
| Less: Contribution from Norman (£40 × 12) (Note) | (480) | |
| | 6,120 | 3,718 |

Employment income = (£20,000 + £6,120 + £3,718) = £29,838

**Note:** There is no deduction from the fuel benefit for partial contributions towards the cost of the fuel provided for private use.

## Clive Scott

### Answer 2 – Chapter 4

(a) (i) **Maximum pension contributions – 2009/10**

If Clive sets up a personal pension scheme in 2009/10 the maximum gross pension contributions that Clive can make into the scheme are restricted to the higher of:
– £3,600, or
– 100% of his earned income = £15,000.

Note that the dividend income does not count as earnings and is not relevant in determining the level of pension contribution.

To obtain relief in the current 2009/10 tax year the contributions need to be paid by 5 April 2010.

This will mean that Clive can make a maximum gross contribution of £15,000 by 5 April 2010.

### (ii) **Method of obtaining tax relief**

Tax relief for contributions into pension schemes is given as follows.

– Basic rate tax relief is given at source. Assuming the maximum contribution possible is paid, Clive will actually pay £12,000 (£15,000 × 80%) to the pension provider.

– Higher rate tax relief is given by extending his basic rate tax band by £15,000 (i.e. the gross amount of the pension contribution paid).

The effect of making such contributions on his 2009/10 income tax liability will be a £15,000 reduction in his dividend income liable to the higher 32.5% tax rate applicable to dividend income. As a result his income tax liability will be reduced by £3,375 (W).

### (iii) **Tax implications of the company making pension contributions**

It is possible to set up the scheme such that Scott Engineering Limited pays all or some of the pension contributions. If this is the case the total combined contributions that may be paid by the employee and his employer on which tax relief can be obtained is restricted to the annual allowance of £245,000 for 2009/10.

If Scott Engineering Limited pays any contributions, these will be paid gross and the company will obtain corporation tax relief on the contributions at its marginal tax rate.

Providing the personal scheme is a registered scheme, these contributions will not be treated as employee benefits or be liable to Class 1 National Insurance contributions.

If total combined contributions in excess of the annual allowance are made, Clive will be liable to income tax at 40% on the excess contributions.

Whether direct contributions by Scott Engineering Limited are more beneficial than personal contributions by Clive will depend upon several factors.

These include:

(1) whether Clive's income is reduced to reflect the contributions paid by the company

(2) if income is so reduced whether this is the dividend income (for which no corporation tax deduction is available) or his salary (which already obtains corporation tax relief and is liable to employer's Class 1 NIC), and

(3) the marginal tax rates of Clive and the company.

(b) **Alternative registered pension arrangements**

As Clive is an employee of Scott Engineering Limited the principal alternative pension arrangement that could be made would be for the company to set up an occupational pension scheme.

This is usually set up in the form of an irrevocable trust to ensure that the scheme assets are held independently of the employer.

The amount of tax relief that can be obtained is the same under either a PPP or an occupational scheme. However the method of obtaining the tax relief is different.

The method of relief for such schemes is as follows:

– employee contributions are deducted from employment income and tax relief is given at both the basic and higher rates via the PAYE system.

– employer contributions are tax deductible for corporation tax purposes and are not regarded as employee benefits nor are they liable to Class 1 National Insurance contributions.

**Working: Income tax relief via the income tax computation**

|  | £ |
|---|---|
| Employment income | 15,000 |
| UK dividends received (£46,350 x 100/90) | 51,500 |
|  | ——— |
| Total income | 66,500 |
| Less PA | (6,475) |
|  | ——— |
| Taxable income | 60,025 |
|  | ——— |

Analysis of income:

| **Dividends** | **Savings** | **Other income** |
|---|---|---|
| £51,500 | £Nil | (£60,025 – £51,500) = £8,525 |

**Income tax before pension contribution**

| | £ | £ |
|---|---|---|
| 8,525 x 20% (other income) | | 1,705 |
| 28,875 x 10% (dividends) | | 2,887 |
| | _____ | |
| 37,400 | | |
| 22,625 x 32½% (dividends) | | 7,353 |
| | _____ | |
| 60,025 | | |
| | | _____ |
| Income tax liability | | 11,945 |

**Income tax after pension contribution**

| | £ | £ |
|---|---|---|
| 8,525 x 20% (other income) | | 1,705 |
| 28,875 x 10% (dividends) | | 2,887 |
| 15,000 x 10% Basic rate band extension | | 1,500 |
| | _____ | |
| 52,400 | | |
| 7,625 x 32½% (dividends) | | 2,478 |
| | _____ | |
| 60,025 | | |
| | | _____ |
| Income tax liability | | 8,570 |
| | | _____ |
| Income tax reduction = (£11,945 – £8,570) | | 3,375 |
| | | _____ |

Alternative calculation: £15,000 x (32.5% – 10%) = £3,375

### Ethel Jones

### Answer 1 – Chapter 6

(a) **Income tax computation – 2009/10**

|  | £ | £ |
|---|---|---|
| Employment income |  | 10,900 |
| Loan stock interest | 5,000 |  |
| (£100,000 x 10% x ½) (Note) |  |  |
| Interest on cash deposits (£4,200 x 100/80) | 5,250 |  |
|  | ——— | 10,250 |
| UK dividends received (10,000 x 25p x 100/90) |  | 2,778 |
| Total income |  | 23,928 |
| Less PAA (W) |  | (8,976) |
| Taxable income |  | 14,952 |

Analysis of income:
**Dividends Savings Other income**
£2,778     £10,250  (£14,952– £2,778 – £10,250) = £1,924

|  | £ |
|---|---|
| 1,924 × 20% (other income) | 385 |
| 516 × 10% (savings) | 52 |
| 2,440 |  |
| 9,734 × 20% (savings) | 1,947 |
| 2,778 × 10% (dividends) | 278 |
| 14,952 |  |
| Income tax liability | 2,662 |

**Note:** In the absence of a declaration of beneficial entitlement,the interest income on the Chaffinch plc shares will be shared equally between Ethel and George.

**Working: Personal age allowance**

| | | £ | £ |
|---|---|---|---|
| PAA (Aged 69) | | | 9,490 |
| Abatement | Total income | 23,928 | |
| | Limit | (22,900) | |
| | | 1,028   x ½ | (514) |
| Revised PAA | | | 8,976 |

(b) **Declaration of beneficial interest**

The effect of making a declaration of beneficial interest in respect of the loan stock in Chaffinch plc would be that Ethel would only be taxed upon her 25% beneficial entitlement with her husband George being taxed on the remaining 75%.

This would reduce Ethel's taxable income from this source to £2,500 and hence her total income for 2009/10 would reduce to £21,428 (£23,928 – £2,500). This in turn would mean that her age allowance for this tax year would no longer be abated, leaving other income of £1,410 (££10,900 – £9,490)

More of the new starting rate band for savings would be available (i.e. £1,030 = £2,440 – £1,410). Therefore an additional £514 (£1,030 – £516) of savings income would be taxed at 10% instead of 20%.

But the effect for George would also need to be considered. This is because if he is a higher rate taxpayer the effect of the declaration would increase his income tax payable by 20% (i.e. 40% less 20% tax credit) of the gross income transferred, which would negate the benefits or lower tax payable by Ethel.

**Julie**

**Answer 1 – Chapter 7**

**Capital gains tax – 2009/10**

| | £ |
|---|---:|
| Piano (W1) | 3,750 |
| Car (Exempt asset) | Nil |
| Property (W2) | 322,225 |
| Business asset (W3) | 33,000 |
| Less Capital loss brought forward | (3,250) |
| | |
| Total chargeable gains | 355,725 |
| Less Annual exemption | (10,100) |
| | |
| Taxable gains | 345,625 |
| | |
| Capital gains tax liability (£345,625 × 18%) | 62,212 |

**Note:** The capital losses brought forward are offset against the capital gains in 2009/10

**Workings**

**(W1) Piano**

| | £ |
|---|---:|
| Sale proceeds (June 2009) | 12,500 |
| Less Cost (September 1997) | (8,750) |
| | |
| Chargeable gain | 3,750 |

**(W2) Property**

| | £ |
|---|---:|
| Sale proceeds (December 2009) | 485,000 |
| Less Costs of sale | (4,075) |
| | |
| Net sale proceeds | 480,925 |
| Less Cost (August 2003) | (156,000) |
| Costs of acquisition | (2,700) |
| | |
| Chargeable gain | 322,225 |

| (W3) **Business asset** | £ |
|---|---|
| Sale proceeds (January 2010) | 37,000 |
| Less Cost (October 2007) | (4,000) |
| Chargeable gain | 33,000 |

The asset does not qualify for Entrepreneurs' relief as it is not part of the sale of the whole of the business.

## Spangle

### Answer 1 – Chapter 7

**Capital gains tax – 2009/10**

| | £ |
|---|---|
| Desk (W1) | 17,000 |
| House (W2) | 158,000 |
| Antique table (W3) | 7,200 |
| Greyhound (W4) | Nil |
| Land (W6) | 96,667 |
| Less Capital loss (W5) | (1,500) |
| Total chargeable gains | 277,367 |
| Less Annual exemption | (10,100) |
| Taxable gains | 267,267 |

| | £ |
|---|---|
| Capital gains tax liability (£267,267 × 18%) | 48,108 |
| Due date for payment | 31 January 2011 |

**Workings**

**(W1) Desk**

|  | £ |
|---|---|
| Proceeds (Dec 2009) | 24,000 |
| Less: Cost (April 1983) | (7,000) |
| Chargeable gain | 17,000 |

**(W2) House**

|  | £ |
|---|---|
| Proceeds (Dec 2009) | 220,000 |
| Less: Cost – April 1983 | (58,000) |
| – October 1985 | (4,000) |
| Chargeable gain | 158,000 |

**(W3) Antique table**

|  | £ |
|---|---|
| Proceeds (Dec 2009) | 17,200 |
| Less Cost (July 1985) | (10,000) |
| Chargeable gain | 7,200 |

**(W4) Greyhound**

A greyhound is a wasting chattel which is exempt from CGT

**(W5) Unquoted shares**

|  | £ |
|---|---|
| Proceeds | 6,000 |
| Less Probate value (July 1985) | (7,500) |
| Allowable loss | (1,500) |

**(W6) Remaining interest in land**

|  | £ |
|---|---|
| Proceeds (Dec 2009) | 205,000 |
| Less: Deemed cost (W7) | (108,333) |
| Chargeable gain | 96,667 |

(W7) **Deemed cost of part disposal**

Disposal in June 2008 – Deemed cost
Cost (4 acres of 24 acres)
= £130,000 x £30,000/£180,000                                £21,667
_____

Disposal in December 2009 – Deemed cost
(£130,000 – £21,667)                                        £108,333
_____

## Darren

### Answer 2 – Chapter 7

**Capital gains tax – 2009/10**

|                                                  | £        |
|--------------------------------------------------|----------|
| Land (W1)                                        | 11,212   |
| Motor Car (exempt)                               | Nil      |
| Painting (W3)                                    | 41,000   |
| Ring (exempt) (W4)                               | Nil      |
| Lease (W5)                                       | 87,954   |
|                                                  |          |
| Total chargeable gains                           | 140,166  |
| Less Annual exemption                            | (10,100) |
|                                                  |          |
| Taxable gains                                    | 130,066  |
|                                                  |          |
| Capital gains tax liability (£130,066 × 18%)     | 23,412   |

## Workings

### (W1) Land

| | £ |
|---|---|
| Proceeds (May 2009) | 15,000 |
| Less: Deemed cost (W2) | (3,788) |
| Chargeable gain | 11,212 |

### (W2) Deemed cost of remaining land

Disposal in March 1994 – Deemed cost

| | |
|---|---|
| Cost (4 acres) = £5,000 x £4,000/(£4,000 + £12,500) | £1,212 |

Disposal in December 2009 – Deemed cost

| | |
|---|---|
| (£5,000 – £1,212) | £3,788 |

### (W3) Painting

| | £ |
|---|---|
| Proceeds (December 2009) | 50,000 |
| Less: Cost (May 1993) | (9,000) |
| Chargeable gain | 41,000 |

### (W4) Antique ring

The antique ring is a chattel. As it was sold for less than £6,000, and cost less than £6,000, the gain is exempt.

### (W5) Short lease

| | £ |
|---|---|
| Disposal proceeds (October 2009) | 275,000 |
| Less: Deemed cost (W6) | (187,046) |
| Chargeable gain | 87,954 |

Entrepreneurs' relief is not available as this is not a disposal of the entire business.

### (W6) **Deemed lease cost**

| | | |
|---|---|---|
| Years left to run at acquisition | 39 years | 12/02/02 |
| Years left to run at disposal | 31 years 4 months | 19/10/09 |

The percentage for 31 years 4 months is:

88.371 + ((89.354 − 88.371) x 4/12) = 88.699

The allowable cost to deduct in the computation is therefore deemed to be:

Cost x % for life of the lease left on disposal date % for life of the lease left on acquisition date

= £200,000 x 88.699 (% for 31 years 4 months)/94.842 (% for 39 years) = £187,046

---

## Emma

### Answer 1 – Chapter 8

**Capital gains tax – 2009/10**

| | £ |
|---|---|
| Apple plc shares (W1) | 74,000 |
| Willow Ltd shares (W2) | 49,700 |
| NS Certificates (Exempt) | Nil |
| Bridge plc takeover (W3) | 26,950 |
| Total chargeable gains | 150,650 |
| Less Annual exemption | (10,100) |
| Taxable gains | 140,550 |
| Capital gains tax liability (£140,550 × 18%) | 25,299 |

**Workings**

(W1) **Shares in Apple plc**

| Share pool | Number | Cost £ |
|---|---|---|
| March 2006: Purchase | 400 | 10,000 |
| January 2007: Rights issue | | |
| 1:4 @ £30 per share | 100 | 3,000 |
| December 2008: Purchase | 200 | 8,000 |
| January 2009: Bonus issue 1:2 | 350 | Nil |
| | 1,050 | 21,000 |
| Disposal | (1,050) | (21,000) |
| Balance to c/f | Nil | Nil |

| | £ |
|---|---|
| Disposal proceeds | 95,000 |
| Less Cost | (21,000) |
| Chargeable gain | 74,000 |

(W2) **Willow Ltd**

| | £ |
|---|---|
| Proceeds (March 2009) | 50,000 |
| Less Cost (see below) | (300) |
| Chargeable gain | 49,700 |

| Share Pool | Number | Cost £ |
|---|---|---|
| February 1988: Purchase | 10 | 1,000 |
| Disposal | (3) | (300) |
| Balance c/f | 7 | 700 |

## (W3) **Bridge plc takeover**

For 100 Bridge plc shares:

|  | January 2010 |
|---|---|
|  | £ |
| Loan notes in Poker plc (100 x £50) | 5,000 |
| Cash (100 x £350) | 35,000 |
| Consideration received | 40,000 |

The loan notes are qualifying corporate bonds (QCBs).

Where a QCB is received in exchange for shares, the gain attributable to these shares is computed as if the bond were cash and this gain is frozen until the corporate bond is disposed of at a later date.

The only gain chargeable in 2009/10 is the gain attributable to the cash received.

The cash consideration is not small and therefore the part disposal rules apply.

| Allocation of cost: | | £ |
|---|---|---|
| Loan notes | (£9,200 x 5/40) | 1,150 |
| Cash consideration | (£9,200 x 35/40) | 8,050 |
|  |  | 9,200 |

Gain re cash consideration:

|  | £ |
|---|---|
| Cash proceeds | 35,000 |
| Less Deemed cost (above) | (8,050) |
| Chargeable gain | 26,950 |

**Mr Harry**

## Answer 1 – Chapter 9

(a) **Capital gains tax – 2009/10**

| | £ |
|---|---|
| **With Gift Relief claim** | |
| X Ltd shares (W1) | 23,413 |
| House (W3) | Nil |
| | ——— |
| Total chargeable gains | 23,413 |
| Less Annual exemption | (10,100) |
| | ——— |
| Taxable gains | 13,313 |
| | ——— |

| | £ |
|---|---|
| **Without Gift relief claim** | |
| X Ltd shares (W1) | 163,889 |
| House (W3) | Nil |
| | ——— |
| Total chargeable gains | 163,889 |
| Less Annual exemption | (10,100) |
| | ——— |
| Taxable gains | 153,789 |
| | ——— |

The decision to claim gift relief, depends on the intention of Mr Harry's daughter in the future.

On the subsequent disposal of the shares by the daughter she will be entitled to Entrepreneurs' relief provided the conditions are satisfied.

Therefore, if the daughter satisfies the conditions, Mr Harry and his daughter will benefit from both the gift relief and Entrepreneurs' relief claims.

If, however, she does not intend to own the shares for at least 12 months and/or not work for the company, Entrepreneurs' relief will not be available to her. In this case it would be beneficial for Mr Harry and his daughter not to claim gift relief on the original gift as she will be liable to tax at 18% on the gain, but Mr Harry would only be liable at an effective rate of 10% on the gain arising now.

(b) **Notes for meeting with Mr Harry**

– Rollover relief may be available to Mr Harry.

– This means that he can make a claim to defer the gain on the building he sold to X Ltd in April 2009, against the base cost of the new commercial property.

– As a result, he will
  – obtain a repayment of the CGT paid in respect of the building, and
  – defer the gain until the new commercial property is sold.

– However, conditions must be satisfied to obtain the relief.

– Mr Harry has disposed of a freehold property which is a qualifying business asset (QBA) for rollover relief purposes.

– The replacement commercial building can be either freehold or leasehold, but must be occupied and used for trading purposes.

– The replacement property must be acquired before 1 April 2012 (i.e. within the four year qualifying period beginning one year before, and ending three years after the date of sale of the old asset).

– A claim needs to be made for rollover relief by 5 April 2013, i.e. within 4 years from the end of the tax year in which the disposal occurred (2008/09 disposal).

– If all of the proceeds from the sale of the old asset are reinvested, full rollover relief is available (i.e. all of the gain is deferred).

However, where there is partial reinvestment of the proceeds only part of the gain may be deferred.

– Mr Harry could plan his reinvestment to ensure that a rollover relief claim will leave a gain to be taxed which utilises his capital losses and the annual exemption.

– If the new commercial property is a leasehold interest in land and buildings with 60 years or less to run on the lease, the gain is held over rather than rolled over.

– This means that the gain will be taxable on 1 April 2019 (i.e. ten years after the date of sale) or earlier if the replacement building is sold or ceases to be used in the trade before then.

– Adjustments need to be made to the calculation of the amount of rollover / holdover relief available if there is an element of non-business use.

– Entrepreneurs' relief would not be available on any remaining gain on a disposal in 2008/09, if Mr Harry rented the buidling to the company. If no rent was charged then relief would be available if the conditions are satisfied as this would be an associated disposal.

**Workings**

**(W1) X Ltd shares**

|  | £ |
|---|---|
| Market value | 365,000 |
| Less: Cost | (70,000) |
|  | |
| Capital gain before reliefs | 295,000 |
| Less Gift relief (W2) | (252,857) |
|  | |
|  | 42,143 |
| Less Entrepreneurs' relief (4/9 × £42,143) | (18,730) |
|  | |
| Chargeable gain | 23,413 |

Entrepreneurs' relief is available as Mr Harry is disposing of a shareholding in a personal trading company. The relief is not restricted for investments in the company balance sheet.

If Mr Harry and his daughter do not claim gift relief then Mr Harry will have the following capital gain:

|  | £ |
|---|---|
| Capital gain before reliefs (per W1) | 295,000 |
| Less Entrepreneurs' relief (4/9 × £295,000) | (131,111) |
|  | |
| Chargeable gain | 163,889 |

**(W2) Gift relief**

Proportion of gain eligible for gift relief

= (MV of total CBA / MVof total CA) x £295,000

= [£480,000 / (£480,000 + £80,000)] x £295,000 = £252,857

### (W3) Principal private residence

The sale of the home is fully covered by the PPR relief.

Although Mr Harry did not live in the house for one year, any period or periods which together do not total more than three years is exempt under the PPR rules provided the property was owner occupied at some time both before and after the period of absence.

## Bangle

### Answer 2 – Chapter 9

#### (a) (i) Chargeable gain on the disposal of the business

|  | £ | Gains/(losses) £ |
|---|---|---|
| Freehold premises: | | |
| Deemed proceeds (MV) | 165,000 | |
| Less Cost | (65,000) | |
| Chargeable gain | | 100,000 |
| Shop fittings – exempt | | Nil |
| Shop front and canopy: | | |
| Deemed proceeds (MV) | 8,000 | |
| Less Cost | (13,165) | |
| Allowable loss | | (5,165) |
| Net chargeable gains before reliefs | | 94,835 |
| Less Incorporation relief | | (94,385) |
| Chargeable gain in 2009/10 | | Nil |

**Note 1:** As all of the consideration is received in the form of shares, all of the net gains can be deferred with incorporation relief.

**Note 2:** The net chargeable gains are deferred. Entrepreneurs' relief is postponed until the sale of the shares providing the conditions are met when the shares are sold.

**Base cost of shares received by Barbara Bangle**

|  | £ |
|---|---|
| Market value of 200,000 shares allotted | 200,000 |
| Less Rolled over gain | (94,835) |
| Base cost | 105,165 |

(ii) **Sale of shares in Bangle Ltd**

| Share pool | Number | Cost £ |
|---|---|---|
| Shares acquired | 200,000 | 105,165 |
| Disposal | (80,000) | (42,066) |
| Balance carried forward | 120,000 | 63,099 |

|  | £ |
|---|---|
| Sale proceeds | 90,000 |
| Less Cost (see above) | (42,066) |
| Chargeable gain | 47,934 |
| Less Annual exemption | (10,100) |
| Taxable gain | 37,834 |

As the shares have been held for less than 12 months, there is no Entrepreneurs' relief available.

(b) (i) **Chargeable gain on disposal of the business**

|  | £ |
|---|---|
| Net chargeble gains before reliefs (as before) | 94,835 |
| Less Incorporation relief | |
| – limited to proportion of consideration received in the form of shares: | |
| (£94,835 × 150,000/200,000) | (71,126) |
| | 23,709 |
| Less Entrepreneurs' relief (4/9 × £23,709) | (10,537) |
| Chargeable gain | 13,172 |

**Base cost of shares received by Barbara Bangle**

|  | £ |
|---|---|
| Market value of 150,000 shares allotted | 150,000 |
| Less Rolled over gain | (71,126) |
| Base cost | 78,874 |

(ii) **Sale of shares in Bangle Ltd**

| Share pool | Number | Cost |
|---|---|---|
|  |  | £ |
| Shares acquired | 150,000 | 78,874 |
| Disposal | (80,000) | (42,066) |
| Balance c/f | 70,000 | 36,808 |

|  | £ |
|---|---|
| Market value |  |
| (as sale at under-value to connected person) | 90,000 |
| Less Cost | (42,066) |
|  | 47,934 |
| Less Gift relief (balancing figure) | (9,000) |
| Chargeable gain (W) | 38,934 |

Entrepreneurs' relief is not available as the shares have been owned for less than 12 months.

|  | £ |
|---|---|
| Chargeable gain – 2009/10 (£13,172 + £38,934) | 52,106 |
| Less Annual exemption | (10,100) |
| Taxable gain | 42,006 |

**Working: Sale of shares**

If there is a sale at undervaluation, a gain arises at the time if the actual consideration received is in excess of the original cost.

|  | £ |
|---|---|
| Actual consideration | 81,000 |
| Less Original cost | (42,066) |
| Gain after gift relief | 38,934 |

### (c) Alternative method of deferring gains on incorporation

Barbara can defer gains on incorporation by using the gift relief provisions instead of incorporation relief.

She can do so by either:

- ensuring she does not satisfy the conditions for incorporation relief, or
- she can satisfy the conditions and elect to disapply incorporation relief.

If the gift relief route is taken, Barbara can gift the individual business assets to the company.

The gain on the freehold premises could be held over against the market value of the freehold premises at acquisition. The gain on the shop-fitting is exempt. There is an allowable loss on the shop front and canopy which would be set against other gains.

The property could be retained by Barbara personally, to avoid double charges to CGT in the future, but should not be rented to the company as this will deny Entrepreneurs' relief on a future disposal of the property if sold as part of the disposal of the company shares.

## Simon White

### Answer 1 - Chapter 10

#### (a) Income tax computation – 2009/10

| | £ |
|---|---|
| Employment income – UK duties only | 1,600 |
| UK property income | 12,600 |
| Total income | 14,200 |
| Less Personal allowance | (6,475) |
| Taxable income | 7,725 |
| Income tax (£7,725 × 20%) | 1,545 |

As Simon's eighteen month secondment abroad covers a complete tax year (1.2.09 – 31.7.10), by concession HMRC will treat Simon as not resident and not ordinary resident in the UK for the whole of his secondment abroad.

Therefore, in this period, Simon will only be taxed on his UK income.

As a British subject he can make a claim for his personal allowances, despite being non-UK resident in 2009/10.

(b) **Peter's tax position in 2009/10 if the secondment to Paris was from 1 October 2008 to 31 March 2010**

Simon is again absent for 18 months but this time from 1 October 2008 to 31 March 2010.

As this period does not cover an entire tax year, Simon will be treated as remaining UK resident throughout and thus will be taxable on this worldwide income in 2009/10.

**Income tax computation – 2009/10**

|  | £ |
|---|---:|
| Employment income – UK duties | 1,600 |
| Employment income – overseas duties (£3,500 × 12) | 42,000 |
| UK property income | 12,600 |
| | ——— |
| Total income | 56,200 |
| Less Personal allowance | (6,475) |
| | ——— |
| Taxable income | 49,725 |
| | ——— |
| Income tax: | |
| £37,400 × 20% | 7,480 |
| £12,325 × 40% | 4,930 |
| | ——— |
| | 12,410 |
| Less DTR (W) | (8,400) |
| | ——— |
| Income tax payable | 4,010 |
| | ——— |

**Working: DTR**

| | £ |
|---|---|
| Deduct the lower of | |
| (i) Overseas tax suffered (£42,000 20%) | 8,400 |
| (ii) UK tax on overseas income | |
| Total tax including overseas income | 12,410 |
| Less Total tax excluding overseas income | |
| (£49,725 – £42,000) × 20% | (1,545) |
| | ——— |
| | 10,865 |
| | ——— |

## Mr and Mrs Posh

### Answer 2 - Chapter 10

Mr Posh will be better off if he pays tax on the arising basis:

| | Arising basis | Remittance basis |
|---|---|---|
| | £ | £ |
| Income | 39,500 | 15,640 |
| Less Personal allowance | (6,475) | Nil |
| | ——— | ——— |
| Taxable income | 32,725 | 15,640 |
| | ——— | ——— |
| Income tax | | |
| £32,725 / £15,640 × 20% | 6,545 | 3,128 |
| Plus Additional charge | | 30,000 |
| | ——— | ——— |
| Income tax liability | 6,545 | 33,128 |
| | ——— | ——— |

Mrs Posh will be better off if she claims the remittance basis and pays tax on £108,900 as well as paying the £30,000 charge:

| | Arising basis | Remittance basis |
|---|---|---|
| | £ | £ |
| Income | 423,000 | 108,900 |
| Less Personal allowance | (6,475) | Nil |
| | ——— | ——— |
| Taxable income | 416,525 | 108,900 |
| | ——— | ——— |

Income tax

| £ | £ | | | |
|---|---|---|---|---|
| 37,400 | 37,400 | × 20% | 7,480 | 7,480 |
| 379,125 | 71,500 | × 40% | 151,650 | 28,600 |
| 416,525 | 108,900 | | | |

| | | |
|---|---|---|
| Plus Additional charge | | 30,000 |
| Income tax liability | 159,130 | 66,080 |

## Darwin

### Answer 3 – Chapter 10

**Income tax computation – 2009/10**

| | £ | £ |
|---|---|---|
| Employment income (W1) | | 53,437 |
| Bank interest (£2,840 x 100/80) | 3,550 | |
| Foreign interest (gross) | 1,265 | |
| | | 4,815 |
| Foreign property income (gross) | | 690 |
| Total income | | 58,942 |
| Less PA | | (6,475) |
| Taxable income | | 52,467 |

Analysis of income:

| Dividends | Savings | Other income |
|---|---|---|
| £Nil | £4,815 | (£52,467 – £4,815) = £47,652 |

|  | £ |  | £ |
|---|---|---|---|
| 47,652 x 20% | (other income) |  | 9,530 |
| 2,048 x 20% | (savings) |  | 410 |
| 49,700 | Extended band (W3) |  |  |
| 2,767 x 40% | (savings) |  | 1,107 |
| 52,467 |  |  |  |
|  |  |  | 11,047 |

Less Double taxation relief (W4) (£506 + £104)                    (610)

| Income tax liability | 10,437 |
|---|---|
| Less Tax credits |  |
| Interest (20% x £3,550) | (710) |
| PAYE | (6,105) |
| Income tax payable | 3,622 |

**Workings**

(W1) **Employment income**

|  | £ |
|---|---|
| Salary | 37,000 |
| Company car benefit (W2) | 10,560 |
| Fuel benefit (W2) | 5,577 |
| Goods (Cost) | 300 |
| Employment income | 53,437 |

**(W2) Car and fuel benefit**

$CO_2$ emission 213 g/km, available all year

Appropriate percentage:

$(210 - 135) \div 5 = 15\% + 18\%$ (diesel car) = 33%

| | |
|---|---:|
| Car benefit = 33% x £32,000 | £10,560 |
| Fuel benefit = 33% x £16,900 | £5,577 |

**(W3) Extension of basic rate band**

| | £ |
|---|---:|
| Basic rate band threshold | 37,400 |
| Add Personal pension premium (£9,840 x 100/80) | 12,300 |
| Extended basic rate band threshold | 49,700 |

**(W4) Double taxation relief**

**DTR on Erewhon income**

The Erewhon income has suffered the higher rate of overseas tax and therefore relief is calculated in respect of this source of income first. The amount of credit cannot exceed the UK tax attributable.

DTR = lower of

| | | |
|---|---|---|
| (a) UK tax | (£1,265 x 40%) | = £506 |
| (b) Overseas tax | (£1,265 x 45%) | = £569 |

**DTR on Narnian income**

The relief for overseas tax is computed on a source by source basis, therefore the relief for Narnian tax must be separately computed, treating it as the next slice of income.

DTR = lower of

| | | |
|---|---|---|
| (a) UK tax | (£690 x 40%) | = £276 |
| (b) Overseas tax | (£690 x 15%) | = £104 |

**Peter Singer**

## Answer 4 – Chapter 10

(i) **Tax status of Peter**

### Residence (R)

An individual will be treated as Resident in the UK if they are present for 6 months or more in any tax year. As Peter will be based in the UK for the whole of this year he will be treated as UK resident.

### Ordinarily Resident (OR)

To be OR it is necessary to be in the UK for 3 years or more. The question does not state how long Peter intends to stay in the UK but if he arrived with the intention of staying in excess of 3 years he will be regarded as R and OR for the duration of his stay.

The fact that the company has bought a flat for his use would be a strong indicator to HMRC that he intends to stay for a substantial period. It may be that the company has decided to buy rather than rent, as it feels that it can currently buy property at a bargain price. If this is the case, they should be able to refute that argument if Peter is staying for less than 3 years.

If it is not certain how long he will be here when he arrives, he will not be treated as OR until the beginning of the fourth year after his arrival, assuming he is still in the UK at that time.

### Domicile

Domicile is the place a person regards as their permanent home. As Peter was born and lived in Portugal until his move to England this will be his domicile of origin.

As his wife has stayed in Portugal the implication would be that he intends to return there, and so will retain his Portuguese domicile for UK tax purposes.

### Effect on Tax Computation

All Peter's UK income will be taxable. With regard to his overseas income the amount taxable in the UK will depend on his tax status.

His investment income and overseas salary will be taxable on an arising basis if he acquired UK domicile as well.

However, if, as appears likely here, he remains non UK domiciled, he can elect to be taxed on the remittance basis for his overseas income as his unremitted income is in excess of £2,000 (unremitted dividends of £1,300, rental income of £1,600 and employment income of £28,000 paid into his Portuguese bank account).

The election will result in Peter only being assessed on overseas investment income and salary remitted to the UK, but with the loss of his personal allowance.

Note that he will not be subject to the £30,000 remittance basis charge as he has not been resident in the UK for more than 7 years.

**Basis of taxation**

Where overseas income is taxed on a remittance basis, regardless of the source of income, it is treated as non-savings income for the purposes of identifying how much UK tax is payable and for calculating the DTR available.

(ii) **Income tax computation – 2009/10**

Peter will elect to be taxed on the remittance basis as the saving from omitting the non remitted foreign income (£30,900) outweighs the loss of the personal allowance (£6,475).

|  | £ |
|---|---:|
| Salary – UK | 44,000 |
| Salary – overseas (none remitted) | Nil |
| Benefits (W1) | 40,682 |
|  | |
| Employment income | 84,682 |
| UK dividends (£3,600  100/90) | 4,000 |
| UK bank interest (£880 × 100/80) | 1,100 |
| Overseas dividends (amount remitted grossed up) | |
| (£2,250 × 100/90) | 2,500 |
| Overseas rent (amount remitted) | 1,300 |
|  | |
| Total income | 93,582 |
| Less PA (none as remittance basis claimed) | (Nil) |
|  | |
| Taxable income | 93,582 |
|  | |
| Analysis of income: | |
| Savings income (UK only) | 1,100 |
| Dividends (UK) | 4,000 |
| Dividends (overseas) | 2,500 |
| Other income | 85,982 |
| (rest of UK income and all overseas income remitted) | |

| | £ |
|---|---|
| Income tax | |
| £37,400 × 20% (other income) | 7,480 |
| £48,582 × 40% (other income) | 19,433 |
| £1,100 × 40% (savings income) | 440 |
| £4,000 × 32.5% (UK dividend income) | 1,300 |
| £2,500 × 40% (overseas dividends remitted) | 1,000 |
| | 29,653 |
| Plus Remittance basis charge (not applicable) | Nil |
| | 29,653 |
| Less DTR (W2) (£3,550 × 10%) | (355) |
| Income tax liability | 29,298 |

**Workings**

**(W1) Benefits**

| | | £ |
|---|---|---|
| Company car | | |
| Appropriate percentage | | |
| = (203 – 135) / 5 + 15 = 28% | | |
| Car benefit (£28,000 × 28%) | | 7,840 |
| Fuel benefit (£16,900 × 28%) | | 4,732 |
| Medical insurance | | 1,800 |
| Living accomodation | | |
| Reteable value | 4,500 | |
| Expensive accomodation charge | | |
| (£187,000 – £75,000) × 4.75% | 5,320 | |
| Running costs | 5,700 | |
| Use of furniture (£49,000 × 20%) | 9,800 | |
| | 25,320 | |
| Less rent paid (£1,300 × 12) | (15,600) | |
| | | 9,720 |
| Nursery costs (£1,250 × 7) | | 8,750 |
| Mobile phone – exempt | | Nil |
| Health club (£220 × 12) | | 2,640 |
| Wife's travel (£650 × 8) (two trips = tax free) | | 5,200 |
| Total benefits | | 40,682 |

**(W2) DTR**

For the purposes of DTR each source of overseas income must be dealt with separately.

The tax on the overseas income is then compared with the UK tax on that source, and relief given for the lower of the two.

In this example both sources of income had 10% overseas tax deducted at source, and the UK rate is clearly higher, therefore the computation has taken the shortcut of just deducting DTR as the 10% overseas tax suffered.

Where the UK tax rate is clearly in excess of the overseas tax rate, an approach like this would be acceptable in the exam providing the answer is suitably annotated to explain why the answer was done in that way.

## Roberta

### Answer 5 – Chapter 10

2006/07 = Year of departure = R, OR and D in UK

- taxable on worldwide gains
- both before and after the date of departure

2007/08 to 2010/11 inclusive = abroad = 4 complete tax years = NR and NOR in UK

- not taxable on any gains at the time

2011/12 = Year of return

- on re-entry into the UK within 5 complete tax years = taxable on any gains relating to assets owned before departure from the UK, and
- gains in that year arising after the return to the UK

Therefore the gains on the disposal in both May 2009 and July 2010 will become chargeable in 2011/12 when Roberta returns to the UK.

| Disposals: | May 2009 | July 2010 |
|---|---|---|
| | £ | £ |
| Sale proceeds | 195,000 | 26,500 |
| Less Cost | (76,000) | (54,000) |
| Chargeable gain / (Allowable loss) | 119,000 | (27,500) |
| Net chargeable gains – taxed in 2011/12 | 91,500 | |

## Mary Day

### Answer 1 – Chapter 12

Mary's previous chargeable lifetime transfer for £335,000 will have fully utilised her nil rate band of £325,000.

(a) **Holiday cottage**

Where an individual makes a gift of property but reserves a benefit, the special gift with reservation (GWR) rules will apply.

Short holiday visits to the cottage would not be caught by the rules, however six months free use would make the gift a GWR.

The gift of the cottage will be a PET of £100,000, ignoring AEs per question but Mary will still be treated as beneficially entitled to the cottage.

It will therefore be included as part of her estate when she dies, and will be included at its value on the date of death.

This might give rise to a double charge to IHT, since the cottage is a PET and also part of Mary's estate.

Relief for the double charges will be given if this is the case.

Mary could avoid the GWR rules by paying a commercial rent for the use of the cottage.

(b) **Antique clock**

The gift of the clock is in consideration of marriage by a grandparent to a grandchild. It will therefore qualify for a wedding gift exemption of £2,500.

The balance of the gift will be a PET of £7,500 (ignoring AEs per question).

(c) **DEF Ltd shares**

The gift of 20,000 shares in DEF Ltd out of an existing shareholding of 30,000 shares into a discretionary trust will be a CLT.

|  | £ |
|---|---|
| Value of estate before the gift: | |
| 30,000 shares valued at £16 each | 480,000 |
| Value of estate after the gift: | |
| 10,000 shares valued at £10 each | (100,000) |
| | ———— |
| Transfer of value | 380,000 |
| | ———— |

BPR is not available because Mary has owned the shares for less than two years. Therefore the chargeable amount of the CLT is £380,000 (ignoring AEs per question).

As Mary is to pay the lifetime IHT liability and there is no nil rate band available, she will have to pay IHT of £95,000 (£380,000 × 25%) within six months of the end of the month of the gift.

The gross chargeable amount of the transfer is therefore £475,000 (£380,000 + £95,000).

(d) **Agricultural land**

The gift of agricultural land will be a PET with a transfer of value of £280,000.

The increase in the value of David's land is irrelevant.

If the PET becomes chargeable as a result of Mary dying within seven years, APR at the rate of 100% should be available as Mary has owned the land for seven years.

However, APR will only be available on the agricultural value of £160,000.

The relief will only be available if David still owns the land, and it is still agricultural property, at the date of Mary's death.

**Gerry Generous**

### Answer 2 – Chapter 12

**IHT implications of lifetime gifts**

**4 June 2002 – Gift to discretionary trust**

| CLT | £ | £ |
| --- | --- | --- |
| Transfer of value | | 331,000 |
| AE – 2002/03 | | (3,000) |
| – 2001/02 b/f | | (3,000) |
| | | ——— |
| Net chargeable amount | | 325,000 |
| NRB at date of gift | 325,000 | |
| GCTs in 7 yrs pre-gift (4.6.95 – 4.6.02) | (Nil) | |
| | ——— | |
| NRB available | | (325,000) |
| | | ——— |
| Taxable amount | | Nil |
| | | ——— |
| Lifetime IHT due | | Nil |
| | | ——— |
| GCT c/f | | 325,000 |
| | | ——— |

**4 March 2004 – Gift to son**

The wedding gift of £10,000 to Jack, being made from one individual to another, will be a PET. There is no IHT payable during Gerry's life time and providing Gerry survives until 4 March 2011 no IHT will arise in relation to this gift.

However, if Gerry dies before 4 March 2011, the PET will become chargeable.

As the gift was made in consideration of marriage, a marriage exemption of £5,000 will be available for gifts from a parent to their child. As there is another gift on the same day (see below) Gerry's 2003/04 annual exemption may need to be apportioned by reference to the value of the gifts made on the same day. The annual exemption is, however, only used after other exemptions and reliefs.

The gift of shares in GG Ltd made on the same day to Jill is likely to qualify for 100% BPR (see below). It is likely therefore that the entire AE for 2003/04 will be allocated against the wedding gift to the son.

The PET is therefore valued at £2,000 (£10,000 – £5,000 – £3,000). Note that the previous year AE for 2002/03 has already been utilised.

If Gerry dies before 4 March 2011 the gross PET of £2,000 becomes chargeable. Death IHT is due at 40% but taper relief will reduce the IHT by 20% per annum if Gerry survives for more than 3 years.

### 4 March 2004 – Gift to daughter

The gift of shares to Jill, being made from one individual to another, will again be a PET.

As annual exemptions are allocated in strict chronological order, and the exemption for 2003/04 and 2002/03 have already been allocated, no annual exemption will be available to reduce this transfer.

The shares will be valued applying the loss to the donor's estate principle. Before the gift Gerry owned an 80% holding (see tutorial note) and after the gift Gerry owned a 60% holding. The value of the transfer is therefore £150,000 (£600,000 – £450,000).

As the GG Ltd shares are unquoted trading company shares and Gerry owned the shares for the minimum qualifying period of two years prior to the gift, BPR at the rate of 100% is likely to be available.

Therefore no IHT is payable on this PET at the time of the gift.

In addition, IHT is not payable on the death of Gerry within seven years unless, upon Gerry's death before 4 March 2011, Jill has ceased to own the shares gifted to her or GG Ltd has ceased to be a qualifying company.

**Note:** The question says Gerry currently (in 2010) owns a 60% holding. At the time of the gift in March 2004, he must therefore have had an 80% holding.

**4 June 2008 – Gift to discretionary trust**

| CLT | £ | £ |
|---|---|---|
| Transfer of value | | 100,000 |
| AE – 2008/09 | | (3,000) |
|    – 2007/08 b/f | | (3,000) |
| | | ——— |
| Net chargeable amount | | 94,000 |
| NRB at date of gift | 325,000 | |
| GCTs in 7 yrs pre-gift (4.6.01 – 4.6.08) | (325,000) | |
| | ——— | |
| NRB available | | (Nil) |
| | | ——— |
| Taxable amount | | 94,000 |
| | | ——— |
| Lifetime IHT due (£94,000 x 25%) (net gift) | | 23,500 |
| | | ——— |
| GCT c/f (£94,000 + £23,500) | | 117,500 |
| | | ——— |

Should Gerry die before 4 June 2015, additional IHT at death rates of 40% may become payable. Taper relief may be available and the lifetime tax paid is an allowable deduction.

## Martin

### Answer 1 – Chapter 13

**Estate computation – Death on 31 July 2009**

|  | £ | £ |
|---|---|---|
| Shares in ABC Ltd (W1) |  | 195,000 |
| Less BPR (W1) |  | (162,500) |
|  |  | 32,500 |
| Shares in DEF plc (W2) |  | 210,000 |
| Holiday cottage |  | 120,000 |
| Bank and cash balances |  | 150,000 |
| Other assets |  | 208,000 |
|  |  | 720,500 |
| Less Exempt legacy – wife (Note) |  | (55,000) |
| Free estate |  | 665,500 |
| Settled property |  | 88,000 |
| Gross chargeable estate |  | 753,500 |
| NRB at death | 325,000 |  |
| GCTs in 7 yrs pre-death (31.7.02 – 31.7.09) | (Nil) |  |
| NRB available |  | (325,000) |
| Taxable amount |  | 428,500 |
| IHT due on death (£428,500 x 40%) |  | 171,400 |
| Less Quick succession relief (W3) |  | (13,500) |
| IHT payable |  | 157,900 |

**Note:** Only £55,000 of the legacy to Martin's wife is exempt since she is not domiciled in the UK.

**IHT payable by the trustees of the IIP trust**

Average rate of IHT on estate

= £157,900/£753,500 x 100 = 20,956%

Trustees liability = £88,000 x 20.956% = £18,441

**Workings**

(W1) **ABC Ltd shares**

The shares in ABC Ltd are valued using the related property rules, and the value is therefore based on a 30% shareholding.

(15,000 x £13) = £195,000

BPR is available at 100% but not on the value of the excepted assets.

BPR = £195,000 x £2,500,000/£3,000,000 x 100% = £162,500

(W2) **DEF plc shares**

The shares in DEF plc are valued at:

Lower of:

(i) quarter up method = 208 + 1/4 x (216 − 208) = 210p

(ii) average of highest and lowest marked bargains = ½ x (196 + 228) = 212p

The valuation is therefore = £210,000 (100,000 at 210p).

(W3) **Quick succession relief**

QSR = Appropriate % x IHT paid on earlier death

= 80% x £22,500/£90,000 x £67,500 = £13,500

## Jane Macbeth

### Answer 2 – Chapter 13

(a) (i) **IHT payable as a result of Jane's death**

**Lifetime IHT payable**

| **28 November 2001 – CLT** | £ | £ |
|---|---|---|
| Transfer of value | | 105,000 |
| AE – 2001/02 | | (3,000) |
| – 2000/01 b/f | | (3,000) |
| | | |
| Net chargeable amount | | 99,000 |
| NRB at date of gift | 325,000 | |
| GCTs in 7 yrs pre-gift (28.11.94 – 28.11.01 ) | (Nil) | |
| | | |
| NRB available | | (325,000) |
| | | |
| Taxable amount | | Nil |
| | | |
| Lifetime IHT due | | Nil |
| | | |
| GCT c/f (99,000 + £Nil) | | 99,000 |

| **15 April 2005 – PET** | | £ |
|---|---|---|
| Transfer of value | | 155,000 |
| BPR (£155,000 x 100% x 80%) (Note) | | (124,000) |
| Marriage exemption | | (5,000) |
| AE – 2005/06 | | (3,000) |
| – 2004/05 b/f | | (3,000) |
| | | |
| Gross chargeable amount | | 20,000 |
| | | |
| Lifetime IHT due | | Nil |

**Note:** As Shakespeare Ltd owns quoted shares (i.e. excepted assets), BPR is only available on 80% (100% – 20%) of the value of the shares.

| 10 March 2006 – CLT | £ | £ |
|---|---|---|
| Transfer of value | | 268,000 |
| AE – 2005/06 and 2004/05 (already used) | | (Nil) |
| Net chargeable amount | | 268,000 |
| NRB at date of gift | 325,000 | |
| GCTs in 7 yrs pre-gift (10.3.99 – 10.3.06) (ignore PETs in lifetime calculations) | (99,000) | |
| NRB available | | (226,000) |
| Taxable amount | | 42,000 |
| Lifetime IHT due (£42,000 x 25%) (net gift) | | 10,500 |
| GCT c/f (£268,000 + £10,500) | | 278,500 |

**IHT payable on death**

| Date of death: | 20 November 2009 |
|---|---|
| Seven years before: | 20 November 2002 |

**Gift on 28 November 2001**

This gift is more than seven years before death, therefore there is no IHT payable on death.

| 15 April 2005 – PET | £ | £ |
|---|---|---|
| GCT b/f (above) | | 20,000 |
| NRB at death | 325,000 | |
| GCTs in 7 yrs pre-gift (15.4.98 – 15.4.05) | (99,000) | |
| NRB available | | (226,000) |
| Taxable amount | | Nil |
| IHT due on death | | Nil |

### 10 March 2006 – CLT

| | £ | £ |
|---|---|---|
| GCT b/f (above) | | 278,500 |
| NRB at death | 325,000 | |
| GCTs in 7 yrs pre-gift (10.3.99 – 10.3.06) (£99,000 + £20,000) (Include PET as chargeable on death) | (119,000) | |
| NRB available | | (206,000) |
| Taxable amount | | 72,500 |

| | £ |
|---|---|
| IHT due on death (£72,500 x 40%) | 29,000 |
| Less Taper relief (10.3.06 to 20.11.09) (3 – 4 years) (20%) | (5,800) |
| Chargeable (80%) | 23,200 |
| Less IHT paid in lifetime (CLT) | (10,500) |
| IHT payable on death | 12,700 |
| Payable by | Trustees |
| Due date | 31.5.2010 |

### IHT on Estate at death – 20 November 2009

| | £ | £ |
|---|---|---|
| Main residence | | 235,000 |
| Mortgage | | (40,000) |
| | | 195,000 |
| Agricultural land | 168,000 | |
| APR (Note) | (110,000) | |
| | | 58,000 |
| Building society deposits | | 87,000 |
| Ordinary shares in Banquo plc (W1) | | 94,800 |
| Life assurance policy | | 104,000 |
| Gross chargeable estate | | 538,800 |

| | £ | £ |
|---|---|---|
| Gross chargeable estate | | 538,800 |
| | | |
| NRB at death | 325,000 | |
| GCTs in 7 yrs pre-death (20.11.02 – 20.11.09) (£20,000 + £278,500) (first gift is too old, Include PET as chargeable on death) | (298,500) | |
| | | |
| NRB available | | (26,500) |
| | | |
| Taxable amount | | 512,300 |
| | | £ |
| IHT due on death (£512,300 x 40%) | | 204,920 |
| Less QSR (£68,000 x £54,000/£360,000 x 60%) | | (6,120) |
| | | |
| IHT payable on estate | | 198,800 |

**Note:** APR is available since the property is let out for the purposes of agriculture, and has been owned for at least seven years.

(a) (ii) **Payment of IHT liability**

The additional IHT of £12,700 in respect of the gift made on 10 March 2006 will be payable by the trustees of the discretionary trust by 31 May 2010.

The IHT liability of the estate will (in practice) be payable by the executors of Jane's estate on the earlier of 31 May 2010 or the delivery of their account.

It will be possible to pay IHT of £93,349 (W2) in respect of the main residence and agricultural land in ten equal instalments commencing on 31 May 2010.

**Inheritance received by Jane's children**

Jane's children will inherit £350,000 (W3).

**Workings:**

**(W1) Value of Banquo plc shares**

Lower of

(1)  Quarter up method = 945 + (957 − 945) x ¼ = 948p
(2)  Average of marked bargains = (937+ 961) x ½ = 949p

Value of 10,000 £1 ordinary shares = (10,000 x 948p) = £94,800

**(W2) Payment by instalments**
Average estate rate = (£198,800/£538,800) x 100 = 36.897%

|  | £ |
|---|---|
| Main residence | 195,000 |
| Agricultural property | 58,000 |
|  | 253,000 |
| Payment by instalments (£253,000 x 36.897%) | 93,349 |

**(W3) Inheritance to children**

|  | £ |
|---|---|
| Chargeable estate | 538,800 |
| Plus APR | 110,000 |
| Value of assets in estate | 648,800 |
| Less Specific gift to brother | (100,000) |
| IHT payable on the estate (Note) | (198,800) |
| Estate value to be shared between the children | 350,000 |

**Note:** The IHT payable on the whole estate comes out of the residue of the estate and is therefore borne by the residual legatees (i.e. the children). This is because specific gifts of UK property (e.g. £100,000 to the brother) do not normally carry their own tax.

## (b) Variation of the terms of Jane's will

### Conditions to be met

Jane's will can be varied by a deed of variation (or deed of family arrangement) within two years of the date of her death.

The deed must be in writing, and be signed by Duncan, the children, and Jane's brother (i.e. those who benefit from the original will and the revised variations).

It must include a declaration that the will should be treated as being effective for IHT purposes.

The children could not enter into the deed of variation if they were still minors.

### Proposed plan

Under the revised terms of Jane's will, the entire estate is left to Duncan. This will be an exempt transfer, and so the IHT liability of £198,800 will no longer be payable.

The gifts from Duncan to the children and Jane's brother will be PETs, and these will be completely exempt if Duncan lives for seven years after making the gifts.

Should the PETs become chargeable, taper relief will be available after three years.

Duncan's annual exemptions of £3,000 for 2008/09 to 2011/12 may also be available.

Even if Duncan dies within three years of the gift, the IHT liability should not be greater than £198,800 (subject to APR being available), and the IHT liability will be postponed until six months after the end of the month of his death. As a result tax savings will be achieved.

The transfer to Duncan will mean that £26,500 of Nil rate band will not be utilised against Jane's death estate.

This can be used on her husband's death estate, in addition to his own Nil rate band available, on his subsequent death.

**Paul**

### Answer 3 – Chapter 13

(a) **IHT liabilities if Paul dies on 31 December 2009**

#### 1 November 2001 – CLT

This gift to the discretionary trust is more than seven years before the date of Paul's death, and therefore no further IHT is due.

It is, however, within seven years of the other lifetime transfers, and will reduce the nil rate band available by £197,000 (£203,000 – £3,000 AE for 2001/02 – £3,000 AE for 2000/01).

#### 1 October 2006 – PET

This wedding gift was originally a PET, and no IHT would have been due at that time. As a result of Paul's death within seven years it now becomes a chargeable transfer, and IHT will be due on 30 June 2010 as follows:

|  | £ | £ |
|---|---|---|
| Transfer of value |  | 150,000 |
| Marriage exemption |  | (5,000) |
| AE – 2006/07 |  | (3,000) |
|   – 2005/06 b/f |  | (3,000) |
|  |  | ———— |
| Gross chargeable amount |  | 139,000 |
| NRB at death | 325,000 |  |
| GCTs in 7 yrs pre-gift (1.10.99 – 1.10.06) | (197,000) |  |
|  | ———— | (128,000) |
|  |  | ———— |
| Taxable amount |  | 11,000 |
|  |  | ———— |
|  |  | £ |
| IHT due on death (£11,000 x 40%) |  | 4,400 |
| Less Taper relief (1.10.06 to 31.12.09) |  |  |
|     (3 – 4 years) (20%) |  | (880) |
|  |  | ———— |
| Chargeable (80%) |  | 3,520 |
| Less IHT paid in lifetime (PET) |  | (Nil) |
|  |  | ———— |
| IHT payable on death |  | 3,520 |
|  |  | ———— |

## 1 November 2006 – PET

This gift of the business will qualify for 100% BPR, and no IHT liability therefore arises.

### NRB at date of death

Only the gift on 1 October 2006 is relevant when calculating the NRB available to Paul's estate as the gift on 1 November 2001 is more than seven years before the date of death.

### Estate at death

|  | £ | £ |
|---|---|---|
| Value of estate |  | 645,000 |
| Less BPR (£65,000 x 100%) |  | (65,000) |
|  |  | ——— |
| Gross chargeable estate |  | 580,000 |
| NRB at death | 325,000 |  |
| GCTs in 7 yrs pre-death (31.12.02 – 31.12.09) (first gift is too old, but include PET as chargeable on death) | (139,000) |  |
|  | ——— | (186,000) |
|  |  | ——— |
| Taxable amount |  | 394,000 |
|  |  | ——— |
| IHT due on death (£394,000 x 40%) |  | 157,600 |
|  |  | ——— |
| Due date |  | 30.6.2010 |

(b) **Advice relating to changing the terms of Paul's will**

At present, Paul has left all of his estate to his son.

The following tax planning points should be considered:

(1) Paul should leave £325,000 of his estate to his wife. In due course this will utilise her NRB which would otherwise be wasted, and will save IHT of £130,000 (£325,000 x 40%). It would only be transferable to Paul if his wife were to die first.

(2) If Paul left an additional amount to his wife, then she could use her annual exemptions of £3,000 by making gifts to the son or grandchildren.

(3) Paul could leave some property to his grandchildren, and thus miss out a generation.

It would also be possible to put this tax planning into effect after Paul's death by making a deed of variation.

This must be made within two years of the date of death and must be signed by all the beneficiaries affected (probably just Paul's son).

### (c) Implications of selling the business

If the business was sold before the date of Paul's death, it would no longer qualify for business property relief.

On Paul's death, the gift would become chargeable, with the charge being based on the sale proceeds of £175,000. This is because relief can be claimed for the fall in the value of a lifetime gift.

The IHT liability will be £70,000 (£175,000 x 40%). The Nil Rate band would have been utilised as Gross changeable transfers in the previous 7 years amount to £336,000 (£197,000 + £139,000)

Additional IHT of £74,400 (£186,000 x 40%) will also be due on Paul's estate, since none of the NRB would then be available.

### (d) (i) Main advantages in lifetime giving for IHT purposes

Possible advantages of lifetime giving include:

– Making use of lifetime IHT exemptions in reducing a taxpayer's chargeable estate at death. In particular, gifts between individuals will not become liable to IHT unless the donor dies within seven years of making the gift.

– If the donor does die prematurely there may still be an IHT advantage in lifetime giving because usually:

– The value of the asset for calculating any additional IHT arising upon death is fixed at the time the gift is made.

– The availability of tapering relief (providing the donor survives at least three years) may help reduce the effective IHT rate.

### (ii) Main factors to consider in choosing assets to gift

The main factors to consider include:

– Whether or not a significant CGT liability will arise upon making the gift.

Lifetime gifting therefore needs to be balanced against the fact that no CGT liability will arise upon death (which results in the 'tax free' uplift of the chargeable assets included in the deceased's estate).

The availability of CGT reliefs (primarily gift relief for business assets or if there is an immediate charge to IHT) and CGT exemptions (e.g. AE) is therefore relevant in selecting assets.

– Whether an asset is appreciating in value.

Because any additional IHT arising as a result of death will be based on the (lower) value of the asset at the date of gift it may be advantageous to select assets that are likely to significantly appreciate in value.

– Whether the donor can afford to make the gift.

Whilst lifetime gifting can result in significant IHT savings this should not be at the expense of the taxpayer's ability to live comfortably, particularly in old age.

– The availability of significant IHT reliefs, particularly BPR. There may be little point in selecting an asset that already qualifies for 100% relief.

## Henry

### Answer 4 – Chapter 13

#### (a) Income tax in the year of death

The basic rule determining the taxation of a taxpayer's income in the tax year of death is that only income due and payable up to the date of death will be included in the deceased's income tax computation.

This will include Henry's retirement pension and annuity income as well as the investment income actually received prior to his death. Apportionments of investment income are not generally required.

However, the following should be noted:

– The accrued income scheme will not apply to the 10% Government stock as the transfer results from Henry's death.

– Interest received on the ISA account is exempt from income tax.

Henry will therefore only be taxed on the following interest:

|  | Date received |
|---|---|
| 10% Government stock | 30 April 2009 |
| Building Society | 30 June 2009 |

**Income tax computation: 2009/10 (date of death 5.10.2009)**

|  | £ | £ |
|---|---|---|
| State pension | | 5,460 |
| Gross annuity | | 7,200 |
| Building society interest (£320 x 100/80) | 400 | |
| Government interest (gross) (£20,000 x 10% x 6/12) | 1,000 | |
| | | 1,400 |
| UK dividends (100,000 x 9p x 100/90) | | 10,000 |
| Total income | | 24,060 |
| Less PAA (W) | | (8,910) |
| Taxable income | | 15,150 |

Analysis of income:

**Dividends Savings Other income**

£10,000    £1,400    (£15,150 − £10,000 − £1,400) = £3,750

|  | £ |
|---|---|
| 3,750 x 20% (other income): | 750 |
| 1,400 x 20% (savings) | 280 |
| 10,000 x 10% (dividends) | 1,000 |
| 15,150 | |
| Income tax liability | 2,030 |
| Less Tax credits | |
|    Dividends (10% x £10,000) | (1,000) |
|    Interest (20% x £400) | (80) |
|    Annuity (20% x £7,200) | (1,440) |
| Income tax repayable | (490) |

**Working: Personal age allowance**

|  | £ | £ |
|---|---|---|
| PAA (age 70) |  | 9,490 |
| Abatement: Total income | 24,060 |  |
| Limit | (22,900) |  |
|  | ———— |  |
|  | 1,160 × ½ | (580) |
|  | ———— | ———— |
| Reduced PAA |  | 8,910 |
|  |  | ———— |

(b) **Inheritance tax liabilities**

**Lifetime IHT payable**

| **1 January 2002 – CLT** | £ | £ |
|---|---|---|
| Transfer of value |  | 181,000 |
| AE – 2001/02 |  | (3,000) |
| – 2000/01 b/f |  | (3,000) |
|  |  | ———— |
| Net chargeable amount |  | 175,000 |
| NRB at date of gift | 325,000 |  |
| GCTs in 7 yrs pre-gift (1.1.95 – 1.1.02) | (Nil) |  |
|  | ———— | (325,000) |
|  |  | ———— |
| Taxable amount |  | Nil |
|  |  | ———— |
| Lifetime IHT due |  | Nil |
|  |  | ———— |
| GCT c/f (£175,000 + £Nil) |  | 175,000 |
|  |  | ———— |

| **1 January 2005 – CLT** | £ | £ |
|---|---|---|
| Transfer of value | | 164,000 |
| AE – 2004/05 | | (3,000) |
|     – 2003/04 b/f | | (3,000) |
| Net chargeable amount | | 158,000 |
| NRB at date of gift | 325,000 | |
| GCTs in 7 yrs pre-gift (1.1.98 – 1.1.05) | (175,000) | |
| | | (150,000) |
| Taxable amount | | 8,000 |
| Lifetime IHT due (£8,000 x 25%) (net gift) | | 2,000 |
| GCT c/f (£158,000 + £2,000) | | 160,000 |

**IHT payable on death**

| Date of death: | 5 October 2009 |
|---|---|
| Seven years before: | 5 October 2002 |

**Gift on 1 January 2002**

This gift is more than seven years before death, therefore there is no IHT payable on death.

| **1 January 2005 – CLT** | £ | £ |
|---|---|---|
| GCT b/f (above) | | 160,000 |
| NRB at death | 325,000 | |
| GCTs in 7 yrs pre-gift (1.1.98 to 1.1.05) | (175,000) | |
| | | (150,000) |
| Taxable amount | | 10,000 |

|  | £ |
|---|---|
| IHT due on death (£10,000 x 40%) | 4,000 |
| Less Taper relief (1.1.05 to 5.10.09) (4 – 5 years) (40%) | (1,600) |
| Chargeable (60%) | 2,400 |
| Less IHT paid in lifetime (CLT) | (2,000) |
| IHT payable on death | 400 |

**Henry's estate computation**

|  | Workings | £ |
|---|---|---|
| Shares – Peel plc | (1) | 202,000 |
| Government stock | (2) | 20,100 |
| Cash (£25,000 + £18,000) |  | 43,000 |
| Income tax refund due (part (a)) |  | 490 |
| Accrued interest | (3) | 331 |
| Home |  | 450,000 |
|  |  | 715,921 |
| Less Exempt legacy to spouse (balancing figure) |  | (675,921) |
| Gross chargeable estate (£20,000 x 2) |  | 40,000 |
| NRB at death | 325,000 |  |
| GCTs in 7 yrs pre-death (5.10.02 – 5.10.09) (first gift is too old) | (160,000) |  |
|  |  | (165,000) |
| Taxable amount |  | Nil |
| IHT due on death |  | Nil |

**Workings:**

**(W1) Value of Peel plc shares**

Lower of

(1) Quarter up method = 200 + ((208 – 200) x ¼) = 202p
(2) Average of recorded bargains = (201 + 207) x ½ = 204p

Value of 100,000 shares = (100,000 x £2.02) = £202,000

BPR is not available on these shares as they are quoted shares and Henry does not have a controlling interest.

(W2) **Value of Government stock**

Quarter up method = 95 + (97 – 95) x ¼ = 95.5p

| | £ |
|---|---:|
| 20,000 × 95.5p | 19,100 |
| Next interest receipt due (20,000 × 10% × 6/12) | 1,000 |
| Value of stock | 20,100 |

(W3) **Accrued interest**

Accrued interest arises on the building society account and ISA deposit as follows:

(£304 + £358) × 3/6 = £331

(c) **Action to reduce or defer IHT liabilities**

Henry's will resulted in the balance of the estate above £40,000 being an exempt transfer to his wife. This has left £125,000 (£165,000 – £40,000) of his nil band unused.

This can be transferred to Sally and utilised against her death estate, in addition to her own available NRB. The executors of Sally's estate must claim the transferable NRB on submission of Sally's IHT return within 2 years of her death.

As Henry's children are already reasonably wealthy, consideration might have been given to transferring the £40,000 directly to Henry's grandchildren. The idea here is to avoid a charge to IHT arising on any transfers that Cecil and Ida may make to their children.

**Deed of variation**

Providing various conditions are satisfied it is possible to vary a will after the testator's death and make more tax efficient provisions as outlined above by entering into a deed of variation.

The main conditions to be satisfied as follows:

(i)   The deed of variation must be in writing.

(ii)  It must be signed by all the beneficiaries that are affected.

(iii) It must be executed within two years of the date of death.

(iv)  It must not be made for a consideration.

(v)   The deed should include a statement that the variation is to be effective for IHT (and/or CGT) purposes.

The effect of making such a variation is that for IHT purposes the deceased's will is treated as rewritten. In this particular case an appropriate deed variation needs to be drafted by 5 October 2011.

### Lifetime gifts by Sally

Sally could make lifetime gifts to her children or grandchildren (for the reason outlined above) to reduce the IHT payable on her death.

If she survives seven years, the gifts will be exempt. However, she is in a frail condition and is possibly not likely to live seven years. Nevertheless, if the survives at least three years taper relief will be available to at least partially mitigate any IHT arising on potentially exempt transfers becoming chargeable within seven years of death.

If she does not survive seven years, the PETs will become chargeable, however PETs are valued at the time of the gift and annual exemptions are available. Therefore, the chargeable amount will be less than valuing the assets in Sally's estate (assuming the assets will appreciate in value between the date of the gift and Sally's death). The IHT position would certainly be no worse than if she had not made any lifetime transfers.

Sally should also make use of her IHT exemptions as follows: immediate gifts of £6,000 could be made in 2009/10 (to make use of her two annual exemptions) which would potentially save £2,400 (£6,000 x 40%). Thereafter annual gifts of £3,000 would save £1,200 (£3,000 x 40%) for each tax year that she survives.

Consideration should be given to personal circumstances. She may wish to gift her main asset (i.e. her home) to her children, but still live in it. However, this will give rise to 'gift with reservation of benefit' problems unless she pays full market rent while living in the house.

Substantial lifetime giving and paying full market rent for living in her home may not be desirable as she may wish to retain sufficient income bearing assets to maintain herself during her lifetime.

## Thelma

### Answer 5 – Chapter 13

(i) **Thelma retains assets until death**

**IHT implications**

**Cash gift – September 2008**

The cash gift made to Louise in September 2008 is a PET which will become chargeable if Thelma dies within seven years of making the gift. There are no other lifetime gifts.

If Thelma therefore dies in four years time (i.e. June 2014) IHT will become payable on the PET as follows:

|  | £ | £ |
|---|---|---|
| Gross chargeable amount (after exemptions per question) |  | 360,000 |
| NRB at death | 325,000 |  |
| GCTs in 7 yrs pre-gift (Sept 2001 – Sept 2008) | (Nil) |  |
|  |  | (325,000) |
| Taxable amount |  | 35,000 |

|  | £ |
|---|---|
| IHT due on death (£35,000 x 40%) | 14,000 |
| Less Taper relief (Sept 2008 to June 2014) (5 – 6 years) (60%) | (8,400) |
| Chargeable (40%) | 5,600 |
| Less IHT paid in lifetime (PET) | (Nil) |
| IHT payable on death | 5,600 |

### Estate on death – 30 June 2014

| | £ | £ |
|---|---|---|
| Residence | | 600,000 |
| Blackbird plc shares | | 200,000 |
| Robin plc loan stock – Thelma's share | | 25,000 |
| (£100,000 × 25%) | | |
| Cash deposits | | 160,000 |
| Antique plates | | 10,000 |
| Other chattels | | 20,000 |
| | | ———— |
| | | 1,015,000 |
| Less: Exempt estate (£600,000 + £20,000) | | (620,000) |
| | | ———— |
| Gross chargeable estate | | 395,000 |
| | | |
| NRB at death | 325,000 | |
| GCTs in 7 yrs pre-death (30.6.07 – 30.6.14) | | |
| (Include PET as chargeable on death) | (360,000) | |
| | ———— | (Nil) |
| | | ———— |
| Taxable amount | | 395,000 |
| | | ———— |
| IHT due on death (£395,000 x 40%) | | 158,000 |
| | | ———— |

### CGT implications

Death is not a chargeable event for the purposes of CGT. Therefore there is no CGT payable if Thelma retains the assets and gifts them in her will.

The recipients of the assets will receive them at their probate value which will form their base cost for future CGT purposes.

### (ii) Thelma gifts selected assets to Louise now

### IHT implications

### Cash gift – September 2008

The implications for the PET made in September 2008 are as above with £5,600 of IHT becoming payable as a result of Thelma's expected death in four years time.

### Gifts to Louise now

Assume the gift is made on 6 July 2010. The gifts of assets to Louise will be further PETs likely to become chargeable on Thelma's death, with further IHT arising as follows:

| | Notes | £ | £ |
|---|---|---|---|
| Blackbird plc shares | (1) | | 146,200 |
| Robin plc loan stock | (2) | | 25,750 |
| Antique plates | (3) | | 6,333 |
| Cash deposits | | | 145,000 |
| | | | 323,283 |
| AE – 2010/11 | | | (3,000) |
|   – 2009/10 b/f | | | (3,000) |
| Gross chargeable amount | | | 317,283 |
| NRB at death | | 325,000 | |
| GCTs in 7 yrs pre-death (30.6.07 – 30.6.14) | | | |
| (Include PET as chargeable on death) | | (360,000) | |
| | | | (Nil) |
| Taxable amount | | | 317,283 |

| | £ |
|---|---|
| IHT due on death (£317,283 x 40%) | 126,913 |
| Less Taper relief (6.7.10 to 30.6.14) | |
|   (3 – 4 years) (20%) | (25,383) |
| Chargeable (80%) | 101,530 |
| Less IHT paid in lifetime (PET) | (Nil) |
| IHT payable on death | 101,530 |

### Notes:

(1) Blackbird plc shares

Quarter up method = (1,460p + (1,468p – 1,460p) x ¼)
= £14.62 per share

Value of 10,000 shares = (10,000 × £14.62) = £146,200

There is no BPR available as the shares are quoted shares and Thelma does not have a controlling interest.

(2) Robin plc loan stock

Quarter up method = (102p + (106p – 102p) x ¼)
= 103p per share

Value of loan stock = £100,000 x £1.03 x 25% = £25,750

(3) Value of the plates

Valued under related party valuation rules, taking account of the fact that Thelma and Gordon own five plates between them (the daughter Louise's plate does not count as related property).

Value of 3 plates/Value of 3 + 2 plates
= [£3,800/(£3,800 + £2,200)] x £10,000 = £6,333

**Estate on death**

When Thelma dies the transfers of the house and personal chattels to Gordon will be exempt under the inter-spouse provisions.

Therefore there is no IHT payable on the estate at death.

**CGT implications**

**Gift of cash and loan stock**

The gifts of cash deposits and loan stock (a qualifying corporate bond) are exempt from CGT.

**Gift of plates**

Whilst the plates form a set, because Thelma has never in the past owned the plates which are owned by her husband and daughter there is no need to treat the gift of her plates to Louise as a part disposal nor to amalgamate the gift with any previous gifts.

The value of the consideration for CGT purposes will simply be the market value of the three plates gifted by Thelma (i.e. £3,800). As their value is less than £6,000 and they cost less than £6,000, any gain arising will also be exempt under the CGT chattels rules.

### Gift of Blackbird plc shares

The gift of these shares will, however, give rise to a chargeable gain. Assuming the gift is made on 6 July 2010, the CGT will be:

| | £ |
|---|---|
| Market value (connected persons) | 146,200 |
| Less: Indexed cost (£25,000 + £50,000) | (75,000) |
| Chargeable gain | 71,200 |

Entrepreneurs' relief is not available as Thelma owns 1% of the shareholding. Gift relief is not available as the shares are quoted and Thelma has a <5% interest in the company.

| | £ |
|---|---|
| Total chargeable gains | 71,200 |
| Less: Annual exemption | (10,100) |
| Taxable gains | 61,100 |
| CGT (£61,100 × 18%) | 10,998 |

### Conclusion

The tax payable under both options is as follows:

| | IHT £ | CGT £ | Total £ |
|---|---|---|---|
| Retention of Assets (£5,600 + £158,000) | 163,600 | Nil | 163,600 |
| Gifting assets now (£5,600 + £101,530) | 107,130 | 10,988 | 118,128 |

It would therefore appear that, providing the key assumptions hold (i.e. asset values in four years, Thelma survives four years), it is preferable to make the gifts to Louise now giving a tax saving of £45,472 (£163,600 − £118,128).

## The Wood Discretionary Trust

### Answer 1 – Chapter 14

**Notes for meeting with trustees**

**Income tax in relation to the Wood Discretionary Trusts**

(1) **Basis of assessment**

- All trusts are assessed to income tax on trust income received on a tax year basis.

- Trustees of all trusts are subject to self-assessment under the same system applying to individuals.

- When income payments are made to a beneficiary, the trustees pay the income net of 40% tax credit.

(2) **Payment of income made to a beneficiary**

If a discretionary payment is made in the tax year:

- The beneficiary is taxed on the gross income actually received in the tax year.

- The income received is grossed up at 100/60, and included in the beneficiary's IT computation.

- A tax credit of 40% is deducted in the beneficiary's IT liability computation.

- A 'statement of trust income' form must be completed for HMRC to show the gross, tax and net amounts distributed to the beneficiary in that tax year.

**CGT in relation to the Wood Discretionary Trust**

(1) **Occasions of charge**

Trustees are chargeable persons for the purposes of CGT and therefore a liability to tax may arise where a trustee makes a chargeable disposal of a chargeable asset.

There are three main occasions of charge to CGT:

- When assets are put into trust (this is a charge on the individual settlor, not the trust itself)

- Disposals of trust assets by the trustees to persons other than the beneficiaries when they are managing the trust assets

- When capital assets are distributed to the beneficiaries.

(2) **Assets put into trust on death**

– Not a chargeable disposal as trust set up on death in a will.

– No CGT payable.

– Trustees acquire assets at probate value.

(3) **Disposals of trust assets by trustees to persons other than the beneficiaries**

– Chargeable disposals of chargeable assets give rise to chargeable gains.

– CGT payable by the trustees on a tax year basis under self assessment.

(4) **Distribution of capital assets out of the trust to beneficiaries**

– Chargeable disposal of asset at full market value

– Gift relief available on any asset as there is an immediate charge to IHT

– Beneficiary acquires the assets at base cost = market value less hold over relief.

**IHT in relation to The Wood Discretionary trust**

(1) **Basis of assessment**

– Taxed as a separate entity with its own nil rate band.

(2) **Occasions of charge**

There will be three key occasions of charge to IHT as follows:

– When assets are put into trust

– The principal charge every ten years following the creation of the trust

– When capital assets are distributed out of the trust to the beneficiaries.

(3) **Assets put into trust on death**

– Assets form part of settlor's estate on death

– IHT payable on the estate

Note there is no difference in IHT payable on the estate if an individual puts his estate into a trust on death or leaves the estate directly to another individual

– Trust established after the estate IHT has been paid (i.e. out of post-tax assets).

## (4) **The principal charge**

- An anniversary charge every tenth anniversary of the creation of the trust is levied on the market value of all of the assets in the trust on the anniversary date

- The maximum rate of IHT is 6%.

## (5) **Distribution of capital assets out of the trust to beneficiaries**

- Exit charge arises

- The maximum rate of IHT is 6%.

## Fred Foyle

### Answer 1 - Chapter 16

### (a) **Reasons for investigation**

HMRC will probably have enquired into Fred's 2009/10 return because of the fall in the gross profit (GP%) and turnover compared to the accounts of the previous owner.

Fred's GP% is 30% (£150,000/(£400,000 + £100,000) x 100), compared to 41.7% (£300,000/(£600,000 + £120,000) x 100) for the previous owner.

The fall in the GP% has arisen because Fred's cash sales are £400,000 compared to an expected £500,000 (£600,000 x 10/12), which is a shortfall of £100,000.

HMRC will therefore assume that cash sales of £100,000 have not been recorded. The adjustment will increase Fred's GP% to the required 41.7%.

Fred could put forward the following points to justify the fall in GP%:

(1) He may be selling goods at a lower margin than the previous owner.

(2) He may be selling a different mix of goods.

(3) He may have suffered an increase in theft or wastage.

**(b) Interest on overdue tax**

Interest will run from 31 January 2011 to 30 August 2011, and will be as follows:

£100,000 @ 40% = £40,000 x 2.5% x 7/12 = £583

**(c) Maximum penalty**

The penalty is determined in the same way as penalties on incorrect income tax and corporation tax returns, according to:

– The amount of tax understated
– The reason for the understatement
– The extent of disclosure by the taxpayer.

The level of the penalty is a percentage of the revenue lost as a result of the inaccuracy or under assessment and depends on the behaviour of the taxpayer as follows:

| Taxpayer behaviour | Maximum penalty (% of revenue lost) |
|---|---|
| Genuine mistake | No Penalty |
| Failure to take reasonable care | 30% |
| Serious or deliberate understatement | 70% |
| Serious or deliberate understatement with concealment | 100% |

The penalties may be reduced depending on the type of penalty and whether the taxpayer makes an unprompted disclosure.

Where the return is incorrect through deliberate intention of a third party, the penalty can be charged on the third party.

**Lucinda Luck**

## Answer 1 – Chapter 17

### (a) Trading income assessments

| Tax year | Basis period | | £ |
|---|---|---|---|
| 2008/09 | Actual profits 1.6.08 to 5.4.09 (10 month period) | p/e 31.12.08 = £13,960 plus 3 months of y/e 31.12.09 (3/12 x £38,164 (W1)) = £9,541 | 23,501 |
| 2009/10 | 12 mths ending in second year | y/e 31.12.09 | 38,164 |
| Overlap profits | | | |
| 1.1.09 to 5.4.09 (3/12 x £38,164) | | | 9,541 |

### Workings:

#### (W1) Adjusted profits after capital allowances

| | 7 m/e 31.12.08 £ | y/e 31.12.09 £ |
|---|---|---|
| Adjusted profits before CAs (W2) | 18,960 | 42,664 |
| Less Capital allowances | (5,000) | (4,500) |
| | 13,960 | 38,164 |

#### (W2) Adjusted profits before capital allowances – y/e 31.12.09

| | £ |
|---|---|
| Net profit per accounts | 26,990 |
| Add back: | |
| Repairs – alterations to wall | 4,650 |
| Depreciation of vans and equipment | 2,000 |
| Amortisation of lease | 220 |
| Professional charges | |
| Costs of obtaining new lease | 460 |
| Sundry expenses | |
| Parking fine | 60 |
| Entertaining customers | 1,336 |
| Salary – Lucinda | 12,000 |
| Goods withdrawn by Lucinda (W3) | 480 |
| | 48,196 |

| | |
|---|---:|
| Less: | |
| Profit on sale of equipment | (400) |
| Interest from the reserve account | (610) |
| Bank deposit interest | (160) |
| Dividends | (262) |
| Proportion of lease premium (W4) | (4,100) |
| | ————— |
| Adjusted profits before capital allowances | 42,664 |
| | ————— |

### (W3) **Goods withdrawn by Lucinda**

Goods have been taken for the proprietor's own use = treated as a 'sale' for tax purposes at full market price.

Therefore add back selling price £480 (£240 x 100/50).

### (W4) **Lease premium deduction**

Lease premium assessed on landlord as property business income:

| | |
|---|---:|
| Property income assessment = £50,000 x [(51 – 10)/50] | £41,000 |
| | ———— |
| Allowed over period of lease: | |
| Amount allowed each year (£41,000 ÷ 10) | £4,100 |
| | ———— |

### (b) **Lucinda Luck**
### **Income tax computation – 2009/10**

| | £ | £ |
|---|---:|---:|
| Trading income | | 38,164 |
| Bank interest | | |
| – reserve account (£610 x 100/80) | 762 | |
| – deposit account (£160 x 100/80) | 200 | |
| | ——— | |
| | | 962 |
| UK dividends received (£262 x 100/90) | | 291 |
| | | ——— |
| Total income | | 39,417 |
| Less PA | | (6,475) |
| | | ——— |
| Taxable income | | 32,942 |
| | | ——— |

Analysis of income:

| Dividends | Savings | Other income |
|-----------|---------|--------------|
| £291 | £962 | (£32,942 – £291 – £962) = £31,689 |

Income tax:

| £ | £ |
|---|---|
| 31,689 x 20% (other income) | 6,338 |
| 962 x 20% (savings) | 192 |
| 291 x 10% (dividends) | 29 |
| ——— | |
| 32,942 | |
| ——— | ——— |
| Income tax liability | 6,559 |
| Less Tax credits | |
| Dividends (10% x £291) | (29) |
| Interest (20% x £962) | (192) |
| | ——— |
| Income tax payable | 6,338 |
| | ——— |

---

## William

### Answer 2 – Chapter 17

**Trading income assessments**

Tax year  Basis period

| | | | £ |
|---|---|---|---|
| 2008/09 | Actual profits 1.3.09 to 5.4.09 | £31,280 (W1) x 1/14 | 2,234 |
| 2009/10 | Actual profits (Note) 6.4.09 to 5.4.10 | £31,280 x 12/14 | 26,811 |
| 2010/11 | 12 months to 30.4.10 | £31,280 x 12/14 | 26,811 |
| | | | |
| Overlap profits (1.5.09 to 5.4.10) | | £31,280 x 11/14 | 24,577 |

**Note:** As there are no accounts ending in the second tax year, the assessment is the actual profits of the second tax year (i.e. from 6 April 2009 to 5 April 2010).

**Workings:**

**(W1) Adjusted profits after capital allowances – 14 m/e 30.4.09**

|  | £ |
|---|---|
| Adjusted profits before capital allowances | 71,440 |
| Less Capital allowances (W2) | (40,160) |
| Adjusted profits after capital allowances | 31,280 |

**(W2) Capital allowances computation – 14 m/e 30.4.09**

|  | General pool | Car 1 (B.U 85%) | Car 2 (B.U 85%) | Total allowances |
|---|---|---|---|---|
|  | £ | £ | £ | £ | £ |
| TWDV b/f | Nil |  |  |  |
| Additions: |  |  |  |  |
| No AIA or FYA – Cars |  | 13,100 | 30,000 |  |
| Qualifying for AIA: |  |  |  |  |
| Plant | 31,150 |  |  |  |
| AIA (Note) | (31,150) |  |  | 31,150 |
|  | Nil |  |  |  |
| Sale proceeds |  | (6,000) |  |  |
|  | Nil | 7,100 | 30,000 |  |
| BA |  | (7,100) ×85% |  | 6,035 |
| WDA (10% × 14/12) | Nil |  | (3,500) ×85% | 2,975 |
| TWDV c/f | Nil | Nil | 26,500 |  |
| Total allowances |  |  |  | 40,160 |

**Note:** The AIA available is £58,333 (£50,000 × 14/12). Any excess not used in the accounting period is wasted.

**Ali**

## Answer 3 – Chapter 17

Loss relief options available:

### – Relief against total income

This relief allows trading losses to be set against the total income of the current and /or the previous tax year. For a loss arising in 2009/10 an extended carryback can be made against trading profits of the previous 3 years.

### – Relief against gains

This relief is allowed after a claim against total income has been made.It allows relief to be claimed against chargeable gains.The trading loss is 'converted' into a current year capital loss.

### – Carry forward relief

This relief is automatic if no other claim is made. It allows trading losses to be carried forward and set against the first available trading profits of the same trade.

## Optimum use of losses:

### – If relief against total income and gains is claimed:

If relief is claimed against total income and gains, the trading loss incurred in 2009 (£18,000 relating to y/e 31.12.09) can be set against total income and gains in 2009/10 and/or 2008/09.

### Allocated against the current year – 2009/10

If the trading loss of £18,000 is set against the other income of 2009/10 (£11,870 see below), this would utilise most of the loss but leave the personal allowance wasted. The rate of tax saving is at 10% on savings income and a small amount at 20% on other non savings income.

There would be £6,130 of loss left to allocate against the capital gains. However, when considering whether to allocate a loss against the capital gain, consideration should be given to the other reliefs that may be wasted such as the annual exemption of £10,100.

Before considering relief against gains, it should be noted that the gain is almost covered by the capital losses brought forward and the annual exemption (£19,400 – £8,750 = £10,650).

A claim against gains is an "all or nothing" relief. This means that you can not choose how much of the loss can be utilised. If a claim is made, the maximum amount possible must be used.

As a result, a small amount of tax is saved at 18% and the claim would waste part of the annual exemption for CGT.

Therefore, claims against total income and gains in 2009/10 are not an attractive option.

### Allocated against the previous year – 2008/09

If the loss was to be set against the other income of the previous year (£72,890 see below), the loss would clearly receive income tax relief at 40% and would not waste any personal allowances. The tax saving is £7,200 (£18,000 x 40%). The extended carryback against the trading profit would give the same result.

This method utilises the loss as quickly as possible and will help Ali's cash flow position.

### – If losses are carried forward:

If the loss is carried forward, the loss of £18,000 would be set against the next available profits from the same trade of £26,000 in 2010/11.

The total taxable income for the year would be £14,840 (£26,000 – £18,000 + £6,840). Personal allowances would not be wasted, however the rate of tax relief is only at 20%.

### – Conclusion:

Ali should claim relief against his total income of 2008/09.

## Taxable income computation

|  | 2007/08 £ | 2008/09 £ | 2009/10 £ |
|---|---|---|---|
| Trading income | 55,000 | Nil | 26,000 |
| Less: Loss relief b/f | (–) | (–) | (–) |
|  | 55,000 | Nil | 26,000 |
| Bank interest | 8,690 | 5,050 | Nil |
| Property income | 9,200 | 6,820 | 6,840 |
| Total income before reliefs | 72,890 | 11,870 | 32,840 |
| Less: Loss relief | (18,000) | (–) | |
| Net income after reliefs | 54,890 | 11,870 | 32,840 |
| Less: PA | (6,475) | (6,475) | (6,475) |
| Taxable income | 48,415 | 5,395 | 26,365 |

## Taxable gain computation – 2009/10

|  | £ |
|---|---|
| Gain in the year | 19,400 |
| Less: Trading loss relief | (–) |
|  | 19,400 |
| Less: Capital loss b/f | (8,750) |
| Net chargeable gain | 10,650 |
| Less Annual exemption | (10,100) |
| Taxable gain | 550 |

**Jane Seemore**

## Answer 1 – Chapter 18

**(a)  (i)  Capital allowance implications on transfer of business**

If Jane incorporates her business, balancing adjustments will be made in the final capital allowance computations, calculated by reference to the market value (restricted to cost if lower) of the assets at cessation compared to the tax WDV at that date.

There is no possibility of making an election to transfer the assets at their tax written down values in this case, as Jane will not control Hollywood Ltd.

The capital allowances for the final accounting period are:

| 1.9.09 – 31.3.10 | General pool | Van | Allowances |
|---|---|---|---|
| | £ | £ | £ |
| TWDV b/f | 15,050 | 4,130 | |
| Additions | 820 | | |
| Disposals | (10,000) | (4,700) | |
| | 5,870 | (570) | |
| Balancing allowance | (5,870) | | 5,870 |
| Balancing charge | | 570 × 85% | (484) |
| Net balancing allowance | | | 5,386 |

**(ii)  Trading income assessments**

Trading loss – period to 31 March 2010

| | £ |
|---|---|
| Trading loss before adjustment | (21,500) |
| Profit on sale of stock (£8,300 x 5/105) | 395 |
| Capital allowances (from (i)) | (5,386) |
| Trading loss | (26,491) |

| | Trading loss £ | Income assessment £ |
|---|---|---|
| 2006/07 Y/e 31.8.06 | | 15,000 |
| 2007/08 Y/e 31.8.07 | | 6,000 |
| 2008/09 Y/e 31.8.08 | | 15,000 |
| 2009/10 1.9.08 – 31.3.10 | | |
| Y/e 31.8.09 | 10,000 | |
| P/e 31.3.10 | (26,491) | |
| Less | | |
| Overlap profits | (2,815) | |
| | (19,306) | Nil |

(iii) **Options available for relief of loss**

Jane has made a trading loss in 2009/10 which is at the end of her trading cycle. The following represent the possible ways she can relieve this loss.

**Relief against total income**

The trading loss can be used in 2009/10 and/or 2008/09 against Jane's total income.

| | 2008/09 | 2009/10 |
|---|---|---|
| Total income | £15,000 | £Nil |

By using the loss in 2008/09, Jane will waste her personal allowance. The rest of the loss will save tax at 20%, but part of the loss will remain unrelieved.

**Relief against capital gains**

After making a claim against total income in a particular tax year, it is also possible to make a further claim in the same year to reduce capital gains tax.

Depending on the consideration received, Jane may have a capital gain in 2009/10 realised on the disposal of the business and can use the loss to reduce this gain.

However, this will only save capital gains tax at 18%.

### Terminal loss relief

As the loss arises in the last 12 months of trading, it can be carried back for three years on a LIFO basis and reduce trading profits of the previous three fiscal years.

|  | 2006/07 | 2007/08 | 2008/09 |
|---|---|---|---|
| Trading profits | £15,000 | £6,000 | £15,000 |

The loss would be used in 2008/09, then 2007/08, wasting two personal allowances and saving tax on the balance of the loss at 20%.

### Incorporation relief

Special incorporation loss relief will be available if the consideration for the business is at least 80% in the form of shares.

The trading loss can be carried forward to 2010/11 and offset against the first available future income that Jane receives from the company.

|  | £ |
|---|---|
| Employment income | 30,000 |
| Investment income | 40,000 |
| Total income in 2010/11 | 70,000 |

In Jane's case, the loss will be offset against her employment income of £30,000, saving tax at 40% with no wasted PA.

### Conclusion

The most tax efficient use of the loss would be to carry it forward against Jane's employment income to save tax at 40%, although there would be a slight cash flow disadvantage as relief would not be obtained until 2010/11.

(b) **Capital gains implications of incorporation**

Where all of the assets of Jane's business are transferred to Hollywood Ltd as a going concern wholly in exchange for shares, any capital gains arising are relieved via incorporation relief such that no capital gains tax liability arises.

However, where part of the payment received from the company is in the form of cash, Jane will have chargeable gains arising.

For Jane to have no liability to capital gains tax in 2010/11, assuming she has no other capital gains in the year, her chargeable gains (after Entrepreneurs' relief) must be covered by her annual exemption of £10,100.

| | £ |
|---|---|
| Gain on premises (£365,000 – £335,000) | 30,000 |
| Gain on goodwill | 50,000 |
| | |
| Total capital gains before reliefs | 80,000 |

| | £ |
|---|---|
| Chargeable gains after Entrepreneurs' relief must be: | 10,100 |
| Chargeable gains before Entrepreneurs' relief must therefore be: | |
| (£10,100 × 9/5) · | 18,180 |
| Incorporation relief should therefore be: | |
| (£80,000 – £18,180) | 61,820 |

Therefore the MV of the shares to be accepted should be:

$$£61,820 = £80,000 \times \frac{\text{MV of shares}}{£438,000}$$

MV of shares = £338,465

Therefore the cash to accept as part of the consideration can be up to the value of £99,535 (£438,000 – £338,465) and there will be no capital gains tax arising on the transfer.

The shares will have a capital gains tax base cost of:

| | £ |
|---|---|
| MV of shares (see above) | 338,465 |
| Less: Incorporation relief | (61,820) |
| | |
| Base cost of shares | 276,645 |

However, if Jane wants to carry forward her losses, as explained above, then she must take at least 80% of the value as shares.

She should therefore take cash of no more than £87,600 (20% x £438,000) if she wants to be able to carry her losses forward to obtain maximum relief.

## Alf and Bob

### Answer 1 – Chapter 19

#### (a) Chargeable gains assessed on the partners

The capital gains of £197,000 arising on the disposal of the business will be split between the partners in their PSR:

|  | £ |
|---|---|
| Alf (40%) | 78,800 |
| Bob (60%) | 118,200 |

Alf's chargeable gains for 2009/10 are as follows:

|  | £ |
|---|---|
| Share of capital gains | 78,800 |
| Less Entrepreneurs' relief (4/9 × £78,800) | (35,022) |
| Chargeable gain on disposal of partnership | 43,778 |

Bob's chargeable gains for 2009/10 are as follows:

|  | £ |
|---|---|
| Share of capital gains | 118,200 |
| Less Entrepreneurs' relief (4/9 × £118,200) | (52,533) |
| Net chargeable gain on disposal of partnership | 65,667 |

#### (b) Loss relief options

There are two possible ways that the partnership loss can be relieved.

(i)  A claim can be made against total income for 2009/10 and/or 2008/09.

Subject to this claim being made, it would then be possible to extend the claim against chargeable gains of the same year.

(ii) Terminal loss relief (TLR) can be claimed.

The final trading income assessments will be split between the partners as follows:

|  | Alf 40% | Bob 60% |
|---|---|---|
|  | £ | £ |
| 2006/07 | 6,000 | 9,000 |
| 2007/08 | 5,600 | 8,400 |
| 2008/09 | 4,480 | 6,720 |
| 2009/10 | (13,400) | (20,100) |

The most beneficial loss relief claim available to Alf would appear to be a terminal loss claim to save income tax at 20%. He could make a claim against his total income of £13,480 (£4,480 + £9,000) for 2008/09, but this would waste his PA. A claim against his capital gains for 2009/10 would only save 18% tax.

Bob could also make a terminal loss claim, but this would waste his PAs for several years. He would be advised to make a claim against his total income of £3,850 (bank interest) for 2009/10, and then claim against his capital gains for 2009/10 (i.e. £5,500 cottage and £65,667 partnership share).

### Alf – taxable income and taxable gains

|  | 2006/07 | 2007/08 | 2008/09 | 2009/10 |
|---|---|---|---|---|
|  | £ | £ | £ | £ |
| Trading income | 6,000 | 5,600 | 4,480 | Nil |
| Less: TLR | (3,320) | (5,600) | (4,480) | – |
|  | 2,680 | Nil | Nil | Nil |
| Employment income | 5,000 | 7,000 | 9,000 | – |
|  | 7,680 | 7,000 | 9,000 | Nil |
| Less: PA | (6,475) | (6,475) | (6,475) | – |
| Taxable income | 1,205 | 525 | 2,525 | Nil |
| Chargeable gains |  |  |  | 43,778 |
| Less: Capital loss b/f |  |  |  | (25,000) |
| Net chargeable gains |  |  |  | 18,778 |
| Less: Annual exemption |  |  |  | (10,100) |
| Taxable gains |  |  |  | 8,678 |

## Bob – taxable income and taxable gain

| | 2006/07 £ | 2007/08 £ | 2008/09 £ | 2009/10 £ |
|---|---|---|---|---|
| Trading income | 9,000 | 8,400 | 6,720 | Nil |
| Bank interest | – | – | – | 3,850 |
| | 9,000 | 8,400 | 6,720 | 3,850 |
| Less: Loss relief | | | | (3,850) |
| Less: PA | (6,475) | (6,475) | (6,475) | (wasted) |
| Taxable income | 2,525 | 1,925 | 245 | Nil |

| | £ |
|---|---|
| Net chargeable gain on partnership | 65,667 |
| Capital gain on cottage | 5,500 |
| Total chargeable gains | 71,167 |
| Less Trading loss relief | (16,250) |
| | 54,917 |
| Less Annual Exemption | (10,100) |
| Taxable gains | 44,817 |

## Ken and Cindy

### Answer 1 – Chapter 20

(a) **Ken's VAT registration**

Traders become liable to register for VAT at the end of any month if the value of taxable supplies in the previous 12 months > £68,000.

| Month to | £ |
|---|---|
| 31 March 2009 | 35,000 |
| 30 April 2009 (£51,000 ÷ 3) | 17,000 |
| 31 May 2009 (£51,000 ÷ 3) | 17,000 |
| | 69,000 |

Ken will therefore be liable to register for VAT from 31 May 2009, and he must notify HMRC by 30 June 2009. Ken will be registered from 1 July 2009.

(b) **Cindy**

| | Total £ | Recover £ | Disallow £ |
|---|---|---|---|
| Relating to taxable supplies | 25,575 | 25,575 | |
| Relating to exempt supplies | 15,400 | | 15,400 |
| Relating to overheads (W) | 30,800 | 21,560 | 9,240 |
| | 71,775 | 47,135 | 24,640 |

Cindy's deductible input VAT is therefore £47,135.

**Working: split of non-attributable VAT**

Taxable % apportionment = £275,000 ÷ (£275,000 + £120,000) x 100 = 70% (rounded up to whole %)

**De minimis test**

The exempt input tax is £24,640 and as this amounts to more than £625 per month on average none of it is recoverable.

## Alan and Roger

### Answer 1 – Chapter 21

Date of liability to register for VAT

| Year | Month | Fees invoiced £ | Annual cumulation £ |
|---|---|---|---|
| 2009 | February | 3,950 | 3,950 |
| | March | 6,200 | 10,150 |
| | April | 3,900 | 14,050 |
| | May | 3,700 | 17,750 |
| | June | 3,500 | 21,250 |
| | July | 2,200 | 23,450 |
| | August | 6,100 | 29,550 |
| | September (Note) | 6,800 | 36,350 |
| | October | 8,200 | 44,550 |
| | November | 10,200 | 54,750 |
| | December | 13,400 | 68,150 |
| 2010 | January | – | 68,150 |
| | February | 35,700 | 103,850 |
| | March | 29,400 | 133,250 |

**Note:** Capital assets of the business are disregarded.

The statutory tests for registration liability are set out as follows:

(i) If, at the end of any month, the value of taxable supplies in the period of one year ending exceeds £68,000, liability to register applies.

(ii) If, at the end of any time, there are reasonable grounds for believing that the taxable supplies in the period of 30 days then beginning will exceed £68,000, liability to register applies.

Under (i) above liability can be avoided if HMRC are satisfied that for the period of one year just beginning the limit of £66,000 will not be exceeded i.e. the turnover has been uncharacteristically high.

If (i) above applies the trader must notify HMRC within 30 days of the end of the relevant month and is registered from the end of the month following the relevant month or from an earlier date if agreed. The relevant month is the month at the end of which the trader became liable to be registered.

If (ii) above applies the trader must notify HMRC before the end of the 30-day period in which his taxable supplies are likely to exceed £68,000. He will then be registered from the start of the 30 days.

Applying these tests to Alan and Roger it is clear that they should be registered following the period to 31 December 2009.

Notification should be made by 30 January 2010.

Registration would then be effective from 1 February 2010.

As they have registered late, they will be subject to a penalty.

## Sandy Brick

### Answer 2 – Chapter 21

(a) **Supply of services**

    (1)  The basic tax point for services is the date that they are completed.

    (2)  If an invoice is issued or payment received before the basic tax point, then this becomes the actual tax point.

    (3)  If an invoice is issued within 14 days of the basic tax point, the invoice date will usually replace the basic tax point date and becomes the actual tax point.

(b) **VAT invoices**

    (1)  A VAT invoice must be issued when a standard rated supply is made to a VAT registered person.

    (2)  A VAT invoice should be issued within 30 days of the date that the taxable supply of services is treated as being made.

(c) **VAT Returns – Quarter ended 31 March 2010**

|  | £ | £ |
|---|---|---|
| **Output VAT** | | |
| Sales to VAT registered customers (Note 1) | | |
| (£44,000 × 95% (100 – 5) × 17.5%) | | 7,315 |
| Sales to non-VAT registered customers | | |
| (£16,920 – £5,170 = £11,750 × 17.5/117.5) | | 1,750 |
| Advance payment (£5,000 × 17.5/117.5) | | 745 |
| | | _____ |
| | | 9,810 |
| **Input VAT** | | |
| Materials (£11,200 – £800 = £10,400 × 17.5%) | 1,820 | |
| Office equipment (Note 3) | 189 | |
| (£120 × 9 = £1,080 × 17.5%) | | |
| Telephone (Note 4) | 49 | |
| (£400 × 70% (100 – 30) × 17.5%) | | |
| Motor repairs (Note 5) (£920 × 17.5%) | 161 | |
| Equipment (£6,000 × 17.5) | 1,050 | |
| | _____ | |
| | | (3,269) |
| | | _____ |
| VAT payable | | 6,541 |
| | | _____ |

**Notes:**

(1) The calculation of output VAT on sales must take into account the discount for prompt payment, even if customers do not take it.

(2) Input VAT cannot be claimed in respect of the materials used in constructing Sandy's private residence since the goods are not used for business purposes.

(3) Input VAT can be recovered on services supplied in the six months prior to registration, so the office equipment claim can be backdated to July 2009.

(4) An apportionment is made where a service such as the use of a telephone is partly for business purposes and partly for private purposes.

(5) However, no apportionment is necessary for motor expenses provided there is some business use.

## Springvale Ltd

### Answer 1 – Chapter 23

**Profits chargeable to corporation tax – y/e 31 March 2010**

|  | £ |
|---|---:|
| Trading profit (W1) | 274,950 |
| Interest income: | |
|     Bank deposit interest receivable | 359 |
|     Loan stock interest receivable | 1,200 |
|     Chargeable gain | 51,160 |
| | 327,669 |
| Less: Gift Aid | (4,150) |
| PCTCT | 323,519 |

### Workings

**(W1) Trading profit – y/e 31.3.10**

|  | £ |
|---|---:|
| Net profit per accounts | 243,163 |
| Add back | |
| Depreciation | 44,400 |
| Entertaining | 420 |
| Gift Aid to charity | 4,150 |
| Trade expenses – Gifts of alcohol | 320 |
| | 292,453 |
| Less | |
| Loan stock interest received | (1,200) |
| Bank deposit interest received | (359) |
| Dividend received | (400) |
| Capital allowances (W2) | (15,544) |
| Trading profit | 274,950 |

**(W2) Capital allowances – y/e 31.3.10**

|  | General pool | Total allowances |
|---|---|---|
|  | £ | £ | £ |
| TWDV b/f |  | 24,220 |  |
| Additions: |  |  |  |
| No AIA or FYA: |  |  |  |
|    Car (111 – 160 g/km) |  | 13,000 |  |
| Qualifying for AIA: |  |  |  |
|   Plant | 8,400 |  |  |
|   Less AIA | (8,400) |  | 8,400 |
|  | ——— | Nil |  |
| Disposal proceeds |  | (1,500) |  |
|  |  | ——— |  |
|  |  | 35,720 |  |
| WDA (20% × £35,720) |  | (7,144) | 7,144 |
|  |  | ——— |  |
| TWDV c/f |  | 28,576 |  |
|  |  | ——— |  |
| Total allowances |  |  | 15,544 |
|  |  |  | ——— |

## Excel Holidays Ltd

## Answer 2 – Chapter 23

**Corporation tax computations**

|  | y/e 31.3.08 £ | y/e 31.3.09 £ | 6 m/e 30.9.09 £ |
|---|---|---|---|
| Adjusted profit (W1) | 129,000 | 110,000 | 55,000 |
| Less: Capital allowances (W2) | (25,000) | (41,000) | (3,125) |
| Trading profit | 104,000 | 69,000 | 51,875 |
| Bank deposit interest receivable | 1,000 | 1,100 | 1,900 |
| PCTCT | 105,000 | 70,100 | 53,775 |
| Corporation tax @ 20%/21%/21% | 21,000 | 14,721 | 11,293 |
| Due date | 1.1.09 | 1.1.10 | 1.7.10 |

**(W1) Adjusted profit computation before capital allowances**

|  | 12 m/e 31.3.08 £ | 18 m/e 30.9.09 £ |
|---|---|---|
| Profits per accounts | 122,000 | 156,000 |
| Add: Depreciation | 8,000 | 10,000 |
| Fine/entertaining | – | 2,000 |
|  | 130,000 | 168,000 |
| Less: Interest received | (1,000) | (3,000) |
| Adjusted profit | 129,000 | 165,000 |

No adjustment is necessary for the repairs accrual, since the accruals basis is the correct method of calculating the trading profit.

The adjusted profit for the 18 month period ended 30.9.09 needs to be time apportioned between the two accounting periods.

(i) y/e 31.3.09    12/18 x £165,000 =    £110,000

(ii) 6 m/e 30.9.09    6/18 x £165,000 =    £55,000

**(W2) Capital allowances**

|  | General pool | Total allowances |
|---|---|---|
|  | £ | £ | £ |

**Y/e 31 March 2008**

| TWDV b/f | | Nil | |
|---|---|---|---|
| Additions: | | | |
| Qualifying for AIA: | | | |
| Plant | 25,000 | | |
| Less AIA | (25,000) | | 25,000 |
| | —— | Nil | |
| | | —— | |
| TWDV c/f | | Nil | |
| | | —— | |
| Total allowances | | | 25,000 |
| | | | —— |

**Y/e 31 March 2009**

| Additions: | | | |
|---|---|---|---|
| Qualifying for AIA: | | | |
| Plant | 41,000 | | |
| Less AIA | (41,000) | | 41,000 |
| | —— | Nil | |
| | | —— | |
| TWDV c/f | | Nil | |
| | | —— | |
| Total allowances | | | 41,000 |
| | | | —— |

**Y/e 30 September 2009**

| Additions: | | | |
|---|---|---|---|
| Qualifying for AIA: | | | |
| Plant | 3,125 | | |
| Less AIA (Note) | (3,125) | | 3,125 |
| | —— | Nil | |
| | | —— | |
| TWDV c/f | | Nil | |
| | | —— | |
| Total allowances | | | 3,125 |
| | | | —— |

**Note:** The maximum AIA available in p/e 30 September 2009 is £25,000 (£50,000 × 6/12)

## Iris Ltd

### Answer 1 – Chapter 24

#### PCTCT computations

|  | Year to 31.12.08 £ | 8 m/e 31.8.09 £ | Year to 31.8.10 £ |
|---|---|---|---|
| Trading profit | 170,000 | 78,000 | Nil |
| Less: Loss relief b/f | ( – ) | ( – ) | ( – ) |
|  | 170,000 | 78,000 | Nil |
| Property income | 10,000 | 11,000 | 12,000 |
| Interest income | 2,500 | 3,600 | 4,100 |
| Total profits | 182,500 | 92,600 | 16,100 |
| Less: Loss relief | (60,833) | (92,600) | (16,100) |
| extended carryback | (6,567) |  |  |
|  | 115,100 | Nil | Nil |
| Less: Gift Aid | (3,000) | (wasted) | (wasted) |
| PCTCT | 112,100 | Nil | Nil |
| Unrelieved Gift Aid | Nil | 3,000 | 3,000 |

#### Loss memorandum

|  | £ |
|---|---|
| Loss for y/e 31.8.10 | 176,100 |
| Less: Loss relief: |  |
| y/e 31.8.10 | (16,100) |
| Eight months to 31.8.09 | (92,600) |
| y/e 31.12.08 (£182,500 x 4/12) | (60,833) |
| Extended relief against y/e 31.12.08 (Max £50,000) | (6,567) |
| Loss available to carry forward | Nil |

**Note:** The full loss may be carried back against profits of the 12 months before 1 September 2009. The loss may therefore be set against all of the total profits (before Gift Aid) for the 8 m/e 31.8.09 and 4/12 of the total profits (before Gift Aid) for the y/e 31.12.08. As the loss is made in an accounting period ending between 24 November 2008 and 23 Novemeber 2010, extended relief is available enabling a maximum of £50,000 to be carried back for 36 months. Therefore, the remaining £6,567 loss can be set against total profits (before Gift Aid) for y/e 31 December 2008.

## Cosmet Ltd

### Answer 2 – Chapter 24

(a) (i) **Corporation tax payable – after loss relief**

|  | y/e 31.5.07 £ | y/e 31.5.08 £ | p/e 31.12.08 £ | y/e 31.12.09 £ |
|---|---|---|---|---|
| Trading profit | 750,250 | 500,500 | 101,999 | Nil |
| Property income | 10,000 | 10,000 | 10,000 | 11,000 |
| Bank interest | 8,460 | 7,526 | 5,076 | 5,275 |
| Net chargeable gains (W) | 1,622 | Nil | Nil | 59,390 |
|  | 770,332 | 518,026 | 117,075 | 75,665 |
| Less: Loss relief | – | (40,050) | (117,075) | (75,665) |
| PCTCT | 770,332 | 477,976 | Nil | Nil |

**Loss memorandum**

|  | £ |
|---|---|
| Loss for y/e 31.12.09 | 232,790 |
| Less: Loss relief: |  |
| Current period claim: y/e 31.12.09 | (75,665) |
| Carry back 12 months: 7 m/e 31.12.08 | (117,075) |
| y/e 31.5.08 (max £518,026 x 5/12 = £215,844) |  |
| restricted to amount of loss left | (40,050) |
| Loss available to carry forward | Nil |

### (ii)  Tax saving p/e 31.12.08

|  | £ |
|---|---|
| PCTCT before loss relief | 117,075 |

There is no FII, therefore 'profits' = PCTCT

|  | |
|---|---|
| Upper limit (£1,500,000 x 7/12) | 875,000 |
| Lower limit (£300,000 x 7/12) | 175,000 |

Therefore the company is taxed at 21%

|  | |
|---|---|
| Tax repayment (21% x £117,075) | £24,586 |

### y/e 31.5.08

|  | £ |
|---|---|
| PCTCT before loss relief | 518,026 |

There is no FII, therefore 'profits' = PCTCT

|  | |
|---|---|
| Upper limit | 1,500,000 |
| Lower limit | 300,000 |

Therefore the company is taxed at 32.04% in the marginal band
(32.5% × 10/12 + 29.75% + 2/12)

|  | |
|---|---|
| Tax repayment (32.04% x £40,050) | £12,832 |

### Working: Net chargeable gains

| y/e 31.5.08: | Capital loss to carry forward £4,000 |
|---|---|
| p/e 31.12.08: | Net chargeable gain = (£2,990 – £2,990 capital loss b/f) = £Nil |
| | Capital loss remaining to c/f = (£4,000 – £2,990) = £1,010 |
| y/e 31.12.09: | Net chargeable gain = (£60,440 – £1,010 capital loss b/f) = £59,390 |

## (b)  Notes for meeting

### (1)  Merging with another company

–  There are anti-avoidance provisions that restrict the carry forward of trading losses when there is both a change in the ownership and a major change in the nature and conduct of trade within a three year period.

–  The three year period can be either before or after the change of ownership.

- Trading losses arising before the change in ownership cannot be carried forward to periods after the change, nor can losses arising after a change in ownership be carried back to periods before the change.

- A change in ownership means that more than one half of the ordinary share capital of the company is acquired by a person or persons, ignoring any person acquiring 5% or less.

- A major change in the nature or conduct of the trade includes:

  - a major change in the type of property dealt in or services provided; and

  - a major change in customers, outlets or markets.

(2) **Changing the products and trading in a more lucrative market**

  - Carry forward relief is only available against future trading income of the same trade.

  - If the nature of the trade changes to such an extent that the original trade ceases and a new trade commences, carry forward relief is denied for losses of the original trade.

### Bream

### Answer 1 – Chapter 26

**The effect of the transactions on Test Valley Ltd:**

| June 2007 (y/e 31/12/07) | • | Company liable to pay tax equal to 25% of the loan outstanding on corporation tax due date | |
| | • | within 9 months of the end of the AP (i.e. on 1.10.08) | |
| | • | £72,000 x 25% | £18,000 |
| | | | |
| January 2009 (y/e 31/12/09) | • | Company becomes entitled to repayment of tax | |
| | • | to extent loan repaid (i.e. £20,000 x 25%) | |
| | • | repayment is due on 1 October 2010 | £5,000 |

| March 2010 (y/e 31/12/10) | • | Company becomes entitled to repayment of tax | |
| | • | on the loan w/off (i.e. £52,000 x 25%) | |
| | • | repayment is due 1 October 2011 | £13,000 |

**The effect of the transactions on Bream:**

| June 2007 | • | If interest is charged at less than the official rate of 4.75%, the difference is treated as a dividend | |
| January 2009 | • | As above | |
| March 2010 | • | Loan waived = treated as dividend payment in 2009/10 | |
| | • | Gross up amount written off at 100/90 | |
| | • | Include in income tax computation as dividends (i.e. £52,000 x 100/90) | £ 57,778 |
| | • | Tax at 32.5% (£57,778 x 32.5%) | 18,778 |
| | • | Deemed tax credit available of 10% | (5,778) |
| | • | Income tax payable | 13,000 |

### Joe

### Answer 2 – Chapter 26

(a) **Transaction treated as a distribution**

| | £ |
|---|---|
| Dividend plus tax credit (£630,000 x 100/90) | 700,000 |
| Income tax @ 32.5% | 227,500 |
| Less: Tax credit (£700,000 @ 10%) | (70,000) |
| Income tax payable | 157,500 |

The amount to be treated as a net distribution is the difference between the sale proceeds and the amount originally subscribed. The net distribution is therefore £630,000 (100,000 x £7.30 = £730,000 – £100,000).

**Note:** For a higher rate taxpayer an alternative method of finding income tax payable = net dividend x 25% (i.e. £630,000 × 25%) = £157,500.

(b) **Transaction not treated as a distribution**

|  | £ |
|---|---|
| Proceeds | 730,000 |
| Less: Cost | (100,000) |
| | |
| Capital gain (Note) | 630,000 |
| Less: Annual exemption | (10,100) |
| | |
| Taxable amount | 619,900 |
| | |
| Capital gains tax @ 18% | 111,582 |

**Note:** As Joe did not work for the company, Entrepreneurs' relief is not available.

(c) **Effect of satisfying the exemption**

The exemption for the purchase by a company of its own shares effectively converts income into capital. As can be seen by the question, this is advantageous as CGT is only charged at 18% compared to 40% for income tax.

In an exam question, consider the effects of both situations.

**John**

## Answer 3 – Chapter 26

(a) (i) **Taxation as a sole trader**

| | | £ |
|---|---|---|
| John's income tax: | | |
| Trading income | | 100,000 |

| Income tax | | | |
|---|---|---|---|
| £ | | £ | £ |
| 37,400 | x 20% | | 7,480 |
| 62,600 | x 40% | | 25,040 |
| | | | 32,520 |
| 100,000 | | | |

| John's National Insurance contributions: | | |
|---|---|---|
| Class 2 (52 x £2.40) | | 125 |
| Class 4 | | |
| (£43,875 – £5,715) x 8% | 3,053 | |
| (£100,000 – £43,875) x 1% | 561 | |
| | | 3,614 |
| | | |
| John's total IT and NIC payable | | 36,259 |

**Note:** The personal allowance is offset against John's property business income of £6,475.

### Taxation as a company, drawing net dividend of £20,000

| | £ | £ |
|---|---|---|
| Company's corporation tax | | |
| Profits chargeable to corporation tax | 100,000 | |
| | | |
| Corporation tax at 21% | | 21,000 |
| John's income tax: | | |
| Dividend income (£20,000 x 100/90) | 22,222 | |
| | | |
| Income tax (£22,222 x 10%) | 2,222 | |
| Less: Tax credit | (2,222) | |
| | | |
| Income tax payable | | Nil |
| | | |
| Total tax payable | | 21,000 |

National insurance:

No NICs is payable on dividends

**Taxation as a company, drawing gross salary of £28,074**

Company's corporation tax:

|  | £ | £ |
|---|---|---|
| Trading income | 100,000 | |
| Less: Salary | (28,074) | |
| Employer's NIC (£28,074 – £5,715) × 12.8% | (2,862) | 2,862 |
| Profits chargeable to corporation tax | 69,064 | |
| Corporation tax at 21% | | 14,503 |
| John's income tax: | | |
| Employment income | 28,074 | |
| Income tax (£28,074 × 20%) | | 5,615 |
| John's National Insurance: | | |
| Class 1 (£28,074 – £5,715) × 11% | | 2,459 |
| Total tax payable | | 25,439 |

**Comparison of taxation**

The main difference between the taxation of a sole trader and a company is that income tax and National Insurance contributions are due on all of the profits of a sole trader, whereas although all of the profits of a company are charged to corporation tax, only profits withdrawn from the company are charged to income tax.

Additionally, NICs are only payable on salary, not on dividends.

**Tutorial note**

John will need to take a gross salary of £28,074 to receive a net salary of £20,000.

This is because the net salary is after deducting income tax of 20% on the gross salary (G) and after deducting National Insurance contributions of (11% on G – £5,715).

Therefore the gross salary is calculated as follows:

$$G - (G \times 20\%) - ((G - £5,715) \times 11\%)) = £20,000$$

$$G - 0.2G - 0.11G + £629 = £20,000$$

$$0.69G = £19,371$$

$$G = £28,074$$

**Note:** The question gives you the gross salary to use in the computation. The above computation is for tutorial purposes only to prove that the net income John will receive is £20,000 (i.e. the same as paying a net dividend of £20,000).

(ii) **From the company's point of view**

**Equity**

(1) Fees incurred in issuing share capital are not an allowable deduction against trading profits

(2) The cost of making distributions to shareholders are disallowable.

(3) The dividends themselves are not allowable.

**Loan Finance**

(1) Interest on loans taken out to finance the business is deductible from trading profits.

(2) Capital costs, for example loans issued at a discount, are deductible from trading profits, where the loan finance is used for trade purposes.

(3) Incidental costs of obtaining medium or long term business loans and for issuing loan stock where the funds are used for trade purposes are deductible from trading profits.

**From an individual investor's point view**

**Equity**

(1) If the investor is an individual, the dividends received are only taxable (at 32.5%) to the extent that the investor is a higher rate taxpayer. The tax credit of 10% is deductible from any tax liability, but never repayable in cash.

For a higher rate taxpayer this gives an effective rate of 25% on dividends received.

(2) There will be a chargeable gain or loss on the disposal of the shareholding.

**Loan Finance**

(1) If the investor is an individual, interest received will be charged to income tax at 40%, to the extent that the individual is a higher rate taxpayer. A tax credit of 20% is deductible from any tax liability, and is repayable to non-taxpayers.

(2) Usually the original creditor will not realise a gain or loss when the debt is disposed of, however a debt on a security can result in a capital gain or a capital loss.

(iii) **Pension options available**

(1) John could invest in a personal pension. He can invest up to a maximum of £25,000 (100% of earnings) in 2009/10 and obtain tax relief.

This amount is paid net of basic rate tax, and the basic rate band is extended by the gross payment when calculating his income tax liability to obtain higher rate relief.

(2) The company could set up a small self administered scheme (SSAS). Loans may be made to the company from the funds. Property can be purchased from the fund. However the costs of setting up and administering the scheme would probably cancel any advantages this option may have.

(3) John could set up a self invested personal pension scheme (SIPPS). It is possible to purchase commercial property with the fund. Again the costs of setting up and administering the scheme would probably cancel any advantages this option may have.

## Longbow

### Answer 1 – Chapter 27

#### (a) One-third of Minnow Ltd's share capital acquired

| Minnow Ltd | £ |
|---|---|
| Chargeable gain | 50,000 |
| Less: Loss relief | (50,000) |
| PCTCT | Nil |

| Longbow Ltd | £ |
|---|---|
| Trading profit | 220,000 |
| Interest income (£150,000 @ 7% x 8/12) | 7,000 |
| | 227,000 |
| Less: Consortium relief | |
| (£140,000 – £50,000 = £90,000 x 1/3 x 6/12) | (15,000) |
| PCTCT | 212,000 |
| Corporation tax liability (£212,000 x 21%) | 44,520 |

**Note:**

(1) Minnow Ltd is a consortium company, and one-third of its trading loss can therefore be surrendered to Longbow Ltd. Minnow Ltd must take into account its own current year profits when calculating the loss to surrender, and this is restricted to the overlapping period of 1 October 2009 to 31 March 2010.

(2) Minnow Ltd's brought forward trading loss will be carried forward, as will the trading loss not used in y/e 31/03/10 of £75,000 (£140,000 – £50,000 – £15,000) against the first available trading profits arising in Minnow Ltd.

#### (b) Two-thirds of Minnow Ltd's share capital acquired

**Minnow Ltd**

The company's PCTCT will be the same as above.

| **Longbow Ltd** | £ |
|---|---|
| Trading profit | 220,000 |
| Interest income | 7,000 |
| | 227,000 |
| Less: Consortium relief | |
| (£140,000 – £50,000 = £90,000 x 2/3 x 6/12) | (30,000) |
| PCTCT | 197,000 |
| Corporation tax (£197,000 × 28%) | 55,160 |
| Less: Marginal relief | |
| (7/400 x (£750,000 – £197,000)) | (9,678) |
| Corporation tax liability | 45,482 |

### Note:

(1) Minnow Ltd is an associated company, and so the relevant lower and upper limits for corporation tax purposes are reduced to £150,000 (£300,000/2) and £750,000 (£1,500,000/2).

(2) The remaining loss of £60,000 and the trading loss b/f of £9,000 will be carried forward in Minnow Ltd for use against first available trading profit subject to no major change in the nature and conduct of trade following the change in ownership.

### (c) All of Minnow Ltd's share capital acquired

**Minnow Ltd**

| | £ |
|---|---|
| Chargeable gain (Note 2) | 12,500 |
| Less: Loss relief | (12,500) |
| PCTCT | Nil |

| **Longbow Ltd** | £ |
|---|---|
| Trading profit | 220,000 |
| Interest income | 7,000 |
| | 227,000 |
| Less: Group relief (£140,000 x 6/12) | (70,000) |
| PCTCT | 157,000 |

| | |
|---|---|
| Corporation tax @ 28% | 43,960 |
| Less: Marginal relief | |
| 7/400 x (£750,000 – £157,000)) | (10,378) |
| Corporation tax liability | 33,582 |

**Notes:**

(1) Minnow Ltd is a 75% subsidiary.

(2) Rollover relief could be claimed based on the freehold factory to be purchased by Longbow Ltd. As all of the sale proceeds relating to the business use is reinvested (i.e. £120,000 > 75% x £150,000 = £112,500), all of the business proportion of the gain can be rolled over. The gain rolled over would be 75% x £50,000 = £37,500.

A rollover claim is likely to be beneficial, as the rolled over gain is only chargeable when Longbow Ltd sells the new asset, and may be rolled over again if further reinvestment is made in qualifying assets. Relief for the trading loss carried forward in Minnow Ltd will be against the first available trading profits arriving in Minnow Ltd, subject to no major change in the nature and conduct of trade following the change in ownership.

An alternative to the rollover claim would be to leave the £50,000 gain chargeable in Minnow Ltd and offset £50,000 of Minnow Ltd's trading losses against it in the current year. This would leave a smaller loss to carry forward in Minnow Ltd, but may avoid a higher tax charge on the gain in future when there may not be losses available to set against it.

Assuming the rollover claim is made, the trade loss to carry forward in Minnow Ltd will be:

| | £ |
|---|---|
| Trading loss arising y/e 31/3/10 | 140,000 |
| Less: Group relief | (70,000) |
| Current year offset | (12,500) |
| Available to c/f | 57,500 |
| Add: Trading loss b/f | 9,000 |
| Total available to c/f | 66,500 |

## Willow Group

### Answer 2 – Chapter 27

### Corporation tax computations – y/e 31 March 2010

| | Ash Ltd £ | Pine Ltd £ | Willow Ltd £ | Oak Ltd £ | Fig Ltd £ | Cherry Ltd £ |
|---|---|---|---|---|---|---|
| Trading profits | Nil | 158,000 | 153,000 | Nil | 294,000 | Nil |
| Group relief (W2) | | | (103,000) | | (15,000) | |
| | | | | | (4,000) | |
| Consortium relief | | (71,100) | | | | |
| | | ——— | ——— | | ——— | |
| PCTCT | Nil | 86,900 | 50,000 | Nil | 275,000 | Nil |
| FII | Nil | Nil | Nil | Nil | Nil | Nil |
| | | ——— | ——— | ——— | ——— | ——— |
| 'Profits' | Nil | 86,900 | 50,000 | Nil | 275,000 | Nil |
| | | | | | | |
| Corporation tax | £ | £ | £ | £ | £ | £ |
| £86,900 x 28% | | 24,332 | | | | |
| Less: | | | | | | |
| Marginal relief | | | | | | |
| (7/400 x (£250,000 – £86,900)) | | (2,854) | | | | |
| £50,000 x 21% | | | 10,500 | | | |
| £275,000 x 28% | | | | | 77,000 | |
| | | ——— | ——— | ——— | ——— | ——— |
| Corporation tax | Nil | 21,478 | 10,500 | Nil | 77,000 | Nil |
| | | ——— | ——— | ——— | ——— | ——— |

### Workings

#### (1) Analysis of group structure

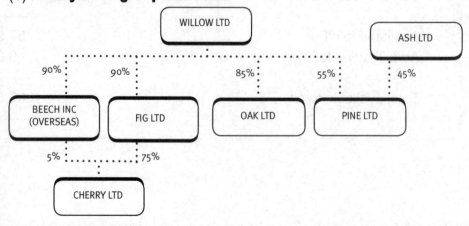

| | | |
|---|---|---|
| Number of associated companies | = | 6 |
| Upper limit = 1,500,000/6 | = | £250,000 |
| Lower limit =300,000/6 | = | £50,000 |
| Number of 75% groups | = | 2 |
| Group 1 | = | Willow Ltd, Beech Inc, Fig Ltd, Oak Ltd (but Beech Inc is an overseas company and cannot surrender its losses to the UK) |
| Group 2 | = | Fig Ltd, Cherry Ltd |
| Consortium | = | 1 |
| Members | = | Ash Ltd, Willow Ltd |
| Consortium owned company | = | Pine Ltd |

(2) **Losses memo**

Deal with the most restrictive losses first:

(i) Consortium relief    Ash Ltd can only give its loss to Pine Ltd

(ii) Group relief    Cherry Ltd can only give its loss to Fig Ltd

(iii) Group relief    Oak Ltd can give its loss to Fig Ltd and Willow Ltd

Aim of loss relief: to bring the companies in the group down to the lower profit limit to save tax at the highest marginal rate.

Therefore, Oak Ltd will give its loss to Willow first to reduce its profits down to £50,000 and save tax at 29.75%, then give the rest to Fig Ltd and save tax at 28%.

**Note:** Beech Inc is an overseas company and cannot surrender its losses to the UK

| | Ash Ltd £ | Oak Ltd £ | Cherry Ltd £ |
|---|---|---|---|
| Loss in the year | 160,000 | 107,000 | 15,000 |
| Consortium relief to Pine Ltd (W3) | (71,100) | | |
| Group relief to Fig Ltd | | | (15,000) |
| Group relief to Willow Ltd | | (103,000) | |
| Group relief to Fig Ltd | | (4,000) | |
| Loss to carry forward | 88,900 | Nil | Nil |

(3) Consortium relief

Lower of: £

| | | |
|---|---|---|
| (1) | Available loss of Ash Ltd | 160,000 |
| (2) | Percentage of Pine Ltd's profit/(loss) (45% x £158,000) | 71,100 |

## X Ltd

### Answer 1 – Chapter 28

**To:** Board of Directors
**From:** Tax Advisor
**Date:** July 2009
**Subject:** Taxation implications of establishing a factory overseas

The factory would be a 'permanent establishment' overseas and the profits will suffer foreign tax. Relief will be given for the foreign tax up to the full amount of UK corporation tax on that income.

### Overseas branch of UK company

(1) The company would be liable to UK corporation tax on all profits of the branch.

(2) Since the branch is considered as part of the UK company, UK capital allowances are available and any branch losses would automatically be relieved.

(3) Capital gains arising would be subject to UK corporation tax.

(4) The overseas branch would not affect the upper and lower limits for starting rate or small companies' rate purposes.

### Foreign based subsidiary

(1) The parent company will only be liable to UK corporation tax on amounts received as rent or interest from the subsidiary, but not dividends.

(2) Capital allowances and relief for losses would not be available between the parent and a non-resident subsidiary, unless the company is established in an EEA country and the losses cannot be utilised in the overseas subsidiary.

(3) Capital gains arising in a non-resident subsidiary would not be subject to UK corporation tax.

(4) Management control must be exercised overseas for the subsidiary to be accepted as a non UK resident.

(5) The overseas company will be an associated company for small company rate purposes, and therefore affect the upper and lower limits.

## Bertie Overseas

### Answer 2 – Chapter 28

Client Address                                          Firm address

Date

Dear Bertie,

### Re: Overseas Expansion

Further to our recent meeting I am writing to set out the principal business tax issues regarding the setting up of Bertie Overseas in the country of Picea.

These would appear to be as follows:

- The basis of taxation of overseas profits and relief for overseas losses.
- Whether Bertie Overseas should take the form of an overseas branch or a limited company.
- Whether relief can be obtained in the UK for any overseas taxes paid.
- Whether there is any relevant anti-avoidance legislation which may apply.

Dealing with each of these in turn.

### Basis of Taxation and the Branch v Limited Company Decision

Subject to the anti-avoidance measures detailed below, when Bertie Overseas starts making profits the 'usual' rules are as follows:

If Bertie Overseas takes the form of a non-UK resident limited company then dividends payable to Bertie Ltd will not be assessable in the UK.

This will be beneficial as corporate taxes in Picea are only 10%.

On the other hand if Bertie Overseas is set up as an overseas branch of Bertie Ltd, which is controlled from the UK, it is likely that all of the overseas profits generated (whether or not they are remitted to the UK) will be treated as part of the profits of Bertie Ltd and therefore entirely taxable in the UK. In these circumstances, however, the vehicles and equipment acquired will qualify for UK capital allowances.

It should be noted that these rules could be used to your advantage.

Your business plan anticipates that Bertie Overseas will make a loss in its first year of operation which will then be followed by progressively stronger profits.

If Bertie Overseas takes the form of a non-UK resident limited company in year one then it is unlikely that Bertie Ltd will be able to offset the losses generated against its own profits. The use of these losses will therefore be determined by Picean tax law. It is stated that Picea has no facility to carry losses backwards or forwards and presumably therefore these losses would remain unrelieved.

If, however, Bertie Overseas takes the form of an overseas branch this is effectively regarded by UK tax law as an extension of the UK trade. Any overseas losses generated are likely therefore to be automatically offset against UK source profits generated by Bertie Ltd. As Bertie Ltd currently pays corporation tax at the full rate it seems probable that these will therefore all be relieved as incurred.

This would only be of benefit in year one of the overseas operations. To prevent 100% of eventual overseas profits being taxed in the UK after year one the overseas branch could then be incorporated as a non-UK resident limited company.

Some relevant points to note here are:

(a) It may be necessary to secure the consent of the Treasury for the incorporation to proceed. It is generally illegal for a UK resident company to permit a non-UK resident company over which it has control to create or issue any shares. However, providing full market value consideration is given this transaction may be covered by published Treasury General Consents and so, in these circumstances, specific consent may not be required.

(b) The conversion will be a disposal of the branch assets at market value.

   (i) In the case of the equipment and vehicles this will give rise to a balancing adjustment which (if a balancing charge) may increase the profits subject to UK corporation tax.

   If the Picean limited company is not chargeable to UK corporation tax after the incorporation, a succession election, which is normally possible where such assets are passed between connected persons, will not be possible.

   (ii) In the case of the freehold premises a chargeable gain may arise. It is possible, by election, to defer this in circumstances where all the branch assets (with the exception of cash) are transferred to the Picean limited company in return for ordinary shares.

   If such an election is made the deferred gain will become taxable when the shares in the foreign company are sold or the foreign company disposes of any chargeable assets within six years of the incorporation.

## Relief for overseas taxes paid on branch profits

To prevent the taxation of overseas income twice (once in the UK and once in the overseas territory) UK legislation allows for double tax relief.

In the absence of a double tax treaty this works by allowing any Picean corporation tax paid on branch profits from Bertie Overseas to be credited against Bertie Ltd's UK corporation tax.

Double tax relief is, however, restricted to the lower of the overseas corporation tax paid and the UK corporation tax on the taxable profits from the overseas source.

As Picean corporation tax rates are 10% which is lower than the rate of UK corporation tax currently being paid (i.e. 28%), all of the Picean tax should be available as a credit against Bertie Ltd's corporation tax liability.

## Anti-Avoidance Legislation

The fact that the use of an overseas subsidiary paying dividends allows companies to avoid UK corporation tax on remittances to the UK is of concern to HMRC. As a result a variety of anti-avoidance legislation exists to protect the UK Treasury position.

The principal pieces of such legislation are as follows:

### Transfer Pricing

In circumstances where sales are made by a large UK resident company to another company which it controls, at an undervalue (thus depressing UK profits), HMRC can substitute a market value price. This is known as transfer pricing.

Assuming that Bertie Ltd is classified as a large company under the transfer pricing legislation it would appear that this legislation is in point.

This is because the proposed mark up to Bertie Overseas is lower than HMRC might expect (80% compared to 85%). We are aware that Bertie Overseas will be responsible for all of its sale and distribution costs therefore it may be possible to explain the reduction in mark up if Bertie Overseas is required to undertake further responsibilities. This is an area that can be further explored at our next meeting.

It is likely that a transfer pricing liability may also exist relating to the differential in interest rates that will be charged of 2%.

Bertie Ltd must self assess its liability under transfer pricing within its corporation tax return. Penalties can be levied if HMRC are successful in arguing that adjustments should have been made but were not.

For this reason it is recommended that Bertie Ltd sets out in advance its proposed transfer pricing arrangements to HMRC under a statutory procedure known as Advance Pricing Arrangements and negotiate their acceptance with them.

### Residence Status of Overseas Limited Company

The exemption from the UK corporation tax will only apply to dividends received from non-UK resident companies. If HMRC can successfully argue that Bertie Overseas is in fact UK resident then all of its profits will be subject to UK corporation tax (with double tax relief available for tax paid in Picea).

A company will be UK resident if it is incorporated in the UK or it is managed and controlled from the UK. Clearly the former is not a problem but the latter may be. This is because the test is not where day to day control is exercised but rather the highest level of strategic control. If this is exercised by the UK Board of Bertie Ltd it is likely that HMRC will regard control as being UK based thus making Bertie Overseas UK resident.

This is something that will need to be explored in greater depth when we next meet.

**Controlled Foreign Company**

In certain circumstances HMRC have powers to apportion profits of controlled foreign companies ('CFC') to a UK resident company.

A CFC exists where a foreign company under UK control is resident in a low tax area (less than 75% of UK corporation tax) and is set up with a view to avoid UK tax.

On the face of it, it would appear that Bertie Overseas will be caught by this legislation but this is considered unlikely as various exemptions exist. In particular the 'exempt activities' exemption means that companies deriving all of their trading income from unconnected parties (as in this case) will not be caught. As Bertie Overseas is considered to have a genuine commercial presence in Picea this is therefore not considered further.

It is perhaps worthwhile pointing out that this anti-avoidance legislation is of no relevance if Bertie Overseas is a branch controlled from the UK as in this case all of its profits are UK taxable in any event.

I hope the above adequately summarises the position but should you have any queries please do not hesitate to contact me.

Meanwhile I look forward to hearing from you further in the near future.

Yours sincerely,

A Accountant

### North and South

## Answer 1 – Chapter 29

(a) **Corporation tax computations**

**North Limited**

| Year ended 31 March | 2010 | 2011 |
|---|---|---|
| | £ | £ |
| Trading profit | 10,000 | |
| Less: Additional goodwill amortisation (Note 1) | (400) | |
| | 9,600 | Nil |
| Chargeable gain (£120,000 – £80,000) | | 40,000 |
| Less: loss relief – current year | | (40,000) |
| – carried back | (9,600) | |
| PCTCT & Corporation tax liability | Nil | Nil |

| Loss working: | £ |
|---|---|
| Loss per question | (114,000) |
| Less: Goodwill (Note 2) | 20,400 |
| Profit on sale of stock | 4,000 |
| (£10,000 – £6,000) | |
| Revised loss | (89,600) |
| Current year offset | 40,000 |
| Carry back relief | 9,600 |
| Carried forward as at 31 March 2011 | (40,000) |

**Notes**

(1) Corporation tax relief for goodwill amortisation is given in line with amounts charged in the accounts under FRS 10.

However, as in this case, if the accounting rate is less than 4% per year then a figure of 4% may be used for tax purposes. North Limited is therefore entitled to a deduction of £400 (£10,000 x 4%).

(2) The sale of the goodwill will be taxed as a trading profit:

|  |  | £ | £ |
|---|---|---:|---:|
| Proceeds |  |  | 30,000 |
| Less: | Tax cost | 10,000 |  |
|  | Tax amortisation | (400) |  |
|  |  |  | (9,600) |
| Trading profit |  |  | 20,400 |

**South Limited**

| Year ended 31 March | 2010 | 2011 |
|---|---:|---:|
|  | £ | £ |
| Trading profit | 160,000 | 200,000 |
| Less: Abortive expenditure |  | (2,000) |
| Additional amortisation (£20,000 x 4%) |  | (800) |
|  | 160,000 | 197,200 |
| Corporation tax liability: |  |  |
| (£160,000 x 28%) (£197,200 x 28%) | 44,800 | 55,216 |
| Less: Marginal relief |  |  |
| (£750,000 – £160,000) x 7/400 | (10,325) |  |
| (£750,000 – £197,200) x 7/400 |  | (9,674) |
| Corporation tax liability | 34,475 | 45,542 |

South Limited and North Limited are associated by common ownership although they will not form a group for 'group relief' purposes as they are not under the 75% control of a third company.

Total corporation tax payable by South Limited is therefore £80,017 (£34,475 + £45,542).

(b) **Weaknesses of the group structure**

North and South Limited are owned personally by Bertrand and do not therefore form a 75% group for both group relief and chargeable gains purposes.

As a consequence:

(i) The forecast trading losses of North Limited for the y/e 31 March 2011 cannot be relieved against the profits made by South Limited for this accounting period. South Limited is forecast to be a marginal rate corporation tax payer for this year.

(ii) The group rollover relief provisions are not available. As a result, North Limited is unable to relieve its gain of £40,000 by rolling this (at least partially) into the proposed acquisition of the freehold property by South Limited in the y/e 31 March 2011.

(iii) The intangible asset rollover provisions will also not be available. As a result North Limited is unable to relieve its profit of £20,400 by rolling this (at least partially) into the proposed acquisition of the goodwill by South Limited in the y/e 31 March 2011.

### Improvement of group structure

To improve the group structure a 75% relationship therefore needs to be established for North Limited and South Limited. This could be achieved either by placing North Limited and South Limited beneath a holding company or (more simply) by placing North Limited beneath South Limited (or vice versa).

### Procedures to alter the group structure

Either route would involve Bertrand making a disposal of (at least some of) his shares. For example if South Limited becomes the holding company of North Limited this would involve Bertrand transferring his shares in North Limited to South Limited.

This transfer is a chargeable disposal for capital gains tax purposes. However, providing the conditions for a 'paper for paper' share exchange are satisfied this gain will not be taxable.

The main conditions are;

(a) that the consideration received for the shares transferred is shares;

(b) that the acquiring company acquires more than a 25% interest as a result of the transaction, and;

(c) that the transaction is undertaken for bona fide commercial purposes.

It is possible (and advisable) that Bertrand obtains a clearance from HMRC that this transaction will be relieved under these provisions. Providing Bertrand can provide a sound commercial reason this should not prove too difficult. If the provisions apply the original base cost for CGT purposes of the shares that Bertrand transfers will become the base cost of the new shares that he acquires.

The transaction should be exempt from stamp duty under the 'group reconstruction relief' provisions.

This is because:

(a) it is likely that the whole of the share capital of North Limited will be acquired by South Limited and;

(b) there is unlikely to be a change in the ultimate ownership after the reconstruction.

It should be noted, however, that this relief will only apply if the transaction is undertaken for bona fide commercial purposes.

If desired, following this group restructuring the shop acquired by South Limited could be transferred on a no gain/no loss basis to North Limited (including the goodwill).

(c) **Revised corporation tax computations**

**North Limited**

| Year ended 31 March | 2010 | 2011 |
|---|---|---|
| | £ | £ |
| Trading profit | 10,000 | |
| Less: Additional goodwill amortisation | (400) | |
| | 9,600 | Nil |
| Chargeable gain (Note 2) | | 20,000 |
| Less: Loss relief – current year (Note 3) | – | (20,000) |
| – carried back (Note 3) | (9,600) | – |
| PCTCT | Nil | Nil |
| Corporation tax | Nil | Nil |

| Loss working | £ |
|---|---:|
| Loss per question | (120,000) |
| Less: Goodwill (Note 1) | 10,400 |
| Profit on stock | 10,000 |
| | |
| Revised loss | (99,600) |
| Current year offset | 20,000 |
| Carry back offset | 9,600 |
| Group relief | 70,000 |
| | |
| Carried forward as at 31 March 2011 | Nil |

**South Limited**

| Year ended 31 March | 2010 | 2011 |
|---|---:|---:|
| | £ | £ |
| Trading profit | 160,000 | 200,000 |
| Less: Abortive expenditure | | (2,000) |
| Additional amortisation (Note 1) | | (400) |
| Group relief (Note 3) | | (70,000) |
| | | |
| PCTCT | 160,000 | 127,600 |
| | | |
| Corporation tax liability: | | |
| (as before)/(£127,600 x 21%) | 34,475 | 26,796 |

Total corporation tax payable by South Limited and North Limited is therefore £61,271 (£34,475 + £26,796) a saving of £18,746 (£80,017 − £61,271).

**Notes:**

(1) Intangible asset rollover relief will be available as follows:

| | £ |
|---|---:|
| Original taxable 'credits' | 20,400 |
| Less: Relief (see below) | (10,000) |
| | |
| Taxable amount | 10,400 |

Relief is restricted to the amount that the proceeds or the amount reinvested if lower exceeded the original cost i.e. £10,000 (£20,000 – £10,000).

The revised goodwill tax cost for South Limited = £10,000 (£20,000 – £10,000).

As a result amortisation relief will be available to South Limited for the year ended 31 March 2011 and later years in respect of this goodwill at 4% £10,000 = £400 p.a.

(2)  Group rollover relief will be available as follows:

|  | £ |
|---|---|
| Original gain on freehold property | 40,000 |
| Less: Proceeds not reinvested | (20,000) |
| | |
| Taxable now | 20,000 |

(3)  As South Limited pays tax at the highest marginal rate it will be beneficial to maximise group relief for the y/e 31 March 2011. Further a carryback in North Limited to y/e 31 March 2010 will be beneficial from a cashflow perspective as this will result in a repayment of tax.

Loss relief allocation is maximised as follows:

|  | £ |
|---|---|
| South Limited (group relief) (see below) | 47,200 (at 29.75%) |
| North Limited (current year) | 20,000 (at 21%) |
| North Limited (carry back) | 9,600 (at 21%) |
| South Limited (group relief) | 22,800 (at 21%) |
| | |
| | 99,600 |

Group relief at highest marginal rate = (£197,200 – £150,000) = £47,200.

**Tutorial note:**

Taxable credits on the disposal of intangible fixed assets (IFA) can be deferred if new IFA are acquired by any company in a 75% group (as defined for capital gains) within 12 months before and up to 36 months after the disposal of the original IFA.

The maximum amount that can be deferred is restricted to the amount to which proceeds (or the amount reinvested if lower) exceed the original cost.

The credit deferred is deducted from the taxable credit, with only the balance subject to corporation tax in the period of disposal.

The credit deferred is also deducted from the acquisition cost of the new IFA to calculate the amortisation for tax purposes and the cost on a future disposal.

# Index

# Index

# Index

# Index

# Index

# Index

# Index

# Index